AMERICA
IN THE SIXTIES—
RIGHT, LEFT, AND CENTER

America
in the Sixties—
Right, Left, and Center

A DOCUMENTARY HISTORY

Edited by
PETER B. LEVY

PRAEGER

Westport, Connecticut
London

The Library of Congress has cataloged the hardcover edition as follows:

America in the sixties—right, left, and center : a documentary
   history / edited by Peter B. Levy.
      p. cm.
    Includes bibliographical references and index.
    ISBN 0–313–29936–6 (alk. paper)
     1. United States—History—1961–1969—Sources. 2. United States—
   Politics and government—1961–1963—Sources. 3. United States—
   Politics and government—1963–1969—Sources. 4. Right and left
   (Political science)—History—20th century—Sources. I. Levy,
   Peter B.
   E841.A47   1998
   973.922—dc21   98–22911

British Library Cataloguing in Publication Data is available.

A hardcover edition of *America in the Sixties—Right, Left, and Center* is
available from Greenwood Press, an imprint of Greenwood Publishing
Group, Inc. (ISBN: 0–313–29936–6).

Library of Congress Catalog Card Number: 98–22911
ISBN: 0–275–95516–8 (pbk.)

First published in 1998

Praeger Publishers, 88 Post Road West, Westport, CT 06881
An imprint of Greenwood Publishing Group, Inc.

Printed in the United States of America

∞™

The paper used in this book complies with the
Permanent Paper Standard issued by the National
Information Standards Organization (Z39.48–1984).

P

CONTENTS

CONTENTS

INTRODUCTION

Few periods in American history have captured the imagination as much as the "sixties," a term that refers both to a specific decade and a mood. Offer a college course on the 1960s, and students will pack the classroom. Peruse journals and magazines generally devoid of historical analysis, and you will uncover a unique fixation with the era. For conservatives, the sixties represent the bogeyman, the source of nearly all current social ills, the time when America got off track. For leftists and old-fashioned liberals, the sixties stand as an emblem of idealism and reform and as an inventory of unfinished agendas.

Not surprisingly, the sixties have already generated a great deal of attention, rivaled perhaps only by the outpouring of literature on the American Civil War. Contemporaries poured out tracts on the "generation gap," the assassination of John F. Kennedy, the tragedy at Kent State, and numerous other extraordinary events. In the immediate aftermath of the sixties, academics and nonacademics maintained a steady flow of publications on these and additional developments. Even as the decade passes from memory to history, bookstores and libraries continue to stock their shelves with memoirs, biographies, and oral histories on or by the decade's most notable figures, from Kennedy to King, and surveys of the Vietnam War and the civil rights movement, as well as scholarly treatises on more narrowly defined subjects. Filmmakers, television producers, musicians, and playwrights similarly have tapped and continue to tap the sixties as a dramatic setting for their works of fact and fiction. Even cyberspace has Web sites on a variety of sixties subjects, from the Black Panther Party to Woodstock.

In spite of this bevy of publications, a need still exists for a balanced documentary history of the sixties that is accessible to a general audience, is effective in college and high-school classrooms, and makes use of recent scholarship and takes advantage of the passage of time and historical hindsight. Documentary histories encourage active learning and pave the way for fresh and original interpretations of the past. By immersing readers in the period and engaging them with the most eloquent and profound speeches and writings of the time, documentary histories encourage further interest and investigation. Unfortunately, existent documentary histories on the sixties tend to be narrowly conceived and biased. Many concentrate almost exclusively on the New Left, the term used to describe the social movements of the era, and the bulk of these overemphasize the role played by male white leaders at the expense of minorities, women, and grass-roots activists.

In contrast, *America in the Sixties* presents a broad sampling of documents that engage the reader in the variety, complexity, and richness of the decade; it contains selections by New Leftists, liberals, and conservatives. It provides insight into the civil rights, women's, and antiwar movements and offers glimpses of both the tragic and triumphant moments of the times. Whereas other documentary histories leave their readers clueless as to the roots of the New Right and confused as to what made liberalism so attractive, this work presents pieces that help readers better understand both subjects. In addition to the ''Port Huron Statement'' and Mario Savio's ''An End to History,'' two classic texts of the New Left, which are justly included in nearly every reader on the period, *America in the Sixties* contains Ronald Reagan's ''A Time for Choosing,'' Richard Nixon's ''Forgotten American'' acceptance speech at the 1968 Republican convention, and Lyndon Johnson's eulogy to John F. Kennedy, in which he first effectively mobilized support for the Great Society. Finally, wanting to prompt the reader to move beyond clichéd and simplistic recollections of the 1960s, such as the notion that the Grateful Dead was *the* representative sound, *America in the Sixties* reflects the breadth of opinion, lifestyles, and fads that constituted sixties culture. Hence the chapter ''American Culture at a Crossroads'' includes an article from the *San Francisco Oracle* announcing the first ''Human Be-In'' as well as a newspaper story on a Christian rally aimed at offering an alternative to a Beatles concert in Memphis, Tennessee. The chapter also contains pieces by some of the most influential purveyors of culture whose views are difficult to pigeonhole as radical, mainstream, or conservative, namely, Hugh Hefner and Helen Gurley Brown.

Of course, wanting to keep this volume succinct, I could not include every writing, speech, and ephemeron that I considered important. Foremost, I sought to provide some sense of balance on the decade's major themes, to offer documents that depict both historical discontinuity and continuity. Thus, for example, while I would have liked to include more examples of the thinking and actions of the antiwar movement, I felt that it was more important to include an assortment of prowar selections as well as texts that displayed the ways in which the views of some changed over time. Likewise, I sought to include pieces by prominent figures while not shortchanging the voices of ordinary Americans. Some classic texts have been omitted, in part because they can be accessed easily elsewhere and also to allow space to introduce readers to lesser-known but equally significant documents. I did not include President John F. Kennedy's inaugural address, but I did include an excerpt from his 1960 televised debates with Richard Nixon. While the book does not contain the Student Nonviolent Coordinating Committee's declaration against the war in Vietnam (available in almost every anthology on the Vietnam War and numerous readers on the post-war period), it does include CBS news anchor Walter Cronkite's somber and influential report on the Tet offensive, which to my knowledge has been repro-duced on only one other occasion. I also sought to present a broad range of selections in terms of their sources as well as ideology. There are documents that come from mainstream as well as underground newspapers, New Left and New Right magazines, and congressional committees and presidential papers; that were written in the privacy of jail cells and were spoken before massive audiences; and that originate from unpublished manuscript collections and from books that were best-sellers. Regrettably, the cost of reprinting some pieces proved prohibitive. In such cases, I attempted to make references to these items in the headnotes and to replace them with material that covers the same general subject.

The book is arranged into nine roughly chronological and thematic chapters. Editorial headnotes introduce and tie together the documents, but I have kept my editorial remarks to a minimum so as to allow the documents to speak for themselves. The text of the reader is followed by a statistical appendix that includes information helpful to understanding key developments, from the steady growth in the economy to the rise of rock music, that are only briefly discussed in the text. The book also includes a bibliographic essay on suggested readings and a subject index.

The sixties began and ended at different points in time depending on one's conceptualization of the period. For those who define the 1960s in strictly chronological terms, the sixties began on January 1, 1960, and ended on De-cember 31, 1969. For those who envision the sixties as a mood distinct from the conservative and complacent fifties and from the seventies, when, as Peter Carroll put it, "it seemed like nothing happened," the sixties began before the decade and continued afterwards (*It Seemed Like Nothing Happened* [1982]). According to this view, the Beats, early stirrings of the peace and civil rights movements, and, to a lesser extent, rock music are considered manifestations of the sixties, while libertarian economic and conservative or orthodox cultural views are clumped together with the rise of the New Right of the 1970s, 1980s, and 1990s.

Even if one favors a strictly chronological definition or approach, one must concede that from very early on in the decade a new mood seemed to take hold.

On February 1, 1960, four black students from North Carolina Agricultural and Technical College in Greensboro, North Carolina, ordered a cup of coffee at a Woolworth's lunch counter. When they were refused service because they were black and the lunch counters were segregated, the four remained seated. Their action marked the first sit-in, which ushered in a wave of similar protests across the South and inspired many in the North to demand racial reform. The sit-ins also signaled that youths, who had been called the "silent generation" during the 1950s, would play a seminal role during the 1960s and hinted that blacks would occupy a vanguard position.

During the spring and fall of 1960 other indicators of a new mood appeared, ranging from student-led protests against the House Committee on Un-American Activities (HUAC), a symbol of the anti-Communist fifties, in San Francisco to the Kennedy campaign for the presidency, which included the first televised presidential debate. Young and energetic, Kennedy pledged to establish a New Frontier and to get the nation moving again. His election conveyed a sense of the new age, distinct from the staid and grandfatherly leadership of Eisenhower. To a lesser extent, so too did the cultural scene. Even though Percy Faith's "Theme from 'A Summer Place' " was the best-selling song in 1960, the rest of the music charts revealed the ascendancy of rock 'n' roll as the new sound, with three songs by Elvis Presley making the top ten and Chubby Checker's "The Twist" briefly hitting number one. On the silver screen, Burt Lancaster won an Oscar for his role in *Elmer Gantry*. Based on Sinclair Lewis's 1920s novel, the film not only satirized the religious fundamentalism of the twenties but shrewdly critiqued the religious revival of the fifties, embodied by the Reverend Billy Graham. Even in the world of fashion, the new mood was evident as the bikini, aided by the release of Brian Hyland's hit tune "Itsy Bitsy Teenie Weenie Yellow Polkadot Bikini," became the vogue. More significant yet in terms of the sexual revolution was the first commercial introduction of the birth-control pill.

Regardless of one's definition of the starting point for the sixties, nearly all analysts of the era agree on the decade's essential narrative. The first half of the 1960s witnessed the rise of the civil rights movement, the birth of youth-led protest, and the simultaneous triumph of liberalism, symbolized by President Johnson's landslide victory in 1964 and the enactment of "Great Society" and civil rights reforms too numerous to list in a brief introduction. The mid-sixties witnessed a growing rift between the New Left and liberals, due in part to the heightened but unfulfilled expectations of the former and to the escalation of the war in Vietnam, which began in the spring of 1965. Generational forces reinforced this rift, with many youths drifting farther and farther away from mainstream culture and adopting increasingly militant means to end the war and combat racial injustice. Yet the blossoming of the counterculture alongside militant protests gave rise to backlash, especially among many "Middle Americans" who had supported the Great Society and civil rights acts of the mid-1960s. Ironically, liberals often caught the brunt of the backlash because conservatives blamed them for encouraging and abetting the New Left in the first place.

Perhaps the backlash would have proved short-lived and liberals would have persevered if it had not been for several factors. The civil rights movement inspired new movements for liberation among women, gays, and Mexican and Native Americans and Puerto Ricans. Sensationalized by the mass media, the counterculture and the threat of radical violence appeared much more dangerous than either ever was. Paradoxically, some New Leftists believed much of what was written and were possessed by delusions of staging a revolution, which further fostered backlash. Just as important, the economy, which had been growing at a steady pace for over twenty years, with the exception of two brief recessions during Eisenhower's presidency, began to misfire. Throughout the 1960s, economic growth bolstered expectations about what could be achieved. Liberals argued that we could have both guns and butter, or domestic reforms and intervention abroad. New Leftists complained that a nation that could afford to send a man to the moon could eradicate poverty. Some cultural radicals even dreamed of creating a utopian society in which work virtually disappeared. The shift in the economy's gears, hence, produced a crisis for both liberals and New Leftists, undermining many of their basic assumptions while giving a boost to conservatives, who were ready to blame liberals and New Leftists for the nation's economic and social woes.

No single event marked the end of the sixties. Richard Nixon's election in 1968 hinted at a changing mood. Large student protests, which took place in 1969 and 1970, and the women's, gay, and environmental movements, which did not take off until the tail end of the decade, however, indicated that the sixties were not yet over. Nixon's defeat of George McGovern in the presidential election of 1972 stands as a better end marker for the era. Yet as resounding as McGovern's defeat was, the fact that he garnered the nomination in the first place suggests that a very significant proportion of the population was not in a conservative mood. Perhaps, then, the Watergate scandal and Nixon's resignation stand as the most accurate ending point for the sixties, closing the door on a period marked by idealism and protest and opening the door to an era distinguished by cynicism and conservative politics. Regardless of which starting and ending points of the sixties one prefers, there is general agreement that the decade was one of the most fascinating and significant in American history. Hopefully, this book will help us to better understand the era, to escape the trap of oversimplification, and to avoid the allure of nostalgia. In addition, this book will enable the reader to capture the passion of the sixties. Indeed, as I readied this book for publication, I was reminded that passionate times give rise to powerful words.

Numerous individuals helped me complete this work, and I have the space to thank only a few of them. My editors at Greenwood Press, especially Cynthia Harris and Betty Pessagno, have been a delight to work with. Similarly, I have received a great deal of aid from my colleagues at York College. Let me particularly thank Phil Avillo, who as my chair helped me secure release time and shared with me his memories of the sixties; Paul Doutrich, whose insight into sixties culture proved invaluable; and Mel Kulbicki, who offered numerous leads on conservative thought. Let me also thank Dean Jean Wyld, the Faculty Enhancement and Research and Publication committees, and the research assistants and work-study students who worked on this project, especially Cathy Hoult and Adam Doutrich. For several years I have taught a course on the 1960s, and my students have worked with me in searching out primary sources. Let me thank them collectively for tracking down a bevy of gems. Finally, let me once again thank my family for laboring with me on this project or, as was often the case, doing the other work I was not doing because I was working on this book.

Chapter One

THE 1950s: HAPPY DAYS AND THEIR DISCONTENTS

The documents in this chapter, culled from the late 1950s and the early 1960s, introduce several of the main themes of the post–World War II era: economic prosperity and optimism, the cold war and the fear of communism it bred, and the emergence of struggles for racial and sexual equality. The documents also hint at several of the undercurrents of the 1950s. Taken together, the selections prompt the reader to reconsider several of the accepted truths about these times. Did the 1960s represent a sharp break from the 1950s, or did the two decades share much in common? Is it accurate to describe the 1950s as "Happy Days" and to characterize the 1960s as an era of turmoil and trouble? If the sixties signified marked change, what accounted for the shift?

Between 1950 and 1960 the gross national product (GNP) nearly doubled; between 1960 and 1970 it nearly doubled again. Throughout this period, inflation remained low, real wages rose, the middle class grew in size, and the number of poor declined. **Document 1.1,** *the text of a General Electric advertisement that appeared in* Harper's *in August 1956, provides a sense of the optimism that flowed from the economy's performance. Accompanied by a photograph of a GE shareholders' meeting, the largest shareholders' meeting in history, the advertisement asserted that the average worker now lived in a world of permanent high wages, had remarkable opportunities for advancement and fulfillment, and enjoyed unprecedented leisure time and technology. Part of a larger Advertising Council campaign sponsored by the United States Information Agency, the advertisement emphasized the shared interest of labor and capital. Of added note, one of General Electric's spokesmen during this time period was Ronald Reagan, who introduced each episode of GE's "Death Valley Days" with a similar upbeat message.*

Document 1.1   General Electric, "People's Capitalism—What Makes It Work for You?" (text of advertisement), *Harper's Weekly,* **213, no. 1275 (August 1956), pp. 18–19.**

Around the world, the term "capitalism" has been applied to economic systems which bear little resemblance to each other.

Our American brand of capitalism is distinctive and unusually successful because it is a "people's capitalism": *all* the people share in its responsibilities and benefits. As we see it, these are its distinguishing characteristics.

1. We in America believe in providing opportunities for each individual to develop himself to his maximum potential.

2. We in America believe in high volume, and prices within the economic reach of all—not low volume, and prices only a few can pay.

3. We in America believe in high wages, high productivity and high purchasing power. They must occur together. One without the others defeats its own ends, but together they spell dynamic growth and progress.

4. We in America believe in innovation and in scrapping the obsolete. By reinvesting earnings in research and in new production facilities, American business is creating more jobs, better products and high living standards for everyone.

5. We in America believe in consumer credit, and have developed and used installment sales techniques to a degree unparalleled elsewhere in the world. Without it our economic indices would be at a fraction of their present level, and new industries like television would still be in their infancy.

6. We in America believe in leisure for our people through a comparatively short and highly productive work week. And the very fact of extensive leisure has produced great new industries which provide means for entertainment, for cultural pursuits, for sports of all kinds and for the do-it-yourself enthusiasts.

7. We in America believe in broad share ownership of American business. Millions of American families now participate directly in the risks and rewards of businesses as share owners; and almost everyone indirectly owns shares through insurance policies, savings banks, pension plans, mutual funds, trust accounts or other investments.

8. And finally, we in America believe deeply in competition versus the cartel. Competition is the spark plug of our economy. It keeps us endlessly, urgently searching and researching for new and better products, more efficient methods of production and improved marketing techniques.

As we see it, the more the principles of America's distinctive brand of capitalism become known and understood, the more certain everyone can be of continued progress—progress which is shared by consumers, employees, share owners, all businesses—large and small, and the nation.

Progress Is Our Most Important Product
GENERAL ELECTRIC

Whereas Americans would come to see academics and the media as bastions of criticism, this was not the case in the 1950s and early 1960s. **Document 1.2,** *an excerpt from* People of Plenty *by David M. Potter, a professor of history at Stanford University, was one of many works that argued that affluence and economic progress were the building blocks to understanding American history and society. Part of the larger "consensus" school of history, Potter downplayed conflict in America's past, focusing instead on those things that made America exceptional, defined as both different and superior. According to Potter, not only did "plenty" inform the modern era, but it stood as the distinguishing characteristic of the American experience.* **Document 1.3** *consists of the introduction to a special issue of* Life *magazine entitled "The Good Life." Hitting the newsstands as the new decade dawned, the issue complemented Potter's argument. Packed with glossy photographs of Americans enjoying themselves and gushing articles on America's "playgrounds" and leisure-time activities, the special issue did not contain an inkling of any of the troubles that would come to characterize the sixties. With a circulation of over 30 million,* Life's *articles and photographs both captured and shaped middle-class attitudes and sensibilities and had a significant reach and impact at the time, probably greater than those of the nightly news, which was still only fifteen minutes in length.*

Document 1.2 David Potter, *People of Plenty: Economic Abundance and the American Character* (Chicago: University of Chicago Press, 1954), pp. 80–84.

Throughout our national experience, the most varied types of observers have agreed in emphasizing America's bounty. Explorers have marveled at wealth previously undiscovered; travelers have contrasted the riches of America with the scarcity of the lands from which they came; millions of inhabitants of the Old World have responded as immigrants to the lure of the land of plenty, the land of promise, where they could "dwell like kings in fairyland, lords of the soil"; politicians have urged the voter to vote himself a farm or a check for thirty dollars every Thursday or an old age pension or a war bonus, in the confident assurance that the country can meet the draft; exploiters have parried demands for conservation by contending that the sources of our wealth are unlimited; a whole battalion of statisticians has been deployed on the task of measuring the abundance of natural resources—our cultivable soil, our hydroelectric potential, our timber, our coal, our iron, our copper, our petroleum, our natural gas, and so on; while another battalion has concentrated upon showing how the potential wealth of natural resources has been translated into an unexampled standard of living.

In every aspect of economic welfare the national differentials between the United States and other countries are immense, and some of these differentials, which have been conveniently summarized by Karl W. Deutsch, are illustrated in Figures 1 and 2. Figure 1 shows that the wages per hour of unskilled laborers in the United States, Canada, and New Zealand, for the year 1940, were about 60 per cent greater than the wages of similar workers in such advanced countries as Great Britain, Australia, and Switzerland and about 400 per cent greater than wages in most of Latin America. Figure 2 shows, by the height of the blocks, per capita incomes in seventy countries in 1949, in dollars of 1949 purchasing power. It shows that per capita income for the United States was $1,453, with no other country exceeding $900. Canada, New Zealand, and Switzerland were in the $800–$900 range; Sweden and the United Kingdom at the $700–$800 level; and no others exceeded $700. That is, no others reached a level half as high as that of the United States. The figure for the Soviet Union was $308. Argentina's $346 was the highest in Latin America, and Haiti's and Ecuador's $40 were the lowest, while the lowest world figure was for China, with a per capita income of $21 per year, or $1.75 per month.

Other data, cited by Deutsch, show that the United States, with 7 per cent of the world's population, has 42 per cent of the world's income, which means that a world population about fourteen times as great as that of the United States enjoys a collective income which is only 38 per cent greater than the income of the United States.

We may measure this differential in the human terms of nourishment rather than in the economic terms of income. In 1949 reliable computations showed that the average American consumed 3,186 calories daily. This was unquestionably the highest nutritional standard in the world. The consumption in England was estimated at more than 2,700, but in France, Italy, and Western Germany it was between 2,201 and 2,700. In Algeria, the Philippines, Japan, and India in the Old World, as well as in El Salvador in the New, it was below 1,800. It obviously must be a factor of immense importance in the daily lives of people that some habitually have more than enough to eat, while others are habitually hungry, and students of personality who regard relations within the family and practices of infant training as critical might surely find in these data a stunning opportunity to apply Gerth and Mills's proposition that "the structural and historical features of modern society must be connected with the most intimate features of man's self."

The compilation of statistics might be extended endlessly, but it would only prove repetitively that in every aspect of material plenty America possesses unprecedented riches and that these are very widely distributed among one hundred and fifty million American people. If few can cite the figures, everyone knows that we have, per capita, more automobiles, more telephones, more radios, more vacuum cleaners, more electric lights, more bathtubs, more supermarkets and movie palaces and hospitals, than any other nation. Even at mid-century prices we can afford college educations and T-bone steaks for a far higher proportion of our people than receive them anywhere else on the globe.

It approaches the commonplace, then, to observe that the factor of relative abundance is, by general consent, a basic condition of American life. As to the fact itself, we have demonstrated it in a thousand measurements of our own plenty. But it may be that we have emphasized this too much as an economic fact and not enough as a social one—that we have not sufficiently considered the pervasive influence of abundance upon many aspects of our lives which have no obvious relation to the standard of living. For certainly it is an influence that impinges upon all American social conditions and contributes in the most fundamental way to the shaping of the American culture and the American character.

Document 1.3 "A Special Double Issue on the Good Life," *Life* 47, no. 26 (December 28, 1959), pp. 4–5.

The Good Life! It's two swimming pools in every backyard, and a jet weekend to Bali. Or is it? Opinions differ. Differing opinions make good horse races and good material for *Life*, week by week. And when a situation affects practically all our readers, a special year-end double issue is called for. So this year's subject is our new-found good life, growing out of our new-found leisure.

On one count there is no real argument. The new leisure is here. For the first time a civilization has reached a point where most people are no longer pre-occupied exclusively with providing food and shelter. The shrinking work week now gives us about 75 free, waking hours as compared with a bare 55 two generations ago. Almost every employe in the land gets a two-day weekend and a vacation. Furthermore, people have the cash to enjoy their time off. But how the new leisure got here and whether it's boon or bane are the questions we take up.

Your Good Life is so much a matter of individual choice that we will merely suggest here that you address yourself to it as *Life* has, by going through the issue from here to the last page. After that, as to what you think about it and what you do about it, you are strictly on your own.

There was a time when only the rich had much leisure (aside from unem-ployment). So the flamboyant way in which they enjoyed their privileges makes a good point of departure. Then came mass production and automation—and suddenly what used to be the small leisured class became the big leisured masses.

How this has affected us we found out when we descended on two U.S. Elm Streets to see how plain Americans spend Saturday morning. Famous people spend it (*pp. 76–82*) on anything from steamboats to elephants, and whether or not they—or you—rate as leisure aristocrats or peasants is charted by an arm-chair sociologist. In "U.S. Playground" you'll find a spectacular example of play and, even if Sloan Wilson (*pp. 117–123*) finds that we may be playing for all the wrong reasons, we've turned up a couple of million Americans who are spending their spare time, in the summer anyhow, wisely and well.

So we didn't get to that jet weekend in Bali. But we do glimpse the goodies in store for 1975 and remind you of some eternal human needs, solitude and love, that no material blessings can replace. And to show what you may get in the way of tomorrow's good life today, we take you on a different kind of weekend—no traffic fumes, or even roads. Have a nice trip, everybody, and if you want a more detailed roadmap of the issue, see below.

Document 1.4, *a reproduction of the Help Wanted section of the* Atlanta Journal-Constitution, *reminds us that abundance and prosperity did not necessarily translate into equal opportunity for all Americans. Job advertisements in the* Journal-Constitution *and numerous other newspapers were divided by race and gender. Some jobs were explicitly reserved for white men, others for white women, still others for "colored" men and women. While northern newspapers did not always explicitly segregate their classified sections, they often contained code words that made clear the preferred gender and/or race of job applicants, such as "girl Friday," "messenger boy," and "salesman." Not surprisingly, the jobs reserved for white men paid better than those for white women or black men and women, confirming the prevailing view that men were supposed to be the breadwinners and that it was proper for whites to enjoy caste privileges over nonwhites.*

Document 1.4   "Want Ads," *Atlanta Journal-Constitution,* January 2, 1960, pp. 17–18.

EMPLOYMENT
Help Wanted Male

APPRENTICE

Young man wanted for outside serviceman trainee. No experience necessary. Must have good automobile. $75 per week with car allowance, plus gas, oil and expenses. Apply after 10 a.m. to Mr. Whitman, 85 Alabama Street, SW.

ARE YOU A
Securities Salesman?

Are you licensed? Will YOU WORK? If so, a new Georgia corporation is looking for YOU. This is not a usual securities salesman ad where YOU will be looking for another job in a matter of a few months. This is a LIFETIME CONNECTION FOR YOU with opportunity for DISTRICT MANAGER'S COMPENSATION WHEN MERITED. YOUR ANNUAL EARNINGS can be well into the FIVE FIGURE BRACKET IF YOU work. It's up to YOU. We have the securities. Do YOU have the ability? If so, telephone JA 4–6674 or CE 7-0535 for appointment and interview.

BAKERY ROUTE MEN

WE can use 2 men, married, age 22 to 40. High school graduate preferred. This is route sales work, 6-day week. Good pay, no lay-offs. Apply Highland Bakery, 655 Highland Ave., NE.

DISTRICT MANAGER

MAJOR Rubber Company will employ a well-experienced, well-qualified man for District assignment in Atlanta, Georgia. Knowledge of tire marketing in the Georgia, South Carolina and Alabama area helpful but not essential. A clean, successful past record a requirement. Excellent income, bonus, and expenses available. All replies will be treated strictly confidential. Write to C. P. Geddie, 1822 Rosemont St., Mesquite, Texas.

MECHANIC for heavy duty earth-moving equipment. Sober and reliable. References required. Phone Sherwood 2–3691, Macon, Ga., between 8:30 a.m. and 4 p.m. for appointment.

MACHINIST AND ELECTRICIAN
MUST be able to set up and run lathe shaper and milling machines. Prefer those with tool and die experience. Electrician familiar with all phases of plant maintenance. Permanent job. Good pay. Apply Swico, 3707 E. Ponce de Leon Ave.

SALESMAN
NATIONAL manufacturer of Venetian blinds, awnings and woven aluminum window treatment, desires salesman to contact manufacturers in South Carolina, Georgia, Florida Territory, well established. Liberal drawing account against commissions. Must have car. Experience in this field helpful but not essential. Write R. Y. 69, Journal-Constitution, giving resume of background.

TV SERVICEMAN
PERMANENT position, paid vacation, hospitalization, major medical and insurance, profit-sharing plan. Good opportunity for the right man. Apply Friedman's Jewelers, 37 Peachtree.

Help Wanted Female
GIRLS
With College Training
If you have graduated or do not plan to return to college contact Miss Adams. RETAIL CREDIT CO. Permanent positions of interesting and varied nature. Good opportunities available, many employee benefits. 1600 Peachtree.

HOSPITAL POSITIONS
NURSES' AIDES
18 to 45, 10th grade education, good health. Will train.
CLERK–TYPISTS
20 to 45, high school graduate, medical experience preferred but not necessary.
FOOD SUPERVISORS
24–45, high school graduates. Will train.
PBX OPERATOR
25 to 50, experience necessary.
APPLY Personnel, Georgia Baptist Hospital, 8:30 to 12 weekday mornings. Do not phone.

PUBLISHING firm in Buckhead area needs young lady experienced in light bookkeeping and office routine. Good typing required. 5-day week. Phone CE 3-5461, 9 till 5.

STENO–CLERK to replace one retiring person at age 45. Prefer mature lady. Must be able to get along with other employees. Reply in own handwriting, giving age, salary expected, and employment references for past 10 years. 112 Journal-Const.

SALESLADIES
NEEDED (6) for immediate employment. Apply Ben Franklin 5 and 10 Store. 3697 Campbeliton Rd., SW.

TEACHERS WANTED—The Cobb County school system needs a girl physical education teacher, a high school English teacher, and a Glee Club director. Contact W. P. Sprayberry, Marietta 8-1596.

WAITRESSES
EXPERIENCED. Apply in person. Jake's Fine Foods. Rear Trailways Bus Station.

COL. EMPLOYMENT
Help Wanted Male, Colored
MINT Car Wash. 1834 P'dmt, 308 T'wood, 536 P. de L., 2280 P'ree Rd.
FIRST-CLASS broiler and roast cook wanted. Salary open. Apply Atlanta Athletic Club, 166 Carnegie Way, N.W. JA 2–7430.

Help Wanted Female, Colored
MAID
MAID to live in, housework and child care. Must have health card and reference. $30 week. BL 5–5690.
EXPERIENCED women's specialty store, marking and pressing. Starting salary $22.50. Apply in person. Norman's. 3224 Peachtree Rd.
CHRISTIAN maid, experienced, high school education, day work, Tuesday and Friday, $5.50 day. BL 5–1262.

SALAD GIRL
EXPERIENCED person under 35, dependable, excellent pay. Apply The Pickrick, 891 Hemphill Ave., Northwest.
EXPERIENCED wool presser on the West side, for Marietta, Ga. Transportation furnished. Apply 3956 Buford Hwy. One Hour Martinizing.

Document 1.5 *consists of excerpts from Adlai Stevenson's 1955 commencement address to graduates of Smith College, one of the elite all-female colleges in the nation. Like* **Document 1.4,** *the speech reveals the consensus that existed in America over the "proper place" for women. Stevenson, the Democratic nominee for president in 1952 and 1956, the favorite of many liberals, including Eleanor Roosevelt, did not expect highly educated women, like those graduating from Smith, to participate in the work force. Rather, he, like most Americans, liberal and conservative, felt that they had a distinct, more "feminine" role to play. One of those who heard Stevenson's remarks was Betty Friedan, an alumna of Smith College, who was researching a story on the attitudes of the graduates of her alma mater. Stevenson's views and the seeming indifference to them by so many of the graduates helped convince Friedan to take a deeper look into the role of women in American society. Indeed, she included excerpts from this speech in her seminal book* The Feminine Mystique *as a foil to her argument that women were suffering from the traditional role to which they had been confined.*

Document 1.5 Adlai Stevenson, "Commencement Address," Smith College, Northampton, Massachusetts, June 6, 1955, reprinted in *Woman's Home Companion* 82 (September 1955), pp. 29–31.

COUNTLESS commencement speakers are rising these days on countless platforms all over the world to tell thousands of helpless young captives how important they are—as citizens in a free society, as educated, rational, privileged participants in a great historic crisis. But for my part I want merely to tell you young ladies that I think there is much you can do about that crisis in the humble role of housewife—which, statistically, is what most of you are going to be whether you like the idea or not just now—and you'll like it!

To explain what I mean I must ask you to step a long way back and recall with me that over vast periods of history and over most of the globe the view has prevailed that man is no more than a unit in the social calculus. Tribal life—the way of life pursued by man for by far the longest period of his history, of which there are many remnants today in Africa—knows no individuals, only groups with disciplines and group sanctions. But then at a certain point in time and place there took place the most momentous revolution yet achieved by mankind—a revolution compared with which such achievements as the discovery of fire or the invention of the wheel seem modest. In the origins of our Western civilization, among two small peoples of the eastern Mediterranean, the Greeks and the Jews, the great Copernican revolution of politics began: the discovery that the state exists for man, not man for the state, and that the individual human personality, spirit, soul—call it what you will—contains within itself the meaning and measure of existence and carries as a result the full range of responsibility and choice. . . .

The peoples of the West are still struggling with the problems of a free society and, just now, are in dire trouble. For to create a free society is at all times a precarious and audacious experiment. Its bedrock is the concept of man as an end in himself, as the ultimate reason for the whole apparatus of government, and the institutions of free society fulfill their task only in so far as this primary position of the free citizen—the *homo liber et legalis*—is not lost to sight. But violent pressures are constantly battering away at this concept, reducing man once again to subordinate status, limiting his range of choice, abrogating his responsibility, and returning him to his primitive status of anonymity in the social group. And it is to these pressures in their contemporary forms that I want to call your attention because I think you can be more helpful in identifying, isolating, and combating these pressures, this virus, than you girls perhaps today realize. . . .

Thus this typical Western man—or typical Western husband!—operates well in the realm of means, as the Romans did before him. But outside his specialty, in the realm of ends, he is apt to operate poorly or not at all. And this neglect of the cultivation of more mature values can only mean that his life, and the life of the society he determines, will lack valid purpose, however busy and even profitable it may be.

And here's where you come in: to restore valid, meaningful purpose to life in your home; to beware of instinctive group reaction to the forces which play upon you and yours; to watch for and arrest the constant gravitational pulls to which we are all exposed, your workaday husband especially, in our specialized, fragmented society that tends to widen the breach between reason and emotion, between means and ends.

And let me also remind you that you will live, most of you, in an environment in which "facts," the data of the senses, are glorified, and value judgments are assigned inferior status as mere "matters of opinion." It is an environment in which art is often regarded as an adornment of civilization rather than a vital element of it, while philosophy is not only neglected but deemed faintly disreputable, because "it never gets you anywhere." Even religion, you will find, commands a lot of earnest allegiance that is more verbal than real, more formal than felt.

You may be hitched to one of these creatures we call "Western man," and I think part of your job is to keep him Western, to keep him truly purposeful, to keep him whole. In short—while I have had very little experience as a wife or mother—I think one of the biggest jobs for many of you will be to frustrate the crushing and corrupting effects of specialization, to integrate means and ends, to develop that balanced tension of mind and spirit which can be properly called "integrity."

This assignment for you, as wives and mothers, has great advantages. In the first place, it is home work—you can do it in the living room with a baby in your lap, or in the kitchen with a can opener in your hands. If you're really clever, maybe you can even practice your saving arts on that unsuspecting man while he's watching television. And, secondly, it is important work worthy of you, whoever you are, or your education, whatever it is—even Smith College— because we will defeat totalitarian, authoritarian ideas only by better ideas; we will frustrate the evils of vocational specialization only by the virtues of intellectual generalities. Since Western rationalism and Eastern spiritualism met in

Athens and that mighty creative fire broke out, collectivism in various forms has collided with individualism time and again. This twentieth-century collision, this "crisis" we are forever talking about, will be won at last not on the battlefield but in the head and heart.

If the Colosseum at Rome is, as some say, the symbol of Roman failure to integrate mind and spirit, or means and ends, the hydrogen bomb, we might say, is the symbol of our own very similar self-betrayal. And one may hope that Hiroshima, like Rome's bloody arena, may be remembered at some distant day as a scene symbolizing a new beginning for mankind.

So you see, I have some rather large notions about you young ladies and what you have to do to rescue us wretched slaves of specialization and group thinking from further shrinkage and contraction of mind and spirit. But you will have to be alert or you may get caught yourself—even in the kitchen or the nursery—by the steady pressures with which you will be surrounded.

Prosperity notwithstanding, two developments created an underlying unease during the 1950s—the threat of communism and the burgeoning black freedom struggle. **Documents 1.6** *through* **1.10** *touch on these subjects, though at times in some subtle and contradictory ways.* **Document 1.6,** *an excerpt from one of Dwight D. Eisenhower's press conferences, contains the president's response to Sputnik, the Soviet Union's successful launch of the first unmanned satellite into space, and to the budding school-desegregation crisis in Little Rock, Arkansas, a byproduct of the 1954* Brown v. Board of Education *decision that had ruled segregation in public education unconstitutional. In both instances, characteristic of his demeanor and administration, Eisenhower responded in a remarkably measured manner. He did not view Sputnik with alarm, nor did he expect to involve the federal government in Little Rock. On the contrary, he described the Sputnik launch in tepid, mechanistic terms and provided no clear sense of his intentions regarding the desegregation of schools in the South. In contrast, many liberals and conservatives reacted with alarm to Sputnik.* Time's *article on the event was headlined "Nothing Startling, My Foot!" Edward Teller, the father of the hydrogen bomb, declared that the United States had "suffered a very serious defeat." Moving beyond criticism, many liberals used Sputnik to pressure the Eisenhower administration to support federal funding for education so that the United States could catch up in the race for space. Similarly, as events heated up in Little Rock, liberals made sure that Eisenhower enforced the law, which he did when he sent federal troops to desegregate Central High School against the wishes of Arkansas governor Orval Faubus and many other conservatives.*

Document 1.6 Dwight D. Eisenhower "Press Conference on Sputnik and Little Rock," September 3, 1957, *Public Papers of the Presidents of the United States: Dwight D. Eisenhower, 1957* (Washington, D.C.: GPO, 1958), pp. 639–646.

THE PRESIDENT. Good morning. Please sit down.

I have no announcements.

Q. Marvin L. Arrowsmith, Associated Press: Mr. President, is there anything that you can tell the American people in the light of the Russian announcement last week, and just what the status of development of our program for an intercontinental ballistic missile is at this point?

THE PRESIDENT. Any answer to your question, Mr. Arrowsmith, must observe the limits that are established by considerations of national security. And if you will read the Russian statement carefully, you will see that it is more notable for what it didn't say than for what it did say. Whenever it talked about the future, the translation is most evasive.

I can say a few things about this. First of all, let's remember this: the Russians never made any statement yet except for their own purposes, their own special purposes, and I don't know of any reason for giving it greater credence than many of the statements of the past, where they have been shown to be less than completely reliable.

Now, in this whole field, let us remember there are a number of things. There is a long distance between proving that you can fire one test instrument in a particular direction and achieve one result, and acquiring that instrument in sufficient numbers and sufficient reliability to be worthwhile tactically.

For a long time, the long-range missile is not going to provide the best means of delivering an explosive charge, and that is all it is for.

For a long time, there will be a changeover as they become perfected.

In our own case, we have spent many, many millions of dollars, as have other nations. We are continuing to do so on what is the highest priority that can possibly be devoted to the capacity of our scientific advancement and to the capacity of our whole, you might say, arrangements and organization to bring the thing forward; that is, testing, plans, and organization and the development, manufacture, and so on.

But the big thing to remember is that a mere tested vehicle is a long ways from actual production.

Q. Merriman Smith, United Press: Mr. President, over quite a wide section of the South today and this week, children are going back to school under difficult circumstances, in places where integration is being attempted for the first time.

We have a case in Arkansas this morning where the Governor has ordered State troops around a school that a Federal court had ordered integrated. I just wonder what you think of this situation.

THE PRESIDENT. Well, first, to say "what you think about it" is sort of a broad subject that you are giving me.

Actually, this particular incident came to my attention the first thing this morning. I have been in contact with the Attorney General's office. They are taking a look at it. They are going to find out exactly what has happened, and discuss this with the Federal judge. As of this moment, I cannot say anything further about the particular point, because that is all I know about it.

Now, time and again a number of people—I, among them—have argued that you cannot change people's hearts merely by laws. Laws presumably express the conscience of a nation and its determination or will to do something. But the laws here are to be executed gradually, according to the dictum of the Supreme Court, and I understand that the plan worked out by the school board of Little Rock was approved by the district judge. I believe it is a ten-year plan.

Now there seems to have been a road block thrown in the way of that plan, and the next decision will have to be by the lawyers and jurists. . . .

Q. Anthony Lewis, New York Times: As to school integration, Mr. President, do you have any plans to take a personal part in the problem this fall, for example, by speaking on it or getting in touch with Governor Faubus of Arkansas?

THE PRESIDENT. My speaking will be always on this subject, as I have always done, urging Americans to recognize what America is, the concepts on which it is based, and to do their part so far as they possibly can to bring about the kind of America that was visualized by our forebears. Now, it is for this reason, because I know this is a slow process. The Supreme Court in its decision of '54 pointed out the emotional difficulties that would be encountered by Negroes if given equal but separate schools, and I think probably their reasoning was correct, at least I have no quarrel with it.

But there are very strong emotions on the other side, people that see a picture of a mongrelization of the race, they call it. They are very strong emotions, and we are going to whip this thing in the long run by Americans being true to themselves and not merely by law.

Sputnik and the growing influence of the Soviet Union in the developing world under the lead of its new premier, Nikita Khrushchev, served as the backdrop of Vice President Richard Nixon's journey to the Soviet Union in 1959. Figuring that he would be the Republican nominee for president in 1960, Nixon sought to stand firm against the Soviets while at the same time convincing moderate Americans of his wisdom and flexibility. In many ways he did both in his impromptu "debate" with Soviet leader Nikita Khrushchev, the transcript of which is excerpted in Document 1.7. *Of added interest, the debate took place at the site of an exhibit of American goods, sponsored by the U.S. Information Agency, of which General Electric's "People's Capitalism" advertisement,* Document 1.1, *was also a part. Given the tone of Nixon's and Khrushchev's exchange, it is worthwhile to consider whether relations between the United States and the Soviet Union would have improved earlier if Nixon had been elected president in 1960.*

Document 1.7   Richard M. Nixon and Nikita Khrushchev, "The Kitchen Debate," *New York Times,* July 25, 1959, p. 1.

Khrushchev: "We want to live in peace and friendship with Americans because we are the two most powerful countries, and if we live in friendship then other countries will also live in friendship. But if there is a country that is too war-minded we could pull its ears a little and say: 'Don't you dare; fighting is not allowed now; this is a period of atomic armament; some foolish one could start a war and then even a wise one couldn't finish the war. Therefore, we are governed by this idea in our policy—internal and foreign. How long has America existed? Three hundred years?"

Nixon: "One hundred and fifty years."

Khrushchev: "One hundred and fifty years? Well, then, we will say America has been in existence for 150 years and this is the level she has reached. We have existed not quite forty-two years and in another seven years we will be on the same level as America. When we catch you up, in passing you by, we will wave to you. Then if you wish we can stop and say: Please follow up. Plainly speaking, if you want capitalism you can live that way. That is your own affair and doesn't concern us. We can still feel sorry for you but since you don't understand us—live as you do understand. . . .''

Nixon (pointing to American workmen): "With men like that we are strong. But these men, Soviet and American, work together well for peace, even as they have worked together in building this exhibition. This is the way it should be. Your remarks are in the tradition of what we have come to expect—sweeping and extemporaneous. Later on we will both have an opportunity to speak and consequently I will not comment on the various points that you raised, except to say this—this color television is one of the most advanced developments in communication that we have. I can only say that if this competition in which you plan to outstrip us is to do the best for both of our people and for peoples everywhere, there must be a free exchange of ideas. After all, you don't know everything."

Khrushchev: "If I don't know everything, you don't know anything about communism except fear of it."

Nixon: "There are some instances where you may be ahead of us, for example, in the development of the thrust of your rockets for the investigation of outer space; there may be some instances in which we are ahead of you—in color television, for instance."

Khrushchev: "No, we are up with you on this, too. We have bested you in one technique and also in the other."

Nixon: "You see, you never concede anything."

Khrushchev: "I do not give up. . . ."

Nixon (halting Khrushchev at model kitchen in model house): "You had a very nice house in your exhibition in New York. My wife and I saw and enjoyed it very much. I want to show you this kitchen. It is like those of our houses in California."

Khrushchev (after Nixon called attention to a built-in panel-controlled washing machine): "We have such things."

Nixon: "This is the newest model. This is the kind which is built in thousands of units for direct installation in the houses." He added that Americans were interested in making life easier for women. Mr. Khrushchev remarked that in the Soviet Union they did not have "the capitalist attitude toward women."

Nixon: "I think that this attitude toward women is universal. What we want to do is make easier the life of our housewives." He explained that the house could be built for $14,000 and that most veterans had bought houses for between $10,000 and $15,000. "Let me give you an example you can appreciate. Our steel workers, as you know are on strike. But any steel worker could buy this house. They earn $3 an hour. This house costs about $100 a month to buy on a contract running twenty-five to thirty-five years.''

Khrushchev: "We have steel workers and we have peasants who also can afford to spend $14,000 for a house.'' He said American houses were built to last only twenty years, so builders could sell new houses at the end of that period. "We build firmly. We build for our children and grandchildren.''

Mr. Nixon said he thought American houses would last more than twenty years, but even so, after twenty years many Americans want a new home or a new kitchen, which would be obsolete by then. The American system is designed to take advantage of new inventions and new techniques, he said.

Khrushchev: "This theory does not hold water.'' He said some things never got out of date—furniture and furnishings, perhaps, but not houses. He said he did not think that what Americans had written about their houses was strictly accurate.

Nixon (pointing to television screen): "We can see here what is happening in other parts of the home.''

Khrushchev: "This is probably always out of order.''

Nixon: "Da [yes].''

Khrushchev: "Don't you have a machine that puts food into the mouth and pushes it down? Many things you've shown us are interesting but they are not needed in life. They have no useful purpose. They are merely gadgets. We have a saying, if you have bedbugs you have to catch one and pour boiling water into the ear. . . .''

Nixon (hearing jazz music): "I don't like jazz music.''

Khrushchev: "I don't like it either.''

Nixon: "But my girls like it.'' Mr. Nixon apologized for being "a poor host at the exposition and allowing a ceremonial visit to turn into a hot foreign policy discussion.''

Khrushchev (apologizing): "I always speak frankly.'' He said he hoped he had not offended Mr. Nixon.

Nixon: "I've been insulted by experts. Everything we say is in good humor.''

Khrushchev: "The Americans have created their own image of the Soviet man and think he is as you want him to be. But he is not as you think. You think the Russian people will be dumbfounded to see these things, but the fact is that newly built Russian houses have all this equipment right now. Moreover, all you have to do to get a house is to be born in the Soviet Union. So I have a right to a house. In America if you don't have a dollar—you have a right to choose between sleeping in a house or on the pavement. Yet you say that we are slaves of communism. . . .''

Khrushchev (noting Nixon gazing admiringly at young women modeling bathing suits and sports clothes): "You are for the girls too.''

Nixon (indicating a floor sweeper that works by itself and other appliances): "You don't need a wife.''

Khrushchev chuckled.

Nixon: "We do not claim to astonish the Russian people. We hope to show our diversity and our right to choose. We do not wish to have decisions made at the top by government officials who say that all homes should be built in the same way. Would it not be better to compete in the relative merits of washing machines than in the strength of rockets? Is this the kind of competition you want?"

Khrushchev: "Yes, that's the kind of competition we want. But your generals say: 'Let's compete in rockets. We are strong and we can beat you.' But in this respect we can also show you something."

Nixon: "To me you are strong and we are strong. In some ways, you are stronger than we are. In others, we are stronger. We are both strong not only from the standpoint of weapons but from the standpoint of will and spirit. Neither should use the strength to put the other in a position where he in effect has an ultimatum. In this day and age that misses the point. With modern weapons it does not make any difference if war comes. We both have had it."

Khrushchev: "For the fourth time I have to say I cannot recognize my friend Mr. Nixon. If all Americans agree with you, then who don't we agree [with]? This is what we want."

Nixon: "Anyone who believes the American Government does not reflect the people is not an accurate observer of the American scene. I hope the Prime Minister understands all the implications of what I have just said. Whenever you place either one of the powerful nations or any other in a position so that it has no choice but to accept dictation or fight, then you are playing with the most destructive force in the world. This is very important in the present world context. It's very dangerous. When we sit down at a conference table it cannot all be one way. One side cannot put an ultimatum to another. It is impossible. But I shall talk to you about this later."

During the 1960 presidential campaign, John F. Kennedy, the Democratic nominee, sought to portray the Eisenhower and Nixon administration as having been soft on communism. Claiming that the Republicans had allowed the development of a missile gap, Kennedy promised to get the nation moving again. Kennedy most forcefully made this case in a series of unprecedented televised debates with Richard Nixon, the Republican nominee for president. Kennedy's opening remarks in the first debate are excerpted in **Document 1.8.** *Many considered these debates the key to Kennedy's extremely narrow victory in November. Ironically, Nixon agreed to them because, as a master debater, he expected to win. However, Nixon did not fully consider or understand the impact that the new medium of television would have on the audience. On words alone, Nixon did not lose the debates, but he clearly lost the battle of images to the much younger-looking Kennedy (who was actually only four years his junior). Of added note, after Kennedy won the presidency, it became clear that* *there was no missile gap, yet tensions between the Soviet Union and the United States increased, in part because of Kennedy's bombastic rhetoric and his need to prove himself to the Soviets and the American people.*

Document 1.8 John F. Kennedy, "Presidential Debate: Opening Remarks," September 26, 1960, U.S. Senate, Committee on Commerce: Subcommittee of the Subcommittee on Communications, *Freedom of Communications: Final Report,* part 3 (Washington, D.C.: GPO, 1961), pp. 73–75.

Mr. SMITH. Good evening.

The television and radio stations of the United States and their affiliated stations are proud to provide facilities for a discussion of issues in the current political campaign by the two major candidates for the Presidency.

The candidates need no introduction. The Republican candidate, Vice President Richard M. Nixon, and the Democratic candidate, Senator John F. Kennedy.

According to rules set by the candidates themselves, each man shall make an opening statement of approximately 8 minutes' duration and a closing statement of approximately 3 minutes' duration.

In between the candidates will answer or comment upon answers to questions put by a panel of correspondents.

In this, the first discussion in a series of four joint appearances, the subject matter, it has been agreed, will be restricted to internal or domestic American matters.

And now, for the first opening statement by Senator John F. Kennedy.

Mr. KENNEDY. Mr. Smith, Mr. Nixon.

In the election of 1860, Abraham Lincoln said the question was whether this Nation could exist half slave or half free.

In the election of 1960, and with the world around us, the question is whether the world will exist half slave or half free, whether it will move in the direction of freedom, in the direction of the road that we are taking or whether it will move in the direction of slavery.

I think it will depend in great measure upon what we do here in the United States, on the kind of society that we build, on the kind of strength that we maintain.

We discuss tonight domestic issues, but I would not want that to be—any implication to be given that this does not involve directly our struggle with Mr. Khrushchev for survival.

Mr. Khrushchev is in New York and he maintains the Communist offensive throughout the world because of the productive power of the Soviet Union, itself.

The Chinese Communists have always had a large population but they are important and dangerous now because they are mounting a major effort within their own country; the kind of country we have here, the kind of society we have, the kind of strength we build in the United States will be the defense of freedom.

If we do well here, if we meet our obligations, if we are moving ahead, then I think freedom will be secure around the world. If we fail, then freedom fails.

Therefore, I think the question before the American people is: Are we doing as much as we can do? Are we as strong as we should be? Are we as strong as we must be if we are going to maintain our independence, and if we're going to maintain and hold out the hand of friendship to those who look to us for assistance, to those who look to us for survival. I should make it very clear that I do not think we're doing enough, that I am not satisfied as an American with the progress that we are making.

This is a great country, but I think it could be a greater country, and this is a powerful country but I think it could be a more powerful country.

I'm not satisfied to have 50 percent of our steel mill capacity unused.

I'm not satisfied when the United States had last year the lowest rate of economic growth of any major industrialized society in the world—because economic growth means strength and vitality. It means we're able to sustain our defenses. It means we're able to meet our commitments abroad.

I'm not satisfied, when we have over $9 billion worth of food, some of it rotting even though there is a hungry world and even though 4 million Americans wait every month for a food package from the Government which averages 5 cents a day per individual.

I saw cases in West Virginia, here in the United States, where children took home part of their school lunch in order to feed their families, because I don't think we are meeting our obligations toward these Americans.

I'm not satisfied when the Soviet Union is turning out twice as many scientists and engineers as we are.

I'm not satisfied when many of our teachers are inadequately paid or when our children go to school part-time shifts. I think we should have an educational system second to none.

I'm not satisfied when I see men like Jimmy Hoffa, in charge of the largest union in the United States, still free.

I'm not satisfied when we are failing to develop the natural resources of the United States to the fullest. Here in the United States, which developed the Tennessee Valley and which built the Grand Coulee and the other dams in the Northwest United States, at the present rate of hydropower production—and that is the hallmark of an industrialized society—the Soviet Union by 1975 will be producing more power than we are.

These are all the things I think in this country that can make our society strong or can mean that it stands still.

I'm not satisfied until every American enjoys his full constitutional rights. If a Negro baby is born, and this is true also of Puerto Ricans and Mexicans in some of our cities, he has about one-half as much chance to get through high school as a white baby. He has one-third as much chance to get through college as a white student. He has about a third as much chance to be a professional man, and about half as much chance to own a house. He has about four times as much chance that he'll be out of work in his life as the white baby. I think we can do better. I don't want the talents of any American to go to waste.

I know that there are those who say that we want to turn everything over to the Government. I don't at all. I want the individuals to meet their responsibilities and I want the States to meet their responsibilities. But I think there is also a national responsibility.

The argument has been used against every piece of social legislation in the last 25 years. The people of the United States individually could not have developed the Tennessee Valley. Collectively, they could have.

A cotton farmer in Georgia or a peanut farmer or a dairy farmer in Wisconsin or Minnesota—he cannot protect himself against the forces of supply and demand in the marketplace, but working together in effective governmental programs, he can do so.

Seventeen million Americans who live over 65 on an average social security check of about $78 a month—they're not able to sustain themselves individually, but they can sustain themselves through the social security system.

I don't believe in big government, but I believe in effective governmental action, and I think that's the only way that the United States is going to maintain its freedom; it's the only way that we're going to move ahead. I think we can do a better job. I think we're going to have to do a better job if we are going to meet the responsibilities which time and events have placed upon us.

We cannot turn the job over to anyone else. If the United States fails, then the whole cause of freedom fails, and I think it depends in great measure on what we do here in this country.

The reason Franklin Roosevelt was a good neighbor in Latin America was because he was a good neighbor in the United States, because they felt that the American society was moving again. I want us to recapture that image. I want people in Latin America and Africa and Asia to start to look to America to see how we're doing things, to wonder what the President of the United States is doing, and not to look at Khrushchev or look at the Chinese Communists. That is the obligation upon our generation.

In 1933 Franklin Roosevelt said in his inaugural that this generation of Americans has a "rendezvous with destiny." I think our generation of Americans has the same "rendezvous." The question now is: Can freedom be maintained under the most severe attack it has ever known? I think it can be, and I think in the final analysis it depends upon what we do here. I think it's time America started moving again.

Numerous right-wing groups, which proliferated in the 1950s, not only expressed their concern about the Soviet Union's military threat, more so than the Eisenhower administration and much more so than liberal Democrats, but expressed their dismay over the Communist threat at home. Put differently, even though Senator Joe McCarthy died in May 1957, several years after he was condemned by the Senate, McCarthyism remained a prominent aspect of American life. For example, in **Document 1.9,** *the American Nationalist, a small right-wing group from Southern California, lambasts Hollywood for promoting a subversive and Communist agenda. While right-wing attacks on the entertainment capital of America were commonplace, this diatribe contained a new twist, linking subversives in Hollywood to seemingly unrelated efforts to promote racial equality. While the American Nationalist was not a large organization, its views were shared by many who belonged to other right-wing organizations, most notably the White Citizens' Councils, which sprang up in the South following the* Brown *decision, and to a lesser extent the John*

Birch Society. Moreover, several of the themes raised by this broadside have re-mained part of the conservative critique. Thus while blatant racism and anticom-munism have diminished in importance, Hollywood, cast as a purveyor of untraditional values and as a prime example of the liberal establishment, has re-mained a principal target of conservative venom.

Document 1.9 American Nationalist, "Fixed Entertainment . . . Inter-racial Style," undated, Radical Right Collection, Hoover Institution on War, Revolution, and Peace, Stanford, California.

The radio and TV quiz scandals have revealed to the American people just how rotten our alien-owned entertainment industry really is. One result is that the public is now thoroughly cognizant of the fact that virtually all the so-called quiz programs were rigged, and that numerous deceptive devices (including dubbed-in laughter and canned applause) have been utilized by practically all types of programs to fool the viewing audiences. It has also been disclosed that the music industry has been controlled from behind the scenes by financial interests which have used "payola" (bribery) to popularize offensive rock-and-roll music, thereby driving good wholesome music practically off the market. Fraud, deception, rigging, bribery and deceit have become the order of the day in the TV and music industries.

But there is yet another aspect of the situation which most Americans are still unfamiliar with—the racial angle. For it is an indisputable fact that the enter-tainment industry (TV, radio, recordings, movies, etc.) has also been "fixed" in such a manner as to popularize race-mixing and integration. Most of the rigged quiz shows, for example, were rigged deliberately to let numerous colored "contestants" win, the idea being to convince the American people that Negroes are extremely intelligent and cultured. . . . In similar fashion Negroes have been raised to stardom and adulation as a result of the fictitious popularity of rock-and-roll music—popularity purchased through "payola". To their dismay, mil-lions of parents have belatedly come to the realization that their own children have been force fed this musical garbage, and this realization is especially acute in those families whose teen-age daughters are squealing and drooling over Negroidal crooners. . . .

Equally offensive is the inter-racial filth with which Hollywood is literally swamping the theatres and TV networks. These films variously portray Negroes as heroic soldiers, as romantic lovers, as suffering martyrs of white bigotry and even as heroes of westerns—but always the propaganda message is there. The illustrations on this page will give you an idea of what is going on:

ITEM 1: The CBS network (Zane Gray Theatre) has cast the Negro, Sammy Davis, as the hero of a western. Davis, incidentally, recently made news when his engagement to a blond white girl was announced.

ITEM 2: A Negro plays the role of a war hero in the new propaganda movie, "Pork Chop Hill", by UNITED ARTISTS.

ITEM 3: In the film "Odds Against Tomorrow", UNITED ARTISTS has produced a hate picture against white Americans. Hero of the story is the mulatto, Harry Belafonte. The white "punk" (and "bigot") is played by Robert Ryan.

ITEM 4: "End of the World" is also an argument for integration. In it the Negro, Belafonte, plays opposite white actress, Inger Stevens. Incidentally, Harry Belafonte is also married to a white woman.

ITEM 5: In "Moment of Danger" the mulatto actress, Dorothy Dandridge, publically kisses a white boy friend for the first time. In real life she is married to a white.

ITEM 6: The Negro agitator and film actor, Sidney Poitier, recently accepted a special award (from a white woman, naturally) for the race picture, "The Defiant Ones". Poitier has made several "integrated" propaganda films of late.

ITEM 7: As a follow-up to the vicious interracial propaganda picture, "Kings Go Forth", Frankie (I love the NAACP) Sinatra is doing it again. This time it's a picture called "Hole in the Head", with the Negro, Sammy Davis, as co-star.

ITEM 8: In a publicity photo released by MGM for the Negro press, Harry Belafonte is shown below fondling the jewelry of a white actress in an advertisement for a forthcoming movie—interracial, of course.

ITEM 9: At the New York Jazz Festival, an arrogant Negro musician, "Count" Basie, was photographed using a white girl's shoulder as a "desk" to sign autographs on . . .

These are not isolated instances: they are part of a well defined pattern. Without exception every part of the entertainment industry (music, pictures, TV, etc.) is being deliberately utilized to popularize and glamourize racial integration to the American public. And if you want to see the ultimate goal they are aiming for, then take a close look at the photo below right. It shows the mulatto musician, Herb Jeffrey, kissing his new white bride, Tempest Storm, at their wedding a short time ago . . .

WHAT CAN BE DONE TO STOP THIS MASSIVE PROPAGANDA DRIVE TO DESTROY THE WHITE RACE?

The answer is: plenty! Whenever a TV station presents offensive interracial propaganda or "mixed" entertainment, *write the sponsor*! When a radio station features Negroidal entertainment or rock-and-roll music, protest! Protest to the radio station and also to the sponsor of the program. *Also*: see that you never patronize coin machines featuring such music. And finally: never allow your children to purchase recordings made by Negroidal entertainers. . . . Discourage your local record shop from handling such trash. As for interracial movies: speak to your local theatre manager. If that doesn't work, arrange a *boycott* if possible. Write protests to your local newspaper. *ANOTHER THING*: Be sure to distribute extra copies of this tract to newspapers, to friends, to parents, to radio stations, to churches. . . . *LET'S FIGHT BACK*!

Document 1.10, *an article from the liberal magazine* The Reporter, *sheds light on the "Beats," the name given to a cluster of avant-garde artists and writers, most notably Allen Ginsberg and Jack Kerouac. In particular, the article describes the trial of Lawrence Ferlinghetti, the owner of the City Lights bookstore, a Beat hangout in San Francisco, and the publisher of "Howl," Ginsberg's famous poem. The Beats did not share* Life *magazine's or GE's assessment of American society and voluntarily chose a life of poverty, which they saw as more fulfilling than the mass consumerism of the day. Nor did the Beats share the right wing's cultural values, but experimented with drugs and flaunted sexual taboos in such a way as to make Hollywood appear tame. While local authorities sought to stop the publication and distribution of "Howl," deeming it obscene, Judge Clayton W. Horn ruled that Ginsberg's poem was protected by the First Amendment. Ironically, as often would be the case, the prosecution of Ferlinghetti gained Ginsberg and the Beats more attention than if they had been left alone and lent them notoriety and influence, especially among youths, who were intrigued by their rebellion against authority. Furthermore, the decision in the "Howl" trial was one of several important decisions reached during this time period that broadened the range of permissible speech, marking one other way in which the Beats served as a springboard to the cultural rebellion of the sixties.*

Document 1.10　David Perlman, "How Captain Hanrahan Made 'Howl' a Best-Seller," *The Reporter* 17, no. 10 (December 12, 1957), pp. 37–39.

San Francisco, an easy-going, tolerant, and highly literate community, was surprised not long ago to learn that two officers of the police department's Juvenile Bureau had made a purchase in a local bookstore and had promptly sworn out warrants for the proprietor and his clerk on charges that they "did willfully and lewdly publish and sell obscene and indecent writings."

The warrants were served, and the defendants duly arrested, fingerprinted, and freed on bail. They pleaded not guilty and the stage was set for the first test of California's obscenity law since the Supreme Court's ruling, last June, that the law itself is Constitutional.

The preparations for the trial produced a certain amount of concern in both legal and literary circles. Captain William Hanrahan, chief of the department's Juvenile Bureau, announced, "We will await the outcome of this case before we go ahead with other books." He did not reveal what books he had in mind, but he made it clear he had quite a list. He also disclosed that his men had been taking a look around the shelves of the city's bookstores—of which there are far more per capita than in any other metropolis outside New York.

A JUDGMENT OF SOLOMON

When Captain Hanrahan was asked what standards he used to judge a book, his reply was brief but vague: "When I say filthy I don't mean suggestive, I mean filthy words that are very vulgar." He was also asked whether he was planning to send his men out to confiscate the Bible. His denial was vehement.

"Let me tell you, though," the captain added, "what King Solomon was doing with all those women wouldn't be tolerated in San Francisco!"

The City Lights Pocket Bookshop, where Captain Hanrahan's men had dragged their net for filth, is not an ordinary emporium of literature. Its owner, and the principal defendant in the case, is Lawrence Ferlinghetti, a poet himself, a painter, and a canny and relatively affluent citizen of a San Francisco district called North Beach, which is a largely Italian neighborhood near the waterfront, between Telegraph and Russian Hills. Ferlinghetti's store is right in the center of the district, where ravioli factories, Italian steamship agencies, *caffé espresso* bars, grocery stores redolent of salami and gorgonzola, and crowded blocks of old frame apartment buildings surround small islands of Bohemia.

The islands contain warrens of artistically decorated back-alley studios with north light and no heat, off-beat night clubs, and hangouts with such names as the Purple Onion, the Old Spaghetti Factory and Excelsior Coffee House, and the Coexistence Bagel Shop. There are a number of cellar joints where Ferlinghetti and poets like the renowned Kenneth Rexroth read their verse to the accompaniment of cool jazz. The jazz-and-poetry medium is currently the rage—and quite successful in commercial terms, too. Kenneth Patchen, another widely known poet, has drawn down as much as two hundred dollars a week reciting his poems to the paying customers at a more tony establishment called the Blackhawk which is situated well outside the undefined city limits of Bohemia . . .

Ferlinghetti is also a publisher. He has issued, under the City Lights imprint, a "Pocket Poets" series, retailing for seventy-five cents each. The first three works offered were Ferlinghetti's own *Pictures of the Gone World*, Rexroth's *Thirty Spanish Poems of Love and Exile*, and Patchen's *Poems of Humor and Protest*. The fourth was a forty-four-page volume called *Howl and Other Poems* by Allen Ginsberg, a thirty-one-year-old member of what Jack Kerouac, author of *On the Road*, must be given credit for naming the "Beat Generation."

Ginsberg's title poem starts: "I saw the best minds of my generation destroyed by madness, starving hysterical naked." In what follows there is a great deal of anger, despair, four-letter words, and grotesque sexual imagery. There are also explicit promises of redemption from the gutter purgatory.

OYEZ! OYEZ!

This was the poem that aroused the San Francisco Police Department and was the actual defendant in the case of *People* vs. *Ferlinghetti*. Ginsberg himself was far away on a trip to Europe, and the owner of the bookstore never took the stand, nor was any evidence presented against him beyond the fact that he had published "Howl." His clerk, Shigeyetsu Murao, was even less involved. The prosecutor conceded that there was no evidence to show the clerk even knew what was in the book, and it was quickly agreed that Murao should be acquitted. It was also agreed that the trial would be held without a jury.

The judge was Clayton W. Horn of the San Francisco Municipal Court, who functions primarily as one of the city's four police magistrates. Judge Horn, who regularly teaches Bible class at a Sunday school, was under something of a cloud when he mounted the bench for the "Howl" case. He had just been raked over by the local press for a decision in which he had sentenced five lady shoplifters to attend *The Ten Commandments* and write penitential essays on the supercolossal epic's moral lesson.

The chief defense counsel was J. W. Ehrlich, known for thirty years in San Francisco as "Jake The Master." Small, wiry, and intense, with dark, lugubrious eyes, Ehrlich is at fifty-seven the city's most famous criminal lawyer. He has defended such varied clients as Sally Rand, the fan dancer; Fritz Weidemann, the Nazi; Walter Wanger, the producer; and Caryl Chessman, the kidnaper and author of *Death Row*. Ehrlich has never been particularly interested in political cases, but when the American Civil Liberties Union asked him to take Ferlin-ghetti as a free client, "The Master" agreed.

Ehrlich's opponent was Ralph McIntosh, an elderly assistant district attorney who had studied law at night while working as a linotype operator on a news-paper. McIntosh has been an assistant district attorney for most of his career, and he has become something of a specialist in smut cases. Pornographic mov-ies, nudist magazines, and Jane Russell's appearance in *The Outlaw* have all been targets of his zeal. . . .

MARK SCHORER ON THE STAND

The first major encounter of the trial came when Ehrlich carefully pitted McIntosh against the defense's principal witness, Mark Schorer. Schorer is pro-fessor of English and chairman of graduate studies at the University of Califor-nia; he is one of America's leading critics, is a textbook consultant to the U.S. Army, has published three novels and seventy-five short stories, and has been awarded a Fulbright and three Guggenheim fellowships.

In his characteristically imperturbable drawl, Schorer testified on direct ex-amination by Ehrlich: "I think that 'Howl,' like any work of literature, attempts and intends to make a significant comment on or interpretation of human ex-perience as the author knows it."

He said the theme and structure "create the impression of a nightmare world in which the 'best minds of our generation' are wandering like damned souls in hell." Much of the content, Schorer said, is "a series of what one might call surrealistic images."

Judge Horn, having carefully read the evolving common law on the subject, ruled that while Schorer and other experts could not testify whether or not they thought the poem obscene, they could state whether they thought the contro-versial language contained in the poem was "relevant" to the intent and theme of the poet.

"Ginsberg uses the rhythms of ordinary speech and also the diction of ordi-nary speech," Schorer said. "I would say the poem uses necessarily the lan-guage of vulgarity."

Then came the cross-examination. For an hour McIntosh pecked at Schorer, stormed at him, and read him nearly every questionable line in the book. The prosecutor railed at the poem too, and it was sometimes difficult to tell which he objected to more, its dirt or its incomprehensibility.

"I presume you understand the whole thing, is that right?" McIntosh asked Schorer at one point, a dare in his voice.

Schorer smiled. "I hope so," he said. "It's not always easy to know that one understands exactly what a contemporary poet is saying, but I think I do."

McIntosh flourished the book triumphantly. "Do you understand," he demanded, "what 'angelheaded hipsters burning for the ancient heavenly connection to the starry dynamo in the machinery of night' means?"

"Sir, you can't translate poetry into prose," Schorer answered. "That's why it's poetry."

The audience, among whom were North Beach writers, downtown booksellers, and a few criminal-court regulars, roared. The judge smiled tolerantly, but McIntosh would not give up.

"In other words," he asked, "you don't have to understand the words?"

"You don't understand the individual words taken out of their context," Schorer explained patiently. "You can no more translate it back into logical prose English than you can say what a surrealistic painting means in words because it's *not* prose."

This still didn't satisfy McIntosh, who kept reading the poem's opening lines and demanding a literal explanation. Finally Schorer said: "I can't possibly translate, nor, I am sure, can anyone in this room translate the opening part of this poem into rational prose."

For some reason, this testimony set McIntosh up immensely. "That's just what I wanted to find out," he declared with the air of one who has just clinched his case. . . .

The judge declined to instruct the witness to enlighten McIntosh on the poem's meaning, so the prosecutor tried another tack. He read a few more vivid phrases into the record and then asked Schorer: "Now couldn't that have been worded some other way? Do they have to put words like that in there?"

But Judge Horn disallowed the question, and offered a bit of literary criticism himself: "I think it is obvious," he said, "that the author could have used another term; whether or not it would have served the same purpose is another thing; that's up to the author." . . .

The defense placed nine expert witnesses on the stand in all, and with each one of them McIntosh went through the same maneuvers: bewilderment at the poem, contempt for the expert on the stand, and glee at the extraction of four-letter words. But no jury was present to see his act.

From Luther Nichols, book critic of the San Francisco *Examiner*, he learned that "Ginsberg's life is a vagabond one; it's colored by exposure to jazz, to Columbia University, to a liberal and Bohemian education, to a certain amount of bumming around. The words he has used are valid and necessary if he's to be honest with his purpose. I think to use euphemisms in describing this would be considered dishonest by Mr. Ginsberg.''

From Walter Van Tilburg Clark, author of *The Ox Bow Incident*, came this statement: ''They seem to me, all of the poems in the volume, to be the work of a thoroughly honest poet, who is also a highly competent technician.''

''Do you classify yourself as a liberal?'' McIntosh asked Clark. But that was as far as he got. Judge Horn barred the question the instant it was uttered.

It was from Kenneth Rexroth—who described himself as a ''recognized American poet of recognized competence, and a poetry critic of recognized competence''—that Ehrlich drew the highest qualitative judgment on ''Howl.'' ''Its merit is extraordinarily high,'' Rexroth said. ''It is probably the most remarkable single poem published by a young man since the second war.''

THE SUMMING UP

McIntosh made an effort to discredit the poem by bringing in two expert witnesses of his own to testify in rebuttal.

One was David Kirk, assistant professor of English at the University of San Francisco, a Catholic school. Kirk condemned ''Howl'' as a ''poem apparently dedicated to a long-dead movement called Dadaism'' and as a ''weak imitation of a form that was used eighty or ninety years ago by Walt Whitman.''

The second was a blonde named Gail Potter who passed out little printed brochures announcing that she gives private lessons in speech and diction, and who offered a formidable array of qualifications as an expert. She had, she said, rewritten *Faust* from its forty original versions; she had written thirty-five feature articles; she had written a pageant for what she called ''one of the big affairs in Florida''; and she had taught at a business college, a church school for girls, and the College of Southern Florida at Lakeland.

''You feel like you are going through the gutter when you have to read that stuff,'' Miss Potter said of ''Howl.'' Then she shuddered in distaste and added: ''I didn't linger on it too long, I assure you.''

Jake Ehrlich bowed Miss Potter off the stand without a question, and that was the prosecution's case.

In the arguments of opposing counsel as the trial wound up, the debate ran true to form. McIntosh cried aloud that San Francisco was in dire danger:

''I would like you to ask yourself, Your Honor, in determining whether or not these books are obscene, would you like to see this sort of poetry printed in your local newspaper? Or would you like to have this poetry read to you over the radio as a diet? In other words, Your Honor, how far are we going to license the use of filthy, vulgar, obscene, and disgusting language? How far can we go?''

For Jake Ehrlich, ''Howl'' was honest poetry, written by an honest poet, and dirty only to the dirty-minded. As for its potential tendency to arouse lustful thoughts in readers, ''The Master'' dismissed that key question in a sentence. ''You can't think common, rotten things just because you read something in a book unless it is your purpose to read common, rotten things and apply a common, rotten purpose to what you read.''

Judge Horn took two weeks to deliberate before reaching a verdict. He took the trouble to read *Ulysses* and the famous court decisions that are part of its publishing history. He read other works that were once attacked as obscene. He read the law, both statute and common.

He found ''Howl'' not obscene and Ferlinghetti not guilty. His written opinion, although it comes from the state's lowest-ranking bench, must now stand as a major codification of obscenity law in California. ''The freedoms of speech and press are inherent in a nation of free people,'' wrote this municipal-court judge. ''These freedoms must be protected if we are to remain free, both individually and as a nation.'' As to the controversial phrasing, Judge Horn declared: ''The people state that it is not necessary to use such words and that others would be more palatable to good taste. The answer is that life is not encased in one formula whereby everyone acts the same or conforms to a particular pattern. No two persons think alike. We are all made from the same mould, but in different patterns. Would there be any freedom of press or speech if one must reduce his vocabulary to vapid innocuous euphemism? An author should be real in treating his subject and be allowed to express his thoughts and ideas in his own words.''

Nothing has been heard from Captain Hanrahan since, and ''Howl'' is now a best-seller throughout San Francisco.

Throughout the postwar era, the Reverend Billy Graham has been one of the most famous and influential evangelical ministers in America, if not the most famous. In the 1950s, he gained adherents in part by peppering his sermons with diatribes against the atheistic Soviet Union. Yet even after he shed his sermons of such anti-Communist rhetoric, he remained exceptionally popular with millions of Americans while at the same time exhibiting unique political ties with and influence on the nation's presidents, from Eisenhower through at least Richard Nixon. Most studies of the postwar era present Graham as part of the political right and deal with him, chronologically, as part of the 1950s. Yet as the bulk of **Document 1.11,** *a sermon that was reprinted in the* Congressional Record *in June 1960, suggests, Graham shared some of the Beats' and the budding New Left's discontents, especially their unease with modernity, conformity, and crass materialism. Indeed, for those who look back nostalgically upon the 1950s as a golden age, Graham's diagnosis of American society in this sermon suggests that there were great troubles in the Garden of Eden. Of course, unlike the Beats or the New Left, Graham offered a different prescription to the problems that he identified, namely, the acceptance of Christ in one's life. Graham is of additional significance because he served as an important bridge between traditional fundamentalists, who were largely apolitical, and the new Christian right, which grew increasingly political in the 1970s, 1980s, and 1990s.*

Document 1.11 Billy Graham, "The National Purpose: Moral and Spiritual Cancer Found in Stress on Personal Comfort," *Congressional Record,* **86th Congress, 2nd Session, 106, part 9 (June 6, 1960), pp. 11859–11860.**

A few months ago I played golf with a man who looked and acted as though he enjoyed perfect health. Today he is dead. In spite of outward appearance he had a virulent form of cancer which within a short time took his life.

I am convinced that regardless of the outward appearance of prosperity within the corporate life of America today there is present a form of moral and spiritual cancer which can ultimately lead to our destruction unless the disease is treated and the trend reversed.

Many thoughtful Americans are disturbed because as a nation we seem bereft of a sense of purpose. We have the mood and stance of a people who have arrived and have nowhere to go.

Some of our most outstanding citizens are warning us with statements that are reminiscent of the flaming prophets of old who prophesied the doom of nations that refused to change their moral course. . . .

Many American leaders have serious doubts concerning the Nation's moral and spiritual capability to match the challenge of a dedicated, disciplined communism. I am convinced that unless we heed the warning, unless we bring Americans back to an awareness of God's moral laws, unless a moral fiber is put back into the structure of our Nation, we are headed for a national disaster.

No patient is willing to take the doctor's medicine until he has heard the diagnosis, and no one should try to prescribe a national purpose for America until he has listened to her heart.

It has been my privilege to travel and preach in nearly all the States of the country for 10 years. I have talked personally with thousands of Americans from every walk of life. My own feeling is that the heart of America is still basically sound but that the bloodstream is being poisoned with the toxins of modern life.

America is in desperate need of a moral and spiritual transfusion that will cause her to recapture some of the strength of individualism. Mass-produced machinery has given rise to mass-produced man. We are inclined to think like the Joneses, dress like the Joneses, build houses like the Joneses, and talk like the Joneses. We have become status conscious and have built for ourselves sets of status symbols.

A few weeks ago, in a visit to the Holy Land, I followed in the steps of some of the great nonconformists of the Bible, men such as Elijah, Amos, and Micah. I stood on top of Mount Carmel, overlooking the beautiful Israeli city of Haifa, and prayed, "Lord, help me not to be a conformist."

Psychologists tell us that we are shaped by heredity and by environment. The prophets of Israel were part of their environment, yet they were not shaped by it.

They reacted against it. They had the courage to stand for moral right—alone if necessary. We need men who will live up to their idealism and who refuse to be moral copycats.

Second, we need to recapture the Spirit of '76. While we encourage nationalism for ambitious smaller nations abroad, we discourage it at home.

Patriotism in America seems to be "old hat." If a man gets out and waves the American flag, he is now suspect or called a reactionary.

We applaud the nationalistic demonstrations in other countries. Perhaps we need a few demonstrations for America.

The Soviet Communist Party recently published 97 slogans for May Day with the accent on complete liquidation of colonialism and a production drive to overtake the United States. Where are the American slogans?

Comdr. Vincent J. Lonergan, a Roman Catholic chaplain, warned participants at the White House Conference on Children and Youth recently that "far too many of [our youth] have been led to believe that patriotism is a phony virtue, that military service is an intolerable burden to be avoided as a plague, or if imposed upon them to be carried out grudgingly, without pride, without honor. It is extremely important that we imbue them with the spirit of intelligent sacrifice that is our heritage as Americans."

What a heartening thing it would be to see the people of America making the spirit of '76 the spirit of 1960.

Third, we need to recapture hardness and discipline in our national life. Our excessive allotment of leisure in an affluent society is making dullards out of us. Thousands of our young men are not even able to pass the Army physical examination. We play too much and work too little. We overeat, overdrink, oversex, and overplay, but few of us are ever overexercised.

We have become surfeited in this land of plenty. Our sedentary way of life has brought an alarming rash of coronaries and related illnesses. We may be the richest people in the world, but we are far from being the sturdiest.

The Bible warns: "Woe to them that are at ease in Zion." We need to recapture the love and dedication of hard work.

Fourth, we must recapture the courage of our fathers. The chairman of the history department of one of our great universities recently confided in me, "We have become a nation of cowards."

I challenged him on this statement, but his arguments were convincing. The great courage that once was so characteristic of America and Americans seems to be going. Many of our military leaders are deeply concerned about the disappearance of the will to fight for what we believe. We seem to be content to sit within the security of our homes and watch the brave western heroes on television doing the things that inwardly we wish we had the courage to do.

What boldness we may have is vicarious and reflected in the fictional acts on the screen. We are content to live in a world of fantasy and cringe at the thought of becoming personally involved with life.

We are so intent on saving our own skins that we are in danger of losing our souls . . .

Fifth, we must recapture the American challenge. William James 50 years ago observed that America needs ''a moral equivalent of war'' to challenge it. The rise of the beatniks is at least a pitiful attempt to find a challenge. Dr. Robert Lindner, the late Baltimore psychoanalyst, wrote the book ''Rebel Without a Cause.''

Dr. Lindner found that American youth feel they are so surrounded by conformity that they rebel for the sake of rebelling. This is the psychological basis of our teenage delinquency.

We need a challenge such as our forefathers had when they transformed this wilderness into a civilized nation. While the challenge of the present hour may take different forms, I believe it is even greater than what the early Americans faced.

What is the American challenge? What is our reason for existence? There are a thousand challenges that should stir our emotions and demand the dedication of every fiber of our being. Some of them may be:

The challenge to be on the side of the little people of the world, the hungry, the homeless, the friendless, the oppressed, the discriminated against, the captives and those who live in countries where there is not freedom.

The challenge to throw political expediency to the wind if necessary and to do what we know is morally right because it is right.

The challenge of sharing our immense wealth with others.

The challenge of electing men with moral courage to high office who will be ruthless with the gangsters that operate on such a wide scale throughout the Nation.

The challenge of selling the American dream and ideals to the world.

The challenge of humility to admit our failures, to repent of our sins, and to unashamedly serve God.

The challenge of solving the worldwide problems of ignorance, disease, and poverty. . . .

America still has a glorious future if we rise to the challenges, opportunities, and responsibilities of the hour. If we fail, may God help us.

Sixth, we must recapture our moral strength and our faith in God.

Some surveys of American life have been alarming and discouraging. We now know that cheating is accepted practice in our society. Morals have become irrelevant or relative—no longer are there moral absolutes. Success at any price is our maxim. We excuse our immorality by saying, ''Everybody is doing it.''

Many of our modern educators have decreed that we are what we are because of external pressures and that each of us is a victim of environment or inherent tendencies and that we cannot help what we are.

This is totally contrary to the teachings of the Holy Scripture. The Bible teaches that we are responsible for our moral choices.

We cannot possibly exist if we reject the time-honored absolutes of the Ten Commandments and the Sermon on the Mount. The Scripture says:

''Righteousness exalteth a nation, but sin is a reproach to my people.''

The Nation is no longer shocked at exposes. Our conscience is being hardened and the Scriptures warn against a hardening conscience. . . .

It is absolutely impossible to change society and reverse the moral trend unless we ourselves are changed from the inside out. Man needs transformation or conversion. Unless we Americans are willing to humbly accept the diagnosis of the "Book" upon which our culture was largely founded—and to accept its remedy—we are going to continue along the road to disaster and ruin.

The Scriptures warn: "To whom much is given, much is required." Because our privileges have been greater, our responsibilities are greater; thus, a Holy God requires more of the American people than of any nation in the history of the world with the possible exception of Israel. Our only way to moral reform is through repentance of our sins and a return to God.

Chapter Two

THE END OF AMERICAN INNOCENCE

The 1960s began with Americans in an optimistic mood, with public opinion polls reflecting the nation's sense that it was experiencing a modern-day Camelot. In early 1962, according to a Gallup poll, 80 percent of Americans approved of the job President Kennedy was doing. While his numbers dipped during the summer of 1962, they rebounded to a remarkably healthy 75 percent following the October 1962 missile crisis. Paradoxically, the early 1960s also witnessed a groundswell of political protest and gave rise to a number of bleak assessments about the times. Perhaps the best way to reconcile these seemingly contradictory trends is to suggest that Kennedy raised the expectations of some to the point that they could not be met. In addition, while the young president's youth and vigor gave rise to idealism, his inexperience and lofty rhetoric generated fears that the nation might be heading for the abyss. Put differently, whereas the Eisenhower administration exuded a spirit of complacency that bred apathy, the Kennedy administration exuded a spirit of activism that in turn shook people out of their complacency.

Nowhere was the process of raised hopes and unmet expectations more clear than among African Americans, who beginning with the Montgomery bus boycott of 1955 displayed their determination to challenge the racial status quo. To an extent, Kennedy profited from this development. Campaigning as the candidate who could best move forward the civil rights agenda, he narrowly defeated Richard Nixon by winning a significantly larger percentage of the black vote than had Adlai Stevenson, the Democratic nominee in 1952 and 1956. Yet once elected, Kennedy felt compelled to go slow on civil rights lest he lose the support of southern whites, one of the core constituents of the Democratic Party.

Documents 2.1 *and* **2.2** *provide a glimpse of the budding civil rights movement,* *especially the nonviolent direct-action wing of the movement that blossomed in the early 1960s, in part due to a frustration with the ability of the mainstream civil rights movement, embodied by the National Association for the Advancement of Colored People (NAACP) to gain real change (as opposed to favorable court decisions). In* **Document 2.1,** *the Reverend James Lawson, one of the organizers of the civil rights movement in Nashville, defines the objectives of the Student Nonviolent Coordinating Committee (SNCC), which was formed in the wake of the sit-ins. SNCC, as Lawson made clear, sought much more than the desegregation of lunch counters. In his words, it sought to raise the moral issue, and it demanded that the pace of change be quickened.*

One of those who was deeply moved by the sit-ins and SNCC's vision was Robert Moses. A graduate of Hamilton College, Moses, who had been accepted to enroll in a Ph.D. program at Harvard University, was working as a math teacher in New York City when the sit-ins erupted. As soon as he could, Moses journeyed south to join the budding freedom movement. After a brief stint in SNCC's headquarters in Atlanta, he set out to organize a voter–education/registration campaign in one of the most repressive and racist regions of the nation, rural Mississippi. Not long after he began his work in McComb, Mississippi, however, one of those he recruited to his campaign, Herbert Lee, was shot to death in broad daylight. Undeterred, Moses and others conducted a freedom march, for which Moses and several other activists were arrested. While serving the prison sentence that followed his conviction, Moses wrote a letter, **Document 2.2.** *Although brief, the letter is one of the most profound documents of the entire period. After his release from prison, Moses continued to build a freedom movement in Mississippi that arguably produced more fundamental change in the way people lived than any other movement of the era.*

Document 2.1   James M. Lawson, Jr., "From a Lunch-Counter Stool," April 1960, Student Nonviolent Coordinating Committee Papers, Martin Luther King, Jr., Center for Nonviolent Social Change, Atlanta, Georgia.

These are exciting moments in which to live. Reflect how over the last few weeks, the "sit-in" movement has leaped from campus to campus, until today hardly any campus remains unaffected. At the beginning of the decade, the student generation was "silent," "uncommitted," or "beatnik." But after only four months, these analogies largely used by adults appear as hasty cliches which should not have been used in the first place. The rapidity and drive of the movement indicates that all the while American students were simply waiting in suspension; waiting for the cause, that ideal, that event, that "actualizing of their faith" which would catapult their right to speak powerfully to their nation and world. . . .

But as so frequently happens, these are also enigmatic moments. Enigmatic, for like man in every age who cannot read the signs of the times, many of us are not able to see what appears before us, or hear what is spoken from lunch-counter stools, or understand what has been cried behind jail cell bars.

Already the paralysis of talk, the disobedience of piety, the frustration of false ambition, and the insensitivity of an affluent society yearns to diffuse the meaning and flatten the thrust of America's first non-violent campaign.

One great university equates the movement to simply another student fad similar to a panty raid, or long black stockings. . . . Amid this welter of irrelevant and superficial reactions, the primary motifs of the movement, the essential message, the crucial issues raised are often completely missed. So the Christian student who has not yet given his support or mind to the movement might well want to know what the issue is all about. Is it just a lot of nonsense over a hamburger? Or is it far more?

To begin, let us note what the issue is not. . . .

Police partiality is not the issue. Nashville has been considered one of those "good" cities where racial violence has not been tolerated. Yet, on a Saturday in February, the mystique of yet another popular myth vanished. For only police permissiveness invited young white men to take over store after store in an effort to further intimidate or crush the "sit-in." Law enforcement agents accustomed to viewing crime, were able to mark well-dressed students waiting to make purchases, as loitering on the lunch-counter stools, but they were unable even to suspect and certainly not to see assault and battery. . . . Such partiality, however, is symptomatic of the diagnosis only—an inevitable by-product—another means of avoiding the encounter. But the "sit-in" does not intend to make such partiality the issue.

Already many well-meaning and notable voices are seeking to define the problem in purely legal terms. But if the students wanted a legal case, they had only to initiate a suit. But not a single sit-in began in this fashion. No one planned to be arrested or desired such. The legal battles which will be fought as a consequence of many arrests never once touch on the matter of eating where you normally shop, or on segregation *per se*. . . .

Let us admit readily that some of the major victories gained for social justice have come through the courts. . . . The Negro has been a law-abiding citizen as he has struggled for justice against many unlawful elements.

But the major defeats have occurred when we have been unable to convince the nation to support or implement the Constitution, when a court decision is ignored or nullified by local and state action. A democratic structure of law remains democratic, remains lawful only as the people are continuously persuaded to be democratic. Law is always nullified by practice and disdain unless the minds and hearts of a people sustain law. . . .

Eventually our society must abide by the Constitution and not permit any local law or custom to hinder freedom or justice. But such a society lives by more than law. In the same respect the sit-in movement is not trying to create a legal battle, but points to that which is more than law.

Finally, the issue is not integration. This is particularly true of the Christian oriented person. Certainly the students are asking in behalf of the entire Negro community and the nation that these eating counters become places of service for all persons. But it would be extremely short-sighted to assume that integration is the problem or the word of the "sit-in." To the extent to which the movement reflects deep Christian impulses, desegregation is a necessary next step. But it cannot be the end. If progress has not been at a genuine pace, it is often because the major groups seeking equal rights tactically made desegregation the end and not the means.

The Christian favors the breaking down of racial barriers because the redeemed community of which he is already a citizen recognizes no barriers dividing humanity. The Kingdom of God, as in heaven so on earth, is the distant goal of the Christian. That Kingdom is far more than the immediate need for integration. . . .

In the first instance, we who are demonstrators are trying to raise what we call the "moral issue." That is, we are pointing to the viciousness of racial segregation and prejudice and calling it evil or sin. The matter is not legal, sociological or racial, it is moral and spiritual. Until America (South and North) honestly accepts the sinful nature of racism, this cancerous disease will continue to rape all of us. . . .

In the second instance, the non-violent movement is asserting, "get moving." The pace of social change is too slow. At this rate it will be at least another generation before the major forms of segregation disappear. All of Africa will be free before the American Negro attains first-class citizenship. Most of us will be grandparents before we can live normal human lives.

The choice of the non-violent method, "the sit-in," symbolizes both judgment and promise. It is a judgment upon middle-class conventional, half-way efforts to deal with radical social evil. It is specifically a judgment upon contemporary civil rights attempts. As one high school student from Chattanooga exclaimed, "We started because we were tired of waiting for you to act. . . ."

But the sit-in is likewise a sign of promise: God's promise that if radical Christian methods are adopted the rate of change can be vastly increased. Under Christian non-violence, Negro students reject the hardship of disobedient passivity and fear, but embrace the hardship (violence and jail) of obedience. Such non-violence strips the segregationalist power structure of its major weapon: the manipulation of law or law-enforcement to keep the Negro in his place.

Document 2.2   Robert Moses, "Letter from a Mississippi Jail Cell" (1961), Howard Zinn, *SNCC: The New Abolitionists* (Boston: Beacon Press, 1964), p. 76.

We are smuggling this note from the drunk tank of the county jail in Magnolia, Mississippi. Twelve of us are here, sprawled out along the concrete bunker; Curtis Hayes, Hollis Watkins, Ike Lewis and Robert Talbert, four veterans of the bunker, are sitting up talking—mostly about girls; Charles McDew ("Tell the story") is curled into the concrete and the wall; Harold Robinson, Stephen Ashley, James Wells, Lee Chester Vick, Leotus Eubanks, and Ivory Diggs lay cramped on the cold bunker; I'm sitting with smuggled pen and paper, thinking a little, writing a little; Myrtis Bennett and Janie Campbell are across the way wedded to a different icy cubicle.

Later on Hollis will lead out with a clear tenor into a freedom song; Talbert and Lewis will supply jokes; and McDew will discourse on the history of the black man and the Jew. McDew—a black by birth, a Jew by choice and a revolutionary by necessity—has taken on the deep hates and deep loves which America, and the world, reserve for those who dare to stand in a strong sun and cast a sharp shadow.

In the words of Judge Brumfield, who sentenced us, we are "cold calculators" who design to disrupt the racial harmony (harmonious since 1619) of McComb into racial strife and rioting; we, he said, are the leaders who are causing young children to be led like sheep to the pen to be slaughtered (in a legal manner). "Robert," he was addressing me, "haven't some of the people from your school been able to go down and register without violence here in Pike county?" I thought to myself that Southerners are most exposed when they boast.

It's mealtime now: we have rice and gravy in a flat pan, dry bread and a "big town cake"; we lack eating and drinking utensils. Water comes from a faucet and goes into a hole.

This is Mississippi, the middle of the iceberg. Hollis is leading off with his tenor, "Michael, row the boat ashore, Alleluia; Christian brothers don't be slow, Alleluia; Mississippi's next to go, Alleluia." This is a tremor in the middle of the iceberg—from a stone that the builders rejected.

Among those shaken out of their complacency by the civil rights movement was Tom Hayden. A journalism student at the University of Michigan, Hayden traveled to Mississippi to report on Moses' efforts for his college newspaper the Michigan Daily. *Upon returning to campus, Hayden became deeply involved with the Students for a Democratic Society (SDS), which at the time was a relatively small left-liberal student group with a nucleus of activists at the University of Michigan. In 1962, when SDS decided to write a mission statement, it turned to Hayden to serve as its prime author. Called the "Port Huron Statement" because it was adopted by a convention of SDSers at the United Automobile Workers' Port Huron retreat, the manifesto, excerpted in* **Document 2.3,** *expressed the group's deep concern over the failure of the nation to deliver on the promise of equality for all, the ever-present threat of atomic war, the problem of apathy, and the disappearance of real participatory democracy in the body politic. By the end of the decade, SDS had tens of thousands of members and stood as the most prominent radical organization in the nation.*

Document 2.4, *"The Sharon Statement," written by the Young Americans for Freedom (YAF), reminds us that the 1960s gave rise to organizing efforts among conservative as well as left-leaning students. Like SDS, YAF sought to spell out its beliefs in a succinct manifesto as a means to attract adherents. YAF's statement was written in the living room of William F. Buckley's Sharon estate. Buckley had founded the* National Review *in the 1950s, the most important conservative journal in the nation. While neither "The Sharon Statement" nor YAF gained as much attention or as many adherents as the "Port Huron Statement" and SDS, respec-*

tively, many YAF members remained committed to their goals. Even after the Gold-water debacle of 1964, YAF continued to promote its conservative agenda, an effort that in some ways finally paid dividends with the rise of the New Right and the election of Ronald Reagan in 1980.

Document 2.3   Students for a Democratic Society, "Port Huron Statement" (1962), Students for a Democratic Society Papers, State Historical Society of Wisconsin, Madison, Wisconsin.

INTRODUCTION: AGENDA FOR A GENERATION

We are people of this generation, bred in at least modest comfort, housed now in universities, looking uncomfortably to the world we inherit.

When we were kids the United States was the wealthiest and strongest country in the world; the only one with the atom bomb, the least scarred by modern war, an initiator of the United Nations that we thought would distribute Western influence throughout the world. Freedom and equality for each individual, government of, by, and for the people—these American values we found good, principles by which we could live as men. Many of us began maturing in complacency.

As we grew, however, our comfort was penetrated by events too troubling to dismiss. First, the permeating and victimizing fact of human degradation, symbolized by the Southern struggle against racial bigotry, compelled most of us from silence to activism. Second, the enclosing fact of the Cold War, symbolized by the presence of the Bomb, brought awareness that we ourselves, and our friends, and millions of abstract "others" we knew more directly because of our common peril, might die at any time. We might deliberately ignore, or avoid, or fail to feel all other human problems, but not these two, for these were too immediate and crushing in their impact, too challenging in the demand that we as individuals take the responsibility for encounter and resolution.

While these and other problems either directly oppressed us or rankled our consciences and became our own subjective concerns, we began to see complicated and disturbing paradoxes in our surrounding America. The declaration "all men are created equal . . ." rang hollow before the facts of Negro life in the South and the big cities of the North. The proclaimed peaceful intentions of the United States contradicted its economic and military investments in the Cold War status quo.

We witnessed, and continue to witness, other paradoxes. With nuclear energy whole cities can easily be powered, yet the dominant nation-states seem more likely to unleash destruction greater than that incurred in all wars of human history. Although our own technology is destroying old and creating new forms of social organization, men still tolerate meaningless work and idleness. While two-thirds of mankind suffers undernourishment, our own upper classes revel amidst superfluous abundance. Although world population is expected to double in forty years, the nations still tolerate anarchy as a major principle of international conduct and uncontrolled exploitation governs the sapping of the earth's physical resources. Although mankind desperately needs revolutionary leadership, America rests in national stalemate, its goal ambiguous and tradition-bound instead of informed and clear, its democratic system apathetic and manipulated rather than "of, by, and for the people."

Not only did tarnish appear on our image of American virtue, not only did disillusion occur when the hypocrisy of American ideals was discovered, but we began to sense that what we had originally seen as the American Golden Age was actually the decline of an era. The worldwide outbreak of revolution against colonialism and imperialism, the entrenchment of totalitarian states, the menace of war, overpopulation, international disorder, supertechnology—these trends were testing the tenacity of our own commitment to democracy and freedom and our abilities to visualize their application to a world in upheaval.

Our work is guided by the sense that we may be the last generation in the experiment with living. But we are a minority—the vast majority of our people regard the temporary equilibriums of our society and world as eternally-functional parts. In this is perhaps the outstanding paradox: we ourselves are imbued with urgency, yet the message of our society is that there is no viable alternative to the present. Beneath the reassuring tones of the politicians, beneath the common opinion that America will "muddle through," beneath the stagnation of those who have closed their minds to the future, is the pervading feeling that there simply are no alternatives, that our times have witnessed the exhaustion not only of Utopias, but of any new departures as well. Feeling the press of complexity upon the emptiness of life, people are fearful of the thought that at any moment things might be thrust out of control. They fear change itself, since change might smash whatever invisible framework seems to hold back chaos for them now. For most Americans, all crusades are suspect, threatening. The fact that each individual sees apathy in his fellows perpetuates the common reluctance to organize for change. The dominant institutions are complex enough to blunt the minds of their potential critics, and entrenched enough to swiftly dissipate or entirely repel the energies of protest and reform, thus limiting human expectancies. Then, too, we are a materially improved society, and by our own improvements we seem to have weakened the case for further change.

Some would have us believe that Americans feel contentment amidst prosperity—but might it not better be called a glaze above deeply-felt anxieties about their role in the new world? And if these anxieties produce a developed indifference to human affairs, do they not as well produce a yearning to believe there *is* an alternative to the present, that something *can* be done to change circumstances in the school, the workplaces, the bureaucracies, the government? It is to this latter yearning, at once the spark and engine of change, that we direct our present appeal. The search for truly democratic alternatives to the present, and a commitment to social experimentation with them, is a worthy and fulfilling human enterprise, one which moves us and, we hope, others today. On such a basis do we offer this document of our convictions and analysis: as an effort in understanding and changing the conditions of humanity in the late twentieth century, an effort rooted in the ancient, still unfulfilled conception of man attaining determining influence over his circumstances of life.

Document 2.4   Young Americans for Freedom, "The Sharon Statement" (1960), http://ualvm.va.edu: 80/~bamayaf4/

ADOPTED IN CONFERENCE AT SHARON, CONNECTICUT, ON 11 SEPTEMBER 1960.

In this time of moral and political crises, it is the responsibility of the youth of America to affirm certain eternal truths.

We, as young conservatives, believe:

That foremost among the transcendent values is the individual's use of his God-given free will, whence derives his right to be free from the restrictions of arbitrary force;

That liberty is indivisible, and that political freedom cannot long exist without economic freedom;

That the purpose of government is to protect those freedoms through the preservation of internal order, the provision of national defense, and the administration of justice;

That when government ventures beyond these rightful functions, it accumulates power, which tends to diminish order and liberty;

That the Constitution of the United States is the best arrangement yet devised for empowering government to fulfill its proper role, while restraining it from the concentration and abuse of power;

That the genius of the Constitution—the division of powers—is summed up in the clause that reserves primacy to the several states, or to the people, in those spheres not specifically delegated to the Federal government;

That the market economy, allocating resources by the free play of supply and demand, is the single economic system compatible with the requirements of personal freedom and constitutional government, and that it is at the same time the most productive supplier of human needs;

That when government interferes with the work of the market economy, it tends to reduce the moral and physical strength of the nation; that when it takes from one man to bestow on another, it diminishes the incentive of the first, the integrity of the second, and the moral autonomy of both;

That we will be free only so long as the national sovereignty of the United States is secure; that history shows periods of freedom are rare, and can exist only when free citizens concertedly defend their rights against all enemies;

That the forces of international Communism are, at present, the greatest single threat to these liberties;

That the United States should stress victory over, rather than coexistence with, this menace; and

That American foreign policy must be judged by this criterion: does it serve the just interests of the United States?

Document 2.5, *which comes from the testimony of two members of Women Strike for Peace (WSP) before the House Committee on Un-American Activities (HUAC), provides further insight into some of the political trends of the early 1960s. Throughout the late 1940s and 1950s, HUAC stood as one of the most prominent governmental watchdogs against communism and internal subversion. While its influence waned in the latter part of the 1950s, it still remained a formidable force, stultifying much dissent. In 1962, it held hearings to determine the extent of Communist influence in the burgeoning peace movement. Topping its list of suspects were the leaders of Women Strike for Peace. To the surprise of many, the leaders of WSP refused to be cowed by the committee. Insisting that they joined WSP because of their motherly interest in securing a safe and healthy environment for their children, Blanche Posner, Dagmar Wilson, and other WSPers disarmed the all-male committee, which did not know how to respond to such a counterattack. The testimony of the WSP members also displays the rising tide of anti-anticommunism, which bound together many New Left groups, and suggests that the threat of the atomic bomb, which SDS listed as one of the two major problems facing the world, shook some adults out of their complacency as well.*

Document 2.5   Women Strike for Peace, "Testimony before the House Committee on Un-American Activities," *Hearings: Communist Activities in the Peace Movement,* **December 11–13, 1962 (Washington, D.C.: GPO, 1963), pp. 2073–2075, 2187–2201.**

TESTIMONY OF BLANCHE HOFRICHTER POSNER, ACCOMPANIED BY COUNSEL, VICTOR RABINOWITZ

Mr. NITTLE. Would you state your full name and address for the record?

Mrs. POSNER. Blanche Hofrichter Posner, 67 Sprain Valley Road, Scarsdale, N.Y.

Mr. NITTLE. Are you represented by counsel?

Mrs. POSNER. Yes, sir.

Mr. NITTLE. Would counsel kindly identify himself for the record, stating his name and office address?

Mr. RABINOWITZ. Victor Rabinowitz, 30 East 42d Street, New York.

Mr. NITTLE. Mrs. Posner, would you state the date and place of your birth, please?

Mrs. POSNER. Is the date material? After all, I am a woman, you know. I shall say, though, I am over 21. I was born in Vienna, Austria, quite a number of years ago.

Mr. NITTLE. That will suffice.

Mrs. POSNER. Thank you.

Mr. NITTLE. Was your maiden name Hofrichter?

Mrs. POSNER. Yes, sir.

Mr. NITTLE. Are you a citizen of the United States?

Mrs. POSNER. Yes, sir.

Mr. NITTLE. How and when did you become a citizen?

Mrs. POSNER. Through my father, who became a citizen.

Mr. NITTLE. Mrs. Posner, would you relate the extent of your formal education?

Mrs. POSNER. Well, I got a B.A. degree from Hunter College. I took postgraduate work at New York University, City College, and Columbia, where I almost got an M.A., but I got bored.

Mr. NITTLE. What is your present occupation?

Mrs. POSNER. Housewife.

Mr. NITTLE. Prior to that, were you occupied as a teacher?

Mrs. POSNER. Yes, sir.

Mr. NITTLE. Do you hold an official position in an organization known as Women Strike for Peace?
(Witness conferred with counsel.)

Mrs. POSNER. I must decline to answer that question and I should be very grateful if you would let me say why.

Mr. NITTLE. We are only interested in whether or not you are presenting a legal reason and basis for your refusal to testify. Therefore, I will ask you simply this, and ask you not to make a statement but to respond to the inquiry: Do you assign as your basis for your refusal to testify the constitutional privilege of the fifth amendment?
(Witness conferred with counsel.)

Mrs. POSNER. I should like to decline to answer the question, but I must please plead with you to let me say why. I have———

Mr. NITTLE. Mr. Chairman, I respectfully request that the witness be directed to answer the question addressed to her.

Mr. DOYLE. I instruct the witness to answer the question. We believe it is a pertinent question and entirely proper.
(Witness conferred with counsel.)

Mrs. POSNER. I don't know, sir, why I am here, but I do know why you are here. I think———

Mr. NITTLE. Mr. Chairman, I must ask for regular order.

Mrs. POSNER.———because you don't quite understand the nature of this movement. This movement was inspired and motivated by mothers' love for their children.

Mr. NITTLE. Mr. Chairman?

Mrs. POSNER. When they were putting their breakfast on the table, they saw not only wheaties and milk, but they also saw strontium 90 and iodine 131.

Mr. DOYLE. Just a moment.

Mrs. POSNER. They feared for the health and life of their children. That is the only motivation.

Mr. DOYLE. Witness! Now, Witness——

Mrs. POSNER. If you gentlemen have children or grandchildren, you should be grateful to the Women Strike for Peace, or whatever peace movement is working to stop nuclear testing. Every nuclear test has resulted in malformations, has resulted in stillbirths, has resulted in leukemia, has resulted in cancer, has resulted in the possibility of a nuclear holocaust.

I have given to you gentlemen this statement which presents some of the reasons why women are concerned.

Mr. DOYLE. Now, Witness, just a minute. I will have to declare you out of order. If you insist on interrupting the hearing, we will have to ask that you be removed from the hearing room. I do not want to do that, and you do not want it. So please cooperate. You have made your little speech. Now proceed and either cooperate with the committee or not, just as you choose.

(Witness conferred with counsel.)

Mr. DOYLE. I order and direct you to answer that question. We believe it is pertinent, legally. You have made your speech, and we have been glad to give you 2 or 3 minutes to make it. But that is it.

(Witness conferred with counsel.)

Mrs. POSNER. By virtue of the statement, this will be just the one sentence, Mr. Doyle, by virtue of the statement that you read at this hearing, I must at this point decline to cooperate with the committee and thank God that the framers of our Constitution and the Bill of Rights included the fifth amendment, which I now invoke. . . .

TESTIMONY OF DAGMAR WILSON, ACCOMPANIED BY COUNSEL, LAWRENCE SPEISER

Mr. NITTLE. Would you state your name and address for the record, please.

Mrs. WILSON. My name is Dagmar Wilson. I live at 1413 29th Street, NW., Washington, D.C.

Mr. NITTLE. You are represented by counsel?

Mrs. WILSON. I am.

Mr. NITTLE. Would counsel kindly identify himself, stating his name and office address.

Mr. SPEISER. Lawrence Speiser, offices at the American Civil Liberties Union, 1101 Vermont Avenue, NW., Washington, D.C.

Mr. NITTLE. Mrs. Wilson, at the outset the committee wishes to make clear just why you have been subpenaed [*sic*] to appear and testify in this hearing. I believe you understand that the committee is presently investigating Communist infiltration of peace groups in this country, with particular attention to Women Strike for Peace, an organization of which, from published reports, you are the recognized leader. These hearings have also been particularly directed to the Metropolitan New York, New Jersey, and Connecticut section of Women Strike for Peace movement.

The committee has no evidence of Communist Party membership, or activity in support of front groups or of pro-Communist sympathies on your part, and this we wish to emphasize.

However, several of the witnesses who have already been heard by the committee and who have occupied leadership positions in the New York section of this movement have refused to divulge certain pertinent information about their organization, its formation, its leadership, and its activities.

The committee believes that you, as a leader of the movement and as a patriotic American citizen, will cooperate in this inquiry. I wish to make it clear that the committee is not interested in your beliefs or opinions and will not make inquiry into them. It is concerned only with factual information relative to the subject under inquiry.

With that introductory statement, would you please state the date and place of your birth?

As to the date of your birth, you may simply state that you are over 21 years of age, if you wish.

Mrs. WILSON. Thank you. I don't mind telling you. I was born in 1916 in New York City.

Mr. NITTLE. Would you relate the extent of your formal education?

Mrs. WILSON. Yes. I completed high school in London in 1934 and in the autumn of that year I went to the Slate School, which is the Art Department of London University. There I spent 4 years.

Mr. NITTLE. Are you the leader or coordinator of a movement known as Women Strike for Peace, which has its headquarters at 1822 Massachusetts Avenue, NW., Washington 6, D.C.?

Mrs. WILSON. It is rather a hard question to answer. People like to call me leader. I regard it as more a term of endearment or, shall we say, an honorary title. I think I can best qualify it in this way.

It was as a result of my initiative that this grassroots movement sprang into being.

Mr. NITTLE. The *New York Times* of November 22, 1961, quoted you as follows: "I think it's about time I stop being head of this. We have many excellent volunteers. I just happened to be the starter."

Apparently at one time you did refer to yourself as being the head of Women Strike for Peace?

Mrs. WILSON. I think we were all kind of groping for what to call me, largely because the press wanted an answer to this, and I have been given various titles such as coordinator, leader. We knew I wasn't the president. We didn't have an organization.

But I think I better just assume the honorary title, although I have no special function. We are really all leaders, you know.

Mr. NITTLE. And I am judging by what you say that the New York group would be under its own steam and the leaders of that group would not be controlled by you as the "head" of the national movement. Is that right?

Mrs. WILSON. Well, nobody is controlled by anybody in the Women Strike for Peace. We do have, however, communication with each other constantly, and I can explain how we do that later if you would like me to. . . .

Mr. NITTLE. Now I want to refer to the picketing of the United Nations on February 20, 1962, which was for the announced purpose of protesting President Kennedy's decision to resume nuclear testing. Was that your idea?

Mrs. WILSON. I think we all demonstrated on that day. We were most disturbed.

Mr. NITTLE. What I mean to say is, Did you call for that particular demonstration and did you initiate it?

Mrs. WILSON. I am not quite sure about that specific one, but it would have worked in exactly the same way as all our other demonstrations did. One area would think of an idea for an action, shall we say, and will then communicate with other groups throughout the country, and in each city where they want to take this action they will do so. Now, in this city it was of course in front of the White House that we demonstrated. In New York it was in front of the United Nations.

Mr. NITTLE. Do you know whether the idea in this particular instance originated from any member of the New York group of Women Strike for Peace?

Mrs. WILSON. Well, I am quite sure you know that this one originated spontaneously in many areas, because one of the things that we are violently against is nuclear testing.

Mr. NITTLE. Now, of course, Mrs. Wilson, I think you will agree that coordinated activities participated in by many people in many parts of the country on the same day do not occur "spontaneously." There must be a suggestion and some kind of communication.

Mrs. WILSON. Certainly, all communications.

Mr. NITTLE. I also want to refer to a very spectacular instance, and that was the sending of 51 delegates to the Geneva disarmament conference in April 1962. I would like to ask whether the idea for doing this was originally conceived by you.

Mrs. WILSON. No. Again, I wish I had thought of it.

Mr. NITTLE. Could you tell the committee, if you know, whether this idea originated from any member of the New York group?

Mrs. WILSON. Well, I think this time it was really New York's baby and I think they should be proud of it. . . .

Mr. NITTLE. The Communist newspaper, *The Worker*, of February 25, 1962, reported that you took part in and spoke at the Women Strike for Peace picketing of the United Nations headquarters in New York City on February 20, 1962. You did speak at the New York U.N. picketing on that date, did you not?

Mrs. WILSON. I prefer you to call it a demonstration. Picketing sounds so hostile. Yes, I spoke there.

Mr. NITTLE. That newspaper reported:

> When Mrs. Dagmar Wilson, a Washington D.C. housewife who initiated this woman's movement for peace rose to speak there was silence. It was the first time Mrs. Wilson had participated in a New York peace action.

Was that journal correct in saying that this was the first time you had participated in any Women Strike for Peace action in New York?

Mrs. WILSON. Well, it was the first time I had participated in a public peace action.

Mr. NITTLE. Was your participation in that demonstration your own idea, or did you do that at the request of the New York group?

Mrs. WILSON. They kindly invited me, and I felt very pleased.

Mr. NITTLE. Prior to that February 20 demonstration, had you at any time consulted with the leadership of the New York group concerning the activities of Women Strike for Peace in that area?

Mrs. WILSON. Again I would like to qualify the word "leadership." We are all leaders. I had met with large numbers of ladies in New York before that, yes.

Mr. NITTLE. Had you at any time, prior to February 20, at least exercised any direction or control of the activities of the New York group?

Mrs. WILSON. I think I already said that nobody controls anybody.

Mr. NITTLE. And since that time you have not directed or controlled any of the New York group's activity?

Mrs. WILSON. No, but cooperated; cooperated, yes. . . .

Mr. NITTLE. I am about to conclude the staff interrogation, with the permission of the Chair, and I would like to pose a few remaining questions in concluding. I think you have observed during the course of your attendance at these hearings that numerous Communist directives, and evidence produced in these hearings, indicate that a present major objective of the Communist Party is the infiltration of peace groups. I would like to ask whether you would knowingly permit or encourage a Communist Party member to occupy a leadership position in Women Strike for Peace?

Mrs. WILSON. Well, my dear sir, I have absolutely no way of controlling, do not desire to control, who wishes to join in the demonstrations and the efforts that the women strikers have made for peace.

In fact I would also like to go even further. I would like to say that unless everybody in the whole world joins us in this fight, then God help us.

Mr. NITTLE. Would you knowingly permit or welcome Nazis or Fascists to occupy leadership positions in Women Strike for Peace?

Mrs. WILSON. Whether we could get them or not, I don't think we could.[1]

Mr. NITTLE. Am I correct, then, in assuming that you plan to take no action designed to prevent Communists from assuming positions of leadership in the movement or to eliminate Communists who may have already obtained such positions?

Mrs. WILSON. Certainly not.

Mr. NITTLE. The staff has no further questions, Mr. Chairman.

In 1962, Rachel Carson burst on the public scene with the publication of Silent Spring, *her analysis of the dangers posed to the environment and to the health of her family by DDT and other chemicals. Although much of the agricultural-industrial complex sought to discredit Carson as a nonscientist, a Communist, and a hysterical woman, she found a very receptive audience among the public at large.* **Document 2.6** *consists of excerpts from her testimony to the Ribicoff Committee, which was established to investigate and ultimately recommend environmental regulations. Unlike HUAC, Ribicoff's committee was friendly to Carson and used her testimony to build support for several environmental laws that were passed in the latter half of the 1960s.*

Document 2.6   Rachel Carson, "Testimony before the Ribicoff Committee," Senate Subcommittee on Reorganization and International Organization, June 4, 1963, in *Interagency Coordination in Environmental Hazards* (Washington, D.C.: GPO, 1964), pp. 206–246.

PESTICIDES ONLY A PART OF THE LARGER PROBLEM OF ENVIRONMENTAL CONTAMINATION

Miss CARSON. Contamination of various kinds has now invaded all of the physical environment that supports us—water, soil, air, and vegetation. It has even penetrated that internal environment that lies within the bodies of animals and of men. It comes from many sources: radioactive wastes from reactors, laboratories, and hospitals; fallout from nuclear explosions; domestic wastes from cities and towns; chemical wastes from factories; detergents from homes and industries.

When we review the history of mankind in relation to the earth we cannot help feeling somewhat discouraged, for that history is for the most part one of the blind or shortsighted despoiling of the soil, forests, waters, and all the rest of the earth's resources. We have acquired technical skills on a scale undreamed of even a generation ago. We can do dramatic things and we can do them quickly; by the time damaging side effects are apparent it is often too late, or impossible, to reverse our actions. These are unpleasant facts, but they have given rise to the disturbing situations that this committee has now undertaken to examine.

1. Despite the fact that this is the response recorded by the official reporter for the hearings, newspapermen covering the hearings reported—and members of the committee and its staff distinctly recall—that Mrs. Wilson's actual reply to the preceding question was: "If only we could get them on our side."

I have pointed out before, and I shall repeat now, that the problem of pesticides can be properly understood only in context, as part of the general introduction of harmful substances into the environment. In water and soil, and in our own bodies, these chemicals are mingled with others, or with radioactive substances. There are little understood interactions and summations of effect. No one fully understands, for example, what happens when pesticide residues stored in our bodies interact with drugs repeatedly taken. And there are some indications that detergents, which are often present in our drinking water, may affect the lining of the digestive tract so that it more readily absorbs cancer-causing chemicals. . . .

INTELLIGENT USE—NOT ELIMINATION—THE OBJECTIVE

Senator RIBICOFF. Thank you very much for this most enlightening testimony, and for what is even more important, your recommendations. Miss Carson, there can be no doubt that you are the person most responsible for the current public concern over pesticide hazards.

It also appears to me that in the public mind the issue has been reduced to a sharp conflict between Rachel Carson on one hand and the manufacturers of agricultural chemicals on the other. It seems to me the issues here can't be drawn that sharply.

I wonder whether your position has been somewhat misunderstood or perhaps misinterpreted. I think it would be helpful if we could have the basis of your outline made clear for the record, and also for the future guidance of this committee. For instance, isn't it fair to say that you are not trying to stop the use of chemical poisons?

Miss CARSON. That is a fair statement; yes. It would not be possible, even if we wished to do so, to eliminate all chemicals tomorrow.

A great deal of the discussion of "Silent Spring" and of the issues has, as you say, been placed on an all-or-none basis, which is not correct. This is not what I advocated, sir.

Senator RIBICOFF. In other words, you recognize that many of these chemical poisons have produced many benefits both to public health in combating disease, and to nutritional health in improving the quality of our food supply.

Miss CARSON. They have produced benefits. My concern is about the serious side effects.

I think that we have had our eyes too exclusively on the benefits, and we have failed to recognize that there are also many side effects which must be taken into consideration. However, what I have advocated is not the complete abandonment of chemical control. I think chemicals do have a place. In fact, I have cited with great approval the coordination of chemical and biological controls such as is applied, for example, in the apple orchards of Nova Scotia. . . .

Senator RIBICOFF. And am I correct, then, that your primary objective is against the indiscriminate use of pesticides and use where they are not necessary, and their excessive use even where they are necessary?

Miss CARSON. That is correct, and I think that instead of automatically reaching for the spray gun or calling in the spray planes, we must consider the whole problem. We must find out first whether there is any other method that can be used.

If there is not, then we should use chemicals as sparingly and as selectively as we can, and we should use them in such a way that we do not destroy the controls that are built into the environment.

Senator RIBICOFF. In other words, you do not believe that next spring will be the silent spring, but that injury to wildlife and to man himself will become an ever-increasing threat in the years ahead, unless proper safeguards are developed and new techniques, such as biological controls, are put into practice.

Miss CARSON. I think we must begin now to take account of the hazards and to change our methods where and when we can. . . .

Senator GRUENING. Miss Carson, every once in a while in the history of mankind a book has appeared which has substantially altered the course of history. I think that sometimes those books are in fiction form and sometimes not.

One can think of many examples, such as Uncle Tom's Cabin, for instance. Your book is of that important character, and I feel you have rendered a tremendous service.

I want to ask you one or two questions bearing on answers you have just given which appear to me to be somewhat in contrast to what you have said if not in your prepared testimony today, then in contrast with what appears in your book, "Silent Spring," which I think is a tremendously important piece of research. . . .

Well, now it is obvious that we are facing a very, very difficult problem of regulation here. You have on the one hand a tremendous investment and profit motive of those who manufacture these chemicals, as against the nonprofitable introduction of parasites.

There is no money in introducing parasites to destroy the evil insects. So you have this tremendous conflict.

Miss CARSON. Yes; but I think you balance the public interest there against the other.

Senator GRUENING. Well, I think it is up to those who are concerned with the public interest to try to achieve that, but that isn't always easy.

What would you think of creating in one of the agencies—you see, there are several agencies that are concerned with this. There is the Department of Health, Education, and Welfare, which is concerned primarily with the health of human beings. You have the Department of Agriculture, which is concerned with agricultural production and elimination of pests that destroy vegetation, food and fiber and you have the Department of the Interior, which is concerned with fish and wildlife.

What would you think of creating a department of ecology that would have an overall supervision of these functions, or at least an agency of ecology in one of those departments that would try to coordinate these conflicting interests?

There certainly would be conflict on the one hand between the people who want to preserve animals, wildlife, fish, and those who want to preserve agricultural products, and overall, of course, the effect on human beings, which is the most important of all.

Miss CARSON. This department you are thinking of would also include the ecology of man?

Senator GRUENING. Yes, indeed, primarily the ecology of man. It seems to me that we are dealing essentially with an ecological problem here.

Miss CARSON. Well, it certainly is a good objective. Whether it is feasible to do this I don't really know. . . .

MISS CARSON'S BACKGROUND AND EXPERIENCE

Senator PEARSON. If I were an attorney interrogating an expert witness, I would just waive your qualifications as a brilliant writer, which are apparent. But we are dealing with a subject here which is quite confusing for one such as myself. The correct identification of certain compounds and the degree of effect of them is extremely important. I wonder—you described yourself in your testimony as a biologist—if for the benefit of the committee and the record you would further state your studies and qualifications.

Miss CARSON. Yes, I will be glad to.

Senator PEARSON. Besides your own research for this book.

Miss CARSON. Yes. To go back to my background, I was graduated from college with a major in zoology. I went on to Johns Hopkins University in Baltimore, where I took my master's degree in zoology, there specializing in embryology and genetics.

I then became quite interested in ecological matters or the basic relation between organisms and their environment.

I carried on studies at the Marine Biological Laboratory in Woods Hole, and then in 1936, I believe, I became a biologist on the staff of what was then called the U.S. Bureau of Fisheries. I was for 16 years a Government biologist with the Bureau of Fisheries, and with its successor, the Fish and Wildlife Service.

I resigned from the Service in 1952, in order to devote my further time to writing. But before I left the Service, as you will remember, in the mid-1940's the new synthetic insecticides had come into use, and we in the Service were faced with the problem of trying to determine the effect of these pesticides on birds and fishes and other wildlife. That was a concern felt by many people in the Service in those years, and I shared it.

About 5 years ago then I came back to this subject, to begin a study of what had happened in the more than a decade of use—about a decade and a half of use of this great variety of new and very toxic chemicals.

So about 5 years ago I began this survey of the problem, which I have continued and which led to the writing of "Silent Spring."

A number of startling events tested America's sense of optimism during the latter part of John F. Kennedy's tenure as president. In South Vietnam, Buddhist monks set themselves on fire in protest against the American-backed Diem regime. In Oxford, Mississippi, whites went on a rampage to protest against the enrollment of a black man, James Meredith, at the University of Mississippi. In Birmingham, Alabama, Sheriff "Bull" Connor attacked nonviolent demonstrators with water cannon and vicious guard dogs. Even more disturbing, the missile crisis of October 1962 left many fearing that the world was on the verge of a nuclear holocaust. On October 15, U.S. spy planes uncovered the establishment of missile bases on the island of Cuba, presumably capable of firing Soviet-built nuclear warheads at the United

States. Ever since Fidel Castro had taken power in the late 1950s, relations between Cuba and the United States had been poor. The Bay of Pigs fiasco, in which the Kennedy administration had attempted to overthrow Castro, only worsened the situation, further driving Cuba into the Soviet orbit. **Document 2.7** *consists of President Kennedy's nationally televised address on the missile crisis, in which the public first became aware of the existence of missiles and the administration's decision to risk war with the Soviets in order to get the missiles removed. Ultimately the crisis was resolved peacefully. The Soviets chose not to challenge the U.S. blockade or quarantine of the island and removed the missile pads. In return, the United States secretly agreed not to invade Cuba and to remove its missiles from Turkey.*

Document 2.7   John F. Kennedy, "Address to the Nation on the Missile Crisis," October 22, 1962, *Public Papers of the Presidents of the United States, John F. Kennedy, 1962* (Washington, D.C.: GPO, 1963), pp. 806–809.

Good evening, my fellow citizens:

This Government, as promised, has maintained the closest surveillance of the Soviet military buildup on the island of Cuba. Within the past week, unmistakable evidence has established the fact that a series of offensive missile sites is now in preparation on that imprisoned island. The purpose of these bases can be none other than to provide a nuclear strike capability against the Western Hemisphere.

Upon receiving the first preliminary hard information of this nature last Tuesday morning at 9 A.M., I directed that our surveillance be stepped up. And having now confirmed and completed our evaluation of the evidence and our decision on a course of action, this Government feels obliged to report this new crisis to you in fullest detail.

The characteristics of these new missile sites indicate two distinct types of installations. Several of them include medium range ballistic missiles, capable of carrying a nuclear warhead for a distance of more than 1,000 nautical miles. Each of these missiles, in short, is capable of striking Washington, D.C., the Panama Canal, Cape Canaveral, Mexico City, or any other city in the southeastern part of the United States, in Central America, or in the Caribbean area.

Additional sites not yet completed appear to be designed for intermediate range ballistic missiles—capable of traveling more than twice as far—and thus capable of striking most of the major cities in the Western Hemisphere, ranging as far north as Hudson Bay, Canada, and as far south as Lima, Peru. In addition, jet bombers, capable of carrying nuclear weapons, are now being uncrated and assembled in Cuba, while the necessary air bases are being prepared.

This urgent transformation of Cuba into an important strategic base—by the presence of these large, long-range, and clearly offensive weapons of sudden mass destruction—constitutes an explicit threat to the peace and security of all the Americas, in flagrant and deliberate defiance of the Rio Pact of 1947, the traditions of this Nation and hemisphere, the joint resolution of the 87th Congress, the Charter of the United Nations, and my own public warnings to the Soviets on September 4 and 13. This action also contradicts the repeated assurances of Soviet spokesmen, both publicly and privately delivered, that the arms buildup in Cuba would retain its original defensive character, and that the Soviet Union had no need or desire to station strategic missiles on the territory of any other nation.

The size of this undertaking makes clear that it has been planned for some months. Yet only last month, after I had made clear the distinction between any introduction of ground-to-ground missiles and the existence of defensive anti-aircraft missiles, the Soviet Government publicly stated on September 11 that, and I quote, "the armaments and military equipment sent to Cuba are designed exclusively for defensive purposes," that, and I quote the Soviet Government, "there is no need for the Soviet Government to shift its weapons . . . for a retaliatory blow to any other country, for instance Cuba," and that, and I quote their government, "the Soviet Union has so powerful rockets to carry these nuclear warheads that there is no need to search for sites for them beyond the boundaries of the Soviet Union." That statement was false.

Only last Thursday, as evidence of this rapid offensive buildup was already in my hand, Soviet Foreign Minister Gromyko told me in my office that he was instructed to make it clear once again, as he said his government had already done, that Soviet assistance to Cuba, and I quote, "pursued solely the purpose of contributing to the defense capabilities of Cuba," that, and I quote him, "training by Soviet specialists of Cuban nationals in handling defensive armaments was by no means offensive, and if it were otherwise," Mr. Gromyko went on, "the Soviet Government would never become involved in rendering such assistance." That statement also was false.

Neither the United States of America nor the world community of nations can tolerate deliberate deception and offensive threats on the part of any nation, large or small. We no longer live in a world where only the actual firing of weapons represents a sufficient challenge to a nation's security to constitute maximum peril. Nuclear weapons are so destructive and ballistic missiles are so swift, that any substantially increased possibility of their use or any sudden change in their deployment may well be regarded as a definite threat to peace.

For many years, both the Soviet Union and the United States, recognizing this fact, have deployed strategic nuclear weapons with great care, never upsetting the precarious status quo which insured that these weapons would not be used in the absence of some vital challenge. Our own strategic missiles have never been transferred to the territory of any other nation under a cloak of secrecy and deception; and our history—unlike that of the Soviets since the end of World War II—demonstrates that we have no desire to dominate or conquer any other nation or impose our system upon its people. Nevertheless, American citizens have become adjusted to living daily on the bull's-eye of Soviet missiles located inside the U.S.S.R. or in submarines.

In that sense, missiles in Cuba add to an already clear and present danger—

although it should be noted the nations of Latin America have never previously been subjected to a potential nuclear threat.

But this secret, swift, and extraordinary buildup of Communist missiles—in an area well known to have a special and historical relationship to the United States and the nations of the Western Hemisphere, in violation of Soviet assurances, and in defiance of American and hemispheric policy—this sudden, clandestine decision to station strategic weapons for the first time outside of Soviet soil—is a deliberately provocative and unjustified change in the status quo which cannot be accepted by this country, if our courage and our commitments are ever to be trusted again by either friend or foe.

The 1930's taught us a clear lesson: aggressive conduct, if allowed to go unchecked and unchallenged, ultimately leads to war. This nation is opposed to war. We are also true to our word. Our unswerving objective, therefore, must be to prevent the use of these missiles against this or any other country, and to secure their withdrawal or elimination from the Western Hemisphere.

Our policy has been one of patience and restraint, as befits a peaceful and powerful nation, which leads a worldwide alliance. We have been determined not to be diverted from our central concerns by mere irritants and fanatics. But now further action is required—and it is under way; and these actions may only be the beginning. We will not prematurely or unnecessarily risk the costs of worldwide nuclear war in which even the fruits of victory would be ashes in our mouth—but neither will we shrink from that risk at any time it must be faced.

Acting, therefore, in the defense of our own security and of the entire Western Hemisphere, and under the authority entrusted to me by the Constitution as endorsed by the resolution of the Congress, I have directed that the following *initial* steps be taken immediately:

First: To halt this offensive buildup, a strict quarantine on all offensive military equipment under shipment to Cuba is being initiated. All ships of any kind bound for Cuba from whatever nation or port will, if found to contain cargoes of offensive weapons, be turned back. This quarantine will be extended, if needed, to other types of cargo and carriers. We are not at this time, however, denying the necessities of life as the Soviets attempted to do in their Berlin blockade of 1948.

Second: I have directed the continued and increased close surveillance of Cuba and its military buildup. The foreign ministers of the OAS, in their communique of October 6, rejected secrecy on such matters in this hemisphere. Should these offensive military preparations continue, thus increasing the threat to the hemisphere, further action will be justified. I have directed the Armed Forces to prepare for any eventualities; and I trust that in the interest of both the Cuban people and the Soviet technicians at the sites, the hazards to all concerned of continuing this threat will be recognized.

Third: It shall be the policy of this Nation to regard any nuclear missile launched from Cuba against any nation in the Western Hemisphere as an attack by the Soviet Union on the United States, requiring a full retaliatory response upon the Soviet Union.

Fourth: As a necessary military precaution, I have reinforced our base at Guantanamo, evacuated today the dependents of our personnel there, and ordered additional military units to be on a standby alert basis.

Fifth: We are calling tonight for an immediate meeting of the Organ of Consultation under the Organization of American States, to consider this threat to hemispheric security and to invoke articles 6 and 8 of the Rio Treaty in support of all necessary action. The United Nations Charter allows for regional security arrangements—and the nations of this hemisphere decided long ago against the military presence of outside powers. Our other allies around the world have also been alerted.

Sixth: Under the Charter of the United Nations, we are asking tonight that an emergency meeting of the Security Council be convoked without delay to take action against this latest Soviet threat to world peace. Our resolution will call for the prompt dismantling and withdrawal of all offensive weapons in Cuba, under the supervision of U.N. observers, before the quarantine can be lifted.

Seventh and finally: I call upon Chairman Khrushchev to halt and eliminate this clandestine, reckless, and provocative threat to world peace and to stable relations between our two nations. I call upon him further to abandon this course of world domination, and to join in an historic effort to end the perilous arms race and to transform the history of man. He has an opportunity now to move the world back from the abyss of destruction—by returning to his government's own words that it had no need to station missiles outside its own territory, and withdrawing these weapons from Cuba—by refraining from any action which will widen or deepen the present crisis—and then by participating in a search for peaceful and permanent solutions.

Even more than the missile crisis, President Kennedy's assassination threw nearly the entire nation into a state of shock. Decades later, the members of nearly an entire generation could remember where they were at the time. The fact that people heard about the assassination instantaneously, saw pictures of it, and viewed his funeral on television added to their dismay. As Life *magazine observed, "it is as though the entire nation had been in Ford's Theater" when Lincoln was shot. Hoping to quell the nation's fears, President Johnson appointed a commission to determine if a plot or conspiracy against the government accounted for Kennedy's assassination or if Lee Harvey Oswald, the alleged assassin, had acted alone. (The fact that Oswald was shot while in police custody by Jack Ruby, a man with reputed Mafia contacts, added to public concerns over the nature of the shooting.) Even though the commission was headed by Supreme Court Chief Justice Earl Warren, an Eisenhower nominee, and included a bipartisan group of prominent public figures, such as future president Gerald Ford, and even though the published part of the commission's report, excerpted in* **Document 2.8,** *ran to nearly one thousand pages, its findings never satisfied many Americans. Perhaps because they could not accept* *the argument that a single lone gunman could kill the most powerful man in the world, perhaps because they vested in Kennedy all that was good about America, or perhaps because of their increasing distrust of the government, many lent credence to much more conspiratorial explanations for his murder.*

Document 2.8 Warren Commission, *Report of the President's Commission on the Assassination of President John F. Kennedy* (Washington, D.C.: GPO, 1964), pp. 1–25.

SUMMARY AND CONCLUSIONS

The assassination of John Fitzgerald Kennedy on November 22, 1963, was a cruel and shocking act of violence directed against a man, a family, a nation, and against all mankind. A young and vigorous leader whose years of public and private life stretched before him was the victim of the fourth Presidential assassination in the history of a country dedicated to the concepts of reasoned argument and peaceful political change. This Commission was created on November 29, 1963, in recognition of the right of people everywhere to full and truthful knowledge concerning these events. This report endeavors to fulfill that right and to appraise this tragedy by the light of reason and the standard of fairness. It has been prepared with a deep awareness of the Commission's responsibility to present to the American people an objective report of the facts relating to the assassination.

Narrative of Events

At 11:40 a.m., c.s.t., on Friday, November 22, 1963, President John F. Kennedy, Mrs. Kennedy, and their party arrived at Love Field, Dallas, Tex. Behind them was the first day of a Texas trip planned 5 months before by the President, Vice President Lyndon B. Johnson, and John B. Connally, Jr., Governor of Texas. After leaving the White House on Thursday morning, the President had flown initially to San Antonio where Vice President Lyndon B. Johnson joined the party and the President dedicated new research facilities at the U.S. Air Force School of Aerospace Medicine. Following a testimonial dinner in Houston for U.S. Representative Albert Thomas, the President flew to Fort Worth where he spent the night and spoke at a large breakfast gathering on Friday.

Planned for later that day were a motorcade through downtown Dallas, a luncheon speech at the Trade Mart, and a flight to Austin where the President would attend a reception and speak at a Democratic fundraising dinner. From Austin he would proceed to the Texas ranch of the Vice President. Evident on this trip were the varied roles which an American President performs—Head of State, Chief Executive, party leader, and, in this instance, prospective candidate for reelection.

The Dallas motorcade, it was hoped, would evoke a demonstration of the President's personal popularity in a city which he had lost in the 1960 election. Once it had been decided that the trip to Texas would span 2 days, those responsible for planning, primarily Governor Connally and Kenneth O'Donnell, a special assistant to the President, agreed that a motorcade through Dallas would be desirable. The Secret Service was told on November 8 that 45 minutes had been allotted to a motorcade procession from Love Field to the site of a luncheon planned by Dallas business and civic leaders in honor of the President. After considering the facilities and security problems of several buildings, the Trade Mart was chosen as the luncheon site. Given this selection, and in accordance with the customary practice of affording the greatest number of people an opportunity to see the President, the motorcade route selected was a natural one. The route was approved by the local host committee and White House representatives on November 18 and publicized in the local papers starting on November 19. This advance publicity made it clear that the motorcade would leave Main Street and pass the intersection of Elm and Houston Streets as it proceeded to the Trade Mart by way of the Stemmons Freeway.

By midmorning of November 22, clearing skies in Dallas dispelled the threat of rain and the President greeted the crowds from his open limousine without the "bubbletop," which was at that time a plastic shield furnishing protection only against inclement weather. To the left of the President in the rear seat was Mrs. Kennedy. In the jump seats were Governor Connally, who was in front of the President, and Mrs. Connally at the Governor's left. Agent William R. Greer of the Secret Service was driving, and Agent Roy H. Kellerman was sitting to his right.

Directly behind the Presidential limousine was an open "followup" car with eight Secret Service agents, two in the front seat, two in the rear, and two on each running board. These agents, in accordance with normal Secret Service procedures, were instructed to scan the crowds, the roofs, and windows of buildings, overpasses, and crossings for signs of trouble. Behind the "followup" car was the Vice-Presidential car carrying the Vice President and Mrs. Johnson and Senator Ralph W. Yarborough. Next were a Vice-Presidential "followup" car and several cars and buses for additional dignitaries, press representatives, and others.

The motorcade left Love Field shortly after 11:50 a.m., and proceeded through residential neighborhoods, stopping twice at the President's request to greet well-wishers among the friendly crowds. Each time the President's car halted, Secret Service agents from the "followup" car moved forward to assume a protective stance near the President and Mrs. Kennedy. As the motorcade reached Main Street, a principal east-west artery in downtown Dallas, the welcome became tumultuous. At the extreme west end of Main Street the motorcade turned right on Houston Street and proceeded north for one block in order to make a left turn on Elm Street, the most direct and convenient approach to the Stemmons Freeway and the Trade Mart. As the President's car approached the intersection of Houston and Elm Streets, there loomed directly ahead on the intersection's northwest corner a seven-story, orange brick warehouse and office building, the Texas School Book Depository. Riding in the

Vice President's car, Agent Rufus W. Youngblood of the Secret Service noticed that the clock atop the building indicated 12:30 p.m., the scheduled arrival time at the Trade Mart.

The President's car which had been going north made a sharp turn toward the southwest onto Elm Street. At a speed of about 11 miles per hour, it started down the gradual descent toward a railroad overpass under which the motorcade would proceed before reaching the Stemmons Freeway. The front of the Texas School Book Depository was now on the President's right, and he waved to the crowd assembled there as he passed the building. Dealey Plaza—an open, landscaped area marking the western end of downtown Dallas—stretched out to the President's left. A Secret Service agent riding in the motorcade radioed the Trade Mart that the President would arrive in 5 minutes.

Seconds later shots resounded in rapid succession. The President's hands moved to his neck. He appeared to stiffen momentarily and lurched slightly forward in his seat. A bullet had entered the base of the back of his neck slightly to the right of the spine. It traveled downward and exited from the front of the neck, causing a nick in the left lower portion of the knot in the president's necktie. Before the shooting started, Governor Connally had been facing toward the crowd on the right. He started to turn toward the left and suddenly felt a blow on his back. The Governor had been hit by a bullet which entered at the extreme right side of his back at a point below his right armpit. The bullet traveled through his chest in a downward and forward direction, exited below his right nipple, passed through his right wrist which had been in his lap, and then caused a wound to his left thigh. The force of the bullet's impact appeared to spin the Governor to his right, and Mrs. Connally pulled him down into her lap. Another bullet then struck President Kennedy in the rear portion of his head, causing a massive and fatal wound. The President fell to the left into Mrs. Kennedy's lap.

Secret Service Agent Clinton J. Hill, riding on the left running board of the "followup" car, heard a noise which sounded like a firecracker and saw the President suddenly lean forward and to the left. Hill jumped off the car and raced toward the President's limousine. In the front seat of the Vice-Presidential car, Agent Youngblood heard an explosion and noticed unusual movements in the crowd. He vaulted into the rear seat and sat on the Vice President in order to protect him. At the same time Agent Kellerman in the front seat of the Presidential limousine turned to observe the President. Seeing that the President was struck, Kellerman instructed the driver, "Let's get out of here; we are hit." He radioed ahead to the lead car, "Get us to the hospital immediately." Agent Greer immediately accelerated the Presidential car. As it gained speed, Agent Hill managed to pull himself onto the back of the car where Mrs. Kennedy had climbed. Hill pushed her back into the rear seat and shielded the stricken President and Mrs. Kennedy as the President's car proceeded at high speed to Parkland Memorial Hospital, 4 miles away.

At Parkland, the President was immediately treated by a team of physicians who had been alerted for the President's arrival by the Dallas Police Department as the result of a radio message from the motorcade after the shooting. The doctors noted irregular breathing movements and a possible heartbeat, although they could not detect a pulsebeat. They observed the extensive wound in the President's head and a small wound approximately one-fourth inch in diameter in the lower third of his neck. In an effort to facilitate breathing, the physicians performed a tracheotomy by enlarging the throat wound and inserting a tube. Totally absorbed in the immediate task of trying to preserve the President's life, the attending doctors never turned the President over for an examination of his back. At 1 p.m., after all heart activity ceased and the Last Rites were administered by a priest, President Kennedy was pronounced dead. Governor Connally underwent surgery and ultimately recovered from his serious wounds.

Upon learning of the President's death, Vice President Johnson left Parkland Hospital under close guard and proceeded to the Presidential plane at Love Field. Mrs. Kennedy, accompanying her husband's body, boarded the plane shortly thereafter. At 2:38 p.m., in the central compartment of the plane, Lyndon B. Johnson was sworn in as the 36th President of the United States by Federal District Court Judge Sarah T. Hughes. The plane left immediately for Washington, D.C., arriving at Andrews AFB, Md., at 5:58 p.m., e.s.t. The President's body was taken to the National Naval Medical Center, Bethesda, Md., where it was given a complete pathological examination. The autopsy disclosed the large head wound observed at Parkland and the wound in the front of the neck which had been enlarged by the Parkland doctors when they performed the tracheotomy. Both of these wounds were described in the autopsy report as being "presumably of exit." In addition the autopsy revealed a small wound of entry in the rear of the President's skull and another wound of entry near the base of the back of the neck. The autopsy report stated the cause of death as "Gunshot wound, head," and the bullets which struck the President were described as having been fired "from a point behind and somewhat above the level of the deceased." . . .

Conclusions

This Commission was created to ascertain the facts relating to the preceding summary of events and to consider the important questions which they raised. The Commission has addressed itself to this task and has reached certain conclusions based on all the available evidence. No limitations have been placed on the Commission's inquiry; it has conducted its own investigation, and all Government agencies have fully discharged their responsibility to cooperate with the Commission in its investigation. These conclusions represent the reasoned judgment of all members of the Commission and are presented after an investigation which has satisfied the Commission that it has ascertained the truth concerning the assassination of President Kennedy to the extent that a prolonged and thorough search makes this possible.

1. The shots which killed President Kennedy and wounded Governor Connally were fired from the sixth floor window at the southeast corner of the Texas School Book Depository. This determination is based upon the following:

(*a*) Witnesses at the scene of the assassination saw a rifle being fired from the sixth floor window of the Depository Building, and some witnesses saw a rifle in the window immediately after the shots were fired.

(*b*) The nearly whole bullet found on Governor Connally's stretcher at Parkland Memorial Hospital and the two bullet fragments found in the front seat of the Presidential limousine were fired from the 6.5-millimeter Mannlicher-Carcano rifle found on the sixth floor of the Depository Building to the exclusion of all other weapons.

(*c*) The three used cartridge cases found near the window on the sixth floor at the southeast corner of the building were fired from the same rifle which fired the above-described bullet and fragments, to the exclusion of all other weapons.

(*d*) The windshield in the Presidential limousine was struck by a bullet fragment on the inside surface of the glass, but was not penetrated.

(*e*) The nature of the bullet wounds suffered by President Kennedy and Governor Connally and the location of the car at the time of the shots establish that the bullets were fired from above and behind the Presidential limousine, striking the President and the Governor as follows:

(1) President Kennedy was first struck by a bullet which entered at the back of his neck and exited through the lower front portion of his neck, causing a wound which would not necessarily have been lethal. The President was struck a second time by a bullet which entered the right-rear portion of his head, causing a massive and fatal wound.

(2) Governor Connally was struck by a bullet which entered on the right side of his back and traveled downward through the right side of his chest, exiting below his right nipple. This bullet then passed through his right wrist and entered his left thigh where it caused a superficial wound.

(*f*) There is no credible evidence that the shots were fired from the Triple Underpass, ahead of the motorcade, or from any other location.

2. The weight of the evidence indicates that there were three shots fired.

3. Although it is not necessary to any essential findings of the Commission to determine just which shot hit Governor Connally, there is very persuasive evidence from the experts to indicate that the same bullet which pierced the President's throat also caused Governor Connally's wounds. However, Governor Connally's testimony and certain other factors have given rise to some difference of opinion as to this probability but there is no question in the mind of any member of the Commission that all the shots which caused the President's and Governor Connally's wounds were fired from the sixth floor window of the Texas School Book Depository.

4. The shots which killed President Kennedy and wounded Governor Connally were fired by Lee Harvey Oswald. This conclusion is based upon the following:

(*a*) The Mannlicher-Carcano 6.5-millimeter Italian rifle from which the shots were fired was owned by and in the possession of Oswald.

(*b*) Oswald carried this rifle into the Depository Building on the morning of November 22, 1963.

(*c*) Oswald, at the time of the assassination, was present at the window from which the shots were fired.

(*d*) Shortly after the assassination, the Mannlicher-Carcano rifle belonging to Oswald was found partially hidden between some cartons on the sixth floor and the improvised paper bag in which Oswald brought the rifle to the Depository was found close by the window from which the shots were fired.

(*e*) Based on testimony of the experts and their analysis of films of the assassination, the Commission has concluded that a rifleman of Lee Harvey Oswald's capabilities could have fired the shots from the rifle used in the assassination within the elapsed time of the shooting. The Commission has concluded further that Oswald possessed the capability with a rifle which enabled him to commit the assassination. . . .

9. The Commission has found no evidence that either Lee Harvey Oswald or Jack Ruby was part of any conspiracy, domestic or foreign, to assassinate President Kennedy. The reasons for this conclusion are:

(*a*) The Commission has found no evidence that anyone assisted Oswald in planning or carrying out the assassination. In this connection it has thoroughly investigated, among other factors, the circumstances surrounding the planning of the motorcade route through Dallas, the hiring of Oswald by the Texas School Book Depository Co. on October 15, 1963, the method by which the rifle was brought into the building, the placing of cartons of books at the window, Oswald's escape from the building, and the testimony of eyewitnesses to the shooting.

(*b*) The Commission has found no evidence that Oswald was involved with any person or group in a conspiracy to assassinate the President, although it has thoroughly investigated, in addition to other possible leads, all facets of Oswald's associations, finances, and personal habits, particularly during the period following his return from the Soviet Union in June 1962.

(*c*) The Commission has found no evidence to show that Oswald was employed, persuaded, or encouraged by any foreign government to assassinate President Kennedy or that he was an agent of any foreign government, although the Commission has reviewed the circumstances surrounding Oswald's defection to the Soviet Union, his life there from October of 1959 to June of 1962 so far as it can be reconstructed, his known contacts with the Fair Play for Cuba Committee, and his visits to the Cuban and Soviet Embassies in Mexico City during his trip to Mexico from September 26 to October 3, 1963, and his known contacts with the Soviet Embassy in the United States.

(*d*) The Commission has explored all attempts of Oswald to identify himself with various political groups, including the Communist Party, U.S.A., the Fair Play for Cuba Committee, and the Socialist Workers Party, and has been unable to find any evidence that the contacts which he initiated were related to Oswald's subsequent assassination of the President.

(e) All of the evidence before the Commission established that there was nothing to support the speculation that Oswald was an agent, employee, or informant of the FBI, the CIA, or any other governmental agency. It has thoroughly investigated Oswald's relationships prior to the assassination with all agencies of the U.S. Government. All contacts with Oswald by any of these agencies were made in the regular exercise of their different responsibilities.

(f) No direct or indirect relationship between Lee Harvey Oswald and Jack Ruby has been discovered by the Commission, nor has it been able to find any credible evidence that either knew the other, although a thorough investigation was made of the many rumors and speculations of such a relationship.

(g) The Commission has found no evidence that Jack Ruby acted with any other person in the killing of Lee Harvey Oswald.

(h) After careful investigation the Commission has found no credible evidence either that Ruby and Officer Tippit, who was killed by Oswald, knew each other or that Oswald and Tippit knew each other.

Because of the difficulty of proving negatives to a certainty the possibility of others being involved with either Oswald or Ruby cannot be established categorically, but if there is any such evidence it has been beyond the reach of all the investigative agencies and resources of the United States and has not come to the attention of this Commission.

10. In its entire investigation the Commission has found no evidence of conspiracy, subversion, or disloyalty to the U.S. Government by any Federal, State, or local official.

11. On the basis of the evidence before the Commission it concludes that Oswald acted alone. Therefore, to determine the motives for the assassination of President Kennedy, one must look to the assassin himself. Clues to Oswald's motives can be found in his family history, his education or lack of it, his acts, his writings, and the recollections of those who had close contacts with him throughout his life. The Commission has presented with this report all of the background information bearing on motivation which it could discover. Thus, others may study Lee Oswald's life and arrive at their own conclusions as to his possible motives.

Five days after Kennedy was killed, Lyndon Johnson, the new president, delivered a moving speech to a special joint session of Congress and to the nation. In this speech, **Document 2.9,** *Johnson shrewdly cast a number of liberal reforms as the martyred president's will. Johnson followed up on this masterful use of the moment by using his political skills to ensure passage of a number of bills that had been stalled in Congress at the time of Kennedy's death, including a tax cut and the Civil Rights Act of 1964. Subsequently, Johnson proposed and got enacted a slew of* *reforms that President Kennedy had only begun to formulate and that might not have been passed as long as he was president. Nonetheless, many of Kennedy's closest aides, including his brother Robert, never trusted Johnson, nor he them, and Johnson never enjoyed the public support Kennedy did.*

Document 2.9 Lyndon B. Johnson, "Address to Joint Session of the House and Senate," *Congressional Record,* 88th Congress, 1st Session, 109, part 17 (November 27, 1963), pp. 22838–22839.

The PRESIDENT. Mr. Speaker, Mr. President, Members of the House, Members of the Senate, my fellow Americans, all I have I would have given gladly not to be standing here today.

The greatest leader of our time has been struck down by the foulest deed of our time. Today John Fitzgerald Kennedy lives on in the immortal words and works that he left behind. He lives on in the mind and memories of mankind. He lives on in the hearts of his countrymen.

No words are sad enough to express our sense of loss. No words are strong enough to express our determination to continue the forward thrust of America that he began. [Applause.]

The dream of conquering the vastness of space—the dream of partnership across the Atlantic, and across the Pacific as well—the dream of a Peace Corps in less developed nations—the dream of education for all of our children—the dream of jobs for all who seek them and need them—the dream of care for our elderly—the dream of an all-out attack on mental illness—and above all, the dream of equal rights for all Americans, whatever their race or color [applause]—these and other American dreams have been vitalized by his drive and by his dedication.

Now the ideas and the ideals which he so nobly represented must and will be translated into effective action. [Applause.]

Under John Kennedy's leadership, this Nation has demonstrated that it has the courage to seek peace, and it has the fortitude to risk war. We have proved that we are a good and reliable friend to those who seek peace and freedom. We have shown that we can also be a formidable foe to those who reject the path of peace and those who seek to impose upon us or our allies the yoke of tyranny.

This Nation will keep its commitments from South Vietnam to West Berlin. [Applause.] We will be unceasing in the search for peace; resourceful in our pursuit of areas of agreement, even with those with whom we differ—and generous and loyal to those who join with us in common cause.

In this age when there can be no losers in peace and no victors in war, we must recognize the obligation to match national strength with national restraint. [Applause.] We must be prepared at one and the same time for both the confrontation of power and the limitation of power. We must be ready to defend the national interest and to negotiate the common interest. This is the path that we shall continue to pursue. Those who test our courage will find it strong and those who seek our friendship will find it honorable. We will demonstrate anew that the strong can be just in the use of strength—and the just can be strong in the defense of justice. And let all know we will extend no special privilege and impose no persecution.

We will carry on the fight against poverty and misery, ignorance and disease—in other lands and in our own.

We will serve all of the Nation, not one section or one sector, or one group, but all Americans. [Applause.] These are the United States—a united people with a united purpose.

Our American unity does not depend upon unanimity. We have differences; but now, as in the past, we can derive from those differences strength, not weakness, wisdom, not despair. Both as a people and as a Government we can unite upon a program, a program which is wise, just, enlightened, and constructive.

For 32 years, Capitol Hill has been my home. I have shared many moments of pride with you—pride in the ability of the Congress of the United States to act; to meet any crisis; to distill from our differences strong programs of national action.

An assassin's bullet has thrust upon me the awesome burden of the Presidency. I am here today to say I need your help, I cannot bear this burden alone. I need the help of all Americans in all America. [Applause.] This Nation has experienced a profound shock and in this critical moment it is our duty—yours and mine—as the Government of the United States—to do away with uncertainty and doubt and delay and to show that we are capable of decisive action [applause]—that from the brutal loss of our leader we will derive not weakness but strength—that we can and will act and act now.

From this Chamber of representative government let all the world know, and none misunderstand, that I rededicate this Government to the unswerving support of the United Nations [applause]—to the honorable and determined execution of our commitments to our allies [applause]—to the maintenance of military strength second to none—to the defense of the strength and stability of the dollar [applause]—to the expansion of our foreign trade [applause]—to the reinforcement of our programs of mutual assistance and cooperation in Asia and Africa [applause]—and to our Alliance for Progress in this hemisphere. [Applause.]

On the 20th day of January, in 1961, John F. Kennedy told his countrymen that our national work would not be finished "in the first thousand days, nor in the life of this administration, nor even perhaps in our lifetime on this planet. But"—he said—"let us begin."

Today in this moment of new resolve, I would say to my fellow Americans, let us continue. [Applause.]

This is our challenge—not to hesitate, not to pause, not to turn about and linger over this evil moment but to continue on our course so that we may fulfill the destiny that history has set for us. Our most immediate tasks are here on this Hill.

First, no memorial oration or eulogy could more eloquently honor President Kennedy's memory than the earliest possible passage of the civil rights bill for which he fought so long. [Applause.] We have talked long enough in this country about equal rights. We have talked for 100 years or more. It is time now to write the next chapter—and to write it in the books of law. [Applause.]

I urge you again, as I did in 1957, and again in 1960, to enact a civil rights law so that we can move forward to eliminate from this Nation every trace of discrimination and oppression that is based upon race or color. [Applause.] There could be no greater source of strength to this Nation both at home and abroad.

And second, no act of ours could more fittingly continue the work of President Kennedy than the early passage of the tax bill for which he fought all this long year. [Applause.] This is a bill designed to increase our national income and Federal revenues, and to provide insurance against recession. That bill, if passed without delay means more security for those now working, more jobs for those now without them, and more incentive for our economy.

In short, this is no time for delay. It is time for action [applause]—strong, forward-looking action on the pending education bills to help bring the light of learning to every home and hamlet in America, strong, forward-looking action on youth employment opportunities, strong, forward-looking action on the pending foreign aid bill, making clear that we are not forfeiting our responsibilities to this hemisphere or to the world, nor erasing executive flexibility in the conduct of our foreign affairs [applause]—and strong, prompt, and forward-looking action on the remaining appropriation bills. [Applause.]

In this new spirit of action the Congress can expect the full cooperation and support of the executive branch. And in particular I pledge that the expenditures of your Government will be administered with the utmost thrift and frugality. [Applause.] I ask your help. I will insist that the Government get a dollar's value for a dollar spent. The Government will set an example of prudence and economy. [Applause.] This does not mean that we will not meet our unfilled needs or that we will not honor our commitments. We will do both.

As one who has long served in both Houses of the Congress, I firmly believe in the independence and the integrity of the legislative branch. [Applause.] I promise you that I shall always respect this. It is deep in the marrow of my bones.

With equal firmness, I believe in the capacity and I believe in the ability of the Congress, despite the divisions of opinion which characterize our Nation, to act—to act wisely, to act vigorously, to act speedily when the need arises.

The need is here. The need is now.

We meet in grief; but let us also meet in renewed dedication and renewed vigor. Let us meet in action, in tolerance and in mutual understanding.

John Kennedy's death commands what his life conveyed—that America must move forward. [Applause.] The time has come for Americans of all races and creeds and political beliefs to understand and to respect one another. [Applause.] So let us put an end to the teaching and preaching of hate and evil and violence. [Applause.] Let us turn away from the fanatics of the far left and the far right, from the apostles of bitterness and bigotry, from those defiant of law, and those who pour venom into our Nation's bloodstream. [Applause.]

I profoundly hope that the tragedy and the torment of these terrible days will bind us together in new fellowship, making us one people in our hour of sorrow. So let us here highly resolve that John Fitzgerald Kennedy did not live—or die—in vain. [Applause.] And on this Thanksgiving eve, as we gather together to ask the Lord's blessing, and give Him our thanks, let us unite in those familiar and cherished words:

> America, America,
>   God shed His grace on thee,
> And crown thy good
>   With brotherhood
> From sea to shining sea.

Chapter Three

THE BLACK FREEDOM STRUGGLE

The struggle for racial equality was central to the history of the 1960s. Sit-ins staged by black students prefigured a larger youth rebellion; the March on Washington of 1963 paved the way for numerous other protests in the nation's capital; grass-roots organizing and demonstrations produced some of the most significant legal legislation of the era, not to mention dramatic shifts in personal attitudes; urban riots and the assassination of Martin Luther King, Jr., muted the idealism of the times and gave rise to visions of a revolution and conservative backlash.

Martin Luther King, Jr.'s "Letter from a Birmingham City Jail," **Document 3.1,** *stands as one of the classic statements of the civil rights movement. On Good Friday, April 12, 1963, King and his closest associate, the Reverend Ralph Abernathy, openly defied a court injunction against marching in Birmingham, Alabama, where he and his organization, the Southern Christian Leadership Conference, were busy orchestrating a massive campaign for civil rights. For violating the injunction, King was placed under arrest and incarcerated. While in jail, he wrote this letter. In part, King's argument represented a direct response to a letter written by a group of white clergymen who urged him and Birmingham's blacks to stop demonstrating. In addition to calling for restraint, the clergymen condemned the entrance of outsiders, like King, into their community and their practice of civil disobedience. King retorted that as a Christian and as an American he had the right and responsibility to protest against injustice wherever it existed. Ironically, King's "Letter" initially received little attention. Over a month passed before a small liberal magazine, the* New Leader, *published it.*

Document 3.1   Martin Luther King, Jr., "Letter from a Birmingham City Jail," reprinted in *New Leader,* June 24, 1963, pp. 3–11.

My Dear Fellow Clergymen,

While confined here in the Birmingham City Jail, I came across your recent statements calling our present activities "unwise and untimely." . . . Since I feel that you are men of genuine good will . . . I would like to answer your statement in what I hope will be patient and reasonable terms.

I think I should give the reason for my being in Birmingham, since you have been influenced by the argument of "outsiders coming in." I have the honor of serving as president of the Southern Christian Leadership Conference. . . . We have some 85 affiliate organizations all across the South—one being the Alabama Christian Movement for Human Rights. . . . Several months ago our local affiliate here in Birmingham invited us to be on call to engage in a nonviolent direct action program if such were deemed necessary. We readily consented and when the hour came we lived up to our promises. So I am here. . . . Beyond this, I am in Birmingham because injustice is here. Just as the 8th century prophets left their little villages and carried their "thus saith the Lord" far beyond the boundaries of their home town, and just as the Apostle Paul left his little village of Tarsus and carried the gospel of Jesus Christ to practically every hamlet and city of the Graeco-Roman world, I too am compelled to carry the gospel of freedom beyond my particular home town. . . .

Moreover . . . I cannot sit idly by in Atlanta and not be concerned about what happens in Birmingham. Injustice anywhere is a threat to justice everywhere. We are caught in an inescapable network of mutuality tied in a single garment of destiny. Whatever affects one directly affects all indirectly. Never again can we afford to live with the narrow, provincial "outside agitator" idea. Anyone who lives inside the United States can never be considered an outsider anywhere in this country.

You deplore the demonstrations that are presently taking place in Birmingham. But I am sorry that your statement did not express a similar concern for the conditions that brought the demonstrations into being. I am sure that each of you would want to go beyond the superficial social analyst who looks merely at effects, and does not grapple with underlying causes. I would not hesitate to say that it is unfortunate that so-called demonstrations are taking place in Birmingham at this time, but I would say in more emphatic terms that it is even more unfortunate that the white power structure of this city left the Negro community with no other alternative. . . .

We know through painful experience that freedom is never voluntarily given by the oppressor; it must be demanded by the oppressed. Frankly I have never yet engaged in a direct action movement that was "well timed," according to the timetable of those who have not suffered unduly from the disease of segregation. For years now I have heard the word "Wait!" It rings in the ear of every Negro with piercing familiarity. This "wait" has almost always meant "never." . . . We must come to see with the distinguished jurist of yesterday that "justice too long delayed is justice denied." We have waited for more than 340 years for our constitutional and God-given rights. The nations of Asia and Africa are moving with jet-like speed toward gaining political independence, but we still creep at horse-and-buggy pace toward gaining a cup of coffee at a lunch counter. Perhaps it is easy for those who have never felt the stinging darts of segregation to say, "Wait." But when you have seen vicious mobs lynch your mothers and fathers at will and drown your sisters and brothers at whim; when you have seen hate-filled policemen curse, kick and even kill your black brothers and sisters; when you see the vast majority of your twenty million Negro brothers smothering in an airtight cage of poverty in the midst of an affluent society; when you suddenly find your tongue twisted and your speech stammering as you seek to explain to your six-year-old daughter why she can't go to the public amusement park that has just been advertised on television, and see tears welling up in her eyes when she is told that Funtown is closed to colored children, and see ominous clouds of inferiority beginning to distort her personality by developing an unconscious bitterness toward white people; when you have to concoct an answer for a five-year-old son who is asking: "Daddy, why do white people treat colored people so mean?"; when you take a cross-country drive and find it necessary to sleep night after night in the uncomfortable corners of your automobile because no motel will accept you; when you are humiliated day in and day out by nagging signs reading "white" and "colored"; when your first name becomes "boy" (however old you are) and your last name becomes "John," and your wife and mother are never given the respected title "Mrs."; when you are harried by day and haunted by night by the fact that you are a Negro, living constantly at tiptoe stance, never quite knowing what to expect next, and are plagued with inner fears and outer resentments; when you are forever fighting a degenerating sense of "nobodi-ness"—then you will understand why we find it difficult to wait. There comes a time when the cup of endurance runs over, and men are no longer willing to be plunged into the abyss of despair. I hope sirs, you can understand our legitimate and unavoidable impatience.

You express a great deal of anxiety over our willingness to break laws. This is certainly a legitimate concern. Since we so diligently urge people to obey the Supreme Court's decision of 1954 outlawing segregation in the public schools, it is rather strange and paradoxical to find us consciously breaking laws. One may well ask, "How can you advocate breaking some laws and obeying others?" The answer is found in the fact that there are *just* laws and there are *unjust* laws. I would be the first to advocate obeying just laws. One has not only a legal but a moral responsibility to obey just laws. Conversely, one has a moral responsibility to disobey unjust laws. I would agree with Saint Augustine that "An unjust law is no law at all."

. . . We can never forget that everything Hitler did in Germany was "legal" and everything the Hungarian freedom fighters did in Hungary was "illegal."

It was "illegal" to aid and comfort a Jew in Hitler's Germany. But I am sure that, if I had lived in Germany during that time, I would have aided and comforted my Jewish brothers even though it was illegal. If I lived in a Communist country today where certain principles dear to the Christian faith are suppressed, I believe I would openly advocate disobeying these anti-religious laws.

I must make two honest confessions to you, my Christian and Jewish brothers. First I must confess that over the last few years I have been gravely disappointed with the white moderate. I have almost reached the regrettable conclusion that the Negroes' great stumbling block in the stride toward freedom is not the White Citizens' "Councilor" or the Ku Klux Klaner, but the white moderate who is more devoted to "order" than to justice; who prefers a negative peace which is the absence of tension to a positive peace which is the presence of justice; who constantly says "I agree with you in the goal you seek, but I can't agree with your methods of direct action"; who paternalistically feels that he can set the timetable for another man's freedom; who lives by myth of time and who constantly advises the Negro to wait until a "more convenient season." Shallow understanding from people of good will is more frustrating than absolute misunderstanding from people of ill will. . . .

I had hoped that the white moderate would understand that law and order exist for the purpose of establishing justice, and that when they fail to do this they become the dangerously structured dams that block the flow of social progress. . . .

In your statement you asserted that our actions, even though peaceful, must be condemned because they precipitate violence. But can this assertion be logically made? Isn't this like condemning the robbed man because his possession of money precipitated the evil act of robbery? . . . Isn't this like condemning Jesus because His unique God consciousness and never-ceasing devotion to His will precipitated the evil act of crucifixion? . . .

You spoke of our activity in Birmingham as extreme. At first I was rather disappointed that fellow clergymen would see my nonviolent efforts as those of the extremist. I started thinking about the fact that I stand in the middle of two opposing forces in the Negro community. One is a force of complacency made up of Negroes who, as a result of long years of oppression, have been so completely drained of self-respect and a sense of "somebodiness" that they have adjusted to segregation, and of a few Negroes in the middle class who, because of a degree of academic and economic security, and because at points they profit by segregation, have unconsciously become insensitive to the problems of the masses. The other force is one of bitterness and hatred and comes perilously close to advocating violence. It is expressed in the various black nationalist groups that are springing up over the nation. . . . This movement is nourished by the contemporary frustration over the continued existence of racial discrimination. It is made up of people who have lost faith in America, who have absolutely repudiated Christianity, and who have concluded that the white man is an incurable "devil." . . .

I must admit that I was initially disappointed in being so categorized. . . . But as I continued to think about the matter I gradually gained a bit of satisfaction from being considered an extremist. Was not Jesus an extremist in love? . . . Was not Martin Luther an extremist? . . . Was not Abraham Lincoln? . . . Thomas Jefferson? . . .

So the question is not whether we will be extremist but what kind of extremist will we be. Will we be extremists for hate or will we be extremists for love? Will we be extremists for the preservation of injustice—or will we be extremists for the cause of justice? . . .

Before closing I am impelled to mention one other point in your statement that troubled me profoundly. You warmly commended the Birmingham police force for keeping "order" and "preventing violence." I don't believe you would have so warmly commended the police force if you had seen its angry violent dogs literally biting six unarmed, nonviolent Negroes. . . . It is true that they have been rather disciplined in their public handling of the demonstrations. In this sense they have been rather publicly "nonviolent." But for what purpose? To preserve the evil system of segregation. . . .

I wish you had commended the Negro sit-inner and demonstrators for their sublime courage, their willingness to suffer, and their amazing discipline in the midst of the most inhuman provocation. One day the South will recognize its real heroes. They will be the James Merediths, courageously and with a majestic sense of purpose, facing jeering and hostile mobs. . . . They will be old, oppressed, battered Negro women, symbolized in a 72-year-old woman of Montgomery, Alabama, who rose up with a sense of dignity and with her people decided not to ride the segregated buses, and responded to one who inquired about her tiredness with ungrammatical profundity: "My feets is tired, but my soul is rested. . . ." One day the South will know that . . . they were in reality standing up for the best in the American dream and the most sacred values in our Judeo-Christian heritage.

During the spring of 1963, civil rights protests erupted across the nation; the Justice Department estimated that at least 758 demonstrations in 186 cities in 11 southern states, in which nearly 15,000 persons were arrested, took place in a period of just 10 weeks. In mid-June, a major crisis occurred when Alabama governor George Wallace vowed to personally block the desegregation of the University of Alabama. Faced with Wallace's open defiance of the law in combination with the swelling tide of indignation against segregation, President Kennedy decided that he could no longer avoid engaging the issue of civil rights. For most of his first two years in office, Kennedy had evaded taking a strong stance because he did not want to alienate southern voters and politicians, whose support he needed to enact the rest of his domestic and foreign policy agenda. But his inability to squelch the protest convinced him that he had to act. In a nationally televised address, excerpted in **Document 3.2,** *Kennedy delivered the strongest pro–civil rights speech by a president in modern American history. Proclaiming that the nation had a moral obligation to*

*combat racism, Kennedy proposed sweeping civil rights legislation that would out-
law discrimination in public accommodations and provide protection for civil rights
activists. Such legislation, in the form of the Civil Rights Act of 1964, was enacted
after Kennedy's assassination.*

Document 3.2   John F. Kennedy, "Address to Congress," June 11, 1963, *Public Papers of the Presidents of the United States, John F. Kennedy, 1963* (Washington, D.C.: GPO, 1964), pp. 468–471.

Good evening, my fellow citizens:

This afternoon, following a series of threats and defiant statements, the presence of Alabama National Guardsmen was required on the University of
Alabama to carry out the final and unequivocal order of the United States District Court of the Northern District of Alabama. That order called for the admission of two clearly qualified young Alabama residents who happened to have
been born Negro.

That they were admitted peacefully on the campus is due in good measure to
the conduct of the students of the University of Alabama, who met their responsibilities in a constructive way.

I hope that every American, regardless of where he lives, will stop and examine his conscience about this and other related incidents. This Nation was
founded by men of many nations and backgrounds. It was founded on the principle that all men are created equal, and that the rights of every man are diminished when the rights of one man are threatened.

Today we are committed to a worldwide struggle to promote and protect the
rights of all who wish to be free. And when Americans are sent to Viet-Nam
or West Berlin, we do not ask for whites only. It ought to be possible, therefore,
for American students of any color to attend any public institution they select
without having to be backed up by troops.

It ought to be possible for American consumers of any color to receive equal
service in places of public accommodation, such as hotels and restaurants and
theaters and retail stores, without being forced to resort to demonstrations in the
street, and it ought to be possible for American citizens of any color to register
and to vote in a free election without interference or fear of reprisal.

It ought to be possible, in short, for every American to enjoy the privileges
of being American without regard to his race or his color. In short, every American ought to have the right to be treated as he would wish to be treated, as one
would wish his children to be treated. But this is not the case.

The Negro baby born in America today, regardless of the section of the Nation
in which he is born, has about one-half as much chance of completing a high
school as a white baby born in the same place on the same day, one-third as
much chance of completing college, one-third as much chance of becoming a
professional man, twice as much chance of becoming unemployed, about one-
seventh as much chance of earning $10,000 a year, a life expectancy which is
7 years shorter, and the prospects of earning only half as much.

This is not a sectional issue. Difficulties over segregation and discrimination exist in every city, in every State of the Union, producing in many cities a rising tide of discontent that threatens the public safety. Nor is this a partisan issue. In a time of domestic crisis men of good will and generosity should be able to unite regardless of party or politics. This is not even a legal or legislative issue alone. It is better to settle these matters in the courts than on the streets, and new laws are needed at every level, but law alone cannot make men see right.

We are confronted primarily with a moral issue. It is as old as the scriptures and is as clear as the American Constitution.

The heart of the question is whether all Americans are to be afforded equal rights and equal opportunities, whether we are going to treat our fellow Americans as we want to be treated. If an American, because his skin is dark, cannot eat lunch in a restaurant open to the public, if he cannot send his children to the best public school available, if he cannot vote for the public officials who represent him, if, in short, he cannot enjoy the full and free life which all of us want, then who among us would be content to have the color of his skin changed and stand in his place? Who among us would then be content with the counsels of patience and delay?

One hundred years of delay have passed since President Lincoln freed the slaves, yet their heirs, their grandsons, are not fully free. They are not yet freed from the bonds of injustice. They are not yet freed from social and economic oppression. And this Nation, for all its hopes and all its boasts, will not be fully free until all its citizens are free.

We preach freedom around the world, and we mean it, and we cherish our freedom here at home, but are we to say to the world, and much more importantly, to each other that this is a land of the free except for the Negroes; that we have no second-class citizens except Negroes; that we have no class or cast system, no ghettoes, no master race except with respect to Negroes?

Now the time has come for this Nation to fulfill its promise. The events in Birmingham and elsewhere have so increased the cries for equality that no city or State or legislative body can prudently choose to ignore them.

The fires of frustration and discord are burning in every city, North and South, where legal remedies are not at hand. Redress is sought in the streets, in demonstrations, parades, and protests which create tensions and threaten violence and threaten lives.

We face, therefore, a moral crisis as a country and as a people. It cannot be met by repressive police action. It cannot be left to increased demonstrations in the streets. It cannot be quieted by token moves or talk. It is a time to act in the Congress, in your State and local legislative body and, above all, in all of our daily lives.

It is not enough to pin the blame on others, to say this is a problem of one section of the country or another, or deplore the fact that we face. A great change is at hand, and our task, our obligation, is to make that revolution, that change, peaceful and constructive for all.

Those who do nothing are inviting shame as well as violence. Those who act boldly are recognizing right as well as reality.

Next week I shall ask the Congress of the United States to act, to make a commitment it has not fully made in this century to the proposition that race has no place in American life or law. The Federal judiciary has upheld that proposition in a series of forthright cases. The executive branch has adopted that proposition in the conduct of its affairs, including the employment of Federal personnel, the use of Federal facilities, and the sale of federally financed housing.

But there are other necessary measures which only the Congress can provide, and they must be provided at this session. The old code of equity law under which we live commands for every wrong a remedy, but in too many communities, in too many parts of the country, wrongs are inflicted on Negro citizens and there are no remedies at law. Unless the Congress acts, their only remedy is in the street.

I am, therefore, asking the Congress to enact legislation giving all Americans the right to be served in facilities which are open to the public—hotels, restaurants, theaters, retail stores, and similar establishments.

This seems to me to be an elementary right. Its denial is an arbitrary indignity that no American in 1963 should have to endure, but many do.

I have recently met with scores of business leaders urging them to take voluntary action to end this discrimination and I have been encouraged by their response, and in the last 2 weeks over 75 cities have seen progress made in desegregating these kinds of facilities. But many are unwilling to act alone, and for this reason, nationwide legislation is needed if we are to move this problem from the streets to the courts.

I am also asking Congress to authorize the Federal Government to participate more fully in lawsuits designed to end segregation in public education. We have succeeded in persuading many districts to desegregate voluntarily. Dozens have admitted Negroes without violence. Today a Negro is attending a State-supported institution in every one of our 50 States, but the pace is very slow.

Too many Negro children entering segregated grade schools at the time of the Supreme Court's decision 9 years ago will enter segregated high schools this fall, having suffered a loss which can never be restored. The lack of an adequate education denies the Negro a chance to get a decent job.

The orderly implementation of the Supreme Court decision, therefore, cannot be left solely to those who may not have the economic resources to carry the legal action or who may be subject to harassment.

Other features will be also requested, including greater protection for the right to vote. But legislation, I repeat, cannot solve this problem alone. It must be solved in the homes of every American in every community across our country.

In this respect, I want to pay tribute to those citizens North and South who have been working in their communities to make life better for all. They are acting not out of a sense of legal duty but out of a sense of human decency.

Like our soldiers and sailors in all parts of the world they are meeting freedom's challenge on the firing line, and I salute them for their honor and their courage.

My fellow Americans, this is a problem which faces us all—in every city of the North as well as the South. Today there are Negroes unemployed, two or three times as many compared to whites, inadequate in education, moving into the large cities, unable to find work, young people particularly out of work without hope, denied equal rights, denied the opportunity to eat at a restaurant or lunch counter or go to a movie theater, denied the right to a decent education, denied almost today the right to attend a State university even though qualified. It seems to me that these are matters which concern us all, not merely Presidents or Congressmen or Governors, but every citizen of the United States.

This is one country. It has become one country because all of us and all the people who came here had an equal chance to develop their talents.

We cannot say to 10 percent of the population that you can't have that right; that your children can't have the chance to develop whatever talents they have; that the only way that they are going to get their rights is to go into the streets and demonstrate. I think we owe them and we owe ourselves a better country than that.

Therefore, I am asking for your help in making it easier for us to move ahead and to provide the kind of equality of treatment which we would want ourselves; to give a chance for every child to be educated to the limit of his talents.

As I have said before, not every child has an equal talent or an equal ability or an equal motivation, but they should have the equal right to develop their talent and their ability and their motivation, to make something of themselves.

We have a right to expect that the Negro community will be responsible, will uphold the law, but they have a right to expect that the law will be fair, that the Constitution will be color blind, as Justice Harlan said at the turn of the century.

This is what we are talking about and this is a matter which concerns this country and what it stands for, and in meeting it I ask the support of all our citizens.

Thank you very much.

In January 1963, prior to the beginning of demonstrations in Birmingham, George Corley Wallace was inaugurated as the governor of Alabama. In his "Inaugural Address," **Document 3.3,** *Wallace threw down the gauntlet in opposition to racial reform, declaring, "segregation now ... segregation tomorrow ... segregation forever." In the 1950s, Wallace had run for governor as a populist. After losing, he vowed never to be "out-niggered again." A fiery orator and a masterful politician, Wallace not only defended segregation in the South, he reached out to whites in the North with subtle and not-so-subtle racist appeals. In January 1964, he entered several Democratic presidential primaries, performing remarkably well in a handful of*

border and northern states. In 1968, running as an independent candidate for pres-
ident, he won a larger percentage of the vote than any third-party candidate for
president since Theodore Roosevelt. Four years later, running as a Democrat, he
strung together a series of primary victories, only to have his campaign cut short by
a bullet from a would-be assassin that left Wallace paralyzed and unable to complete
his run for the White House. Even though he never won national office, Wallace
had a profound impact on American politics, standing in the forefront of the con-
servative backlash that grew in strength in the 1960s. In addition to placing the issues
of law and order and smaller government at the center of the political debate, Wal-
lace imparted a tone of political discourse, both populist and nationalistic, that
served as the model for many office seekers.

Document 3.3   George C. Wallace, "Inaugural Address," January 14, 1963, Alabama Department of Archives and History, Montgomery, Alabama.

Governor Patterson, Governor Barnett . . . fellow Alabamians:

. . . This is the day of my Inauguration as Governor of the State of Alabama.
And on this day I feel a deep obligation to renew my pledges, my covenants
with you . . . the people of this great state.

General Robert E. Lee said that "duty" is the sublimest word in the English
language and I have come, increasingly, to realize what he meant. I SHALL do
my duty to you, God helping . . . to every man, to every woman . . . yes, and to
every child in this State. . . .

Today I have stood, where once Jefferson Davis stood, and took an oath to
my people. It is very appropriate then that from this Cradle of the Confederacy,
this very Heart of the Great Anglo-Saxon Southland, that today we sound the
drum for freedom as have our generations of forebearers before us done, time
and again down through history. Let us rise to the call of freedom-loving blood
that is in us and send our answer to the tyranny that clanks its chains upon the
South. In the name of the greatest people that ever trod the earth, I draw the
line in the dust and toss the gauntlet before the feet of tyranny . . . and I say . . .
segregation now . . . segregation tomorrow . . . segregation forever.

The Washington, D.C. school riot report is disgusting and revealing. We will
not sacrifice our children to any such type of school system—and you can write
that down. The federal troops in Mississippi could better be used guarding the
safety of the citizens of Washington, D.C., where it is even unsafe to walk or
go to a ball game—and that is the nation's capital. I was safer in a B-29 bomber
over Japan during the war in an air raid, than the people of Washington are
walking in the White House neighborhood. A closer example is Atlanta. The
city officials fawn for political reasons over school integration and THEN build
barricades to stop residential integration—what hypocrisy!

Let us send this message back to Washington . . . that from this day we are
standing up, and the heel of tyranny does not fit the neck of an upright man . . .
that we intend to take the offensive and carry our fight for freedom across the

nation, wielding the balance of power we know we possess in the Southland. . . . that WE, not the insipid bloc voters of some sections will determine in the next election who shall sit in the White House . . . that from this day, from this minute, we give the word of a race of honor that we will not tolerate their boot in our face no longer. . . .

Hear me, Southerners! You sons and daughters who have moved north and west throughout this nation. We call on you from your native soil to join with us in national support and vote and we know wherever you are, away from the hearths of the Southland, that you will respond, for though you may live in the farthest reaches of this vast country, your heart has never left Dixieland.

And you native sons and daughters of old New England's rock-ribbed patriotism, and you sturdy natives of the great Mid-West, and you descendants of the far West flaming spirit of pioneer freedom, we invite you to come and be with us, for you are of the Southern mind, and the Southern spirit, and the Southern philosophy. You are Southerners too and brothers with us in our fight. . . .

To realize our ambitions and to bring to fruition our dreams, we as Alabamians must take cognizance of the world about us. We must re-define our heritage, re-school our thoughts in the lessons our forefathers knew so well, first hand, in order to function and to grow and to prosper. We can no longer hide our head in the sand and tell ourselves that the ideology of our free fathers is not being attacked and is not being threatened by another idea, for it is. We are faced with an idea that if centralized government assumes enough authority, enough power over its people that it can provide a utopian life, that if given the power to dictate, to forbid, to require, to demand, to distribute, to edict and to judge what is best and enforce that will of judgment upon its citizens from unimpeachable authority, then it will produce only "good" and it shall be our father and our God. It is an idea of government that encourages our fears and destroys our faith, for where there is faith, there is no fear, and where there is fear, there is no faith. . . .

Not so long ago men stood in marvel and awe at the cities, the buildings, the schools, the autobahns that the government of Hitler's Germany had built . . . but it could not stand, for the system that built it had rotted the souls of the builders and in turn rotted the foundation of what God meant that God should be. Today that same system on an international scale is sweeping the world. It is the "changing world" of which we are told. It is now called "new" and "liberal." It is as old as the oldest dictator. It is degenerate and decadent. As the national racism of Hitler's Germany persecuted a national minority to the whim of a national majority so the international racism of liberals seek to persecute the international white minority to the whim of the international colored majority, so that we are footballed about according to the favor of the Afro-Asian bloc. But the Belgian survivors of the Congo cannot present their case to the war crimes commission . . . nor the survivors of Castro, nor the citizens of Oxford, Mississippi.

It is this theory of international power politics that led a group of men on the Supreme Court for the first time in American history to issue an edict, based not on legal precedent, but upon a volume, the editor of which has said our Constitution is outdated and must be changed and the writers of which, some had admittedly belonged to as many as half a hundred communist front organizations. It is this theory that led this same group of men to briefly bare the ungodly core of the philosophy in forbidding little school children to say a prayer. . . .

This nation was never meant to be a unit of one but a unit of the many, that is the exact reason our freedom-loving forefathers established the states, so as to divide the rights and powers among the many states, insuring that no central power could gain master control.

In united effort we were meant to live under this government, whether Baptist, Methodist . . . or whatever one's denomination or religious belief, each respecting the other's right to a separate denomination. And so it was meant in our political lives . . . each . . . respecting the rights of others to be separate and work from within the political framework. . . .

And so it was meant in our racial lives, each race, within its own framework has the freedom to teach, to instruct, to develop, to ask for and receive deserved help from others of separate racial stations. This is the great freedom of our American founding fathers. But if we amalgamate into the one unit as advocated by the communist philosophers, then the enrichment of our lives, the freedom for our development, is gone forever. We become, therefore, a mongrel unit of one under a single all powerful government and we stand for everything and for nothing.

The true brotherhood of America, of respecting separateness of others and uniting in effort, has been so twisted and distorted from its original concept that there is small wonder that communism is winning the world.

We invite the negro citizen of Alabama to work with us from his separate racial station, as we will work with him, to develop, to grow. . . . But we warn those, of any group, who would follow the false doctrine of communistic amalgamation that we will not surrender our system of government, our freedom of race and religion. That freedom was won at a hard price and if it requires a hard price to retain it, we are able and quite willing to pay it. . . .

We remind all within hearing of the Southland that . . . Southerners played a most magnificent part in erecting this great divinely inspired system of freedom, and as God is our witness, Southerners will save it.

Let us, as Alabamians, grasp the hand of destiny and walk out of the shadow of fear and fill our divine destiny. Let us not simply defend but let us assume the leadership of the fight and carry our leadership across the nation. God has placed us here in this crisis. Let us not fail in this our most historical moment.

In the summer of 1964, civil rights forces, spearheaded by the Student Nonviolent Coordinating Committee, organized a massive campaign known as Mississippi Sum-

*mer or Freedom Summer. According to many historians, this campaign, which at-
tracted nearly one thousand volunteers, represented a turning point in the history of
the sixties in general. Following a summer of violence, which included the murder
of James Chaney, Michael Schwerner, and Andrew Goodman, the campaign came
to a climax in August, with the appearance of Fannie Lou Hamer, a member of the
Mississippi Democratic Party, before the credentials committee of the Democratic
National Convention in Atlantic City, New Jersey* (**Document 3.4**). *With the support
of Joe Rauh, the general counsel of the United Automobile Workers and a leader
of the Americans for Democratic Action, a prominent liberal organization, the Mississippi Freedom Democratic Party (MFDP), one of the main foci of the summer,
argued that it, not the all-white Regular Democrats, deserved to be recognized as
the legitimate delegation from the state. Hamer personified the grass-roots strength
of the movement. She was a sharecropper and mother, and her courage was leg-
endary. Her description of the ordeals she had to endure simply for registering to
vote proved particularly forceful. However, unwilling to risk a walkout of southern
delegates, President Johnson pressured the party's leaders to offer the MFDP a
"compromise" of two at-large delegates and the promise of future reforms. Not only
did MFDP reject this token offer, many of its members and allies left the convention
feeling betrayed by liberals who acceded to Johnson's demands. Some activists
would never trust liberals again.*

Document 3.4 Fannie Lou Hamer, "Testimony before the Credentials Committee of the Democratic National Convention," Atlantic City, New Jersey, August 22, 1964, Democratic National Committee, Washington, D.C.

Mr. Chairman, and the Credentials Committee, my name is Mrs. Fannie Lou
Hamer, and I live at 626 East Lafayette Street, Ruleville, Mississippi, Sunflower
County, the home of Senator James O. Eastland, and Senator Stennis.

It was the 31st of August in 1962 that 18 of us traveled 26 miles to the county
courthouse in Indianola to try to register to try to became first-class citizens.
We was met in Indianola by Mississippi men, Highway Patrolmen and they
allowed two of us in to take the literacy test at the time. After we had taken
the test and started back to Ruleville, we was held up by the City Police and
the State Highway Patrolmen and carried back to Indianola where the bus driver
was charged that day with driving a bus the wrong color.

After we paid the fine among us, we continued on to Ruleville, and Reverend
Jeff Sunny carried me the four miles in the rural area where I had worked as a
time-keeper and sharecropper for 18 years. I was met there by my children, who
told me the plantation owner was angry because I had gone down to try to
register.

After they told me, my husband came, and said the plantation owner was
raising cain because I had tried to register and before he quit talking the plantation owner came, and said, "Fannie Lou, do you know—did Pap tell you what
I said?" And I said, "Yes sir." He said, "I mean that. . . . If you don't go down

and withdraw . . . well—you might have to go because we are not ready for that.'' . . .

And I addressed him and told him and said, "I didn't try to register for you. I tried to register for myself.''

I had to leave that same night.

On the 10th of September, 1962, 16 bullets was fired into the home of Mr. and Mrs. Robert Tucker for me. That same night two girls were shot in Ruleville, Mississippi. Also Mr. Joe McDonald's house was shot in.

And in June, the 9th, 1963, I had attended a voter registration workshop, was returning back to Mississippi. Ten of us was traveling by the Continental Trailways bus. When we got to Winona, Mississippi, which is Montgomery County, four of the people got off to use the washroom. . . . I stepped off the bus to see what was happening and somebody screamed from the car that four workers was in and said, "Get that one there," and when I went to get in the car, when the man told me I was under arrest, he kicked me.

I was carried to the county jail and put in the holding room. They left some of the people in the booking room and began to place us in cells. I was placed in a cell with a young woman called Miss Euvester Simpson. After I was placed in the cell I began to hear sounds of licks and screams. I could hear the sounds of licks and horrible screams, and I could hear somebody say, "Can you say, yes, sir, nigger?" "Can you say yes, sir?"

And they would say horrible names. She would say. "Yes, I can say yes, sir." . . . They beat her, I don't know how long, and after a while she began to pray and asked God to have Mercy on those people. And it wasn't too long before three white men came to my cell. One of these men was a State Highway Patrolmen and he asked me where I was from, and I told him Ruleville; he said, "We are going to check this."

And they left my cell and it wasn't too long before they came back. He said, "You are from Ruleville all right," and he used a curse word, he said, "We are going to beat you until you wish you was dead."

I was carried out of that cell into another cell where they had two Negro prisoners. The State Highway Patrolmen ordered the first Negro to take the blackjack. The first Negro prisoner ordered me, by orders from the State Highway Patrolmen, for me to lay down on a bunk bed on my face, and I laid on my face.

The first Negro began to beat, and I was beat by the first Negro until he was exhausted, and I was holding my hands behind at this time on my left side because I suffered polio when I was six years old. After the first Negro had beat until he was exhausted the State Highway Patrolman ordered the second Negro to take the blackjack. The second Negro began to beat and I began to work my feet, and the State Highway Patrolman ordered the first Negro who had beat to set on my feet to keep me from working my feet. I began to scream and one white man got up and began to beat me in my head and tell me to hush.

One white man—my dress had worked up high, he walked over and pulled my dress down and he pulled my dress back, back up. . . .

All of this on account we want to register, to become first-class citizens, and if the freedom Democratic Party is not seated now, I question America, is this America, the land of the free and the home of the brave where we have to sleep with our telephones off the hooks because our lives be threatened daily because we want to live as decent human beings, in America?

Document 3.5 *consists of a speech by Malcolm X, one of the most prominent African Americans during the 1960s. Born Malcolm Little in Omaha, Nebraska, in 1925, Malcolm X spoke in a more militant voice than King. While King advocated nonviolence and integration, Malcolm X called for black nationalism and utilizing "any means necessary" to achieve equality. Partly due to the influence of Malcolm X, SNCC and the Congress of Racial Equality (CORE) jettisoned their commitment to nonviolence and integration in favor of self-defense and black nationalism in the latter part of the 1960s. Around the same time, SNCC and CORE, which had been founded as multiracial organizations, purged themselves of their remaining white members. Whether Malcolm, who repudiated some of his antiwhite views following his break with the Nation of Islam, would have endorsed these developments remains unclear, as he was assassinated shortly before black power took off as the new rallying cry of the movement. Clearly Stokely Carmichael, who coined the slogan "black power," and other black radicals felt that they were espousing and building on Malcolm X's views.*

Document 3.5   Malcolm X, "Address to a Meeting in New York" (1964), in *Two Speeches by Malcolm X,* ed. George Breitman (New York: Pathfinder Press, 1965), pp. 7–21.

Friends and enemies, tonight I hope that we can have a little fireside chat with as few sparks as possible tossed around. Especially because of the very explosive condition that the world is in today. Sometimes, when a person's house is on fire and someone comes in yelling fire, instead of the person who is awakened by the yell being thankful, he makes the mistake of charging the one who awakened him with having set the fire. I hope that this little conversation tonight about the black revolution won't cause many of you to accuse us of igniting it when you find it at your doorstep.

I'm still a Muslim, that is, my religion is still Islam. I still believe that there is no god but Allah and that Mohammed is the apostle of Allah. That just happens to be my personal religion. But in the capacity which I am functioning in today, I have no intention of mixing my religion with the problems of 22,000,000 black people in this country. . . .

I'm still a Muslim, but I'm also a nationalist, meaning that my political philosophy is black nationalism, my economic philosophy is black nationalism, my social philosophy is black nationalism. And when I say that this philosophy is black nationalism, to me this means that the political philosophy for black nationalism is that which is designed to encourage our people, the black people, to gain complete control over the politics and the politicians of our own people.

Our economic philosophy is that we should gain economic control over the economy of our own community, the businesses and the other things which create employment so that we can provide jobs for our own people instead of having to picket and boycott and beg someone else for a job.

And, in short, our social philosophy means that we feel that it is time to get together among our own kind and eliminate the evils that are destroying the moral fiber of our society, like drug addiction, drunkenness, adultery that leads to an abundance of bastard children, welfare problems. We believe that we should lift the level or the standard of our own society to a higher level wherein we will be satisfied and then not inclined toward pushing ourselves into other societies where we are not wanted. . . .

Just as we can see that all over the world one of the main problems facing the West is race, likewise here in America today, most of your Negro leaders as well as the whites agree that 1964 itself appears to be one of the most explosive years yet in the history of America on the racial front, on the racial scene. Not only is the racial explosion probably to take place in America, but all of the ingredients for this racial explosion in America to blossom into a world-wide racial explosion present themselves right here in front of us. America's racial powder keg, in short, can actually fuse or ignite a world-wide powder keg.

And whites in this country who are still complacent when they see the possibilities of racial strife getting out of hand and you are complacent simply because you think you outnumber the racial minority in this country, what you have to bear in mind is wherein you might outnumber us in this country, you don't outnumber us all over the earth.

Any kind of racial explosion that takes place in this country today, in 1964, is not a racial explosion that can be confined to the shores of America. It is a racial explosion that can ignite the racial powder keg that exists all over the planet that we call the earth. Now I think that nobody would disagree that the dark masses of Africa and Asia and Latin America are already seething with bitterness, animosity, hostility, unrest, and impatience with the racial intolerance that they themselves have experienced at the hands of the white West.

And just as they themselves have the ingredients of hostility toward the West in general, here we also have 22,000,000 African-Americans, black, brown, red, and yellow people in this country who are also seething with bitterness and impatience and hostility and animosity at the racial intolerance not only of the white West but of white America in particular. . . .

1964 will be America's hottest year; her hottest year yet; a year of much racial violence and much racial bloodshed. But it won't be blood that's going to flow only on one side. The new generation of black people that have grown up in this country during recent years are already forming the opinion, and it's just opinion, that if there is to be bleeding, it should be reciprocal—bleeding on both sides. . . .

So today, when the black man starts reaching out for what America says are his rights, the black man feels that he is within his rights—when he becomes the victim of brutality by those who are depriving him of his rights—to do whatever [is] necessary to protect himself. . . .

There are 22,000,000 African-Americans who are ready to fight for independence right here. When I say fight for independence right here, I don't mean any non-violent fight, or turn-the-other-cheek fight. Those days are gone. Those days are over.

If George Washington didn't get independence for this country non-violently, and if Patrick Henry didn't come up with a non-violent statement, and you taught me to look upon them as patriots and heroes, then it's time for you to realize that I have studied your books well. . . .

Every time a black man gets ready to defend himself some Uncle Tom tries to tell us, how can you win? That's Tom talking. Don't listen to him. This is the first thing we hear: the odds are against you. You're dealing with black people who don't care anything about odds. . . .

Again I go back to the people who founded and secured the independence of this country from the colonial power of England. . . . They didn't care about the odds. . . .

Our people are becoming more politically mature. . . . The Negro can see that he holds the balance of power in this country politically. It is he who puts in office the one who gets in office. Yet when the Negro helps that person get in office the Negro gets nothing in return. . . .

The present administration, the Democratic administration, has been there for four years. Yet no meaningful legislation has been passed by them that proposes to benefit black people in this country, despite the fact that in the House they have 267 Democrats and only 177 Republicans. . . . In the Senate there are 67 Democrats and only 33 Republicans. The Democrats control two thirds of the government and it is the Negroes who put them in a position to control the government. Yet they give the Negroes nothing in return but a few handouts in the form of appointments that are only used as window-dressing to make it appear that the problem is being solved.

No, something is wrong. And when these black people wake up and find out for real the trickery and the treachery that has been heaped upon us you are going to have revolution. And when I say revolution I don't mean that stuff they were talking about last year about "We Shall Overcome." . . .

And the only way without bloodshed that this [revolution] can be brought about is that the black man has to be given full use of the ballot in every one of the 50 states. But if the black man doesn't get the ballot, then you are going to be faced with another man who forgets the ballot and starts using the bullet. . . .

So you have a people today who not only know what they want, but also know what they are supposed to have. And they themselves are clearing the way for another generation that is coming up that not only will know what it wants and know what it should have, but also will be ready and willing to do whatever is necessary to see what they should have materializes immediately. Thank you.

Documents **3.6** *and* **3.7** *provide a further sense of the wave of black militancy that took hold in the latter part of the 1960s. In* **Document 3.6,** *the Black Panther Party summarizes its views. The best known of several militant organizations, the Panthers won the hearts of many blacks and the support of much of the New Left by meshing fiery rhetoric with down-to-earth programs such as free breakfast for poor school-children. At the same time, the Panthers were hated by much of the law-enforcement community. FBI director J. Edgar Hoover, for one, termed them the most dangerous group in America.* **Document 3.7** *consists of a compilation of recordings of a speech delivered by SNCC leader H. Rap Brown in Cambridge, Maryland, in 1967. While Stokely Carmichael argued that black-power advocates favored self-defense, not violence, Brown's speech rang with violent overtones. Indeed, shortly after he finished delivering it, a riot erupted in Cambridge that he was arrested for inciting. Even though he was never convicted on this charge (he was imprisoned on a separate charge), Congress attached a rider to the 1968 open-housing bill, known as the Brown Amendment, that made it a crime to cross state boundaries to incite a riot, a reflection of the growing backlash fomented by black power.*

Document 3.6   Black Panther Party, "Ten Point Program and Party Platform" (1967), Sixties Project: Primary Documents Collection, Institute of Advanced Technology in the Humanities, University of Virginia, Charlottesville.

1. We want freedom. We want power to determine the destiny of our Black Community.
We believe that Black people will not be free until we are able to determine our destiny.

2. We want full employment for our people.
We believe that the federal government is responsible and obligated to give every man and woman employment or a guaranteed income. We believe that if the white American businessmen will not give full employment, then the means of production should be taken from the businessmen and placed in the community so that the people of the community can organize and employ all of its people and give a high standard of living.

3. We want an end to the robbery by the white man of our Black community.
We believe that this racist government has robbed us and now we are demanding the overdue debt of forty acres and two mules. This was promised 100 years ago as restitution for slave labor and mass murder of Black people. We will accept the payment in currency which will be distributed to our many communities. The Ger-

mans are now aiding the Jews in Israel for the genocide of the Jewish people. The Germans murdered six million Jews. The American racist has taken part in the slaughter of over 50 million Black people; therefore, we feel that this is a modest demand that we make.

4. We want decent housing fit for shelter of human beings.
We believe that if the white landlords will not give decent housing to our Black community then the housing and the land should be made into cooperatives so that our community, with government aid can build and make decent housing for its people.

5. We want education for our people that exposes the true nature of this decadent American society. We want education that teaches us our true history and our role in the present day society.
We believe in an educational system that will give to our people a knowledge of self. If a man does not have knowledge of himself and his position in society and the world, then he has little chance to relate to anything else.

6. We want all Black men to be exempt from military service.
We believe that Black people should not be forced to fight in the military service to defend a racist government that does not protect us. We will not fight and kill other people of color in the world who, like Black people are being victimized by the white racist government of America. We will protect ourselves from the force and violence of the racist police and the racist military, by whatever means necessary.

7. We want an immediate end to POLICE BRUTALITY and murder of Black people.
We believe we can end police brutality in our Black community by organizing Black self defense groups that are dedicated to defending our Black community from racist police oppression and brutality. The second Amendment to the Constitution of the United States gives a man a right to bear arms. We therefore believe that all black people should arm themselves for self-defense.

8. We want freedom for all Black men held in federal, state, county and city prisons and jails.
We believe that all Black people should be released from the many jails and prisons because they have not received a fair and impartial trial.

9. We want all Black people when brought to trial to be tried in court by a jury of their peer group or people from their black communities as defined by the Constitution of the United States.
We believe that the courts should follow the United States Constitution so that Black people will receive fair trials. The 14th amendment of the U.S. Constitution gives a man a right to be tried by his peer group. A peer is a person from a similar economic, social, religious, geographical, environmental, historical and racial background. To do this the court will be forced to select a jury from the Black community from which the Black defendant came. We have been, and are being tried by all white juries that have no understanding of the average reasoning man of the Black community.

10. We want land, bread, housing, education, clothing, justice and peace. And as our major political objective, a United Nations supervised plebiscite to be held throughout the Black colony in which only black colonial subjects will be allowed to participate for the purpose of determining the will of the black people as to their national destiny.

When in the course of human events it becomes necessary for one people to dissolve the political bands, which have connected them with another, and to assume, among the powers of the earth, the separate and equal station to which the laws of nature and nature's God entitle them, a decent respect to the opinions of mankind requires that they should declare the causes which impel them to the separation. We hold these truths to be self-evident that all men are created equal; that they are endowed by their creator with certain unalienable rights; that among these are life, liberty, and the pursuit of happiness. That to secure these rights, governments are instituted among men deriving their just powers from the consent of the governed; that whenever any form of government becomes destructive of these ends, it is the right of the people to alter or to abolish it, and to institute a new government laying its foundation on such principles and organizing its powers in such form, as to them shall seem most likely to effect their safety and happiness. Prudence, indeed, will dictate that governments long established should not be changed for light and transient causes; and, accordingly, all experience hath shown that mankind are more disposed to suffer, while evils are sufferable than to right themselves by abolishing the forms to which they are accustomed. But, when a long train of abuses and usurpations, pursuing invariably the same object evinces a design to reduce them under absolute despotism, it is their right, it is their duty, to throw off such government, and to provide new guards for their future security.

Document 3.7   H. Rap Brown, "Speech in Cambridge, Maryland," July 24, 1967, Documents for the Classroom: "Is Baltimore Burning?" Maryland State Archives, Annapolis, Maryland.

[A great black man named Winston [sic] Hughes wrote a poem one time called A Dream Deferred] A poem *went* [which said]: "What happens to a dream that *were* [deferred]? Does it dry up like a raisin in the sun? Or does it fester like a sore [?]—and then run? Or does it sag like a heavy load? Or does it explode?" Uh . . . that question was never answered. Detroit answer*s* [ed] that question. Detroit exploded. *New York* [Newark] exploded. Harlem exploded. Dayton exploded. Cincinnati exploded. It's time for Cambridge to explode, *ladies and gentlemen* [baby].

They say [I heard someone up in Dayton once say, they say] "If Dayton don't come around, we are *gonna* [going to] burn Dayton down." Black folks built America. If America don't come around, we *going* [should] burn it down, brother. [And] We are going to burn it down if we don't get our share of it.

It's [It is] time *black folks stopped* [to stop] talking about being non-violent 'cause *we* [you] ain't non-violent *towards* [to] each other. Every Friday and Saturday you prove that. You cut up more people among your race than any other race.

As for being [If you are going to be] violent, (you) don't be violent to your brother. Be non-violent in your *communities* [community] and let it end right there.

"Take your violen*t* [ce] to the hunkies. Take it to the (loud cheering blurred word) [cracker].

(It takes a lot of effort . . .) It takes a lot of effort to love black in America. You'*ve* [have] been told all your life if you'*re* [are] black, you'*re* [are] wrong. *If you're black, there's something wrong with you.* [Something wrong with you, if you're black.] They tell you black cows don't give good milk; black hens don't lay eggs. Devil's food cake(s). You know, [when] you put on black *to* [you] go to funerals. When you put on white you go to weddings. They talk about flesh-colored band-aids. *You* [I] ain't never seen a black [colored]-flesh-colored band-aid. *So* [But] they tell you (there's) something wrong with (being) black.

You'*ve* got to be proud *of being* [to be] black. You'*ve* got to be proud of being black. You can't run around here calling yourself (colored. And calling yourself) Negroes. That['s] a word the honkies gave you. You'*re* [are] black, brother, and be proud of it. *It's beautiful* [Just be proud] to be black. [It's beautiful to be black]. Black folks got to understand that. We built this country. They tell you you('re) lazy. *They tell you* [And that] you stink. Brother, [do] you realize *what the state be of this country if we was lazy?* [that the slaves built this country? If we was lazy how we built this country?]

(Brother,) they captured us *in* [from] Africa and brought us over here to work for them. Now, who('s) lazy? [Who is lazy?]

He *walks* [runs] around and tells you: [that] "You Lazy." You don't want to *work* [do nothing]. All you want to do is lay *around* [down]. Hell! You can't do nothing but lay down after he done work[ed] you to death. I tell you what—[I tell you what. Old Sam, before he died, he made a record saying change is going to come] (first thing I'm ( ) representing the change gonna come. Now) *w*[W]e got to make the change come, see? *'Cause it's* [That become] our job. Now, [cause you see,] my mother. She worked from *kin to kate* [can till can't] every day of her life. My old man *Tommed* [Tom] so I wouldn't have to. Brother, [we ain't got no excuse] the streets belong to us. We got to take them.

They ain't *gonna* [going to] give it to us. We got to take *'em* [them]. (There) ain't no reason in the world *why* [for] on the other side of Race Street the honky pecker-wood "cracker" owns all the stores [and he takes our money from us. If I can't own, If I can't own my stores over here.] If I can't control my community over here, he ain't *gonna* [going to] control his over there. [He ain't going to control his over there.]

They run around and [they] tell you [, they say,]: "Don't start no fight with the honky *pecker* [cracker] 'cause *he* [you] can't win. He outnumber you. Hell! Don't you know they always outnumber us [, always they outnumber us]. David was outnumbered when he fought (the) Goliath. He was outnumbered. [Hell!] Daniel in the lion's den was outnumbered. Moses was outnumbered. All of us *is* [are] outnumbered. That don't make no difference. 'Cause let me tell you, brother, we work[ing] in their houses. They ain't got to leave home [, they ain't got to leave home]. When they want to do work *they* [and] let us come in their house (and) that shows you how stupid the honky is. *Cause* [Because] he ain't got to leave home.

And [Now] we look at what the man does to black people. A 10-year old boy in Newark (is) dead! A 19-year old boy shot 39 times, 4 times in the head. It don't take but one bullet to kill you. So they'*re* [are] (really) trying to tell you something else. [They tell you] How much they hate you. How much they hate black folks. [They had a poke in the paper (unclear).] When they shot him 39 times they said: ["This nigger ain't dead,] "Die, nigger, die." And they shot him some more. [He was] 19-years old—he's dead today. But we go over to Vietnam and fight the *races crapper* [racist cracker] war. We got to be crazy. Something's got to be wrong with black men. Our war is here.

If I can die defending my Mother land, I can die defending my mother. And that's *what I'm going* [the one I want] to die defending first. See, you are less than a man if you can't *defend* [protect] your mother, [and] your brother and your family. You ain't doing nothing, brother. That war over there in Vietnam is not the war *of* [for] the black man. This is our war.

(You've) got to understand what they are doing, though. America has laid out a plan to eliminate all black people who go against them. America is killing people down south by starving them to death in Alabama. Babies die. 500 *people* [kids] die a year for lack of [proper] food and nourishment. (And) yet we got enough money to go to the moon. Think about that. People in New York and Harlem *go rife and bites to death* [die from the bites of rats]. Big old rats bite them (to) death and you tell [the man] about it and the honkey say: "Hell, man, [he say] we can't do nothing about them rats." Do you realize this is the [same] man who exterminated the buffalo? [He killed the buffalo.] Hell, If he wanted to *kill the* [get rid of the] rats he could do it. . . .

He run around and he talk(s) about black people looting. Hell, he [is] the *biggest* [greatest] looter in the world. He looted us from Africa. He looted America from [the] Indians. *Man can you* [How can he] tell me about looting? You can't steal from a thief. This is the biggest thief going. So don't you worry about [that], but look what the brothers did in Plainfield. The brothers got their stuff. They got 46 automatic weapons [, 46 automatic weapons]. So the peckerwood goes down there [and wants] to take the weapons and they stomp one of them to death. They stomp the cop to death. Good. He('s) dead! They stomped him to death. They stomped him. You all might think that's brutal, but it ain't no more brutal than killing a pregnant woman. And that's what the honkey does. He kill[s] pregnant black women. They stomped him to death and threw a shopping basket on his head, took his pistol and shot him and then cut him. [And] You know he was hurt. [Yes] They don't like to hear about niggers cutting. They don't never want to hear about niggers cutting. *But* [And] they cut [him]. *And* [But] then they went back to their community with the(ir) 46 weapons and they told that peckerwood cop, they *say* [said]: "Don't you come in(to) my community." We going to control our community. And the peckerwood cop says: "(Huh), well, we got to come down there and get them weapons." The brother(s) told him, "Don't come in my community." He didn't come. And the only reason he didn't come *is* [was 'cause] he didn't want to get killed. And the brothers had the material to do it. They had 46 carbines down there. That's what he respects. Power. He respect[s] that kind of power. So, the next day they *were* [was] looking *back* [bad all] across the country, so they say, well, we going to go down there and take them guns. We going to search the houses. So the brothers say, "Cool." and they hid the guns. And they *say we'll* [said, we'll,] go [ahead] down there and look. So, when he went down there he started kicking down doors and tearing up brothers' property. and the brothers saw what was going on and the brothers told him: "If you kick down one more door, I'*m* [am] going to shoot your leg off." And look what the honky did. He left. That's the kind of force he respects.

Brothers, *you've got to* [you better] get some guns. I don't care if *its B-B guns* [it is a B-B gun] with poison(ed) B-Bs. *He's done* [The man has] declared war on (the) black people. [He has declared war on black people and] He don't mind killing them. It might be your son he kills next. (Or) it might be your daughter. Or it might be you. So, *wherever* [whenever] you go, brother, take some of them with you. That's what you do, (brother.) An eye for an eye; a tooth for a tooth. Tit for tat, brother, that's the only kind of war that man knows. That's the only thing he recognizes. Ain't no need in the world for me to come to Cambridge and I see all (of) them stores sitting *up* [over] there *and* [with] all them honkies *own* [over there owning] them. You got to own some of them stores. I don't care if you have to burn *him* [them] down and run *him* [them] out. *You'd better* [You got to] take over them stores. The streets are yours. (Take 'em.) They gave you the streets a long time ago; before they gave you houses. They gave you the streets. So, we own the streets. Take *'em* [them]. *You've* [You] got to take *'em* [them]. They *ain't going to* [won't] give them to you.

Freedom is not a welfare commodity. It ain't like that old bad food they give you. They can't give you no freedom. You got to take your freedom. You were born free. You got to exercise that right though, brother, cause the honkey got you where he want(s) you. . . .

Like I said in the beginning, if this town don't come [a]round, this town should be burned down. It should be burned down, brother. They('re) going to have to live in the same stuff I live in [be]'cause I ain't *going to* [gonna] make it no better for them. [I ain't gonna make it no better for them.] But do this brother—don't burn up your own stuff. Don't tear up your own stuff. Whenever you decide to fight the man, take it to his battleground. (It's) one thing that man respects. *It's* [That's] money. That's his god. When you tear down his store, you hit[ting] his religion. You hit him right where it hurt(s) him on Sunday. In his pocket. [That's the only god that man got.] That's his best friend. In his pocket. So, when you move to get him, don't tear up your stuff, don't tear up your brother's *stuff, hear?* [store here.]

Document 3.8, *an excerpt from the* Report of the National Advisory Commission on Civil Disorders, *was issued in 1968 by a special commission created by President*

Johnson in the wake of the worst spate of rioting in American history. The com-mission concluded that the riots were caused by social conditions, themselves the outgrowth of white racism, and called for massive social programs to address the needs of blacks who lived in America's urban ghettos. Despite the report's alarmist tone, President Johnson did not follow its suggestions. Shell-shocked by develop-ments in Vietnam, as well as by the deterioration of the liberal coalition, he offered only a lukewarm response to the commission's findings. Hubert Humphrey, John-son's vice president and the Democratic Party's nominee for president in 1968, kept his distance from its recommendations as well. More important, Republican leaders, including Richard Nixon, the Republican presidential nominee in 1968, harshly crit-icized the Kerner Commission, declaring that the government should coddle the militants less and enforce the law more.

Document 3.8 National Advisory Commission on Civil Disorders (Kerner Commission), *Report* (Washington, D.C.: GPO, 1968), pp. 1–2.

The summer of 1967 again brought racial disorders to American cities, and with them shock, fear and bewilderment to the nation.

The worst came during a two-week period in July, first in Newark and then in Detroit. Each set off a chain reaction in neighboring communities.

On July 28, 1967, the President of the United States established this Com-mission and directed us to answer three basic questions:

What happened?

Why did it happen?

What can be done to prevent it from happening again?

To respond to these questions, we have undertaken a broad range of studies and investigations. We have visited the riot cities; we have heard many wit-nesses; we have sought counsel of experts across the country.

This is our basic conclusion: Our nation is moving toward two societies, one black, one white—separate and unequal.

Reaction to last summer's disorders has quickened the movement and deep-ened the division. Discrimination and segregation have long permeated much of American life; they now threaten the future of every American. The deepening racial division is not inevitable. The movement apart can be reversed. Choice is still possible. Our principle task is to define that choice and to press for a national resolution.

To pursue the present course will involve the continuing polarization of the American community and, ultimately, the destruction of basic democratic values. The alternative is not blind repression or capitulation to lawlessness. It is the realization of common opportunities for all within a single society.

This alternative will require a commitment to national action—compassionate, massive and sustained, backed by the resources of the most powerful and the richest nation on this earth. From every American it will require new attitudes, new understanding, and, above all, new will.

The vital needs of the nation must be met; hard choices must be made, and, if necessary, new taxes enacted.

Violence cannot build a better society. Disruption and disorder nourish repression, not justice. They strike at the freedom of every citizen. The community cannot—it will not—tolerate coercion and mob rule. Violence and destruction must be ended—in the streets of the ghetto and in the lives of people.

Segregation and poverty have created in the racial ghetto a destructive environment totally unknown to most white Americans.

What white Americans have never fully understood—but what the Negro can never forget—is that the white society is deeply implicated in the ghetto. White institutions created it, white institutions maintain it, and white society condones it. . . .

It is time to make good the promises of American democracy to all citizens— urban and rural, black and white, Spanish-surname, American Indian, and every minority group.

Documents 3.9 *and* **3.10** *display Richard Nixon's and the Republican Party's somewhat ambiguous civil rights record. In 1968, Richard Nixon pursued a "southern strategy," whereby he courted white southern voters by suggesting that he would put an end to the civil rights revolution. A key element of this strategy was his decision to nominate Maryland governor Spiro T. Agnew as his running mate.* **Document 3.9** *consists of a speech that Agnew, an unknown political leader at the time, delivered to local civil rights leaders in the wake of riots that erupted in Baltimore following Martin Luther King, Jr.,'s assassination. Agnew's forthright condemnation of black radicals caught the attention of Nixon and landed him a place on the Republican ticket in 1968. Paradoxically, at least up until he delivered this address, Agnew considered himself a "Rockefeller Republican," meaning that he viewed himself as a moderate on racial issues. In fact, he had been elected governor of Maryland in 1966 by winning the vast majority of black votes, defeating George P. Mahoney, who had run on the slogan, "Your Home Is Your Castle," a not-so-thinly-veiled criticism of proposed fair-housing legislation.*

In **Document 3.10,** *Arthur Fletcher, the assistant secretary of labor, discusses the "Philadelphia Plan," which displayed a more moderate side of Nixon's civil rights policy. Much less well known than the* Brown *decision, which ruled segregated schools unconstitutional, or the Civil Rights or Voting Rights acts of 1964 and 1965, the "Philadelphia Plan" introduced affirmative action as a federal policy. In other words, it helps us better grapple with one of the central contradictions of the Nixon years. While Nixon condemned busing and called for law and order, his administration crafted numerous measures aimed at addressing ongoing racial inequity, to the point where some have argued that he was more liberal in terms of race than most of his predecessors.*

Document 3.9 Spiro T. Agnew, "Statement at Conference with Civil Rights and Community Leaders," Baltimore, Maryland, April 11, 1968, in *Addresses and State Papers of Spiro T. Agnew, Governor of Maryland, 1967–69,* ed. Frank L. Burdette (Annapolis: State of Maryland, 1975), pp. 758–763.

Ladies and Gentlemen:

Hard on the heels of tragedy come the assignment of blame and the excuses. I did not invite you here for either purpose. I did not ask you here to recount previous deprivations, or to hear me enumerate prior attempts to correct them. I did not request your presence to bid for peace with the public dollar.

Look around you and you may notice that every one here is a leader—and that each leader present has *worked* his way to the top. If you'll observe, the ready-mix, instantaneous type of leader is not present. The circuit-riding, Hanoi-visiting type of leader is missing from this assembly. The caterwauling, riot-inciting, burn-America-down type of leader is conspicuous by his absence. That is no accident, ladies and gentlemen, it is just good planning. And in the vernacular of today—"that's what it's all about, baby."

Some weeks ago, a reckless stranger to this City, carrying the credentials of a well-known civil rights organization, characterized the Baltimore Police as "enemies of the black man." Some of you here, to your eternal credit, quickly condemned this demagogic proclamation. You condemned it because you recognized immediately that it was an attempt to undermine lawful authority—the authority under which you were elected and under which you hold your leadership position. You spoke out against it because you knew it was false and was uttered to attract attention and inflame.

When you, who courageously slapped hard at irresponsibility, acted, you did more for civil rights than you realize. But when white leaders openly complimented you for your objective, courageous action, you immediately encountered a storm of censure from parts of the Negro community. The criticism was born of a perverted concept of race loyalty and inflamed by the type of leader who, as I earlier mentioned, is not here today.

And you ran. You met in secret with that demagogue and others like him—and you agreed, according to published reports that have not been denied, that you would not openly criticize any black spokesman, regardless of the content of his remarks. You were beguiled by the rationalizations of unity; you were intimidated by veiled threats; you were stung by insinuations that you were Mr. Charlie's boy, by epithets like "Uncle Tom." God knows I cannot fault you who spoke out for breaking and running in the face of what appeared to be overwhelming opinion in the Negro community. But actually it was only the opinion of those who depend upon chaos and turmoil for leadership—those who deliberately were not invited today. It was the opinion of a few, distorted and magnified by the *silence* of most of you here today.

Now, parts of many of our cities lie in ruins. You need not leave these City limits to verify the destruction and the resulting hardship to our citizens. And you know whom the fires burned out just as you know who lit the fires. They were not lit in honor of your great fallen leader. Nor were they lit from an overwhelming sense of frustration and despair. Those fires were kindled at the suggestion and with the instruction of the advocates of violence. It was no accident that one such advocate appeared at eight separate fires before the fire chief could get there.

The looting and rioting which has engulfed our City during the past several days did not occur by chance. It is no mere coincidence that a national disciple of violence, Mr. Stokely Carmichael, was observed meeting with local black power advocates and known criminals in Baltimore on April 3, 1968—three days before the Baltimore riots began.

It is deplorable and a sign of sickness in our society that the lunatic fringes of the black and white communities speak with wide publicity while we, the moderates, remain continuously mute. I cannot believe that the only alternative to white racism is black racism.

Somewhere the objectives of the civil rights movement have been obscured in a surge of emotional oversimplification. Somewhere the goal of equal opportunity has been replaced by the goal of instantaneous economic equality. This country does not guarantee that every man will be successful but only that he will have an equal opportunity to achieve success. I readily admit that this equal opportunity has not always been present for Negroes—that it is still not totally present for Negroes. But I say that we have come a long way. And I say that the road we have trodden is built with the sweat of the Roy Wilkinses and the Whitney Youngs—with the spiritual leadership of Dr. Martin Luther King—and not with violence.

Tell me one constructive achievement that has flowed from the madness of the twin priests of violence, Stokely Carmichael and Rap Brown. They do not build—they demolish. They are agents of destruction and they will surely destroy us if we do not repudiate them and their philosophies—along with the white racists such as Joseph Carroll and Connie Lynch—the American Nazi Party, the John Birchers, and their fellow travelers.

The bitterness of past and present days has been brewed by words like these:

We have to retaliate for the deaths of our leaders. The execution for those deaths will not be in the court rooms. They're going to be in the streets of the United States of America. . . . Black people know that they have to get guns.
—Stokely Carmichael: Washington, D.C., April 5, 1968.

And:

To hell with the laws of the United States. . . . Your brothers in the ghettos are going to wake up with matches . . . if a white man tries to walk over you, kill him . . . one match and you can retaliate. Burn, baby, burn . . . We're going to tear the cities up. . . .
—Stokely Carmichael: Miles College, April 4, 1967.

And:

> Get yourselves some guns. The honky is your enemy. The brothers are now calling Detroit destroyed. You did a good job here. [This City's riot will] look like a picnic [after black people unite] to take their due.
> —Rap Brown: Detroit, August 27, 1967.

And:

> Black people are being forced to become both judge and jury. We must arm ourselves with rifles, shotguns, pistols, bow and arrows (with poison arrows), BB guns (with poison BBs), gas, rags, bottles and knives. The only way to get justice in this evil land is to kill the white devil before he kills you.
> —Willard Dixon in a publication, "The Black Dispatch, a voice of the Black Ghetto."

What possible hope is there for peace in our community if these apostles of anarchy are allowed to spew hatred unchallenged?

If we are to learn from bitter experience, if we are to progress in the battle for equal opportunity, we must plan together and execute those plans together. To do this we must be able to communicate. We cannot communicate and progress if the lunatic fringes are included in the problem-solving team.

I publicly repudiate, condemn and reject all white racists. I call upon you to publicly repudiate, condemn and reject all black racists. This, so far, you have not been willing to do.

I call upon you as Americans to speak out now against the treason and hate of Stokely Carmichael and Rap Brown. If our nation is not to move toward two separate societies—one white and one black—you have an obligation, too.

I submit to you that these men and others like them represent a malignancy out of control; that they will lead us to a devastating racial civil war. I submit to you that there can be no winner from such a conflict and that the heaviest losers will be the Negro citizens of America.

It is not too late to return to the true target of the crusade for equality. The target is the elimination of all prejudice against Negroes in America and the provision of an equal opportunity to reach the top. That target will be realized when every man is judged on his own individual merit and only on his merit. Divisiveness and the doctrine of apartheid are impenetrable barriers between us and that target. With your help they can be torn down.

I am sure that these remarks come as somewhat of a surprise to you; that you expected nebulous promises and rationalizations and possibly a light endorsement of the Kerner report. This I could not do. Some hard things needed to be said. The desperate need to confront the problem squarely justified the political risk in saying them.

I need your help, but your help would be of little value if you did not know and subscribe to the objectives for which I seek it. We can do much together—little apart. Blind militancy must be converted into constructive purpose. This cannot occur so long as you or I condone or cling to racism, black or white. We do not deserve the mantle of leadership unless we are prepared to wear it proudly and, if need be, defiantly.

Above all, I believe you represent the views of the overwhelming majority of Maryland's Negro citizens—responsible, hard-working, decent people who are as horrified by the events of the past days as you or I. These are the people who will be unjustly victimized by a hardening of attitudes in the responsible, decent white community—white people who clearly repudiated racism in the 1966 election—white people who could normally be expected to endorse the 1967 open housing legislation on referendum this November.

My greatest fear is this polarization of attitudes as an aftermath of violence. Next I fear that we cannot endure continuous tension over the next months—that our community cannot live in constant fear that any irrational provocation may cause racial war.

Together we must work first to prevent polarization and second to reduce tension. I will need your vision and your voice. Now as never before your articulate, responsible leadership is needed. I am prepared to do whatever I can to aid the innocent victims of last weekend's rampage, to alleviate clear abuses and to enlarge opportunity within the inner city.

We must do this—as I said in my report to the people last Sunday night—"not out of fear of reprisal but out of certain faith that it is right."

So let us begin to rebuild now—to rebuild our City and to rebuild the image of Baltimore. Let us work together—not as black and white—but as responsible citizens of Maryland who uphold the law; as concerned citizens who are united in their dedication to eliminate prejudice and poverty or any conditions which create hopelessness and despair.

Let us promptly and publicly renounce any who counsel or condone violence. Let us acknowledge that we have a real stake in our society. Let us proudly acclaim our patriotism and our recognition that no other nation in the world offers such opportunity. The fiction that Negroes lack any opportunity in this country is dispelled by the status of those of you in this room.

As Thomas Jefferson said, nearly two centuries ago, "With all the imperfections of our present government, it is without comparison the best existing, or that ever did exist."

Document 3.10   Arthur Fletcher, "Remarks on the Philadelphia Plan," June 27, 1969, Philadelphia Plan Documents, United States Department of Labor, no. 6.

It is most appropriate that a plan for equal employment opportunity should bear the title "Philadelphia Plan" and should be inaugurated in this city. Philadelphia and its people have a great heritage of freedom which is rich in historical events known to every school child throughout the Nation. It was here in this city that the Declaration of Independence was signed and it was here freedom's ring was heard for the first time. It was here that the Constitution of our country guaranteeing freedom for all was drafted.

A vital freedom guaranteed by our Constitution is the right to equal participation in the economic processes of our society. This freedom has been denied to groups within our country. This denial of fundamental participation in the advantages of capitalism has even been institutionalized in our society.

The Federal Government cannot contribute to this denial of rights through blind acceptance of customs and traditions which eliminate the contributions and talents of groups of people. The Federal Government has an obligation to see that every citizen has an equal chance at the most basic freedom of all—the right to succeed.

Millions of dollars at every level of Government are being spent to correct the symptoms of the denial of this right in our society but almost no effort has been made in the past to affect this problem at its source—where Federal dollars enter the area economy.

These Federal dollars—part of which are Black, Puerto Rican, Mexican-American, and others—enter local economy primarily through Federal contracts. Once these dollars pass the "Gateway" of contracting procedures—the Federal Government has no further control over them. Through the "multiplier" effect experienced by imported money in the regional economy and the existence of institutionalized segregation—the Federal Government can be pictured as contributing to the denial of the right to succeed for substantial groups of people. No amount of money spent by whatever level of Government to correct this situation can be justified after the fact.

The most fair, economical and effective point to address this problem is at the beginning—the time of contracting.

My office is dedicated to this proposition. I view this concept as being in harmony with the highest principles guaranteed by our Constitution and the sound economic cornerstones of our capitalist system. It is good business for the Government, for industry, for labor and for all the people of this country.

With this background firmly in mind, I now want to tell you about the Philadelphia Plan.

The Philadelphia Plan applies to all Federal and federally-assisted construction contracts for projects in excess of $500,000. The plan at the present time is to apply to the Philadelphia area including Bucks, Chester, Delaware, Montgomery, and Philadelphia counties, and goes into effect on July 18, 1969. It is also anticipated that the plan will be put into effect in all the major cities across the Nation as soon as possible.

The plan is aimed at increasing minority participation in designated trades. These trades are:

Iron workers
Plumbers, pipefitters

Steam fitters
Sheetmetal workers
Electrical workers
Roofers and water proofers
Elevation construction workers

The named trades have been singled out for special emphasis because in the past these trades, at least in the Philadelphia area, have been operating without significant minority participation.

Within the plan's presently established geographical boundaries, the Office of Federal Contract Compliance will, with the assistance of representatives from the Federal contracting agencies, determine definite standards for minority participation in each of the trades named and to be used on a construction project. The standard for each trade will be included in the invitation for bids or other solicitations used for every Federally-involved construction contract. The standards will specify the range of minority manpower utilization expected for each of the named trades and such standards must be maintained during the performance of the construction contract. . . .

Perhaps I should pause at this point to discuss the concept of goals or standards for percentages of minority employees contained in the Philadelphia Plan.

Let me start by saying it would have been much better in our history if segregation had not occurred. But it has. This is a fact. None of us—white or black—like to talk about it—much less admit it. But there it remains— it won't go away.

Segregregation [sic] didn't occur naturally—it was imposed. In that process quotas, limits, boundaries were set. Sometimes written—sometimes unpublished. But official or informal the effect was total, decisive, and I might add— contrary to the American sense of fair play.

Large segments of our society were oppressed by these rules and institutions until they believed it was impossible to change them. With the increasing wealth of our economic system—the gap—visible to any thinking man—between white and black—employed and unemployed—rich and poor—was growing wider and wider.

Contrary to the poet—hope does *not* spring eternal. Hope—and, therefore, the commitment to try to succeed—is directly related to the chances of success. Impossible dreams are not long sustained by anyone—white or black. . . .

Fair play and definitive agreements concerning working conditions, promotional opportunities, ratios of skilled craftsmen to trainees, recognition of bargaining groups and seniority security are now an acceptable and respected tradition in our world of commerce. This was not always so. It developed in stormy times and created great feelings of anxiety, threat and insecurity.

The disadvantaged of this country are now asking that the opportunities achieved through this great movement be extended to include them. No more. No less.

It might be better, admittedly, if specific goals were not required—certainly the black people of America understand taboos—but it is imperative that we face facts and dedicate ourselves to ending discrimination in employment in this country.

What is at stake here is something more than equal employment opportunity in a specific industry or named trades. What is at stake is our basic system of Government itself. Persons in the minority communities must be assured that results can be obtained by working within the framework of the existing governmental system. The Office of Federal Contract Compliance must translate the dreams and ambitions of a large segment of our population into every day realities. This means job opportunities in at least every trade and industry which does substantial business with the Federal Government. The time for speculation has ended and the hour for action is now.

Every Government contractor must realize that he has the responsibility to provide equal access to money spent by the Federal Government. This is true in Philadelphia and is equally true in every city and town throughout the United States. This is why the Philadelphia Plan is important not only to this area but is a forerunner of the direction my Administration is going to take.

Chapter Four

THE GREAT SOCIETY AND ITS CRITICS

In the 1930s, in the midst of the Great Depression, Franklin D. Roosevelt trans-formed the role of the federal government and American politics. Arguing that the United States faced an emergency situation, similar to war, he convinced Congress to enact many sweeping programs, from federal relief for the unemployed to Social Security. World War II reinforced this transformation of the government. Yet the war also ended the economic emergency that had created the underlying justification for expanding the power of the federal government in the first place. After the war, numerous factors, from the expansion of the economy to the cold war, cooled the nation's fervor for further reforms. While Dwight Eisenhower did not repeal the New Deal, neither did he enact new measures. John Kennedy's election signaled a greater willingness of the nation to enact liberal measures. Nonetheless, most liberal proposals, from tax reforms to civil rights, remained bottled up in Congress.

Numerous concurrent developments helped break this deadlock. Several seminal books awakened the nation to a number of pressing problems. In The Other Amer-ica, *Michael Harrington demonstrated that in spite of the nation's overarching af-fluence, large segments of America remained mired in poverty. Rachel Carson revealed the dangers to the environment and public health posed by certain widely used insecticides. Somewhat paradoxically, the continued expansion of the economy convinced many that the United States could afford massive programs aimed at overcoming its remaining domestic problems. As President Lyndon Johnson de-clared: "I'm sick of all the people who talk about the things we can't do. Hell, we're the richest country in the world, the most powerful. We can do it all."[1] Keynesian economic theories bolstered the claim that increased federal spending would not harm the economy; in fact, it might help. President Kennedy's assassination, com-*

bined with President Johnson's deft use of the moment and his and the Democratic Party's landslide victory in the 1964 elections, provided further impetus for breaking the legislative deadlock.

In **Document 4.1,** *President Johnson outlined his Great Society. While he had used the term prior to this occasion, he most fully fleshed out his vision in this commencement address to the University of Michigan. Note Johnson's attempt to address both the quantitative and qualitative needs of the American people and his emphasis on urban America. One of the cornerstones of the Great Society, and the one that has retained its popularity, was Medicare, a federal program that provided health insurance to the elderly. At the time, it faced greater opposition, in particular in the form of a massive lobbying effort spearheaded by the American Medical Association (AMA), than programs that subsequently became much more controversial.* **Document 4.2** *contains excerpts from AFL-CIO president George Meany's congressional testimony in support of the program. Meany argued that Medicare was necessary because the private sector had failed to provide adequate health insurance for the elderly. Meany added that the program would allow America's senior citizens to maintain their dignity. He did not need to state that most within organized labor, which was about 25 percent of the work force, as well as most senior citizens, favored the proposal, and that large numbers of both groups voted.*

Document 4.1   Lyndon B. Johnson, "Commencement Address—The Great Society," University of Michigan, Ann Arbor, Michigan, May 22, 1964, in *Public Papers of the Presidents of the United States, Lyndon B. Johnson, 1963–64* (Washington D.C.: GPO, 1965), pp. 704–707.

I have come today from the turmoil of your Capital to the tranquility of your campus to speak about the future of our country. The purpose of protecting the life of our Nation and preserving the liberty of our citizens is to pursue the happiness of our people. Our success in that pursuit is the test of our success as a nation. For a century we labored to settle and to subdue a continent. For half a century, we called upon unbounded invention and untiring industry to create an order of plenty for all our people. The challenge of the next half century is whether we have the wisdom to use that wealth to enrich and elevate our national life, and to advance the quality of our American civilization.

Your imagination, your initiative, and your indignation will determine whether we build a society where progress is the servant of our needs, or a society where old values and new visions are buried under unbridled growth. For in your time we have the opportunity to move not only toward the rich society and the powerful society, but upward to the Great Society. The Great Society rests on abundance and liberty for all. It demands an end to poverty and racial injustice, to which we are totally committed in our time. But that is just the beginning. The Great Society is a place where every child can find knowledge to enrich his mind and to enlarge his talents. It is a place where leisure is a welcome chance to build and reflect, not a feared cause of boredom and restlessness. It is a place where the city of man serves not only the needs of the body and the demands of commerce, but the desire for beauty and the hunger for community.

It is a place where man can renew contact with nature. It is a place which honors creation for its own sake and for what it adds to the understanding of the race. It is a place where men are more concerned with the quality of their goals than the quantity of their goods. But most of all, the Great Society is not a safe harbor, a resting place, a final objective, a finished work. It is a challenge constantly renewed, beckoning us toward a destiny where the meaning of our lives matches the marvelous products of our labor.

So I want to talk to you today about three places where we begin to build the Great Society—in our cities, in our countryside, and in our classrooms. Many of you will live to see the day, perhaps 50 years from now, when there will be 400 million Americans; four-fifths of them in urban areas. In the remainder of this century urban population will double, city land will double, and we will have to build homes, highways and facilities equal to all those built since this country was first settled. So in the next 40 years we must rebuild the entire urban United States.

Aristotle said, "Men come together in cities in order to live, but they remain together in order to live the good life."

It is harder and harder to live the good life in American cities today. The catalogue of ills is long: There is the decay of the centers and the despoiling of the suburbs. There is not enough housing for our people or transportation for our traffic. Open land is vanishing and old landmarks are violated. Worst of all, expansion is eroding the precious and time-honored values of community with neighbors and communion with nature. The loss of these values breeds loneliness and boredom and indifference. Our society will never be great until our cities are great. Today the frontier of imagination and innovation is inside those cities, and not beyond their borders. New experiments are already going on. It will be the task of your generation to make the American city a place where future generations will come, not only to live but to live the good life.

I understand that if I stay here tonight I would see that Michigan students are really doing their best to live the good life.

This is the place where the Peace Corps was started. It is inspiring to see how all of you, while you are in this country, are trying so hard to live at the level of the people.

A second place where we begin to build the Great Society is in our countryside. We have always prided ourselves on being not only America the strong and America the free, but America the beautiful. Today that beauty is in danger. The water we drink, the food we eat, the very air that we breathe, are threatened with pollution. Our parks are overcrowded. Our seashores overburdened. Green fields and dense forests are disappearing.

A few years ago we were greatly concerned about the Ugly American. Today we must act to prevent an Ugly America.

For once the battle is lost, once our natural splendor is destroyed, it can never be recaptured. And once man can no longer walk with beauty or wonder at nature, his spirit will wither and his sustenance be wasted.

A third place to build the Great Society is in the classrooms of America. There your children's lives will be shaped. Our society will not be great until every young mind is set free to scan the farthest reaches of thought and imagination. We are still far from that goal. Today, eight million adult Americans, more than the entire population of Michigan, have not finished five years of school. Nearly 20 million have not finished 8 years of school. Nearly 54 million, more than one-quarter of all America, have not even finished high school.

Each year more than 100,000 high school graduates, with proven ability, do not enter college because they cannot afford it. And if we cannot educate today's youth, what will we do in 1970 when elementary school enrollment will be 5 million greater than 1960? And high school enrollment will rise by 5 million. College enrollment will increase by more than 3 million. In many places, classrooms are overcrowded and curricula are outdated. Most of our qualified teachers are underpaid, and many of our paid teachers are unqualified. So we must give every child a place to sit and a teacher to learn from. Poverty must not be a bar to learning, and learning must offer an escape from poverty.

But more classrooms and more teachers are not enough. We must seek an educational system which grows in excellence as it grows in size. This means better training for our teachers. It means preparing youth to enjoy their hours of leisure as well as their hours of labor. It means exploring new techniques of teaching, to find new ways to stimulate the love of learning and the capacity for creation.

These are three of the central issues of the Great Society. While our government has many programs directed at those issues, I do not pretend that we have the full answer to those problems. But I do promise this: We are going to assemble the best thought and the broadest knowledge from all over the world to find those answers for America. I intend to establish working groups to prepare a series of White House conferences and meetings on the cities, on natural beauty, on the quality of education, and on other emerging challenges. And from these meetings and from this inspiration and from these studies we will begin to set our course toward the Great Society.

The solution to these problems does not rest on a massive program in Washington, nor can it rely solely on the strained resources of local authority. They require us to create new concepts of cooperation, a creative federalism, between the national Capitol and the leaders of local communities.

Woodrow Wilson once wrote: "Every man sent out from this university should be a man of his nation as well as a man of his time."

Within your lifetime powerful forces, already loosed, will take us toward a way of life beyond the realm of our experience, almost beyond the bounds of our imagination. For better or for worse, your generation has been appointed by history to deal with those problems and to lead America toward a new age. You have the chance never before afforded to any people in any age. You can help build a society where the demands of morality, and the needs of the spirit, can be realized in the life of the Nation. So will you join in the battle to give every citizen the full equality which God enjoins and the law requires, whatever his belief, or race, or the color of his skin? Will you join in the battle to give every citizen an escape from the crushing weight of poverty? Will you join in the battle to make it possible for all nations to live in enduring peace as neighbors and not as mortal enemies? Will you join in the battle to build the Great Society, to prove that our material progress is only the foundation on which we will build a richer life of mind and spirit?

There are those timid souls who say this battle cannot be won, that we are condemned to a soulless wealth. I do not agree. We have the power to shape the civilization that we want. But we need your will, your labor, your hearts, if we are to build that kind of society.

Those who came to this land sought to build more than just a new country. They sought a free world.

So I have come here today to your campus to say that you can make their vision our reality. Let us from this moment begin our work so that in the future men will look back and say: It was then, after a long and weary way, that man turned the exploits of his genius to the full enrichment of his life.

Thank you. Goodbye.

Document 4.2   George Meany, "Testimony on Medicare," U.S. House, Committee on Ways and Means, *Hearings: Medical Care for the Aged, January 20, 1964* (Washington, D.C.: GPO, 1964), pp. 1205–1213.

Mr. Chairman, my name is George Meany. I am president of the American Federation of Labor and Congress of Industrial Organizations, and I am appearing here on behalf of that organization.

This statement was originally scheduled for November 26 and it was postponed when this committee interrupted the hearings after the tragic assassination of President Kennedy. This is a measure which was close to the heart of our late President. It seems to me fitting indeed that it is the first piece of major legislation to be considered by this committee in the 2d session of the 88th Congress. I trust, I hope, I pray it will be adopted by this Congress.

I am going to try to present our case in terms of people, with a minimum of statistics. All the statistics are already in the record. This is a human issue; that is the way President Johnson views it as he told the Congress in his state of the Union message, and that is exactly the way we look at this matter too.

More than 6 years have passed since Congressman Forand rose in the House of Representatives to introduce the bill which was the prototype of the one you are presently considering. From the very beginning, this idea—health insurance, and primarily hospital insurance, for the aged as part of the social security and railroad retirement systems—had the warm support of the labor movement. We said then, and we say now, that this is the kind of program we must have to round out our social security concept—to plug up its biggest loophole.

In the beginning, there were many who honestly disagreed with us. Some of them did not realize the scope of the problem. Others believed, or at least hoped, that it could be met by other means. But by now, the facts are clear. . . .

So it is now agreed that the aged get sick oftener, and for longer periods of time; that they require much more institutional care; and that they have much less money to meet the costs of illness. There is no real dispute about that.

The only things that have happened in this respect, in the last 6 years, are that the number of aged has increased; that the cost of hospital care has risen far faster than their incomes; and that their life expectancy has been lengthened. In other words, they are worse off now than they were 6 years ago when it comes to the threat of a catastrophic illness.

Second, there is now a broad range of experience with alternative remedies, both public and private. Let us see what that experience has been.

There are only two basic proposals that have been offered as alternatives to the social security approach. One is private insurance, commercial or nonprofit. The second is public assistance, or as it was generally known 30 years ago, public relief. I will discuss them in that order.

Your committee is well aware that private insurance companies have reacted violently to the social security proposal. They began by claiming that the Federal Government was cutting into their business.

Then, after it was pointed out that they had let this particular section of their business go by default, they began promoting—with great fanfare and high-priced advertising—a whole range of health insurance policies for the aged. This latter process is still going on.

Speaking for myself, and I am sure for the great majority of Americans, I would be delighted if these private plans could meet the need. We do not want a Federal plan for its own sake. We do not have any ideological stake in extending the operations of the Government. On this issue, as on others we press for Government action only when other means have proved to be inadequate.

Such is the case here. I am willing to assume that the insurance companies have made a sincere effort; but the actuarial facts doomed them to failure. The nature of the problem, as I described it earlier, makes it impossible for any commercial insurance carrier or nonprofit health plan to devise a policy that will adequately protect the aged, at a cost they can afford to pay.

The proof of this lies in the policies now on the market. Let us look behind the inviting headlines on their advertisements and see what they really offer.

About half of all the aged who hold commercial health insurance are covered by one of two policies—Continental Casualty 65-Plus or Mutual of Omaha Senior Security. These policies did cost $78 and $102 a year, respectively, for each insured person. Continental has now announced that effective next week the rates for its policy will be hiked by 23 percent. It will now cost $98 per year. While even these amounts would be burdensome to many of the aged, they are admittedly within the reach of many others.

But what do they get for the money? They get hospital room and board payments of $10 a day—for a maximum of 31 days in one case, and 60 days in the other. Yet the average daily charge for semiprivate hospital accommodations is $20 nationwide, and exceeds $35 a day in some cities.

This means that a Continental Casualty policyholder who was unlucky enough to be hospitalized for 45 days—not an unusual length of time for an older person—would have to pay 66 percent of the room and board out of his own pocket, assuming the average rate of $20 a day. That would amount to $590. And if he happened to live in Cleveland, Los Angeles, or San Francisco, which are among the higher cost cities, his personal share would be more than 80 percent.

Is this insurance? It may be better than nothing—but not by much. . . .

Since I am sure that the insurance company actuaries are able, hard-headed men, it is hard to understand why the industry keeps insisting it can do a job which its own figures must prove to be impossible. I have reluctantly concluded that there is a political motive involved. . . .

What makes us suspect a political motive is the timing of these advertising campaigns. They have been heaviest, as a rule, just before elections, or at times when the social insurance proposal was under active discussion in Congress. In 1962, for example, we were actually informed in advance, by a source inside the insurance industry, that a national campaign was being planned for the period just before the congressional elections. That is exactly what happened.

Are these campaigns really designed to sell insurance to the aged? Or are they designed as propaganda to influence the political attitude of Congress and the American people?

Let me repeat, we are not opposed to private health insurance, sold by either the commercial carriers or Blue Cross. On the contrary, we believe it has a great future, a great role to play, in protecting the aged. But we do say, and the record proves it, that private insurance cannot do the whole job.

I am not implying that some of the aged should be protected by a Federal program and that others should be left to the private companies. That would be completely unsound. Inevitably, the private companies would siphon off the people in the best health, leaving the bad risks to the Government. And that is not the only objection. . . .

Many of you know from personal experience, as I do, that the great majority of these pensioners are proud of their independence—proud that they have earned it. Yet when a severe and costly illness strikes, that pride and independence can be destroyed overnight, not to mention the modest store of personal goods, the little luxuries, accumulated by a lifetime of honest work. . . .

I would like to say just a few words about financing—the increase in social security taxes that would finance this program. Opposition to the King bill based on this point takes two different lines.

The first is that the American people in general, and workers in particular, will revolt against higher social security taxes. This is one of the enduring myths of our time.

We in the labor movement have been pressing for improvements in the social security system since it first came into being. We have been pressing for this particular improvement for 6 years. And in every statement, every speech, every leaflet, we have always been careful to say what the cost will be to workers, both the average and the maximum amounts.

The American Medical Association, the insurance industry, and certain candidates for public office have all complained about this terrible tax burden we were trying to saddle on wage earners. Even some of our liberal friends have expressed concern about it. Almost everyone seems to be worried but the workers themselves.

True, we hear from union members about this legislation. I assure you that Congressmen are not the only ones who get mail from their constituents. Our members complain about the deductibles. They complain that there is no surgical coverage. They say there ought to be more emphasis on preventive care. All they say about money is that we're not asking for a high enough tax to pay for these other things.

I have never had a letter from a union member protesting against social security taxes. There are very few issues—possibly no other issues—about which I could make such a statement.

It seems that workers have somehow mastered an economic point that has escaped a good many others, including some with higher educational status. They know that old-age security—whether pensions or health care—has to be paid for. And they are convinced that the best way to do it is in a working lifetime of small installments. . . .

What happens when an elderly, retired person, of modest means, becomes seriously ill?

The first call goes out to his children. That is natural enough, the family is still at the heart of our society.

And the children, in most cases, are willing to do whatever they can to help out. But generally they are not children any more—not in a chronological sense. They are men and women of 35, or 40, or 50. They have their own lives, their own obligations—their own children.

Yes, they will go to great lengths to keep a father or mother, or a father-in-law or mother-in-law, from going on relief—from becoming a public charge. But is it fair to demand so much?

Much is said about education, and the importance of making it available to all young people, to the limit of their abilities. I wonder how many young people lost their chance to go to college because their grandfather died a lingering death. We do not have statistics on that; we do not know how many carefully gathered college funds, saved in dimes and quarters and half dollars over the years, went to pay a hospital bill instead. All we know is that there have been a great many.

These sacrifices, it may be argued, are a part of family life. They ought to be taken in good spirit, or at least with resignation. That would be true—and in practice, it is indeed true today—if there were no alternative.

But there is an alternative. We can prevent these personal tragedies that strike the old, the middle aged, and the young alike. The alternative is now before you—a comprehensive program of hospital insurance for the aged, as part of the social security system, paid for, in pennies a week, by those who will reap its benefits.

Mr. Chairman, I urge you and your committee to give this just and simple remedy, explored and refined over 6 years of examination, your prompt and favorable action.

Document 4.3 *consists of a speech delivered by Vice President Hubert H. Humphrey in Tampa, Florida, on the first anniversary of the enactment of the Economic Opportunity Act, the cornerstone of the War on Poverty. Humphrey, one of the nation's most prominent liberal Democrats, celebrated the achievements of the War on Poverty, arguing that it was creating and would continue to create millions of productive, taxpaying citizens. Notably, Aid to Families with Dependent Children (AFDC), which would later be seen as the symbol of the War on Poverty, was only a small part of the effort at the time. Most of the War on Poverty sought to offer, as Humphrey and other advocates of the War on Poverty put it, a hand up rather than a handout. Ironically, it was these parts of the War on Poverty, especially the Community Action Projects, that initially proved most controversial, in part because they sought to break the impoverished person's dependence on government. Put differently, Democratic Party bosses saw efforts to empower the poor as a threat to their political base, essentially because they undercut the power they gained via patronage. As a result, they lobbied aggressively to obtain control over War on Poverty funds and programs. Closely allied with these bosses, neither Humphrey nor Johnson was able to thwart their efforts, and while federal antipoverty spending remained high, innovative efforts to empower the poor faded away.*

Document 4.3 Hubert H. Humphrey, "Speech on the First Anniversary of the War on Poverty," Tampa, Florida, August 27, 1965, *Congressional Digest* 45, no. 3 (March 1966), pp. 76–80.

It was my privilege to be present when President Lyndon Johnson signed into law the Economic Opportunity Act of 1964.

At that time our President told this Nation: ''I firmly believe that as of this moment a new day of opportunity is dawning, and a new era of progress is opening for us all.''

It is my privilege to report on the first year of that ''new era of progress''—to report on how we are doing in the War on Poverty.

As the general coordinator, with Sargent Shriver, of the war on poverty, I have been asked by the President to maintain a close watch on the efforts of the Americans—in Government and out—who are fighting this war not only against poverty, but for equality of opportunity, for hope, for human dignity.

We in America enjoy today an unprecedented peacetime economic expansion. That expansion—created through a positive partnership for prosperity between

Government and the private sector—gives us the opportunity to make basic investments to strengthen our American society for the great long-term responsibilities we face at home and in the world. We are moving ahead in seizing that opportunity.

In the midst of our rich society there is an "other America." There are some 30 million Americans in it. They have been shunted aside or lost in the backwaters. For them our national prosperity is something seen but seldom shared. These Americans belong to families earning an average $1,800 a year from all sources. That is $35 a week—to feed that family, to clothe that family, to house that family, to provide education and transportation and health care for that family.

But the poverty of these 30 million Americans is not to be measured in dollar terms alone. It must be measured in hopelessness and helplessness, in resentment and rejection, in despair and distrust, in loss to our Nation of valuable human resources.

The costs of welfare are a continuing drain on American communities.

The "other Americans" are taxeaters and not taxpayers.

There are estimates which indicate that hundreds of millions of dollars each year could be added to our economy; that hundreds of millions of dollars could be subtracted from our public budgets through greater investment to break the other Americans' cycle of poverty.

What if these people could become productive citizens—could become, for our communities, pluses and not minuses? These are challenges facing all Americans today. These are challenges we seek to meet with our war on poverty.

What are the dimensions—in numbers—of our first year's program under the Economic Opportunity Act itself? At the heart of our efforts, under the Economic Opportunity Act, is the community action program. In the past year, more than 800 separate grants have been made to nearly 750 cities and counties in all 50 American States, directly benefiting some 3 million people.

Two complementary programs—the Neighborhood Youth Corps and the Job Corps—together seek to find an answer to one of America's most urgent challenges: the challenge of finding useful, productive, gainful employment for our young people.

The Neighborhood Youth Corps will have more than 300,000 American youngsters working by the end of this year.

Over 300,000 men and women have already applied for the Job Corps. The first 10,000 enrollees are now learning and working in 50 centers across the land.

There is VISTA, the Volunteers in Service to America. VISTA has already attracted the volunteered services of more than 20,000 Americans of all ages, of all backgrounds, and from all parts of our land. The first 1,000 of our Nation's finest citizens are now on the job or in training—in Appalachian hollows, on Indian reservations, in urban and rural slums. By the end of the year they will number 2,000—working in 40 States.

There is Project Head Start, developed only in February of this year. This program is based on the simple proposition that if we give some special attention to those four- and five-year-olds entering school for the first time this fall—youngsters who might otherwise have difficulty adjusting—we cannot only alleviate some of the problems already afflicting these children, but can prevent their tragic accumulation in the years immediately ahead. We hoped Head Start would reach, its first year, 100,000 children. But Head Start reached this summer more than half a million of these children in 13,000 child development centers across the Nation.

There is the college work-study program, under which 40,000 students from 750 colleges worked this summer.

There is the work experience program, under which 88,000 unemployed parents are participating in projects in 42 States.

There is the adult basic education program, under which 37,000 persons are receiving literacy training.

And there is aid to migrants and the rural loan program.

The Small Business Administration has helped, too, in the war on poverty.

In communities across the Nation, local citizens have formed small business development centers as the focal point for local efforts to expand jobs and boost economic development through the creation of new small firms or the upgrading of existing businesses.

I have given, on this anniversary, some statistics to show the scope of what is already being done under the Economic Opportunity Act. But the Economic Opportunity Act—important as it is—is only a beginning. And the progress made in the past year under that act is only a part of the progress our Nation has made in awakening to the task at hand and in turning this country's will and resources to poverty's final elimination.

In this past year, the conscience of America has been aroused and disturbed. We now, as a Nation, believe the fact of poverty in our affluent midst.

There is greater understanding, too, that the war on poverty and civil rights are tied directly together. We recognize that the granting of legal rights must be matched with economic opportunity. The tragedy of Los Angeles has made this painfully clear.

We have placed on the Federal statute books a series of vital programs.

The Congress has approved a doubling of the economic opportunity program. But this is only one battleground of our struggle. Congress has also passed historic legislation granting aid to education, it has passed Medicare, a voting rights law, a new housing program, aid to Appalachia, the Older Americans Act, and other laws aimed at one or another of poverty's causes and symptoms.

Hundreds of communities have organized their own wars on poverty. More than 500 American communities have organized on their own. Tens of thousands of community leaders and citizens have joined the battle at home. The poor themselves have been mobilized for their own help.

Unlike previous programs, we look today to the poor themselves for a substantial effort on their own behalf. They are no longer apart, as spectators.

Literally tens of thousands of poor Americans are not [sic] at work helping themselves.

All parts of our society have joined in this task. Hundreds of American corporations have undertaken affirmative programs of job recruitment and training. Business organizations, including the U.S. Chamber of Commerce and National Association of Manufacturers, have joined the effort as organizations and through their members. The AFL-CIO, and its member unions, have opened the way for greater job opportunity.

All levels of American Government, business, and labor have become directly involved and are working in cooperation. Our efforts have touched the lives of millions of individual Americans.

I have reported the progress made in programs authorized only a year ago. Today, in America, there are hundreds of thousands of our citizens who have played a role in civic action, in training programs, in volunteer work. There are other hundreds of thousands who know for the first time that their poverty is not inevitable and that there are ways to be helped, trained, educated—ways to reach upward.

Yes, over the past year we have implemented a new law. But, even more important, we have mobilized our country for work too long delayed and pushed aside.

The people who came to this continent and built this Nation set out to create a society in which each citizen would have unfettered opportunity to lift himself and his family to something better.

If we really believe in our past—and our future—we must dedicate ourselves to making each man, each woman, each child in America a full participant in American life. I mean a life not just of prosperity and security, but a life in which self-expression and self-fulfillment are within the reach of all.

I came to Washington seventeen years ago as a freshman Senator. During that first year a scene took place in a Senate hearing room that symbolized just what we mean by the Great Society.

A woman from Tennessee, a garment worker, was testifying before seven U.S. Senators on behalf of raising the minimum wage to 75 cents an hour. At one point, this is what she said:

"My youngest girl she's nine now, goes straight to the piano when we go to a house where they have one. She does want to play the piano so bad. I've thought that maybe I could save 50 cents or a dollar a week to buy a second-hand piano for her, but I haven't found a way to do it yet. Maybe I've been foolish to talk to you people about music for one of my children when the main question is getting enough to eat and wear, or blankets for the bed, or a chair to sit on. But down in Tennessee we love music, and factory workers don't live by bread alone any more than anyone else does."

Piano lessons for a little Tennessee girl; full, productive lives for our citizens and the places where they live—these are what the war on poverty is all about, what the Great Society is all about. This is what we work for.

For the elderly, sick, and disabled—compassion and concern. For the young—an equal start in life. For all Americans—the opportunity to raise themselves not only to wealth and productivity, but to a life of satisfaction and fulfillment.

In 20th century America we have come to realize that the worth of a nation is, as John Stuart Mill said, no more than "the worth of the individuals composing it."

Thus we are determined to free millions of Americans from the bondage of that tragic equation which has too often decreed that poor shall beget poor and ignorance shall beget misery.

Thus it is that we seek to heal for all time the emotional scars of the experience which the Book of Job so poignantly describes: "The poor of the earth hide themselves together."

And thus it is that we are increasingly aware that, of those to whom much is given, much is expected—that as the abundance of worldly goods provides us with the tools to wage this war, so does it also impose upon us the moral imperative, the obligation, to wage it—and to wage it with resolution.

And cooperation must be the keynote—cooperation between public and private sectors; among Federal, State, and local governments; among all interested parties. Together there is little we cannot do, divided there is little that we can.

Yes, we wage war on poverty because it will make America stronger economically. But we attack poverty, too, in the spirit expressed by the author Thomas Wolfe: "To every man his chance, to every man regardless of his birth, his shining golden opportunity—to every man the right to live, to work, to be himself, and to become whatever thing his manhood and his vision can combine to make him—this . . . is the promise of America."

Even though Johnson won in a landslide in 1964, it is important to remember that a core of conservatives opposed the Great Society from the start. In 1964, the hopes and dreams of these conservatives were represented by Barry Goldwater, a lifelong foe of liberalism. After Goldwater lost the presidential election, many conservatives began to focus their attention on a new political figure, Ronald Reagan. A longtime actor, Reagan became an overnight political sensation during the 1964 presidential campaign when he delivered the nationally televised speech "A Time for Choosing" (**Document 4.4**). *Reagan's views were very similar to Goldwater's, but as many observed, he delivered them much more effectively than the Republican nominee. In part because of this speech, Reagan won the Republican nomination for governor of California in 1966. Fourteen years later, essentially making the same argument he did in "A Time for Choosing," he was elected president of the United States.*

Document 4.4   Ronald Reagan, "Televised Address—A Time for Choosing," reprinted in *Human Events* 24, no. 48 (November 28, 1964), pp. 8–9.

I have spent most of my life as a Democrat. I recently have seen fit to follow another course. I believe that the issues confronting us cross party lines. Now, one side in this campaign has been telling us that the issues of this election are the maintenance of peace and prosperity. The line has been used, ''We've never had it so good!''

But I have an uncomfortable feeling that this prosperity isn't something upon which we can base our hopes for the future. No nation in history has ever survived a tax burden that reached a third of its national income. Today 37 cents out of every dollar earned in this country is the tax collector's share, and yet our government continues to spend $17 million a day more than the government takes in.

We haven't balanced our budget 28 out of the last 34 years. We have raised our debt limit three times in the last 12 months, and now our national debt is one and a half times bigger than all the combined debts of all the nations of the world. We have $15 billion in gold in our treasury—we don't own an ounce. Foreign dollar claims are $27.3 billion, and we have just had announced that the dollar of 1939 will now purchase 45 cents in its total value.

As for the peace that we would preserve, I wonder who among us would like to approach the wife or mother whose husband or son has died in Viet Nam and ask them if they think this is a peace that should be maintained indefinitely. Do they mean we just want to be left in peace? There can be no real peace while one American is dying some place in the world for the rest of us.

We are at war with the most dangerous enemy that has ever faced mankind in his long climb from the swamp to the stars, and it has been said if we lose that war, and in so doing lose this way of freedom of ours, history will record with the greatest astonishment that those who had the most to lose did the least to prevent its happening.

Well, I think it's time to ask ourselves if we still know the freedoms intended for us by the Founding Fathers.

Not too long ago two friends of mine were talking to a Cuban refugee, a businessman who had escaped from Castro, and in the midst of his story one of my friends turned to the other and said, ''We don't know how lucky we are.'' And the Cuban stopped and said, ''How lucky *you* are! I had some place to escape to.''

In that sentence he told us the entire story. If we lose freedom here, there is no place to escape to. This is the last stand on earth, and this idea that government is beholden to the people, that it has no other source of power except the sovereign people, is still the newest and most unique idea in all the long history of man's relation to man.

This is the issue of this election, whether we believe in our capacity for self-government or whether we abandon the American Revolution and confess that a little intellectual elite in a far-distant capital can plan our lives for us better than we can plan them ourselves.

You and I are told increasingly that we have to choose between a left or right, but I would like to suggest that there is no such thing as a left or right. There is only an up or down—up to man's age-old dream—the ultimate in individual freedom consistent with law and order—or down to the ant heap of totalitarianism, and, regardless of their sincerity, their humanitarian motives, those who would trade our freedom for security have embarked on this downward course.

In this vote-harvesting time they use terms like "the Great Society," or, as we were told a short time ago by the President, we must accept a "greater government activity in the affairs of the people." But they have been a little more explicit in the past, and among themselves—and all of these things that I now will quote have appeared in print. These are not Republican accusations.

For example, they have voices that say "the cold war will end through our acceptance of a not undemocratic socialism." Another voice says that the profit motive has become outmoded; it must be replaced by the incentives of the welfare state, or our traditional system of individual freedom is incapable of solving the complex problems of the 20th Century.

Sen. Fulbright has said at Stanford University that the Constitution is outmoded. He referred to the President as our moral teacher, and our leader, and he said he is hobbled in his task by the restrictions in power imposed on him by this antiquated document. He must be freed so that he can do for us what he knows is best.

And Sen. Clark of Pennsylvania, another articulate spokesman, defines liberalism as "meeting the material needs of the masses through the full power of centralized government." Well, I for one resent it when a representative of the people refers to you and me—the free men and women of this country—as "the masses." This is a term we haven't applied to ourselves in America.

But beyond that, "the full power of centralized government"—this was the very thing the Founding Fathers sought to minimize. They knew that governments don't control things. A government can't control the economy without controlling people. And they know when a government sets out to do that, it must use force and coercion to achieve its purpose.

They also knew, those Founding Fathers, that outside of its legitimate functions, government does nothing as well or as economically as the private sector of the economy. Now, we have no better example of this than the government's involvement in the farm economy over the last 30 years. Since 1955 the cost of this program has nearly doubled. One-fourth of farming in America is responsible for 85 per cent of the farm surplus, three-fourths of farming is out on the free market and has shown a 21 per cent increase in the per capita consumption of all its produce. You see that one-fourth of farming that's regulated and controlled by the federal government?

In the last three years we have spent $43 in the feed grain program for every dollar bushel of corn we don't grow. Sen. Humphrey last week charged that Barry Goldwater as President would seek to eliminate farmers. He should do his homework a little better, because he will find out that we have had a decline of 5 million in the farm population under these government programs. . . .

Meanwhile, back in the city, under urban renewal, the assault on freedom carries on. Private property rights are so diluted that public interest is almost anything that a few government planners decide it should be. In a program that takes from the needy and gives to the greedy, we see such spectacles as in Cleveland, Ohio, a million and a half dollar building, completed only three years ago, must be destroyed to make way for what government officials call a "more compatible use of the land."

The President tells us he is now going to start building public housing units in the thousands where heretofore we have only built them is [sic] the hundreds. But FHA and the Veterans Administration tell us that they have 120,000 units they've taken back through mortgage foreclosures.

For three decades we have sought to solve the problems of unemployment through government planning, and the more the plans fail, the more planners plan. The latest is the Area Redevelopment Agency. They have just declared Rice County, Kan., a depressed area. Rice County, Kan., has 200 wells, and the 14,000 people there have over $30 million on deposit in personal savings in their banks. When the government tells you you are depressed, lie down and be depressed!

We have so many people who can't see a fat man standing beside a thin one without coming to the conclusion that the fat man got that way by taking advantage of the thin one! So they are going to solve all the problems of human misery through government and government planning.

Well, now, if the government planning and welfare had the answer, and they've had almost 30 years of it, shouldn't we expect the government to read the score to us once in a while?

Shouldn't they be telling us about the decline each year in the number of people needing help? . . . The reduction in the need for public housing? But the reverse is true. Each year the need grows greater, the problem grows greater. We were told four years ago that 17 million people went to bed hungry each night. Well, that was probably true. They were all on a diet!

But now we are told that 9.3 million families in this country are poverty-stricken on the basis of earning less than $3,000 a year. Welfare spending is ten times greater than in the dark depths of the depression. We are spending $45 billion on welfare. Now do a little arithmetic and you will find that if we divided $45 billion up equally among those 9 million poor families, we would be able to give each family $4,600 a year, and this, added to their present income, should eliminate poverty!

Direct aid to the poor, however, is running only about $600 per family. It seems that someplace there must be some overhead. So now we declare "War on Poverty," or "You, Too, Can Be a Bobby Baker!"

Now, do they honestly expect us to believe that if we add $1 billion to the $45 billion we are spending . . . one more program to the 30-odd we have (and remember, this new program doesn't replace any, it just duplicates existing programs). . . . Do they believe that poverty is suddenly going to disappear by magic? . . .

Well, in all fairness I should explain that there is one part of the new program that isn't duplicated. This is the youth feature. We are now going to solve the dropout problem, juvenile delinquency, by reinstituting something like the old CCC camps, and we are going to put our young people in camps; but again we do some arithmetic, and we find that we are going to spend each year just on room and board for each young person that we help $4,700 a year!

We can send them to Harvard for $2,700! Don't get me wrong. I'm not suggesting that Harvard is the answer to juvenile delinquency.

But seriously, what are we doing to those we seek to help? Not too long ago, a judge called me here in Los Angeles. He told me of a young woman who had come before him for a divorce.

She had six children, was pregnant with her seventh. Under his questioning, she revealed her husband was a laborer earning $250 a month. She wanted a divorce so that she could get an $80 raise. She is eligible for $330 a month in the aid to dependent children program. She got the idea from two women in her neighborhood who had already done that very thing.

Yet any time you and I question the schemes of the do-gooders, we are denounced as being against their humanitarian goals. They say we are always "against" things, never "for" anything. Well, the trouble with our liberal friends is not that they are ignorant, but that they know so much that is not so! . . .

No government ever voluntarily reduces itself in size. Government programs, once launched, never disappear. Actually, a government bureau is the nearest thing to eternal life we'll ever see on this earth!

Federal employees number 2.5 million. These proliferating bureaus with their thousands of regulations have cost us many of our constitutional safeguards. How many of us realize that today federal agents can invade a man's property without a formal hearing, let alone a trial by jury, and they can seize and sell his property in auction to enforce the payment of that fine? . . .

They say we offer simple answers to complex problems. Well, perhaps there is a simple answer . . . not an easy one . . . but a simple one. If you and I have the courage to tell our elected officials that we want our national policy based upon what we know in our hearts is morally right, we cannot buy our security, our freedom from the threat of the bomb by committing an immorality so great as saying to a billion human beings now in slavery behind the Iron Curtain, "Give up your dreams of freedom, because, to save our own skin, we are willing to make a deal with your slave master."

Alexander Hamilton said, "A nation which can prefer disgrace to danger is prepared for a master, and deserves one!" Let's set the record straight. There is no argument over the choice between peace and war, but there is only one guaranteed way you can have peace . . . and you can have it in the next second . . . surrender!

Admittedly there is a risk in any course we follow. Either course we follow other than this [sic], but every lesson in history tells us that the greater risk lies in appeasement, and this is the specter our well-meaning liberal friends refuse to face . . . that their policy of accommodation is appeasement, and it gives no choice between peace and war, only between fight or surrender. If we continue to accommodate, continue to back and retreat, eventually we have to face the final demand—the ultimatum.

And what then, when Nikita Khrushchev has told his people he knows what our answer will be? He has told them that we are retreating under the pressure of the cold war and some day when the time comes to deliver the ultimatum, our surrender will be voluntary because by that time we will have been weakened from within, spiritually, morally, and economically.

He believes this because from our side he has heard voices pleading for a "peace at any price," or "better Red than dead." Or as one commentator put it, he would rather "Live on his knees than die on his feet."

And therein lies the road to war, because those voices don't speak for the rest of us. You and I know and do not believe that life is so dear and peace so sweet as to be purchased at the price of chains and slavery.

If nothing in life is worth dying for, when did this begin. . . . Just in the face of the enemy . . . or should Moses have told the children of Israel to live in slavery under the Pharaohs? Should Christ have refused the cross? Should the patriots at Concord Bridge have thrown down their guns and refused to fire the shot heard 'round the world?

The martyrs of history were not fools, and our honored dead who gave their lives to stop the advance of the Nazis didn't die in vain! Where, then, is the road to peace? Well, it's a simple answer after all. You and I have the courage to say to our enemies, "There is a price we will not pay." There is a point beyond which they must not advance! This is the meaning in the phrase of Barry Goldwater's "peace through strength!"

Winston Churchill said that the destiny of man is not measured by material computation. When great forces are on the move in the world, we learn we are spirits, not animals. And he said there is something going on in time and space, and beyond time and space, which, whether we like it or not, spells duty.

You and I have a rendezvous with destiny. We will preserve for our children this, the last best hope for man on earth, or we will sentence them to take the last step into a thousand years of darkness.

We will keep this in mind and remember that Barry Goldwater has faith in us. He has faith that you and I have the ability and the dignity and the right to make our own decisions and determine our own destiny.

While the "Great Society" referred specifically to the domestic reforms proposed by the Johnson administration, many Americans associated it with several other reforms, especially those fostered by the Warren Court. Under the lead of Earl Warren, who served as chief justice from 1953 to 1969, the Supreme Court handed down numerous decisions that revolutionized the law. In addition to Brown v. Board of Education *(1954), which desegregated public schools, the Court expanded civil lib-*

erties, tightened criminal procedures, established the principle of "one man, one vote," and overturned state laws that banned the distribution of contraceptives. One of the Court's most controversial decisions involved freedom of religion. **Document 4.5** *contains Justice Hugo Black's majority opinion in* Engel v. Vitale *(1962), in which the Court ruled that official prayer in public schools was unconstitutional. In* **Document 4.6,** *South Carolina senator Strom Thurmond railed at this ruling, warning that the Court threatened to undermine American society and values. Barry Goldwater, the Republican candidate for president in 1964, echoed Thurmond's sentiments. So too did numerous other public figures, including Senators Preston Bush and Willis Robertson, the fathers of George Bush and Pat Robertson, the founder of the Christian Coalition, respectively. While the Supreme Court won the day, as suggested by Thurmond's speech,* Engel v. Vitale *helped catalyze conservative opposition to the Great Society and liberalism in general. Moreover, as the twentieth century draws to a close, it is difficult to judge who won the battle. While Thurmond, who still sits in the Senate, has been unable to gain passage of a constitutional amendment to allow for prayer in schools, in recent years the Supreme Court, whose membership has been influenced by the Judiciary Committee on which Thurmond sits, has begun to break down the wall between church and state and other reforms decreed by the Warren Court.*

Document 4.5 *Engel v. Vitale,* 370 U.S. 421 (1962).

MR. JUSTICE BLACK delivered the opinion of the Court:

. . . We think that by using its public school system to encourage recitation of the Regents' prayer, the State of New York has adopted a practice wholly inconsistent with the Establishment Clause. There can, of course, be no doubt that New York's program of daily classroom invocation of God's blessings as prescribed in the Regents' prayer is a religious activity. It is a solemn avowal of divine faith and supplication for the blessings of the Almighty. The nature of such a prayer has always been religious, none of the respondents has denied this and the trial court expressly so found:

> "The religious nature of prayer was recognized by Jefferson and has been concurred in by theological writers, the United States Supreme Court and State courts and administrative officials, including New York's Commissioner of Education. A committee of the New York Legislature has agreed.
>
> "The Board of Regents as *amicus curiae*, the respondents and intervenors all concede the religious nature of prayer, but seek to distinguish this prayer because it is based on our spiritual heritage. . . ."

The petitioners contend among other things that the state laws requiring or permitting use of the Regents' prayer must be struck down as a violation of the Establishment Clause because that prayer was composed by governmental officials as a part of a governmental program to further religious beliefs. For this reason, petitioners argue, the State's use of the Regents' prayer in its public school system breaches the constitutional wall of separation between Church and State. We agree with that contention since we think that the constitutional prohibition against laws respecting an establishment of religion must at least mean that in this country it is no part of the business of government to compose official prayers for any group of the American people to recite as a part of a religious program carried on by government.

It is a matter of history that this very practice of establishing governmentally composed prayers for religious services was one of the reasons which caused many of our early colonists to leave England and seek religious freedom in America. The Book of Common Prayer, which was created under governmental direction and which was approved by Acts of Parliament in 1548 and 1549, set out in minute detail the accepted form and content of prayer and other religious ceremonies to be used in the established, tax-supported Church of England. The controversies over the Book and what should be its content repeatedly threatened to disrupt the peace of that country as the accepted forms of prayer in the established church changed with the views of the particular ruler that happened to be in control at the time. Powerful groups representing some of the varying religious views of the people struggled among themselves to impress their particular views upon the Government and obtain amendments of the Book more suitable to their respective notions of how religious services should be conducted in order that the official religious establishment would advance their particular religious beliefs. Other groups, lacking the necessary political power to influence the Government on the matter, decided to leave England and its established church and seek freedom in America from England's governmentally ordained and supported religion.

It is an unfortunate fact of history that when some of the very groups which had most strenuously opposed the established Church of England found themselves sufficiently in control of colonial governments in this country to write their own prayers into law, they passed laws making their own religion the official religion of their respective colonies. Indeed, as late as the time of the Revolutionary War, there were established churches in at least eight of the thirteen former colonies and established religions in at least four of the other five. But the successful Revolution against English political domination was shortly followed by intense opposition to the practice of establishing religion by law. This opposition crystallized rapidly into an effective political force in Virginia where the minority religious groups such as Presbyterians, Lutherans, Quakers and Baptists had gained such strength that the adherents to the established Episcopal Church were actually a minority themselves. In 1785–1786, those opposed to the established Church, led by James Madison and Thomas Jefferson, who, though themselves not members of any of these dissenting religious groups, opposed all religious establishments by law on grounds of principle, obtained the enactment of the famous "Virginia Bill for Religious Liberty" by which all religious groups were placed on equal footing so far as the State was concerned. Similar though less far-reaching legislation was being considered and passed in other States.

By the time of the adoption of the Constitution, our history shows that there was a widespread awareness among many Americans of the dangers of a union of Church and State. These people knew, some of them from bitter personal experience, that one of the greatest dangers to the freedom of the individual to worship in his own way lay in the Government's placing its official stamp of approval upon one particular kind of prayer or one particular form of religious services. They knew the anguish, hardship and bitter strife that could come when zealous religious groups struggled with one another to obtain the Government's stamp of approval from each King, Queen, or Protector that came to temporary power. The Constitution was intended to avert a part of this danger by leaving the government of this country in the hands of the people rather than in the hands of any monarch. But this safeguard was not enough. Our Founders were no more willing to let the content of their prayers and their privilege of praying whenever they pleased be influenced by the ballot box than they were to let these vital matters of personal conscience depend upon the succession of monarchs. The First Amendment was added to the Constitution to stand as a guarantee that neither the power nor the prestige of the Federal Government would be used to control, support or influence the kinds of prayer the American people can say—that the people's religions must not be subjected to the pressures of government for change each time a new political administration is elected to office. Under that Amendment's prohibition against governmental establishment of religion, as reinforced by the provisions of the Fourteenth Amendment, government in this country, be it state or federal, is without power to prescribe by law any particular form of prayer which is to be used as an official prayer in carrying on any program of governmentally sponsored religious activity.

There can be no doubt that New York's state prayer program officially establishes the religious beliefs embodied in the Regents' prayer. The respondents' argument to the contrary, which is largely based upon the contention that the Regents' prayer is "non-denominational" and the fact that the program, as modified and approved by state courts, does not require all pupils to recite the prayer but permits those who wish to do so to remain silent or be excused from the room, ignores the essential nature of the program's constitutional defects. Neither the fact that the prayer may be denominationally neutral nor the fact that its observance on the part of the students is voluntary can serve to free it from the limitations of the Establishment Clause, as it might from the Free Exercise Clause, of the First Amendment, both of which are operative against the States by virtue of the Fourteenth Amendment. Although these two clauses may in certain instances overlap, they forbid two quite different kinds of governmental encroachment upon religious freedom. The Establishment Clause, unlike the Free Exercise Clause, does not depend upon any showing of direct governmental compulsion and is violated by the enactment of laws which establish an official religion whether those laws operate directly to coerce nonobserving individuals or not. This is not to say, of course, that laws officially prescribing a particular form of religious worship do not involve coercion of such individuals. When the power, prestige and financial support of government is placed behind a particular religious belief, the indirect coercive pressure upon religious minorities to conform to the prevailing officially approved religion is plain. But the purposes underlying the Establishment Clause go much further than that. Its first and most immediate purpose rested on the belief that a union of government and religion tends to destroy government and to degrade religion. The history of governmentally established religion, both in England and in this country, showed that whenever government had allied itself with one particular form of religion, the inevitable result had been that it had incurred the hatred, disrespect and even contempt of those who held contrary beliefs. That same history showed that many people had lost their respect for any religion that had relied upon the support of government to spread its faith. The Establishment Clause thus stands as an expression of principle on the part of the Founders of our Constitution that religion is too personal, too sacred, too holy, to permit its "unhallowed perversion" by a civil magistrate. Another purpose of the Establishment Clause rested upon an awareness of the historical fact that governmentally established religions and religious persecutions go hand in hand. The Founders knew that only a few years after the Book of Common Prayer became the only accepted form of religious services in the established Church of England, an Act of Uniformity was passed to compel all Englishmen to attend those services and to make it a criminal offense to conduct or attend religious gatherings of any other kind—a law which was consistently flouted by dissenting religious groups in England and which contributed to widespread persecutions of people like John Bunyan who persisted in holding "unlawful [religious] meetings . . . to the great disturbance and distraction of the good subjects of this kingdom. . . ." And they knew that similar persecutions had received the sanction of law in several of the colonies in this country soon after the establishment of official religions in those colonies. It was in large part to get completely away from this sort of systematic religious persecution that the Founders brought into being our Nation, our Constitution, and our Bill of Rights with its prohibition against any governmental establishment of religion. The New York laws officially prescribing the Regents' prayer are inconsistent with both the purposes of the Establishment Clause and with the Establishment Clause itself.

It has been argued that to apply the Constitution in such a way as to prohibit state laws respecting an establishment of religious services in public schools is to indicate a hostility toward religion or toward prayer. Nothing, of course, could be more wrong. The history of man is inseparable from the history of religion. And perhaps it is not too much to say that since the beginning of that history many people have devoutly believed that "More things are wrought by prayer than this world dreams of." It was doubtless largely due to men who believed this that there grew up a sentiment that caused men to leave the cross-currents of officially established state religions and religious persecution in Europe and come to this country filled with the hope that they could find a place in which they could pray when they pleased to the God of their faith in the language they chose. And there were men of this same faith in the power of prayer who led the fight for adoption of our Constitution and also for our Bill of Rights with the very guarantees of religious freedom that forbid the sort of governmental activity which New York has attempted here. These men knew that the First Amendment, which tried to put an end to governmental control of religion and of prayer, was not written to destroy either. They knew rather that it was written to quiet well-justified fears which nearly all of them felt arising out of an awareness that governments of the past had shackled men's tongues to make them speak only the religious thoughts that government wanted them to speak and to pray only to the God that government wanted them to pray to. It is neither sacrilegious nor antireligious to say that each separate government in this country should stay out of the business of writing or sanctioning official prayers and leave that purely religious function to the people themselves and to those the people choose to look to for religious guidance.

It is true that New York's establishment of its Regents' prayer as an officially approved religious doctrine of that State does not amount to a total establishment of one particular religious sect to the exclusion of all others—that, indeed, the governmental endorsement of that prayer seems relatively insignificant when compared to the governmental encroachments upon religion which were commonplace 200 years ago. To those who may subscribe to the view that because the Regents' official prayer is so brief and general there can be no danger to religious freedom in its governmental establishment, however, it may be appropriate to say in the words of James Madison, the author of the First Amendment:

"[I]t is proper to take alarm at the first experiment on our liberties. . . . Who does not see that the same authority which can establish Christianity, in exclusion of all other Religions, may establish with the same ease any particular sect of Christians, in exclusion of all other Sects? That the same authority which can force a citizen to contribute three pence only of his property for the support of any one establishment, may force him to conform to any other establishment in all cases whatsoever?"

The judgment of the Court of Appeals of New York is reversed and the cause remanded for further proceedings not inconsistent with this opinion.

Document 4.6 Strom Thurmond, "Address on the Supreme Court Decision on Prayer in the Public Schools," with additional "Remarks" by Barry Goldwater, *Congressional Record,* 87th Congress, 2nd Session, 108, part 9 (June 28, 1962), pp. 12175–12179.

Mr. THURMOND. Mr. President, the Supreme Court of the United States has overstepped its bounds in loose and distorted interpretations of the United States Constitution on many occasions, particularly in recent years. No Court decision, however, has shocked the conscience of the American people as has the ruling in the now famous school prayer decision of Engle [sic] against Vitale, on June 25, 1962. The Court ruled in this case that a simple, nondenominational prayer as devised by the New York State Board of Regents for schoolchildren without compulsion is offensive to the Constitution. The prayer reads as follows:

Almighty God, we acknowledge our dependence upon Thee, and we beg Thy blessings upon us, our parents, our teachers, and our country.

The constitutional provision which this simple prayer purportedly violates is a portion of the first amendment, which reads as follows:

Congress shall make no law respecting an establishment of religion, or prohibiting the free exercise thereof.

It should be difficult for any American to find much, if anything, to quarrel with in that brief school prayer which merely acknowledges the existence of a Supreme Being, recognizing in a small way our national religious heritage and traditions. The constitutional provision appears to carry little or no ambiguity as to its meaning, particularly if one studies the contemporaneous events leading up to its adoption as a part of the Constitution. It is clear that the framers of this provision were concerned about the establishment of a national religion which would suppress all other religions. They were, as Dr. Billy Graham has so ably pointed out, concerned with maintaining freedom of religion, not freedom from religion. In fact, the late Justice Joseph Story informs us in his famous "Commentaries on the Constitution" that "an attempt to level all religion and to make it a matter of state policy to hold all in utter indifference, would have created universal disapprobation, if not universal indignation." Another expert on constitutional law, Mr. Cooley, made the point in his important work, "Principles of Constitutional Law," that "it was never intended by the Constitution that the Government should be prohibited from recognizing religion, where it might be done without drawing any invidious distinctions between different religious beliefs, organizations, or sects."

What the Court found to be invidious or dangerous in this case was the New York board's attempt to establish a religion with this simple, nondenominational prayer. The Wall Street Journal has stated in an editorial comment of June 27 that "this attitude bespeaks considerable confusion and no abundance of commonsense." It is indeed the height of legal absurdity and distortion to state or even imply that the State of New York was attempting to establish a State religion by use of this noncompulsory, 22-word prayer which was carefully worded to avoid making any "invidious distinctions" so as to give preference to one religion over another. . . .

Besides, the constitutional provision contains a prohibition not against the States, but against the Congress establishing a religion or interfering with the free exercise of religion. Justice Story also made a strong point when he stated in his "Commentaries" that "the whole power over the subject of religion is left exclusively to the State governments, to be acted upon according to their own sense of justice and the State constitutions; and the Catholic and the Protestant, the Calvinist and the Arminian, the Jew and the infidel, may sit down at the common table of the national councils without any inquisition into their faith or mode of worship."

The Supreme Court, however, has attempted to tie the 14th amendment into the 1st amendment in another loose interpretation of the Constitution, and this combination of the "no establishment" clause with the "equal protection and immunities" clause has been used to rule out the action of the New York State Board of Regents in authorizing this school prayer.

Americans all across this great land of ours are concerned about this decision because it reflects a pattern of national actions designed, as Dr. Billy Graham warned in the February 17, 1962, issue of the Saturday Evening Post, "to take the traditional concept of God out of our national life." This is the disturbing fact about this lamentable decision. It signals the come-on of more antireligion decisions to follow in the wake of the precedent set in this judicial amendment to the Constitution. If this decision stands, then any action in public schools or in our national life carrying the "taint" of religion or acknowledgment of a Supreme Being can be swept away. Justice Hugo Black in a footnote to the majority opinion tried to "pooh-pooh" the idea that congressionally approved acts, such as establishment of our national motto, "In God we trust," or the addition to the "Pledge of Allegiance to the Flag" of the words "under God," might be affected. But, if the Court can interpret a constitutional provision which plainly states that the prohibition is only against congressional action as applying to a State action, then the Court could, with more validity—if there be any validity here at all—rule out these and other congressional enactments of recent and past years. . . .

The American people are proud of our national heritage and traditions, especially our spiritual ties to a Supreme Being. The history of America has been marked by religious features from the very beginning, just as the map of America is marked with names of religious origin and meaning. The first discoverers and settlers of the Americas came with the Bible and the cross. From each country of the Old World with each expedition or attempted colony went missionaries, ministers, priests, for the conversion of the pagan Indians and to provide the ministrations of religion for the colonists.

Many of the colonists came to the New World to escape religious persecution and to worship in freedom. They determined to establish a new world whose government would be based on religious foundations but which would retain for each individual the right to worship in freedom and determine his own destiny. . . .

After proclaiming our independence in the Declaration of Independence and winning it in the American Revolution, our forefathers sought to secure our independence and newly won liberties for all our people for generations to come. When they met in Philadelphia in 1787 at the Constitutional Convention, the Founding Fathers determined to establish a government which would be separate from any religious faith and one which would place a premium on individual liberty, individual initiative, and individual responsibility. In making certain that church and state would not be mixed, they did not rule God out of our national life as the Supreme Court is attempting to do today. Indeed, they based their ideals as a nation on those given us by Christ.

For it was Christ, Himself, who ordained the preeminence of the individual, and Christian individualism was the very bedrock on which our Nation was founded. The Founding Fathers intended that each man should be free to determine his own religion and his own destiny, but by their example and the foundations which they laid for our Government they made it crystal clear that individually and as a nation we would have to look to God for guidance and blessings to ourselves and our Nation.

At one point in its proceedings when the Constitutional Convention was at the point of breaking up, the venerated and wise Benjamin Franklin suggested prayer. . . .

Down through the years since the founding of our great Republic, each President has asked the protection and help of God in taking his oath of office, as have Members of the Congress and most other National, State, and local officeholders. In the dissenting opinion in Engel against Vitale, Justice Potter Stewart has pointed out that even in the Supreme Court there has been a traditional recognition of God—the wisdom of which is specifically questioned by Justice William Douglas—by the Crier of the Court, in opening each session with the petition: "God save the United States and this honorable Court." . . .

The irrational—and, I think, irreverent—decision in Engel against Vitale comes, Mr. President, at a time when the world is locked in a cold war struggle between the forces of freedom which look to a Supreme Being for divine guidance and supplication and the forces of tyranny which are presided over by an ideology which does not recognize true freedom or any god except man himself and the worship of materialism. In this time of the most critical period in our national life, we need to increase rather than decrease individual and national attention to spiritual and moral values which undergird our Nation in this struggle, which is essentially a fight between those who do and do not believe in a Supreme Being. Every time we turn our young people—or any of our people for that matter—away from God, we turn them down the road toward the enemy camp of reliance on man and devotion to materialism. . . .

The American people expect the Congress to act decisively to correct this erroneous decision based on illogical reason and distorted interpretation of a constitutional provision which was meant to insure that our religious heritage and traditions would always be a vital part not just of our individual lives but also our national life. The Court has on this occasion "bitten off more than it can chew," and I trust that the American people will soon have the Congress take the necessary action to reverse this decision.

In closing, I commend Justice Stewart for taking a stand—albeit a lonesome stand on the Court—in favor of fostering and promoting our religious heritage and traditions rather than joining in the action which attempts to interpret God out of our national life. In the end his dissent will prevail, not only because his position is supported by the overwhelming majority of the American people, who still hold the reins of Government, but because it is right. . . .

Mr. GOLDWATER. I take this occasion to thank the distinguished Senator from South Carolina for so eloquently and brilliantly calling to the attention of the Senate the error of the Supreme Court in its recent decision. . . .

In concluding my commendation of the Senator from South Carolina, I make this observation: The unhappiness and concern with this unwise decision must be unanimous. I am sure the Senator from South Carolina will remember that on previous occasions when the Supreme Court has rendered decisions that have tended to destroy States rights and take away the individual liberties of our people, the liberal Members of this body have risen up in defense of the Court.

I have not heard any liberal Member of this body rise to defend the Court in its recent action. I wonder about that inconsistency. I wonder if finally they are not agreeing with the conservative Members of this body that the Supreme Court of the United States has been in error and continues to be in error. If it continues to make the mistakes it has made, this legislative body will be sorely pressed to overcome them in order that we may perpetuate our constitutional Republic and protect the rights of the people.

Mr. THURMOND. I thank the distinguished Senator from Arizona for his complimentary remarks about my address. He has made a great contribution in the statement he has just made.

I feel very strongly about this. I concur wholeheartedly with the statement the Senator has made. I believe that a majority of the Congress, as well as the majority of the American people, also concur. It is my sincere hope that action will be taken promptly by the Congress to offset and reverse this unconstitutional and unwise decision of the Supreme Court in the school prayer case.

While the Vietnam War became the bête noire of the "New Left," large student protests first took place over other issues prior to the escalation of the war. In the fall of 1964, a cluster of students, some of whom had been active in the civil rights movement, protested against restrictions on their freedom of speech and against the bureaucratization of the University of California at Berkeley. Initially joined by members of the Young Americans for Freedom, who similarly found the university's regulations banning political activity on campus unacceptable, the Free Speech Movement, as it became known, energized students all across the nation, many of whom wrote that they too felt repressed by "the system." Mario Savio's "An End to History," **Document 4.7,** *stands as the classic text of the Free Speech Movement. A veteran of Mississippi Summer and a graduate student in philosophy at the University of California at Berkeley, Savio drew an analogy between the civil rights movement and the student movement and called upon students to play a role similar to that being played by freedom fighters in the South. As he put it at a large rally, "There comes a time when the operation of the machine becomes so odious, makes you so sick at heart, that you can't take part, you can't even tacitly take part. And you've got to put your bodies on the gears and upon the wheels, upon the levers, upon all the apparatus, and you've got to make it stop."*

Document 4.7 Mario Savio, "An End to History," *Humanity*, no. 2 (December 1964).

Last summer I went to Mississippi to join the struggle there for civil rights. This fall I am engaged in another phase of the same struggle, this time in Berkeley. The two battlefields may seem quite different to some observers, but this is not the case. The same rights are at stake in both places—the right to participate as citizens in democratic society and the right to due process of law. Further, it is a struggle against the same enemy. In Mississippi an autocratic and powerful minority rules, through organized violence, to suppress the vast, virtually powerless majority. In California, the privileged minority manipulates the university bureaucracy to suppress the students' political expression. That "respectable" bureaucracy masks the financial plutocrats; that impersonal bureaucracy is the efficient enemy in a "Brave New World."

In our free-speech fight at the University of California, we have come up against what may emerge as the greatest problem of our nation—depersonalized, unresponsive bureaucracy. We have encountered the organized status quo in Mississippi, but it is the same in Berkeley. Here we find it impossible usually to meet with anyone but secretaries. Beyond that, we find functionaries who cannot make policy but can only hide behind the rules. We have discovered total lack of response on the part of the policy makers. To grasp a situation which is truly Kafkaesque, it is necessary to understand the bureaucratic mentality. And we have learned quite a bit about it this fall, more outside the classroom than in.

As bureaucrat, an administrator believes that nothing new happens. He occupies an a-historical point of view. In September, to get the attention of this bureaucracy which had issued arbitrary edicts suppressing student political expression and refused to discuss its action, we held a sit-in on the campus. We sat around a police car and kept it immobilized for over thirty-two hours. At last, the administrative bureaucracy agreed to negotiate. But instead, on the following Monday, we discovered that a committee had been appointed, in accordance with usual regulations, to resolve the dispute. Our attempt to convince any of the administrators that an event had occurred, that something new had happened, failed. They saw this simply as something to be handled by normal university procedures.

The same is true of all bureaucracies. They begin as tools, means to certain legitimate goals, and they end up feeding their own existence. The conception that bureaucrats have is that history has in fact come to an end. No events can occur now that the Second World War is over which can change American society substantially. We proceed by standard procedures as we are.

The most crucial problems facing the United States today are the problem of automation and the problem of racial injustice. Most people who will be put out of jobs by machines will not accept an end to events, this historical plateau, as the point beyond which no change occurs. Negroes will not accept an end to history here. All of us must refuse to accept history's final judgment that in America there is no place in society for people whose skins are dark. On campus students are not about to accept it as fact that the university has ceased evolving and is in its final state of perfection, that students and faculty are respectively raw material and employees, or that the university is to be autocratically run by unresponsive bureaucrats.

Here is the real contradiction: the bureaucrats hold history has ended. As a result significant parts of the population both on campus and off are dispossessed, and these dispossessed are not about to accept this a-historical point of view. It is out of this that the conflict has occurred with the university bureaucracy and will continue to occur until that bureaucracy becomes responsive or until it is clear the university cannot function.

The things we are asking for in our civil-rights protests have a deceptively quaint ring. We are asking for the due process of law. We are asking for our actions to be judged by committees of our peers. We are asking that regulations ought to be considered as arrived at legitimately only from the consensus of the governed. These phrases are all pretty old, but they are not being taken seriously in America today, nor are they being taken seriously on the Berkeley campus.

I have just come from a meeting with the Dean of Students. She notified us that she was aware of certain violations of university regulations by certain organizations. University friends of Student Non-violent Coordinating Committee, which I represent, was one of these. We tried to draw from her some statement on these great principles, consent of the governed, jury of one's peers, due process. The best she could do was to evade or to present the administration party line. It is very hard to make any contact with the human being who is behind these organizations.

The university is the place where people begin seriously to question the conditions of their existence and raise the issue of whether they can be committed to the society they have been born into. After a long period of apathy during the fifties, students have begun not only to question but, having arrived at answers, to act on those answers. This is part of a growing understanding among many people in America that history has not ended, that a better society is possible, and that it is worth dying for.

This free-speech fight points up a fascinating aspect of contemporary campus life. Students are permitted to talk all they want so long as their speech has no consequences.

One conception of the university, suggested by a classical Christian formulation, is that it be in the world but not of the world. The conception of Clark Kerr by contrast is that the university is part and parcel of this particular stage in the history of American society; it stands to serve the need of American industry; it is a factory that turns out a certain product needed by industry or government. Because speech does often have consequences which might alter this perversion of higher education, the university must put itself in a position of censorship. It can permit two kinds of speech, speech which encourages continuation of the status quo, and speech which advocates changes in it so radical as to be irrelevant in the foreseeable future. Someone may advocate radical change in all aspects of American society, and this I am sure he can do with impunity. But if someone advocates sit-ins to bring about changes in discriminatory hiring practices, this cannot be permitted because it goes against the status quo of which the university is a part. And that is how the fight began here.

The administration of the Berkeley campus has admitted that external, extralegal groups have pressured the university not to permit students on campus to organize picket lines, not to permit on campus any speech with consequences.

And the bureaucracy went along. Speech with consequences, speech in the area of civil rights, speech which some might regard as illegal, must stop.

Many students here at the university, many people in society, are wandering aimlessly about. Strangers in their own lives, there is no place for them. They are people who have not learned to compromise, who for example have come to the university to learn to question, to grow, to learn—all the standard things that sound like clichés because no one takes them seriously. And they find at one point or other that for them to become part of society, to become lawyers, ministers, businessmen, people in government, that very often they must compromise those principles which were most dear to them. They must suppress the most creative impulses that they have; this is a prior condition for being part of the system. The university is well structured, well tooled, to turn out people with all the sharp edges worn off, the well-rounded person. The university is well equipped to produce that sort of person, and this means that the best among the people who enter must for four years wander aimlessly much of the time questioning why they are on campus at all, doubting whether there is any point in what they are doing, and looking toward a very bleak existence afterward in a game in which all of the rules have been made up, which one cannot really amend.

It is a bleak scene, but it is all a lot of us have to look forward to. Society provides no challenge. American society in the standard conception it has of itself is simply no longer exciting. The most exciting things going on in American today are movements to change America. America is becoming ever more the utopia of sterilized, automated contentment. The "futures" and "careers" for which American students now prepare are for the most part intellectual and moral wastelands. This chrome-plated consumers' paradise would have us grow up to be well-behaved children. But an important minority of men and women coming to the front today have shown that they will die rather than be standardized, replaceable and irrelevant.

NOTE

1. Robert M. Collins, "Growth Liberalism in the Sixties," in *The Sixties: From Memory to History*, ed. David Farber (Chapel Hill: University of North Carolina Press, 1994), p. 19.

Vice President Richard M. Nixon and Soviet Premier Nikita Khrushchev at "Kitchen Debate," July 1959. National Archives.

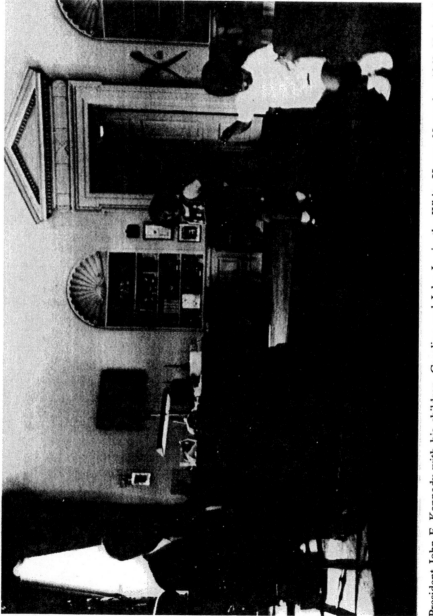

President John F. Kennedy with his children, Caroline and John Jr., in the White House, November 1962. National Archives.

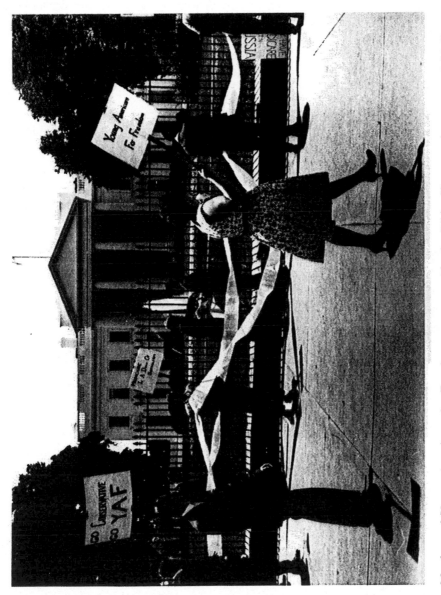

Members of Young Americans for Freedom protest outside the White House against proposed Medicare program, July 11, 1962. National Archives.

President Lyndon B. Johnson and Thurgood Marshall, prior to Marshall's appointment to Supreme Court. National Archives.

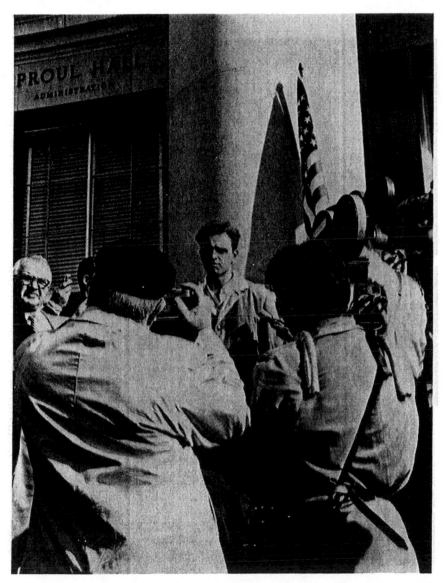

Mario Savio, leader of the Free Speech Movement, on the steps of Sproul Hall, University of California at Berkeley, 1964. Courtesy, The Bancroft Library, University of California, Berkeley. 24B:14.

Two soldiers of the 173rd Airborne Brigade await helicopter to evacuate them following a firefight in Long Kanh Province, Vietnam, 1966. National Archives.

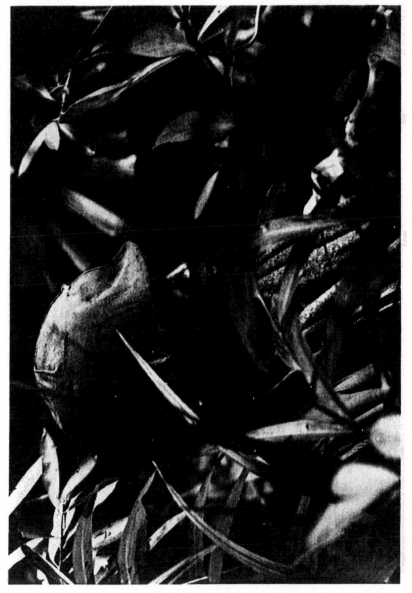

U.S. soldier awaits action in South Vietnam, undated. National Archives.

Betty Friedan speaks at Equal Rights Amendment Rally, undated. National Archives.

Topless woman dances in People's Park, Berkeley, California, 1969. Courtesy, The Bancroft Library, University of California, Berkeley. 24A:10.

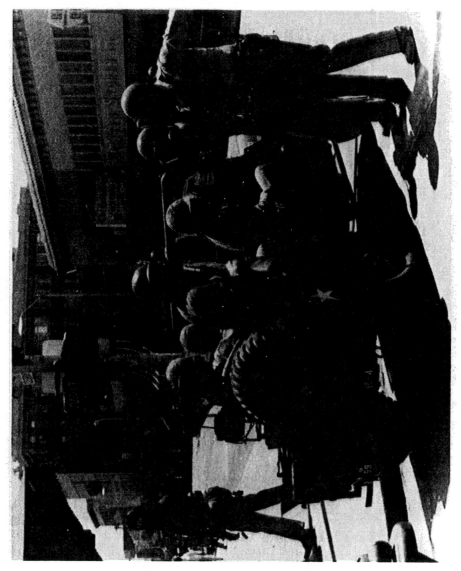

National Guard troops and police occupy Berkeley during battle over People's Park, 1969. Courtesy, The Bancroft Library, University of California, Berkeley. 24A:34.

Black Panther Party poster, featuring Bobby Seale and Huey Newton. Library of Congress.

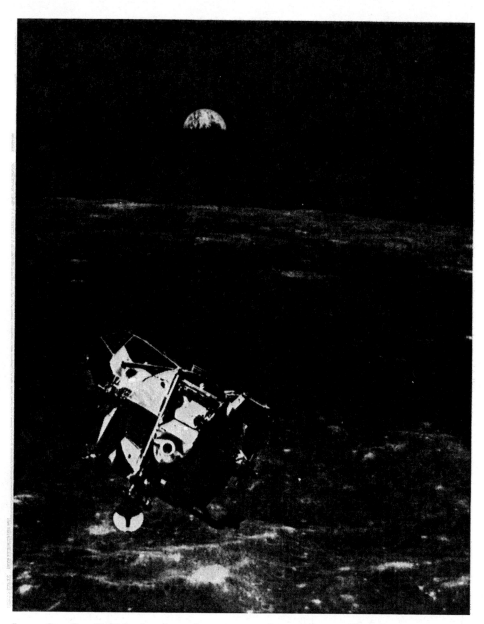

Lunar Landing Vehicle rises from the moon to rejoin Apollo 11 following the first "walk on the moon," with Earth in the background, July 12, 1969. National Archives.

Chapter Five

VIETNAM

For many Americans, Vietnam and the sixties are synonymous. While the U.S. involvement in Southeast Asia stretched back to the latter half of the 1940s, Johnson's escalation of the war in 1965 transformed the nature of the conflict. Ironically, few Americans initially understood the implications of the expansion of the war in Vietnam; most figured that U.S. involvement would be brief and uneventful. Only after neither assumption proved true did support for Johnson's policies decline.

Document 5.1, the Gulf of Tonkin Resolution, enacted by Congress on August 7, 1964, granted President Johnson the power to expand the war in Vietnam. Although the president did not submit concrete evidence verifying the North Vietnamese attack on the U.S.S. Maddox, and information gathered later would cast doubt on nearly all of his assertions regarding the incident, the resolution was passed unanimously by the House of Representatives and by a 98–2 margin in the Senate. As a sign of the public's lack of concern over Vietnam, very few Americans objected to the resolution at the time. In fact, one of the two senators who voted against the resolution was defeated in his bid for reelection.

In February 1965, acting on the authority granted to him by the Gulf of Tonkin Resolution, Johnson escalated the air war against the communists in retaliation against a Viet Minh (often called the Vietcong) attack on an American airbase in Pleiku, Vietnam. At first Johnson claimed that the use of air power would obviate the need to increase the number of ground troops in Vietnam, but later that summer he increased the number of marines and army troops in Southeast Asia in order to protect the air bases and to follow up on the air attacks. By the end of 1966, 375,000 troops were stationed in Vietnam; by 1968, the number had grown to roughly 500,000, and General William Westmoreland was calling for more. In **Document**

5.2, *a speech that Johnson delivered at Johns Hopkins University on April 7, 1965, the president spelled out the reason behind the war effort. Emphasizing the need to maintain the nation's credibility and commitments, he painted the military objective as one of turning back an invasion by North Vietnam's Communist troops so as to protect the free people of South Vietnam. This rationale was repeated throughout the war, although the extent to which it was valid became and remains a point of contention.*

Document 5.1   "The Gulf of Tonkin Resolution" (1964), *Congressional Record,* 88th Congress, 2nd Session, 110, part 14 (August 5, 1964), p. 18133.

Whereas naval units of the Communist regime in [North] Vietnam, in violation of the principles of the Charter of the United Nations and of international law, have deliberately and repeatedly attacked United States naval vessels lawfully present in international waters, and have thereby created a serious threat to international peace;

Whereas these attacks are part of a deliberate and systematic campaign of aggression that the Communist regime in North Vietnam has been waging against its neighbors and the nations joined with them in the collective defense of their freedom; and

Whereas the United States is assisting the peoples of southeast Asia to protect their freedom and has no territorial, military or political ambitions in that area, but desires only that these peoples should be left in peace to work out their own destinies in their own way: Now, therefore, be it

Resolved by the Senate and House of Representatives of the United States of America in Congress assembled, That the Congress approves and supports the determination of the President, as Commander in Chief, to take all necessary measures to repel any armed attack against the forces of the United States and to prevent further aggression.

Sec. 2. The United States regards as vital to its national interest and to world peace the maintenance of international peace and security in southeast Asia. Consonant with the Constitution of the United States and the Charter of the United Nations and in accordance with its obligations under the Southeast Asia Collective Defense Treaty, the United States is, therefore, prepared, as the President determines, to take all necessary steps, including the use of armed force, to assist any member or protocol state of the Southeast Asia Collective Defense Treaty requesting assistance in defense of its freedom.

Sec. 3. This resolution shall expire when the President shall determine that the peace and security of the area is reasonably assured by international conditions created by action of the United Nations or otherwise, except that it may be terminated earlier by concurrent resolution of the Congress.

Document 5.2 Lyndon B. Johnson, "Address at Johns Hopkins University—We Have Promises to Keep," April 7, 1965, reprinted in *Department of State Bulletin* **52, no. 1348 (April 26, 1965), pp. 607–609.**

... Why are we in South Viet-Nam?

We are there because we have a promise to keep. Since 1954 every American President has offered support to the people of South Viet-Nam. We have helped to build, and we have helped to defend. Thus, over many years, we have made a national pledge to help South Viet-Nam defend its independence.

And I intend to keep that promise.

To dishonor that pledge, to abandon this small and brave nation to its enemies, and to the terror that must follow, would be an unforgivable wrong.

We are also there to strengthen world order. Around the globe, from Berlin to Thailand, are people whose well-being rests in part on the belief that they can count on us if they are attacked. To leave Viet-Nam to its fate would shake the confidence of all these people in the value of an American commitment and in the value of America's word. The result would be increased unrest and instability, and even wider war.

We are also there because there are great stakes in the balance. Let no one think for a moment that retreat from Viet-Nam would bring an end to conflict. The battle would be renewed in one country and then another. The central lesson of our time is that the appetite of aggression is never satisfied. To withdraw from one battlefield means only to prepare for the next. We must say in Southeast Asia—as we did in Europe—in the words of the Bible: "Hitherto shalt thou come, but no further."

There are those who say that all our effort there will be futile—that China's power is such that it is bound to dominate all Southeast Asia. But there is no end to that argument until all of the nations of Asia are swallowed up.

There are those who wonder why we have a responsibility there. Well, we have it there for the same reason that we have a responsibility for the defense of Europe. World War II was fought in both Europe and Asia, and when it ended we found ourselves with continued responsibility for the defense of freedom.

Our objective is the independence of South Viet-Nam and its freedom from attack. We want nothing for ourselves—only that the people of South Viet-Nam be allowed to guide their own country in their own way. We will do everything necessary to reach that objective. And we will do only what is absolutely necessary.

In recent months attacks on South Viet-Nam were stepped up. Thus, it became necessary for us to increase our response and to make attacks by air. This is not a change of purpose. It is a change in what we believe that purpose requires.

We do this in order to slow down aggression.

We do this to increase the confidence of the brave people of South Viet-Nam who have bravely borne this brutal battle for so many years with so many casualties.

And we do this to convince the leaders of North Viet-Nam—and all who seek to share their conquest—of a simple fact:

We will not be defeated.

We will not grow tired.

We will not withdraw, either openly or under the cloak of a meaningless agreement.

We know that air attacks alone will not accomplish all of these purposes. But it is our best and prayerful judgment that they are a necessary part of the surest road to peace. . . .

This war, like most wars, is filled with terrible irony. For what do the people of North Viet-Nam want? They want what their neighbors also desire—food for their hunger, health for their bodies, a chance to learn, progress for their country, and an end to the bondage of material misery. And they would find all these things far more readily in peaceful association with others than in the endless course of battle.

These countries of Southeast Asia are homes for millions of impoverished people. Each day these people rise at dawn and struggle through until the night to wrest existence from the soil. They are often wracked by disease, plagued by hunger, and death comes at the early age of 40.

Stability and peace do not come easily in such a land. Neither independence nor human dignity will ever be won, though, by arms alone. It also requires the works of peace. The American people have helped generously in times past in these works, and now there must be a much more massive effort to improve the life of man in that conflict-torn corner of our world.

The first step is for the countries of Southeast Asia to associate themselves in a greatly expanded cooperative effort for development. We would hope that North Viet-Nam would take its place in the common effort just as soon as peaceful cooperation is possible.

The United Nations is already actively engaged in development in this area, and as far back as 1961 I conferred with our authorities in Viet-Nam in connection with their work there. And I would hope tonight that the Secretary-General of the United Nations could use the prestige of his great office and his deep knowledge of Asia to initiate, as soon as possible, with the countries of that area, a plan for cooperation in increased development.

For our part I will ask the Congress to join in a billion-dollar American investment in this effort as soon as it is underway. And I would hope that all other industrialized countries, including the Soviet Union, will join in this effort to replace despair with hope and terror with progress.

The task is nothing less than to enrich the hopes and the existence of more than a hundred million people. And there is much to be done.

The vast Mekong River can provide food and water and power on a scale to dwarf even our own TVA. The wonders of modern medicine can be spread through villages where thousands die every year from lack of care. Schools can be established to train people in the skills that are needed to manage the process of development. And these objectives, and more, are within the reach of a co-operative and determined effort.

I also intend to expand and speed up a program to make available our farm surpluses to assist in feeding and clothing the needy in Asia. We should not allow people to go hungry and wear rags while our own warehouses overflow with an abundance of wheat and corn, rice and cotton.

Prior to 1965, Students for a Democratic Society (SDS) focused most of its attention on domestic issues. In the summer of 1964, for example, many of its members went to live in poor urban communities as part of its Economic Research and Action Projects (ERAPs). Even though SDS's leaders opposed the escalation of the Vietnam War from the start, many of them did not want SDS to assume a leading role in the budding antiwar movement, fearing (somewhat correctly) that to do so would sidetrack it from its fight against poverty. Not wanting to cede leadership of the New Left to several smaller leftist organizations, most of which had ties to the Old Left, however, it decided to sponsor an antiwar demonstration in Washington, D.C., in April 1965. Much to its surprise, over twenty thousand protesters showed up, most firmly committed to opposing the war in Vietnam. In **Document 5.3,** *SDS president Paul Potter challenged Johnson's rationale for the war. Potter not only implored the audience to question the assumptions of American foreign policy, but prompted it to consider the nature of the system that conducted immoral and undemocratic actions in pursuit of that policy.*

Document 5.3   Paul Potter, "We Must Name the System," Washington, D.C., April 17, 1965, Students for a Democratic Society Papers, State Historical Society of Wisconsin, Madison, Wisconsin.

Most of us grew up thinking that the United States was a strong but humble nation, that involved itself in world affairs only reluctantly, that respected the integrity of other nations and other systems, and that engaged in wars only as a last resort. This was a nation with no large standing army, with no design for external conquest, that sought primarily the opportunity to develop its own resources and its own mode of living. If at some point we began to hear vague and disturbing things about what this country had done in Latin America, China, Spain and other places, we somehow remained confident about the basic integrity of this nation's foreign policy. The Cold War with all of its neat categories and black and white descriptions did much to assure us that what we had been taught to believe was true.

But in recent years, the withdrawal from the hysteria of the Cold War era and the development of a more aggressive, activist foreign policy have done much to force many of us to rethink attitudes that were deep and basic sentiments about our country. The incredible war in Vietnam has provided the razor, the terrifying sharp cutting edge that has finally severed the last vestige of illusion that morality and democracy are the guiding principles of American foreign policy. The saccharine self-righteous moralism that promises the Vietnamese a billion dollars of economic aid at the very moment we are delivering billions for economic and social destruction and political repression is rapidly losing what power it might ever have had to reassure us about the decency of our foreign policy. The further we explore the reality of what this country is doing and planning in Vietnam the more we are driven toward the conclusion of Senator Morse that the United States may well be the greatest threat to peace in the world today. That is a terrible and bitter insight for people who grew up as we did—and our revulsion at that insight, our refusal to accept it as inevitable or necessary, is one of the reasons that so many people have come here today.

The President says that we are defending freedom in Vietnam. Whose freedom? Not the freedom of the Vietnamese. The first act of the first dictator, Diem, the United States installed in Vietnam, was to systematically begin the persecution of all political opposition, non-Communist as well as Communist. The first American military supplies were not used to fight Communist insurgents; they were used to control, imprison or kill any who sought something better for Vietnam than the personal aggrandizement, political corruption and the profiteering of the Diem regime. The elite of the forces that we have trained and equipped are *still* used to control political unrest in Saigon and defend the latest dictator from the people.

And yet in a world where dictatorships are so commonplace and popular control of government so rare, people become callous to the misery that is implied by dictatorial power. The rationalizations that are used to defend political despotism have been drummed into us so long that we have somehow become numb to the possibility that something else might exist. And it is only the kind of terror we see now in Vietnam that awakens conscience and reminds us that there is something deep in us that cries out against dictatorial suppression.

The pattern of repression and destruction that we have developed and justified in the war is so thorough that it can only be called cultural genocide. I am not simply talking about napalm or gas or crop destruction or torture, hurled indiscriminately on women and children, insurgent and neutral, upon the first suspicion of rebel activity. That in itself is horrendous and incredible beyond belief. But it is only part of a larger pattern of destruction to the very fabric of the country. We have uprooted the people from the land and imprisoned them in concentration camps called "sunrise villages." Through conscription and direct political intervention and control, we have destroyed local customs and traditions, trampled upon those things of value which give dignity and purpose to life.

What is left to the people of Vietnam after 20 years of war? What part of themselves and their own lives will those who survive be able to salvage from the wreckage of their country or build on the "peace" and "security" our Great Society offers them in reward for their allegiance? How can anyone be surprised that people who have had total war waged on themselves and their culture rebel in increasing numbers against that tyranny? What other course is available? And still our only response to rebellion is more vigorous repression, more merciless opposition to the social and cultural institutions which sustain dignity and the will to resist.

Not even the President can say that this is a war to defend the freedom of the Vietnamese people. Perhaps what the President means when he speaks of freedom is the freedom of the American people.

What in fact has the war done for freedom in America? It has led to even more vigorous governmental efforts to control information, manipulate the press and pressure and persuade the public through distorted or downright dishonest documents such as the White Paper on Vietnam. It has led to the confiscation of films and other anti-war material and the vigorous harassment by the FBI of some of the people who have been most outspokenly active in their criticism of the war. As the war escalates and the administration seeks more actively to gain support for any initiative it may choose to take, there has been the beginnings of a war psychology unlike anything that has burdened this country since the 1950s. How much more of Mr. Johnson's freedom can we stand? How much freedom will be left in this country if there is a major war in Asia? By what weird logic can it be said that the freedom of one people can only be maintained by crushing another? . . .

Thus far the war in Vietnam has only dramatized the demand of ordinary people to have some opportunity to make their own lives, and of their unwillingness, even under incredible odds, to give up the struggle against external domination. We are told, however, that the struggle can be legitimately suppressed since it might lead to the development of a Communist system, and before that ultimate menace all criticism is supposed to melt.

This is a critical point and there are several things that must be said here—not by way of celebration, but because I think they are the truth. First, if this country were serious about giving the people of Vietnam some alternative to a Communist social revolution, that opportunity was sacrificed in 1954 when we helped to install Diem and his repression of non-Communist movements. There is no indication that we were serious about that goal—that we were ever willing to contemplate the risks of allowing the Vietnamese to choose their own destinies. Second, those people who insist now that Vietnam can be neutralized are for the most part looking for a sugar coating to cover the bitter pill. We must accept the consequences that calling for an end of the war in Vietnam is in fact allowing for the likelihood that a Vietnam without war will be a self-styled Communist Vietnam. Third, this country must come to understand that creation of a Communist country in the world today is not an ultimate defeat. If people are given the opportunity to choose their own lives it is likely that some of them will choose what we have called "Communist systems." We are not powerless in that situation. Recent years have finally and indisputably broken the myth that the Communist world is monolithic and have conclusively shown that American power can be significant in aiding countries dominated by greater powers to become more independent and self-determined. And yet the war that we are creating and escalating in Southeast Asia is rapidly eroding the base of independence of North Vietnam as it is forced to turn to China and the Soviet Union, involving them in the war and involving itself in the compromises that that implies. Fourth, I must say to you that I would rather see Vietnam Communist than see it under continuous subjugation of the ruin that American domination has brought.

But the war goes on; the freedom to conduct that war depends on the dehumanization not only of Vietnamese people but of Americans as well; it depends on the construction of a system of premises and thinking that insulates the President and his advisors thoroughly and completely from the human consequences of the decisions they make. I do not believe that the President or Mr. Rusk or Mr. McNamara or even McGeorge Bundy are particularly evil men. If asked to throw napalm on the back of a ten-year-old child they would shrink in horror—but their decisions have led to mutilation and death of thousands and thousands of people.

What kind of system is it that allows good men to make those kinds of decisions? What kind of system is it that justifies the United States or any country seizing the destinies of the Vietnamese people and using them callously for its own purpose? What kind of system is it that disenfranchises people in the South, leaves millions upon millions of people throughout the country impoverished and excluded from the mainstream and promise of American society, that creates faceless and terrible bureaucracies and makes those the place where people spend their lives and do their work, that consistently puts material values before human values—and still persists in calling itself free and still persists in finding itself fit to police the world? What place is there for ordinary men in that system and how are they to control it, make it bend itself to their wills rather than bending them to its?

We must name that system. We must name it, describe it, analyze it, understand it and change it. For it is only when that system is changed and brought under control that there can be any hope for stopping the forces that create a war in Vietnam today or a murder in the South tomorrow or all the incalculable, innumerable more subtle atrocities that are worked on people all over—all the time.

How do you stop a war then? If the war has its roots deep in the institutions of American society, how do you stop it? Do you march to Washington? Is that enough? Who will hear us? How can you make the decision makers hear us, insulated as they are, if they cannot hear the screams of a little girl burnt by napalm? . . .

There is no simple plan, no scheme or gimmick that can be proposed here. There is no simple way to attack something that is deeply rooted in the society. If the people of this country are to end the war in Vietnam, and to change the institutions which create it, then the people of this country must create a massive social movement—and if that can be built around the issue of Vietnam then that is what we must do.

By a social movement I mean more than petitions or letters of protest, or tacit support of dissident Congressmen; I mean people who are willing to change their lives, who are willing to challenge the system, to take the problem of change seriously. By a social movement I mean an effort that is powerful enough to make the country understand that our problems are not in Vietnam, or China or Brazil or outer space or at the bottom of the ocean, but are here in the United States. What we must do is begin to build a democratic and humane society in which Vietnams are unthinkable, in which human life and initiative are precious. The reason there are twenty thousand people here today and not a hundred or none at all is because five years ago in the South students began to build a social movement to change the system. The reason there are poor people, Negro and white, housewives, faculty members, and many others here in Washington is because that movement has grown and spread and changed and reached out as an expression of the broad concerns of people throughout the society. The reason the war and the system it represents will be stopped, if it is stopped before it destroys all of us, will be because the movement has become strong enough to exact change in the society. Twenty thousand people, the people here, if they were serious, if they were willing to break out of their isolation and to accept the consequences of a decision to end the war and commit themselves to building a movement wherever they are and in whatever way they effectively can, would be, I'm convinced, enough.

To build a movement rather than a protest or some series of protests, to break out of our insulations and accept the consequences of our decisions, in effect to change our lives, means that we can open ourselves to the reactions of a society that believes it is moral and just, that we open ourselves to libeling and persecution, that we dare to be really seen as wrong in a society that doesn't tolerate fundamental challenges.

It means that we desert the security of our riches and reach out to people who are tied to the mythology of American power and make them part of our movement. We must reach out to every organization and individual in the country and make them part of our movement.

Donald Duncan's "The Whole Thing Was a Lie!" **(Document 5.4)** *was published in* Ramparts *magazine, the New Left's most prominent publication, in February 1966. As a former member of the Special Forces in Vietnam, Duncan lent credibility to the antiwar movement's claim that the United States was not fighting for freedom in Southeast Asia and that it was acting in an immoral manner, analogous to the role played by Russian tanks that put down a rebellion in Hungary in 1956. Duncan's article contained some of the most riveting firsthand descriptions of the fighting, which contrasted sharply with the largely favorable coverage the war was receiving at the time by the mainstream media. Indeed, although the antiwar movement has often been portrayed as anti-GI, this article suggests that the relationship between active soldiers, Vietnam veterans, and the antiwar movement was quite com-*

plex and certainly should not be caricatured as one of antiwar protesters spitting on GIs, as has often been the case.

In addition to disillusioned veterans, the antiwar movement attracted a number of prominent figures, such as the author Norman Mailer, Dr. Martin Luther King, Jr., Dr. Benjamin Spock, and J. William Fulbright, head of the Senate Foreign Relations Committee. Fulbright's investigations into America's conduct in Vietnam revealed that President Johnson had intentionally misled the American people in order to gain passage of the Gulf of Tonkin Resolution. In "A Sick Society" (1967) **(Document 5.5)** *and other speeches and writings, Fulbright argued that the Vietnam War was poisoning American society. Martin Luther King, Jr., Benjamin Spock, and many other antiwar statesmen made the same claim. Although Fulbright did not participate in public protests, his findings lent legitimacy to the antiwar movement.*

Document 5.4 Donald Duncan, "The Whole Thing Was a Lie!" *Ramparts* 4, no. 10 (February 1966), pp. 12–24.

When I was drafted into the Army, ten years ago, I was a militant anti-Communist. Like most Americans, I couldn't conceive of anybody choosing communism over democracy. The depths of my aversion to this ideology was, I suppose, due in part to my being Roman Catholic, in part to the stories in the news media about communism, and in part to the fact that my stepfather was born in Budapest, Hungary. Although he had come to the United States as a young man, most of his family had stayed in Europe. From time to time, I would be given examples of the horrors of life under communism. Shortly after Basic Training, I was sent to Germany. I was there at the time of the Soviet suppression of the Hungarian revolt. Everything I had heard about communism was verified. Like my fellow soldiers I felt frustrated and cheated that the United States would not go to the aid of the Hungarians. Angrily, I followed the action of the brute force being used against people who were armed with sticks, stolen weapons, and a desire for independence.

While serving in Germany, I ran across the Special Forces. I was so impressed by their dedication and élan that I decided to volunteer for duty with this group. By 1959 I had been accepted into the Special Forces and underwent training at Fort Bragg. I was soon to learn much about the outfit and the men in it. A good percentage of them were Lodge Act people—men who had come out from Iron Curtain countries. Their anti-communism bordered on fanaticism. Many of them who, like me, had joined Special Forces to do something positive, were to leave because "things" weren't happening fast enough. They were to show up later in Africa and Latin America in the employ of others or as independent agents for the CIA.

Initially, training was aimed at having United States teams organize guerrilla movements in foreign countries. Emphasis was placed on the fact that guerrillas can't take prisoners. We were continuously told "You don't have to kill them yourself—let your indigenous counterpart do that." In a course entitled, "Countermeasures to Hostile Interrogation," we were taught NKVD (Soviet Security) methods of torture to extract information. It became obvious that the title was only camouflage for teaching us "other" means of interrogation when time did not permit more sophisticated methods, for example, the old cold water–hot water treatment, or the delicate operation of lowering a man's testicles into a jeweler's vise. When we asked directly if we were being told to use these methods the answer was, "We can't tell you that. The Mothers of America wouldn't approve." This sarcastic hypocrisy was greeted with laughs. Our own military teaches these and even worse things to American soldiers. They then condemn the Viet Cong guerrillas for supposedly doing those very things. I was later to witness firsthand the practice of turning prisoners over to ARVN for "interrogation" and the atrocities which ensued.

Throughout the training there was an exciting aura of mystery. Hints were continually being dropped that "at this very moment" Special Forces men were in various Latin American and Asian countries on secret missions. The anti-Communist theme was woven throughout. Recommended reading would invariably turn out to be books on "brainwashing" and atrocity tales—life under communism. The enemy was THE ENEMY. There was no doubt that THE ENEMY was communism and Communist countries. There never was a suggestion that Special Forces would be used to set up guerrilla warfare against the government in a Fascist-controlled country.

It would be a long time before I would look back and realize that this conditioning about the Communist conspiracy and THE ENEMY was taking place. Like most of the men who volunteered for Special Forces, I wasn't hard to sell. We were ready for it. Artur Fisers, my classmate and roommate, was living for the day when he would "lead the first 'stick' of the first team to go into Latvia." "How about Vietnam, Art?" "To hell with Vietnam. I wouldn't blend. There are not many blue-eyed gooks." This was to be only the first of many contradictions of the theory that Special Forces men cannot be prejudiced about the color or religion of other people. . . .

My first impressions of Vietnam were gained from the window of the jet while flying over Saigon and its outlying areas. As I looked down I thought, "Why, those could be farms anywhere and that could be a city anywhere." The ride from Tan Son Nhut to the center of town destroyed the initial illusion.

My impressions weren't unique for a new arrival in Saigon. I was appalled by the heat and humidity which made my worsted uniform feel like a fur coat. Smells. Exhaust fumes from the hundreds of blue and white Renault taxis and military vehicles. Human excrement; the foul, stagnant, black mud and water as we passed over the river on Cong Ly Street; and overriding all the others, the very pungent and rancid smell of what I later found out was *nuoc mam*, a sauce made much in the same manner as sauerkraut, with fish substituted for cabbage. No Vietnamese meal is complete without it. People—masses of them! The smallest children, with the dirty faces of all children of their age, standing on the sidewalk unshod and with no clothing other than a shirtwaist that never quite reached the navel on the protruding belly. Those a little older wearing overall-type trousers with the crotch seam torn out—a practical alteration that eliminates the need for diapers. Young grade school girls in their blue butterfly sun hats, and boys of the same age with hands out saying, "OK—Salem," thereby exhausting their English vocabulary. The women in *ao dais* of all colors, all looking beautiful and graceful. The slim, hipless men, many walking hand-in-hand with other men, and so misunderstood by the newcomer. Old men with straggly Fu Man Chu beards staring impassively, wearing wide-legged, pajama-like trousers.

Bars by the hundreds—with American-style names (Playboy, Hungry i, Flamingo) and faced with grenade-proof screening. Houses made from packing cases, accommodating three or four families, stand alongside spacious villas complete with military guard. American GI's abound in sport shirts, slacks, and cameras; motorcycles, screaming to make room for a speeding official in a large, shiny sedan, pass over an intersection that has hundreds of horseshoes impressed in the soft asphalt tar. Confusion, noise, smells, people—almost overwhelming.

My initial assignment was in Saigon as an Area Specialist for III and IV Corps Tactical Zone in the Special Forces Tactical Operations Center. And my education began here. The officers and NCO's were unanimous in their contempt of the Vietnamese.

There was a continual put-down of Saigon officials, the Saigon government, ARVN (Army Republic of Vietnam), the LLDB (Luc Luong Dac Biet—Vietnamese Special Forces) and the Vietnamese man-in-the-street. The government was rotten, the officials corrupt, ARVN cowardly, the LLDB all three, and the man-in-the-street an ignorant thief. (LLDB also qualified under "thief.")

I was shocked. I was working with what were probably some of the most dedicated Americans in Vietnam. They were supposedly in Vietnam to help "our Vietnamese friends" in their fight for a democratic way of life. Obviously, the attitude didn't fit.

. . . [W]henever anybody questioned our being in Vietnam—in light of the facts—the old rationale was always presented: "We have to stop the spread of communism somewhere . . . if we don't fight the commies here, we'll have to fight them at home . . . if we pull out, the rest of Asia will go Red . . . these are uneducated people who have been duped; they don't understand the difference between democracy and communism. . . ."

Being extremely anti-Communist myself, these "arguments" satisfied me for a long time. In fact, I guess it was saying these very same things to myself over and over again that made it possible for me to participate in the things I did in Vietnam. But were we stopping communism? Even during the short period I had been in Vietnam, the Viet Cong had obviously gained in strength; the government controlled less and less of the country every day. The more troops and money we poured in, the more people hated us. Countries all over the world were losing sympathy with our stand in Vietnam. Countries which up to now had preserved a neutral position were becoming vehemently anti-American. A village near Tay Ninh in which I had slept in safety six months earlier was the center of a Viet Cong operation that cost the lives of two American friends. A Special Forces team operating in the area was almost decimated over a period of four months. United States Operations Mission (USOM), civilian representatives, who had been able to travel by vehicle in relative safety throughout the countryside, were being kidnapped and killed. Like the military, they now had to travel by air.

The real question was, whether communism is spreading in spite of our involvement or because of it.

The attitude that the uneducated peasant lacked the political maturity to decide between communism and democracy and ". . . we are only doing this for your own good," although it had a familiar colonialistic ring, at first seemed to have merit. Then I remembered that most of the villages would be under Viet Cong control for some of the time and under government control at other times. How many Americans had such a close look at both sides of the cloth? The more often government troops passed through an area, the more surely it would become sympathetic to the Viet Cong. The Viet Cong might sleep in the houses, but the government troops ransacked them. More often than not, the Viet Cong helped plant and harvest the crops; but invariably government troops in an area razed them. Rape is severely punished among the Viet Cong. It is so common among the ARVN that it is seldom reported for fear of even worse atrocities.

I saw the Airborne Brigade come into Nha Trang. Nha Trang is a government town and the Vietnamese Airborne Brigade are government troops. They were originally, in fact, trained by Special Forces, and they actually had the town in a grip of terror for three days. Merchants were collecting money to get them out of town; cafes and bars shut down.

The troops were accosting women on the streets. They would go into a place—a bar or cafe—and order varieties of food. When the checks came they wouldn't pay them. Instead they would simply wreck the place, dumping over the tables and smashing dishes. While these men were accosting women, the police would just stand by, powerless or unwilling to help. In fact, the situation is so difficult that American troops, if in town at the same time as the Vietnamese Airborne Brigade, are told to stay off the streets at night to avoid coming to harm.

The whole thing was a lie. We weren't preserving freedom in South Vietnam. There was no freedom to preserve. To voice opposition to the government meant jail or death. Neutralism was forbidden and punished. Newspapers that didn't say the *right* thing were closed down. People are not even free to leave and Vietnam is one of those rare countries that doesn't fill its American visa quota. It's all there to see once the Red film is removed from the eyes. We aren't the freedom fighters. We are the Russian tanks blasting the hopes of an Asian Hungary. . . .

When I returned from Vietnam I was asked, "Do you resent young people who have never been in Vietnam, or in any war, protesting it?" On the contrary, I am relieved. I think they should be commended. I had to wait until I was 35 years old, after spending 10 years in the Army and 18 months personally witnessing the stupidity of the war, before I could figure it out. That these young people were able to figure it out so quickly and so accurately is not only a credit to their intelligence but a great personal triumph over a lifetime of conditioning and indoctrination. I only hope that the picture I have tried to create will help other people come to the truth without wasting 10 years. Those people protesting the war in Vietnam are not against our boys in Vietnam. On the contrary. What they are against is our boys *being* in Vietnam. They are not unpatriotic. Again the opposite is true. They are opposed to people, our own and others, dying for a lie, thereby corrupting the very word democracy.

Document 5.5   J. William Fulbright, "A Sick Society," *Congressional Record,* **90th Congress, 1st Session, 113, part 16 (1967), pp. 22126–22129.**
Standing in the smoke and rubble of Detroit, a Negro veteran said: "I just got back from Vietnam a few months ago, but you know, I think the war is here."

There are in fact two wars going on. One is the war of power politics which our soldiers are fighting in the jungles of southeast Asia. The other is a war for America's soul which is being fought in the streets of Newark and Detroit and in the halls of Congress, in churches and protest meetings and on college campuses, and in the hearts and minds of silent Americans from Maine to Hawaii. I believe that the two wars have something to do with each other, not in the direct, tangibly causal way that bureaucrats require as proof of a connection between two things, but in a subtler, moral and qualitative way that is no less real for being intangible. Each of these wars might well be going on in the absence of the other, but neither, I suspect, standing alone, would seem so hopeless and demoralizing.

The connection between Vietnam and Detroit is in their conflicting and incompatible demands upon traditional American values. The one demands that they be set aside, the other that they be fulfilled. The one demands the acceptance by America of an imperial role in the world, or of what our policy makers like to call the "responsibilities of power," or of what I have called the "arrogance of power." The other demands freedom and social justice at home, an end to poverty, the fulfillment of our flawed democracy, and an effort to create a role for ourselves in the world which is compatible with our traditional values. The question, it should be emphasized, is not whether it is *possible* to engage in traditional power politics abroad and at the same time the perfect democracy at home, but whether it is possible for *us Americans*, with our particular history and national character, to combine morally incompatible roles.

Administration officials tell us that we can indeed afford both Vietnam and the Great Society, and they produce impressive statistics of the gross national product to prove it. The statistics show financial capacity but they do not show moral and psychological capacity. They do not show how a President preoccupied with bombing missions over North and South Vietnam can provide strong and consistent leadership for the renewal of our cities. They do not show how a Congress burdened with war costs and war measures, with emergency briefings and an endless series of dramatic appeals, with anxious constituents and a mounting anxiety of their own, can tend to the workaday business of studying social problems and legislating programs to meet them. Nor do the statistics tell how an anxious and puzzled people, bombarded by press and television with the bad news of American deaths in Vietnam, the "good news" of enemy deaths—and with vividly horrifying pictures to illustrate them—can be expected to support neighborhood anti-poverty projects and national programs for urban renewal, employment and education. . . .

At present much of the world is repelled by America and what America seems to stand for in the world. Both in our foreign affairs and in our domestic life we convey an image of violence; I do not care very much about images as distinguished from the things they reflect, but this image is rooted in reality. Abroad we are engaged in a savage and unsuccessful war against poor people in a small and backward nation. At home—largely because of the neglect from twenty-five years of preoccupation with foreign involvements—our cities are exploding in violent protest against generations of social injustice. America, which only a few years ago seemed to the world to be a model of democracy and social justice, has become a symbol of violence and undisciplined power. . . . By our undisciplined use of physical power we have divested ourselves of a greater power: the power of example. How, for example, can we commend peaceful compromise to the Arabs and the Israelis when we are unwilling to suspend our relentless bombing of North Vietnam? How can we commend democratic social reform to Latin America when Newark, Detroit, and Milwaukee are providing explosive evidence of our own inadequate efforts at democratic social reform? How can we commend the free enterprise system to Asians and Africans when in our own country it has produced vast, chaotic, noisy, dangerous and dirty urban complexes while poisoning the very air and land and water? . . .

While the death toll mounts in Vietnam, it is mounting too in the war at home. During a single week of July 1967, 164 Americans were killed and 1,442 wounded in Vietnam, while 65 Americans were killed and 2,100 were wounded in city riots in the United States. We are truly fighting a two-front war and doing badly in both. Each war feeds on the other and, although the President assures us that we have the resources to win both wars, in fact we are not winning either.

Together the two wars have set in motion a process of deterioration in American society, and there is no question that each of the two crises is heightened by the impact of the other. Not only does the Vietnam war divert human and material resources from our festering cities; not only does it foster the conviction on the part of slum Negroes that their country is indifferent to their plight. In addition the war feeds the idea of violence as a way of solving problems. If, as Mr. Rusk tells us, only the rain of bombs can bring Ho Chi Minh to reason, why should not the same principle apply at home? Why should not riots and snipers' bullets bring the white man to an awareness of the Negro's plight when peaceful programs for housing and jobs and training have been more rhetoric than reality? Ugly and shocking thoughts are in the American air and they were forged in the Vietnam crucible. Black power extremists talk of "wars of liberation" in the urban ghettoes of America. . . .

Priorities are reflected in the things we spend money on. Far from being a dry accounting of bookkeepers, a nation's budget is full of moral implications; it tells what a society cares about and what it does not care about; it tells what its values are.

Here are a few statistics on America's values: Since 1946 we have spent over $1,578 billion through our regular national budget. Of this amount over $904 billion, or 57.29 percent of the total, have gone for military power. By contrast, less than $96 billion, or 6.08 percent, were spent on "social functions" including education, health, labor and welfare programs, housing and community development. The Administration's budget for fiscal year 1968 calls for almost $76 billion to be spent on the military and only $15 billion for "social functions."

I would not say that we have shown ourselves to value weapons five or ten times as much as we value domestic social needs, as the figures suggest; certainly much of our military spending has been necessitated by genuine requirements of national security. I think, however, that we have embraced the necessity with excessive enthusiasm, that the Congress has been too willing to provide unlimited sums for the military and not really very reluctant at all to offset these costs to a very small degree by cutting away funds for the poverty program and urban renewal, for rent supplements for the poor and even for a program to help protect slum children from being bitten by rats. . . .

While the country sickens for lack of moral leadership, a most remarkable younger generation has taken up the standard of American idealism. Unlike so many of their elders, they have perceived the fraud and sham in American life and are unequivocally rejecting it. Some, the hippies, have simply withdrawn, and while we may regret the loss of their energies and their sense of decency, we can hardly gainsay their evaluation of the state of society. Others of our youth are sardonic and skeptical, not, I think, because they do not want ideals but because they want the genuine article and will not tolerate fraud. Others— students who wrestle with their consciences about the draft, soldiers who wrestle with their consciences about the war, Peace Corps volunteers who strive to light the spark of human dignity among the poor of India or Brazil, and VISTA volunteers who try to do the same for our own poor in Harlem or Appalachia— are striving to keep alive the traditional values of American democracy.

They are not really radical, these young idealists, no more radical, that is, than Jefferson's idea of freedom, Lincoln's idea of equality, or Wilson's idea of a peaceful community of nations. Some of them, it is true, are taking what many regard as radical action, but they are doing it in defense of traditional values and in protest against the radical departure from those values embodied in the idea of an imperial destiny for America.

The focus of their protest is the war in Vietnam and the measure of their integrity is the fortitude with which they refused to be deceived about it. By striking contrast with the young Germans who accepted the Nazi evil because the values of their society had disintegrated and they had no normal frame of reference, these young Americans are demonstrating the vitality of American values. . . .

It may be that . . . America will succumb to becoming a traditional empire and will reign for a time over what must surely be a moral if not a physical wasteland, and then, like the great empires of the past, will decline or fall. Or it may be that the effort to create so grotesque an anachronism will go up in flames of nuclear holocaust. But if I had to bet my money on what is going to happen, I would bet on this younger generation—this generation who reject the inhumanity of war in a poor and distant land, who reject the poverty and sham in their own country, this generation who are telling their elders what their elders ought to have known, that the price of empire is America's soul and that price is too high.

The growth of the antiwar movement should not fool us into thinking that everyone opposed the war. On the contrary, public polls and votes in Congress suggest that the majority of Americans supported Johnson's policies in Vietnam at least until the middle of 1967, and even then a good proportion of those who disapproved of his policies felt that the United States should escalate its effort, not withdraw. Among the president's most faithful supporters were the leaders of the AFL-CIO, who, believing that the war was winnable and good for the economy, regularly endorsed the U.S. policy in Southeast Asia. **Document 5.6,** *from the* Proceedings *of the AFL-CIO's December 1965 convention, provides a look at a brief debate over one such endorsement. After Emil Mazey, secretary-treasurer of the United Automobile Workers (UAW), opined that the federation had to respect the right to dissent—an allusion to the appearance of antiwar protesters at the convention—AFL-CIO president George Meany and UAW president Walter Reuther, Mazey's superior, spoke in favor of the labor federation's endorsement of Johnson's policy in Vietnam and against the antiwar movement.*

Document 5.7, *an editorial from the* St. Louis Globe-Democrat *that was reprinted in* Human Events, *a leading conservative journal, provides an even clearer sense than does the AFL-CIO piece of the existence of anti-antiwar sentiment that tended to parallel the growth of the antiwar movement. Most likely written by Pat Buchanan, who later became a speech writer for Richard Nixon, an advisor to Ronald Reagan, and one of the most prominent conservatives in America, the editorial reminds us that many found the antiwar movement's antics, from its adulation of Ho Chi Minh, the leader of North Vietnam, to its defilement of the American flag, revulsive. Along the same lines, many Americans who probably only lukewarmly supported Johnson's policies strongly opposed the antiwar movement because they* *associated it with the counterculture, black militancy, and other radical trends of the era that they disparaged.*

Document 5.6   AFL-CIO, "Support of Viet Nam Policy," *Proceedings of the Constitutional Convention of the AFL-CIO, Vol. 1, Daily Proceedings, San Francisco, CA, December 9–15, 1965* (Washington, D.C.: AFL-CIO), pp. 561–570.

SUPPORT OF VIET NAM POLICY

RESOLUTION NO. 68—By Delegates David Sullivan, George E. Fairchild, George Hardy, Charles C. Levey, Thomas Shortman, Albert G. Hearn, Arthur T. Hare, Thomas G. Young, Peter Ottley, Eugene Moats; Building Service Employees International Union.

WHEREAS, The protests and demonstrations which have been lodged against U.S. policy in South Viet Nam during recent months may have given some foreign nations the impression that the people of the United States are not supporting the government policy in South Viet Nam; therefore, be it

RESOLVED: That the labor movement proclaim to the world that the nation's working men and women do support the Johnson Administration in Viet Nam, and do believe that the United States must continue to support the people of South Viet Nam in their fight for freedom and democracy; and be it further

RESOLVED: That the labor movement again proclaim its support of the Administration's policy to contain imperialistic communism and keep it from spreading through Southeast Asia and the rest of the world; and be it further

RESOLVED: That this convention commend the forthright action of President George Meany and the Executive Council of the AFL-CIO in supporting President Johnson and the Administration on its policy and activities in South Viet Nam.

COMMITTEE SECRETARY ABEL: Mr. Chairman, the committee recommends adoption of the substitute resolution No. 68, and I so move.

. . . The motion was seconded.

PRESIDENT MEANY: You have heard the report on Resolution 68, and the motion is to adopt. The Chair recognizes Secretary Mazey of the Auto Workers.

DELEGATE EMIL MAZEY, United Auto Workers: Mr. Chairman and fellow delegates: In considering the problems of Viet Nam I believe that it is important for us to recognize the basic difference between a democracy and a dictatorship, be it of a Communist, Fascist or military variety. The basic difference between free people and people who are enslaved by the various dictatorship systems of our world is the freedom of expression, the freedom of press, the freedom of religion, the freedom of assembly, and a representative government.

I believe that the most precious freedom we have is the freedom of dissent, the right and the opportunity of expressing a difference of opinion when you feel strongly about it. You don't have the right of dissent in a Communist country or a Fascist country or a country that has a military dictatorship. And the test as to whether or not we believe in freedom and believe in democracy is not whether or not we are willing to let people demonstrate and speak when we agree with them, but whether or not we are willing to listen to people with whom we may disagree.

I was sick with the vulgar display of intolerance that some delegates showed to some college students following Secretary Rusk's remarks here the other day. The labor movement has been the victim of people trying to silence our right of expression. In many places in the South today, our organizers can't pass out handbills without being molested by company guards or by police. Our picket lines in strikes have been disturbed because people didn't agree with our view. And it seems to me that the labor movement has to take the lead and has to demonstrate and fight for the right of people to disagree, whether it is on Viet Nam or on any other subject matter.

I am one of those concerned Americans who is worried about our foreign policy, where we are going in Viet Nam, who is concerned about the role we play in the Dominican Republic. I recognize that foreign policy is probably the most difficult single subject to discuss, because any time you criticize or challenge or question a policy of the government your criticism is immediately equated with treason, appeasement, maybe charged with being soft on communism or even being charged with disloyalty. I do not believe the Viet Nam situation is a black and white situation. . . .

There are a lot of people in our country who are concerned about Viet Nam because they recognize the fact that we have a corrupt military dictatorship in that country today, and we have had a succession of military dictatorships. There isn't any representative government in Viet Nam. Premier Ky has publicly stated that his great hero in this world was Adolph Hitler [sic], that he believed in his methods and his means.

It should be quite easy to understand that when we are fighting for a country we say we are trying to stop Chinese aggression and the advance of their influence. But at the point that we have a country where there aren't any of the elements of democratic society and we have a military dictatorship, we ought to be able to understand why people are concerned and why people picket and why people demonstrate.

I believe that in this very unhappy situation we have one of two choices to follow. One is that we must use every effort possible to find a negotiated settlement of our dispute in Viet Nam in order to cut down the bleeding and the dying and the sacrifices on the part of our own military forces as well as on the part of the Vietnamese people. I believe that we must intensify and give support to President Johnson in his efforts to negotiate, because there are forces in our country that are attempting to escalate this war into World War III, who would like to have a war against China. Therefore, we must put ourselves on the side of our government in its efforts to negotiate so that we can bring a peaceful solution to this problem and avoid having another Korea or, what is even worse, starting World War III, a nuclear holocaust that nobody can possibly win.

I just want to say in conclusion that one of the things the leadership of my union is in total agreement with is that we must intensify our efforts to find a way to seek a negotiated, honorable peaceful settlement of the Viet Nam situation. We must use the machinery of the UN. We ought to consider getting the participants of the Geneva Conference back together again. But we ought to continue to search and seek ways of doing this.

I believe that we ought to call upon the people of North Viet Nam and call upon Red China, if you please, to join the conference table, to accept the invitation of our President for unconditional discussions and negotiations so that we can bring this unhappy conflict to an end, and that we can then begin to use some of our resources to help build and rebuild this country, and give the people the opportunity of living the kind of life that all of us want to live.

Thank you very much. . . .

PRESIDENT MEANY: Is there further discussion?

Before putting the motion to adopt Resolution 68, I would like to just say a few words.

It is true that this is a very difficult situation in which our government finds itself and, of course, it is also true that we believe in the freedom of dissent.

I sat here the other day—and I speak for myself—I thought that we were quite tolerant of those people who were in the balcony. They had signs denouncing our Secretary of State. Several of them carried great big signs reading, "Stop lying; get to the conference table." "Stop lying; negotiate."

I don't know whether Secretary Rusk noticed them or not, but I did and they sat right straight back there. Nobody bothered them; nobody interfered with them. However, when Secretary Rusk was leaving, these college students—well, they don't look too much like students, some of them, but I suppose they are college students—then these college students started to shout and wave their banners.

Now, the reason that they did that was that a newspaper photographer went up to take their picture, and this is their immediate response to that sort of thing. It was then that I suggested that the Sergeant-at-Arms clear them out so that we could go ahead with our work.

I believe in tolerance, but I think there is a limit to peoples' patience. We allowed them in the hall; we didn't interfere with them. We allowed them to sit there with their banners which were insulting; certainly insulting to the President of the United States and to the Secretary of State and, I think, insulting to this convention. But when they started to make noise by shouting and interfering with the work of this convention, I felt that was the place where our tolerance ended. And if Brother Mazey is annoyed, let him be annoyed by me.

(Applause.)

I am satisfied that we treated these people right.

Now, as far as criticizing the government policy on foreign affairs, I think we are free to do this. I think this federation and I think the AFL and the CIO before the merger criticized the government on foreign affairs. We have never deviated from our policy in regard to our government's relationship with Franco's Spain. I don't think any one can say that we tried to shut off criticism. However, when we examine Viet Nam, we find we have a commitment there. We are there because of an international agreement that these people were to have right [sic] to self-determination. And I resent very much, our country being compared to the French exploiters, the colonial exploiters of Viet Nam.

The French were in Viet Nam as a colonial power, ruling these people from the outside. And to say that our present situation there should be compared to the French exploiters is a little bit ridiculous.

One of our unions is spending a couple hundred thousand dollars of its own money to help the transport situation in Viet Nam, to help the workers get a decent wage, to install some modern methods over there. The president of that union has made several trips for that purpose on his own as an American trade unionist. Is this exploitation? We are spending millions of dollars to feed the hungry in Viet Nam, to build hospitals, to take care of the sick, do everything possible to make life a little better for these people. Is this exploitation? It is a strange kind of exploitation. Insofar as the comparison goes, has anyone any doubt when we say we don't want to own or seize a single inch of territory? Are you in doubt that this is true?

Insofar as getting to the conference table, President Johnson has done everything short of begging the people to come to the conference table. He hasn't begged them, but he has done everything short of begging them to come to the conference table.

Every known method of communication has been used. And our government, in communication with the North Vietnamese, in communication with various other governments, the so-called 17 non-aligned nations, the representative of the British Commonwealth of Nations, are all trying to get these people to the conference table.

So there can't be any question on the desire of our government and the desire of this labor movement to get to the conference table. But until the people of Hanoi and Peking understand that they can't have a military victory, until they understand that, it seems they won't get to the conference table. In the meantime, there is no question about what we have to do as Americans. We have to back up every effort our government can make to keep them from that military victory, so that they will see the light and come to the conference table.

The Chair recognizes Vice President Reuther.

VICE PRESIDENT REUTHER: I think this is a very healthy discussion, and I would like to contribute my two cents worth.

I am in support of the resolution because the resolution, I believe, stands behind the position of President Johnson and the policy that he articulated at the historic speech which he gave at Johns Hopkins University.

In that speech the President detailed the basic policy and the attitude of our government. He said we were determined to resist Communist aggression in Viet Nam, but he said while we are doing that, we are going to extend our hand and we are going to make it clear that we are prepared to meet at any time with anyone at any place to try to achieve a resolution of this problem at the conference table.

It seems to me that this is a sound position, because we have learned a long time ago that you cannot appease aggression. And, as Secretary Rusk made it plain the other day, if you try to appease it, it's [sic] appetite gets greater and greater and greater.

The position that we take here today, I think, is a position that stands midpoint between two extreme positions. There is that position of those Americans—and I do not question their loyalty, I question their judgment—who would have us pull out of Viet Nam on the theory that this is a civil war, it is an internal matter that the Vietnamese people should resolve themselves, and therefore we ought to bring the American troops home. I reject that, as does this resolution, as does American foreign policy, because such a policy would create a vacuum which the Communists would fill, and Peiping would be able to say that their concept of world domination pays off. You would have a chain reaction, and no other small country in South Asia would be secure against future subversion, infiltration and Communist penetration. Instead of solving the problem in South Asia, you would have traded one problem for potentially many other problems. Therefore, we reject that policy, even though a lot of well meaning Americans may believe that that is the solution to the problem.

The other extreme is the right wing position. It is the Goldwater position. It is the position of Richard Nixon, who would have us believe that the answer is unlimited escalation of the war.

We reject that because there is no military solution to the forces that are struggling for power in South Asia, and an escalation of the war would ultimately lead to a utilization of nuclear weapons, and the utilization of nuclear weapons means the beginning of the end of human civilization. We believe, as the resolution says, that ultimately the solution to these problems must be found at the conference table, and that ultimately we must begin to deal with the underlying causes of the problems in South Asia which are essentially economic and social in character. And only as we begin to raise the living standards and give the people of that part of the world their share of the fruits of the 20th Century can we begin to lay the foundation upon which you can build a just social order in which democracy must flourish.

We understand in the labor movement, perhaps better than any other group, that the Communists are able to forge human poverty into political power; that everywhere in the world where there is a strong trade union movement that has the capability and the will to struggle to achieve a measure of economic and social justice for the people, the Communists are weak and without influence. It's where they can exploit poverty and insecurity and social injustices that they are able to build their political forces.

Therefore, we recognize that you can't solve this problem with guns; that ultimately it must be solved by economic and social action.

I am happy to report that my own union in the last month has shipped to South Viet Nam, to the trade union movement there that is opening up clinics for children, $250,000 worth of medical supplies and equipment to help them open up the first children's clinic under the sponsorship of the Vietnamese trade union.

But I think it ought to be made clear, as I said to some of these people who carry these signs, "You are demonstrating at the wrong place. Why don't you tell Hanoi and Peking?"

They say, "Well, we can't influence them."

I think that anyone who objectively looks at the situation there must conclude that the full moral responsibility for the continuation of that war rests upon the Communists in Hanoi and Peking, because they are responsible for this war. . . .

I think this convention will make clear on the Vietnamese thing that the war goes on because the Communists are unwilling to sit at the conference table. And I believe that we have no choice but to continue to pursue a policy that says we will resist aggression, because if we do not resist it, then it will be encouraged and in time it will create again the same kind of problem that aggression created when Hitler was responsible.

While we resist aggression on the military front, our government is committed to doing everything possible. I have talked to the President of these United States, as has Brother Meany and other people, and I know that Lyndon Johnson is just as concerned about peace as was Jack Kennedy, because he too can understand that peace transcends every other question. Everything is academic if we do not have peace. If we do not have peace in the world, the human family will not survive.

Document 5.7 "SDS Borders on Treason," *St. Louis Globe-Democrat,* reprinted in *Human Events* 25, no. 40 (October 2, 1965), p. 13.

Students for a Democratic Society, a radical-leftist movement with more than 100 campus chapters, is mapping out plans to encourage and assist thousands of college students who oppose the Viet Nam war to declare as "conscientious objectors" and thus avoid their military obligations.

If the program is successful, it will of course give immense comfort and encouragement to the Communist enemies of this nation—even while we are spending increasing amounts of American blood and treasure in a heroic effort to see to it that the South Vietnamese people do not have a Communist government imposed upon them by force.

In our estimation, the generators of this movement come quite close to being traitors to the United States.

These exponents of a "democratic society" are apparently undisturbed, even delighted, at the prospect of all of Viet Nam falling under the type of "democratic" regime which flourishes in Hanoi and Peking.

If these people were not blind and unreasoning radicals, they could see at a glance that the greatest enemy of the freedom of the human mind, the freedom of the individual, is today in Communist Asia, and that an American pullback from Asia would mean domination for decades of these people by the type of philosophy which quite literally murders dissent.

It is because this is so obvious, because the national debate on Viet Nam has been exhaustive, because the bloody record of the Viet Cong atrocities is so well known, that such efforts to sabotage the American commitment to the Vietnamese people are so stomach-turning.

These are the youth who have been deferred from military service, who have been the beneficiaries of an unrivaled number of scholarships and grants, who have enjoyed more individual freedom and material prosperity than any other students in history—and now they come cackling about "Twentieth Century United States imperialism!"

Anyone but a complete jackass could reason to the conclusion that no truly imperialist power, with as much to lose as the United States, is going to risk a massive land war in Asia just to set up a few military bases or for control of a puppet government of generals in a backward and remote corner of Asia, good only for growing rice.

No, but the United States will risk a major war in Asia, will send more than 125,000 of its sons into the jungles and rice paddies to honor its word to a few million Asian peasants depending on it, because that is the type of government and country this is—and that honorable commitment shines all the brighter when placed alongside the sniveling sedition of a handful of pompous academic parasites.

We have listened to these puling students making their snide derogations at our country and our society for so long that we are tempted to ask them why they don't just get out of the United States and go join their Brave New World in Peking, Hanoi, Havana, Moscow and East Berlin.

There are millions of men and women in these lands quite willing to shed a little blood to swap places and enjoy the freedoms this pack of ingrates is abusing daily.

In 1967, as public sentiment in favor of the Vietnam War began to wane, General William Westmoreland, the top commander in Vietnam, returned to the United States to make an extraordinary appeal for public support. The climax of his stateside journey came with his address to a joint session of Congress, **Document 5.8.** *Both in this address and elsewhere, Westmoreland praised the performance of South Vietnamese troops and suggested that victory was around the corner. The administration's portrayal of the war dovetailed with Westmoreland's, producing a credibility gap between the government, which had largely only positive things to say about the fighting, and much of the public, which found reason to disbelieve the government's claims. It is worthwhile to consider the long-term impact that the credibility gap had on American society, even on those who supported the war in Vietnam.*

Document 5.8   William C. Westmoreland, "Address to Joint Session of Congress," *Congressional Record,* 90th Congress, 1st Session, 113, part 9 (April 28, 1967), pp. 11153–11155.

General WESTMORELAND. Mr. President, Mr. Speaker, Members of Congress:

I am deeply honored to address the Congress of the United States. I stand in the shadow of military men who have been here before me, but none of them could have had more pride than mine in representing the gallant American fighting men in Vietnam today.

These servicemen and women are sensitive to their mission and, as the record shows, they are unbeatable in carrying out that mission.

As their commander in the field, I have seen many of you in Vietnam during the last 3 years. Without exception, you gentleman have shown interest, responsibility, and concern for the commitment which we have undertaken, and for the welfare of our troops.

The Republic of Vietnam is fighting to build a strong nation while aggression—organized, directed, and supported from without—attempts to engulf it. This is an unprecedented challenge for a small nation. But it is a challenge which will confront any nation that is marked as a target for the Communist stratagem called war of national liberation.

I can assure you here and now that militarily this strategy will not succeed in Vietnam.

In 3 years of close study and daily observation, I have seen no evidence that this is an internal insurrection. I have seen much evidence to the contrary—documented by the enemy himself—that it is aggression from the north.

Since 1954, when the Geneva accord was signed, the North Vietnamese have been sending leaders, political organizers, technicians, and experts on terrorism and sabotage into the south. Clandestinely directed from the north, they and their Hanoi-trained southern counterparts have controlled the entire course of the attack against the Republic of South Vietnam.

More than 2 years ago, North Vietnamese divisions began to arrive, and the control was no longer clandestine. Since then, the buildup of enemy forces has been formidable. During the last 22 months, the number of enemy combat battalions in the south has increased significantly, and nearly half of them are now North Vietnamese. In the same period, overall enemy strength has nearly doubled in spite of large combat losses.

Enemy commanders are skilled professionals. In general, their troops are indoctrinated, well trained, aggressive, and under tight control. . . .

For months now we have been successful in destroying a number of main force units. We will continue to seek out the enemy, catch him off guard, and punish him at every opportunity.

But success against his main forces alone is not enough to insure a swift and decisive end to the conflict.

This enemy also uses terror—murder, mutilation, abduction, and the deliberate shelling of innocent men, women, and children—to exercise control through fear. Terror, which he employs daily, is much harder to counter than his best conventional moves.

A typical day in Vietnam was last Sunday. Terrorists near Saigon assassinated a 39-year-old village chief. The same day in the delta they kidnaped 26 civilians, assisting in arranging for local elections. The next day the Vietcong attacked a group of Revolutionary Development workers, killing one and wounding 12 with grenades and machinegun fire in one area, and in another they opened fire on a small civilian bus and killed three and wounded four of its passengers. These are cases of calculated enemy attack on civilians to extend by fear that which they cannot gain by persuasion. One hears little of this brutality here at home. What we do hear about is our own aerial bombing against North Vietnam, and I would like to address this for a moment.

For years the enemy has been blowing bridges, interrupting traffic, cutting roads, sabotaging power stations, blocking canals, and attacking airfields in the south, and he continues to do so. This is a daily occurrence. Bombing in the north has been centered on precisely these same kinds of targets and for the same military purposes—to reduce the supply, interdict the movement, and impair the effectiveness of enemy military forces.

Within his capabilities the enemy in Vietnam is waging total war all day— every day—everywhere. He believes in force, and his intensification of violence is limited only by his resources and not by any moral inhibitions. . . .

Given the nature of the enemy, it seems to me that the strategy that we are following at this time is the proper one, and that it is producing results. While he obviously is far from quitting, there are signs that his morale and his military structure are beginning to deteriorate. The rate of decline will be in proportion to the pressure directed against him.

Faced with this prospect, it is gratifying to note that our forces and those of the other free world allies have grown in strength and profited from experience. In this connection it is well to remember that Korea, Australia, New Zealand, Thailand, and the Philippines all have military forces fighting and working with the Vietnamese and Americans in Vietnam.

It is also worthy of note that 30 other nations are providing noncombat support. All of these free world forces are doing well, whether in combat or in support of nation-building. Their exploits deserve recognition, not only for their direct contribution to the overall effort, but for their symbolic reminder that the whole of free Asia opposes Communist expansion.

As the focal point of this struggle in Asia, the Republic of Vietnam Armed Forces merit special mention.

Before 1954 South Vietnam had no armed forces in being. And there was no tradition of military leadership. The requirement to build an army, navy, and air force in the face of enemy attack and subversion seems, in retrospect, an almost impossible task. Yet, in their determination to resist the Communists, the Vietnamese have built an effective military force. . . .

As you know, we are fighting a war with no front lines, since the enemy hides among the people, in the jungles and mountains, and uses covertly border areas of neutral countries. One cannot measure progress by lines on a map. We therefore have to use other means to chart progress. Several indices clearly point to steady and encouraging success. As an example:

Two years ago the Republic of Vietnam had fewer than 30 combat-ready battalions. Today it has 154.

Then there were three jet-capable runways in South Vietnam. Today there are 14.

In April 1965 there were 15 airfields that could take C-130 transport aircraft. We now have 89.

Then there was one deep-water port for sea-going ships. Now there are seven.

In 1965 ships had to wait weeks to unload. We now turn them around in as little as one week.

A year ago there was no long-haul highway transport. Last month alone 161,000 tons of supplies were moved over the highways. During the last year the mileage of essential highways open for use has risen from about 52 percent to 80 percent.

During 1965 the Republic of Vietnam Armed Forces and its allies killed 36,000 of the enemy at a cost of approximately 12,000 friendly killed and 90 percent of these were Vietnamese. During recent months this 3-to-1 ratio in favor of the allies has risen significantly and in some weeks has been as high as 10- or 20-to-1 in our favor.

In 1965, 11,000 Vietcong defected to the side of the Government. In 1966 there were 20,000. In the first 3 months of 1967 there have been nearly 11,000 ralliers, a figure that equals all of 1965 and more than half of all of 1966.

In 1964 and in the first part of 1965 the ratio of weapons captured was 2-to-1 in favor of the enemy. The ratio for 1966 and the first 3 months of this year is 2 ½-to-1 in favor of the Republic of Vietnam and its allies.

Our President and the representatives of the people of the United States, the Congress, have seen to it that our troops in the field have been well supplied and equipped. When a field commander does not have to look over his shoulder to see whether he is being supported, he can concentrate on the battlefield with much greater assurance of success. I speak for my troops, when I say we are thankful for this unprecedented material support.

As I have said before, in evaluating the enemy strategy it is evident to me that he believes our Achilles' heel is our resolve. Your continued strong support is vital to the success of our mission.

Our soldiers, sailors, airmen, marines, and coastguardsmen in Vietnam are the finest ever fielded by our Nation. In this assessment I include Americans of all races, creeds, and colors. Your servicemen in Vietnam are intelligent, skilled, dedicated, and courageous. In these qualities no unit, no service, no ethnic group, and no national origin can claim priority.

These men understand the conflict and their complex roles as fighters and as builders. They believe in what they are doing. They are determined to provide the shield of security behind which the Republic of Vietnam can develop and prosper for its own sake and for the future and freedom of all Southeast Asia.

Backed at home by resolve, confidence, patience, determination, and continued support, we will prevail in Vietnam over the Communist aggressor.

Mr. President, Mr. Speaker, Members of Congress—I am sure you are as proud to represent our men serving their country and the free world in Vietnam as I am to command them.

[Applause, the Members rising.]

In many ways, the turning point in the war came early in 1968 with the Tet offensive. Even though U.S. and South Vietnamese forces successfully repulsed this risky all-out attack on the South, which included the temporary penetration of the American embassy in Saigon, the offensive undercut Westmoreland's and the government's contention that the war had been going America's way. Perhaps the most telling development during the Tet offensive was a change in the media's outlook. Up until Tet, the major newspapers and broadcast networks rarely directly challenged the official reports of the government. With Tet, the press adopted a more critical stance. Walter Cronkite, the anchor of CBS's nightly news and one of the most respected men in America, journeyed to South Vietnam, where he delivered several special reports on the Tet offensive and the war in general. **Document 5.9** *consists of the transcript of his final report, in which Cronkite delivered a pessimistic summary of the status of the war.*

Document 5.10, *a telegram that UAW president Walter Reuther sent to President Nixon in opposition to the invasion of Cambodia, provides further evidence of the erosion of public support for the war in Vietnam. Through most of the 1960s, Reuther, a very prominent liberal leader, supported the cold war in general and the Vietnam War in particular. In this telegram, however, the last message of his life—he died in an airplane crash—he bemoaned the tragedy of Vietnam and implored the president to "mobilize for peace." Paradoxically, most Americans believed that labor strongly supported the president's policies, a view reinforced by an attack on antiwar protesters in New York City by construction workers. Yet even these workers, who took out their anger on the antiwar movement, wanted American GIs to return home. Aware of the public's declining support for the war, President Nixon reduced the number of U.S. troops in Southeast Asia and did his best to scare the North Vietnamese into negotiating a settlement.*

Document 5.9   Walter Cronkite, "Who, What, When, Where, and Why: Report from Vietnam," CBS News, February 27, 1968, New York.

Cronkite: These ruins are in Saigon, capital and largest city of South Vietnam. They were left here by an act of war, Vietnamese against Vietnamese. Hundreds died here. Here in these ruins can be seen physical evidence of the Vietcong's Tet offensive, but far less tangible is what those ruins mean, and like everything else in this burned and blasted and weary land, they mean success or setback, victory or defeat, depending upon whom you talk to.

President Nguyen Van Thieu: I believe it gives to the VC, it shows first to the VC that the—the Vietnamese people from whom they hoped to have a general uprising, and to welcome the VC in the cities, this is a very bad test for them.

Nguyen Xuan Oanh (critic of government): I think the people have realized now that there [are] no secure areas. Your own home in the heart of the city is not secure. I am stunned myself when I see that the Vietcong can come to your door and open the door and just kill you instantly, without any warning, and without any protection from the government.

Cronkite: There are doubts about the measure of success or setback, but even more, there are doubts about the exact measure of the disaster itself. All that is known with certainty is that on the first two nights of the Tet Lunar New Year, the Vietcong and North Vietnamese Regular Forces, violating the truce agreed on for that holiday, struck across the entire length of South Vietnam, hitting the largest 35 cities, towns, and provincial capitals. How many died and how much damage was done, however, are still but approximations, despite the official figures.

The very preciseness of the figures brings them under suspicion. Anyone who has wandered through these ruins knows that an exact count is impossible. Why, just a short while ago a little old man came and told us that two VC were buried in a hastily dug grave up at the end of the block. Had they been counted? And what about these ruins? Have they gone through all of them for buried civilians and soldiers? And what about those 14 VC we found in the courtyard behind the post office at Hue? Had they been counted and tabulated? They certainly hadn't been buried.

We came to Vietnam to try to determine what all this means to the future of the war here. We talked to officials, top officials, civilian and military, Vietnamese and American. We toured damaged areas like this, and refugee centers. We paid a visit to the Battle at Hue, and to the men manning the northernmost provinces, where the next big communist offensive is expected. All of this is the subject of our report. . . .

How could the Vietnamese communists have mounted this offensive with such complete surprise? After all, the cities were supposed to be secure, except for the occasional, unpreventable attack of terrorism. As a matter of fact, a whole measure of the success of this war has been that we were pushing out from the secure cities, pacifying the countryside around them in an increasingly widening ring. Now all that seemed to be knocked into a cocked hat. How could it happen? Well, let's take a look.

Well, for one thing, there was the enemy's timing, the Tet Lunar holiday. For Asiatics, it's Christmas, New Year's, and Fourth of July all rolled into one, with a little touch of Memorial Day, too. And just like Americans, they all take to the roads to go visit their family and friends. This is a normal day's traffic in Saigon. Imagine it two or three times this big for the Tet holiday. The job of stopping each of these cars, searching them, and checking the people for their papers, why, it staggers the imagination. It staggered the ability of the Vietnamese police to handle, too.

While some residents of Saigon certainly had to be privy to the communist plans, there didn't have to be a lot of them, as some people have charged. Just a few Vietcong sympathizers in whose homes arms could be stored, arms smuggled into town one by one, or even piece by piece. And then on the night of Tet the soldiers, Vietcong and North Vietnamese, slipped into town one by one, rendezvoused at the arms caches, and the offensive was on.

Intelligence people, American and Vietnamese, agree on the same story. They figured the enemy might launch a big attack on Saigon or another South Vietnamese city, but they admit they grossly underestimated the enemy's ability to plan, to provision, to coordinate, to launch such a widespread full-scale attack as this. There are some odd stories about this intelligence failure. High American sources, for instance, say that they warned the Vietnamese, but they let their troops go on Tet leave anyway, until some units were down to just 10 percent of normal strength. Some American newsmen say they tried to reach the Vietnamese General Staff headquarters, and only a sergeant was on duty. There are even stories, believed by many Vietnamese intellectuals, that Chief of Police Loan and Vice

President Ky warned President Thieu, but Thieu thought it was some sort of a trick, perhaps a coup, and ignored the warnings. Thieu himself was at his country home at My Tho outside of town; it took him six hours to get back after the attack, and, in the meantime, Vice President Ky signed the first defensive orders, and many Vietnamese intellectuals thought that indeed Ky had engineered a coup. There was even a suspicion that some of the police on checkpoint duty on the highways outside of town accepted bribes instead of identity papers, all in the spirit of Tet, and that many communists got in that way. . . .

What did the communists hope to achieve by this attack on the cities? As to their ultimate objectives, their maximum goal, prisoner interrogations and captured documents seem to leave no doubt. They hoped, at the best, to bring down the Saigon government and win the war, presumably either by forcing a defeated enemy to the peace table, or by actually capturing his capital. To achieve that knockout victory, the 60,000 or so troops they committed to the battle had two prime targets. First, to seize as much real estate as possible, such as the Presidential Palace, the U.S. Embassy, military headquarters, provincial capitals; and second, to kidnap or assassinate members of the thinning ranks of Vietnamese leadership. But they had shorter-range objectives, about which they could be far more certain of success.

They expected the allies to pull their troops off the pacification campaign in the countryside and bring them in for the defense of the cities. They expected the Americans, too, to commit some of their reserves at least to the defense of the cities, rather than hold them for the big battles expected at the Demilitarized Zone. They expected to create maximum economic confusion and disruption, and to create new hordes of refugees, among which the seeds of discontent against the government could be sown. They expected by destroying the myth of the security of the cities to widen the credibility gap that exists here, too, between what the people are told and what they see about them. And the experts do not agree on the objectives or on the amount of success the communists had in achieving them.

Ellsworth Bunker: They have, certainly, disrupted the pacification effort for the time being, for how long I don't know. We haven't yet the full reports on the situation. They have interrupted—interdicted lines of communication, which are now being opened up again. What other effect they may have had, I don't know, on the population.

Nguyen Xuan Oanh: The war damages, I think, have been tremendous. I have talked to quite a few Vietnamese here who have been in Vietnam during the struggle for independence, during the partition of the country, and they all say, they all concur in the opinion that nothing has been so serious. I think that it will take perhaps weeks, if not much, much more, for the people to realize that we are going back to normal. Production is disturbed. You will have the problem of shortage of jobs in the future. The refugee problem is tremendous. The rehabilitation of the—sort of the damaged areas is a tremendous job, and I think that this is of all the things [sic] which the Vietcong attempt to achieve by this attack.

Cronkite: In that sense, they were successful, then?

Nguyen Xuan Oanh: In that sense, I think they have been very successful. . . .

Cronkite: Pacification is not the only casualty of the Tet offensive. These are refugees, most pathetic of all the victims of the attacks on the cities. Just yesterday the U.S. command in Saigon estimated their number at 470,000, new human flotsam, living in unbelievable squalor, huddled in schools and sheds and shanties. Before Tet there were 800,000 officially listed as refugees. One of the South Vietnamese government's greatest failures had been to provide them with decent food and shelter and a role in the economic life. . . .

Tonight, back in more familiar surroundings in New York, we'd like to sum up our findings in Vietnam, an analysis that must be speculative, personal, subjective. Who won and who lost in the great Tet offensive against the cities? I'm not sure. The Vietcong did not win by a knockout, but neither did we. The referees of history may make it a draw. Another stand-off may be coming in the big battles expected south of the Demilitarized Zone. Khe Sanh could well fall, with a terrible loss in American lives, prestige, and morale, and this is a tragedy of our stubbornness there; but the bastion no longer is a key to the rest of the northern regions, and it is doubtful that the American forces can be defeated across the breadth of the DMZ with any substantial loss of ground. Another stand-off. On the political front, past performance gives no confidence that the Vietnamese government can cope with its problems, now compounded by the attack on the cities. It may not fall, it may hold on, but it probably won't show the dynamic qualities demanded of this young nation. Another stand-off.

We have been too often disappointed by the optimism of the American leaders, both in Vietnam and Washington, to have faith any longer in the silver linings they find in the darkest clouds. They may be right, that Hanoi's winter-spring offensive has been forced by the communist realization that they could not win the longer war of attrition, and that the communists hope that any success in the offensive will improve their position for eventual negotiations. It would improve their position, and it would also require our realization, that we should have had all along, that any negotiations must be that—negotiations, not the dictation of peace terms. For it seems now more certain than ever that the bloody experience of Vietnam is to end in a stalemate. This summer's almost certain stand-off will either end in real give-and-take negotiations or terrible escalation; and for every means we have to escalate, the enemy can match us, and that applies to invasion of the North, the use of nuclear weapons, or the mere commitment of 100-, or 200-, or 300,000 more American troops to the battle. And with each escalation, the world comes closer to the brink of cosmic disaster.

To say that we are closer to victory today is to believe, in the face of the evidence, the optimists who have been wrong in the past. To suggest we are on the edge of defeat is to yield to unreasonable pessimism. To say that we are mired in stalemate seems the only realistic, yet unsatisfactory, conclusion. On the off chance that military and political analysts are right, in the next few months we must test the enemy's intentions, in case this is indeed his last gasp before negotiations. But it is increasingly clear to this reporter that the only rational way out then will be to negotiate, not as victors, but as an honorable people who lived up to their pledge to defend democracy, and did the best they could.

This is Walter Cronkite. Good night.

Document 5.10   Walter P. Reuther, "His Last Message: A Call to Peace," *UAW Solidarity* **13, no. 6 (June 1970).**

Just two days before his death, UAW President Walter P. Reuther sent a telegram to the President of the United States, deploring the invasion of Cambodia and the needless killing of students at Kent State University.

It was to be his last public pronouncement. Characteristically, it was a plea for peace at home and abroad.

Following is the complete text of that telegram:

"On behalf of the UAW, I wish to convey to you our deep concern and distress over your action authorizing the use of United States forces and material in a broadening of the war in Indochina.

"Your decision to invade the territory of Cambodia can only increase the enormity of the tragedy in which our nation is already deeply and unfortunately involved in that region.

"Your action must stand as a repudiation of your oft repeated pledge to bring this tragic war to an end and not to escalate it.

"Widening the war at this point in time once again merely re-enforces the bankruptcy of our policy of force and violence in Vietnam.

"Your action taken without the consultation or authorization by the Congress has created a serious Constitutional crisis at a time when there is growing division in our nation. Many Senators are understandably aroused. Senator Cooper has clearly pointed out that your action represents a turnabout in your policy and Senator Aiken has warned that your escalation of the war means the end of the Vietnamization policy.

"However this dangerous adventure turns out militarily, America has already suffered a moral defeat beyond measure among the people of the world.

"You pledged to bring America together. Yet by your action you have driven the wedge of division deeper and you have dangerously alienated millions of young Americans. The bitter fruits of this growing alienation and frustration among America's youth have been harvested on the campus of Kent State University where the lives of four students involved only in an emotional protest against the war were ended by the needless and inexcusable use of military force.

"At no time in the history of our free society have so many troops been sent to so many campuses to suppress the voice of protest by so many young Americans.

"With the exception of a small minority, the American people, including our young people, reject violence in all its forms as morally repugnant and counterproductive. The problem, Mr. President, is that we cannot successfully preach nonviolence at home while we escalate mass violence abroad.

"It is your responsibility to lead us out of the Southeast Asian War—to peace at home and abroad. We must mobilize for peace rather than for wider theaters of war in order to turn our resources and the hearts, hands and minds of our people to the fulfillment of America's unfinished agenda at home."

Chapter Six

AMERICAN CULTURE AT A CROSSROADS

During the 1950s, many social critics bemoaned the uniformity and tepidness of American culture and society. By the end of the 1960s, in contrast, American culture seemed to have turned upside down. Rather than uniformity and togetherness, chaos and conflict abounded. Radicals heralded a cultural revolution, the dawning of the "Age of Aquarius." Rock music went psychedelic; men wore long hair and women donned pants and stopped wearing bras, not to mention girdles. A sexual revolution swept across the land; young coeds openly touted the virtue of living in sin, while middle-class adults increasingly chose divorce rather than "till death do us part." One Ivy League professor, Timothy Leary, toured the country proselytizing the virtues of LSD, a hallucinogenic drug. Another, Charles Reich, predicted the "greening of America." In response, conservatives delivered the equivalent of Puritan jeremiads in the hope that they could shock the American flock into returning to its senses.

The documents in this chapter present a sense of the cultural turmoil that the nation experienced in the 1960s. Document 6.1 consists of two newspaper articles on the appearance of the Beatles in Memphis, Tennessee. Few musical, theatrical, or artistic groups had as much impact as did the Beatles. They arrived on the American scene with a storm early in 1964, attracting swarms of hysterical teen fans and selling millions of records in a matter of weeks. Their appearance on the "Ed Sullivan Show" drew the largest television audience to that date, 67 million, topping the record 54 million who had tuned in to watch Elvis Presley, from the hips up, also on "Ed Sullivan," in 1956. While many predicted that Beatlemania, like other fads, would quickly pass, the Beatles remained phenomenally popular. At the same time, the Beatles gave a boost to rock music, both commercially and artistically. Controversial from the start, in part because of their hairstyle and in part

*because of their sexual appeal, the Beatles garnered much antipathy in 1966 when
John Lennon, one of the fab four, stated that "Christianity will go. It will vanish
and shrink. . . . We're more popular than Jesus now." In reaction to this statement,
the city council of Memphis, which could be considered the birthplace of rock and
roll, sought to prevent the Beatles from performing. When this action failed, local
conservative Christians and the Ku Klux Klan organized rallies to counter their
appearance.*

Document 6.1   Thomas BeVier, "Show by the Beatles Is a Scream," and Dale Enoch, "Rally Provides 8,000 Answers to Beatle Cries," *Memphis Commercial Appeal,* August 20, 1966, pp. 1, 17.

Emily Strider, hands folded, face emotionless and sweet 16, yawned as The
Remains bounced their music, with the help of seven amplifiers, off the walls
and ceiling of the Coliseum.

And then it happened. The Beatles pranced on stage in their gray, Mod suits
with red vertical stripes and abbreviated jackets. Emily, who drove to Memphis
early yesterday afternoon from her home in Charleston, Miss., started to cry.
Then she started to scream. Then she started shaking her head wildly and pounding her knees with her fists.

It was a commentary on uninhibitedness, just the sort of thing Jerry Leighton
had been talking about earlier when he was trying to figure out the difference
between a nickel and a quarter.

Leighton is a disk jockey from England who is traveling with the Beatles on
their tour of the United States. His is a "pirate station," one of several that
operate on ships off the English coast because commercial stations aren't allowed in England.

"The Beatles are a phenomenon," he said in the studied accent of a true
Englishman. "I asked them once how it felt to be a phenomenon and they said
they didn't feel anything."

With help from the Yankee press, Leighton was able to figure out how to
operate the cigaret machine and just then Brian Epstein, the Beatles' manager,
walked by.

"Give me two seconds," he was asked.

"Two seconds—my life is spent giving people two seconds," he said.

His quick comment was that, "Yes, the Memphis performance is very important to us" because of the John Lennon comment that the group is more
popular than Christ.

The Ku Klux Klan made its opinion known by picketing at the Southern
Avenue entrance to Coliseum grounds. The sheets and hoods lent an incongru-
ous touch to the stream of bell-bottomed trousers, paisley shirts and high heeled
boots worn by the Beatles' faithful who filed by.

There were 7,589—mostly girls and almost all teenagers—at the first performance, and another 12,539 at the second. You couldn't hear the Beatles for
the screaming.

Before they came on stage there were threats that anybody leaving his seat would be thrown out. It worked and Early Maxwell, Memphis promoter of the show, was glad.

"This was a real test," he said. "I've never had so much security (80 policemen) at an event, even Bob Hope."

Security started at 1:45 p.m. when the chartered American Airlines Electra with the Beatles and their entourage touched down on the military side of the airport. Only 10 Beatle bugs managed to slip by guards.

One, Charles Hardy, 19, of 4931 Montgomery, even infiltrated the press corps and got a hurried, almost legible autograph from Paul McCartney for his persistence.

One of those meeting the plane was a harried man of about 45 from Washington. He was Cabell Bowles, the group's advance man.

"No, you can't ride in on the bus with them," he said.

"No, we don't allow exclusive interviews."

"Yes, I'm tired."

Someone asked him his opinion of the Beatles and their music.

"No comment," he said sharply.

* * *

About 8,000 persons, at least half of them adults, crammed The Auditorium Amphitheatre and overflowed into the Music Hall last night to "stand up and be counted" for Christ.

The program, which approached three hours in length, was without mention of the Mid-South Coliseum concert by the Beatles, a rock-and-roll group which had provoked the organization of the "Memphis Christian Youth Rally" by a statement by one that the singers were more popular than Christ.

Jimmy Stroud, director of Memphis Union Mission and an organizer of the rally, told the crowd that the rally was "to show Memphis and the whole world that Christianity will not vanish and that young people will stand up and be counted on the Lord's side. This is not anti-anything."

The crowd was devoid of string-haired girls or mop-topped boys and showed no signs of beatlemania, but they applauded lustily through the tight schedule of singing, testimonies by young people and two 30-minute speeches.

Gregory Walcott, Hollywood television and film star and leading Baptist layman, made no mention of the Beatles or of their remarks on religion.

He and a featured co-speaker, Dave Wilkerson, director of Teen Challenge in New York City, were presented keys to the city mid-way in the program by Mayor William B. Ingram.

But all were not in accord at the rally.

One angry father, who said he had been in on the planning session, walked out with about 30 others as a vocal group, Sing-Out Memphis, swept into another religious song with a beat early in the program.

"Many young people were decoyed into going down there for a Christian testimonial service. We might as well have gone to the Coliseum,'' he said as the vocal group continued singing to a modified "twist" and the accompanying combo maintained a throbbing beat.

Documents 6.2 *and* **6.3** *remind us that some of the most significant cultural challenges of the era were not byproducts of the counterculture. Rather, they grew out of the imperatives of mass consumerism and were promoted by individuals who identified with the broad middle class, not the political left. In* **Document 6.2,** *Hugh Hefner, the founder of Playboy Enterprises, whose* Playboy Magazine *featured naked pinup girls, described his philosophy. Hefner realized that* Playboy *represented a challenge to America's Puritan or Victorian traditions. Yet at no time did Hefner criticize the basic relationship between men and women. On the contrary, as many feminists observed, Hefner objectified women, treating them as playthings for men, not as equals.*

Document 6.3, *from Helen Gurley Brown's* Sex and the Single Girl, *presents an interesting spin on the same theme. Like Hefner, Brown, who took over and rejuvenated* Cosmopolitan *magazine, was one of the progenitors of the sexual revolution. Aided by pharmaceutical breakthroughs, such as the development of the birth-control pill, Brown renounced traditional sexual taboos, especially those that informed women that "nice girls don't do it." Brown argued that single women should take advantage of their sexuality as a means toward advancing themselves, personally and within society. Like Hefner, however, she did not champion a more fundamental change in the role of women in society and could be accused of perpetuating gender inequality.*

Document 6.2   Hugh Hefner, *The Playboy Philosophy* (Chicago: HMH Publishing, 1962), pp. 1–6.

Exactly nine years ago this month, the first issue of *Playboy* was published, with a personal investment of $600 and $6000 begged or borrowed from anyone who would stand still long enough to listen to "a new idea for a men's magazine." Now something of a collector's item, that issue—forged with much youthful zeal by a small group of dedicated iconoclasts who shared a publishing dream—seems almost childishly crude when compared with the magazine you hold in your hands. We have come a long way since then, in editorial scope and polish as well as in circulation, and we are mightily pleased whenever we are complimented on the fact. But when well-wishers sometimes praise us for the way in which our magazine has changed, we must shake our head in disagreement. The fact is that in its basic concepts and its editorial attitude, in its view of itself and its view of life, its feelings about its readers and—we believe—their feelings toward it, the magazine called *Playboy* is the same today as it was nine years ago. Improved—yes, we like to think. Altered in its aims and outlook—definitely no.

Recently, and increasingly in the past year, *Playboy*'s aims and outlook have been given considerable comment in the press, particularly in the journals of social, philosophical and religious opinion, and have become a popular topic of conversation at cocktail parties around the country. While we've been conscious of the virtues in seeing ourselves as others see us, we've also felt the image is occasionally distorted; having listened patiently for so long a time to what others have decided *Playboy* represents and stands for, we've decided—on this ninth anniversary—to state our own editorial credo here, and offer a few personal observations on our present-day society and *Playboy*'s part in it—an effort we hope to make interesting to friends and critics alike.

OPINION ON PLAYBOY

When Professor Archibald Henderson titled his definitive biography of George Bernard Shaw *Playboy and Prophet*, he probably came closer to using the word *playboy* as we conceive it than is common today. Certainly, he did not mean that the highly prolific playwright-critic was an all-play-and-no-work sybarite. He certainly did not mean to suggest that Shaw led a pleasure-seeking life of indolent ease, nor that the platonically inclined vegetarian was leading a secret life of the seraglio. He did mean—and he told us so when he visited our offices on the occasion of the founding of the Shaw Society in Chicago—that Shaw was a man who approached life with immense gusto and relish. As a word, *playboy* has suffered semantic abuse: Its most frequent usage in the press is to characterize those functionless strivers after pleasure whom Federico Fellini, in *La Dolce Vita*, showed to be so joylessly diligent in their pursuit of self-pleasuring as to be more deserving of sympathy than righteous condemnation. *Playboy*, the magazine, has been sometimes tarred with the same brush—usually by those who are more zealous in their criticism than in their reading of it. We have been accused of leadership in a cult of irresponsibility and of aiding in the decline of the Western world. We deny it. . . .

The professional critics and commentators on the contemporary scene could not too long resist supplying a personal analysis of the *Playboy* phenomenon. In *Commentary*—"A journal of significant thought and opinion on Jewish affairs and contemporary issues," Benjamin DeMott, professor of English at Amherst, wrote an article on the subject, "The Anatomy of 'Playboy,' " which he sums up as "the whole man reduced to his private parts."

But in *"Playboy's* Doctrine of Male" by Harvey Cox, first published in *Christianity and Crisis*—"A Christian Journal of Opinion," and reprinted in *The Intercollegian*—"A Journal of Christian Encounter," and the editorial pages of a number of college newspapers, *Playboy* is criticized for being "basically antisexual." Cox describes *Playboy* as "one of the most spectacular successes in the entire history of American journalism," but stamps us "dictatorial taste-makers," decries the emphasis on emotionally uninvolved "recreational sex" and announces that—like the sports car, liquor and hi-fi—girls are just another *"Playboy* accessory." . . .

THE CRITICISM OF CONTENT

There are actually two aspects of *Playboy* that prompt comment today, where previously there was only one. There have always been those who criticized the magazine for its *content*—certain specific features to which they take exception. There is another, newer area for comment now: the philosophical pros and cons of *Playboy*'s *concept*—the overall editorial viewpoint expressed in the magazine. While both are clearly related—the one (content) growing naturally out of the other (concept)—they are quite different and the comment and criticism on them takes different forms, too.

The critics of content are rather easily disposed of. No one who bothers to seriously consider several issues of the magazine can reasonably question the overall excellence of the editorial content. *Playboy* publishes some of the finest, most thought-provoking fiction, satire, articles, cartoons, service features, art and photography appearing in any magazine in America today; *Playboy* pays the highest rates, for both fiction and nonfiction, of any magazine in the men's field; and *Playboy* has received more awards for its art, design, photography, typography and printing over the last half-dozen years than almost any other publication in all the United States. A questioning of the lack of serious "think" pieces in the magazine, as the Unitarian minister did, can only be the result of a superficial scanning of *Playboy*, as the Hugh Russell Fraser critique of the March issue makes clear. But lest the occasional reader consider that March may have been an uncommon issue, in addition to the Arthur C. Clarke science series and the J. Paul Getty series on men, money and values in society today, *Playboy* has published Nat Hentoff's *Through the Racial Looking Glass*, "a perceptive report on the American Negro and his new militancy for uncompromising equality" (July 1962); . . . *The Cult of the Aged Leader*, expressing the need for younger men in our Government before any of us had heard of a John or Robert Kennedy (August 1959); *Eros and Unreason in Detroit*, decrying the ever-increasing size, and emphasis on chrome and fins, in U.S. cars, before the automobile industry reversed the trend and introduced the compacts (August 1958); Philip Wylie's *The Womanization of America*, expressing concern over the feminine domination of our culture (September 1958); and Vance Packard's *The Manipulators*, on the "vanguards of 1984: the men of motivational research" (December 1957). . . .

A MATTER OF SEX

At the heart of most of the criticism of *Playboy*'s contents, we find that ol' devil *sex*. . . .

For some, it is the pictures that offend—the full-color, full-bosomed Playmates and their photographic sisters, who apparently show off too much bare skin to please a part of the public. That another sizable portion of the citizenry, numbering in the several million, is obviously pleased as punch by this display of photogenic pulchritude is—for the moment—beside the point. We'd like to make our case on merits other than mathematical ones.

It was disconcerting when we first discovered that many of those who consider nudity and obscenity nearly synonymous often drag God's name into the act—this struck us, and strikes us still, as a particularly blatant bit of blasphemy. The logic that permits a person to call down God's wrath on anyone for displaying a bit of God's own handiwork does, we must admit, escape us. If the human body—far and away the most remarkable, the most complicated, the most perfect and the most beautiful creation on this earth—can become objectionable, obscene or abhorrent, when purposely posed and photographed to capture that remarkable perfection and beauty, then the world is a far more cockeyed place than we are willing to admit. That there may be some people in this world with rather cockeyed ideas on subjects of this sort—well, that's something else again. . . .

The great majority will agree with what we've just stated, and yet the almost subconscious, guilty feeling persists that there is something evil in the flesh of man—a carryover from a Puritanism of our forefathers (that included such delights as the torturing of those who didn't abide by the strict ethical and moral code of the community and the occasional burning of witches) which we have rejected intellectually, but which still motivates us on subtler, emotional levels. Thus a men's magazine is appealing to "peep-show tastes" when it includes in its contents the photographs of sparsely clad women—a conclusion the *Newsweek* writer could almost certainly never justify intellectually, but a conclusion that he managed to put to paper just the same. . . .

Naturally, *Playboy* includes sex as one of the ingredients in its total entertainment and service package for the young urban male. And far from proving that we suffer from a split editorial personality, it shows that we understand our reader and the things that interest him.

Document 6.3 Helen Gurley Brown, *Sex and the Single Girl* (New York: Bernard Geis Associates, 1962), pp. 3–10.

WOMEN ALONE? OH COME NOW!

I married for the first time at thirty-seven. I got the man I wanted. It *could* be construed as something of a miracle considering how, old *I* was and how eligible *he* was.

David is a motion picture producer, forty-four, brainy, charming and sexy. He was sought after by many a Hollywood starlet as well as some less flamboyant but more deadly types. And *I* got him! We have two Mercedes-Benzes, one hundred acres of virgin forest near San Francisco, a Mediterranean house overlooking the Pacific, a full-time maid and a good life.

I am not beautiful, or even pretty. I once had the world's worst case of acne. I am not bosomy or brilliant. I grew up in a small town. I didn't go to college.

My family was, and is, desperately poor and I have always helped support them. I'm an introvert and I am sometimes mean and cranky.

But *I* don't think it's a miracle that I married my husband. I think I deserved him! For seventeen years I worked hard to become the kind of woman who might interest him. And when he finally walked into my life I was just worldly enough, relaxed enough, financially secure enough (for I also worked hard at my job) and adorned with enough glitter to attract him. He wouldn't have looked at me when I was twenty, and I wouldn't have known what to do with *him*.

There is a tidal wave of misinformation these days about how many more marriageable women there are than men (that part is true enough) and how tough is the plight of the single woman—spinster, widow, divorcee.

I think a single woman's biggest problem is coping with the people who are trying to marry her off! She is so driven by herself and her well-meaning but addlepated friends to become married that her whole existence seems to be an apology for *not* being married. Finding *him* is all she can think about or talk about when (a) she may not be psychologically ready for marriage; (b) there is no available husband for every girl at the time she wants one; and (c) her years as a single woman can be too rewarding to rush out of.

Although many's the time I was sure I would die alone in my spinster's bed, I could never bring myself to marry just to get married. If I had, I would have missed a great deal of misery along the way, no doubt, but also a great deal of fun.

I think marriage is insurance for the *worst* years of your life. During your best years you don't need a husband. You do need a man of course every step of the way, and they are often cheaper emotionally and a lot more fun by the dozen.

I believe that as many women over thirty marry out of fear of being alone someday—not necessarily now but *some* day—as for love of or compatibility with a particular man. The plan seems to be to get someone while the getting's good and by the time you lose your looks he'll be too securely glued to you to get away.

Isn't it silly? A man can leave a woman at fifty (though it may cost him some dough) as surely as you can leave dishes in the sink. He can leave any time *before* then too, and so may you leave *him* when you find your football hero developing into the town drunk. Then you have it all to do over again as if you hadn't gobbled him up in girlish haste.

How much saner and sweeter to marry when you have both jelled. And how much safer to marry with part of the play out of his system *and yours*. It takes guts. It can be lonely out there out of step with the rest of the folks. And you may *not* find somebody later. But since you're not finding somebody *sooner* as things stand, wouldn't it be better to stop driving . . . to stop fretting . . . to start recognizing what you have *now?*

As for marrying to have children, you can have babies until you're forty or older. And if you happen to die before *they* are forty, at least you haven't lingered into their middle age to be a doddering old bore. You also avoid those tiresome years as an unpaid baby sitter.

Frankly, the magazines and their marriage statistics give me a royal pain.

There is a more important truth that magazines never deal with, that single women are too brainwashed to figure out, that married women know but won't admit, that married men *and* single men endorse in a body, and that is that the single woman, far from being a creature to be pitied and patronized, is emerging as the newest glamour girl of our times.

She is engaging because she lives by her wits. She supports herself. She has had to sharpen her personality and mental resources to a glitter in order to survive in a competitive world and the sharpening looks good. Economically she is a dream. She is not a parasite, a dependent, a scrounger, a sponger or a bum. She is a giver, not a taker, a winner and not a loser.

Why else is she attractive? Because she isn't married, that's why! She is free to be The Girl in a man's life or at least his vision of The Girl, whether he is married or single himself.

When a man thinks of a married woman, no matter how lovely she is, he must inevitably picture her greeting her husband at the door with a martini or warmer welcome, fixing little children's lunches or scrubbing them down because they've fallen into a mudhole. She is somebody else's wife and somebody else's mother.

When a man thinks of a single woman, he pictures her alone in her apartment, smooth legs sheathed in pink silk Capri pants, lying tantalizingly among dozens of satin cushions, trying to read but not very successfully, for *he* is in that room—filling her thoughts, her dreams, her life. . . .

Sex—What of It?

Theoretically a "nice" single woman has no sex life. What nonsense! She has a better sex life than most of her married friends. She need never be bored with one man per lifetime. Her choice of partners is endless and they seek *her*. They never come to her bed duty-bound. Her married friends refer to her pursuers as wolves, but actually many of them turn out to be lambs—to be shorn and worn by her.

Sex of course is more than the act of coitus. It begins with the delicious feeling of attraction between two people. It may never go further, but sex it is. And a single woman may promote the attraction, bask in the sensation, drink it like wine and pour it over her like blossoms, with never a guilty twinge. She can promise with a look, a touch, a letter or a kiss—and she doesn't have to deliver. She can be maddeningly hypocritical and, after arousing desire, insist that it be shut off by stating she wants to be chaste for the man she marries. Her pursuer may strangle her with his necktie, but he can't *argue* with her. A flirtatious married woman is expected to Go Through With Things.

Since for a female getting there is at *least* half the fun, a single woman has reason to prize the luxury of taking long, gossamer, attenuated, pulsating trips before finally arriving in bed. A married woman and her husband have precious little time and energy for romance after they've put the house, animals and children to bed. A married woman with her lover is on an even tighter schedule.

During and after an affair, a single woman suffers emotional stress. Do you think a married woman can bring one off more blissfully free of strain? (One of my close friends, married, committed suicide over a feckless lover. Another is currently in a state of fingernail-biting hysteria.) And I would rather be the other woman than the woman who watches a man *stray* from her.

Yet, while indulging her libido, which she has plenty of if she is young and healthy, it is still possible for the single woman to be a lady, to be highly respected and even envied if she is successful in her work.

I did it. So have many of my friends. . . .

Brains are an asset but it doesn't take brainy brains like a nuclear physicist's. Whatever it is that keeps you from saying anything unkind and keeps you asking bright questions even when you don't quite understand the answers will do nicely. A lively interest in people and things (even if you aren't *that* interested) is why bosses trust you with new assignments, why men talk to you at parties . . . and sometimes ask you on to dinner.

Fashion is your powerful ally. Let the "secure" married girls eschew shortening their skirts (or lengthening them) and wear their classic cashmeres and tweeds until everybody could throw up. You be the girl other girls look at to see what America has copied from Paris.

Roommates are for sorority girls. You need an apartment alone even if it's over a garage.

Your figure can't harbor an ounce of baby fat. It never looked good on anybody but babies.

You must cook well. It will serve you faithfully.

You must have a job that interests you, at which you work hard.

I say "must" about all these things as though you were under orders. You don't have to do anything. I'm just telling you what worked for me.

While the sexual revolution led some to contend that marriage was obsolete, many more adopted a less radical stance. They agreed to live together outside of marriage. Yet as is revealed in **Document 6.4,** *an editorial by William Buckley, even this challenge to traditional values raised the ire of conservatives. Buckley, the founder of the* National Review, *disapprovingly recounts the story of Linda LeClair, a student at Barnard College, who lived with her boyfriend in a private apartment. Not only did Buckley berate LeClair for her decision to live with a man outside of wedlock, but he lambasted Barnard administrators and other liberals for tolerating such behavior. While LeClair probably viewed* Playboy's *philosophy as the antithesis of hers, Buckley linked the two together, seeing them as equal parts in the same revolution against time-honored morality. Buckley coupled this editorial with a piece on the student rebellion at Barnard College's male affiliate, Columbia University. Whereas Buckley censured Barnard administrators for tolerating LeClair's violation* *of school rules, he praised Columbia University president Grayson Kirk for cracking down on student rebels who occupied and defiled campus buildings. Indeed, in contrast to many other commentators who demanded Kirk's resignation for allowing New York City police to brutally evict the student demonstrators, Buckley cast the university president as a champion of virtue.*

Document 6.4 William F. Buckley, Jr., "Linda's Crusade," *National Review* 20, no. 2 (May 21, 1968), p. 518.

New York, April 28—It is now a national story that Miss Linda LeClair, twenty, of Barnard College, has been living off campus in New York with Mr. Peter Behr, 22, of Columbia, and that a general story on such practices by the *New York Times* flushed out the cohabitation and put the authorities of Barnard College on the spot. Complications came swift and fast. Dozens upon dozens of Miss LeClair's classmates stepped forward to admit that their living arrangements were similarly loose-minded, and that therefore it would be unfair to penalize Miss LeClair simply because she happened to be the one who was caught, a defensive doctrine which is not exactly airtight.

The authorities, visibly disconcerted, demonstrated from the outset a total lack of conviction about the significance of Miss LeClair's sexual habits, and decided instead to focus on her having lied in the college form she had filled out giving the required details on where she was domiciled. All of a sudden, all of Barnard was rising in indignation over the false entry in the form, which is rather like being indignant at Iago because he was rude to Desdemona. And then, to make opera bouffe of the whole thing, after meeting solemnly to consider the disposition of the LeClair case, the authorities voted to deprive her of access to the school cafeteria, which was joke enough for a public unfamiliar with the school cafeteria, but for those who are forced to patronize it, it was apparently something in the nature of black humor.

Miss LeClair's parents were finally consulted, and it transpires that they, being of the older generation of course, disapprove their daughter's habits, and have gone so far as to cease to send her money. Mr. Behr, who is a draft evader, is apparently unable to take up the slack; so that perhaps the indomitable Miss LeClair will list herself as an unemployed concubine and apply for relief from the City, which has never been known to deny relief to anyone who applies for it: and that should settle the economic exigencies of the matter.

As for the future, we learn from Miss LeClair that it is her intention to continue to live with Mr. Behr after he is let out of prison, to which he expects to repair in consequence of his violation of the statute law if not the moral law. And they will then found a colony where couples can live and bear and raise children, without getting married. Miss LeClair, in other words, desires to abrogate the institution of marriage, which is apparently okay by Barnard, now that she has ceased to lie about it.

The commentary on the case in the urban press is of course more interesting than the delinquency of this pathetic little girl, so gluttonous for sex and publicity. My favorite is Mr. Max Lerner's, ever on his avant garde. Surveying the story, he concludes, "In moral terms, while it says that the sexual code is no longer there, it fails to deal with the question of truthfulness . . ." So much for a code that developed over three thousand years of Judaeo-Christian experience—shot down, in a subordinate phrase, by Mr. Max Lerner.

There isn't anyone around who seems prepared to say to Miss LeClair: Look, it is wrong to do what you have done. Wrong because sexual promiscuity is an assault on an institution that is central to the survival of the hardiest Western ideal: the family. In an age in which the *Playboy* philosophy is taken seriously, as a windy testimonial to the sovereign right of all human appetites, it isn't surprising that the LeClairs of this world should multiply like rabbits, whose morals they imitate. But the fact that everybody does it—even Liberace, as Noel Coward assures us—doesn't make it the right thing to do, and doesn't authorize the wishful conclusion of Mr. Lerner that, like God, the sexual code is dead.

Perhaps the sexual code *is* dead. Question: Should we regret it? Or should we take the position that that which is "no longer there" is no longer missed? That should be a very good argument for saying that, in South Africa, one should not bemoan the fact of apartheid, inasmuch as integration is, indisputably, "no longer there." Many observers are telling us here that our country is so thorough-goingly racist that we have no practicable alternative than to turn to apartheid. Should we, even assuming they were correct, diminish efforts to make things otherwise?

One wonders whether, if Miss LeClair were plopped into the middle of Columbia's Union Theological Seminary, a single seminarian would trouble to argue with her, as Christ did the woman at Jacob's well, that her ways are mistaken?

Much of the public's conception of the counterculture grew out of the media's description of the so-called hippies, self-avowed bohemians who sought to construct an alternative culture. In the latter half of the 1960s, the Haight-Ashbury district of San Francisco came to embody hippy culture, with hundreds if not thousands of men and women migrating there to take part in the Summer of Love (1967). San Francisco, which had been the home of a thriving "Beat" community in the 1950s, gave rise to numerous countercultural institutions, from Bill Graham's Fillmore West, a famous rock-music hall, to the San Francisco Oracle, *one of many underground or independent newspapers that sprang up across the nation.* **Document 6.5** *contains two selections from the* Oracle. *The initial piece advertises the first "Human Be-In" held in Golden Gate Park in San Francisco, where men and women gathered to listen to rock music, most notably the Grateful Dead, heard poetry and political speeches, and dropped acid (LSD), all for free. The second selection consists of excerpts from "The Houseboat Summit," an informal meeting of several of the most prominent cultural radicals of the era, Allen Ginsberg, Timothy Leary, Gary Snyder, and Alan Watts, the owner of the houseboat.*

Document 6.5 "A Gathering of the Tribes," *San Francisco Oracle* 1, no. 5 (January 1967), and "The Houseboat Summit," *San Francisco Oracle* 1, no. 7 (April 1967).

A union of love and activism previously separated by categorical dogma and label mongering will finally occur ecstatically when Berkeley political activists and hip community and San Francisco's spiritual generation and contingents from the emerging revolutionary generation all over California meet for a Gathering of the Tribes for a Human Be-In at the Polo Field in Golden Gate Park on Saturday, January 14, 1967, from 1 to 5 p.m.

Twenty to fifty thousand people are expected to gather for a joyful Pow-Wow and Peace Dance to be celebrated with leaders, guides, and heroes of our generation: Timothy Leary will make his first Bay Area public appearance; Allen Ginsberg will chant and read with Gary Snyder, Michael McClure, and Lenore Kandel; Dick Alpert, Jerry Rubin, Dick Gregory, and Jack Weinberg will speak. Music will be played by all the Bay Area rock bands, including the Grateful Dead, Big Brother and the Holding Co., Quicksilver Messenger Service, and many others. Everyone is invited to bring costumes, blankets, bells, flags, symbols, cymbals, drums, beads, feathers, flowers.

Now in the evolving generation of America's young the humanization of the American man and woman can begin in joy and embrace without fear, dogma, suspicion, or dialectical righteousness. A new concert of human relations being developed within the youthful underground must emerge, become conscious, and be shared so that a revolution of form can be filled with a Renaissance of compassion, awareness, and love in the Revelation of the unity of all mankind. The Human Be-In is the joyful, face-to-face beginning of the new epoch.

* * *

ALAN WATTS: ... Look then, we're going to discuss where it's going ... the whole problem of whether to drop out or take over.

TIMOTHY LEARY: Or anything in between?

WATTS: Or anything in between, sure.

LEARY: Cop out ... drop in ...

GARY SNYDER: I see it as the problem about whether or not to throw all your energies to the subculture or try to maintain some communication network within the main culture.

WATTS: Yes. All right. Now look ... I would like to make a preliminary announcement so that it has a certain coherence.

This is Alan Watts speaking, and I'm this evening, on my ferry boat, the host to a fascinating party sponsored by the San Francisco Oracle, which is our new underground paper, far-outer than any far-out that has yet been seen. And we have here, members of the staff of the Oracle. We have Allen Ginsberg, poet, and rabbinic saddhu. We have Timothy Leary, about whom nothing needs to be said. (laughs) And Gary Snyder, also poet, Zen monk, and old friend of many years.

ALLEN GINSBERG: This swami wants you to introduce him in Berkeley. He's going to have a Kirtan to sanctify the peace movement. So what I said is, he ought to invite Jerry Rubin and Mario Savio, and his cohorts. And he said: "Great, great, great!"

So I said, "Why don't you invite the Hell's Angels, too?" He said: "Great, great, great! When are we gonna get hold of them?"

So I think that's one next feature. . . .

WATTS: You know, what is being said here, isn't it: To sanctify the peace movement is to take the violence out of it.

GINSBERG: Well, to point attention to its root nature, which is desire for peace, which is equivalent to the goals of all the wisdom schools and all the Saddhanas.

A PACIFIST ON THE RAMPAGE

WATTS: Yes, but it isn't so until sanctified. That is to say, I have found in practice that nothing is more violent than peace movements. You know, when you get a pacifist on the rampage, nobody can be more emotionally bound and intolerant and full of hatred.

And I think this is the thing that many of us understand in common, that we are trying to take moral violence out of all those efforts that are being made to bring human beings into a harmonious relationship.

GINSBERG: Now, how much of that did the peace movement people in Berkeley realize?

WATTS: I don't think they realize it at all. I think they're still working on the basis of moral violence, just as Gandhi was.

GINSBERG: Yeah . . . I went last night and turned on with Mario Savio. Two nights ago. . . . After I finished and I was talking with him, and he doesn't turn on very much. . . . This was maybe about the third or fourth time.

He was describing his efforts in terms of the motive power for large mass movements. He felt one of the things that move large crowds was righteousness, moral outrage, and ANGER . . . Righteous anger.

MENOPAUSAL MINDS

LEARY: Well, let's stop right here. The implication of that statement is: we want a mass movement. Mass movements make no sense to me, and I want no part of mass movements. I think this is the error that the leftist activists are making. I see them as young men with menopausal minds.

They are repeating the same dreary quarrels and conflicts for power of the thirties and the forties, of the trade union movement, of Trotskyism and so forth.

I think they should be sanctified, drop out, find their own center, turn on, and above all avoid mass movements, mass leadership, mass followers. I see that there is a great difference—I say completely incompatible difference—between the leftist activist movement and the psychedelic religious movement.

In the first place, the psychedelic movement, I think, is much more numerous. But it doesn't express itself as noisily. I think there are different goals. I think that the activists want power. They talk about student power. This shocks me, and alienates my spiritual sensitivities.

Of, course, there is a great deal of difference in method. The psychedelic movement, the spiritual seeker movement, or whatever you want to call it, expresses itself ... as the Haight-Ashbury group had done ... with flowers and chants and pictures and beads and acts of beauty and harmony ... sweeping the streets. That sort of thing.

WATTS: And giving away free food.

LEARY: Yes ... I think this point must be made straight away, but because we are both looked upon with disfavor by the Establishment, this tendency to group the two together ... I think that such confusion can only lead to disillusion and hard feelings on someone's part. So, I'd like to lay this down as a premise right at the beginning.

GINSBERG: Well, of course, that's the same premise they lay down, that there is an irreconcilable split. Only, their stereotype of the psychedelic movement is that it's just sort of like the opposite. . . . I think you're presenting a stereotype of them.

SNYDER: I think that you have to look at this historically, and there's no doubt that the historical roots of the revolutionary movements and the historical roots of this spiritual movement are identical. This is something that has been going on since the Neolithic as a strain in human history, and one which has been consistently, on one level or another, opposed to the collectivism of civilization toward the rigidities of the city states and city temples. Christian utopianism is behind Marxism.

LEARY: They're outs and they want in.

UTOPIAN, RELIGIOUS DRIVE

SNYDER: . . . but historically it arrives from a utopian and essentially religious drive. The early revolutionary political movements in Europe have this utopian strain in them.

Then Marxism finally becomes a separate, non-religious movement, but only very late. That utopian strain runs right through it all along. So that we do share this. . . .

LEARY: I think we should get them to drop out, turn on, and tune in.

GINSBERG: Yeah, but they don't know what that means even.

LEARY: I know it. No politician, left or right, young or old, knows what we mean by that.

GINSBERG: Don't be so angry!

LEARY: I'm not angry. . . .

GINSBERG: Yes, you are. Now, wait a minute. . . . Everybody in Berkeley, all week long, has been bugging me . . . and Alpert . . . about what you mean by drop out, tune in, and turn on. Finally, one young kid said, "Drop out, turn on, and tune in." Meaning: get with an activity—a manifest worldly activity—that's harmonious with whatever vision he has.

Everybody in Berkeley is all bugged because they think, one: drop-out thing really doesn't mean anything, that what you're gonna cultivate is a lot of freak-out hippies goofing around and throwing bottles through windows when they flip out on LSD. That's their stereotype vision. Obviously stereotyped.

LEARY: Sounds like bullshitting. . . .

GINSBERG: But they're just as intelligent as you are on this fact. They know about what happened in Russia. That's the reason they haven't got a big, active organization.

It's because they, too, are stumped by: How do you have a community, and a community movement, and cooperation within the community to make life more pleasing for everybody—including the end of the Vietnam war? How do you have such a situation organized, or disorganized, just so long as it's effective—without a fascist leadership? Because they don't want to be that either.

See, they are conscious of the fact that they don't want to be messiahs—political messiahs. At least, Savio in particular. Yesterday, he was weeping. Saying he wanted to go out and live in nature.

LEARY: Beautiful.

GINSBERG: So, I mean he's like basically where we are: stoned.

GENIUS OF NON-LEADERSHIP

WATTS: Well, I think that thus far, the genius of this kind of underground that we're talking about is that it has no leadership.

LEARY: Exactly!

WATTS: That everybody recognizes everybody else.

GINSBERG: Right, except that that's not really entirely so.

WATTS: Isn't it so? But it is so to a great extent now. . . .

GINSBERG: There's an organized leadership, say, at such a thing as a Be-In. There is organization; there is community. There are community groups which cooperate, and those community groups are sparked by active people who don't necessarily parade their names in public, but who are capable people . . . who are capable of ordering sound trucks and distributing thousands of cubes of LSD and getting signs posted. . . .

WATTS: Oh yes, that's perfectly true. There are people who can organize things. But they don't assume the figurehead role.

LEARY: I would prefer to call them *foci* of energy. There's no question. You start the poetry, chanting thing. . . .

WATTS: Yes.

LEARY: And I come along with a celebration. Like Allen and Gary at the Be-In.

More than anyone else, Jerry Rubin and Abbie Hoffman gained fame by seeking to combine or join the counterculture with the New Left. To this end, they founded, with the help of Paul Krassner, the Yippies or the Youth International Party in Greenwich Village on New Year's Eve, 1967. Raised during the age of television, both were masters at using the mass media to promote themselves and their views. After bringing the New York Stock Exchange to a temporary halt by throwing dollar bills from the gallery onto the floor of the exchange, they focused their energy on disrupting the Democratic Party's convention in Chicago in August 1968. **Document 6.6,** *from* Do It!, *includes Rubin's commentary on long hair, one of the symbols of rebellion; the Democratic convention in Chicago; and America in general. In the 1980s Rubin turned his back on radical politics, focusing instead on creating "networking" opportunities for young urban professionals, or yuppies. This led many to conclude that Rubin, like many other activists, had always been more interested in personal self-gratification and aggrandizement than radical politics. Whether this was actually the case remains a matter of debate.*

Document 6.6 Jerry Rubin, *Do It! Scenarios of the Revolution* (New York: Simon and Schuster, 1970), pp. 12–13, 92–95, 168–169, 172–173.

1: CHILD OF AMERIKA

I am a child of Amerika.

If I'm ever sent to Death Row for my revolutionary "crimes," I'll order as my last meal: a hamburger, french fries and a Coke.

I dig big cities.

I love to read the sports pages and gossip columns, listen to the radio and watch color TV.

I dig department stores, huge supermarkets and airports. I feel secure (though not necessarily hungry) when I see Howard Johnson's on the expressway.

I groove on Hollywood movies—even bad ones.

I speak only one language—English.

I love rock 'n' roll.

I collected baseball players' cards when I was a kid and wanted to play second base for the Cincinnati Reds, my home team. . . .

My father drove a truck delivering bread and later became an organizer in the Bakery Drivers' Union. He dug Jimmy Hoffa (so do I). He died of heart failure at fifty-two.

My mother had a college degree and played the piano. She died of cancer at the age of fifty-one. . . .

I dodged the draft.

I went to Oberlin College for a year, graduated from the University of Cincinnati, spent 1 ½ years in Israel and started graduate school at Berkeley.

I dropped out.

I dropped out of the White Race and the Amerikan nation.

I dig being free.
I like getting high.
I don't own a suit or tie.
I live for the revolution.
I'm a yippie!
I am an orphan of Amerika. . . .

16: LONG HAIR, AUNT SADIE, IS A COMMUNIST PLOT

My earliest introduction to Communism involved family intrigue and outa-sight chicken soup. Every family has a black sheep. Mine was Aunt Sadie in New York.

"She went to Russia to meet Stalin," members of the family used to gossip to each other.

When I was a kid, my family often visited Aunt Sadie, and she served the best chicken soup in the whole world. She used to say to me, "**Jerry**, you must still be hungry. Please eat some more, **Jerry darling**. Eat some more good chicken soup."

And as she ladled more chicken soup into my already overflowing bowl, she'd whisper into my ear, "The capitalists need unemployment to keep wages down."

I lost contact with Aunt Sadie and meanwhile became a family misfit myself. Then one unexpected afternoon Aunt Sadie knocked on the door of my Lower East Side apartment. I hadn't seen her in ten years.

"Aunt Sadie," I shouted, hugging her. "I'm a commie, too!"

She didn't even smile.

Maybe she was no longer a Communist?

"Aunt Sadie, what's the matter?"

She hesitated. "**Jerry**, why don't you cut your hair?"

So I gave her a big bowl of Nancy's outasight chicken soup and began:

"Aunt Sadie, long hair is a commie plot! Long hair gets people uptight—more uptight than ideology, cause long hair is communication. We are a new minority group, a nationwide community of longhairs, a new identity, new loyalties. We longhairs recognize each other as brothers in the street.

"Young kids identify short hair with authority, discipline, unhappiness, bore-dom, rigidity, hatred of life—and long hair with letting go, letting your hair down, being free, being open.

"Our strategy is to steal the children of the bourgeoisie right away from the parents. Dig it! Yesterday I was walking down the street. A car passed by, parents in the front seat and a young kid, about eight, in the back seat. The kid flashed me the clenched fist sign."

"**But, Jerry** . . ." Aunt Sadie stammered.

"Aunt Sadie, *long hair is our black skin.* Long hair turns white middle-class youth into niggers. Amerika is a different country when you have long hair.

We're outcasts. We, the children of the white middle class, feel like Indians, blacks, Vietnamese, the outsiders in Amerikan history. . . .

"Long hair polarizes every scene, Aunt Sadie. It's instant confrontation. Everyone is forced to become an actor, and that's revolutionary in a society of passive consumers.

"Having long hair is like saying hello to everybody you see. A few people automatically say 'Hi' right back; most people get furious that you disturbed their environment."

"**Jerry**, *you have so much to offer*. If only you'd cut your hair. People laugh at you. They don't take you seriously."

"Listen, Aunt Sadie, *long hair* is what makes them take us seriously! Wherever we go, our hair tells people where we stand on Vietnam, Wallace, campus disruption, dope. We're living TV commercials for the revolution. We're walking picket signs.

"Every response to longhairs creates a moral crisis for straights. We force adults to bring all their repressions to the surface, to expose their real feelings." . . .

29: THE BATTLE OF CZECHAGO

Every Amerikan's first glimpse at the dawning of the 1968 Democratic National Convention:

Two hundred freeks running around the park. Funny-looking, longhaired, crazy yippie boys and girls, practicing Japanese snake-dancing and street-fighting with poles, learning how to defend themselves by kicking a cop in the balls with a well-placed karate blow while shouting:

"WASHOI!"

Czechago police are permanently stationed outside each water main in the city to prevent the yippies from dropping LSD in the water supply. The Democratic Convention is behind barbed wire.

And we are just warming up.

Sunday we looked around Lincoln Park and counted noses—maybe 2,000 to 3,000 freeks—and we organizers looked at each other sadly. We once dreamed 500,000 people would come to Czechago. We expected 50,000. But Daley huffed and puffed, and scared the people away. . . .

But although we were few, we were hard core: after the movement/Daley fear campaign, who but a bad, fearless, strungout, crazy motherfucker would come to Czechago?

And we *were* motherfucking bad. We were dirty, smelly, grimy, foul, loud, dope-crazed, hell-bent and leather-jacketed. We were a public display of filth and shabbiness, living in-the-flesh rejects of middle-class standards.

We pissed and shit and fucked in public; we crossed streets on red rights; and we opened Coke bottles with our teeth. We were constantly stoned or tripping on every drug known to man.

We were the outlaw forces of Amerika displaying ourselves flagrantly on a world stage.

Dig it! *The future of humanity was in our hands!*

Yippie! . . .

The pigs invaded the sanctity of Lincoln Park on Tuesday morning to arrest Tom Hayden and Wolf Lowenthal. We rushed to picket the jail and ended up in an assault on General Logan's statue in Grant Park. We hoisted the Viet Kong flag high upon the statue.

"It's better than Iwo Jima," someone shouted.

Hundreds of pigs rushed up to recapture the hill.

On Tuesday yippie guerrilla strategy scored its greatest victory. Tear gas aimed at yippies floated into the ventilation system of the Hilton Hotel.

The Hump was in bed when he smelled something funny.

It was tear gas! He had to stand under the shower 45 minutes to get all the stinky, stingy tear gas off.

The headlines blared:

HUMPHREY IS TEAR-GASSED.

Our guerrilla strategy was working: if they tear-gas us, they tear-gas themselves too.

Wednesday's rally of sleepy "the war is immoral, illegal" speeches was halted when the pigs saw the Amerikan flag being lowered. The lowering of the red-white-and-blue, while not illegal, is a symbolic attack on the masculinity of every Czechago pig, so they attacked us with gas and clubs and were met with an avalanche of rocks, bags of shit and table benches.

Then 10,000 people began an illegal march to the amphitheater and were stopped by a line of pigs.

We ran through the streets toward the Hilton Hotel, but every bridge to the Hilton was blocked by National Guardsmen who volleyed tear gas at us as we approached.

"HERE! HERE!" someone shouted. "An unguarded bridge." Through some colossal military fuckup by the pigs, we flooded across the undefended bridge to the front door of the Hilton. We filled Michigan Avenue.

The pigs got the order to clear us out and, as TV floodlights turned the dark street into the world's Broadway, cops shot tear gas, clubbed reporters, pushed little old ladies through store windows, smashed faces and tried to annihilate us.

Yippies built barricades, started fires, turned over paddy wagons and spread havoc through the streets. The Hump's nomination took place at the precise moment the Nazi state carried out its brutal attack on the people.

Scenes of pigs beating McCarthy housewives, newsmen and photographers, liberal college kids, yippies, delegates and innocent bystanders were perpetuated on videotape.

Scenes of brave youth battling back flashed over and over again on every TV channel:

infinite replay
of the Fall
of Amerika.

The divisions in American society affected the views and reviews of major figures and productions in the entertainment world. Muhammad Ali and John Wayne, for example, two of the most famous men in sports and the movies, respectively, became symbols of the cultural left and right in America. Ali, who was the heavyweight champion of the world before he was stripped of his title for refusing to be inducted into the army, opposed the war in Vietnam, exuded black pride, and was viewed as a martyr by many New Leftists. In contrast, Wayne, who made millions of dollars acting in Westerns and other old-fashioned films, championed the war, defended white supremacy, and was heralded as a standard-bearer of traditional values by conservatives. **Documents 6.7** *and* **6.8** *consist of a* Ramparts *article on Ali and a speech by Strom Thurmond in which the South Carolina senator criticized the liberal press for its unfavorable treatment of Wayne's prowar film,* The Green Berets. *Thurmond sharpened his argument by comparing the* New York Times' *critical reviews of Wayne's movie to the newspaper's glowing description of* Hair, *the theatrical production that illustrated the arrival of the counterculture. Both selections hint at the complexity and contradictions of American culture. Wayne's popularity warns against exaggerating the significance of the counterculture. Yet at the same time, the fact that Ali is now considered a national treasure by proponents of mainstream culture suggests that the counterculture, or at least the oppositional culture of the 1960s, had a lasting impact on the nation's values and mores.*

Document 6.7   Gene Marine, with Robert Avakian and Peter Collier, "Nobody Knows My Name," *Ramparts* 5, no. 12 (June 1967), pp. 11–16.

Whosoever flieth from his country for the sake of the true religion of Allah, shall find in the earth many forced to do the same, and plenty of provisions.

—The Koran

[A BRAVE RESPECT]

There was once a white man who beat the hell out of Muhammad Ali.

The present heavyweight champion of the world (no matter what any boxing commission says) was not yet champion, nor was he known by his chosen religious name. He was Cassius Marcellus Clay, and he still had not left Louisville, Kentucky, and he was, at the time, eight years old.

Clay's father rescued him that day in the Louisville slum where Muhammad Ali's father still lives; but we ought to remember the cracker who for no known reason was beating the boy. We ought to remember him because you don't have to be black to know that there's a straight line from that white man in Kentucky to all the white men who recoiled in horror 17 years later at the sound of Muhammad Ali saying, "No."

What he said, in full, was, "No, I'm not going ten thousand miles from here to help murder and kill and burn another poor people simply to help continue the domination of white slavemasters over the darker people the world over." . . .

Muhammad Ali's refusal to take the one step forward that constitutes formal induction into the armed forces of the United States is rife with ironies, and not the least of them is that an athlete, representing a feared and outcast group, has committed the act of leadership in the "best educated" nation in the world, while its intellectuals, far from banding together in defense of "treason"—if treason be necessary in pursuit of truth—bicker among themselves while they compete for government grants.

But perhaps the greatest irony is the almost uniform castigation of Ali for being what Americans have always professed most to admire: a man who combines courage and principle. At worst—as in a May 7th diatribe by Melvin Durslag of the Los Angeles Times (who of course calls him "Cassius Clay")—Ali is berated as a coward or a fake or both; at best, newsmen and columnists by the dozens have quoted, with sad, wise approval, a fellow inductee who said, "If I have to go, then he ought to have to go."

None of them, so far as I know, has drawn the obvious corollary: the other guy didn't have to go either. More important, none has taken the time to think out loud about the meaning of Muhammad Ali and his act.

If Ali's act in refusing to step forward for induction was treason, then it was a treason, certainly, which "means a brave respect for what is true," and in which decent men must join or face the fact that we are, morally, valve tenders at Auschwitz. This is not to say that Muhammad Ali is America's Jean-Paul Sartre, much less to say that he holds all the principles and positions that are hastily being attributed to him. He is a symbol of the failure of the rest of us—but he is a person, a human being, before he is any kind of symbol. . . .

And he insists on being called by his chosen name.

It is a funny thing, that name. People in any trade can call themselves anything they want to—Mark Twain, Ross MacDonald, Jack Ruby, Robert Taylor, Fabian—and nobody much gives a damn. People change their names for religious reasons all the time, and few are the Irish sports writers who would insist on referring to Sister Mary Theresa as Annie O'Houlihan. Much less would they be likely to make fun of her religious name—like syndicated buffoon Jim Murray, out of the Los Angeles Times, who has called Ali things like "Abdullah Bull Bull" and "Abou Ben Hernia."

The case of "Muhammad Ali," however, is something else again. "Cassius Clay" is certainly a euphonious enough name, and it was as "Cassius Clay" that the man became famous. But it is not ignorance or forgetfulness that leads almost every sports writer, almost every copy desk, almost every radio or television news-actor to insist, like a spit in the face, on "Cassius Clay." And this has gone on for three years.

Sports writers do not, of course, recognize the Muslims as a religious group, any more than do prison officials across the country, any more than does the Federal government (can you see Ali commissioned a lieutenant and made a chaplain?). No sports writer would poke fun at Floyd Patterson for attending Mass, or at Barney Ross for observing Passover. But all but three or four have for three years insisted on saying every day to the heavyweight champion of the world that he will damned well wear a white name and like it.

That could make a guy a little angry. It could make him think, if he didn't think so already, that he lives in a white racist country. . . .

At 18, young, eager, Cassius Clay returned from the 1960 Olympics in triumph, and they all loved him. He was a "warm, natural young man, totally lacking in sophistication, whose personality could be a refreshing breeze in a becalmed sport"; that was Dick Schaap, writing in The Saturday Evening Post in 1961. He was "an amiable and unsophisticated young man, who loves life and people and success and fame," said Newsweek—and the whites complacently read it, "good, simple, happy nigger."

Amiable, unsophisticated Clay swung his deal with the white Louisville businessmen—they did all the investing, he got more than half the income—and deliberately manufactured his attention-getting "I am the greatest" pose. His corny "poetry" (he writes poetry only a little better than the average sports writer) and his uncanny knack for naming the round in which his opponent would fall, was offensive to a few and misleading to many, but it brought him up the ladder fast.

Clay had only 19 professional fights before he was matched with terrible "Sonny" Liston ("the King of Hip," Norman Mailer called him, "the Ace of Spades"). The underlying racism of the heavyweight world had been showing on the surface more than usual, aimed for a time at Floyd Patterson, who was then thought by the white-hope dreamers to be black. Another amateur champion, Pete Rademacher, had been elevated to a pro and matched with Patterson in his first fight, through a financial guarantee put up by a racist group; Patterson had demolished him. Ingemar Johanssen had come from Scandinavia to prove the superiority of the white man; Patterson took the title back and kept it.

Then—as so often happens—the ringmasters realized that things hadn't been so bad after all. "Sonny" Liston had appeared—a burly, lazy, slow, hulking ex-con, a cool killer, the absolute stereotype of the black man in the white man's nightmares about his sister—and had clobbered Patterson twice, both times in the first round.

Liston could hit like a falling boulder, and he probably wasn't afraid of any *fighter* alive—but Clay convinced Liston that he was facing the completely unpredictable. He pulled up in front of Liston's house at three a.m., stood on

the lawn, and shouted insults. At the weigh-in before the fight, Clay turned up—
somehow—with a pulse rate of 120, convincing the examining physician that
Clay was hysterically frightened. The sports writers—so devoted to the "big
black buck" stereotype that they were convinced Liston was invincible—glee-
fully began to predict that Clay wouldn't show up for the fight.

He showed up—with a steady pulse rate—and he has been champion ever
since. Immediately afterward, he announced his adherence to the Muslim faith,
and in March 1964—after a brief flirtation with "Cassius X" that may have
risen from his friendship with Malcolm—he announced that, as is the custom
in the Nation of Islam, Elijah Muhammad had bestowed on him a "holy name"
because he had fulfilled the requirements of his faith. He wished, he said, to be
known as Muhammad Ali.

Two days later, Ali told reporters, "I know where I'm going and I know the
truth, and I don't have to be what you want me to be; I'm free to be what I
want to be."

Roman Catholic Floyd Patterson immediately metamorphosed from black
threat to dark-skinned white hope. "I disagree with the precepts of the black
Muslims," he said, "just as I disagree with the Ku Klux Klan—in fact so much
that I am willing and desire to fight Cassius X to take the title from the black
Muslim leadership." He offered to fight for no purse. Cassius X turned the offer
aside with a mild put-down of Patterson (mild, possibly, because Patterson
hadn't called him "Clay") and the serious remark, "I don't want no religious
war."

Any non-Muslim, black or white, who has ever read Muhammad Speaks or
listened to Elijah Muhammad's broadcasts is likely to have some reservations
about the Nation of Islam. Aside from the pseudo-science, the improbable so-
ciology and the falsified history, it is at least disconcerting to read about the
hypocritical white man who forces the use of the hated word "Negro"—in a
newspaper you've bought from a black man who said, "Excuse me, sir, would
you buy a paper and help the Negro?"

And there can be little doubt that the Muslims get as much out of Ali as he
ever got out of them. For one thing, they get money; for another, they get a
forum that they could never buy. Probably it is trust rather than understanding
that binds Ali to them.

"Followers of Allah," he has said, "are the sweetest people in the world.
They don't carry knives. They don't tote weapons. They pray. The women wear
dresses that come all the way to the knees and don't commit adultery. All they
want to do is live in peace with the world. They don't hate anybody. They don't
want to stir up any kind of trouble. All the meetings are held in secret, without
any fuss or hate-mongering."

But there is more to be said about the Muslims, and their impact on Ali, than
that. "Muslims are righteous people," Elijah Muhammad said recently (in a
lengthy interview with CBS and ABC reporters, only a small portion of which
was broadcast, on ABC). "They do not believe in making war on anybody—

and senseless aggression against people violates a Muslim's religious belief. . . .
I refused to take part in the war at that time [in 1942] against Japan and Germany, or help America to fight those wars. I considered myself a righteous Muslim, and I teach peace. . . . If it is fighting for truth and righteousness—yes, we go along with that. But if it is fighting for territorial gain, or to master and rule people in their own spheres, no. We think it is an injustice. . . ."

A Catholic bishop could as easily make those statements, in full conformance with his dogma, for the guidance of a Floyd Patterson—but none has. Any leader could stand and trumpet those words—but none has (Martin Luther King is certainly more black leader than Baptist leader). A few lonely Christian pacifists have always resisted war—but no major Christian religion, least of all the Roman Catholic, has dared to step so far outside the "acceptable" on moral grounds.

The irony is not only that a group of black outcasts, hated and feared by white America, leads in taking the one position that upholds the rhetoric of great American ideas, and is willing to sacrifice American material rewards. It is equally ironic that Elijah Muhammad's Muslimism is the only religion in the United States that is willing to say unequivocally that God is higher than Caesar—even if they call him Allah.

Ali had barely become Ali when the World Boxing Association and its president, Ed Wassman, started trying to take his newly won title away. Fewer than 60 days had gone by before Wassman was quoted in the press as saying that the behavior of "Clay" since becoming champion was "detrimental to boxing." Since his only public behavior had been to proclaim his religion and his change of name, the meaning was clear.

On a pretext, they took the title from Ali in September 1964; the importance of the action is evident from the fact that everybody but the WBA ignored it. . . .

When, in November of 1965, Ali finally clobbered Patterson, he infuriated sports writers—not because he won, but because he won so easily, took 12 rounds to do it in, and was quite clear about why. All the pre-fight talk proved costly to Patterson; in the ring, Ali continually taunted Patterson by calling him "Mr. White America." The white writers were outraged, but there must have been some black smiles. . . .

In Ali's next to last fight, Ernie Terrell threw several visibly low blows and rabbit-punched and kidney-punched throughout the fight, but when it was over and he was beaten, he called Ali a "dirty fighter"—and half the writers who covered the fight echoed the charge.

That fight, more than any other, brought down on Ali not only the contempt but the righteous wrath of the sports pages. Already he had been classified 1-A; already he had said that he wasn't going to go. Already he had been barred from fighting in several states because he refused to support the war in Vietnam. Already he had made it clear that he would play no newsman's game, that he would say what he felt like saying and insist on his dignity as a man. And already he had told them, over and over, "My name is Muhammad Ali," and they had ignored him.

Ernie Terrell chose to ignore him too, and to make a public issue out of calling him "Cassius Clay." In February 1967, Ali held Terrell up for 15 rounds while he hit him; there is no more charitable description. And every so often, Ali—the fastest heavyweight who has ever been in a ring—would throw a particularly fast combination of punches, step back, and shout, "What's my name?" . . .

The freedom of the press, these days, is the freedom to be sure that all the propaganda is on one side. Long feature stories dot the Sunday editions about the stars who entertain the troops; the gossip columnists glorify the prizefighters (black and white) who travel in the right chic circles; Steve Canyon grimly flies the comic pages; the sports pages are celebrations of publicity for local heroes. "They tell me it would be a wonderful thing if I married a white woman," Ali once sneered, "because this would be good for brotherhood." It would be good for the gossip columnists, anyway; they'd be very noble, just as the sports writers are very noble about black prizefighters so long as they are content to be brown bombers.

But Ali challenges the sports page picture of America, and for that reason, if for no other, the sports writers must feel compelled to get him. Possibly they are all liberals; possibly they would all insist that the name change is a symbol only of separatism, and that they defy it in the cause of some word-magic variant of integration. But to Ali it must look—as, indeed, it looks to many white Americans—like an attempt to deny him his dignity, his prerogatives of choice, his opportunity to be a man.

They may be liberals; but if they are, they are the same sort of liberals as those who asked actor Ossie Davis in bewilderment why he delivered an oration at the funeral of Malcolm X—the question to which Davis answered, in part, "No Negro has yet asked me that question."

"Malcolm kept snatching our lies away," Davis wrote. "He kept shouting the painful truth we whites and blacks did not want to hear from all housetops. And he wouldn't stop for love or money." And Davis wrote: "White folks do not need anybody to remind them that they are men. We do! This was his one incontrovertible benefit to his people."

Muhammad Ali, alone among athletes, fits Davis' description. "The white men want me hugging on a white woman," Ali said, "or endorsing some whiskey, or some skin bleach. . . . But by my sacrificing a little wealth I'm helping so many others. Little children can come by and meet the champ. Little kids in the alleys and slums of Florida and New York, they can come and see me where they never could walk up on Patterson and Liston. Can't see them niggers when they come to town."

He said: "Jackie Gleason tried to show me why I shouldn't be a Muslim. He said, 'Champ, why don't you think about it?' He's not the onliest one. All the big whiteys are trying. . . . Take those big niggers Floyd Patterson, 'Sonny' Liston. The whites make 'em rich, and in return they brainwash the little Negroes walking around. Liston lives in a white neighborhood, Patterson lives in a white neighborhood. I can live in the Fontainebleau, anywhere I want; but I live here in a slum with my people. I could have taken money from the whites, but it would brainwash all the little black children.''

But Muhammad Ali is not a ''credit to his race''; according to Ring magazine, he is ''not to be held up as an example to the youngsters of the United States.''

''I went in one place in Louisville,'' Ali once said, ''and asked to be served, and the waiter told the boss, 'He's the Olympic champion,' and the boss said, 'I don't give a damn who he is, get him out of here!' ''

[A HIGHER BANNER]

From ''I don't give a damn who he is'' to ''What's my name?'' is not so far as all that. And Olympic champion Cassius Clay, now heavyweight champion Muhammad Ali, once said he wanted ''some type of little mission, something to do with the freedom of the Negro in America.'' He's found it; it has something to do with my freedom, too, and that of a lot of other white Americans.

It started on February 17, 1966, when Muhammad Ali was reclassified 1-A. Nine days later he announced that, as a Muslim, he would not fight in Vietnam. The New York Times quoted him as saying, ''I don't have no personal quarrel with those Vietcong,'' but he actually said it much better than that:

''I ain't got nothing against them Viet Congs.''

If that be treason, it is the kind of treason that rises to a banner above the banner of Caesar: it rises to the banner of truth. Alone, young, uneducated, Ali may not be able to take it by himself; but he certainly isn't getting any help from intellectuals.

The principled act of Muhammad Ali is a tragic-ironic heroism. He stands out not only because he is right but because he is alone, in a position which might be, but isn't, shared by all the intellectuals, the religious leaders, the men and women who by profession or position or announced dedication should today be in the forefront of ''treason.''

It is time, I think, to call Muhammad Ali by his right name.

Document 6.8   Strom Thurmond, "Remarks on John Wayne, *The Green Berets,* and *Hair,*" *Congressional Record,* 90th Congress, 2nd Session, 114, part 14 (June 26, 1968), pp. 18856–18857.

Mr. THURMOND. Mr. President, this afternoon the Town Theater will present the Washington premiere of a new film called ''The Green Berets,'' starring John Wayne and codirected by John Wayne. I have not yet had the opportunity to see this movie, but I am extremely anxious to do so. This is not only the first major studio movie about the Vietnam war, but it also portrays our American heroes in action. But if my admiration for John Wayne were not enough to make me want to see the movie, I became convinced that this must be one of the finest and most admirable movies of our generation, after reading the review which appeared last week in the New York Times when the movie opened there. The first paragraph of this review was enough to convince anyone that this was a good movie. Please listen carefully to what the New York Times reviewer had to say:

> "The Green Berets" is a film so unspeakable, so stupid, so rotten and false in every detail that it passes through being fun, through being funny, through being camp, through being everything and becomes an invitation to grieve not for our soldiers or for Vietnam . . . but for what has happened to the fantasy-making apparatus in this country. Simplicity of the right, simplicity of the left, but this one is beyond the possible. It is vile and insane. On top of that, it is dull.

That last sentence is the tip-off, since I find it hard to believe that John Wayne could ever be dull. But it set me to wondering what on earth the standards of criticism are that are current in the New York Times that a film which is patriotic and pro-American should receive such treatment.

I got a small clue about the New York Times standards when looking back over recent reviews on the entertainment page in the New York Times. I came across a review that begins in ecstatic terms of admiration. This is the review of the recent Broadway musical entitled "Hair." The reviewer says:

> What is so likeable about "Hair," that tribal rock musical that Monday completed its trek from downtown, via a discotheque, and landed, positively panting with love and smelling of sweat and flowers, at the Biltmore Theatre? I think it is simply that it is so likeable. So new, so fresh, and so unassuming, even in its pretensions.

So here we have a review that starts out just the opposite of the review of "The Green Berets." Whereas "The Green Berets" is unspeakable, stupid, rotten, false, vile, and insane, "Hair" is likable, new, fresh, unassuming.

Now what is "Hair" all about? Well, the reviewer goes on to explain why it is so likable and fresh. He says that he cannot spell out what happens on stage because the Times is a "family newspaper." However, he does go on with the following description:

> A great many four-letter words, such as "love", are used very freely. At one point—in what is later affectionately referred to as "the nude scene"—a number of men and women (I should have counted) are seen totally nude and full, as it were, face.
>
> Frequent references—frequent approving references—are made to the expanding benefits of drugs. Homosexuality is not frowned upon—one boy announces that he is in love with Mike Jagger [sic], in terms unusually frank. The American flag is not desecrated—that would be a Federal offense,

wouldn't it?—but it is used in a manner that not everyone would call respectful. Christian ritual also comes in for a bad time, the authors approve enthusiastically of miscegenation, and one enterprising lyric catalogues somewhat arcane sexual practices more familiar to the pages of the "Kama Sutra" than The New York Times. So there—you have been warned. Oh yes, they also hand out flowers.

So there we have the story of "Hair," at least insofar as it is fit to print. This is what is fresh and frank and likable. But a movie about honor and glory and courage and loyalty and duty and country is a film that is unspeakable, stupid, rotten, false, vile, and insane. I think now we have a clear picture of the standards of criticism used by the New York Times reviewers. If the New York Times says that a film is unspeakable, and so forth, it must be pretty good. And if the New York Times says a film about depravity is fresh and likable, we know well enough to avoid it.

Mr. President, there is something utterly perverted with our society's standards of art and entertainment if these examples from the New York Times in any way actually reflect the temper of our time. We have come to the point described by Orwell in "1984," where he talks about newspeak. In newspeak, words are used to mean the opposite of the commonly accepted meaning. Love means hate, peace means war, and so forth. We are now at the point where depravity is fresh and likable, whereas virtue is apparently false and insane. Despite the ecstatic review of "Hair" by the Times, I confess that I have no desire whatsoever to see it. Despite the incredible blast by the Times at "The Green Berets," I am eager to see the film. I trust John Wayne's judgment more than I would trust that of the Times movie critic.

John Wayne is one of the great actors of our time. He is a true and loyal patriot and a great American. It is men of his caliber and stripe who have built America and made it what it is today—the greatest country in the world.

Chapter Seven

WOMEN'S LIBERATION AND OTHER MOVEMENTS

While the happy housewives of television sitcoms, such as June Cleaver of "Leave It to Beaver," were fictional creations that misrepresented the world of millions of American women, exaggerating their sense of fulfillment, as the sixties began, the women's movement showed few signs of life. Even women activists like those who forged Women Strike for Peace did not openly challenge their prescribed role as mothers and homemakers. On the contrary, they justified their activism on the grounds that they were seeking to protect their children. Somewhat similarly, gay men and women who were politically active by and large remained in the closet or at least separated their political and personal lives.

The civil rights movement, however, reenergized the women's movement and inspired liberation movements among other minorities, from gays and lesbians to Mexican and Native Americans. In numerous instances, nascent feminists and gay and minority activists learned critical organizing skills and developed ties to other activists while participating in the civil rights movement. Just as important, the black freedom struggle and the antiwar movement encouraged men and women to question authority and offered theoretical models for understanding their own exploitation.

Document 7.1 contains an excerpt from The Feminine Mystique by Betty Friedan. Often compared to Uncle Tom's Cabin and The Jungle, Friedan's book, published in 1963, helped catalyze the second wave of feminism. While Friedan's argument was not original, she articulated it in such a way as to strike a respondent chord among thousands of women (and some men). Several years later, Friedan cofounded the National Organization for Women (NOW), whose "Statement of Purpose" is excerpted in **Document 7.2.**

Document 7.1   Betty Friedan, *The Feminine Mystique* (New York: W. W. Norton, 1963), pp. 11–27.

The problem lay buried, unspoken, for many years in the minds of American women. It was a strange stirring, a sense of dissatisfaction, a yearning that women suffered in the middle of the twentieth century in the United States. Each suburban wife struggled with it alone. As she made the beds, shopped for groceries, matched slipcover material, ate peanut butter sandwiches with her children, chauffeured Cub Scouts and Brownies, lay beside her husband at night—she was afraid to ask even of herself the silent question—"Is this all?"

For over fifteen years there was no word of this yearning in the millions of words written about women, for women, in all the columns, books and articles by experts telling women their role was to seek fulfillment as wives and mothers. Over and over women heard in voices of tradition and of Freudian sophistication that they could desire no greater destiny than to glory in their own femininity. Experts told them how to catch a man and keep him, how to breastfeed children and handle their toilet training, how to cope with sibling rivalry and adolescent rebellion; how to buy a dishwasher, bake bread, cook gourmet snails, and build a swimming pool with their own hands; how to dress, look, and act more feminine and make marriage more exciting; how to keep their husbands from dying young and their sons from growing into delinquents. They were taught to pity the neurotic, unfeminine, unhappy women who wanted to be poets or physicists or presidents. They learned that truly feminine women do not want careers, higher education, political rights—the independence and the opportunities that the old-fashioned feminists fought for. Some women, in their forties and fifties, still remembered painfully giving up those dreams, but most of the younger women no longer even thought about them. A thousand expert voices applauded their femininity, their adjustment, their new maturity. All they had to do was devote their lives from earliest girlhood to finding a husband and bearing children.

By the end of the nineteen-fifties, the average marriage age of women in America dropped to 20, and was still dropping, into the teens. Fourteen million girls were engaged by 17. The proportion of women attending college in comparison with men dropped from 47 per cent in 1920 to 35 per cent in 1958. A century earlier, women had fought for higher education; now girls went to college to get a husband. By the mid-fifties, 60 per cent dropped out of college to marry, or because they were afraid too much education would be a marriage bar. Colleges built dormitories for "married students," but the students were almost always the husbands. A new degree was instituted for the wives— "Ph.T." (Putting Husband Through). . . .

By the end of the fifties, the United States birthrate was overtaking India's. The birth-control movement, renamed Planned Parenthood, was asked to find a method whereby women who had been advised that a third or fourth baby would be born dead or defective might have it anyhow. Statisticians were especially astounded at the fantastic increase in the number of babies among college women. Where once they had two children, now they had four, five, six. Women who had once wanted careers were now making careers out of having babies. So rejoiced *Life* magazine in a 1956 paean to the movement of American women back to the home.

In a New York hospital, a woman had a nervous breakdown when she found she could not breastfeed her baby. In other hospitals, women dying of cancer refused a drug which research had proved might save their lives: its side effects were said to be unfeminine. "If I have only one life, let me live it as a blonde," a larger-than-life-sized picture of a pretty, vacuous woman proclaimed from newspaper, magazine, and drugstore ads. And across America, three out of every ten women dyed their hair blonde. They ate a chalk called Metrecal, instead of food, to shrink to the size of the thin young models. Department-store buyers reported that American women, since 1939, had become three and four sizes smaller. "Women are out to fit the clothes, instead of vice-versa," one buyer said.

Interior decorators were designing kitchens with mosaic murals and original paintings, for kitchens were once again the center of women's lives. Home sewing became a million-dollar industry. Many women no longer left their homes, except to shop, chauffeur their children, or attend a social engagement with their husbands. Girls were growing up in America without ever having jobs outside the home. In the late fifties, a sociological phenomenon was suddenly remarked: a third of American women now worked, but most were no longer young and very few were pursuing careers. They were married women who held part-time jobs, selling or secretarial, to put their husbands through school, their sons through college, or to help pay the mortgage. Or they were widows supporting families. Fewer and fewer women were entering professional work. The shortages in the nursing, social work, and teaching professions caused crises in almost every American city. Concerned over the Soviet Union's lead in the space race, scientists noted that America's greatest source of unused brainpower was women. But girls would not study physics: it was "unfeminine." A girl refused a science fellowship at Johns Hopkins to take a job in a real-estate office. All she wanted, she said, was what every other American girl wanted—to get married, have four children and live in a nice house in a nice suburb.

The suburban housewife—she was the dream image of the young American women and the envy, it was said, of women all over the world. The American housewife—freed by science and labor-saving appliances from the drudgery, the dangers of childbirth and the illnesses of her grandmother. She was healthy, beautiful, educated, concerned only about her husband, her children, her home. She had found true feminine fulfillment. As a housewife and mother, she was respected as a full and equal partner to man in his world. She was free to choose automobiles, clothes, appliances, supermarkets; she had everything that women ever dreamed of.

In the fifteen years after World War II, this mystique of feminine fulfillment became the cherished and self-perpetuating core of contemporary American culture. Millions of women lived their lives in the image of those pretty pictures of the American suburban housewife, kissing their husbands goodbye in front of the picture window, depositing their stationwagonsful of children at school, and smiling as they ran the new electric waxer over the spotless kitchen floor. They baked their own bread, sewed their own and their children's clothes, kept their new washing machines and dryers running all day. They changed the sheets on the beds twice a week instead of once, took the rug-hooking class in adult education, and pitied their poor frustrated mothers, who had dreamed of having a career. Their only dream was to be perfect wives and mothers; their highest ambition to have five children and a beautiful house, their only fight to get and keep their husbands. They had no thought for the unfeminine problems of the world outside the home; they wanted the men to make the major decisions. They gloried in their role as women, and wrote proudly on the census blank: "Occupation: housewife." . . .

If the woman had a problem in the 1950's and 1960's, she knew that something must be wrong with her marriage, or with herself. Other women were satisfied with their lives, she thought. What kind of a woman was she if she did not feel this mysterious fulfillment waxing the kitchen floor? She was so ashamed to admit her dissatisfaction that she never knew how many other women shared it. . . .

But on an April morning in 1959, I heard a mother of four, having coffee with four other mothers in a suburban development fifteen miles from New York, say in a tone of quiet desperation, "the problem." And the others knew, without words, that she was not talking about a problem with her husband, or her children, or her home. Suddenly they realized they all shared the same problem, the problem that has no name. They began, hesitantly, to talk about it. Later, after they had picked up their children at nursery school and taken them home to nap, two of the women cried, in sheer relief, just to know they were not alone.

Gradually I came to realize that the problem that has no name was shared by countless women in America. As a magazine writer I often interviewed women about problems with their children, or their marriages, or their houses, or their communities. But after a while I began to recognize the telltale signs of this other problem. I saw the same signs in suburban ranch houses and split-levels on Long Island and in New Jersey and Westchester County; in colonial houses in a small Massachusetts town; on patios in Memphis; in surburban and city apartments; in living rooms in the Midwest. Sometimes I sensed the problem, not as a reporter, but as a suburban housewife, for during this time I was also bringing up my own three children in Rockland County, New York. I heard echoes of the problem in college dormitories and semi-private maternity wards, at PTA meetings and luncheons of the League of Women Voters, at suburban cocktail parties, in station wagons waiting for trains, and in snatches of conversation overheard at Schrafft's. The groping words I heard from other women, on quiet afternoons when children were at school or on quiet evenings when husbands worked late, I think I understood first as a woman long before I understood their larger social and psychological implications.

Just what was this problem that has no name? What were the words women used when they tried to express it? Sometimes a woman would say "I feel empty somehow . . . incomplete." Or she would say, "I feel as if I don't exist." Sometimes she blotted out the feeling with a tranquilizer. . . .

It is no longer possible to ignore that voice, to dismiss the desperation of so many American women. This is not what being a woman means, no matter what the experts say. For human suffering there is a reason; perhaps the reason has not been found because the right questions have not been asked, or pressed far enough. I do not accept the answer that there is no problem because American women have luxuries that women in other times and lands never dreamed of; part of the strange newness of the problem is that it cannot be understood in terms of the age-old material problems of man: poverty, sickness, hunger, cold. The women who suffer this problem have a hunger that food cannot fill. It persists in women whose husbands are struggling interns and law clerks, or prosperous doctors and lawyers; in wives of workers and executives who make $5,000 a year or $50,000. It is not caused by lack of material advantages; it may not even be felt by women preoccupied with desperate problems of hunger, poverty or illness. And women who think it will be solved by more money, a bigger house, a second car, moving to a better suburb, often discover it gets worse.

It is no longer possible today to blame the problem on loss of femininity: to say that education and independence and equality with men have made American women unfeminine. I have heard so many women try to deny this dissatisfied voice within themselves because it does not fit the pretty picture of femininity the experts have given them. I think, in fact, that this is the first clue to the mystery: the problem cannot be understood in the generally accepted terms by which scientists have studied women, doctors have treated them, counselors have advised them, and writers have written about them. Women who suffer this problem, in whom this voice is stirring, have lived their whole lives in the pursuit of feminine fulfillment. They are not career women (although career women may have other problems); they are women whose greatest ambition has been marriage and children. For the oldest of these women, these daughters of the American middle class, no other dream was possible. The ones in their forties and fifties who once had other dreams gave them up and threw themselves joyously into life as housewives. For the youngest, the new wives and mothers, this was the only dream. They are the ones who quit high school and college to marry, or marked time in some job in which they had no real interest until they married. These women are very "feminine" in the usual sense, and yet they still suffer the problem. . . .

If I am right, the problem that has no name stirring in the minds of so many American women today is not a matter of loss of femininity or too much education, or the demands of domesticity. It is far more important than anyone recognizes. It is the key to these other new and old problems which have been torturing women and their husbands and children, and puzzling their doctors and educators for years. It may well be the key to our future as a nation and a culture. We can no longer ignore that voice within women that says: "I want something more than my husband and my children and my home."

Document 7.2 National Organization for Women, "Statement of Purpose" (adopted at the organizing conference in Washington, D.C., October 29, 1966), National Organization for Women, Washington, D.C.
We, men and women, who hereby constitute ourselves as the National Organization for Women, believe that the time has come for a new movement toward true equality for all women in America, and toward a fully equal partnership of the sexes, as part of the world-wide revolution of human rights now taking place within and beyond our national borders.

The purpose of NOW is to take action to bring women into full participation in the mainstream of American society now, exercising all the privileges and responsibilities thereof in truly equal partnership with men.

We believe the time has come to move beyond the abstract argument, discussion and symposia over the status and special nature of women which has raged in America in recent years; the time has come to confront, with concrete action, the conditions that now prevent women from enjoying the equality of opportunity and freedom of choice which is their right, as individual Americans, and as human beings.

NOW is dedicated to the proposition that women, first and foremost, are human beings, who, like all other people in our society, must have the chance to develop their fullest human potential. We believe that women can achieve such equality only by accepting to the full the challenges and responsibilities they share with all other people in our society, as part of the decision-making mainstream of American political, economic and social life.

We organize to initiate or support action, nationally, or in any part of this nation, by individuals or organizations, to break through the silken curtain of prejudice and discrimination against women in government, industry, the professions, the churches, the political parties, the judiciary, the labor unions, in education, science, medicine, law, religion and every other field of importance in American society. Enormous changes taking place in our society make it both possible and urgently necessary to advance the unfinished revolution of women toward true equality, now. With a life span lengthened to nearly 75 years it is no longer either necessary or possible for women to devote the greater part of their lives to child-rearing; yet childbearing and rearing which continues to be a most important part of most women's lives—still is used to justify barring women from equal professional and economic participation and advance.

Today's technology has reduced most of the productive chores which women once performed in the home and in mass-production industries based upon routine unskilled labor. This same technology has virtually eliminated the quality of muscular strength as a criterion for filling most jobs, while intensifying American industry's need for creative intelligence. In view of this new industrial revolution created by automation in the mid-twentieth century, women can and must participate in old and new fields of society in full equality—or become permanent outsiders.

Despite all the talk about the status of American women in recent years, the actual position of women in the United States has declined, and is declining, to an alarming degree throughout the 1950's and '60s. Although 46.4% of all American women between the ages of 18 and 65 now work outside the home, the overwhelming majority—75%—are in routine clerical, sales, or factory jobs, or they are household workers, cleaning women, hospital attendants. About two-thirds of Negro women workers are in the lowest paid service occupations. Working women are becoming increasingly—not less—concentrated on the bottom of the job ladder. As a consequence full-time women workers today earn on the average only 60% of what men earn, and that wage gap has been increasing over the past twenty-five years in every major industry group. In 1964, of all women with a yearly income, 89% earned under $5,000 a year; half of all full-time year round women workers earned less than $3,690; only 1.4% of full-time year round women workers had an annual income of $10,000 or more.

Further, with higher education increasingly essential in today's society, too few women are entering and finishing college or going on to graduate or professional school. Today, women earn only one in three of the B.A.'s and M.A.'s granted, and one in ten of the Ph.D.'s.

In all the professions considered of importance to society, and in the executive ranks of industry and government, women are losing ground. Where they are present it is only a token handful. Women comprise less than 1% of federal judges; less than 4% of all lawyers; 7% of doctors. Yet women represent 51% of the U.S. population. And, increasingly men are replacing women in the top positions in secondary and elementary schools, in social work, and in libraries—once thought to be women's fields,

Official pronouncements of the advance in the status of women hide not only the reality of this dangerous decline, but the fact that nothing is being done to stop it. . . .

There is no civil rights movement to speak for women, as there has been for Negroes and other victims of discrimination. The National Organization for Women must therefore begin to speak.

A separate segment of the women's movement, often referred to as the women's liberation movement, traced its roots to the New Left. Paradoxically, as Mary King and Casey Hayden, two white female SNCC veterans, reveal in their "Memo," **Document 7.3,** *many New Leftists initially scoffed at their claim that, like blacks, women had been treated as a separate caste and thus needed to organize their own move-*

ment. Nonetheless, as King later observed, women learned a great deal through their involvement in the movement, from ways to organize and raise the consciousness of others to theories for exploring their own exploitation.

In "No More Miss America!" (**Document 7.4**), *a coalition of feminists called for a protest against one of the symbols of the oppression of women, the annual Miss America Pageant, in Atlantic City, New Jersey. Drawing on tactics used by the antiwar movement, they urged demonstrators to throw their "bras, girdles, curlers, false eyelashes . . . and other symbols of the oppression and objectification" into a trash can to be set on fire. Picking up on this call, the press reported that women burned their bras. In fact, because of an Atlantic City ordinance that barred fires on the boardwalk, no bras were burned, but the claim that feminists burned their bras became part of American lore.*

Often feminists sought to link the personal and political. One prime example of this took place in the field of health when a group of women formed a collective to gain more information about women's health issues. Out of their efforts grew Our Bodies, Ourselves. *Originally published by the small New England Free Press and disseminated freely to health care providers and educators, the book became so popular in such a short period of time that the collective arranged to have it reprinted by Simon and Schuster, one of the largest publishing houses in the world.* **Document 7.5** *contains the preface to the second edition of this best-selling work.*

Document 7.3   Casey Hayden and Mary King, "A Kind of Memo . . . to a Number of Other Women in the Peace and Freedom Movements," reprinted in Mary King, *Freedom Song* (New York: William Morrow, 1987), pp. 571–574.

Sex and caste: There seem to be many parallels that can be drawn between treatment of Negroes and treatment of women in our society as a whole. But in particular, women we've talked to who work in the movement seem to be caught up in a common-law caste system that operates, sometimes subtly, forcing them to work around or outside hierarchical structures of power which may exclude them. Women seem to be placed in the same position of assumed subordination in personal situations too. It is a caste system which, at its worst, uses and exploits women.

This is complicated by several facts, among them: (1) The caste system is not institutionalized by law (women have the right to vote, to sue for divorce, etc.); (2) Women can't withdraw from the situation (à la nationalism) or overthrow it; (3) There are biological differences (even though these biological differences are usually discussed or accepted without taking present and future technology into account so we probably can't be sure what these differences mean). Many people who are very hip to the implications of the racial caste system, even people in the movement, don't seem to be able to see the sexual-caste system and if the question is raised they respond with: "That's the way it's supposed to be. There are biological differences." Or with other statements which recall a white segregationist confronted with integration.

Women and problems of work: The caste-system perspective dictates the roles assigned to women in the movement, and certainly even more to women outside the movement. Within the movement, questions arise in situations ranging from relationships of women organizers to men in the community, to who cleans the freedom house, to who holds leadership positions, to who does secretarial work and to who acts as spokesman for groups. Other problems arise between women with varying degrees of awareness of themselves as being capable as men but are held back from full participation, or between women who see themselves as needing more control of their work than other women demand. And there are problems with relationships between white women and black women.

Women and personal relations with men: Having learned from the movement to think radically about the personal worth and abilities of people whose role in society had gone unchallenged before, a lot of women in the movement have begun trying to apply those lessons to their own relations with men. Each of us probably has her own story of the various results, and of the internal struggle occasioned by trying to break out of very deeply learned fears, needs, and self-perceptions, and of what happens when we try to replace them with concepts of people and freedom learned from the movement and organizing.

Institutions: Nearly everyone has real questions about those institutions which shape perspectives on men and women: marriage, child-rearing patterns, women's (and men's) magazines, etc. People are beginning to think about and even to experiment with new forms in these areas. . . .

Lack of community for discussion: Nobody is writing, or organizing or talking publicly about women in any way that reflects the problems that various women in the movement come across and which we've tried to touch above. . . .

Objectively, the chances seem nil that we could start a movement based on anything as distant to general American thought as a sex-caste system. Therefore, most of us will probably want to work full time on problems such as war, poverty, race. The very fact that the country can't face, much less deal with, the questions we're raising means that the movement is one place to look for some relief. Real efforts at dialogue within the movement and with whatever liberal groups, community women, or students might listen are justified. That is, all the problems between men and women and all the problems of women functioning in society as equal human beings are among the most basic that people face. We've talked in the movement about trying to build a society which would see basic human problems (which are now seen as private troubles), as public problems and would try to shape institutions to meet human needs rather than shaping people to meet the needs of those with power. To raise questions like those above illustrates very directly that society hasn't dealt with some of its deepest problems and opens discussion of why that is so. . . . The second objective reason we'd like to see discussion begin is that we've learned a great deal in the movement and perhaps this is one area where a determined attempt to apply ideas we've learned there can produce some new alternatives.

Document 7.4 "No More Miss America!" (August 1968), in Robin Morgan, ed., *Sisterhood Is Powerful: An Anthology of Writings from the Women's Liberation Movement* (New York: Random House, 1970), pp. 521–524.

On September 7th in Atlantic City, the Annual Miss America Pageant will again crown "your ideal." But this year, reality will liberate the contest auction-block in the guise of "genyooine" de-plasticized, breathing women. Women's Liberation Groups, black women, high-school and college women, women's peace groups, women's welfare and social-work groups, women's job-equality groups, pro–birth control and pro-abortion groups—women of every political persuasion—all are invited to join us in a day-long boardwalk-theater event, starting at 1:00 p.m. on the Boardwalk in front of Atlantic City's Convention Hall. We will protest the image of Miss America, an image that oppresses women in every area in which it purports to represent us. There will be: Picket Lines; Guerrilla Theater; Leafleting; Lobbying Visits to the contestants urging our sisters to reject the Pageant Farce and join us; a huge Freedom Trash Can (into which we will throw bras,* girdles, curlers, false eyelashes, wigs, and representative issues of *Cosmopolitan, Ladies' Home Journal, Family Circle*, etc.—bring any such woman-garbage you have around the house); we will also announce a Boycott of all those commercial products related to the Pageant, and the day will end with a Women's Liberation rally at midnight when Miss America is crowned on live television. Lots of other surprises are being planned (come and add your own!) but we do not plan heavy disruptive tactics and so do not expect a bad police scene. It should be a groovy day on the Boardwalk in the sun with our sisters. In case of arrests, however, we plan to reject all male authority and demand to be busted by policewomen only. (In Atlantic City, women cops are not permitted to make arrests—dig that!)

Male chauvinist-reactionaries on this issue had best stay away, nor are male liberals welcome in the demonstrations. But sympathetic men can donate money as well as cars and drivers.

Male reporters will be refused interviews. We reject patronizing reportage. *Only newswomen will be recognized.*

The Ten Points
We Protest:

1. *The Degrading Mindless-Boob-Girlie Symbol.* The Pageant contestants epitomize the roles we are all forced to play as women. The parade down the runway blares the metaphor of the 4-H Club county fair, where the nervous animals are judged for teeth, fleece, etc., and where the best "specimen" gets the blue ribbon. So are women in our society forced daily to compete for male

*Bras were never burned. Bra-burning was a whole-cloth invention of the media—Ed.

approval, enslaved by ludicrous "beauty" standards we ourselves are conditioned to take seriously.

2. *Racism with Roses*. Since its inception in 1921, the Pageant has not had one Black finalist, and this has not been for a lack of test-case contestants. There has never been a Puerto Rican, Alaskan, Hawaiian, or Mexican-American winner. Nor has there ever been a *true* Miss America—an American Indian.

3. *Miss America as Military Death Mascot*. The highlight of her reign each year is a cheerleader-tour of American troops abroad—last year she went to Vietnam to pep-talk our husbands, fathers, sons and boyfriends into dying and killing with a better spirit. She personifies the "unstained patriotic American womanhood our boys are fighting for." The Living Bra and the Dead Soldier. We refuse to be used as Mascots for Murder.

4. *The Consumer Con-Game*. Miss America is a walking commercial for the Pageant's sponsors. Wind her up and she plugs your product on promotion tours and TV—all in an "honest, objective" endorsement. What a shill.

5. *Competition Rigged and Unrigged*. We deplore the encouragement of an American myth that oppresses men as well as women: the win-or-you're-worthless competitive disease. The "beauty contest" creates only one winner to be "used" and forty-nine losers who are "useless."

6. *The Woman as Pop Culture Obsolescent Theme*. Spindle, mutilate, and then discard tomorrow. What is so ignored as last year's Miss America? This only reflects the gospel of our society, according to Saint Male: women must be young, juicy, malleable—hence age discrimination and the cult of youth. And we women are brainwashed into believing this ourselves!

7. *The Unbeatable Madonna-Whore Combination*. Miss America and Playboy's centerfold are sisters over the skin. To win approval, we must be both sexy and wholesome, delicate but able to cope, demure yet titillatingly bitchy. Deviation of any sort brings, we are told, disaster: "You won't get a man!!"

8. *The Irrelevant Crown on the Throne of Mediocrity*. Miss America represents what women are supposed to be: unoffensive, bland, apolitical. If you are tall, short, over or under what weight The Man prescribes you should be, forget it. Personality, articulateness, intelligence, commitment—unwise. Conformity is the key to the crown—and, by extension, to success in our society.

9. *Miss America as Dream Equivalent To—?* In this reputedly democratic society, where every little boy supposedly can grow up to be President, what can every little girl hope to grow to be? Miss America. That's where it's at. Real power to control our own lives is restricted to men, while women get patronizing pseudo-power, an ermine cloak and a bunch of flowers; men are judged by their actions, women by their appearance.

10. *Miss America as Big Sister Watching You*. The Pageant exercises Thought Control, attempts to sear the Image onto our minds, to further make women

oppressed and men oppressors; to enslave us all the more in high-heeled, low-status roles; to inculcate false values in young girls; to use women as beasts of buying; to seduce us to prostitute ourselves before our own oppression.

NO MORE MISS AMERICA

Document 7.5 Boston Women's Health Collective, "Preface to New Edition," *Our Bodies, Ourselves* (New York: Simon and Schuster, 1976), pp. 11–14.

A GOOD STORY

The history of this book, *Our Bodies, Ourselves*, is lengthy and satisfying.

It began in a small discussion group on "women and their bodies" which was part of a women's conference held in Boston in the spring of 1969, one of the first gatherings of women meeting specifically to talk with other women. For many of us it was the very first time we had joined together with other women to talk and think about our lives and what we could do about them. Before the conference was over, some of us decided to keep on meeting as a group to continue the discussion, and so we did.

In the beginning we called ourselves "the doctors group." We had all experienced similar feelings of frustration and anger toward specific doctors and the medical maze in general, and initially we wanted to do something about those doctors who were condescending, paternalistic, judgmental and non-informative. As we talked and shared our experiences with one another, we realized just how much we had to learn about our bodies. So we decided on a summer project—to research those topics which we felt were particularly pertinent to learning about our bodies, to discuss in the group what we had learned, then to write papers individually or in groups of two or three, and finally to present the results in the fall as a course for women on women and their bodies.

As we developed the course we realized more and more that we really *were* capable of collecting, understanding and evaluating medical information. Together we evaluated our reading of books and journals, our talks with doctors and friends who were medical students. We found we could discuss, question and argue with each other in a new spirit of cooperation rather than competition. We were equally struck by how important it was for us to be able to open up with one another and share our feelings about our bodies. The process of talking was as crucial as the facts themselves. Over time the facts and feelings melted together in ways that touched us very deeply, and that is reflected in the changing titles of the course and then the book—from *Women and Their Bodies* to *Women and Our Bodies* to, finally, *Our Bodies, Ourselves*.

When we gave the course we met in any available free space we could get—in day schools, in nursery schools, in churches, in our homes. We wanted the course to stimulate the same kind of talking and sharing that we who had prepared the course had experienced. We had something to say, but we had a lot to learn as well; we did not want a traditional teacher-student relationship. At the end of ten to twelve sessions—which roughly covered the material in the current book—we found that many women felt both eager and competent to get together in small groups and share what they had learned with other women. We saw it as a never-ending process always involving more and more women.

After the first teaching of the course, we decided to revise our initial papers and mimeograph them so that other women could have copies as the course expanded. Eventually we got them printed and bound together in an inexpensive edition published by the New England Free Press. It was fascinating and very exciting for us to see what a constant demand there was for our book. It came out in several editions, a larger number being printed each time, and the time from one printing to the next becoming shorter. The growing volume of requests began to strain the staff of the New England Free Press. Since our book was clearly speaking to many people, we wanted to reach beyond the audience who lived in the area or who were acquainted with the New England Free Press. For wider distribution it made sense to publish our book commercially.

You may want to know who we are. Our ages range from twenty-five to forty-one, most of us are from middle-class backgrounds and have had at least some college education, and some of us have professional degrees. Some of us are married, some of us are separated, and some of us are single. Some of us have children of our own, some of us like spending time with children, and others of us are not sure we want to be with children. In short, we are both a very ordinary and a very special group, as women are everywhere. We can describe only what life has been for us, though many of our experiences have been shared by other women. We realize that poor and nonwhite women have had greater difficulty in getting accurate information and adequate health care, and have most often been mistreated in the ways we describe in this book. Learning about our womanhood from the inside out has allowed us to cross over some of the socially created barriers of race, color, income and class, and to feel a sense of identity with all women in the experience of being female.

We are eleven individuals and we are a group. (The group has been ongoing for three years, and some of us have been together since the beginning. Others came in at later points. Our current collective has been together for one year.) We know each other well—our weaknesses as well as our strengths. We have learned through good times and bad how to work together (and how not to, as well). We recognize our similarities and differences and are learning to respect each person for her uniqueness. We love each other.

Many, many other women have worked with us on the book. A group of gay women got together specifically to do the chapter on lesbianism. Other chapters were done still differently. For instance, the mother of one woman in the group volunteered to work on menopause with some of us who have not gone through that experience ourselves. Other women contributed thoughts, feelings and comments as they passed through town or passed through our kitchens or workrooms. There are still other voices from letters, phone conversations, and a variety of discussions that are included in the chapters as excerpts of personal experiences. Many women have spoken for themselves in this book, though we in the collective do not agree with all that has been written. Some of us are even uncomfortable with part of the material. We have included it anyway, because we give more weight to accepting that we differ than to our uneasiness. We have been asked why this is exclusively a book about women, why we have restricted our course to women. Our answer is that we are women and, as women, do not consider ourselves experts on men (as men through the centuries have presumed to be experts on us). We are not implying that we think most twentieth-century men are much less alienated from their bodies than women are. But we know it is up to men to explore that for themselves, to come together and share their sense of themselves as we have done. We would like to read a book about men and their bodies.

We are offering a book that can be used in many different ways—individually, in a group, for a course. Our book contains real material about our bodies and ourselves that isn't available elsewhere, and we have tried to present it in a new way—an honest, humane and powerful way of thinking about ourselves and our lives. We want to share the knowledge and power that come with this way of thinking, and we want to share the feelings we have for each other—supportive and loving feelings that show we can indeed help one another grow.

From the very beginning of working together, first on the course that led to this book and then on the book itself, we have felt exhilarated and energized by our new knowledge. Finding out about our bodies and our bodies' needs, starting to take control over that area of our lives, has released for us an energy that has overflowed into our work, our friendships, our relationships with men and women, and for some of us, our marriages and our parenthood. In trying to figure out why this has had such a life-changing effect on us, we have come up with several important ways in which this kind of body education has been liberating for us and may be a starting point for the liberation of many other women.

First, we learned what we learned equally from professional sources—textbooks, medical journals, doctors, nurses—and from our own experiences. The facts were important, and we did careful research to get the information we had not had in the past. As we brought the facts to one another we learned a good deal, but in sharing our personal experiences relating to those facts we learned still more. Once we had learned what the "experts" had to tell us, we found that we still had a lot to teach and to learn from one another. For instance, many of us had "learned" about the menstrual cycle in science or biology classes—we had perhaps even memorized the names of the menstrual hormones and what they did. But most of us did not remember much of what we had learned. This time when we read in a text that the onset of menstruation is a normal and universal occurrence in young girls from ages ten to eighteen, we started to talk about our first menstrual periods. We found that, for many of us, beginning to menstruate had not felt normal at all, but scary, embarrassing, mysterious. We realized that what we had been told about menstruation and what we had not been told—even the tone of voice it had been told in—had all had an effect on our feelings about being female. Similarly, the information from enlightened texts describing masturbation as a normal, common sexual activity did not really become our own until we began to pull up from inside ourselves and share what we had never before expressed—the confusion and shame we had been made to feel, and often still felt, about touching our bodies in a sexual way.

Learning about our bodies in this way is an exciting kind of learning, where information and feelings are allowed to interact. It makes the difference between rote memorization and relevant learning, between fragmented pieces of a puzzle and the integrated picture, between abstractions and real knowledge. We discovered that people don't learn very much when they are just passive recipients of information. We found that each individual's response to information was valid and useful, and that by sharing our responses we could develop a base on which to be critical of what the experts tell us. Whatever we need to learn now, in whatever area of our lives, we know more how to go about it.

A second important result of this kind of learning is that we are better prepared to evaluate the institutions that are supposed to meet our health needs— the hospitals, clinics, doctors, medical schools, nursing schools, public health departments, Medicaid bureaucracies and so on. For some of us it was the first time we had looked critically, and with strength, at the existing institutions serving us. The experience of learning just how little control we had over our lives and bodies, the coming together out of isolation to learn from each other in order to define what we needed, and the experience of supporting one another in demanding the changes that grew out of our developing critique—all were crucial and formative political experiences for us. We have felt our potential power as a force for political and social change.

The learning we have done while working on *Our Bodies, Ourselves* has been a good basis for growth in other areas of life for still another reason. For women throughout the centuries, ignorance about our bodies has had one major consequence—pregnancy. Until very recently pregnancies were all but inevitable, biology *was* our destiny—that is, because our bodies are designed to get pregnant and give birth and lactate, that is what all or most of us did. The courageous and dedicated work of people like Margaret Sanger started in the early twentieth century to spread and make available birth control methods that women could use, thereby freeing us from the traditional lifetime of pregnancies. But the societal expectation that a woman above all else will have babies does not die easily. When we first started talking to each other about this, we found that that old expectation had nudged most of us into a fairly rigid role of wife-and-motherhood from the moment we were born female. Even in 1969, when we first started the work that led to this book, we found that many of us were still getting pregnant when we didn't want to. It was not until we researched carefully and learned more about our reproductive systems, about birth-control methods and abortion, about laws governing birth control and abortion, and not until we put all this information together with what it meant to us to be female, that we began to feel we could truly set out to control whether and when we would have babies.

This knowledge has freed us to a certain extent from the constant, energy-draining anxiety about becoming pregnant. It has made our pregnancies better because they no longer happen to us, but we actively choose them and enthusiastically participate in them. It has made our parenthood better because it is our choice rather than our destiny. This knowledge has freed us from playing the role of mother if it is not a role that fits us. It has given us a sense of a larger life space to work in, an invigorating and challenging sense of time and room to discover the energies and talents that are in us, to do the work we want to do. And one of the things we most want to do is to help make this freedom of choice, this life span, available to every woman. This is why people in the women's movement have been so active in fighting against the inhumane legal restrictions, the imperfections of available contraceptives, the poor sex education, the highly priced and poorly administered health care that keep too many women from having this crucial control over their bodies.

There is a fourth reason why knowledge about our bodies has generated so much new energy. For us, body education is core education. Our bodies are the physical bases from which we move out into the world; ignorance, uncertainty— even, at worst, shame—about our physical selves create in us an alienation from ourselves that keeps us from being the whole people that we could be. Picture a woman trying to do work and to enter into equal and satisfying relationships with other people—when she feels physically weak because she has never tried to be strong; when she drains her energy trying to change her face, her figure, her hair, her smells, to match some ideal norm set by magazines, movies and TV; when she feels confused and ashamed of the menstrual blood that every month appears from some dark place in her body; when her internal body processes are a mystery to her and surface only to cause her trouble (an unplanned pregnancy, or cervical cancer); when she does not understand or enjoy sex and concentrates her sexual drives into aimless romantic fantasies, perverting and misusing a potential energy because she has been brought up to deny it. Learning to understand, accept, and be responsible for our physical selves, we are freed of some of these preoccupations and can start to use our untapped energies. Our image of ourselves is on a firmer base, we can be better friends and better lovers, better *people*, more self-confident, more autonomous, stronger and more whole. March, 1973.

Angry at being treated as second-class citizens, gays and lesbians joined other minorities in voicing their demand for equality. In late June 1969, in response to a raid on the Stonewall Inn, a gay bar in New York City, gay men battled police over what they considered their turf. Gay women joined the protest the following day. Like the sit-ins, Stonewall served as a moment of awakening, spurring assertions of pride elsewhere. One such assertion, "A Gay Manifesto," **Document 7.6,** *was written by Carl Wittman, a onetime leader of SDS. Like many other gays, Wittman had migrated to San Francisco because it was more hospitable to alternative lifestyles than many other cities. Nonetheless, as Wittman observed, gays had been ghettoized, and he called on them to liberate themselves.*

Somewhat similarly, in **Document 7.7,** *Cesar Chavez, the leader of the largely Mexican-American United Farm Workers, called for the liberation of his people. Unlike gays, however, the farm workers garnered the support of a broad coalition of middle-class housewives, blue-collar workers, and New Leftists who otherwise wanted nothing to do with one another. Opposed by powerful agribusinesses and conservative politicians from Reagan to Nixon, the United Farm Workers won unprecedented recognition following a lengthy table-grape boycott, and Chavez became the best-known Mexican American in U.S. history.*

Document 7.6 Carl Wittman, "A Gay Manifesto," *Liberation* 14, no. 11 (February 1970), p. 18.

San Francisco is a refugee camp for homosexuals. We have fled here from every part of the nation, and like refugees elsewhere, we came not because it is so great here, but because it was so bad there. By the tens of thousands, we fled small towns where to be ourselves would endanger our jobs and any hope of a decent life; we have fled from blackmailing cops, from families who disowned or "tolerated" us; we have been drummed out of the armed services, thrown out of schools, fired from jobs, beaten by punks and policemen.

And we have formed a ghetto, out of self-protection. It is a ghetto rather than a free territory because it is still theirs. Straight cops patrol us, straight legislators govern us, straight employers keep us in line, straight money exploits us. We have pretended everything is OK, because we haven't been able to see how to change it—we've been afraid.

In the past year there has been an awakening of gay liberation ideas and energy. How it began we don't know; maybe we were inspired by black people and their freedom movement; we learned how to stop pretending from the hip revolution. Amerika in all its ugliness has surfaced with the war and our national leaders. And we are revulsed by the quality of our ghetto life.

Where once there was frustration, alienation, and cynicism, there are new characteristics among us. We are full of love for each other and are showing it; we are full of anger at what has been done to us. And as we recall all the self-censorship and repression for so many years, a reservoir of tears pours out of our eyes. And we are euphoric, high, with the initial flourish of a movement.

We want to make ourselves clear: our first job is to free ourselves; that means clearing our heads of the garbage that's been poured into them. This article is an attempt at raising a number of issues, and presenting some ideas to replace the old ones. It is primarily for ourselves, a starting point of discussion. If straight people of good will find it useful in understanding what liberation is about, so much the better.

It should also be clear that these are the views of one person, and are determined not only by my homosexuality, but my being white, male, middle class. It is my individual consciousness. Our group consciousness will evolve as we get ourselves together—we are only at the beginning.

I. ON ORIENTATION

1. What homosexuality is: Nature leaves undefined the object of sexual desire. The gender of that object is imposed socially. Humans originally made homosexuality taboo because they needed every bit of energy to produce and raise children: survival of species was a priority. With overpopulation and technological change, that taboo continued only to exploit us and enslave us.

As kids we refused to capitulate to demands that we ignore our feelings toward each other. Somewhere we found the strength to resist being indoctrinated, and we should count that among our assets. We have to realize that our loving each other is a good thing, not an unfortunate thing, and that we have a lot to teach straights about sex, love, strength, and resistance.

Homosexuality is *not* a lot of things. It is not a makeshift in the absence of the opposite sex; it is not hatred or rejection of the opposite sex; it is not genetic; it is not the result of broken homes except inasmuch as we could see the sham of American marriage. *Homosexuality is the capacity to love someone of the same sex.*

2. Bisexuality: Bisexuality is good; it is the capacity to love people of either sex. The reason so few of us are bisexual is because society made such a big stink about homosexuality that we got forced into seeing ourselves as either straight or non-straight. Also, many gays got turned off to the ways men are supposed to act with women and vice-versa, which is pretty fucked-up. Gays will begin to turn on to women when 1) it's something that we do because we want to, and not because we should, and 2) when women's liberation changes the nature of heterosexual relationships.

We continue to call ourselves homosexual, not bisexual, even if we do make it with the opposite sex also, because saying "Oh, I'm Bi" is a cop out for a gay. We get told it's OK to sleep with guys as long as we sleep with women, too, and that's still putting homosexuality down. We'll be gay until everyone has forgotten that it's an issue. Then we'll begin to be complete.

3. Heterosexuality: Exclusive heterosexuality is fucked up. It reflects a fear of people of the same sex, it's anti-homosexual, and it is fraught with frustration. Heterosexual sex is fucked up, too; ask women's liberation about what straight guys are like in bed. Sex is aggression for the male chauvinist; sex is obligation for traditional woman. And among the young, the modern, the hip, it's only a subtle version of the same. For us to become heterosexual in the sense that our straight brothers and sisters are is not a cure, it is a disease.

II. ON WOMEN

1. Lesbianism: It's been a male-dominated society for too long, and that has warped both men and women. So gay women are going to see things differently from gay men; they are going to feel put down as women, too. Their liberation is tied up with both gay liberation and women's liberation.

This paper speaks from the gay male viewpoint. And although some of the ideas in it may be equally relevant to gay women, it would be arrogant to presume this to be a manifesto for lesbians. . . .

III

* * *

4. Gay "stereotypes": The straights' image of the gay world is defined largely by those of us who have violated straight roles. There is a tendency among "homophile" groups to deplore gays who play visible roles—the queens and the nellies. As liberated gays, we must take a clear stand. *1.* Gays who stand out have become our first martyrs. They came out and withstood disapproval before the rest of us did. *2.* If they have suffered from being open, it is straight society whom we must indict, not the queen.

5. Closet queens: This phrase is becoming analogous to "Uncle Tom." To pretend to be straight sexually, or to pretend to be straight socially, is probably the most harmful pattern of behavior in the ghetto. The married guy who makes it on the side secretly; the guy who will go to bed once but who won't develop any gay relationships; the pretender at work or school who changes the gender of the friend he's talking about; the guy who'll suck cock in the bushes but who won't go to bed.

If we are liberated we are open with our sexuality. Closet queenery must end. *Come out.*

But: in saying come out, we have to have our heads clear about a few things: 1) closet queens are our brothers, and must be defended against attacks by straight people; 2) the fear of coming out is not paranoia; the stakes are high: loss of family ties, loss of job, loss of straight friends—these are all reminders that the oppression is not just in our heads. It's real. Each of us must make the steps toward openness at our own speed and on our own impulses. Being open is the foundation of freedom: it has to be built solidly. 3) "Closet queen" is a broad term covering a multitude of forms of defense, self-hatred, lack of strength, and habit. We are all closet queens in some ways, and all of us had to come out—very few of us were "flagrant" at the age of seven! We must afford our brothers and sisters the same patience we afforded ourselves. And while their closet queenery is part of our oppression, it's more a part of theirs. They alone can decide when and how.

IV. ON OPPRESSION

It is important to catalog and understand the different facets of our oppression. There is no future in arguing about degrees of oppression. A lot of "movement" types come on with a line of shit about homosexuals not being oppressed as much as blacks or Vietnamese or workers or women. We don't happen to fit into their ideas of class or caste. Bull! When people feel oppressed, they act on that feeling. We feel oppressed. Talk about the priority of black liberation or ending imperialism over and above gay liberation is just anti-gay propaganda.

1. Physical attacks: We are attacked, beaten, castrated and left dead time and time again. There are half a dozen known unsolved slayings in San Francisco parks in the last few years. "Punks", often of minority groups who look around for someone under them socially, feel encouraged to beat up on "queens" and cops look the other way. That used to be called lynching.

Cops in most cities have harassed our meeting places: bars and baths and parks. They set up entrapment squads. A Berkeley brother was slain by a cop in April when he tried to split after finding out that the trick who was making advances to him was a cop. Cities set up "pervert" registration, which if nothing else scares our brothers deeper into the closet.

One of the most vicious slurs on us is the blame for prison "gang rapes". These rapes are invariably done by people who consider themselves straight. The victims of these rapes are us and straights who can't defend themselves. The press campaign to link prison rapes with homosexuality is an attempt to make straights fear and despise us, so they can oppress us more. It's typical of the fucked-up straight mind to think that homosexual sex involves tying a guy down and fucking him. That's aggression, not sex. If that's what sex is for a lot of straight people, that's a problem they have to solve, not us.

2. Psychological warfare: Right from the beginning we have been subjected to a barrage of straight propaganda. Since our parents don't know any homosexuals, we grow up thinking that we're alone and different and perverted. Our school friends identify "queer" with any nonconformist or bad behavior. Our elementary school teachers tell us not to talk to strangers or accept rides. Television, billboards and magazines put forth a false idealization of male/female relationships, and make us wish we were different, wish we were "in". In family living class we're taught how we're supposed to turn out. And all along, the best we hear if anything about homosexuality is that it's an unfortunate problem.

3. Self-oppression: As gay liberation grows, we will find our uptight brothers and sisters, particularly those who are making a buck off our ghetto, coming on strong to defend the status quo. This is self-oppression: "don't rock the boat"; "things in SF are OK"; "gay people just aren't together"; "I'm not oppressed". These lines are right out of the mouths of the straight establishment. A large part of our oppression would end if we would stop putting ourselves and our pride down.

4. Institutional: Discrimination against gays is blatant, if we open our eyes. Homosexual relationships are illegal, and even if these laws are not regularly enforced, they encourage and enforce closet queenery. The bulk of the social work/psychiatric field looks upon homosexuality as a problem, and treats us as sick. Employers let it be known that our skills are acceptable only as long as our sexuality is hidden. Big business and government are particularly notorious offenders.

The discrimination in the draft and armed services is a pillar of the general attitude toward gays. If we are willing to label ourselves publicly not only as homosexual but as sick, then we qualify for deferment; and if we're not "discreet" (dishonest) we get drummed out of the service. Hell, no, we won't go, of course not, but we can't let the army fuck over us this way, either....

VI. ON OUR GHETTO

We are refugees from Amerika. So we came to the ghetto—and as other ghettos, it has its negative and positive aspects. Refugee camps are better than what preceded them, or people never would have come. But they are still enslaving, if only that we are limited to being ourselves there and only there.

Ghettos breed self-hatred. We stagnate here, accepting the status quo. The status quo is rotten. We are all warped by our oppression, and in the isolation of the ghetto we blame ourselves rather than our oppressors.

Ghettos breed exploitation: Landlords find they can charge exorbitant rents and get away with it, because of the limited area which is safe to live in openly. Mafia control of bars and baths in NYC is only one example of outside money controlling our institutions for their profit. In San Francisco the Tavern Guild favors maintaining the ghetto, for it is through ghetto culture that they make a buck. We crowd their bars not because of their merit but because of the absence of any other social institution. The Guild has refused to let us collect defense funds or pass out gay liberation literature in their bars—need we ask why?

Police or con men who shake down the straight gay in return for not revealing him; the bookstores and movie makers who keep raising prices because they are the only outlet for pornography; heads of "modeling" agencies and other pimps who exploit both the hustlers and the johns—these are the parasites who flourish in the ghetto.

SAN FRANCISCO—Ghetto or Free Territory: Our ghetto certainly is more beautiful and larger and more diverse than most ghettos, and is certainly freer than the rest of Amerika. That's why we're here. But it isn't ours. Capitalists make money off us, cops patrol us, government tolerates us as long as we shut up, and daily we work for and pay taxes to those who oppress us.

To be a free territory, we must govern ourselves, set up our own institutions, defend ourselves, and use our own energies to improve our lives. The emergence of gay liberation communes, and our own paper is a good start. The talk about a gay liberation coffee shop/dance hall should be acted upon. Rural retreats, political action offices, food cooperatives, a free school, unalienating bars and after hours places—they must be developed if we are to have even the shadow of a free territory.

* * *

CONCLUSION: AN OUTLINE OF IMPERATIVES FOR GAY LIBERATION

1. Free ourselves: come out everywhere; initiate self defense and political activity; initiate counter community institutions.

2. Turn other gay people on: talk all the time; understand, forgive, accept.

3. Free the homosexual in everyone: we'll be getting a good bit of shit from threatened latents: be gentle, and keep talking & acting free.

4. We've been playing an act for a long time, so we're consummate actors. Now we can begin *to be*, and it'll be a good show!

Document 7.7   Cesar E. Chavez, "Letter from Delano" (1969), reprinted in *Christian Century* 86 (April 23, 1969), p. 539.

Good Friday 1969.

E. L. Barr, Jr., President
California Grape and Tree Fruit League
717 Market St.
San Francisco, California

Dear Mr. Barr:

I am sad to hear about your accusations in the press that our union movement and table grape boycott have been successful because we have used violence and terror tactics. If what you say is true, I have been a failure and should withdraw from the struggle; but you are left with the awesome moral responsibility, before God and man, to come forward with whatever information you have so that corrective action can begin at once. If for any reason you fail to come forth to substantiate your charges, then you must be held responsible for committing violence against us, albeit violence of the tongue. I am convinced that you as a human being did not mean what you said but rather acted hastily under pressure from the public relations firm that has been hired to try to counteract the tremendous moral force of our movement. How many times we ourselves have felt the need to lash out in anger and bitterness.

Today on Good Friday 1969 we remember the life and the sacrifice of Martin Luther King, Jr., who gave himself totally to the nonviolent struggle for peace and justice. In his "Letter from Birmingham Jail" Dr. King describes better than I could our hopes for the strike and boycott: "Injustice must be exposed, with all the tension its exposure creates, to the light of human conscience and the air of national opinion before it can be cured." For our part I admit that we have seized upon every tactic and strategy consistent with the morality of our cause to expose that injustice and thus to heighten the sensitivity of the American conscience so that farm workers will have without bloodshed their own union and the dignity of bargaining with their agribusiness employers. By lying about the nature of our movement, Mr. Barr, you are working against nonviolent social change. Unwittingly perhaps, you may unleash that other force which our union by discipline and deed, censure and education has sought to avoid, that panacean shortcut: that senseless violence which honors no color, class or neighborhood.

You must understand—I must make you understand—that our membership and the hopes and aspirations of the hundreds of thousands of the poor and dispossessed that have been raised on our account are, above all, human beings, no better and no worse than any other cross-section of human society; we are not saints because we are poor, but by the same measure neither are we immoral. We are men and women who have suffered and endured much, and not only because of our abject poverty but because we have been kept poor. The colors of our skins, the languages of our cultural and native origins, the lack of formal education, the exclusion from the democratic process, the numbers of our slain in recent wars—all these burdens generation after generation have sought to demoralize us, to break our human spirit. But God knows that we are not beasts of burden, agricultural implements or rented slaves; we are men. And mark this well, Mr. Barr, we are men locked in a death struggle against man's inhumanity to man in the industry that you represent. And this struggle itself gives meaning to our life and ennobles our dying.

As your industry has experienced, our strikers here in Delano and those who represent us throughout the world are well trained for this struggle. They have been under the gun, they have been kicked and beaten and herded by dogs, they have been cursed and ridiculed, they have been stripped and chained and jailed, they have been sprayed with the poisons used in the vineyards; but they have been taught not to lie down and die nor to flee in shame, but to resist with every ounce of human endurance and spirit. To resist not with retaliation in kind but to overcome with love and compassion, with ingenuity and creativity, with hard work and longer hours, with stamina and patient tenacity, with truth and public appeal, with friends and allies, with mobility and discipline, with politics and law, and with prayer and fasting. They were not trained in a month or even a year; after all, this new harvest season will mark our fourth full year of strike and even now we continue to plan and prepare for the years to come. Time accomplishes for the poor what money does for the rich.

This is not to pretend that we have everywhere been successful enough or that we have not made mistakes. And while we do not belittle or underestimate our adversaries—for they are the rich and the powerful and they possess the land—we are not afraid nor do we cringe from the confrontation. We welcome it! We have planned for it. We know that our cause is just, that history is a story of social revolution, and that the poor shall inherit the land.

Once again, I appeal to you as the representative of your industry and as a man. I ask you to recognize and bargain with our union before the economic pressure of the boycott and strike takes an irrevocable toll; but if not, I ask you to at least sit down with us to discuss the safeguards necessary to keep our historical struggle free of violence. I make this appeal because as one of the leaders of our nonviolent movement, I know and accept my responsibility for preventing, if possible, the destruction of human life and property. For these reasons and knowing of Gandhi's admonition that fasting is the last resort in place of the sword, during a most critical time in our movement last February 1968 I undertook a 25-day fast. I repeat to you the principle enunciated to the membership at the start of the fast: if to build our union required the deliberate taking of life, either the life of a grower or his child, or the life of a farm worker or his child, then I choose not to see the union built.

Mr. Barr, let me be painfully honest with you. You must understand these things. We advocate militant nonviolence as our means for social revolution and to achieve justice for our people, but we are not blind or deaf to the desperate and moody winds of human frustration, impatience and rage that blow among us. Gandhi himself admitted that if his only choice were cowardice or violence, he would choose violence. Men are not angels, and time and tide wait for no man. Precisely because of these powerful human emotions, we have tried to involve masses of people in their own struggle. Participation and self-determination remain the best experience of freedom, and free men instinctively prefer democratic change and even protect the rights guaranteed to seek it. Only the enslaved in despair have need of violent overthrow.

This letter does not express all that is in my heart, Mr. Barr. But if it says nothing else it says that we do not hate you or rejoice to see your industry destroyed; we hate the agribusiness system that seeks to keep us enslaved, and we shall overcome and change it not by retaliation or bloodshed but by a determined nonviolent struggle carried on by those masses of farm workers who intend to be free and human.

Sincerely yours,
Cesar E. Chavez

United Farm Workers Organizing
  Committee, A.F.L.-C.I.O.
Delano, California.

Perhaps the most famous antifeminist was a woman, Phyllis Stewart Schlafly. Ironically, Schlafly shared much in common with Betty Friedan. Both grew up during the depression, were valedictorians of their high schools, and attended private colleges. Schlafly went to Maryville College in Maryville, Illinois, and then transferred to and graduated with a degree in political science from Washington University of St. Louis; Friedan went to Smith College in Massachusetts. Both had some graduate education and worked—Friedan as a journalist and Schlafly as a congressional researcher. Both married, moved to the suburbs, had children, and remained active— Schlafly as a community volunteer and Republican Party activist. Yet by the second half of the 1960s, Schlafly and Friedan came to represent opposite ends of the political spectrum. While Friedan cofounded NOW, Schlafly spoke out vociferously against the women's movement. In "What's Wrong with 'Equal Rights' for Women?" (Document 7.7), Schlafly denounced the Equal Rights Amendment, one of NOW's primary objectives, arguing that it and the women's movement sought to undermine the family, a charge Friedan, but not all feminists, denied. Schlafly maintained close ties with numerous conservatives and often joined them in attacking other left and liberal causes, ranging from gay rights to the Great Society. Like many other conservatives, Schlafly found numerous adherents among working-class, religious, less educated, and more provincial Americans, who saw the left and liberals as elitist.

Document 7.8 Phyllis Schlafly, "What's Wrong with 'Equal Rights' for Women?" *Phyllis Schlafly Report* 5, no. 7 (February 1972).

Of all the classes of people who ever lived, the American woman is the most privileged. We have the most rights and rewards, and the fewest duties. Our unique status is the result of a fortunate combination of circumstances.

1. We have the immense good fortune to live in a civilization which respects the family as the basic unit of society. This respect is part and parcel of our laws and our customs. It is based on the fact of life—which no legislation or agitation can erase—that women have babies and men don't.

If you don't like this fundamental difference, you will have to take up your complaint with God because He created us this way. The fact that women, not men, have babies is not the fault of selfish and domineering men, or of the establishment, or of any clique of conspirators who want to oppress women. It's simply the way God made us.

Our Judeo-Christian civilization has developed the law and custom that, since women must bear the physical consequences of the sex act, men must be required to bear the *other* consequences and pay in other ways. These laws and customs decree that a man must carry his share by physical protection and financial support of his children and of the woman who bears his children, and also by a code of behavior which benefits and protects both the woman and the children.

THE GREATEST ACHIEVEMENT OF WOMEN'S RIGHTS

This is accomplished by the institution of the family. Our respect for the family as the basic unit of society, which is ingrained in the laws and customs of our Judeo-Christian civilization, is the greatest single achievement in the entire history of women's rights. It assures a woman the most precious and important right of all—the right to keep her own baby and to be supported and protected in the enjoyment of watching her baby grow and develop.

The institution of the family is advantageous for women for many reasons. After all, what do we want out of life? To love and be loved? Mankind has not discovered a better nest for a lifetime of reciprocal love. A sense of achievement? A man may search 30 to 40 years for accomplishment in his profession. A woman can enjoy real achievement when she is young—by having a baby. She can have the satisfaction of doing a job well—and being recognized for it.

Do we want financial security? We are fortunate to have the great legacy of Moses, the Ten Commandments, especially this one: "Honor thy father and thy mother that thy days may be long upon the land." Children are a woman's best social security—her best guarantee of social benefits such as old age pension, unemployment compensation, workman's compensation, and sick leave. The family gives a woman the physical, financial and emotional security of the home—for all her life.

THE FINANCIAL BENEFITS OF CHIVALRY

2. The second reason why American women are a privileged group is that we are the beneficiaries of a tradition of special respect for women which dates from the Christian Age of Chivalry. The honor and respect paid to Mary, the Mother of Christ, resulted in all women, in effect, being put on a pedestal.

This respect for women is not just the lip service that politicians pay to "God, Motherhood, and the Flag." It is not—as some youthful agitators seem to think—just a matter of opening doors for women, seeing that they are seated first, carrying their bundles, and helping them in and out of automobiles. Such good manners are merely the superficial evidences of a total attitude toward women which expresses itself in many more tangible ways, such as money.

In other civilizations, such as the African and the American Indian, the men strut around wearing feathers and beads and hunting and fishing (great sport for men!), while the women do all the hard, tiresome drudgery including the tilling of the soil (if any is done), the hewing of wood, the making of fires, the carrying of water, as well as the cooking, sewing and caring for babies.

This is not the American way because we were lucky enough to inherit the traditions of the Age of Chivalry. In America, a man's first significant purchase is a diamond for his bride, and the largest financial investment of his life is a home for her to live in. American husbands work hours of overtime to buy a fur piece or other finery to keep their wives in fashion, and to pay premiums on their life insurance policies to provide for her comfort when she is a widow (benefits in which he can never share).

In the states which follow the English common law, a wife has a dower right in her husband's real estate which he cannot take away from her during life or by his will. A man cannot dispose of his real estate without his wife's signature. Any sale is subject to her ⅓ interest.

Women fare even better in the states which follow the Spanish and French community-property laws, such as California, Arizona, Texas and Louisiana. The basic philosophy of the Spanish/French law is that a wife's work in the home is just as valuable as a husband's work at his job. Therefore, in community-property states, a wife owns one-half of all the property and income her husband earns during their marriage, and he cannot take it away from her.

In Illinois, as a result of agitation by "equal rights" fanatics, the real-estate dower laws were repealed as of January 1, 1972. This means that in Illinois a husband can now sell the family home, spend the money on his girl friend or gamble it away, and his faithful wife of 30 years can no longer stop him. "Equal rights" fanatics have also deprived women in Illinois and in some other states of most of their basic common-law rights to recover damages for breach of promise to marry, seduction, criminal conversation, and alienation of affections.

THE REAL LIBERATION OF WOMEN

3. The third reason why American women are so well off is that the great American free enterprise system has produced remarkable inventors who have lifted the backbreaking "women's work" from our shoulders.

In other countries and in other eras, it was truly said that "Man may work from sun to sun, but woman's work is never done." Other women have labored every waking hour—preparing food on wood-burning stoves, making flour, baking bread in stone ovens, spinning yarn, making clothes, making soap, doing the laundry by hand, heating irons, making candles for light and fires for warmth, and trying to nurse their babies through illnesses without medical care.

The real liberation of women from the backbreaking drudgery of centuries is the American free enterprise system which stimulated inventive geniuses to pursue their talents—and we all reap the profits. The great heroes of women's liberation are not the straggly-haired women on television talk shows and picket lines, but Thomas Edison who brought the miracle of electricity to our homes to give light and to run all those labor-saving devices—the equivalent, perhaps, of a half-dozen household servants for every middle-class American woman. Or Elias Howe who gave us the sewing machine which resulted in such an abundance of readymade clothing. Or Clarence Birdseye who invented the process for freezing foods. Or Henry Ford, who mass-produced the automobile so that it is within the price-range of every American, man or woman.

A major occupation of women in other countries is doing their daily shopping for food, which requires carrying their own containers and standing in line at dozens of small shops. They buy only small portions because they can't carry very much and have no refrigerator or freezer to keep a surplus anyway. Our American free enterprise system has given us the gigantic food and packaging industry and beautiful supermarkets, which provide an endless variety of foods, prepackaged for easy carrying and a minimum of waiting. In America, women have the freedom from the slavery of standing in line for daily food.

Thus, household duties have been reduced to only a few hours a day, leaving the American woman with plenty of time to moonlight. She can take a full or part-time paying job, or she can indulge to her heart's content in a tremendous selection of interesting educational or cultural or homemaking activities.

THE FRAUD OF THE EQUAL RIGHTS AMENDMENT

In the last couple of years, a noisy movement has sprung up agitating for "women's rights." Suddenly, everywhere we are afflicted with aggressive females on television talk shows yapping about how mistreated American women are, suggesting that marriage has put us in some kind of "slavery," that housework is menial and degrading, and—perish the thought—that women are discriminated against. New "women's liberation" organizations are popping up, agitating and demonstrating, serving demands on public officials, getting wide press coverage always, and purporting to speak for some 100,000,000 American women.

It's time to set the record straight. The claim that American women are down-trodden and unfairly treated is the fraud of the century. The truth is that American women never had it so good. Why should we lower ourselves to "equal rights" when we already have the status of special privilege?

The proposed Equal Rights Amendment states: "Equality of rights under the law shall not be denied or abridged by the United States or by any state on account of sex." So what's wrong with that? Well, here are a few examples of what's wrong with it.

This Amendment will absolutely and positively make women subject to the draft. Why any woman would support such a ridiculous and un-American proposal as this is beyond comprehension. Why any Congressman who had any regard for his wife, sister or daughter would support such a proposition is just as hard to understand. Foxholes are bad enough for men, but they certainly are *not* the place for women—and we should reject any proposal which would put them there in the name of "equal rights."

It is amusing to watch the semantic chicanery of the advocates of the Equal Rights Amendment when confronted with this issue of the draft. They evade, they sidestep, they try to muddy up the issue, but they cannot deny that the Equal Rights Amendment will positively make women subject to the draft. Congresswoman Margaret Heckler's answer to this question was, Don't worry, it will take two years for the Equal Rights Amendment to go into effect, and we can rely on President Nixon to end the Vietnam War before then!

Literature distributed by Equal Rights Amendment supporters confirms that "under the Amendment a draft law which applied to men would apply also to women." The Equal Rights literature argues that this would be good for women so they can achieve their "equal rights" in securing veterans' benefits.

Another bad effect of the Equal Rights Amendment is that it will abolish a woman's right to child support and alimony, and substitute what the women's libbers think is a more "equal" policy, that "such decisions should be within the discretion of the Court and should be made on the economic situation and need of the parties in the case."

Under present American laws, the man is *always* required to support his wife and each child he caused to be brought into the world. Why should women abandon these good laws—by trading them for something so nebulous and un-certain as the "discretion of the Court"?

The law now requires a husband to support his wife as best as his financial situation permits, but a wife is not required to support her husband (unless he is about to become a public charge). A husband cannot demand that his wife go to work to help pay for family expenses. He has the duty of financial support under our laws and customs. Why should we abandon these mandatory wife-support and child-support laws so that a wife would have an "equal" obligation to take a job?

By law and custom in America, in case of divorce, the mother always is given custody of her children unless there is overwhelming evidence of mistreatment, neglect or bad character. This is our special privilege because of the high rank that is placed on motherhood in our society. Do women really want to give up this special privilege and lower themselves to "equal rights", so that the mother gets one child and the father gets the other? I think not. . . .

WHAT "WOMEN'S LIB" REALLY MEANS

Many women are under the mistaken impression that "women's lib" means more job employment opportunities for women, equal pay for equal work, appointments of women to high positions, admitting more women to medical schools, and other desirable objectives which all women favor. We all support these purposes, as well as any necessary legislation which would bring them about.

But all this is only a sweet syrup which covers the deadly poison masquerading as "women's lib." The women's libbers are radicals who are waging a total assault on the family, on marriage, and on children. Don't take my word for it—read their own literature and prove to yourself what these characters are trying to do.

The most pretentious of the women's liberation magazines is called *Ms.*, and subtitled "The New Magazine For Women," with Gloria Steinem listed as president and secretary.

Reading the Spring 1972 issue of *Ms.* gives a good understanding of women's lib, and the people who promote it. It is anti-family, anti-children, and pro-abortion. It is a series of sharp-tongued, high-pitched whining complaints by unmarried women. They view the home as a prison, and the wife and mother as a slave. To these women's libbers, marriage means dirty dishes and dirty laundry. One article lauds a woman's refusal to carry up the family laundry as "an act of extreme courage." Another tells how satisfying it is to be a lesbian. (page 117)

The women's libbers don't understand that most women want to be wife, mother and homemaker—and are happy in that role. The women's libbers actively resent the mother who stays at home with her children and likes it that way. The principal purpose of *Ms.*'s shrill tirade is to sow seeds of discontent among happy, married women so that *all* women can be unhappy in some new sisterhood of frustrated togetherness.

Obviously intrigued by the 170 clauses of exemptions from marital duties given to Jackie Kennedy, and the special burdens imposed on Aristotle Onassis, in the pre-marriage contract they signed, *Ms.* recommends two women's lib marriage contracts. The "utopian marriage contract" has a clause on "sexual rights and freedoms" which approves "arrangements such as having Tuesdays off from one another," and the husband giving "his consent to abortion in advance."

The "Shulmans' marriage agreement" includes such petty provisions as "wife strips beds, husband remakes them," and "Husband does dishes on Tuesday, Thursday and Sunday. Wife does Monday, Wednesday and Saturday, Friday is split..." If the baby cries in the night, the chore of "handling" the baby is assigned as follows: "Husband does Tuesday, Thursday and Sunday. Wife does Monday, Wednesday and Saturday, Friday is split..." Presumably, if the baby cries for his mother on Tuesday night, he would be informed that the marriage contract prohibits her from answering.

Of course, it is possible, in such a loveless home, that the baby would never call for his mother at all.

Who put up the money to launch this 130-page slick-paper assault on the family and motherhood? A count of the advertisements in *Ms.* shows that the principal financial backer is the liquor industry. There are 26 liquor ads in this one initial issue. Of these, 13 are expensive full-page color ads, as opposed to only 18 full-page ads from all other sources combined, most of which are in the cheaper black-and-white.

Another women's lib magazine, called *Women*, tells the American woman that she is a prisoner in the "solitary confinement" and "isolation" of marriage. The magazine promises that it will provide women with "escape from isolation ... release from boredom," and that it will "break the barriers ... that separate wife, mistress and secretary ... heterosexual women and homosexual women."

These women's libbers do, indeed, intend to "break the barriers" of the Ten Commandments and the sanctity of the family. It hasn't occurred to them that a woman's best "escape from isolation and boredom" is—not a magazine subscription to boost her "stifled ego"—but a husband and children who love her.

The first issue of *Women* contains 68 pages of such proposals as "The BITCH Manifesto," which promotes the line that "Bitch is Beautiful and that we have nothing to lose. Nothing whatsoever." Another article promotes an organization called W.I.T.C.H. (Women's International Terrorist Conspiracy from Hell), "an action arm of Women's Liberation."

In intellectual circles, a New York University professor named Warren T. Farrell has provided the rationale for why men should support women's lib. When his speech to the American Political Science Association Convention is stripped of its egghead verbiage, his argument is that men should eagerly look forward to the day when they can enjoy free sex and not have to pay for it. The husband will no longer be "saddled with the tremendous guilt feelings" when he leaves his wife with nothing after she has given him her best years. If a husband loses his job, he will no longer feel compelled to take any job to support his family. A husband can go "out with the boys" to have a drink without feeling guilty. Alimony will be eliminated.

WOMEN'S LIBBERS DO *NOT* SPEAK FOR US

The "women's lib" movement is *not* an honest effort to secure better jobs for women who want or need to work outside the home. This is just the superficial sweet-talk to win broad support for a radical "movement." Women's lib is a total assault on the role of the American woman as wife and mother, and on the family as the basic unit of society.

Women's libbers are trying to make wives and mothers unhappy with their career, make them feel that they are "second-class citizens" and "abject slaves." Women's libbers are promoting free sex instead of the "slavery" of marriage. They are promoting Federal "day-care centers" for babies instead of homes. They are promoting abortions instead of families.

Why should we trade in our special privileges and honored status for the alleged advantage of working in an office or assembly line? Most women would rather cuddle a baby than a typewriter or factory machine. Most women find that it is easier to get along with a husband than a foreman or office manager. Offices and factories require many more menial and repetitious chores than washing dishes and ironing shirts.

Women's libbers do *not* speak for the majority of American women. American women do *not* want to be liberated from husbands and children. We do *not* want to trade our birthright of the special privileges of American women— for the mess of pottage called the Equal Rights Amendment.

Modern technology and opportunity have not discovered any nobler or more satisfying or more creative career for a woman than marriage and motherhood. The wonderful advantage that American women have is that we can have all the rewards of that number-one career, and still moonlight with a second one to suit our intellectual, cultural or financial tastes or needs.

And why should the men acquiesce in a system which gives preferential rights and lighter duties to women? In return, the men get the pearl of great price: a happy home, a faithful wife, and children they adore.

If the women's libbers want to reject marriage and motherhood, it's a free country and that is their choice. But let's not permit these women's libbers to get away with pretending to speak for the rest of us. Let's not permit this tiny minority to degrade the role that most women prefer. Let's not let these women's libbers deprive wives and mothers of the rights we now possess.

Tell your Senators NOW that you want them to vote NO on the Equal Rights Amendment. Tell your television and radio stations that you want equal time to present the case FOR marriage and motherhood.

Chapter Eight

CAN THE CENTER HOLD?

If one were to write a fictional screenplay for the 1960s, one could hardly bring it to a more thrilling climax than the real thing. Early in 1968 the North Vietnamese launched the Tet offensive, which, even though it was rebuffed by U.S. and South Vietnamese forces, shocked Americans who had been led to believe that victory was close at hand. At the end of March, Lyndon Johnson stunned the nation by announcing that he would neither seek nor accept the Democratic Party's presidential nomination. Not long afterwards, Martin Luther King, Jr., was assassinated in Memphis, Tennessee, triggering the worst spate of rioting in modern American history. During the spring of 1968, college campuses all across America erupted in protest. Strife in the United States took place alongside worldwide turmoil, including a rebellion in Czechoslovakia, crushed by Russian tanks, and a joint worker-student uprising in France.

For a brief while, Robert F. Kennedy rekindled the spirit of Camelot with his bid for the presidency, but then the remaining idealism of the decade was snuffed out by another assassin's bullet. Later that summer, the Democratic convention in Chicago turned into a melee as Mayor Richard Daley's police pulverized protesters in the streets while Democratic politicians and delegates jeered at each other inside the convention hall. Deeming their protest a victory, some New Leftists dedicated themselves to toppling the "American empire" via guerrilla tactics. Pledging to restore law and order and bring the nation together, Richard Nixon won the presidency in one of the closest elections ever. Yet when it became clear to members of the antiwar movement that Nixon, who had promised "peace with honor," did not intend to end the war, they staged a series of massive protests. Concomitantly, women, gays, and Chicano and Native Americans demanded equality in some of the most contentious protests of the era, and the environmental movement sprang into action.

The documents in this chapter provide a feel for the tail end of the sixties. **Document 8.1** *consists of one of Robert F. Kennedy's most memorable speeches, delivered in Indianapolis, Indiana, in the immediate aftermath of Martin Luther King, Jr.,'s assassination. From the start of his campaign, Kennedy captured the support of many who hoped to revive the idealism of the early 1960s. Shortly before he arrived in Indianapolis, Kennedy learned that King had been shot. Fearing the outbreak of violence, several of his top aides and Indianapolis mayor Richard Lugar advised Kennedy to call off the appearance. News of King's death had not yet reached Indianapolis's ghetto. Kennedy determined to go ahead with the event anyway, in spite of the risk to his own life. Reminding the audience that, having lost a brother, he could feel its despair, Kennedy called for America to unite to build a better society. While over one hundred cities experienced rioting in the wake of King's assassination, Indianapolis, perhaps because of Kennedy's bravery, did not. A little over two months later, on the night of his victory in California's presidential primary, Robert F. Kennedy was assassinated by Sirhan Sirhan.*

Document 8.1   Robert F. Kennedy, "Speech—On the Death of Martin Luther King, Jr.," Indianapolis, Indiana, April 4, 1968, Robert F. Kennedy, Senate Papers, Speeches, and Press Releases, Box 4, John F. Kennedy Library, Boston, Massachusetts.

I have bad news for you, for all of our fellow citizens, and people who love peace all over the world, and that is that Martin Luther King was shot and killed tonight. Martin Luther King dedicated his life to love and to justice for his fellow human beings, and he died because of that effort.

In this difficult day, in this difficult time for the United States, it is perhaps well to ask what kind of a nation we are and what direction we want to move in. For those of you who are black—considering the evidence there evidently is that there were white people who were responsible—you can be filled with bitterness, with hatred, and a desire for revenge. We can move in that direction as a country, in great polarization—black people amongst black, white people amongst white, filled with hatred toward one another.

Or we can make an effort, as Martin Luther King did, to understand and to comprehend, and to replace that violence, that stain of bloodshed that has spread across our land, with an effort to understand with compassion and love.

For those of you who are black and are tempted to be filled with hatred and distrust at the injustice of such an act, against all white people, I can only say that I feel in my own heart the same kind of feeling. I had a member of my family killed, but he was killed by a white man. But we have to make an effort in the United States, we have to make an effort to understand, to go beyond these rather difficult times.

My favorite poet was Aeschylus. He wrote: "In our sleep, pain which cannot forget falls drop by drop upon the heart until, in our own despair, against our will, comes wisdom through the awful grace of God."

What we need in the United States is not division; what we need in the United States is not hatred; what we need in the United States is not violence or lawlessness; but love and wisdom, and compassion toward one another, and a feeling of justice toward those who still suffer within our country, whether they be white or they be black.

So I shall ask you tonight to return home, to say a prayer for the family of Martin Luther King, that's true, but more importantly to say a prayer for our own country, which all of us love—a prayer for understanding and that compassion of which I spoke.

We can do well in this country. We will have difficult times; we've had difficult times in the past; we will have difficult times in the future. It is not the end of violence; it is not the end of lawlessness; it is not the end of disorder.

But the vast majority of white people and the vast majority of black people in this country want to live together, want to improve the quality of our life, and want justice for all human beings who abide in our land.

Let us dedicate ourselves to what the Greeks wrote so many years ago: to tame the savageness of man and make gentle the life of this world.

Let us dedicate ourselves to that, and say a prayer for our country and for our people.

Not long after King was assassinated, students at Columbia University organized a series of protests that led to the takeover of numerous college buildings. Their protest was part of a broader campaign organized by SDS to "bring the war home." A bit over a month after this confrontation, ex-SDS president Tom Hayden wrote "Two, Three, Many Columbias," Document 8.2. Published in Ramparts, the article heralded the Columbia protest as a model to follow and as an omen of things to come. Ironically, shortly after he wrote this article, Hayden visited Robert F. Kennedy's casket at St. Patrick's Cathedral in New York City, where he privately wept, suggesting that he may have held hopes of rekindling the idealism of the early 1960s. After Kennedy's funeral, however, more disillusioned with the system than ever, Hayden focused on organizing a confrontation at the Democratic convention in Chicago.

Document 8.2   Tom Hayden, "Two, Three, Many Columbias," *Ramparts* (June 15, 1968), p. 40.

The goal written on the university walls was "Create two, three, many Columbias"; it meant expand the strike so that the U.S. must either change or send its troops to occupy American campuses.

At this point the goal seems realistic; an explosive mix is present on dozens of campuses where demands for attention to student views are being disregarded by university administrators.

The American student movement has continued to swell for nearly a decade: during the semi-peace of the early '60s as well as during Vietnam; during the token liberalism of John Kennedy as well as during the bankrupt racism of Lyndon Johnson. Students have responded most directly to the black movement of the '60s: from Mississippi Summer to the Free Speech Movement; from "Black Power" to "Student Power"; from the seizure of Howard University to the seizure of Hamilton Hall. As the racial crisis deepens so will the campus crisis. But the student protest is not just an offshoot of the black protest—it is based on authentic opposition to the middle-class world of manipulation, channeling and careerism. The students are in opposition to the fundamental institutions of society.

The students' protest constantly escalates by building on its achievements and legends. The issues being considered by seventeen-year-old freshmen at Columbia University would not have been within the imagination of most "veteran" student activists five years ago.

Columbia opened a new tactical stage in the resistance movement which began last fall: from the overnight occupation of buildings to permanent occupation; from mill-ins to the creation of revolutionary committees; from symbolic civil disobedience to barricaded resistance. Not only are these tactics already being duplicated on other campuses, but they are sure to be surpassed by even more militant tactics. In the future it is conceivable that students will threaten destruction of buildings as a last deterrent to police attacks. Many of the tactics learned can also be applied in smaller hit-and-run operations between strikes: raids on the offices of professors doing weapons research could win substantial support among students while making the university more blatantly repressive.

In the buildings occupied at Columbia, the students created what they called a "new society" or "liberated area" or "commune," a society in which decent values would be lived out even though university officials might cut short the communes through use of police. The students had fun, they sang and danced and wisecracked, but there was continual tension. There was no question of their constant awareness of the seriousness of their acts. Though there were a few violent arguments about tactics, the discourse was more in the form of endless meetings convened to explore the outside political situation, defense tactics, maintenance and morale problems within the group. Debating and then determining what leaders should do were alternatives to the remote and authoritarian decision-making of Columbia's trustees.

The Columbia strike represented more than a new tactical movement, however. There was a political message as well. The striking students were not holding onto a narrow conception of students as a privileged class asking for inclusion in the university as it now exists. This kind of demand could easily be met by administrators by opening minor opportunities for "student rights" while cracking down on campus radicals. The Columbia students were instead taking an internationalist and revolutionary view of themselves in opposition to the imperialism of the very institutions in which they have been groomed and educated. They did not even want to be included in the decision-making circles of the military-industrial complex that runs Columbia: *they want to be included only if their inclusion is a step toward transforming the university.* They want a new and independent university standing against the mainstream of American society, or they want no university at all. They are, in Fidel Castro's words, "guerrillas in the field of culture."

How many other schools can be considered ripe for such confrontations? The question is hard to answer, but it is clear that the demands of black students for cultural recognition rather than paternalistic tolerance, and radical white students' awareness of the sinister paramilitary activities carried on in secret by the faculty on many campuses, are hardly confined to Columbia. Columbia's problem is the American problem in miniature—the inability to provide answers to widespread social needs and the use of the military to protect the authorities against the people. This process can only lead to greater unity in the movement.

Support from outside the university communities can be counted on in many large cities. A crisis is foreseeable that would be too massive for police to handle. It can happen; whether or not it will be necessary is a question which only time will answer. What is certain is that we are moving toward power— the power to stop the machine if it cannot be made to serve humane ends.

American educators are fond of telling their students that barricades are part of the romantic past, that social change today can only come about through the processes of negotiation. But the students at Columbia discovered that barricades are only the beginning of what they call "bringing the war home."

By 1969, SDS had over 100,000 members, and the number of students who identified themselves as radicals mushroomed to an all-time high. Yet, beset by internal divisions, SDS splintered into rival factions, each bent on developing the proper strategy for leading the revolution that they perceived was around the corner. The best-known faction, the Weathermen, named after a line in a Bob Dylan song, issued a manifesto, **Document 8.3,** *which called for American youths to occupy a vanguard position in the worldwide rebellion against the "mother country." Compare the Weathermen's manifesto to the "Port Huron Statement" and consider what factors led SDS, or at least segments of it, to adopt such a revolutionary posture. Did the Weathermen represent a natural outgrowth of the New Left, as some have argued, or could SDS have taken a different direction?*

Document 8.3   Weathermen, "You Don't Need a Weatherman to Know Which Way the Wind Blows," June 1969, Students for a Democratic Society Papers, State Historical Society of Wisconsin, Madison, Wisconsin.

1. INTERNATIONAL REVOLUTION

"The contradiction between the revolutionary peoples of Asia, Africa and Latin America and the imperialists headed by the United States is the principal contradiction in the contemporary world. The development of this contradiction is promoting the struggle of the people of the whole world against US imperialism and its lackeys."
—Lin Piao, *Long Live the Victory of People's War!*

People ask, what is the nature of the revolution that we talk about? Who will it be made by, and for, and what are its goals and strategy?

The overriding consideration in answering these questions is that the main struggle going on in the world today is between US imperialism and the national liberation struggles against it. This is essential in defining political matters in the whole world: because it is by far the most powerful, every other empire and petty dictator is in the long run dependent on US imperialism, which has unified, allied with, and defended all of the reactionary forces of the whole world. Thus, in considering every other force or phenomenon, from Soviet imperialism or Israeli imperialism to "workers struggle" in France or Czechoslovakia, we determine who are our friends and who are our enemies according to whether they help US imperialism or fight to defeat it.

So the very first question people in this country must ask in considering the question of revolution is where they stand in relation to the United States as an oppressor nation, and where they stand in relation to the masses of people throughout the world whom US imperialism is oppressing.

The primary task of revolutionary struggle is to solve this principal contradiction on the side of the people of the world. It is the oppressed peoples of the world who have created the wealth of this empire and it is to them that it belongs; the goal of the revolutionary struggle must be the control and use of this wealth in the interests of the oppressed peoples of the world.

It is in this context that we must examine the revolutionary struggles in the United States. We are within the heartland of a world-wide monster, a country so rich from its world-wide plunder that even the crumbs doled out to the enslaved masses within its borders provide for material existence very much above the conditions of the masses of people of the world. The US empire, as a worldwide system, channels wealth, based upon the labor and resources of the rest of the world, into the United States. The relative affluence existing in the United States is directly dependent upon the labor and natural resources of the Vietnamese, the Angolans, the Bolivians and the rest of the peoples of the Third World. All of the United Airlines Astrojets, all of the Holiday Inns, all of Hertz's automobiles, your television set, car and wardrobe already belong, to a large degree, to the people of the rest of the world.

Therefore, any conception of "socialist revolution" simply in terms of the working people of the United States, failing to recognize the full scope of interests of the most oppressed peoples of the world, is a conception of a fight for a particular privileged interest, and is a very dangerous ideology. While the control and use of the wealth of the Empire for the people of the whole world is also in the interests of the vast majority of the people in this country, if the goal is not clear from the start we will further the preservation of class society, oppression, war, genocide, and the complete emiseration of everyone, including the people of the US.

The goal is the destruction of US imperialism and the achievement of a classless world: world communism. Winning state power in the US will occur as a result of the military forces of the US overextending themselves around the world and being defeated piecemeal; struggle within the US will be a vital part of this process, but when the revolution triumphs in the US it will have been made by the people of the whole world. For socialism to be defined in national terms within so extreme and historical an oppressor nation as this is only imperialist national chauvinism on the part of the "movement. . . ."

VI. INTERNATIONAL STRATEGY AND THE BLACK VANGUARD

What is the strategy of this international revolutionary movement? What are the strategic weaknesses of the imperialists which make it possible for us to win? Revolutionaries around the world are in general agreement on the answer, which Lin Piao describes in the following way:

"US imperialism is stronger, but also more vulnerable, than any imperialism of the past. It sets itself against the people of the whole world, including the people of the United States. Its human, military, material and financial resources are far from sufficient for the realization of its ambition of domination over the whole world. US imperialism has further weakened itself by occupying so many places in the world, overreaching itself, stretching its fingers out wide and dispersing its strength, with its rear so far away and its supply lines so long."
—Lin Piao, *Long Live the Victory of People's War!* p. 122

The strategy which flows from this is what Che called "creating two, three, many Vietnams"—to mobilize the struggle so sharply in so many places that the imperialists cannot possibly deal with it all. Since it is essential to their interests, they will try to deal with it all, and will be defeated and destroyed in the process.

In defining and implementing this strategy, it is clear that the vanguard (that is, the section of the people who are in the forefront of the struggle and whose class interests and needs define the terms and tasks of the revolution) of the "American Revolution" is the workers and oppressed peoples of the colonies of Asia, Africa and Latin America. Because of the level of special oppression of black people as a colony they reflect the interests of the oppressed people of the world from within the borders of the United States; they are part of the Third World and part of the international revolutionary vanguard.

The vanguard role of the Vietnamese and other Third World countries in defeating US imperialism has been clear to our movement for some time. What has not been so clear is the vanguard role black people have played, and continue to play, in the development of revolutionary consciousness and struggle within the United States. Criticisms of the black liberation struggle as being "reactionary" or of black organizations on campus as being conservative or "racist" very often express this lack of understanding. These ideas are incorrect and must be defeated if a revolutionary movement is going to be built among whites.

The black colony, due to its particular nature as a slave colony, never adopted a chauvinist identification with America as an imperialist power, either politically or culturally. Moreover, the history of black people in America has consistently been one of the greatest overall repudiation of and struggle against the state. From the slave ships from Africa to the slave revolts, the Civil War, etc., black people have been waging a struggle for survival and liberation. In the history of our own movement this has also been the case: the civil rights struggles, initiated and led by blacks in the South; the rebellions beginning with Harlem in 1964 and Watts in 1965 through Detroit and Newark in 1967; the campus struggles at all-black schools in the south and struggles led by blacks on campuses all across the country. As it is the blacks—along with the Vietnamese and other Third World people—who are most oppressed by US imperialism, their class interests are most solidly and resolutely committed to waging revolutionary struggle through to its completion. Therefore it is no surprise that time and again, in both political content and level of consciousness and militancy, it has been the black liberation movement which has upped the ante and defined the terms of the struggle.

What is the relationship of this "black vanguard" to the "many Vietnams" around the world? Obviously it is an example of our strategy that different fronts reinforce each other. The fact that the Vietnamese are winning weakens the enemy, advancing the possibilities for the black struggle, etc. But it is important for us to understand that the interrelationship is more than this. Black people do not simply "choose" to intensify their struggle because they want to help the Vietnamese, or because they see that Vietnam heightens the possibilities for struggle here. The existence of any one Vietnam, especially a winning one, spurs on others not only through consciousness and choice, but through need, because it is a political and economic, as well as military, weakening of capitalism, and this means that to compensate, the imperialists are forced to intensify their oppression of other people.

Thus the loss of China and Cuba and the loss now of Vietnam not only encourages other oppressed peoples (such as the blacks) by showing what the alternative is and that it can be won, but also costs the imperialists billions of dollars which they then have to take out of the oppression of these other peoples. Within this country increased oppression falls heavier on the most oppressed sections of the population, so that the condition of all workers is worsened through rising taxes, inflation and the fall of real wages, and speedup. But this increased oppression falls heaviest on the most oppressed, such as poor white workers and, especially, the blacks, for example through the collapse of state services like schools, hospitals, and welfare, which naturally hits the hardest at those most dependent on them.

This deterioration pushes people to fight harder to even try to maintain their present level. The more the ruling class is hurt in Vietnam, the harder people will be pushed to rebel and to fight for reforms. Because there exist successful models of revolution in Cuba, Vietnam, etc., these reform struggles will provide a continually larger and stronger base for revolutionary ideas. Because it needs to maximize profits by denying the reforms, and is aware that these conditions and reform struggles will therefore lead to revolutionary consciousness, the ruling class will see it more and more necessary to come down on any motion at all, even where it is not yet highly organized or conscious. It will come down faster on black people, because their oppression is increasing fastest, and this makes their rebellion most thorough and most dangerous, and fastest growing. It is because of this that the vanguard character and role of the black liberation struggle will be increased and intensified, rather than being increasingly equal to and merged into the situation and rebellion of oppressed white working people and youth. The crises of imperialism (the existence of Vietnam and especially that it's winning) will therefore create a "black Vietnam" within the US. . . .

VIII. WHY A REVOLUTIONARY YOUTH MOVEMENT?

. . . In general, young people have less stake in a society (no family, fewer debts, etc.), are more open to new ideas (they have not been brainwashed for so long or so well), and are therefore more able and willing to move in a revolutionary direction. Specifically in America, young people have grown up experiencing the crises in imperialism. They have grown up along with a developing black liberation movement, with the liberation of Cuba, the fights for independence in Africa, and the war in Vietnam. Older people grew up during the fight against Fascism, during the cold war, the smashing of the trade unions, McCarthy, and a period during which real wages consistently rose—since 1965 disposable real income has decreased slightly, particularly in urban areas where inflation and increased taxation have bitten heavily into wages. This crisis in imperialism affects all parts of the society. America has had to militarize to protect and expand its Empire; hence the high draft calls and the creation of a standing army of three and a half million, an army which still has been unable to win in Vietnam. Further, the huge defense expenditures—required for the defense of the empire and at the same time a way of making increasing profits for the defense industries—have gone hand in hand with the urban crisis around welfare, the hospitals, the schools, housing, air, and water pollution. The State cannot provide the services it has been forced to assume responsibility for, and needs to increase taxes and to pay its growing debts while it cuts services and uses the pigs to repress protest. The private sector of the economy can't provide jobs, particularly unskilled jobs. The expansion of the defense and education industries by the State since World War II is in part an attempt to pick up the slack, though the inability to provide decent wages and working conditions for "public" jobs is more and more a problem.

As imperialism struggles to hold together this decaying social fabric, it inevitably resorts to brute force and authoritarian ideology. People, especially young people, more and more find themselves in the iron grip of authoritarian institutions. Reaction against the pigs or teachers in the schools, welfare pigs or the army is generalizable and extends beyond the particular repressive institution to the society and the State as a whole. The legitimacy of the State is called into question for the first time in at least 30 years, and the anti-authoritarianism which characterizes the youth rebellion turns into rejection of the State, a refusal to be socialized into American society. Kids used to try to beat the system from inside the army or from inside the schools; now they desert from the army and burn down the schools.

The crisis in imperialism has brought about a breakdown in bourgeois social forms, culture and ideology. The family falls apart, kids leave home, women begin to break out of traditional "female" and "mother" roles. There develops a "generation gap" and a "youth problem." Our heroes are no longer struggling businessmen, and we also begin to reject the ideal career of the professional and look to Mao, Che, the Panthers, the Third World, for our models, for motion. We reject the elitist, technocratic bullshit that tells us only experts can rule, and look instead to leadership from the people's war of the Vietnamese. Chuck Berry, Elvis, the Temptations brought us closer to the "people's culture" of Black America. The racist response to the civil rights movement revealed the depth of racism in America, as well as the impossibility of real change through American institutions. And the war against Vietnam is not "the heroic war against the Nazis"; it's the big lie, with napalm burning through everything we had heard this country stood for. Kids begin to ask questions: Where is the Free World? And who do the pigs protect at home?

The breakdown in bourgeois culture and concomitant anti-authoritarianism is fed by the crisis in imperialism, but also in turn feeds that crisis, exacerbates it so that people no longer merely want the plastic '50s restored, but glimpse an alternative (like inside the Columbia buildings) and begin to fight for it. We don't want teachers to be more kindly cops; we want to smash cops, and build a new life. . . .

The above arguments make it clear that it is both important and possible to reach young people wherever they are—not only in the shops, but also in the schools, in the army, and in the streets—so as to recruit them to fight on the side of the oppressed peoples of the world. Young people will be part of the International Liberation Army. The necessity to build this International Liberation Army in America leads to certain priorities in practice for the revolutionary youth movement which we should begin to apply this summer.

Throughout much of the 1960s, developments in Berkeley, California, predicted and shaped the trajectory of the New Left. Evidence of a student rebellion appeared there early in the decade in the form of anti-HUAC, anti–death penalty, and pro–civil rights demonstrations. The University of California's Free Speech Movement signaled the birth of a massive student movement. Berkeley activists were among the first to protest against the Vietnam War, and the counterculture flourished there, with Telegraph Avenue rivaling the Haight-Ashbury district in San Francisco as a magnet of the "hippie" lifestyle. Berkeley also served as a lightning rod for conservatives. While running for and later serving as governor of the state of California, Ronald Reagan gained much attention and public support by denouncing student rebels and liberal academics who, in his words, should have known better. Edwin Meese, who became one of Reagan's top aides and his U.S. attorney general, first gained fame when, while serving as the Alameda County district attorney, he pledged to crack down on disruptive students. In 1969, Berkeley experienced one of the most harrowing confrontations of the decade, over "People's Park." Robert Scheer's "Who Ripped Off the Park?" (**Document 8.4**)*, published in* Ramparts, *describes and analyzes the clash. Similar confrontations took place at numerous campuses in 1969, at San Francisco State University, the University of Wisconsin, and Cornell University, to name just a few.*

Document 8.4   Robert Scheer, "Who Ripped Off the Park?" *Ramparts* 8, no. 2 (August 1969), pp. 42–43.

[INTRODUCTION]

"The pigs are ripping off the People's Park." With this frantic message, thousands of Berkeley students, street people, radicals, Free Church Christians, conservationists, student government leaders, and even pom-pon girls and fraternity men were alerted to the fact that the plot of ground they had come to accept as their own was in danger. One of those sounding the alarm was "Big Bill" Miller. He had been sleeping guard in the park along with about a hundred others, when the combined forces of the Berkeley police, the California Highway Patrol, and the Alameda County Sheriff's Department invaded the area and sealed off traffic for an eight-block square, while a fence was quickly thrown up. Miller rushed down to the Red Square dress shop (about 20 feet from the southwest tip of the park) to warn Mike Delacour, the man who had come up with the idea of a People's Park and supervised its early development. Delacour tried calling Reverend York of the Free Church; he was going to hold a sunrise service in the park at 5 a.m. Others activated the "telephone tree," an early warning system of chain phone calls set up in anticipation of a move by the authorities. Within the hour, the streets in the area began to come alive with people bitter and frustrated over this swift display of establishment power.

Nine hours later, more than 100 demonstrators had been injured, 13 of them requiring hospitalization due to shotgun wounds. One was dying from 1/3-inch buckshot which had ripped open his belly, and another was blind from being blasted in the face with birdshot. Tear gas hung heavy over much of the city, and people milled about in bewilderment over the incredible and unprecedented overkill used to punish those who had attempted to plant a park on one square block of land owned by the University of California.

Thousands of people had passed by People's Park that morning, apparently needing to bear personal witness to the process of destruction. They had watched as iron fence poles were set three feet deep in concrete and bulldozers ripped up the shrubbery which they had so carefully planted. They watched the heavy equipment rolling over the newly-planted sod and the police cynically cavorting on the slides and swings in the park, which was now off-limits to ordinary citizens. But there were no incidents of confrontation during the morning hours of the day which became known as "Bloody Thursday."

The crowd at the traditional Berkeley campus noon rally in Sproul plaza, the largest of the year, had gathered to do something about the fence. At one point in the rally, student body president-elect Dan Siegel, a second-year law student, said, ". . . Let's go down there and take the park." Without waiting for any qualifications he might make, the crowd, to the amazement of the political activists still waiting to speak, roared its approval and spontaneously began to move down Telegraph Avenue toward the park three blocks away. It could have been another line from another speaker that launched them, or it could have been no line at all. It didn't matter. They were getting ready to go anyway; they could not just accept the fence.

At first everything seemed to be following a familiar Berkeley pattern—a chanting crowd moving down Telegraph, once again breaking the front window of the Bank of America building. They encountered the police lines that had been thrown up across Haste and Dwight streets to block access to the park, and in a matter of minutes tear gas canisters and rocks had crossed paths and someone had opened a water hydrant to spray cops standing across the street. Then the police charged, clubs swinging, and a Berkeley police car shot down the Avenue, zigzagging from one side of the street to the other, shooting tear gas out the windows. *Ramparts* reporter Art Goldberg recalls, "A number of us walked down Ellsworth and turned up Durant to get back to the campus. A girl ran towards us, yelling hysterically, 'They're shooting people. Three people have been shot.' We told her to cool it, that tear gas canisters were the only things getting shot off."

Reports of other shootings began to circulate, and for the next few hours there was horrified disbelief. When hospital reports began to confirm serious shotgun injuries to demonstrators and bystanders alike, the police released accounts implying that the shootings had occurred in the heat of the battle and as a result of frantic self-defense rather than a deliberate police riot. But as a result of careful research by trained investigators, *Ramparts* is now able to document . . . the identity and movements of a "death squad" of Alameda County Deputy Sheriffs, which, as it moved in a circular path through the area of protest, used its shotguns to cause almost all the serious injuries as well as the one death. At no point that day or in the next week of demonstrations was there a single reported instance of an officer being fired upon, nor did a single officer sustain a serious injury. In fact, only 18 policemen required any hospital treatment— all for superficial cuts, mostly from flying glass—and none had an injury serious enough to require hospitalization. Commenting on the scores of civilians who were brought in for treatment, Dr. Henry Brean, Chief Radiologist at Berkeley's Herrick Hospital, said: "The indiscriminate use of shotguns is sheer insanity."

He listed a partial toll of the casualties: One death, three punctured lungs, two eyes blinded and a third damaged, a shatter-fracture of the lower leg and a rupture complicated by a massive internal infection.

Alan Blanchard, father of a three-month-old child, was by all reliable accounts an observer on a roof when he was blinded by birdshot; James Rector, who later died from being shot with size "00" buckshot (used to kill deer, each charge containing 9 or 12 of the ⅓-inch pellets), was also looking on. The surgeon who treated Rector at Herrick later gave this account to the San Francisco Examiner: "This young boy had picked up three slugs—the sort of thing you'd expect from a machine gun. But it wasn't. It was buckshot from 30 feet. His belly was just ripped apart." One victim arrived at the hospital with 125 pellets of birdshot in his body. Two newsmen, Don Wegars of the San Francisco Chronicle and Daryl Lembke of the Los Angeles Times, were also hit by shotgun blasts.

Berkeley's nightmare wasn't big national news at first. As one New York editor said, no one outside the Bay Area could believe that a civil war had broken out over grass being planted in a homemade park. Only when Governor Reagan stationed 2000 National Guardsmen in the area the next day was the national press alerted to some of the bizarre developments that would follow—the tear gas air strike against demonstrators on the campus by a National Guard helicopter, or the fact that over 1000 people were to be arrested in Berkeley that week, including 200 booked on felony charges.

The blowup at Berkeley ultimately got coverage, but there has still been little recognition that what happened is more than a particularly bad riot in a college town. Few have seen the battle over People's Park for what it really is: a preview of the confrontations of the '70s.

The crisis in Berkeley was not simply the result of right-wing excess or backlash; rather, it represented a fundamental conflict between a generation which was the product of ten years of Berkeley revolts and was now coming into its own, and the "enlightened" authorities of the University of California, who had spent the past 20 years attempting to prevent such a generation from developing, and had ended up provoking it instead.

The park confrontation was a battle in a war between the mainstream of society, as represented by the University of California's administration, and the counter-community of revolt which thrives in the South Campus–Telegraph Avenue area, with the People's Park site at its heart. The Berkeley crisis was never over whether the University would be able to stop one "people's park," but rather over whether it would succeed in what had been a long-term strategy of eliminating the culture of protest by denying it its turf.

[II.]

The U.C. Regents decided to take over the heart of Berkeley's South Campus area as early as 1952, when they originally produced the current Long Range

Development Plan for the University. Their thinking at the time appeared more bureaucratic than political. It was simply easier and cheaper to move into the South Campus area, "blighted" as it was by a jumble of bookstores, coffee shops and older houses used by students and others who were not at that time likely to mobilize significant opposition.

But the bureaucratic motive was based on assumptions about the purpose of the University and the role of its students. South Campus expansion was based on the presumed need to sanitize and control the University environment. The University community which the Development Plan envisioned was one of a total environment in which every need—classrooms, housing, office space, recreation and parking—was programmed for ten years into the future. Students would literally be forced to dwell within an ivory tower of concrete and glass dormitories which—along with other official buildings, churches and a few spanking new store fronts properly up to code—would be the only structures permitted in the central South Campus area. All others would be pushed out by the University Regents exercising their power of eminent domain. This would, as the Development Plan (1956 revision) noted, provide "a well-rounded life for students. . . ." If the Multiversity was to be a knowledge factory, South Campus Berkeley would be a company town.

At the time of its conception, it looked as if there could be no possible opposition to the Development Plan. Those were the "silent '50s" and "Cal" was as caught up in McCarthyite hysteria as the rest of the country. But disaffection simmered, and it began to move into the open in 1957, when Telegraph Avenue came to rival San Francisco's North Beach as the vital center of the Beat Generation, with Allen Ginsberg and Gregory Corso denouncing the sterile social order and calling for liberation from their forum at Robbie's Chinese-American restaurant on Telegraph. Slowly this mood began to slip into the campus itself, and in 1958 a group of about 100 students organized a political party which would be a *bête noire* for California citizens over the next few years. This party, called SLATE, organized a left-liberal coalition and uncovered a broad base of student concerns. Before being banned from campus, it managed to win two student senate seats and eventually the student body presidency on a campus thought safely de-politicized.

There is, as on most questions of theory, little agreement among New Leftists as to where and when the Movement began; but certainly one can make a strong case for the Berkeley of ten years ago. In 1959, there were large protests against the execution of Caryl Chessman. In 1960, several thousand students, mostly from Berkeley, stormed a hearing of the House Un-American Activities Committee being held in the San Francisco City Hall. Soon there were massive protests over U.S. policy toward Cuba, sit-ins at San Francisco hotels to protest discriminatory hiring practices and demonstrations at the 1964 Republican Convention at San Francisco's Cow Palace. Local reactionaries like Oakland Tribune publisher William Knowland had already learned to hate and mistrust students, and in the fall of 1964, when the administration tried to accommodate them by putting the lid on, the FSM erupted, setting a model for the next few years of campus protest.

The non-student community—including both cultural and political dropouts—grew rapidly. Each successive student generation seemed more hell-bent than the last on breaking new ideological or tactical ground. After the FSM it was the Vietnam Day Committee (VDC), which departed from the liberals of the Peace Movement by insisting that imperialism, not foreign policy blunders, was the cause of the war. But the VDC was forced to fight the university issue as well: criticized for using the campus as a "staging ground" for its actions, the VDC replied that the University was itself a staging ground for weapons research and defense contracts; that it had in fact perfected a technique for giving priority to non-students like Dow Chemical and the Defense Department.

While the Weathermen cast their strategy in Marxist-Leninist terms and while some Berkeley activists sought to recruit workers to their side, little evidence exists to suggest that either group made much headway with them. Does this mean, however, that labor was in the forefront of the political backlash that developed in the wake of the 1960s? Or did workers remain in the political middle, dedicated to retaining liberal programs, such as Medicare, and to maintaining the power of the federal government? **Document 8.5,** *an editorial by M. A. Hutcheson, the president of the Carpenters' Union, suggests that while labor found the youth rebellion appalling, it was not yet ready to jettison many of Franklin Roosevelt's and Lyndon Johnson's reforms. On the contrary, to a degree labor adopted the language of what some scholars have termed "rights-consciousness," with Hutcheson asserting that older Americans had certain rights that had not been fulfilled and that, implicitly, could be met only by the federal government.*

Document 8.5 M. A. Hutcheson, "Rebellion Road Is Not the Oldsters' Road," *The Carpenter* 89, no. 7 (July 1969), p. 40.

When the history of this age is written it could well be labeled "The Age of Rebellion." Rebellion seems to be an integral part of every-day life for many social, ethnic, and economic groups.

The young are rebelling against the old; the blacks are challenging the white establishment; the priests are defying the church hierarchy; college students are locking horns with the college administrations.

It must be difficult for some youngsters to keep their rebellions straight. For example, a young black Catholic priest taking extra work at a college would have at least four rebellions to participate in if he supported all the above-mentioned causes.

I only bring this up to emphasize one point; namely, if there is one group which has ample cause for rebellion, it is people in the over-60 age bracket.

We lived through the rigors of two world wars and survived a depression which kept most of us broke, frustrated, and unemployed for the better part of ten years. However, we maintained our faith in the institutions which built America, with the result that today we enjoy the highest standard of living ever achieved by mankind.

With our tax money we built the universities which the hippies and yippies are seeking to destroy. Our contributions erected the churches the dissidents now want to take over. Our hard work and thrift over the years made possible the checks from home which the college students and hippies now get to keep them going while they are trying to destroy the society that made it all possible.

I believe that the over-60 generation really has cause for rebellion if they are inclined in that direction.

The entire society is youth oriented. All the emphasis is on helping the young. For example, an analysis of the current budget shows that among individuals participating in manpower programs in 1968, 64% were age 21 or under. On the other hand, only 4% were 55 or over.

Consider also that those 65 or older make up only 12 or 15% of the population, yet one-third of the nation's poor are in the 65 and over category.

Currently, wage increases are running as high as 9%. On the other hand Social Security recipients will be lucky if they secure a 7% increase in benefits this year. It could be nothing at all.

Adding all these things together, it seems to me that the over-60 generation which was short-changed in the 1930's is getting short-changed again. All the affluence that has been achieved has been spark-plugged by the efforts of this now tired generation, and it is my thinking that the time has come for Congress, the state legislatures, and society as a whole to accord them a better break.

Long ago, however, we learned that it does not pay to burn the house down to get rid of the roaches nor throw the baby out with the bath water. We know whatever inequities we may be smarting under can be cured by political action.

It may be old fashioned and decidedly "square" to pursue the course of redressing grievances by persuasion, education and political action, but this is the road we know best.

It is a road we have traveled all our lives, and I am sure most of us are convinced it can lead us to the goals we aim for.

Richard Nixon, who just barely lost to John F. Kennedy in 1960, crafted his political comeback on the premise that he needed to win the support of the political middle. A sense of Nixon's strategy can be gleaned from **Document 8.6,** *his acceptance speech at the Republican convention, where he cast himself as the champion of these "forgotten Americans." Unlike those on the right, who sought to shrink government, cut taxes, and stand tall against Russia, Nixon steered a more moderate course. While he talked tough on crime and denounced some of the social engineering of the Johnson administration, as president he extended numerous Great Society programs, instituted affirmative action and wage and price controls, and flirted with national health insurance, not to mention commencing talks with China and detente with the Soviet Union.*

Document 8.6   Richard M. Nixon, "Acceptance Speech at the Republican National Convention," Miami Beach, Florida, August 8, 1968, *Congressional Record*, 90th Congress, 2nd Session, 114, part 20 (September 16, 1968), pp. 26881–26883.

Mr. Chairman, delegates to this convention, my fellow Americans.

Sixteen years ago I stood before this convention to accept your nomination as the running mate of one of the greatest Americans of our time or of any time, Dwight D. Eisenhower.

Eight years ago I had the highest honor of accepting your nomination for President of the United States.

Tonight, I again proudly accept the nomination for President of the United States.

But I have news for you; this time there's a difference. This time we're going to win.

We're going to win for a number of reasons. First, a personal one. General Eisenhower, as you know, lies critically ill in the Walter Reed Hospital tonight. I have talked, however, to Mrs. Eisenhower on the telephone. She tells me that his heart is with us, and she says that there is nothing that would lift him more than for us to win in November. And I say, let's win this one for Ike.

We're going to win because this great convention has demonstrated to the nation that the Republican Party has the leadership, the platform and the purpose that America needs.

We're going to win because you have nominated as my running mate a statesman of the first rank, who will be a great campaigner and one who is fully qualified to undertake the new responsibilities that I shall give to the next Vice President of the United States. And he is a man who fully shares my conviction and yours that after a period of forty years when power has gone from the cities and the states to the Government in Washington, D.C., it's time to have power go back from Washington to the states and the cities of this country all over America.

We're going to win because at a time when America cries out for the unity that this Administration has destroyed, the Republican Party after a spirited contest for its nomination for President and Vice President stands united before the nation tonight. . . .

A Party that can unite itself will unite America.

My fellow Americans, most important, we're going to win because our cause is right.

We make history tonight, not for ourselves but for the ages. The choice we make in 1968 will determine not only the future of America but the future of peace and freedom of the world for the last third of the Twentieth Century. And the question that we answer tonight—can America meet this great challenge?

For a few moments, let us look at America, let us listen to America, to find the answer to that question.

As we look at America we see cities enveloped in smoke and flame. We hear sirens in the night. We see Americans dying on distant battlefields abroad. We see Americans hating each other; fighting each other; killing each other at home. And as we see and hear these things, millions of Americans cry out in anguish. Did we come all this way for this? Did American boys die in Normandy, Korea and in Valley Forge for this?

Listen to the answer to those questions.

It is another voice. It is a quiet voice, in the tumult of the shouting. It is the voice of the great majority of Americans, the forgotten Americans, the non-shouters, the non-demonstrators.

They are not racist or sick; they are not guilty of the crime that plagues the land. They are black and they are white. They are native-born and foreign-born. They are young and they are old. They work in America's factories. They run America's businesses. They serve in the Government. They provide most of the soldiers who died to keep us free. They give drive to the spirit of America. They give life to the American dream. They give steel to the backbone of America. They are good people, they are decent people, they work and they save and they pay their taxes and they care. Like Theodore Roosevelt, they know that this country will not be a good place for any of us to live in unless it's a good place for all of us to live in.

And this, I say to you tonight, is the real voice of America. In the year 1968 this is the message that will be broadcast to America and the world.

Let's never forget that despite her faults, America is a great nation. America is great because her people are great.

With Winston Churchill we say, "We have not journeyed all this way across the centuries, across the oceans, across the mountains, across the prairies because we are made of sugar candy."

America is in trouble today not because her people have failed, but because her leaders have failed. What America needs are leaders to match the greatness of her people.

And this great group of Americans, the forgotten Americans and others, know the great question Americans must answer by their votes in November, is this: Whether we shall continue for four more years the policies of the last five years.

This is their answer and this is my answer to that question.

When the strongest nation in the world can be tied down for four years in a war in Vietnam with no end in sight; when the richest nation in the world can't manage its own economy; when the nation with the greatest tradition of rule of the law is plagued by unprecedented lawlessness; when a nation that has been known for a century for equality of opportunity is torn by unprecedented racial violence; and when the President of the United States cannot travel abroad or to any major city at home without fear of a hostile demonstration, then it's time for new leadership for the United States of America.

My fellow Americans, tonight I accept the challenge and the commitment to provide that new leadership for America. I ask you to accept it with me.

Let us accept this challenge not as a grim duty but as an exciting adventure in which we are privileged to help a great nation realize its destiny. Let us begin by committing ourselves to the truth, to see it like it is and tell it like it is. To find the truth, to speak the truth and to live the truth. That's what we will do.

We've had enough of big promises and little action. The time has come for honest Government in the United States of America. So tonight I do not promise the millennium in the morning. I don't promise that we can eradicate poverty and end discrimination and eliminate all danger of war in the space of four or even eight years. But I do promise action, a new policy for peace and progress and justice at home.

Look at our problems abroad. Do you realize that we face the stark truth that we are worse off in every area of the world tonight than we were eight years ago? That's the record. There is only one answer to such a record of failure, and that is a complete housecleaning of those responsible for the failures and that record. The answer is the complete re-appraisal of America's policies in every section of the world.

We shall begin with Vietnam. We all hope in this room that there's a chance that current negotiations may bring an honorable end to that war, and we will say nothing during this campaign that might destroy that chance. If the war is not ended when the people choose in November, the choice will be clear.

For four years the Administration has had at its disposal the greatest military and economic advantage that one nation has ever had over another in a war in history. For four years, America's fighting men have set a record for courage and sacrifice unsurpassed in history. For four years this Administration has had the support of the Loyal Opposition for the objective of seeking an honorable end of the struggle.

Never has so much military and economic and diplomatic power been used so ineffectively. If after all of this time and all of this sacrifice and all of this support there is still no end in sight, then I say the time has come for the American people to turn to new leadership not tied to the mistakes and the policies of the past.

That is what we offer to America. And I pledge to you tonight that the first priority foreign policy objective of our next Administration will be to bring an honorable end to the war in Vietnam. We shall not stop there. We need a policy to prevent more Vietnams.

All of America's peace-keeping institutions and all of America's foreign commitments must be re-appraised. Over the past 25 years America has provided more than 150 billion dollars in foreign aid to nations abroad. In Korea and now again in Vietnam, the United States furnished most of the money, most of the arms, most of the men to help the people of those countries defend themselves against aggression. We're a rich country, we're a strong nation, we're a populous nation, but there are 200 million Americans and there are 2 billion people that live in the free world and I say the time has come for other nations in the free world to bear their fair share of the burden of defending peace and freedom around the world.

What I call for is not new isolationism, it's a new internationalism, in which

America enlists its allies and its friends around the world in those struggles in which their interest is as great as ours.

And now to the leaders of the Communist world we say: After an era of confrontation, the time has come for negotiation. Where the world's super powers are concerned, there is no acceptable alternative to peaceful negotiation. Because this will be a period of negotiation, we shall restore the strength of America, so that we shall always negotiate from strength and never from weakness.

As we seek peace through negotiation, let our goals be clear: We do not seek domination over any other country. We believe deeply in our ideas, but we believe they should travel on their own power and not on the power of our arms. We shall never be belligerent but we shall be as firm in defending our system as they are in expanding theirs. We believe this should be an era of peaceful competition, not only in the productivity of our factories but in the quality of our ideas. We extend the hand of friendship to all people, to the Russian people, to the Chinese people, to all people in the world, and we shall work toward the goal of an open world, open skies, open cities, open hearts, open minds. . . .

As we commit to new policies for America tonight, let me make one further pledge: For five years hardly a day has gone by when we haven't read or heard a report of the American flag being spit on; an embassy being stoned; a library being burned; or an ambassador being insulted someplace in the world. Each incident reduced respect for the United States until the ultimate insult inevitably occurred.

I say to you tonight that when respect for the United States of America falls so low that a fourth rate military power like North Korea will seize an American naval vessel on the high seas, it's time for new leadership to restore respect for the United States of America.

My friends, America is a great nation. It is time we started to act like a great nation around the world. It is ironic to note that when we were a small nation, weak militarily and poor economically, America was respected. The reason was that America stood for something more powerful than military strength and economic wealth.

The American Revolution was a shining example of freedom in action which caught the imagination of the world. Today too often America is an example to be avoided and not followed.

A nation that can't keep the peace at home won't be trusted to keep the peace abroad. A President who isn't treated with respect at home will not be treated with respect abroad. A nation which can't manage its own economy can't tell others how to manage theirs. If we are to restore prestige and respect for America abroad, the place to begin is at home in the United States of America.

My friends, we live in an age of revolution in America and in the world. To find the answers to our problems let us turn to a revolution, a revolution that will never grow old, the world's greatest continuing revolution, the American

Revolution. The American Revolution was and is dedicated to progress, but our founders recognized that the first requisite of progress is order. There is no quarrel between progress and order because neither can exist without the other. So let us have order in America. Not the order that suppresses dissent and discourages change, but the order which guarantees the right to dissent and provides the basis for peaceful change. . . .

Let us always respect as I do our courts and those who serve on them. But let us also recognize that some of our courts in their decisions have gone too far in weakening the peace forces against the criminal forces in this country. Let those who have responsibility to enforce our laws and our judges who have the responsibility to interpret them be dedicated to the great principles of civil rights. Let them also recognize that the first civil right of every American is to be free from domestic violence. And that right must be guaranteed in this country. . . .

The wave of crime is not going to be the wave of the future in the United States of America. We shall re-establish freedom from fear in America so that America can take the lead in re-establishing freedom from fear in the world.

To those who say that law and order is the code word for racism, here is a reply: Our goal is justice, justice for every American. If we are to have respect for law in America, we must have laws that deserve respect. . . .

This brings me to the clearest choice among the great issues of this campaign. For the past five years we have been deluged by the program for the unemployed; programs for the cities; programs for the poor. And we have reaped from these programs an ugly harvest of frustration, violence and failure across the land.

Now our opponents will be offering more of the same, more billions for government jobs, government housing, government welfare. I say it's time to quit pouring billions of dollars into programs that have failed in the United States of America.

To put it bluntly, we're on the wrong road and it's time to take a new road to progress.

Again we turn to the American Revolution for our answer. The war on poverty didn't begin five years ago in this country. It began when the country began. It's been the most successful war on poverty in the history of nations. There's more wealth in America today more broadly shared than in any nation in the world. We are a great nation, and we must never forget how we became great.

America is a great nation today not because of what government did for people, but because of what people did for themselves over 190 years in this country. It is time to apply the lesson of the American Revolution to our present problem. . . .

Let us build bridges, my friends, build bridges to human dignity across that gulf that separates black America from white America. Black Americans no more than white Americans do not want more government programs to perpetuate dependency. They don't want to be a colony in a nation. They want the pride and the self-respect and the dignity that can only come if they have an equal chance to own their own homes, to own their own businesses, to be managers and executives as well as workers, to have a piece of the action in the exciting ventures of private enterprise. I pledge to you tonight that we shall have new programs which will provide the equal chance. . . .

My fellow Americans, I believe that historians will record that 1968 marked the beginning of the American generation in world history. Just to be alive in America, at this time, is an experience unparalleled in history. Here is where the action is.

Think. Thirty-two years from now most of Americans living will celebrate a New Year that comes once in a thousand years. Eight years from now, in the second term of the next President, we will celebrate the 200th anniversary of the American Revolution. By our decision in this election, we—all of us here, all of you listening on television and the radio—will determine what kind of nation America will be on its 200th birthday. We will determine what kind of world America will live in in the year 2000.

This is the kind of day I see for America on that glorious Fourth eight years from now. I see a day when Americans are once again proud of their flag. When once again at home and abroad, it is honored as the world's greatest symbol of liberty and justice. I see a day when the President of the United States is respected and his office is honored because it is worthy of respect and worthy of honor. I see a day when every child in this land, regardless of his background, has a chance for the best education that our wisdom and schools can provide. . . . I see a day when life in rural America attracts people to the country, rather than driving them away. I see a day when we can look back on massive breakthroughs in solving the problems of slums, pollution and traffic which are choking our cities to death. I see a day when our senior citizens and millions of others can plan for the future with the assurance that their government is not going to rob them of their savings by destroying the value of the dollar. . . .

None of the old hatreds mean anything when you look down into the faces of our children. In their faces is our hope, our love and our courage.

Tonight I see the face of a child. He lives in a great city. He is black. He is white. He is Mexican, Italian, Polish. None of that matters. What matters is that he is an American child. That child in that great city is more important than any politician's promise. He is America. He is a poet, he's a scientist. He is a great teacher, he's a proud craftsman; he's everything we ever hoped to be and everything we dare to dream to be. He sleeps the sleep of childhood; he dreams the dreams of a child. Yet when he awakens, he awakens to a living nightmare of poverty, neglect and despair.

He fails in school. He ends up on welfare. For him the American system is one that feeds his stomach and starves his soul. It breaks his heart and in the end it may take his life on some distant battlefield. To millions of children in this rich land, this is their prospect for the future.

But this is only part of what I see in America. I see another child tonight.

He hears the train go by at night and he dreams of far away places he would like to go. It seems like an impossible dream, but he is helped on his journey through life. A father who had to go to work before he finished the sixth grade, sacrificed everything he had so that his sons could go to college. A gentle Quaker mother, with a passionate concern for peace, quietly wept when he went to war, but she understood why he had to go. A great teacher, a remarkable football coach, an inspirational minister encouraged him on his way.

A courageous wife and loyal children stood by him in victory and also in defeat. And in his chosen profession of politics, first there were scores, then hundreds, then thousands, and finally millions who worked for his success. Tonight he stands before you nominated for President of the United States of America. You can see why I believe so deeply in the American dream.

For most of us the American Revolution has been won; the American dream has come true. What I ask you to do tonight is to help me make that dream come true for millions to whom it is an impossible dream today.

One hundred eight years ago, the newly elected President of the United States, Abraham Lincoln, left Springfield, Illinois, never to return again. He spoke to his friends gathered at the railroad station. Listen to his words:

"Today I leave you. I go to assume a greater task than devolved on General Washington. The great God which helped him must help me. Without that great assistance, I will surely fail. With it, I cannot fail."

Abraham Lincoln lost his life but he did not fail. The next President of the United States will face challenges which in some ways will be greater than those of Washington or Lincoln. For the first time in our nation's history an American President will face not only the problem of restoring peace abroad, but of restoring peace at home. Without God's help and your help, we will surely fail; but with God's help and your help, we shall surely succeed.

My fellow Americans, the long dark night for America is about to end. The time has come for us to leave the valley of despair and climb the mountain so that we may see the glory of the dawn—a new day for America, a new dawn for peace and freedom in the world.

In July 1969, several days after blasting off from Cape Kennedy, Florida, Apollo 11 successfully completed its historic mission when Neil Armstrong stepped off the lunar module and onto the surface of the moon. While some cynically dismissed the moon walk as a waste of money, the majority of Americans reacted otherwise. To them, the mission to the moon transcended the political conflict and social turmoil that marked the sixties. Indeed, such conflict notwithstanding, the space program reflected many of the themes of the decade. Economic prosperity and scientific and technological progress made the space program possible. The cold war sped up the race to the moon. Faith in the capabilities of the federal government informed the effort. Moreover, many baby boomers grew up with the space program, watching it progress from its infant stages to its triumphant moment, with some of them, per-

haps, dreaming of traveling in space themselves. **Document 8.7** *consists of speeches that Apollo 11's three astronauts delivered to a special session of Congress following their return to earth. Without dismissing the troubles that beset the nation, the astronauts hoped that the space program would serve as a mechanism for reuniting Americans around a common set of goals, or at least around the vision that the impossible was possible.*

Document 8.7   Neil A. Armstrong, Michael Collins, and Edwin E. Aldrin, Jr., "Remarks to a Special Session of Congress," *Congressional Record,* 91st Congress, 1st Session, 115, part 19 (September 16, 1969), pp. 25609–25611.

Mr. ARMSTRONG. Mr. Speaker, Mr. President, Members of Congress, distinguished guests, we are greatly honored that you have invited us here today. Only now have we completed our journey to land on and explore the moon, and return. It was here in these Halls that our venture really began. Here the Space Act of 1958 was framed, the chartering document of the National Aeronautics and Space Administration. And here in the years that followed the key decisions that permitted the successive steps of Mercury and Gemini and Apollo were permitted.

Your policies and the marvels of modern communication have permitted people around the world to share the excitement of our exploration. And, although you have been informed of the results of the Apollo 11, we are particularly pleased to have this opportunity to complete our work by reporting to you and through you to the American people. My colleagues share the honor of presenting this report. First, it is my pleasure to present Col. Edwin Aldrin.

Colonel ALDRIN. Distinguished ladies and gentlemen, it is with a great sense of pride as an American and with humility as a human being that I say to you today what no men have been privileged to say before: "We walked on the moon." But the footprints at Tranquillity Base belong to more than the crew of Apollo 11. They were put there by hundreds of thousands of people across this country, people in Government, industry, and universities, the teams and crews that preceded us, all who strived throughout the years with Mercury, Gemini, and Apollo. Those footprints belong to the American people and you, their representatives, who accepted and supported the inevitable challenge of the moon. And, since we came in peace for all mankind those footprints belong also to all people of the world. As the moon shines impartially on all those looking up from our spinning earth so do we hope the benefits of space exploration will be spread equally with a harmonizing influence to all mankind.

Scientific exploration implies investigating the unknown. The result can never be wholly anticipated. Charles Lindbergh said, "Scientific accomplishment is a path, not an end; a path leading to and disappearing in mystery."

Our steps in space have been a symbol of this country's way of life as we open our doors and windows to the world to view our successes and failures and as we share with all nations our discovery. The Saturn, Columbia, and Eagle, and the extravehicular mobility unit have proved to Neil, Mike, and me that this Nation can produce equipment of the highest quality and dependability. This should give all of us hope and inspiration to overcome some of the more difficult problems here on earth. The Apollo lesson is that national goals can be met where there is a strong enough will to do so.

The first step on the moon was a step toward our sister planets and ultimately toward the stars. "A small step for a man," was a statement of fact, "a giant leap for mankind," is a hope for the future.

What this country does with the lessons of Apollo apply [*sic*] to domestic problems, and what we do in further space exploration programs will determine just how giant a leap we have taken.

Thank you.

Mr. ARMSTRONG. Now I should like to present Col. Michael Collins.

Colonel COLLINS. Mr. President, Members of Congress, and distinguished guests: One of the many things I have very much enjoyed about working for the Space Agency, and for the Air Force, is that they have always given me free rein, even to the extent of addressing this most august assemblage without coaching, without putting any words in my mouth. Therefore, my brief remarks are simply those of a free citizen living in a free country and expressing free thoughts that are purely my own.

Many years before there was a space program my father had a favorite quotation: "He who would bring back the wealth of the Indies must take the wealth of the Indies with him." This we have done. We have taken to the moon the wealth of this Nation, the vision of its political leaders, the intelligence of its scientists, the dedication of its engineers, the careful craftsmanship of its workers, and the enthusiastic support of its people. We have brought back rocks. And I think it is a fair trade. For just as the Rosetta stone revealed the language of ancient Egypt, so may these rocks unlock the mystery of the origin of the moon, of our earth, and even of our solar system.

During the flight of Apollo 11, in the constant sunlight between the earth and the moon, it was necessary for us to control the temperature of our spacecraft by a slow rotation not unlike that of a chicken on a barbecue spit. As we turned, the earth and the moon alternately appeared in our windows. We had our choice. We could look toward the Moon, toward Mars, toward our future in space—toward the new Indies—or we could look back toward the Earth, our home, with its problems spawned over more than a millennium of human occupancy.

We looked both ways. We saw both, and I think that is what our Nation must do.

We can ignore neither the wealth of the Indies nor the realities of the immediate needs of our cities, our citizens, or our civics. We cannot launch our planetary probes from a springboard of poverty, discrimination, or unrest. But neither can we wait until each and every terrestrial problem has been solved. Such logic 200 years ago would have prevented expansion westward past the Appalachian Mountains, for assuredly the eastern seaboard was beset by problems of great urgency then, as it is today.

Man has always gone where he has been able to go. It is that simple. He will continue pushing back his frontier, no matter how far it may carry him from his homeland.

Someday in the not-too-distant future, when I listen to an earthling step out onto the surface of Mars or some other planet, just as I listened to Neil step out onto the surface of the Moon, I hope I hear him say: "I come from the United States of America."

Mr. ARMSTRONG. We landed on the Sea of Tranquillity, in the cool of the early lunar morning, when the long shadows would aid our perception.

The sun was only 10° above the horizon. While the earth turned through nearly a full day during our stay, the sun at Tranquillity Base rose barely 11°—a small fraction of the month-long lunar day. There was a peculiar sensation of the duality of time—the swift rush of events that characterizes all our lives—and the ponderous parade which marks the aging of the universe.

Both kinds of time were evident—the first by the routine events of the flight, whose planning and execution were detailed to fractions of a second—the latter by rocks around us, unchanged throughout the history of man—whose 3-billion-year-old secrets made them the treasure we sought.

The plaque on the Eagle which summarized our hopes bears this message:

Here men from the planet earth first set foot upon the moon July 1969 A.D.

We came in peace for all mankind. Those nineteen hundred and sixty-nine years had constituted the majority of the ages of Pisces, a 12th of the great year. That is measured by the thousand generations the precession of the earth's axis requires to scribe a giant circle in the heavens.

In the next 20 centuries, the age of Aquarius of the great year, the age for which our young people have such high hopes, humanity may begin to understand its most baffling mystery—where are we going?

The earth is, in fact, traveling many thousands of miles per hour in the direction of the constellation Hercules—to some unknown destination in the cosmos. Man must understand his universe in order to understand his destiny.

Mystery however is a very necessary ingredient in our lives. Mystery creates wonder and wonder is the basis for man's desire to understand. Who knows what mysteries will be solved in our lifetime, and what new riddles will become the challenge of the new generations?

Science has not mastered prophesy. We predict too much for next year yet far too little for the next 10. Responding to challenge is one of democracy's great strengths. Our successes in space lead us to hope that this strength can be used in the next decade in the solution of many of our planet's problems. Several weeks ago I enjoyed the warmth of reflection on the true meanings of the spirit of Apollo.

I stood in the highlands of this Nation, near the Continental Divide, introducing to my sons the wonders of nature, and pleasures of looking for deer and for elk.

In their enthusiasm for the view they frequently stumbled on the rocky trails, but when they looked only to their footing, they did not see the elk. To those of you who have advocated looking high we owe our sincere gratitude, for you have granted us the opportunity to see some of the grandest views of the Creator.

To those of you who have been our honest critics, we also thank, for you have reminded us that we dare not forget to watch the trail. We carried on Apollo 11 two flags of this Union that had flown over the Capitol, one over the House of Representatives, one over the Senate. It is our privilege to return them now in these Halls which exemplify man's highest purpose—to serve one's fellow man.

We thank you, on behalf of all the men of Apollo, for giving us the privilege of joining you in serving—for all mankind.

[Applause, the Members rising.]

(Thereupon, the flags were presented to the Speaker and to the Vice President.)

The last document in this chapter reminds us of one final remarkable event of the 1960s. While the sports world enjoyed its moments of controversy, in general, sports acted as an agent of continuity and consensus, knitting its consumers together into a common culture, one that celebrated teamwork and individual potential, two quintessentially traditional values. Moreover, sports took on a certain rhythm, with each season raising hopes of a championship and diverting attention away from divisive political, social, and cultural issues. Born in the early 1960s, the New York Mets were arguably the worst team ever. Nonetheless, they won the admiration of millions of New Yorkers, young and old, who were starved for a team following the departure of the Brooklyn Dodgers and the New York Giants to California. Indeed, as the 1969 season heated up, both political radicals and conservatives, long-haired protesters and blue-collar construction workers, dreamed the impossible, that the Mets could win the World Series. On the verge of splintering into several rival revolutionary factions, some SDSers even broke out with the chant "Let's Go Mets." Document 8.8, from George Vecsey's Joy in Mudville, *captures the glory of the Mets' moment of victory.*

Document 8.8 George Vecsey, *Joy in Mudville* (New York: McCall Publishing Company, 1970), p. 3.

They spilled over the barricades like extras in a Genghis Khan movie, all hot-eyed and eager for plunder. The Mets had just won the 1969 World Series, and the fans wanted to take home a talisman piece of Shea Stadium, to secure good fortune for the rest of their lives.

For half an hour they sacked the stadium, clawing at home plate with their fingernails, ripping out great chunks of sod for souvenirs, ransacking the swivel chairs from the box seats. Others pranced merrily over the infield, waving their forefingers in the air, performing for the television cameras, chanting "one-one-one" like some mystical incantation. There always had been something mystical about Met Fans, the way they kept the faith.

The New York Mets had justifiably been called the Worst Team in the History of Baseball. In their first seven lean years, they had won 394 games and lost 737 for a staggeringly poor percentage of .348. They had finished a total of 288½ games out of first place in those seven years.

The Mets were absolutely awful. They didn't try to be. They just were. Anybody can fumble a grounder or give up a long home run, but the Mets were champions at it. They had a first baseman named Marvelous Marv Throneberry, who chased runners to the wrong base when he was in the field and forgot to touch the bases when he was running them. They had a pitcher who gave up a home run on his first pitch as a Met. Most Met pitchers waited at least until their second or third pitch.

Fortunately, there were people who saw the Mets in perspective, right from that dreadful start. Casey Stengel, the manager, used to laugh "It's a joke" when the Mets blew another game. A new breed of New York fans were just plain happy to have a National League team again and would have flipped their wigs for just a Little League team—which, in effect, they did. And a sensitive band of sportswriters sensed this spirit of the people that was more important than winning or losing.

The fans endured the losing for seven years and were prepared for another hundred years of it. New York was getting used to losing. The city had been evacuated by too much of its middle class; it was barren in finances and in spirit. Its mayor was running for reelection as an underdog against two "law and order" candidates. It was a city that badly needed bread and circuses— maybe even a miracle.

Now on October 17, the miracle happened. The Mets had stormed through an unbelievable season to capture the World Series, and the people were piling into the street to celebrate. Tons of paper were streaming out of office windows. People were dancing in the streets, holding hands with strangers, reaching back to their childhood for ways to express their joy.

Over on the East Side, the pastor of St. Agnes Church told his curate to ring the bell in honor of this most secular occasion. It was like the closing minutes of some old Bing Crosby movie, the kind of ending that had become impossible in our world of war and ghettoes.

Yet for a few brief weeks in 1969, the Mets reminded people of love and hope, sentiments that were neither very stylish nor realistic in 1969. If the Mets could win the World Series, people said, anything was possible. It was a joke, sure. But perhaps the Mets' victory had been planned for a long time, maybe for a million years, just so in this one crazy season they could send us all out into the streets, to hold hands and dance in a circle.

Chapter Nine

LOOKING BACKWARD

This chapter contains reminiscences from well-known political activists, scholars, and ordinary Americans, selections from the Internet, and speeches from the floor of Congress. Altogether, they offer a sense of the ongoing debate over the meaning and legacy of the 1960s. Was it the worst or best of times? Is America better off today because of the sixties, or did today's problems take root during the decade? In **Documents 9.1** *and* **9.2,** *Tom Hayden and Peter Collier and David Horowitz advance vastly different answers to these questions. Hayden, in* **Document 9.1,** *from his memoir* Reunion, *champions the 1960s as a time of idealism and historical progress. In contrast, in* **Document 9.2,** *Peter Collier and David Horowitz, former editors of* Ramparts, *renounce the sixties and call upon their former colleagues to do likewise.*

Document 9.1 Tom Hayden, "Epilogue," in *Reunion* (New York: Random House, 1988), pp. 501–507.

Looking back from life's mid-passage, what did the generation of the sixties achieve? What does it mean today?

By the most measurable standards, we accomplished more than we expected, more than most generations ever accomplish. Consider the most obvious:

- Students led the civil rights movement, which destroyed a century-old segregation system and which politically enfranchised twenty million blacks.
- Students were the backbone of the antiwar movement, which forced our government to abandon its policies in Vietnam and the nation to reconsider the Cold War.

- Because of student criticism, most universities retreated from their traditional paternalism toward an acceptance of active student participation in decision making.

- Movement activists were the key factor in making Lyndon Johnson withdraw from the presidency in 1968 and in transforming the political rules that permitted reformers to prevail in the Democratic party, which then endorsed "participatory democracy" in its 1972 platform.

- The same movement was conceded the eighteen-year-old vote by the 1970s.

- These movements were direct catalysts for the reemergence of the women's movement, the birth of environmentalism, and other diverse causes.

In short, we opened up closed systems. From Georgia and Mississippi to the South as a whole, from Newark and Chicago to the cities of the North, from the 1965 Vietnam teach-ins to the 1973 War Powers Act, from the Democratic convention of 1968 to that of 1972, there was a steady evolution from patterns of exclusion toward greater citizen participation in basic decisions.

More generally, the New Left fostered a vision that gradually took hold throughout much of society. At the center of that vision was a moral view of human beings, "ordinary people" in the process of history, a view which held that systems should be designed for human beings and not the other way around. The dignity of the individual in this perspective could only be realized through active citizenship. That in turn required a society of citizens, or a democracy of participation, where individuals had a direct voice in the making of decisions about their own lives. We were expressing a rising dissatisfaction with all institutions, even liberal and expressly humane ones, that absorbed power into their hierarchies. Instead of "taking power," we imagined creating the new power out of the raw material of apathy. At the same time, new measurements of excellence, such as the quality of life and personal relationships, were to take on greater significance than external status symbols and material monuments, in both our lives and the existence of our country.

These perceptions and values are an ongoing legacy of our generation. They do not always prevail in our culture or politics today, nor are they always recognized as arising from the sixties. Yet their enduring and widening impact can be seen in a variety of ways. Enlightened business and labor viewpoints now concur that humane treatment of the worker, including participation in decision making, is not only an ethical good, but a plus for productivity as well. More broadly, the survey researcher Daniel Yankelovich, in his book, *New Rules* concluded that

the campus upheavals of the sixties gave us the first premonitory sign that the plates of American culture, after decades of stability, had begun to shift. ... Then in the seventies the public as a whole began to experience them and the mass reappraisal of American life values was launched.

The Yankelovich study concluded that the mainstream American goal is "to build a more productive economy and at the same time a society in which the cravings of the spirit as well as material well-being can be satisfied."

These findings were also reflected in an extraordinary work of social science, *Habits of the Heart*, published by a UC Berkeley team of researchers in 1985. One of their purposes was to review and revive the nineteenth-century French writer, Alexis de Toqueville [*sic*], whose observations in *Democracy in America* in some ways foreshadowed the theme of participatory democracy. De Toqueville celebrated the town meetings and voluntary associations that constituted the rich political core of early nineteenth-century American society and warned of the dangers of rampant individualism, under which participation could atrophy and be replaced by imperial forms of rule. The authors of *Habits of the Heart*, responding to the resurgent individualism of the religious right of the eighties, cited local chapters of the Campaign for Economic Democracy among the many representative efforts at restoring an emphasis on democracy at the community level, noting that "the morally concerned social movement, informed by republican and biblical sentiments, has stood us in good stead in the past and may still do so again."

These conclusions and many others like them represent nothing less than the maturing of the awkward formulations of *The Port Huron Statement* into the cultural vocabulary of the mainstream of American life.

The logical question then is why the New Left did not succeed in building an organized and permanent leftist presence on the American political spectrum? Why did we produce so few political leaders? Why did we, who were so able to shake existing institutions, leave so little behind? Part of me inclines to the view of the New Left's better administrative leaders, like Paul Booth and Richie Rothstein, that our profound distrust of leadership and structure doomed us to failure on the level of political organization.

But the American political system is inhospitable to third parties, isolating them before gradually absorbing their ideas and activists into the two-party system. The most that could have been organized out of the New Left might have been an "adult" SDS, a kind of American Civil Liberties Union for social justice. Of course, without the Kennedy assassinations the history of our generation would have been different, and I believe most of the New Left would have found itself politically involved as part of a new governing coalition by the end of the sixties, just as Millie Jeffrey's generation became linked with the politics of the New Deal. But it was not to be. Instead, in Jack Newfield's summary phrase, we became "might have beens." . . .

There are such strong feelings of nostalgia on the one hand and loss on the other among so many who went through those times because the sixties were about more than practical reforms. It was a decade not focused simply on specific goals, like the organization of American workers in the thirties or the issue agendas of the Populist and Socialist parties at the century's beginning. The goal of the sixties was a larger transformation. Perhaps the only parallels might have been during the times of the American Revolution and Civil War, when individuals became caught up in remaking America itself. The goal of the sixties was, in a sense, the completion of the vision of the early revolutionaries and the abolitionists, for Tom Paine and Frederick Douglass wanted even more than the Bill of Rights or Emancipation Proclamation. True democrats, they wanted the fulfillment of the American promise through a different quality of relations between people, between government and governed, a participatory democracy within a genuinely human community. The sixties movements were inspired toward that loftier goal and were blocked in the quest by the intervention of fate.

Like the American revolutionary period, the awakening of the early sixties was a unique ingathering of young people—many of them potential leaders— to proclaim and then try to carry out a total redemptive vision. This visionary quest is what bound each of us together in a community, from Gandhian Freedom Riders to disillusioned Marxists. The gods of our parents had failed or become idols. Then a new spiritual force came in 1960, to move in the world. We felt ourselves to be the prophets of that force. When we first used the term *revolution*, it was not about overthrowing power but about overcoming hypocrisy, through a faithfulness to a democratic and spiritual heritage. Then came rejection and both physical and spiritual martyrdom, and later a discovery that we ourselves were not pure. We faltered, lost our way, became disoriented above all by death upon death. What began on a soaring spirit suddenly was over, perhaps to be finished permanently. We who claimed to be masters of our future discovered that we were not.

The sacrifices were many, and there were no distinguished service medals. In writing this book, I found it revealing that there is nowhere a factual summary of all the suffering that people went through—shootings, beatings, firings, expulsions, arrests, not to mention psychological pain—to achieve quite elementary goals in the sixties decade. It is as if the sacrifices were not worthy of record, but should be suppressed and forgotten. With the help of Eric Dey, a UCLA graduate student, I developed a minimal estimate of our untabulated sacrifices:

- During the southern civil rights movement (1960–68), at least 28 activists were killed, and 31,000 people were arrested. There is no calculating the numbers who were beaten, fired, or expelled from schools.
- In the black civil disorders of 1965–70, 188 people were killed, at least 7,612 were injured, and another 52,920 were arrested.
- In the campus and antiwar protests of 1965–71, for which data are woefully unrecorded, at least 14 were killed, thousands were injured or expelled from colleges, and at least 26,358 were arrested.
- It therefore would be safe to estimate that in a society priding itself on its openness, 100,000 arrests of protestors occurred in the decade of the sixties. They were prophets without honor in their time.

For all these reasons, the sixties leave a sense of troubling incompleteness and shortcoming alongside that of proud achievement. But if the time has remained difficult to capture, it is also possible that the sixties are not over. The decade itself was perhaps only the beginning of a time of vast change that is not yet fulfilled. Our generation, after all, has only lived into its middle years. Why conclude that life's most powerful moments already are behind us? If the sixties are not over, it is up to the sixties generation to continue trying to heal our wounds, find our truth, and apply our ideals with a new maturity to our nation's future.

Since 1980, however, the official mood of the nation has been contrary to a spirit of reconciliation. Rather, the tone has been one of escape from bitter realities toward an immortalizing vision of nostalgia proposed by President Reagan. There has been a strong pressure to wipe out the "Vietnam syndrome," which allegedly left us prostrate before our enemies. Thanks to greater military spending, we are told that America is "back," is "standing tall," that the "naysayers" have been vanquished. I find this stance to be an armed reminder of the most rigid view of my parents' generation when they wanted to impose the lessons of their experience on their children and grandchildren. But my personal experience gives me faith that this official obsession with restoring a mythic past will give way to wiser consciousness in the era ahead:

- An emerging generation of voters—about eighty million born since 1945—will seek newer philosophies than those which led to constant government scandal these past two decades.

- Those who experienced the inner reality of Vietnam—from the end of police clubs or in jungle darkness—will unite around a more mature foreign policy, based on the strength of democracy.

- Americans will increasingly look to human merits, rather than color, class, or gender, in choosing those who represent them, even for the presidency.

- The quality of life will replace the quantity of possessions as Americans' standard of excellence in our lifetime.

- A new generation of entrepreneurs will come to learn that human and natural resources require cultivation rather than depletion.

- Democracy and human rights will grow more powerfully contagious in a world linked by satellites and television.

- The assassinations of the sixties left a bleeding and broken connection in our personal lives and political culture; that connection must and will be restored by a new cycle of leadership.

Times filled with tragedy are also times of greatness and wonder, times that really matter, and times truly worth living through. Whatever the future holds, and as satisfying as my life is today, I miss the sixties and always will.

Document 9.2   Peter Collier and David Horowitz, "Lefties for Reagan" (1985), in *Major Problems in American History Since 1945: Documents and Essays,* ed. Robert Griffith (Lexington: D.C. Heath, 1992), pp. 467–474.

When we tell our old radical friends that we voted for Ronald Reagan last November, the response is usually one of annoyed incredulity. After making sure that we are not putting them on, our old friends make nervous jokes about Jerry Falwell and Phyllis Schlafly, about gods that have failed, about ageing yuppies ascending to consumer heaven in their BMWs. We remind them of an old adage: "Anyone under 40 who isn't a socialist has no heart—anyone over 40 who is a socialist has no brain."

Inevitably the talk becomes bitter. One old comrade, after a tirade in which she had denounced us as reactionaries and crypto-fascists, finally sputtered, "And the worst thing is that you've turned your back on the *Sixties!*" That was exactly right: casting our ballots for Ronald Reagan was indeed a way of finally saying goodbye to all that—to the self-aggrandising romance with corrupt Third Worldism; to the casual indulgence of Soviet totalitarianism; to the hypocritical and self-dramatising anti-Americanism which is the New Left's bequest to mainstream politics.

The instruments of popular culture may perhaps be forgiven for continuing to portray the '60s as a time of infectious idealism, but those of us who were active then have no excuse for abetting this banality. If in some ways it was the best of times, it was also the worst of times, an era of bloodthirsty fantasies as well as spiritual ones. We ourselves experienced both aspects, starting as civil-rights and anti-war activists and ending as co-editors of the New Left magazine *Ramparts.* The magazine post allowed us to write about the rough beast slouching through America and also to urge it on through non-editorial activities we thought of as clandestine until we later read about them in the FBI and CIA files we both accumulated.

Like other radicals in those early days, we were against electoral politics, regarding voting as one of those charades used by the ruling class to legitimate its power. We were even more against Reagan, then governor of California, having been roughed up by his troopers during the People's Park demonstrations in Berkeley and tear-gassed by his National Guard helicopters during the University of California's Third World Liberation Front Strike.

But neither elections nor elected officials seemed particularly important compared with the auguries of Revolution the Left saw everywhere by the end of the decade—in the way the nefarious Richard Nixon was widening the war in Indo-China; in the unprovoked attacks by paramilitary police against the Black Panther Party; in the formation of the "Weather Underground", a group willing to pick up the gun or the bomb. It was a time when the apocalypse struggling to be born seemed to need only the slightest assist from the radical midwife.

When we were in the voting booth this past November (in different precincts but of the same mind) we both thought back to the day in 1969 when Tom Hayden came by the office and, after getting a *Ramparts* donation to buy gas masks and other combat issue for Black Panther "guerrillas," announced portentously:

"Fascism is here, and we're all going to be in jail by the end of the year."

We agreed wholeheartedly with this apocalyptic vision and in fact had just written in an editorial:

"The system cannot be revitalised. It must be overthrown. As humanly as possible, but by any means necessary."

Every thought and perception in those days was filtered through the dark and distorting glass of the Viet Nam war.

The Left was hooked on Viet Nam. It was an addictive drug whose rush was a potent mix of melodrama, self-importance, and moral rectitude. Viet Nam was a universal solvent—the explanation for every evil we saw and the justification for every excess we committed. Trashing the windows of merchants on the main streets of America seemed warranted by the notion that these petty-bourgeois shopkeepers were cogs in the system of capitalist exploitation that was obliterating Viet Nam. Fantasising the death of local cops seemed warranted by the role they played as an occupying army in America's black ghettos, those mini-Viet Nams we yearned to see explode in domestic wars of liberation. Viet Nam caused us to acquire a new appreciation for foreign tyrants like Kim Il Sung of North Korea. Viet Nam also caused us to support the domestic extortionism and violence of groups like the Black Panthers, and to dismiss derisively Martin Luther King, Jr. as an "Uncle Tom." (The Left has conveniently forgotten this fact now that it finds it expedient to invoke King's name and reputation to further its domestic politics.)

How naive the New Left was can be debated, but by the end of the '60s we were not political novices. We knew that bad news from Southeast Asia—the reports of bogged-down campaigns and the weekly body counts announced by Walter Cronkite—was good for the radical agenda. The more repressive our government in dealing with dissent at home, the more recruits for our cause and the sooner the appearance of the revolutionary Armageddon.

Our assumption that Viet Nam would be the political and moral fulcrum by which we would tip this country toward revolution foresaw every possibility except one: that the United States would pull out. Never had we thought that the US, the arch-imperial power, would of its own volition withdraw from Indo-China. This development violated a primary article of our hand-me-down Marxism: that political action through normal channels could not alter the course of the war. The system we had wanted to overthrow worked tardily and only at great cost, but it worked.

When American troops finally came home, some of us took the occasion to begin a long and painful re-examination of our political assumptions and beliefs. Others did not. For the diehards, there was a post–Viet Nam syndrome in its own way as debilitating as that suffered by people who had fought there—a sense of emptiness rather than exhilaration, a paradoxical desire to hold on to and breathe life back into the experience that had been their high for so many years.

As the post–Viet Nam decade progressed, the diehards on the left ignored conclusions about the viability of democratic traditions that might have been drawn from America's exit from Viet Nam and from the Watergate crisis that followed it, a time when the man whose ambitions they had feared most was removed from office by the Constitution rather than by a coup. The only "lessons" of Viet Nam the Left seemed interested in were those that emphasised the danger of American power abroad and the need to diminish it, a view that was injected into the Democratic party with the triumph of the McGovernite wing. The problem with this use of Viet Nam as a moral text for American policy, however, was that the pages following the fall of Saigon had been whited out. . . .

Perhaps the leading feature of the Left today is the moral selectivity that French social critic Jean-François Revel has identified as "the syndrome of the cross-eyed Left."

Leftists can describe Viet Nam's conquest and colonialisation of Cambodia as a "rescue mission," while reviling Ronald Reagan for applying the same term to the Grenada operation, although better than 90% of the island's population told independent pollsters they were grateful for the arrival of US troops. Forgetting for a moment that Afghanistan is "Russia's Viet Nam," Leftists call Grenada "America's Afghanistan," although people in Afghanistan (as one member of the resistance there told us) would literally die for the elections held in Grenada.

The Left's memory can be as selective as its morality. When it comes to past commitments that have failed, the Leftist mentality is utterly unable to produce a coherent balance sheet, let alone a profit-and-loss statement. The attitude toward Soviet penetration of the Americas is a good example. Current enthusiasm for the Sandinista régime in Nicaragua should recall to those of us old enough to remember a previous enthusiasm for Cuba 25 years ago. Many of us began our "New Leftism" with the "Fair Play for Cuba" demonstrations. We raised our voices and chanted, *"Cuba Si! Yanqui No!"* We embraced Fidel Castro not only because of the flamboyant personal style of the *barbudos* of his 26th of July Movement but also because Castro assured the world that his revolution belonged to neither Communists nor capitalists, that it was neither red nor black, but Cuban olive-green.

We attributed Castro's expanding links with Moscow to the US-sponsored invasion of the Bay of Pigs, and then to the "secret war" waged against Cuba by US intelligence and paramilitary organisations. But while Castro's apologists in the United States may find it expedient to maintain these fictions, Carlos Franqui and other old Fidelistas now in exile have made it clear that Castro embraced the Soviets even before the US hostility became decisive, and that he steered his country into an alliance with the Soviets with considerable enthusiasm. Before the Bay of Pigs he put a Soviet general in charge of Cuban forces. Before the Bay of Pigs he destroyed Cuba's democratic trade-union movement, although its elected leadership was drawn from his own 26th of July Movement. He did so because he knew that the Stalinists of Cuba's Communist Party would be dependable cheerleaders and efficient policemen of his emerging dictatorship. . . .

Adherents of today's version of radical chic may never take seriously the words of Sandinista directorate member Bayardo Arce when he says that elections are a "hindrance" to the goal of "a dictatorship of the proletariat" and necessary only "as an expedient to deprive our enemies of an argument." They will ignore former Sandinista hero and now Contra leader Eden Pastora, who sees the Junta as traitors who have sold out the revolutionary dream. ("Now that we are occupied by foreign forces from Cuba and Russia, now that we are governed by a dictatorial government of nine men, now more than ever the Sandinista struggle is justified.") They will ignore opposition leader Arturo Cruz, an early supporter of the Sandinista revolution and previously critical of the Contras, when the worsening situation makes him change his mind and ask the Reagan administration to support them in a statement that should have the same weight as Andrei Sakharov's plea to the West to match the Soviet arms build-up.

American Leftists propose solutions for the people of Central America that they wouldn't dare propose for themselves. These armchair revolutionaries project their self-hatred and their contempt for the privileges of democracy—which allow them to live well and to think badly—on to people who would be only too grateful for the luxuries they disdain. Dismissing "bourgeois" rights as a decadent frill that the peoples of the Third World can't afford, Leftists spread-eagle the Central Americans between the dictators of the Right and the dictators of the Left. The latter, of course, are their chosen instruments for bringing social justice and economic well-being, although no Leftist revolution has yet provided impressive returns on either of these qualities and most have made the lives of their people considerably more wretched than they were before.

Voting is symbolic behaviour, a way of evaluating what one's country has been as well as what it might become. We do not accept Reagan's policies chapter and verse (especially in domestic policy, which we haven't discussed here), but we agree with his vision of the world as a place increasingly inhospitable to democracy and increasingly dangerous for America.

One of the few saving graces of age is a deeper perspective on the passions of youth. Looking back on the Left's revolutionary enthusiasms of the last 25 years, we have painfully learned what should have been obvious all along: that we live in an imperfect world that is bettered only with great difficulty and easily made worse—much worse. This is a conservative assessment, but on the basis of half a lifetime's experience, it seems about right.

In **Document 9.3** *Cal Thomas, a syndicated conservative columnist, complements the argument put forth by Collier and Horowitz. Unlike Collier and Horowitz, Thomas was never a radical. Even during the 1960s he espoused conservative views. Thomas blames the sixties for nearly all of the social ills that currently plague America, from high crime and drug use to the breakdown of the family and the persistence of poverty. Thomas originally delivered this diatribe at Hillsdale College, a conservative institution in Michigan. His views are representative of arguments put forth by many others.*

Document 9.3   Cal Thomas, "The Sixties Are Dead: Long Live the Nineties," *Imprimis,* Vol. 24, no. 1 (January 1995), pp. 1–4.

If you slept through the sixties, you woke to a different America. It was the pivotal point of the recent past—an authentic decade of decision. It marked the beginning of a passionate social debate that still divides us. It changed ancient attitudes on matters both public and private. One sixties' radical with second thoughts, Peter Collier, has written, "The stones we threw into the waters of our world in those days caused ripples that continue to lap on our shores today— for better, and more often, for worse." No generation of Americans has ever heard more extravagant promises. Promises of revolution. Promises of utopia. Promises of ecstasy. Promises of justice. Here is a brief look at some of the other features of the sixties' ambitious agenda:

(1) *The promise to end poverty.* In 1962, President John F. Kennedy asked Congress for the creation of a "public welfare program" designed to "attack dependency, juvenile delinquency, family breakdown, illegitimacy, ill health, and disability." During the Great Society, these goals were expanded even further, and President Lyndon B. Johnson assured his fellow Americans, "The final conquest of poverty is within our grasp." This massive government effort led one wag to comment, "God is dead but fifty-thousand social workers have risen to take His place."

(2) *The promise of liberation from the traditional family.* In the 1960s, Betty Friedan mocked the life of a mother and homemaker as consisting of "comfortable, empty, purposeless days" lacking any possibility for a woman to "grow and realize one's full potential." Children and marriage were represented as the sworn enemy of self-fulfillment. Distrust and suspicion were returned by the young: "Don't trust anyone over thirty" were the passwords for entry into the counter-culture. Jim Morrison, lead singer for the brash new musical group, the "Doors," influenced millions of young fans by always referring to his parents as "dead" even though they were still alive.

(3) *The promise of sexual freedom.* In 1966. Masters and Johnson cast the blinding light of research into the "dark corners" of human sexuality. Every-

thing was measured, categorized, and revealed. Most Americans were surprised to learn what went on in suburban bedrooms—and kitchens and closets. The lesson drawn? It was less than profound: "Do your own thing." Meanwhile, the infamous Weathermen pursued their "smash monogamy" campaign. Many committed couples were harangued until they admitted their "political errors" and split apart. Marriage began to replace cohabitation as the unpardonable sin. The youth culture began to experiment with group sex and homosexuality out of a sense of political obligation, as well as a yearning to be trendy.

(4) *The promise of "pharmaceutical enlightenment."* Harvard University Professor Timothy Leary urged students in the *Psychedelic Reader* to "Tune in, turn on, drop out" as a surefire method to expand their mental horizons. Happiness and drug use became synonymous. And, of course, flouting the law and convention on the issue of drugs soon led to a general disrespect for all law and convention.

(5) *The promise of progressive education.* On the sixties-style open campus, students were delighted to find more and more courses without assignments, lectures, or grades. Universities began to abandon their most basic mission of providing liberal arts undergraduate education. As sociologist Robert Nisbet explains, "The ideologies which gained entry into the academy in the sixties claimed that the fundamental intellectual principles of Western culture were illegitimate and must be overthrown. With that destroyed, terms like *truth, good, evil,* and *soul* could be discarded."

(6) *The promise of unrestrained expression.* "Little Richard's First Law of Youth Culture," named after a then-popular singer, set the agenda: Please kids by shocking their parents. Beyond popular culture, even "high culture" led by prestigious artistic figures threw off all convention in an effort to redefine the medium and in so doing opened the floodgates of nihilism and perversion in the name of "art."

(7) *The promise of God's death.* Radical activists and even once-conventional theologians sponsored an escape from traditional religion and morality in an attempt to create "new values" for a new generation. Some merely wanted to make the church seem "hip" and relevant; some desired to tear it down. Few demurred at all when Chicago Seven defendant and militant atheist Abbie Hoffman proclaimed, "God is dead, and we did it for the kids."

BROKEN PROMISES

The attack on authority was frontal and heavy. Jim Morrison spoke for many when he said, "I have always been attracted to ideas that were about revolt against authority. . . . I am interested in anything about revolt, disorder, chaos—especially activity that seems to have no meaning. It seems to me to be the road to freedom."

The mottoes of the time, charged with wild-eyed, unwashed intensity, tell the story of the sixties: "If you see something slipping, push." "Burn baby, burn."

Ideas like personal honor, gentlemanly conduct, loyalty, duty, obligation, and the sacred were all disowned. The past was demolished, like a decaying, outdated historical landmark, to make way for a chrome and glass future.

The decade of the sixties was judged, in its own time, by the height of its aspirations. Today, it can be judged by the depth of its influence. When the evidence is weighed, the verdict is irrefutable: We have lived through the unfolding history of its utter failure. Promises and illusions were shattered like glass. Americans are left to walk carefully among the jagged shards.

To fight poverty, the government has spent beyond the wildest dreams of avarice—let alone Franklin Roosevelt, John F. Kennedy, or Lyndon B. Johnson. For over three decades, we have conducted the greatest social experiment the world has ever seen with *$3.5 trillion* in government funds. Yet poverty is still on the increase, deeply rooted as it is in fragmented families, and welfare is still a trap that eventually destroys the soul.

Feminist disdain for the family and the sexual revolution have given millions of women the chance to realize their full potential—of abandonment and poverty, that is—and has "liberated" countless children from the affection and care of their parents. The results for children are particularly disturbing, because their suffering has been uninvited and undeserved. The Census Bureau estimates, for example, that only 39 percent of children born in 1988 will live with both parents until their 18th birthday.

Other surveys suggest that over 40 percent of all American children have no set goals, a limited education, and a sense of hopelessness about their lives. It is no wonder that psychologist Judith Wallerstein concludes that almost the same number enter "adulthood as worried, underachieving and sometimes angry young men and women." The doctrine of the dispensable two-parent family—so central to the sixties—turned out to be a lie. Those who embraced it have much to answer for; they have sacrificed too many children on the altar of their ideology.

Progressive education, designed to provide enlightenment, has generally left students entirely in the dark. At Vermont's Middlebury College, it is possible to take a class called "Popular Culture, Eroticism, Aesthetics, Voyeurism, and Misogyny in the Films of Brigitte Bardot." "Music Video 454," taught at California State University, uses the *Rolling Stone Book of Rock Video* as its only textbook and places students as extras in rock videos—for credit.

Is it any wonder that stories about the ignorance of college students have become clichés? Recently, a Harvard senior thanked his history professor for explaining World War I, saying, "I never knew why people kept talking about a *second* world war."

Those who once were keepers of the gateways of learning have little left to offer. Their fields have been impoverished by critical theories that reinterpret all knowledge in terms of political and economic power and exploitation. Since the sixties, college professors have taken up political causes as a profession, using the classroom to denounce falsehood and injustice while teaching that truth and justice are illusions. J. Allen Smith, the father of many modern education reforms, confessed: "The trouble with us reformers is that we have made reform a crusade against all standards. Well, we have smashed them all, and now neither we nor anyone else has anything left."

In regard to culture, theories that hate beauty and order have undermined meaning, value, and conscience. Whether it is popular culture or high culture, they have led to ever stranger sins and more startling obscenities. Each year requires more baroque perversions to provoke society's jaded capacity for outrage. The National Endowment for the Arts, official arbiter of the avant garde, illustrates the change. In 1989, the NEA denied a modest request from the New York Academy of Art to provide young painters with skills in drawing the human figure. Susan Lubowsky, director of the NEA's visual arts program, explained, "Teaching students to draw the human figure is revisionist . . . and stifles creativity."

Recently, the distinguished sculptor Frederick Hart, who created "Three Soldiers" at the Vietnam War Memorial, applied for a grant to do a series of sculptures. To his surprise, the endowment turned him down. "The NEA," he said, "told me I was not doing art." Yet the NEA paid $70,000 to fund a show featuring Shawn Eichman's "Alchemy Cabinet," displaying a jar with the fetal remains from the "artist's" own abortion. Around the same time, it authorized $20,000 for a project in Lewiston, New York that was "to create large, sexually explicit props covered with a generous layer of requisitioned Bibles."

On the front line of the drug war, the news is even more grim. Everyone has seen the effect of drugs on the young, who are seldom more than a handshake away from any drug they can afford. The permissive treatment of drugs has spawned a violent subculture of gangs, guns, and random terror. It has squandered lives, talent, and hope in every school and every community.

The escape from religion and the triumph of secularism have left many Americans isolated, confused, and alone. They are disconnected from traditional sources of meaning, value, and love like the family and the church. Sociologists call them "loose individuals" who are free from traditional restraints, obsessed with self-fulfillment, but uncertain of whether anything makes much difference. They are sentenced, in the words of one writer, to "the dark little dungeon of the ego." Novelist George MacDonald once put it another way: "The one principle of hell is, 'I am my own.' "

The ultimate result is a genuine social crisis—a crisis, if you will, of cultural authority. How can we make any moral judgments? How can we draw dividing lines between sane and insane, noble and base, beautiful and hideous? How can we know anything about living a good life? How can we cry for reform when "form" has no meaning? Peter Collier and another former sixties' radical activist, David Horowitz, conclude, "In the inchoate attack against authority, we have weakened our culture's immune system, making it vulnerable to opportunistic diseases. The origins of metaphorical epidemics of crime and drugs could be traced to the sixties, as could literal ones such as AIDS."

Where does this leave us? The promises of the decade of the sixties have been broken. Nearly every victory turned out to be a defeat. The revolution that was meant to solve every problem became *the* problem. If a cultural crimes trial were to be convened today, like the war crime trials of the past, the testimony of the victims would be damning. An abandoned child. An overdosed teenager. A trapped welfare mother. An ignorant student. A victim of venereal disease. Each could ask, "Where was *my* liberation?"

Document 9.4, *written by Philip J. Avillo, Jr., a professor of history at York College, offers a different spin on the era. Not only does he avoid the trap of seeing the sixties in black-and-white terms, he steers clear of one of the most prevalent clichés of the decade, namely, the dysfunctional Vietnam veteran. Instead, Avillo, who shipped over to Vietnam as a marine in 1964, offers a much more subtle insight into the times. For many baby boomers, the period of the sixties was a time of growing up, of coming of age. Regardless of their political views, their experiences shaped their personalities. Indeed, even though Avillo's courses and research emphasize the futility and immorality of the war, in this article he suggests that on a personal level the war was a time of individual growth. Perhaps the same was as true for those who actively opposed the war as for those who fought it.*

Document 9.4   Philip J. Avillo, Jr., "The Marines of '64," *Marine Corps Gazette* (November 1989), p. 62.

August 7, 1989 marked the 25th anniversary of the passage of the Gulf of Tonkin Resolution. President Lyndon Johnson offered the resolution in response to apparent attacks on U.S. naval vessels patrolling the Gulf of Tonkin and the Congress endorsed the document almost unanimously. The resolution empowered Johnson to employ whatever means necessary, including the use of force, to prevent further aggression in Southeast Asia. He did just that, interpreting the resolution as a "blank check" for waging war in Vietnam that cost the lives of more than 58,000 Americans, as many as 1.5 million Vietnamese, and plunged our country into nearly a decade of turmoil and anguish.

Not surprisingly, the Tonkin Gulf Resolution shaped dramatically the lives of many American servicemen. The January 1964 class at The Basic School, G-64, was one group of such men. Most of its members found themselves serving in Vietnam within the next year. Many returned with physical scars; a number died there.

I was a member of that class. When the class began, all of us were newly minted second lieutenants. The six-month course, conducted at Quantico, trained us in the art of command. Among other things, we studied and practiced small-unit infantry tactics, and we were introduced to guerrilla warfare. But we were peacetime Marines. While we may not have ignored completely our instructors' admonitions that Marines in 1950 learning these same lessons suddenly found themselves in Korea, few of us took them very seriously. No matter—we were well trained in spite of our youthful indifference, and when we arrived in Vietnam, we were prepared.

We were not prepared, however, for the opposition to the war, the protests and the demonstrations, which erupted almost immediately in the United States. Nevertheless, these seemed to have little impact on our morale or our performance. We were Marines; our country had sent us here; and what we were doing must be right. What we didn't know, or were only dimly aware of at best, was that many within the Government itself had reservations about that policy.

Two Senators, Democrats Wayne Morse of Oregon and Ernest Gruening of Alaska, criticized the policy from the start, casting the only two ballots against the Tonkin Gulf Resolution. J. W. Fulbright, the chairman of the Senate Foreign Relations Committee, and the man instrumental in steering the Tonkin Resolution through the Senate, developed similar misgivings as Johnson escalated the American military involvement in Vietnam during the early months of 1965. As the year drew to a close, Mike Mansfield, the Senate-majority leader, and four other senators prepared a gloomy report for the President. "The war in Vietnam is just beginning for the United States," Mansfield wrote, and "all the choices open to us are bad choices." Finally, he concluded, the United States "stood to lose far more at home and throughout the world by the more extensive military pursuit of an elusive objective in Vietnam."

The Marines of 1964 knew little of this during their tours in Vietnam. And what they did know was no doubt irrelevant information. Recently when over 50 of us from that class at The Basic School met in Washington and Quantico to commemorate our 25th anniversary, such information still seemed irrelevant. We didn't discuss the war in terms of justice or morality; we didn't criticize the conduct of the war, its tactics or strategy; we didn't condemn the country's leadership. Perhaps that is because even after 25 years we are unable collectively to confront these issues. Or perhaps our very presence at this reunion testified to our own personal resolution of the war's meaning within the context of our Nation's history.

Instead, we talked in terms of what the war and the Marines meant to us. For most of us, they provided the watershed of our lives. We developed in the Marines and in Vietnam in particular a camaraderie unmatched in civilian life. We possessed a common purpose, a selflessness seldom seen or understood in other walks of life. We realized that most of us have never experienced again the exhilaration and excitement of those days, days when as very young men we accepted responsibility for the lives of the 40 to 50 men under our command.

We recognized these truths then; we understand them more fully today. This is not to say that we were without flaws or that we have somehow managed to romanticize the war. Nor is it to diminish the great tragedy of the war in terms of American and Vietnamese lives. We all remembered vividly the mud, the muck, the smell of fear, the pain, and the suffering. Surely, none of us would wish such a war, or any war, for our own children. And yet, we all seemed to comprehend, consciously or unconsciously, this disturbing, paradoxical truth—

that because of the war, because of the pain, the suffering, and the anguish, we appreciate more profoundly the preciousness of life and have glimpsed more clearly its meaning.

Document 9.5 *contains excerpts from a 1983 congressional debate over a proposal to establish a national holiday in honor of Dr. Martin Luther King, Jr. The debate reflects the larger discussion over the meaning of the sixties. In addition to rehashing old accusations that King was a Communist, those who opposed paying tribute to King objected to elevating a symbol of protest and disorder. In contrast, many who favored establishing King's birthday as a national holiday downplayed his activism, emphasizing instead his peacefulness and vision of a color-blind society. They added that establishing a federal holiday in honor of King might provide a means to heal some of the wounds that had been opened during his lifetime. Whether King would want those wounds to be healed as long as racism continued to plague America is problematic.*

Document 9.5 "Congress Debates Designating Birthday of Martin Luther King, Jr., as a Legal Public Holiday," *Congressional Record,* 98th Congress, 1st Session, 129, part 112 (August 2, 1983), pp. 6235–6269.

Mrs. HALL of Indiana. Mr. Speaker, I yield myself such time as I may consume.

Mr. Speaker, H.R. 3345 designates the third Monday in January of each year a legal public holiday to commemorate the birthday of Dr. Martin Luther King, Jr., to take effect on the first January that occurs 2 years after enactment.

Martin Luther King gave to this great Nation a new understanding of equality and justice for all. He taught us that our democratic principles could be seriously impaired if they were not applied equally, and that tailoring these principles through nonviolence would have a lasting effect.

Mr. Speaker, the legislation before us will act as a national commitment to Dr. King's vision and determination for an ideal America, which he spoke of the night before his death, where equality will always prevail.

Next year marks the 20th anniversary of Dr. Martin Luther King's Nobel Peace Prize Award, where he was recognized by all people of the world for bringing about a peaceful social revolution which changed the hearts and minds of men and women everywhere.

Mr. Speaker, the time is before us to show what we believe, that justice and equality must continue to prevail, not only as individuals, but as the greatest Nation in this world. It is America's turn to say thank you to Dr. Martin Luther King, Jr., and it is our duty as elected Representatives to nationalize this tribute. . . .

Mr. DANNEMEYER. Mr. Speaker, I yield myself 5 minutes. . . .

We have nine holidays in this country. Three of them relate to recognition of persons—Washington's Birthday, Columbus Day and Christmas Day. These persons whom we recognize on these 3 days are, of course, noted in history. I question whether or not the contribution of Martin Luther King, Jr., is of equal stature to these three persons. . . .

It has been estimated that the cost of this to the taxpayers, Federal taxpayers, is $225 million in lost productivity in our Federal work force, per year. The private sector loss has been estimated at three times this amount....

Mr. MITCHELL. Mr. Speaker, I cannot really say what I want to say in 1 minute. It is impossible. I can just point out to you that when I was a young man I dreamed that the only way I could participate in this society was by being a revolutionist. I was absolutely convinced that the only way I would achieve equality in this Nation was by armed warfare. I was convinced of that because I was segregated in my schools, I had been segregated in the military, I had been segregated in my neighborhood.

When I was a young man I had absolute contempt for those older blacks who had been so brutalized and debased by this evil thing in this Nation that they were what we called Uncle Toms—stripped away of almost any sense of manhood, personhood, and womanhood.

And then came this man King, who somehow or another took that young militant and said to him: There is another way through nonviolence. He lifted a whole nation, a whole race of people. And more importantly than that, he took the tenets of the Judeo-Christian ethic and turned them into a weapon that changed the face of this Nation, and indeed the world.

What do you mean, "cost"? What was the cost of keeping us blacks where we were? All these extraneous things do not mean a thing to me. I am talking about what is the right and decent thing to do, and to urge a vote for this bill in the form that it is....

Mr. HOYER. Mr. Speaker, I rise in support of passage of this bill.

Mr. Speaker, 20 years ago this month, Dr. Martin Luther King, Jr., led over half a million people to the Nation's Capital to sound a joint declaration of protest: That America had defaulted on a promissory note to which all Americans were to have been heirs. That note contained the promise that all men and women would enjoy the riches of freedom and the security of justice.

But as he spoke the words which have become as integral a part of American history as the Great Lincoln and Douglas debates, Dr. King reminded us that for far too long, the benefits of liberty and opportunity—the basis of our democratic state—had been routinely denied to impoverished Americans, the overwhelming majority of whom were black.

Twenty years ago this month, Dr. Martin Luther King was able to pierce the veil of withering injustice and visualize a nation, his nation, where man's inhumanity to man would not flourish. As he shared with us his vision, he challenged each of us to make ours a world where "we will be able to work together, to pray together, to struggle together, to go to jail together, to stand up for freedom together, knowing that we will be free one day."

In challenging us to work toward greatness, Dr. King planted the seed whose progeny will endure as long as the struggle against injustice endures.

Tragically, we find that 20 years later the disparity between the haves and the have nots is even greater. Within our borders, poverty is more and more a condition suffered by women and minorities and families are feeling the oppression of an economic crisis unparalleled since the Great Depression.

There is much work to be done, and while the dreamer has been silenced by an assassin's bullet, 20 years later his words live on with new applications to new oppression. The challenge is for us now to act in a responsible manner to insure that Dr. King and his dream for his America—our America—are not forgotten. . . .

Mr. FAUNTROY. Mr. Speaker, it was Tchaikovsky who said of Marian Anderson: "A voice like this comes once in a hundred years." In the hearing room, where the Subcommittee on Census and Population marked up H.R. 3345 last month, there hang the pictures of two great Americans who were truly the men of their centuries. The first is that of George Washington, the founding father and first President of our great Republic. No one questions that he was indeed the man of the 18th century. The second is that of Abraham Lincoln. No one questions the fact that the valiant leadership of Abraham Lincoln as saving our Union made him the "Man of the 19th Century."

When the history of the 20th century is written, few will question the fact that Martin Luther King, Jr., was the singularly most important man, with the most important message for this, the most violent century in the history of mankind. That message was this: "We must either learn to live together as brothers or we are all going to perish together as fools."

That message and the life work of Dr. Martin Luther King, Jr., which shaped it, has made the name of Martin Luther King, Jr., a trigger to the deep longings of people in every corner of this globe, particularly those who have survived the savagery of war in Europe, in Asia, and on the continent of Africa. America honors herself when she honors this man of world renown with a legal holiday. . . .

Mr. McDONALD. Mr. Speaker, I rise in strong opposition to H.R. 3706, a bill designating the third Monday in January of each year a legal public holiday to commemorate the birthday of Martin Luther King, Jr.

At best, Martin Luther King, Jr.'s, prior associations and activities are questionable. This fact is reflected in the action taken by Attorney General Robert F. Kennedy, certainly one of the most liberal men to hold that high post, when he authorized wiretaps and other forms of surveillance of Martin Luther King, Jr. after the FBI developed evidence that King was associated with and being manipulated by Communists and secret Communist agents.

Consider the effusion from Political Affairs, official theoretical journal of the Communist Party, U.S.A., for May 1968, a month after King's assassination:

> The Reverend Martin Luther King, Jr., the voice, inspiration and symbol of the Negro people's struggle for freedom and equality, is dead. . . . The man who, more than anyone else, personified the heroic determination of the black people to win their liberation now. One of humanity's great leaders has been silenced forever. . . . We must see that his memory not be desecrated. We must not fail to do all in our power to realize the dream for which he died.

I would like to emphasize that this is not a quote from the Washington Post or the Atlanta Constitution but from an official publication of the Communist Party, U.S.A. . . .

At this point in the Record, I include the following:

[From the Congressional Record, Dec. 8, 1975]

THE KING FILE

(By Robert H. Reeder)

Senator Frank Church (D-Idaho) has turned the Senate Intelligence Committee into a vehicle for smearing the late F.B.I. Director J. Edgar Hoover. Hoover's private files show that he had become convinced that Martin Luther King was a person of low moral character who had fallen under the control of the Communists. Church claims to find this absurd. Attorney General Robert Kennedy, however, did not find it absurd in the least and authorized F.B.I. surveillance of King—including wiretaps, which were maintained between 1963 and 1966.

Those wiretaps and other evidence proved that Martin Luther King was indeed a person of low moral character who had fallen under the control of the Communists. But Senator Church has, like Richard Nixon, ducked the issue by refusing to release the damning tapes. And the "Liberal" press has cooperated by laboring to create the myth that Martin Luther King was an innocent victim of Director Hoover's bad temper. . . .

We do not know what information is in the substantial F.B.I. file on Dr. King but we do know that even the most cursory look at Martin Luther King's public record should convince the merest tyro that there was very good reason for Director Hoover to consider King "dangerous." . . .

If Martin Luther King was "sick and tired of people saying this movement has been infiltrated by Communists and Communist sympathizers," it was because he knew it was true.

And so did J. Edgar Hoover and the F.B.I. Director Hoover spoke out many times to warn of Communist involvement in the "civil rights" movement. On one occasion, he said: "We do know that Communist influence does exist in the Negro movement and it is this influence which is vitally important." Hoover declared that the Communist Party "strives only to exploit what are often legitimate Negro complaints and grievances for the advancement of Communist objectives. . . . Racial incidents are magnified and dramatized by Communists in an effort to generate racial tensions."

Mrs. Julia Brown is a brave and gracious Negro lady who spent more than nine years as a member of the Communist Party in Cleveland, serving as an undercover operative for the Federal Bureau of Investigation. According to Mrs. Brown:

". . . Mr. King was one of the worst enemies my people every [sic] had.

"I know that it is considered poor taste to speak ill of the dead. But when someone served the enemies of our country while alive, and his name is still used by his comrades to promote anti-American activities, shouldn't people who know the truth speak out?"

Mr. KEMP. Mr. Speaker, I appreciate that.

You know, a number of years ago I watched a fascinating documentary, interviewing refugees from Vietnam in refugee camps in Thailand. The network interviewer went up to an old woman of almost 90 years of age and asked, "What keeps you going? What are you hoping to do with your life?"

She said, "I dream of living in the United States of America."

She did not know America from the newspapers. She did not know America from being able to speak very good English. She just knew America from the standpoint of what America means as an idea as a dream. It was an idea and a dream that here was a place in which people were free to be all that God meant them to be. Here was a place in which all people were created equal and that the Government was instituted to help preserve those rights that were given to us, not by the Government, but by an inalienable source.

I just returned with my wife from the Soviet Union. They have beautiful documents about guaranteed rights in the Soviet Union, the right to emigrate, the right to join your family, the right to speak, the right to join a labor union; but unfortunately, the rights which are given to them by the Government are denied by the Government because those rights do not come from that inalienable source. That which the Government gives, it can take away and thus the Russian Revolution was flawed from the beginning.

The Martin Luther King holiday is not just a holiday for a civil rights leader. It is more importantly, as the gentleman from California pointed out, a holiday to commemorate that idea, that dream that all people have all over this country and indeed the world, to live in freedom, justice, dignity, to be able to know that those rights are guaranteed by Government through our Constitution but are given to us by God, that inalienable source.

I have changed my position on this vote because I really think that the American Revolution will not be complete until we commemorate the civil rights revolution and guarantee those basic declarations of human rights for all Americans and remove those barriers that stand in the way of people being what they were meant to be.

The gentleman from California suggested he changed his position and so did I because this is the time in which we must truly say that America is one nation, one people, one family, one country dedicated to rights not only for all Americans, but for all people everywhere. Ending social segregation through constitutional means is as important a contribution to this country and our American Revolution as holding the Union together.

I want to see my party stand for that. If we lose sight of the fact that the Republican Party was founded by Mr. Lincoln as a party of civil rights, of freedom, and hope and opportunity and dreams and a place where all people could be free. If we turn our backs we are not going to be the party of human dignity we want as Republicans to be known for.

I ask that we make this a unanimous vote today and vote for ourselves and for our country and for the future of our children by showing the world this Nation is still the land of opportunity and freedom.

This is a vote to help make the American dream a reality. . . .

The vote was taken by electronic device, and there were—yeas 338, nays 90, not voting 5. . . .

Documents 9.6 *and* **9.7** *are drawn from a new source for historians, the Internet. While the Internet is often touted as a remarkable intellectual tool replete with un-*

imaginable amounts of information, its utility for those doing primary research on historical subjects remains limited. Perhaps one way in which the Internet may prove quite fruitful, however, is as a source of memories of the past, especially of ordinary people who traditionally have left few written records. **Document 9.6** *contains remembrances posted on the homepage of Levittown, New York, on the occasion of its fiftieth anniversary. While the selections might seem more appropriate to our understanding of the 1950s than the 1960s, it should be remembered that Levittown, and thousands of suburban communities like it, served as the place of residence for millions of Americans throughout the postwar era, informing their sensibilities and, quite often, acting as a source of historical continuity as the sixties gave way to the 1970s, 1980s, and 1990s.*

Document 9.7, *similarly drawn from a homepage on the Internet, consists of recollections of one of the most famous events of the decade, the musical concert or happening called Woodstock. Woodstock, which took place in upstate New York in the summer of 1969, attracted close to half a million men and women who listened to an all-star cast of rock musicians, from Jimi Hendrix to Crosby, Stills, Nash, and Young. In addition to enjoying the music, those in attendance saw themselves as living or embodying the counterculture. Undoubtedly, Cal Thomas and Collier and Horowitz would perceive Woodstock as a prime example of the excesses of the decade and remind readers of the results of Altamont, a somewhat similar free concert organized by the rock group the Rolling Stones, where the motorcycle gang the Hells Angels, serving as security guards, beat to death, on stage, a young black man, to the dismay of bandleader Mick Jagger and many others.*

Document 9.6 "Levittown Memories," Levittown 50th Anniversary Web Page, http://www.infosource.com/Levittown.

Senior Citizen Prom Invitation Poem
Written by Candyce Nathanson-Goldstein

Note: The Senior Citizen Prom for senior citizen residents residing in the Levittown school district will be held on Friday, May 2nd at Salk Middle School celebrating Levittown's 50th anniversary. Look for an invitation in the mail and respond.

On seven miles of Hempstead Plains
Some fifty years ago
A new idea came bursting forth
Whose seeds would quickly grow.

Capes and Ranches filled the land
The suburbs gone mainstream
Mass produced, affordably priced
For all, the American Dream.

Veterans came with families
The elite were filled with scorn

But one by one the houses sold
And Levittown was born.

Prospering through these many years
We proved the critics wrong
Sharing in our Levittown pride
We're healthy, alive, and strong.

And so this year we honor all
The players in our cast
Looking to our future years
Remembering our past.

With this in mind we're sending you
A cordial invitation
To join us at your special prom
The Senior Citizens' Celebration.

Levittown marks 50 years as the 'American Dream'
Written by Joann Beattie

This past year, as the baby boomers start to turn 50, so does the town that is synonymous with suburbia, mass-produced housing and veterans—Levittown.

After World War II, the returning veterans came home to a tremendous housing shortage. Addressing this dilemma, in 1947, Abraham Levitt and Sons started to construct Cape Cod (later on, Ranch) style homes using mass production techniques. Within four years, Levitt and Sons built 17,447 houses on seven miles of former potato farms in Hempstead Plains, east of New York City. After the first year, VA mortgages were made available. Veterans were now able to purchase a Levitt home of their very own with no money down. According to veterans and their families, living in Levittown allowed them to live the "American Dream."

Having spoken with some original homemakers, I was grateful for their touching accounts of the beginning of Levittown:

"I was a city gal who never dreamed she would leave Manhattan for a real house in the country," said one woman. "We lived with my father-in-law in his apartment because we could not find an apartment anywhere. An ad in the paper told how veterans only needed $100 deposit down for a Levitt house. The day of the closing we took a cab from the train station to the North Village Green. We even got our $100 back. Afterwards, we attempted to walk to our new home, but no street signs were up yet. The milkman took pity on us and drove us to our new Levitt home. Our families all lived in apartments, they could not believe we owned our own home. It was actually cheaper to buy a Levitt home ($58 per month) than rent an apartment."

"After World War II, I finished college on the GI Bill," said another pioneer. "I accepted a job at Sperry's as an electrical engineer and bought a new 1950 Levitt Ranch home. Each house had GE appliances, a Bendix washer and its own big 12-inch Admiral television set. Wow, this was a real selling feature, especially for me and my wife. To be able to move into a new home with all these new luxury items for no money down was unbelievable.''

"Coming to the states was difficult for me," said one English woman who married a G.I. and settled with her new husband in New York. "The G.I.'s returned home first, the U.S. government paid for all the brides to come over on ship. There was no housing anywhere for all the returning veterans and their families. People were living in in-law's unfinished attics, garages, basements and summer bungalows. Levitt's houses were a blessing! We applied for a rental cape code [*sic*] house in 1947 and moved in January 1948. It sounds silly but it was like going into a palace at that time.''

Living the "American Dream" was what Levittown symbolized. Come share your dreams, memories and help us celebrate Levittown's 50th anniversary by attending our year-long celebrations.

Document 9.7   "Woodstock Memories," Guestbook, Woodstock Home Page, http://www.woodstock69.com.

I was there. I most remember waking up in the morning to Grace Slick (Jefferson Airplane) saying "good morning, its a new day . . ." and launching into song as the sun came up. I remember bumping into friends, which seemed so cosmic in all those thousands of people to actually run into someone you knew. It is an experience I cherish. A turning point in my life, and I enjoy telling my kids about it! I know it was a wonderful spiritual and musical experience that will never be duplicated. Peace, Love and Music. . . .
Diana Thompson Vincelli

Woodstock was a time of social changes in human freedom and expression . . . we learned not to be ashamed of our bodies in the nude, we smoked grass to expand our horizons with the music, we spent time with our kids our pets . . . it was very much focused on a new standard for families . . . the music of the late 60's that appeared in Woodstock 69 was some of the best around, very expressive of its thoughts and messages . . . indeed an experiment . . . but one that worked! That festival set the standard for peace, music, people and expression and showed to the world that all was not just violence and hatred . . . it was LIFE!!
Juan C. Morales

Hi everyone, I was at Woodstock and I'm still alive! I flew out from San Francisco with my 6-month old daughter, Tuesday Jones. My husband, Ron Jones, had been traveling with the festival route that left San Francisco. It all perpetuated around music bookings. Ron had been working on the road crew for several of the music groups and selling hippie candles our friends at The House of the Seventh Angel had made in Nevada City in the California foothills (a group from the Haight who had a candle factory/retreat). The booth cost us

$200, which was a lot of money those days, considering the candles were only $1.00/set—nice drippy ones with the smell of pachoulie, raspberry, frangipani and musk. But Ron was industrious and sold t-shirts and other assundy [*sic*] items as well. His main interest was protesting the Vietnam War. He was an outspoken revolutionary figure and wrote several articles for underground newspapers and hung around with the underground news writers and Black Panthers that ultimately were responsible for "ending the war" in Vietnam. It wasn't the politicians who stopped that war—it was "THE PEOPLE." WE did it! We stood up to the government and risked imprisonment in the name of justice and freedom (just as the revolutionaries and students in Tieniman [*sic*] Square, Beijing did). And the time may come soon when we will be faced with standing up the [*sic*] this oppressive govenment [*sic*] as it continues on its path of ignorance the [*sic*] destruction. For you who have been inspired by the Woodstock Festival, continue looking at the real reason it took place and remember that YOU MAKE A DIFFERENCE when you stand up for your rights! WAR IS NOT THE ANSWER! Imbed it in your brainwaves. And the next time it is proposed, go to your nearest politician and find out what you can do to stop it! If Woodstock did anything for me, it gave me STRENGTH to state my beliefs.
Susan Harnisch-Jones

I was there. I ended the weekend walking away while Jimi played on Monday morning. I had lost my friends, ride, clothes, et al. When I got home two days later, I wasn't even wearing my own clothes. Wish I was older and straighter so I could remember more.
Todd Goodman

I was just tripping around the west coast, being sort of free, when I heard something about a gig back in N.Y. A year later, the movie came out and I realized I was part of something much bigger than myself, and my life changed. I don't think I was ever the same, and have always looked at life a little differently. To [*sic*] bad we can't go back.
Warren Roberts

Woodstock was not a concert. This was a coming together. What the Byrds called a Tribal Gathering. We came together in Bethel. Yes like Bethlehem, this was a meeting of the essence of the thing. The music was just the background music of our lives. We were doing what great men like our High Priest Timothy Leary had led us to do. "All I'm about is empowering individuals to explore with your friends the great wonders and mysteries of life" . . . Tim Leary.

Hippies were at that time visually, small groups of people. On the coasts the cops knew who they were. They would see a few, think it was a squashable problem, and leave us alone. Estimates were that there were about 150,000 hippies world wide. When 500,000 showed up at one place at one time. Exploring with friends the great wonders and mysteries of life. When they saw sympathetic hippies in the bedrooms of there [sic] own homes. They freaked. They sold the look to jocks, and watered the stock.

In hind site [sic] many people see Woodstock as a concert. The press tried to defuse our religious experience. They made people think that Hippies were a bunch of drug users. It was not true. That is not what it was all about. Not all true spiritual hippies did or do drugs.

The Woodstock movie glorified the music. This was the same music at a half a dozen similar concerts that summer. How could the music have had anything to do with it. Some people never even found the main stage. Without the hippies those groups would have been nothing. Nixon wiped the term LSD out of the press and movies for decades to come. The DEA attacked the peace loving Dead Heads. Why? Who had they harmed? There was something much greater that pulled us all together at Woodstock that day in August. Something unformed, only hinted at in Timothy Leary's original Psychedelic Prayers. Something Spiritual, unnamable, unseeable, metaorganic.

Many people dropped out, stopped wearing and eating decaying animals, began to respect our setting. This is not the responcs [sic] of people at a concert. These responses were predicted by Tim before Monterey. Why! What really happened here? How were you effected [sic]? How are you being effected [sic] now?
Dr. Jan Pitts

Among the first to arrive, we got to within yards of the fence with the van and the two VW Bugs. From that place we were privileged to float in a sea of musically charged energy, the nature of which can never again take place. A magical mystical tour of the third kind. . . . I never got a chance to use my tickets. I still have them. They are the only physical evidence I have . . . so it must have been real. Or was it? I still can't say for sure. I'm starting to remember things, a little at a time. . . .
Jeff Ayers

I was there in '69 and loved it. The most amazing thing is that I actually met some friends there who had arrived the night before. We had agreed ahead to meet at the main gate. Ha-Ha. What main gate? Anyway, when I got there I just happened to walk into one of the guys, strolling among 400,000 other people. I went back in '94 for the 25th reunion at Yasgur's Farm. It was just as spontaneous as the first one and equally fun and of course it rained. Peace!
Mark Friend

THE 1960s: A STATISTICAL PROFILE

Table I
The Economy

Year	GNP (1982 $s in billions)	Unemployment Rate (%)	Per Capita Income (1982 $s)	Avg. Hourly Earnings (1982 $s)	Real Annual Growth (%)
1950	1,203.7	5.2	6,216	5.34	8.5
1955	1,494.9	4.3	7,066	6.15	5.6
1960	1,665.3	5.4	7,655	6.79	2.2
1961	1,708.7	6.5	7,756	6.88	2.6
1962	1,779.4	5.4	8,045	7.07	5.3
1963	1,873.3	5.5	8,225	7.17	4.1
1964	1,973.3	5.0	8,577	7.33	5.3
1965	2,087.6	4.4	9,019	7.52	5.8
1966	2,208.3	3.7	9,434	7.62	5.8
1967	2,271.4	3.7	9,711	7.72	2.9
1968	2,365.6	3.5	10,125	7.89	4.1
1969	2,423.3	3.4	10,391	7.98	2.4
1970	2,416.2	4.8	10,455	8.03	−.3
1980	3,187.1	7.0	12,034	7.78	−.2
1990	4,155.8	5.4	14,139	7.54	.9

Table II
Federal Expenditures (in Billions of Current Dollars)

Year	Govt. Expenditures	Surplus or Deficit	National Debt	Defense Spending	Social Welfare Expenditures
1950	41.2	9.2	256.9	13.1	10.5
1955	68.6	4.4	274.4	40.2	14.6
1960	93.9	3.0	290.2	46.0	24.9
1961	102.9	−3.9	292.9	47.4	27.4
1962	111.4	−4.2	303.3	51.1	30.6
1963	115.3	.3	310.8	52.3	32.7
1964	119.5	−3.3	316.8	54.1	34.9
1965	125.3	.5	323.2	49.6	37.7
1966	143.3	−1.8	329.5	56.8	45.3
1967	165.8	−13.2	341.3	70.1	53.2
1968	182.9	−6.0	369.8	80.5	60.3
1969	191.3	8.4	367.1	81.2	68.3
1970	207.8	−12.4	382.6	80.3	77.3
1980	615.1	−61.3	914.3	134.0	NA
1990	1,273.0	−161.3	3,206.3	299.3	NA

Table III
Cost of Selected Goods and Services (in Current Dollars)

	1955	1960	1965	1970	1980
Eggs (one dozen grade A)	.61	.57	.53	.61	.90
Hamburger (1 lb.)	.40	.52	.51	.66	1.16
Chicken (fryer 1 lb.)	.47	.43	.39	.41	.79
Gasoline (one gallon including taxes)	.33	.33	.32	.39	1.27
Television set	NA	250 (23-in. black-and-white)	NA	380 (18-in. color)	NA
Movie ticket (first-run, indoor)	NA	.65	.85	1.55	2.51
Automobiles:					
Cadillac (LE)	3,882	4,892	4,959	5,637	12,899
Volkswagen (LE)	1,495	1,565	1,563	1,839	5,215 (Rabbit)
Corvette	2,934	3,872	4,106	4,849	13,965
College tuition:					
Penn State (in-state students)	NA	NA	525	525	1,368
Notre Dame	NA	NA	1,400	1,900	5,250
Yale	NA	NA	1,800	2,350	6,210
Taxes, average	NA	821	922	1,415	3,387
Taxes, as percent of total taxable income	NA	23%	19.5%	20.9%	19.6%

Table IV
Vital Statistics

	1950	1960	1970	1980
U.S. population (in millions)	150.7	179.3	203.3	226.8
Birth rate (per 1,000 women)	106.2	118.0	87.9	68.5
Marriage rate (per 1,000)	11.1	8.5	10.6	10.6
Divorce rate (per 1,000)	2.6	2.2	3.5	5.4
Life expectancy at birth				
Male	65.6	66.6	67.1	69.9
Female	71.1	73.1	74.8	77.6
New immigrants (legal)	249,187	265,398	373,326	460,348
Total motor vehicle registrations (in millions)	49.2	73.9	108.4	154.7
Households with TV sets (in millions)	3.9	45.8	59.6	NA
Percent of women in work force (age 10 and up)	33.9	37.8	43.4	51.7
High-school graduates	1,199,700	1,864,000	2,896,000	3,147,000
College graduates	432,058	392,440	827,234	921,000
Homicide rate (per 100,000)	5.4	5.2	9.1	10.8

Table V
Presidential Elections

Year	Candidates	Party	Popular Vote (in Millions)	Percentage of Vote	Electoral Vote	Voter Turnout
1960	**John F. Kennedy**	Democrat	34.2	49.7	303	62.8%
	Richard M. Nixon	Republican	34.1	49.5	219	
1964	**Lyndon B. Johnson**	Democrat	43.1	61.1	486	61.7%
	Barry M. Goldwater	Republican	27.2	38.5	52	
1968	**Richard M. Nixon**	Republican	31.8	43.4	301	60.6%
	Hubert H. Humphrey	Democrat	31.3	42.7	191	
	George C. Wallace	American	9.9	13.5	46	
1972	**Richard M. Nixon**	Republican	47.1	60.7	520	55.2%
	George S. McGovern	Democrat	29.2	37.5	17	
	John G. Schmitz	American	1.0	1.4		

Table VI
Party Strength in Congress

Period	Congress	House Majority Party	Minority Party	Senate Majority Party	Minority Party
1959–61	86th	Dem. 283	Rep. 153	Dem. 65	Rep. 35
1961–63	87th	Dem. 263	Rep. 174	Dem. 65	Rep. 35
1963–65	88th	Dem. 258	Rep. 177	Dem. 67	Rep. 33
1965–67	89th	Dem. 295	Rep. 140	Dem. 68	Rep. 32
1967–69	90th	Dem. 247	Rep. 187	Dem. 64	Rep. 36
1969–71	91st	Dem. 243	Rep. 192	Dem. 57	Rep. 43

Source: Congressional Quarterly, *Congressional Quarterly's Guide to U.S. Elections, Second Edition* (Washington, D.C.: Congressional Quarterly, 1985), p. 1116.

Table VII
Justices of the Supreme Court

Name	Term of Service	Nominated by
Hugo L. Black	1937–1971	Franklin D. Roosevelt
Felix Frankfurter	1939–1962	Franklin D. Roosevelt
William O. Douglas	1939–1975	Franklin D. Roosevelt
Tom C. Clark	1949–1967	Harry S. Truman
Earl Warren (Chief)	1953–1969	Dwight D. Eisenhower
John Marshall Harlan	1955–1971	Dwight D. Eisenhower
William J. Brennan, Jr.	1956–1990	Dwight D. Eisenhower
Charles E. Whittaker	1957–1962	Dwight D. Eisenhower
Potter Stewart	1958–1981	Dwight D. Eisenhower
Byron R. White	1962–1993	John F. Kennedy
Arthur J. Goldberg	1962–1965	John F. Kennedy
Abe Fortas	1965–1969	Lyndon B. Johnson
Thurgood Marshall	1967–1991	Lyndon B. Johnson
Warren E. Burger (Chief)	1969–1986	Richard M. Nixon

Table VIII
Major Decisions of the Warren Court

Year	Case	Ruling
1954	*Brown v. Board of Education*	Outlawed segregation in public education.
1957	*Yates v. United States*	Limited prosecution under the Smith Act.
1961	*Mapp v. Ohio*	Established "exclusionary rule," limiting evidence obtained illegally by state.
1962	*Baker v. Carr*	Established principle of "one man, one vote."
1962	*Engel v. Vitale*	Prohibited prayer in public schools.
1963	*Abington v. Schempp*	Banned Bible reading in public schools.
1963	*Gideon v. Wainwright*	Guaranteed defense attorneys for defendants accused of committing a felony.
1963	*Jacobellis v. Ohio*	Broadened ability to publish sexually explicit material.
1964	*New York Times Co. v. Sullivan*	Expanded freedom of the press by limiting libel suits involving public figures.
1965	*Griswold v. Connecticut*	Ruled that laws that prohibited distribution of contraceptives violated right to privacy.
1966	*Miranda v. Arizona*	Increased protections for criminal suspects; must be read their right to remain silent.
1967	*Loving v. Virginia*	Ruled that laws banning interracial marriages are unconstitutional.
1968	*Katzenbach v. Morgan*	Upheld federal law prohibiting literacy requirements for voters.

Table IX
Major Legislation Enacted During the 1960s

Year	Legislation and Description

1964   Tax Reduction Act: Decreased tax rates of corporations and individuals in top tax brackets.

Civil Rights Act of 1964: Outlawed discrimination in public accommodations and employment because of an individual's race, color, or sex.

Economic Opportunity Act: Omnibus "War on Poverty" bill, establishing Office of Economic Opportunity, Head Start, VISTA, Job Corps, Community Action projects.

1965   Elementary and Secondary Education Act: Authorized over $1 billion in federal funds for public and parochial schools.

Voting Rights Act: Provided federal government with power to protect voting rights of African Americans and others who had historically been denied rights.

Medical Care Act: Established Medicare and Medicaid—federal health insurance programs for the elderly and the poor, respectively.

Omnibus Housing Act: Approved approximately $8 billion of federal funds for low-income and middle-income housing and rent subsidies.

Immigration Act: Ended quotas against certain immigrant groups established in the 1920s.

Higher Education Act: Approved $650 million for scholarships and loans to college students and for the building of college facilities.

National Endowment for the Arts and Humanities: Established by the federal government to promote the arts and humanities.

Highway Beautification Act: Encouraged states to remove billboards and other clutter along federally funded freeways.

1966   Demonstration Cities and Metropolitan Development Act: Authorized federal funding for numerous urban projects, from mass transit to slum rehabilitation.

1968   Open (Fair) Housing Act: Prohibited discrimination on the basis of race in the sale or rental of the vast majority of dwellings.

Table X
Entertainment and Culture

Pulitzer Prize Winners in Fiction

1960 Allen Drury, *Advise and Consent*
1961 Harper Lee, *To Kill a Mockingbird*
1962 Edwin O'Connor, *The Edge of Sadness*
1963 William Faulkner, *The Reivers*
1964 Not awarded
1965 Shirley Ann Grau, *The Keepers of the House*
1966 Katherine Anne Porter, *The Collected Stories of Katherine Anne Porter*
1967 Bernard Malamud, *The Fixer*
1968 William Styron, *The Confessions of Nat Turner*
1969 N. Scott Momaday, *House Made of Dawn*
1970 Jean Stafford, *Collected Stories*

Academy Award Winners

	Best Picture	Best Actor	Best Actress
1960	*The Apartment*	Burt Lancaster	Elizabeth Taylor
1961	*West Side Story*	Maximilian Schell	Sophia Loren
1962	*Lawrence of Arabia*	Gregory Peck	Anne Bancroft
1963	*Tom Jones*	Sidney Poitier	Patricia Neal
1964	*My Fair Lady*	Rex Harrison	Julie Andrews
1965	*The Sound of Music*	Lee Marvin	Julie Christie
1966	*A Man for All Seasons*	Paul Scofield	Elizabeth Taylor
1967	*In the Heat of the Night*	Rod Steiger	Katharine Hepburn
1968	*Oliver!*	Cliff Robertson	Katharine Hepburn & Barbra Streisand
1969	*Midnight Cowboy*	John Wayne	Maggie Smith
1970	*Patton*	George C. Scott	Glenda Jackson

Top-Rated TV Shows

	First	Second	Third	Fourth	Fifth
1960	"Gunsmoke"	"Wagon Train"	"Have Gun Will Travel"	"Danny Thomas"	"Red Skelton"
1961	"Gunsmoke"	"Wagon Train"	"Have Gun Will Travel"	"Andy Griffith"	"Real McCoys"
1962	"Wagon Train"	"Bonanza"	"Gunsmoke"	"Hazel"	"Perry Mason
1963	"Beverly Hillbillies"	"Candid Camera"	"Red Skelton"	"Bonanza"	"Lucy Show"
1964	"Beverly Hillbillies"	"Bonanza"	"Dick Van Dyke"	"Petticoat Junction"	"Andy Griffith"
1965	"Bonanza"	"Bewitched"	"Gomer Pyle"	"Andy Griffith"	"The Fugitive"
1966	"Bonanza"	"Gomer Pyle"	"Lucy"	"Red Skelton"	"Batman"

Table X (*cont.*)

Top-Rated TV Shows

	First	Second	Third	Fourth	Fifth
1967	"Bonanza"	"Red Skelton"	"Andy Griffith"	"Lucy"	"Jackie Gleason"
1968	"Andy Griffith"	"Lucy"	"Gomer Pyle"	"Gunsmoke"	"Family Affair"
1969	"Laugh-In"	"Gomer Pyle"	"Bonanza"	"Mayberry R.F.D."	"Family Affair"
1970	"Laugh-In"	"Gunsmoke"	"Bonanza"	"Mayberry R.F.D."	"Family Affair"

Billboard's Top-Rated Singles

Year	Artist	Title	Weeks at Top of Charts
1960	Percy Faith	The Theme from "A Summer Place"	9
1960	Elvis Presley	Are You Lonesome Tonight	6
1960	Elvis Presley	It's Now or Never	5
1961	Bobby Lewis	Tossin' and Turnin'	7
1961	Jimmy Dean	Big Bad John	5
1961	Del Shannon	Runaway	4
1962	Ray Charles	I Can't Stop Loving You	5
1962	The Four Seasons	Big Girls Don't Cry	5
1962	The Four Seasons	Sherry	5
1963	Jimmy Gilmer & the Fireballs	Sugar Shack	5
1963	The Chiffons	He's So Fine	4
1963	The Singing Nun	Dominique	4
1964	The Beatles	I Want to Hold Your Hand	7
1964	The Beatles	Can't Buy Me Love	5
1964	Bobby Vinton	There! I Said It Again	4
1964	The Supremes	Baby Love	4
1965	The Rolling Stones	(I Can't Get No) Satisfaction	4
1965	The Beatles	Yesterday	4
1965	The Byrds	Turn! Turn! Turn!	3
1965	Herman's Hermits	Mrs. Brown You've Got a Lovely Daughter	3
1965	Sonny & Cher	I've Got You Babe	3
1965	The Beatles	Help!	3
1966	The Monkees	I'm a Believer	7
1966	S. Sgt. Barry Sadler	The Ballad of the Green Berets	5
1966	The New Vaudeville Band	Winchester Cathedral	3
1966	The Righteous Bros.	(You're My) Soul and Inspiration	3
1966	The Mamas & The Papas	Monday, Monday	3

Billboard's Top-Rated Singles

Year	Artist	Title	Weeks at Top of Charts
1966	The Beatles	We Can Work It Out	3
1966	The Lovin' Spoonful	Summer in the City	3
1966	The Association	Cherish	3
1967	Lulu	To Sir with Love	7
1967	The Monkees	Daydream Believer	4
1967	The Association	Windy	4
1967	Bobbie Gentry	Ode to Billie Joe	4
1967	Nancy Sinatra & Frank Sinatra	Somethin' Stupid	4
1967	The Young Rascals	Groovin'	4
1967	The Box Tops	The Letter	4
1968	The Beatles	Hey Jude	9
1968	Marvin Gaye	I Heard It through the Grapevine	7
1968	Paul Mauriat	Love Is Blue	5
1968	Bobby Goldsboro	Honey	5
1968	The Rascals	People Got to Be Free	5
1969	The 5th Dimension	Aquarius/Let the Sunshine In	6
1969	Zager & Evans	In the Year 2525 (Exordium & Terminus)	6
1969	The Beatles with Billy Preston	Get Back	5
1970	Simon & Garfunkel	Bridge over Troubled Water	6
1970	The Jackson Five	I'll Be There	5
1970	B. J. Thomas	Raindrops Keep Fallin' on My Head	4
1970	Carpenters	(They Long to Be) Close to You	4
1970	George Harrison	My Sweet Lord	4

Sports Champions

Year	NCAA Basketball	NCAA Football	Pro Football Super Bowl	Pro Baseball World Series
1960	Ohio State	Minnesota	NA	Pittsburgh Pirates
1961	Cincinnati	Alabama	NA	New York Yankees
1962	Cincinnati	USC	NA	New York Yankees
1963	Loyola (Chicago)	Texas	NA	Los Angeles Dodgers
1964	UCLA	Alabama	NA	St. Louis Cardinals
1965	UCLA	Alabama and Michigan State	NA	Los Angeles Dodgers
1966	Texas Western	Notre Dame	NA	Baltimore Orioles
1967	UCLA	USC	Green Bay Packers	St. Louis Cardinals
1968	UCLA	Ohio State	Green Bay Packers	Detroit Tigers
1969	UCLA	Texas	New York Jets	New York Mets
1970	UCLA	Nebraska and Texas	Kansas City Chiefs	Baltimore Orioles

Table XI
Polls and People

Time Man of the Year	Most Admired Man (Gallup Poll)	Most Admired Woman (Gallup Poll)
1960 U.S. Scientists	Dwight D. Eisenhower	Eleanor Roosevelt
1961 John F. Kennedy	John F. Kennedy	Eleanor Roosevelt
1962 Pope John XXIII	John F. Kennedy	Jacqueline Kennedy
1963 Martin Luther King, Jr.	Lyndon B. Johnson	Jacqueline Kennedy
1964 Lyndon B. Johnson	Lyndon B. Johnson	Jacqueline Kennedy
1965 William C. Westmoreland	Lyndon B. Johnson	Jacqueline Kennedy
1966 The 25 and Under Generation	Lyndon B. Johnson	Jacqueline Kennedy
1967 Lyndon B. Johnson	Dwight D. Eisenhower	(NA)
1968 Astronauts Anders, Borman, and Lovell	(NA)	Ethel Kennedy
1969 The Middle Americans	Richard M. Nixon	Mamie Eisenhower
1970 Willy Brandt	Richard M. Nixon	Pat Nixon

The Most Important Problem (Gallup Poll)

Date of Poll	Top Problem	Second Most Important Problem
Feb. 1960	Foreign policy	Missile gap
June 1960	Foreign policy	Relations with Russia
April 1961	War, peace, international tensions	High cost of living, economy
March 1962	Cuba, Castro	International problems: Berlin, Laos
Sept. 1963	Racial problems	International problems, Russia, threat of war
April 1964	Racial problems	International problems, Russia, threat of war
Nov. 1964	International problems, Vietnam	Medical care for the aged
April 1965	Civil rights	Foreign affairs
Nov. 1965	Vietnam	Civil rights
May 1966	Vietnam	High cost of living
Oct. 1966	Vietnam	Civil rights
Oct. 1967	Vietnam	Civil rights
Jan. 1968	Crime	Civil rights
May 1968	Vietnam	Race relations
Jan. 1969	Vietnam	Crime
April 1970	Crime	Pollution
Sept. 1970	Vietnam	Campus violence

Table XII
Presidential Approval Rating (Gallup Poll)

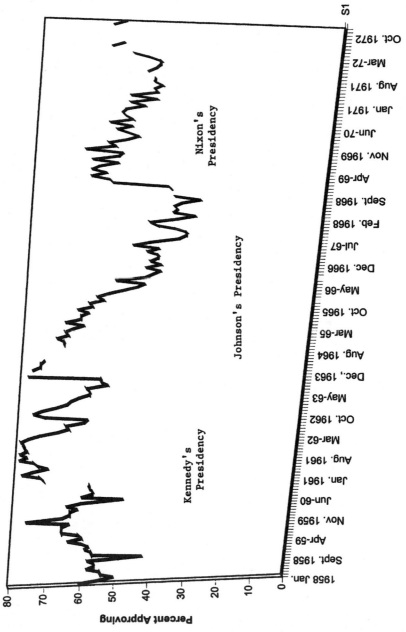

Percent Approving

Kennedy's Presidency

Johnson's Presidency

Nixon's Presidency

1958 Jan. · Sept. 1958 · Apr-59 · Nov. 1959 · Jun-60 · Jan. 1961 · Aug. 1961 · Mar-62 · Oct. 1962 · May-63 · Dec., 1963 · Aug. 1964 · Mar-65 · Oct. 1965 · May-66 · Dec. 1966 · Jul-67 · Feb. 1968 · Sept. 1968 · Apr-69 · Nov. 1969 · Jun-70 · Jan. 1971 · Aug. 1971 · Jan. 1971 · Mar-72 · Oct. 1972

S1

SUGGESTED READINGS

For such a recent era, the 1960s have already generated a great deal of writing. Primary sources can be found in Judith Clavir Albert and Stewart Edward Albert, eds., *The Sixties Papers* (New York: Praeger, 1984); Alexander Bloom and Wini Breines, eds., *"Takin' It to the Streets": A Sixties Reader* (New York: Oxford University Press, 1995); Michael Brown, ed., *The Politics and Anti-Politics of the Young* (Beverly Hills: Glencoe Press, 1969); Bruce Franklin, ed., *From the Movement toward Revolution* (New York: Van Nostrand, 1971); Paul Jacobs and Saul Landau, *The New Radicals: A Report with Documents* (New York: Random House, 1966); Carl Oglesby, ed., *The New Left Reader* (New York: Grove Press, 1969); Massimo Teodori, ed., *The New Left: A Documentary History* (Indianapolis: Bobbs-Merrill, 1969); and Immanuel Wallerstein and Paul Starr, eds., *The University Crisis Reader*, 2 vols. (New York: Random House, 1971). More specialized documentary histories include Philip Foner, ed., *The Black Panthers Speak* (Philadelphia: Lippincott, 1970); Joanne Grant, ed., *Black Protest* (New York: Fawcett, 1968); Peter B. Levy, ed., *Let Freedom Ring* (Westport, Conn.: Praeger, 1992); and Francis L. Broderick and August Meier, eds., *Negro Protest Thought in the Twentieth Century* (Indianapolis: Bobbs-Merrill, 1965), on the civil rights movements, and Jerry Avorn with Andrew Crane, *Up against the Ivy Wall* (New York: Atheneum, 1969); Harold Jacobs, ed., *Weatherman* (Berkeley: Ramparts Press, 1971); and Seymour Martin Lipset and Sheldon Wolin, eds., *The Berkeley Student Revolt* (Garden City, N.Y.: Anchor Books, 1965), on the uprising at Columbia University, the militant Weatherman, and the Free Speech Movement, respectively.

Overviews of the sixties, many of which focus on the New Left, are Terry Anderson, *The Movement and the Sixties* (New York: Oxford University Press, 1995);

Stewart Burns, *Social Movements of the 1960s* (Boston: Twayne, 1990); Joseph Conlin, *The Troubles: A Jaundiced Glance Back at the Movement of the Sixties* (New York: Franklin Watts, 1982); Morris Dickstein, *Gates of Eden: American Culture in the Sixties* (New York: Basic Books, 1977); Todd Gitlin, *The Sixties: Years of Hope, Days of Rage* (New York: Bantam, 1987); Herb Hendler, *Year by Year in the Rock Era* (Westport, Conn.: Greenwood, 1987); Allen Matusow, *The Unravelling of America* (New York: Harper & Row, 1984); William O'Neill, *Coming Apart* (Chicago: Quadrangle, 1971); Irwin Unger, *The Movement* (New York: Dodd Mead, 1974); and Milton Viorst, *Fire in the Streets* (New York: Simon and Schuster, 1979). Even more specialized works on 1960s protests or radical organizations include Paul Buhle, ed., *History and the New Left: Madison, Wisconsin, 1950–1970* (Philadelphia: Temple University Press, 1990); David Farber, *Chicago '68* (Chicago: University of Chicago Press, 1988); Maurice Isserman, *If I Had a Hammer: The Death of the Old Left and the Birth of the New Left* (Urbana: University of Illinois Press, 1993); Peter B. Levy, *The New Left and Labor in the 1960s* (Urbana: University of Illinois Press, 1994); James Miller, *Democracy Is in the Streets: From Port Huron to the Siege of Chicago* (New York: Free Press, 1987); W. J. Rorabaugh, *Berkeley at War* (New York: Oxford University Press, 1989); and Kirkpatrick Sale, *SDS* (New York: Random House, 1973).

Three valuable historiographical articles are Wini Breines, "Whose New Left?" *Journal of American History* 75 (September 1988), pp. 528–545; Alan Brinkley, "Dreams of the Sixties," *New York Review of Books* 34, no. 16 (October 22, 1987), pp. 10–16; and Maurice Isserman, "The Not-So-Dark and Bloody Ground: New Works on the 1960s," *American Historical Review* 94, no. 4 (October 1989), pp. 990–1010. For collections of analytical essays on the 1960s, see Peter Collier and David Horowitz, eds., *Second Thoughts: Former Radicals Look Back at the Sixties* (Lanham, Md.: Madison Books, 1989); Robert Divine, ed., *Exploring the Johnson Years* (Austin: University of Texas Press, 1981); David Farber, ed., *The Sixties: From Memory to History* (Chapel Hill: University of North Carolina Press, 1994); Steve Fraser and Gary Gerstle, eds., *The Rise and the Fall of the New Deal Order, 1930–1980* (Princeton: Princeton University Press, 1989); Sonya Sayres, Anders Stephanson, Stanley Aronowitz, and Fredric Jameson, *The 60s without Apology* (Minneapolis: University of Minnesota Press, 1984); and Michael Shafer, ed., *The Legacy: The Vietnam War in the American Imagination* (Boston: Beacon Press, 1990). Oral histories can be found in Dick Cluster, ed., *They Should Have Served That Cup of Coffee* (Boston: South End Press, 1979); Ronald Fraser, ed., *1968: A Student Generation in Revolt* (New York: Pantheon, 1988); Henry Hampton and Steve Fayer, *Voices of Freedom: An Oral History of the Civil Rights Movement from the 1950s through the 1980s* (New York: Bantam, 1990); Joan Morrison and Robert K. Morrison, *From Camelot to Kent State* (New York: Times, 1987); and Howell Raines, *My Soul Is Rested* (New York: G. P. Putnam's Sons, 1977).

There are hundreds of biographies and autobiographies. Some of the best are Stephen Ambrose, *Nixon: The Triumph of a Politician, 1962–1972* (New York: Simon and Schuster, 1989); Taylor Branch, *Parting the Waters: America in the King Years, 1954–63* (New York: Simon and Schuster, 1988); Carl Brauer, *John F. Kennedy and the Second Reconstruction* (New York: Columbia University Press, 1977); Joseph Califano, *The Triumph and Tragedy of Lyndon Johnson* (New York: Simon and Schuster, 1991); Paul Conkin, *Big Daddy from the Pedernales: Lyndon Baines Johnson* (Boston: Twayne, 1986); David Burner, *John F. Kennedy and a New Generation* (Boston: Little Brown, 1988); James Farmer, *Lay Bare the Heart* (New York: Arbor House, 1985); James Forman, *The Making of Black Revolutionaries: A Personal Account* (New York: Macmillan, 1972); David Garrow, *Bearing the Cross: Martin Luther King, Jr., and the Southern Christian Leadership Conference* (New York: William Morrow, 1986); James Giglio, *The Presidency of John F. Kennedy* (Lawrence: University Press of Kansas, 1991); Malcolm X with the assistance of Alex Haley, *The Autobiography of Malcolm X* (New York: Grove Press, 1964); Tom Hayden, *Reunion: A Memoir* (New York: Random House, 1988); Joan Hoff, *Nixon Reconsidered* (New York: Basic Books, 1994); Doris Kearns, *Lyndon Johnson and the American Dream* (New York: Harper & Row, 1976); Mary King, *Freedom Song* (New York: William Morrow, 1987); Herbert Parmet, *JFK* (New York: Dial Press, 1983); Richard Reeves, *President Kennedy: Profile of Power* (New York: Simon and Schuster, 1993); Arthur Schlesinger, Jr., *Robert Kennedy and His Times* (Boston: Houghton Mifflin, 1978); Bruce Schulman, *Lyndon B. Johnson and American Liberalism* (Boston: Bedford Books, 1995); and Garry Willis, *Nixon Agonistes* (Boston: Houghton Mifflin, 1970).

Five good surveys of the civil rights movement are Manning Marable, *Race, Reform, and Rebellion* (Jackson: University of Mississippi Press, 1984); Peter B. Levy, *The Civil Rights Movement* (Westport, Conn.: Greenwood, 1998); Harvard Stikoff, *The Struggle for Black Equality, 1954–1992*, rev. ed. (New York: Hill and Wang, 1993); Robert Weisbrot, *Freedom Bound* (New York: Plume, 1990); and Juan Williams, *Eyes on the Prize: America's Civil Rights Years, 1954–1965* (New York: Viking, 1987). More specialized works on the civil rights movement include Clayborne Carson, *In Struggle: SNCC and the Black Awakening of the 1960s* (Cambridge: Harvard University Press, 1981); William Chafe, *Civilities and Civil Rights: Greensboro, North Carolina, and the Black Struggle for Freedom* (New York: Oxford University Press, 1980); John Dittmer, *Local People: The Struggle for Civil Rights in Mississippi* (Urbana: University of Illinois Press, 1994); Hugh Davis Graham, *The Civil Rights Era: Origins and Development of National Policy, 1960–1972* (New York: Oxford University Press, 1990); Doug McAdam, *Freedom Summer* (New York: Oxford University Press, 1988); and Robert Norell, *Reaping the Whirlwind: The Civil Rights Movement in Tuskegee* (New York: Viking, 1985).

On the Great Society and the War on Poverty, see Edward Berkowitz, *America's Welfare State from Roosevelt to Reagan* (Baltimore: Johns Hopkins University Press, 1991); Michael Harrington, *The Other America* (New York: Macmillan, 1962); Daniel Moynihan, *Maximum Feasible Misunderstanding: Community Action in the War on Poverty* (New York: Free Press, 1969); Charles Murray, *Losing Ground: American Social Policy, 1950–1980* (New York: Basic Books, 1984); and Frances Fox Piven and Richard Cloward, *Regulating the Poor: The Functions of Public Welfare*, rev. ed. (New York: Vintage Books, 1993).

Works on the women's and other liberation movements include John D'Emilio and Estelle Freedman, *Intimate Matters: A History of Sexuality in America* (New York: Harper & Row, 1988); Alice Echols, *Daring to Be Bad: Radical Feminism in America 1967–1975* (Minneapolis: University of Minnesota Press, 1989); Sara Evans, *Personal Politics: The Roots of Women's Liberation in the Civil Rights Movement and the New Left* (New York: Oxford University Press, 1979); Jo Freeman, *The Politics of Women's Liberation* (New York: David McKay, 1975); Cynthia Harrison, *On Account of Sex: The Politics of Women's Issues, 1945–1968* (Berkeley: University of California Press, 1988); J. Craig Jenkins, *The Politics of Insurgency: The Farm Worker Movement in the 1960s* (New York: Columbia University Press, 1985); and Kristin Luker, *Abortion and the Politics of Motherhood* (Berkeley: University of California Press, 1984).

Studies on the origins of the New Right are just beginning to appear. See Dan Carter, *The Politics of Rage: George Wallace, The Origins of the New Conservatism, and the Transformation of American Politics* (Baton Rouge: Louisiana University Press, 1995); Alan Crawford, *Thunder on the Right: The "New Right" and the Politics of Resentment* (New York: Pantheon, 1980); Thomas Edsall with Mary Edsall, *Chain Reaction: The Impact of Race, Rights, and Taxes on American Politics* (New York: Norton, 1992); Jerome Himmelstein, *To the Right: The Transformation of American Conservatism* (Berkeley: University of California Press, 1990); and Jonathan Rieder, *Canarsie: The Jews and Italians of Brooklyn against Liberalism* (Cambridge: Harvard University Press, 1985).

There are numerous books on foreign policy. Among the best on the Vietnam War are Larry Berman, *Lyndon Johnson's War* (New York: Norton, 1989); George Herring, *America's Longest War: The United States and Vietnam, 1950–1975*, 2nd ed. (New York: Alfred A. Knopf, 1986); Neil Sheehan, *A Bright Shining Lie: John Paul Vann and America in Vietnam* (New York: Random House, 1988); and Marilyn Young, *The Vietnam Wars, 1945–1990* (New York: HarperCollins, 1991). On the draft and the antiwar movement, see Christian Appy, *Working-Class War: American Combat Soldiers and Vietnam* (Chapel Hill: University of North Carolina Press, 1993); Lawrence Baskir and William Strauss, *Chance and Circumstance: The Draft, the War, and the Vietnam Generation* (New York: Knopf, 1978); and Nancy Zaroulis and Gerald Sullivan, *Who Spoke Up? American Protest against the War in Vietnam, 1963–1975* (Garden City, N.Y.: Doubleday, 1984). Other aspects of American foreign policy can be found in Michael Beschloss, *The Crisis Years: Kennedy and Khrushchev, 1960–1963* (New York: Edward Burlingame Books, 1991); and Thomas Paterson, ed., *Kennedy's Quest for Victory: American Foreign Policy, 1961–1963* (New York: Oxford University Press, 1989).

Examinations of recent American culture include Erik Barnouw, *Tube of Plenty: The Evolution of Modern Television* (New York: Oxford University Press, 1975); Randy Roberts and James Olson, *Winning Is the Only Thing: Sports in America since 1945* (Baltimore: Johns Hopkins University Press, 1989); Ed Ward et al., *Rock of Ages: The Rolling Stone History of Rock and Roll* (New York: Rolling Stone Press, 1986); and Jon Wiener, *Come Together: John Lennon in His Time* (New York: Random House, 1984).

Also valuable are numerous books written during the 1950s and 1960s, many of which are excerpted in the text. Among those not excerpted or previously mentioned are Rachel Carson, *Silent Spring* (New York: Fawcett Crest, 1962); Stokely Carmichael and Charles Hamilton, *Black Power: The Politics of Liberation in America* (New York: Vintage Books, 1967); Eldridge Cleaver, *Soul on Ice* (New York: McGraw-Hill, 1967); Paul Goodman, *Growing Up Absurd* (New York: Vintage, 1960); Abbie Hoffman, *Revolution for the Hell of It* (New York: Dial Press, 1968); and Norman Mailer, *The Armies of the Night* (New York: Signet, 1968).

Also see Charles Reich, *The Greening of America* (New York: Random House, 1970); Theodore Roszak, *The Making of a Counter Culture* (Garden City, N.Y.: Doubleday, 1969); and Tom Wolfe, *Radical Chic and Mau-Mauing the Flak Catchers* (New York: Farrar, Straus and Giroux, 1970).

INDEX

About the Editor

PETER B. LEVY is Associate Professor of History and Political Science at York College, Pennsylvania. He is the author of *A Documentary History of the Modern Civil Rights Movement* (1992), *100 Key Documents in American Democracy* (1994), *Encyclopedia of the Reagan-Bush Years* (1996), and *The Civil Rights Movement* (1998), all from Greenwood.

Acknowledgment

It takes a single tragedy to remind us of our blessings.
It takes but a single prayer to thank the Lord
for the little things we all take for granted.
I am blessed for I can walk, I can talk,
I can see, I can hear, and I can feel.
I have food on my table, a dry roof over my head,
a bed to lie in,
and the love of my family and friends.
For all these things, I thank the Lord.

A special thank you also to the special people in my life who understand my journey and know that writing is my raison d'être.

My husband Arnold Mallette who is also my best friend and agent, my son Jared Mallette who is the light of my life, my aunts Jimmie Lee Mosby and Sylvia Turner, my sisters Brenda and Linda Rudolph, my brothers Early and Whirlee Rudolph, my good friends Debbie Buie and Curtis Richard, my sister friends and fellow authors Mary B. Morrison, Tracy Price-Thompson, Hope C. Clarke, Karen E. Quinones Miller, my publicists Marlive Harris and Ann Brown of The GRITS.com Literary Services, book and beauty editor Gerrie Summers, and Customer Service Director/Trade Sales Manager Jessica McClean-Ricketts of Kensington Books.

Prologue

1958

Stephanie Lewis couldn't get the song "How Great Thou Are" out of her head. She hummed it as she walked home. Choir rehearsal had gone well and, although it had run overtime by forty minutes, she would not have minded staying another forty minutes, except she had to walk the four blocks home to the St. Nicolas Housing Project. Her mother told her to come straight home and she did so mainly because she was told to, but more so because she was afraid to be out on the streets alone at night. This was only the second time her mother had left her behind at choir practice to come home alone. Her mother was very protective of her and her little brother Marcus. She always had been, but ever since they moved up to Harlem from Queens, her mother was more strict and cautious. Stephanie could only assume it was because Harlem was rough. It was loud, it was a haven for drug users and for anyone who had a criminal thought in his mind. Stephanie hated living in Harlem, but when her father died and they could no longer afford to live in the house they rented out in South Jamaica, her mother packed them up and moved them into the projects with a promise they'd be out of there in two years. Well, it was going on four years and the way things were going, they'd be there another four.

Stephanie hated Harlem, she hated the projects, and she hated the people. Very few people in her building worked. Most of them were living off of welfare, sleeping their days away, and partying their nights into the wee early morning hours as if nothing else mattered but the good time they seemed to think they deserved.

"Hey, church girl! Baby, you looking good tonight."

"Watch out now!" another boy shouted. "Your mama let you out by yourself? You're a big girl now, huh?"

"Yeah, baby. And I got something big for you, too."

Stephanie ignored the raucous, beer guzzling, cigarette smoking, pot smoking elementary school dropouts and hurried past them. She kept her head high and her eyes straight ahead. That rowdy bunch

was always standing on the corner of 129th Street. They always had something to say, even when her mother and brother were with her. Four nights a week on their way home from church they passed these same bums with nothing better to do but hold up the street lamp and stand in the way of legitimate customers trying to enter Juan's corner store. But then guys with nothing to do with their time stood on every corner in Harlem calling out to girls they thought they were impressing. Stephanie wasn't the least bit impressed.

"I like me some tight ass church girls!" a boy said. "They hot to be laid."

"Hey, baby, come let me preach the gospel to you," another boy said. "I know how to save your soul."

"See, Tyrone, while you preaching, I'll have her calling on the holy ghost," the first boy said. He broke away from his friends and trotted up alongside Stephanie. She walked faster.

"Man, you wasting your time. That girl's a virgin. She's saving herself for a preacher man."

The boy matched Stephanie's pace. "I'm a preacher man, baby. I got the power. I got something to lay on you, and it ain't my hands. You wanna touch my power?"

"Leave me alone!" Stephanie clutched her bible and her hymn book tighter to her chest. She hated the closeness of the boy walking next to her. Walking faster, she skittered to the curb, but he moved with her.

"Baby, don't be like that." The boy suddenly put his arm around Stephanie's shoulder and she pushed it off.

"Don't touch me!" Stephanie ran off up 129th Street leaving the half grown men laughing at her fear of them. She couldn't understand how men could stand around wasting their time like that. She was only sixteen, but even she knew if she wanted something out of life other than a welfare check, she had to get her education and a better job. God, she prayed her mother would get a good job sooner than later.

Breathing a sigh of relief, Stephanie entered her building and ran to catch the elevator. As she approached it, a tall, rangy, older boy was just getting off. In her haste, she bumped into him.

"I'm sorry."

"No problem, sweet cakes." The boy, who was almost a man

although he wore a woman's stocking over his hair, held the door open for Stephanie.

"Thank you." Stephanie stepped onto the elevator and pushed the button for the twelfth floor with the knuckle of her finger. She hated touching the buttons that so many fingers touched. She locked eyes with the boy as he let go of the door and it slowly closed. With her hand covering her nose, she tried to hold her breath against the stench that filled the small space. She stood in the center of the slow moving elevator because she knew better than to stand against the walls because they were as disgusting as the floors were. Dried urine and sometimes fresh urine was everywhere.

The elevator trudged along and stopped on the fourth floor. Stephanie looked up just as the door began to slowly slide open and was ready to move aside to let whomever was getting on inside. To Stephanie's surprise, the boy she had bumped into getting onto the elevator on the first floor was the boy who stepped onto the elevator now. Seeing his eyes, instinctively, Stephanie screamed. In a split second, with a knife in his hand, the boy shoved Stephanie back with such force her head hit the back wall. Stephanie tried to fight back.

"Shut up!" The boy shoved his arm across Stephanie's chest and held the knife to her throat, forcing her to be quiet. With his other hand he pressed the Close Door button and then pressed for them to go to the sixteenth floor. He then pushed Stephanie into the corner. He wedged her in with his body, holding her captive.

"Please don't hurt me. Please let me go. I won't tell nobody."

"Shut up, bitch!"

"I gotta go home. My mother—"

"Shut up! You goin' with me."

Stephanie was scared out of her mind. Her heart was racing. As her eyes darted back and forth from the floor numbers over the door to the crazed eyes of the foul breath, pimply-faced man-child, Stephanie prayed that the elevator door would open on her floor or any floor before the sixteenth floor and that someone would appear to help her. The elevator did stop on her floor, but no one was there to get on. No one was going to help her. Again she screamed.

The boy uppercut Stephanie with his arm and rammed her head into the wall. He then banged on the Close Door button repeatedly until

the door closed.

"I told you to shut up! Now I'm gonna mess your ass up for real."

Still holding the knife to Stephanie's throat, the boy snatched her dress up in the front and, although she tried to pull her dress back down, the boy shoved his hand between her thighs and rubbed her hard in the place that her mother always told her to let no man touch unless he had a ring on his finger to match hers. Stephanie clawed at the boy's hand, but he wouldn't stop.

"Please don't do this. Please, I gotta go home. I gotta go home."

The boy pressed the tip of the knife into Stephanie's throat, which caused her to suck in a big gulp of air.

"Say another word, I'll cut your throat."

On the sixteenth floor the elevator door slid open. The boy shoved Stephanie out of the elevator and pushed her toward the stair-well that led to the roof of the building. There was no doubt in Stephanie's mind what was about to happen to her. She dropped to the floor.

"Noooo! Nooooo!"

1989

For the third time in ten minutes, Stephanie Richards checked her wristwatch. And for the third time, she exhaled a full breath of irri-table impatience.

"This is ridiculous!" Stephanie cared not a bit that her haughty voice rose above the loudest adult speaking in the wide courthouse cor-ridor full of people waiting just as she was. She glanced over eleven-year-old Nadirah Lewis' head at her husband Lester, giving him an aggravated look of absolute annoyance. Of course, it was no surprise to Stephanie that Lester had his signature lackadaisical look of tolerance on his face. Lester never let much excite him beyond his job putting out fires for the City of New York, which was all well and good, but he should have focused more on trying to rekindle the fire he had caused so long ago to be extinguished between them. The day the twins were born, eighteen years ago, was the day their marriage screeched to a halt. The fault was totally Lester's. All these years since, the path they were

on was one of strife and indifference. Love was forever lost. Oh, but Stephanie wasn't pouting or hurting a bit. She was getting all the loving she needed, whenever she wanted it, and however she wanted it. Ironically, Lester being away from home four days a week on the job turned out to be a godsend. Stephanie's body warmed as the memory of her last night, a week ago, with Henry Lakewood filled her mind. She crossed her legs.

"Stephanie."

Stephanie quickly opened her eyes. She hadn't realized that she had not only closed them, but she had also grunted ever so softly.

"What?"

"Are you all right?"

"Do I look like I'm all right? I'm sick and tired of waiting in this damn hallway."

Stephanie re-crossed her legs and went to shaking her right foot. Next to being late for an appointment or work, she hated to be kept waiting for anything or anyone. Why in the world did they have to be made to wait just to speak to some judge? If they were filing legal guardianship papers in New York City instead of in Birmingham, they would have been saying their goodbyes and on their way out of the court building by now. She had to get back to New York, she had a business to run.

Lester Richards wasn't bothered by his wife's constant huffing and puffing nor by the incessant re-crossing of her legs. After twenty-three years of marriage, of which the last eighteen was a living hell, he was used to Stephanie's sharp tongue and extreme lack of patience. One would think by now that Stephanie would have figured out that she made her wait infinitely longer when she kept looking at her watch and fidgeting like a two-year-old. They had to wait, that's all there was to it. He wasn't going to let himself get upset over something as trivial as waiting. His nineteen-year job as a fireman strengthened his mind and body, and as well taught him patience and love for family. He'd seen too many families perish which is why he'd wait forever to not see another fire. So this little wait for their turn to go before a judge was light duty. He could do it standing on his head and never blink an eye.

Lester turned his attention to Nadirah who seemed so small sitting between him and Stephanie. Although he had seen her less than a

handful of times since she'd been born, he liked her. She had good manners and he liked that. His own kids, Lynn and Lester, Jr. or Les as he preferred to be called, were spoiled rotten and never seemed to appreciate the pampered life he gave them. Stephanie's brother Marcus and his wife Rochelle had been well on their way to raising a fine young lady. Nadirah was a sweet little girl, and as much as he hated the circumstances that brought them to this day, he couldn't say he wasn't pleased. He had wanted more children, but Stephanie swore a long time ago that she'd die before she'd have another baby for him. The fact that she was still alive backed up her words. He never told Stephanie how much it pained him that she wouldn't give him more children. He had been an only child and he had always wanted a houseful of children of his own. Since that wasn't to be with Stephanie, he considered going outside his marriage to have more children, but, several times at the eleventh hour, he pulled out of his lover, spilling the seed that would give him the babies he wanted. He'd already hurt Stephanie one time, which is why she no longer loved him. If he lost the love of Les and Lynn, then he'd lose everything. They could never know of his infidelity, and to make sure of that, he let go of his dream of more children, but now here sat Nadirah. Stephanie had no choice but to take her in. Nadirah was Stephanie's dead brother's child.

Lester slid his arm around Nadirah's small shoulders. "How you holding up, kiddo?"

Shrugging just once, Nadirah kept her head lowered. She was on the brink of crying.

"Everything is gonna be okay. You'll see."

"Of course, it is," Stephanie said, patting Nadirah on the thigh. "We're going to take good care of you."

On either side of her, because their chairs were so close, Nadirah could feel the tenseness of her Aunt Stephanie's rigid body at her side, while from her Uncle Lester, although his body was hard, she felt his warmth and was much more comfortable next to him. He felt just as good as her daddy when she used to sit up against him when they watched television together.

Nadirah's eyes welled. Uncle Lester was nice, but she wanted her real daddy.

"These people need to get their act together," Stephanie said.

"This process should not take this long! This is deplorable."

Nadirah eased her hand up to her face and quietly wiped away the tears that wet her cheeks. The more upset Aunt Stephanie got, the more afraid Nadirah became. She folded her hands tightly in her lap. As much as she wanted to steal a glimpse of Aunt Stephanie's face, she didn't. The last thing she wanted to see was cold, angry eyes glaring back at her, blaming her because they had to wait so long. Instead she looked at her aunt's wristwatch when she let her arm again drop to her lap. They had been sitting in the corridor outside courtroom 3B for an hour and twenty-five minutes. A whole hour and ten minutes past their 9:00 o'clock appointment. But they weren't the only ones waiting, the entire corridor was filled with parents to be and children eager to legally have a family and home to call their own. Nadirah was waiting, too, just like everyone else although she already had a family. She was related to Aunt Stephanie who was not only her father's older sister, but his only sister. Her father had no brothers and her mother had no brothers or sisters. So now Aunt Stephanie was going to be her legal guardian. The question was, was Aunt Stephanie still going to be Aunt Stephanie, or was she going to be her mother? If she could, she would tell the judge to not let Aunt Stephanie be her mother. She was too mean.

The clerk once again exited the courtroom. "Mr. and Mrs. Robert Hunt and minor child Gail Johnson."

"Ah, shhh," Stephanie groaned, sucking her teeth.

"The Hunts came in just ahead of us," Lester said, hoping to calm Stephanie. "We're next."

"We better be or I'm going to give that clerk a piece of my mind. I don't know why Marcus moved to this hick 'bama town in the first place."

"Stephanie, Birmingham isn't exactly a hick town," Lester said, hoping that no one heard Stephanie insult their city.

"If it's in the Heart of Dixie," Stephanie said seriously, "then it's a hick town."

Reaching across Nadirah, Lester placed his hand on Stephanie's arm. "Stephanie, we're all nervous. Just hang in there. We'll be next and we'll be out of here in fifteen, twenty minutes at most."

"Yeah, right." Stephanie folded her arms and re-crossed her legs.

Lester knew he was wasting his time. He looked at Nadirah. "Your aunt needs to take lessons on how to be calm and patient from you. I hope she's not upsetting you."

"Don't talk about me like I'm not here," Stephanie said, annoyed. "I'm not upsetting her."

Nadirah gave no hint as to how she was feeling, but inside she was screaming, You are upsetting me! And that was the truth. She was scared and had been from the minute she heard Aunt Betty, her great aunt, crying down in the hallway at the front door. Someone had rang the bell only minutes before and by the time Nadirah and her best friend Cherylee got down the stairs, whomever had been there was gone, but Aunt Betty was crying.

"Aunt Betty, what's wrong? How come you're crying?"

Aunt Betty, still tearing, pulled herself together enough to say, "Cherylee, you have to go home now."

"But I'm supposed to spend the night."

Nadirah held onto Cherylee. "Her mother said she could spend the night and Mommy said she could, too."

"That was before … before—" Aunt Betty couldn't go on. She turned suddenly and opened the front door. "Cherylee, I have to talk to Nadirah. You go on next door to your mother."

"Aww!" Cherylee said, stomping her foot.

"That's not fair!" Nadirah started to cry. "Me and Cherylee was supposed to make cookies and watch a movie."

"I'm sorry, baby," Aunt Betty said, fighting to not cry aloud, "not tonight."

As soon as the door closed behind Cherylee, Betty grabbed Nadirah and hugged her tight to her chest, crying, and scaring Nadirah, who was trying to pull away.

"Aunt Betty!"

Reluctantly letting up on her embrace, Aunt Betty wiped at her tears.

"Come sit with me, child." Aunt Betty took Nadirah's hand and took her into the living room where she, herself, sat on the sofa but pulled Nadirah onto her lap and again held her tight.

Confused, Nadirah protested, "I'm not a baby, Aunt Betty. Why

you holding me?"

"Lord, Lord," Aunt Betty said, "give me the strength to do what I have to do."

That's when it hit Nadirah that something was awfully wrong and it had to do with her. She felt her heart thump.

"What's wrong, Aunt Betty?"

Aunt Betty took a breath. "Nadirah, your … mommy … and … da … dad—"

"What? Tell me, Aunt Betty. What about my mother and father?"

"Oh, God," Betty again took a deep breath. "Baby, your mommy and daddy … they … they aren't coming home."

"Yes, they are. They're coming home late tonight. Mommy told me so this morning. And Mommy has a surprise for me. She said so."

Tears steadily rushed down Aunt Betty's face. "Nadirah, your mommy and daddy have gone on to … to be with the Lord. They…"

Nadirah's eyes widened. She froze. She knew what "Gone on to be with the Lord" meant. The Lord was God and God was in heaven. Everyone knew that and the only way to get to heaven was to die. She began shaking her head. It couldn't be.

"They're dead, Nadirah. Their plane crashed. Your mommy and daddy are dead."

That was three months ago. Nadirah couldn't remember what happened after Aunt Betty said that awful word—dead. When she remembered anything, it was when she woke up and Uncle Lester and Aunt Stephanie were standing at the window in her bedroom talking about taking her back to New York City to live with them. That's when she started screaming, started crying, and started to remember that her mother and father had been killed in the plane that crashed in Mexico.

"Nadirah," Lester said, "I know you miss your mommy and daddy, and you'll miss them for a long time. But you'll get through this. Your Aunt Stephanie and I will help you. You'll be all right."

Still Nadirah didn't raise her head. She knew Uncle Lester meant well, but he was wrong. She'd never get through this and she was never going to be all right.

Lester prompted Stephanie with his eyes to say something to

Nadirah, which annoyed Stephanie to no end.

"My goodness, Lester. Don't worry the girl to death," Stephanie said, speaking low enough for only Lester and Nadirah to hear her. "She'll be okay."

"Yes," Lester agreed with his voice low and tense, "but right now, Stephanie, she needs all of our attention and support."

"And she'll get that, Lester. But as I see it, right now we have to concern ourselves with finalizing Marcus' estate. Thank goodness he was smart enough to put my name on all of his assets along with his and Rochelle's, although in my opinion, Marcus could have left Rochelle's name off of everything."

"Stephanie!"

"Well, it's the truth."

Nadirah was getting the feeling that Aunt Stephanie didn't like her mother and she wanted to know why.

"This is not the time to discuss this," Lester said, signaling with his eyes to Stephanie to consider Nadirah.

"I don't see why not," Stephanie said, disregarding whatever Lester was trying to tell her. "We have nothing else to do but talk. By the way, can you believe that house is selling for four hundred and seventy-five thousand dollars? Marcus really did well for himself. Nadirah, you should be very proud of my brother. He has really looked out for your future."

Nadirah didn't care about her future without her mother and father.

Lester shook his head. Stephanie was really a piece of work. She was nothing like the girl he begged to go out with or the woman he married. God, how can a person change so much?

"Nadirah," Stephanie was saying, "you're too young to understand how well off you are. Between my brother's and your mother's savings …"

Lester didn't bother to try and stop Stephanie. It was useless. She'd do what she wanted no matter what he said.

"… stock portfolio, life insurance policies, and the sale of the house—"

"Please don't sell my daddy's house," Nadirah said, speaking up for the first time since her Aunt Stephanie stormed in and took charge

of everything.

"Your daddy—"

"Stephanie!" Lester said through clinched teeth. "That's enough."

"You don't—"

"I said that's enough, Stephanie. This is not the place."

While both exchanged challenging glares, it was Stephanie who finally shrugged and cut her eyes away. Caught between the two of them, Nadirah scrunched up closer to her uncle.

"Lester, I see nothing wrong with letting the child know that her financial future is set and that she has nothing to worry about. But since you don't want me talking to her—"

"I meant not here, Stephanie."

"I won't ever talk to her about it again. Hell, she won't see a dime of the money anyway until she's thirty. My brother was smart."

Again Lester shook his head. It was no use.

The courtroom door suddenly swung open, drawing Stephanie's attention. The Hunt family was smiling broadly as Mr. and Mrs. Hunt both came out with their arms around their new daughter Gail. Family members who had waited outside the courtroom greeted them with hugs and congratulations.

The clerk announced, "Mr. and Mrs. Lester Richards and minor child Nadirah Lewis."

"Thank God," Stephanie said, quickly standing. She immediately turned to Nadirah. "Look at your hair." Stephanie quickly took a comb from her pocketbook and began to rake hastily through Nadirah's already combed hair, scraping her scalp. Nadirah hunched her shoulders up to her ears and began raising her hand to touch her head when Stephanie popped her hand with the comb.

Nadirah rubbed her stinging hand.

"Her hair looks fine," Lester said in a hushed voice.

"The child has to look right or the judge'll think we're not taking care of her properly." Stephanie stopped combing Nadirah's hair, but then she went to tugging on the collar of her blouse.

"Girl," Stephanie said, "you not only look like your mother, but you're built like her. You have no neck. Your collars are never going to lay right."

Nadirah already felt bad enough, but now she felt worse. It wasn't because she was built like her mother—her mother was beautiful and she was glad she looked like her. She felt bad that Aunt Stephanie didn't think it was a good thing that she looked like her mother. Didn't Aunt Stephanie like her mother at all? Well, if she didn't, she didn't like her either.

Nadirah started to step back from Stephanie, but Stephanie yanked her back by the collar.

"Dammit, Stephanie. That's enough," Lester said in a low, firm voice while trying to not be obvious about pulling Nadirah back from Stephanie. "She looks just fine."

"Now she does." Stephanie headed for the door through which the clerk had already gone.

"Come on, kiddo," Lester said, taking Nadirah's hand. "Everything isn't as bad as it seems."

Stephanie looked back. "She's not a baby, Lester. You don't need to hold her hand."

Ignoring Stephanie, Lester continued to hold Nadirah's hand, while Nadirah, her chin quivering, toddled on rubbery legs in to see the family court judge who would put the final stamp of approval on her going to live with an aunt who didn't much like her or her mother. At least Uncle Lester liked her, but he wasn't the one who was going to be in charge of her, it was Aunt Stephanie. Aunt Stephanie was the one her daddy left her to. She was the one Nadirah wasn't feeling too good about.

Chapter 1

Silent, sorrowful tears slipped endlessly down Nadirah's cheeks onto her black dress and dampened it just below her collarbone. She had given up wiping at her tired, waterlogged eyes, it would be a while yet before she could stop crying. Every time one of Uncle Lester's fellow firemen spoke about how heroic he was, how funny he was, how devoted to his job and to his family he was, more tears flowed. Every kind word said about Lester Richards, who had been much like a father to Nadirah, was true. He had always been a hero to her. He had saved her many a time over the past nine years from Aunt Stephanie's brunt critiques and harsh criticisms. Nadirah's heroic uncle now lay in his American flag-draped casket, closed to all onlookers because he had been burned so badly in the fire. He had rescued two children from a burning house and had run back inside looking to rescue a third child, but he never made it out alive. Nadirah didn't know how she could go on living with the aunt who made her life absolutely miserable. She had to move out. She had to get her own apartment. She had to—

Riiiing! Riiiing! Riiiing!

The harsh, incessant ringing of the brass bell snatched Nadirah from the depths of the grievous dream she'd had at least a handful of times since Uncle Lester died nine years ago. Even in her sleep, Nadirah hated the dreaded ringing of the bell, but more than she hated the ringing of the bell, she hated who was ringing it.

"Nadirah! Nadirah!"

Riiiing! Riiiing! Riiiing!

Groaning, Nadirah pulled the cover up over her head. She tried to shut out the sounds of her aunt's grating voice and the squeal of her hated bell. The single plaster and wood wall that separated their bedrooms seemed to vanish whenever that dreaded bell was ringing and her aunt was calling her name.

"Nadirah!"

Nadirah angrily snatched the cover off her face. "I can't take this anymore!"

"Nadirah! I know you hear me! It's 5:00 o'clock. I do not relish the thought of marinating in my own waste. I need to go to the bathroom! Nadirah! Nadirah!

Riiiing! Riiiing! Riiiing! Riiiing! Riiiing! Riiiing!

"Aww!" Nadirah sat up, flung the cover off onto the floor, threw her legs over the side of the bed, and flicked on the lamp. As it was, she was exhausted from staying up with Aunt Stephanie last night. How inconsiderate the woman was to wake her up so early when she didn't have to get up until six-thirty.

"Nadirah, I have to go to the bathroom!"

Nadirah tried to temper the anger in her voice. "Aunt Stephanie, go to the bathroom! You can do it! You're not paralyzed. You can go on your own!"

"So that's the thanks I get for taking you in and giving you a home? Why do I have to always beg you to help me?"

That familiar pain that always settled at the nape of Nadirah's neck and behind her ears whenever Stephanie started haranguing her suddenly appeared. It was too early in the morning for her to get this upset. Gritting her teeth, Nadirah shot up off the bed and covered her ears with her hands. She did not want to hear her aunt's next words.

"I wouldn't be stuck in this Godawful bed or in a goddamn wheelchair if it wasn't for you! If you hadn't pushed me, I would not have fallen down those damn stairs! Maybe I should have died and then I wouldn't be a burden on you! I wouldn't be a burden on anyone. You don't wanna help me? Don't! I'll make do on my own!"

Nadirah snatched up her bathrobe and yanked it on. She started toward her bedroom door, but couldn't bring herself to open it. She dreaded seeing her aunt's accusatory eyes. She fell back against the door. She couldn't count how many times in the last eighteen years she'd heard her aunt blame her for falling down the stairs. It was hard enough over the years trying to block the memory of Aunt Stephanie tumbling down the stairs from her mind, but to constantly be reminded of it almost daily was driving Nadirah bonkers because that memory was as clear now as it was when she was twelve years old.

"Nadirah, what the hell did you do to my floor? Why does it look

so dull?"

Her heart quaking, Nadirah anxiously looked over the hall floor. Although it didn't shine, the hardwood floor was clean. She'd done her best. She'd washed it like Aunt Stephanie said before she went out. She had gone over the floor with a damp rag like she'd done all the floors downstairs, but she ran out of Floor Shine by the time she got to the upstairs floor.

"All the floors look dull. What the hell did you do?"

Nadirah shrugged.

"Answer me!"

"I ... I ... I did what you told me, Aunt Stephanie. I—"

"No the hell you didn't! I told you to use the Floor Shine only on the hardwood floors. No water, just Floor Shine. Did you do that, Nadirah? Or did you put water on my floors?"

Nadirah could feel her hands shaking. "Aunt Stephanie, you told me to use water first. You—"

"You calling me a liar?"

"No, Aunt Stephanie! I thought—"

"That's just it. Your dumb behind don't think! You messed up my damn floors."

"But, I ... Aunt—"

"Shut up! Don't you say another word! Do you hear me?"

Frozen in fear, Nadirah stared bug-eyed at her aunt. She could swear Aunt Stephanie told her to put a little water on a rag first to get the dust off the floors, then use the Floor Shine. When she left from downstairs the floors were shining, but the truth is Nadirah didn't know what she was doing. She didn't know how to make the floors shine like Alaina made them shine. Since Aunt Stephanie fired Alaina four weeks before, she said or laziness, she hadn't hired a new cleaning lady. Instead, Aunt Stephanie made her do a lot of the cleaning, especially when Uncle Lester wasn't home.

"Nadirah, you will go over every floor in this house, starting with this one, and put the shine back in my expensive-ass wood or I will beat you within an inch of your life. Do you understand me?"

As scared as she was, Nadirah bobbed her head repeatedly.

Stephanie thrust two large white rags and a full bottle of Floor Shine at Nadirah.

"You get your behind down on that floor and do it right this time!"

Nadirah plopped down on her knees and quickly opened the bottle of Floor Shine.

Stephanie stumped off to her bedroom and behind her, slammed the door.

Pouring a large pool of thick, clear, waxy liquid onto the floor at the top of the stairs, Nadirah tried to remember exactly what her aunt had told her. As hard as she tried, she still couldn't remember Aunt Stephanie telling her to use the Floor Shine. It was water she had told her to use first.

With the large rag, Nadirah slowly spread the liquid in a circular motion as far as her arm could reach. The floor began to shine right away. Backing up, Nadirah spread the liquid from side to side in the narrow hallway until she was backed up against the wall. Uh oh. Nadirah had boxed herself in. She should have started at the wall and come out at the top of the stairs. Aunt Stephanie was going to kill her! Nadirah started to cry just as, suddenly, Stephanie's bedroom door opened.

"What are you doing? You haven't started yet?"

Scared, Nadirah's mouth opened, but her words were stuck in her throat.

Stephanie charged at Nadirah, but when her foot hit the wet spot at the top of the stairs, she slipped. While her arms flailed wildly trying to catch hold of the banister to keep from going down, both her feet left the floor sending her airborne. Shrieking once, Stephanie came down hard on the edge of the top step just at the opening to the stairs and tumbled unchecked down the stairs until she landed with a nauseating thud at the bottom of the long flight of stairs.

For so long, that god-awful day gave Nadirah nightmares and woke her gasping for air and in tears. She'll never forget how quiet the house was after Aunt Stephanie landed at the bottom of the stairs, her body twisted, her head at an odd angle facing up the stairs but seeing nothing because her eyes were closed. It was a horrific sight, and by the time Nadirah, now screaming insanely, made her way down the stairs, she just knew Aunt Stephanie was dead. She almost was. All the way to the hospital, it had been touch and go. The paramedics pulled Aunt

Stephanie back from death's clutches twice, and each time Nadirah prayed harder that God would let her live. Well, he did, with everything in tact including her vicious tongue.

After two months in the hospital and rehabilitation, Aunt Stephanie came home in a wheelchair to a house newly carpeted throughout. Her broken leg and back injury were not fatal. The doctors said Aunt Stephanie would, in time, be able to get around just fine with the aid of a cane. Nadirah had never known such guilt. She cried practically every day that Aunt Stephanie was away and even more when she came home in that wheelchair. Uncle Lester didn't blame Nadirah, and neither did Lynn or Les, but Aunt Stephanie did every opportunity she got.

"That evil child pushed me down the stairs!" Aunt Stephanie told everyone when she came to in the hospital. As shocked as she was to hear her aunt accuse her of something so bad, Nadirah couldn't defend herself. She shrank from the cold, ugly looks the nurses gave her until Uncle Lester showed up. He never believed one bad word about her. He took her down to the hospital cafeteria and asked her what happened.

"Your aunt had no business making you shine those floors. No business at all. It's not your fault that she fell. It's hers."

Nadirah could not have loved Uncle Lester more than she already did, but her trust and love for him deepened even more.

When she was eleven and first moved to the Upper East Side of New York City, leaving behind in Birmingham all that she had known and loved, it was Uncle Lester, when he was home, who came to her room at night when she cried or had bad dreams. It was he who called her Kiddo and brought her little presents every week because he said they were a consolation prize for his having to be away from home four days a week on the job, which was horrible for Nadirah. Her cousins Lynn and Les were nice enough to her, but being older by seven years, they were hardly ever around. It was when Nadirah was alone with Aunt Stephanie that she felt like she didn't belong.

"You are not a pretty girl," Stephanie said so frequently that Nadirah had, by the age of twelve, accepted that this had to be true. Why else would her aunt keep telling her that?

"When a girl can't get by on her looks she has to have a brain

that would rival any man, and sadly, you don't have much in the way of smarts either."

Those words stung bitterly, and Nadirah had a hard time understanding why her aunt would not think she was smart. She did very well in school and, in fact, graduated from high school magna cum laude. She had scored 2000 on her SAT, had her B.A. in Education from City College in hand a week after her twenty-first birthday in May, and had her M.A. from Columbia by the time she was twenty-four. How was that not smart? Uncle Lester said she was smart and it was him that Nadirah chose to believe. God, she still missed him and wished that she had moved out when he died, but Lynn and Les convinced her that she was doing the right thing by staying to help Aunt Stephanie deal with Uncle Lester's death.

"Nadirah, it'll only be for a little while," Lynn said. "I'll be down to help as often as I can." Despite Lynn's caring words, Nadirah was never convinced that she would give up her life as a part-time travel agent, working full-time as a mother to her three children, or leave her successful husband Byron, or her beautiful home in Boston to come back to New York City.

"Mama's doctor said she'll be all right, but she can't be alone. I've hired a home attendant. She'll be here eight hours a day. So don't worry, you won't have to be here long."

Long? These nine years since Uncle Lester died had been no picnic and certainly had not been short. Okay, so Lynn wasn't willing to give up her well-ordered comfortable life for her mother, and neither was Les. Les wasn't married and was steadfastly vowing that he was never going to get married. He said he'd die first if he had to live with a woman like his mother. Les met a lot of women through his job as a music producer, and he was always in the company of female singers—some famous, some not—all over the country. He was always on the road and wasn't about to give up his exciting life. Five years ago he stopped coming back altogether. Not even Christmas brought him to his mother's doorstep.

Lynn did try to come every few months or so, but she never stayed long enough to give Nadirah the much needed break she craved. Les told her once that leaving home was liberating, and Nadirah needed desperately to experience that liberation. If she didn't soon, she'd lose

her mind.

    "Nadirah!"

    Thump!

    Nadirah knew that sound. Aunt Stephanie had fallen out of bed again and most likely on purpose because Nadirah didn't respond posthaste to her demands for attention.

    Taking a deep breath, Nadirah yanked open her bedroom door. While walking the too short distance to Aunt Stephanie's bedroom, Nadirah prayed that this wouldn't be the day that she lost all patience and murdered her aunt.

Chapter 2

Nadirah calmly switched on the overhead light in her aunt's bedroom. Stephanie was laying flat on her back with her nightgown pulled demurely below her knees, and while one of her arms will be resting on her round stomach, the other will be raised up and resting above her brow. After all these years, Nadirah knew it was all an act. Nadirah didn't raise a brow or miss a step as she went straight to Stephanie to help her up off the floor. It wasn't an easy task as Stephanie had probably gained as much as sixty pounds since her fall down the stairs, and, of course, it didn't help that Stephanie was now sixty-five and lazy as heck.

Nadirah took hold of Stephanie's arm. "Aunt Stephanie, you have to sit up."

"You can't wait for me to die, can you?" Stephanie said as she used the side of the bed to pull herself upright while Nadirah pulled on her arm, but still Stephanie made no effort to help Nadirah get her all the way up off the floor.

"Aunt Stephanie, you have to help me a little. I can't lift you by myself."

"If you tried harder you could." Stephanie, although grunting, turned her heavy body toward her bed and pulled herself up onto her knees. "If I'd died, I'm sure you would have been happy."

Nadirah hooked her arm under Stephanie's and helped her up off the floor and onto the side of her bed. "If you had died, Aunt Stephanie, perhaps you might've been happy yourself."

Stephanie shot Nadirah a bitter look of disdain. "That's a smart-ass thing to say. What kind of respect is that?"

Nadirah began rubbing the nape of her neck. "Didn't you say you had to go to the bathroom?"

"You don't care about me, you never did. It was Lester you liked. Him you loved."

"Uncle Lester was a great person."

"And I'm not?"

The pain in Nadirah's neck had snaked around to the front of her head making it feel like it would explode.

"Aunt Stephanie, I can't play this game with you this morning. Here, take your walker and go to the bathroom."

Stephanie ignored the walker Nadirah pulled in front of her. "You know, it wasn't Lester's idea to take you in, it was mine out of affinity for my brother. If it was up to Lester, you would have been put in a state home."

Nadirah didn't believe that for one minute, but she shot back, "Maybe that would have been the best thing for all of us."

"You talk big now that you're grown, but when you were eleven—"

"Aunt Stephanie, please!" Nadirah exhaled a heavy breath of exasperation. "Don't you ever get tired of hearing yourself tell this same story over and over again?"

Stephanie smirked. "Humph! Don't you get tired of making me tell it?"

Nadirah felt like screaming. "Aunt Stephanie, I have a long day ahead me. If you're going to the bathroom, please go now."

"Well, don't you think if I could go to the bathroom by myself, I would not've had to call your name?"

Nadirah's headache was so bad it was blinding her. "Aunt Stephanie, please don't do this this morning."

"Do what? Ask you for help? After all I've done for you, I can't expect you to help me now that I'm practically an invalid? You're selfish, Nadirah. And you're ungrateful."

Nadirah's hands shook. She was close to crying. This was a lifelong nightmare that she'd prayed she'd wake up from, but the joke was on her because she was already awake.

"I can see it now," Stephanie said. "One of these days, you're going to leave me on the floor to rot, aren't you?"

Nadirah folded her arms across her chest and tucked her shaking hands. "If you wanna believe that, be my guest, but, truthfully, if I wasn't in the house, you wouldn't allow yourself to fall onto the floor in the first place."

"Allow?"

"That's right, allow, Aunt Stephanie. I find it interesting that Millicent has never mentioned that she has had to help you up off the floor. Why is that?"

"Why don't you ask Millicent? Maybe she'll give you an interesting answer."

"You're playing games, Aunt Stephanie, and I don't like it."

Stephanie leveled a cold look on Nadirah. "I don't like what you're intimating. Either say it straight out or swallow it unsaid."

Stephanie was daring Nadirah to say aloud what she couldn't actually prove as fact, but she wasn't about to back down.

"Aunt Stephanie, what do you do when I'm not home and Millicent hasn't arrived yet? I doubt that you lay on the floor waiting for one of us to get here? The floor isn't that comfortable."

"How dare you, you ungrateful—"

"How dare you!" Nadirah said, determined to not let her aunt scare her down. "Aunt Stephanie, I know you throw yourself out of bed onto the floor just to get to me, to make me kowtow to you like I'm your slave. As long as I'm around, I believe you'd stay down on that floor forever as long as you thought it would torment me."

Stephanie sneered. "Poor, tormented, victimized Nadirah! So you think I've subjected myself to falling onto the floor, sitting in a wheelchair, and hiding away in this house for the last eighteen years just so that I could torment you? Don't flatter yourself. I'd rather be up on my own two feet living my life without the burden of you around my neck. I should have never brought you into my home."

As usual, her aunt's biting words hit their mark. Nadirah turned to leave.

"If it wasn't for you," Stephanie continued, "I'd have full use of both my legs! I could get up off this floor my damn self! You did this to me. You took my life and now you have the nerve to play the victim here. You are a selfish piece of work. My brother couldn't be your father because you're too damn selfish."

Unwanted tears slipped from Nadirah's eyes. She couldn't believe that she was still so sensitive to the mere mention of her father.

"What you gotta say now, smart ass? I'm in a wheelchair because of you."

Nadirah turned back to face her aunt. "If it makes you feel good

to keep blaming me for your injury, then you go right ahead."

"I didn't throw myself down the stairs. I had a lot of help from you."

Nadirah had often wondered about that. How Aunt Stephanie had fallen down the stairs had never made sense to her. True, the floor was wet. That had to be obvious to Aunt Stephanie when she came out of her bedroom. Compared to the rest of the hall floor, the area she had put the Floor Shine on had to be shining brilliantly. Could it be that Aunt Stephanie stepped on that wet, shinny spot because she knew she'd fall and have something else to add to her long list of reasons why she hated her? Just maybe she didn't know how bad her fall would be.

"Humph!" Stephanie sighed. "If Lester were alive, I wonder how he'd feel about you if he knew how terribly you treated me?"

Nadirah again started from the room. She'd had enough.

"Can't take the heat, huh? You never had any backbone."

Nadirah pushed aside the little voice that told her to keep going. "You know something, Aunt Stephanie? I can't figure out for the life of me what Uncle Lester ever saw in you. You're a heartless woman. You were so undeserving of him."

For the first time, Stephanie had no comeback. She stared hatefully at Nadirah.

Nadirah chuckled to herself. Finally, a well aimed bullet that stopped Aunt Stephanie cold. It was true that she often wondered how Uncle Lester had put up with being married to Aunt Stephanie all those years. Nadirah didn't understand a love like that. It didn't make sense. It defied logic. Personality wise, Uncle Lester was so polar opposite to Aunt Stephanie that it was amazing. They rarely agreed on anything, yet Uncle Lester never put Aunt Stephanie down, yelled at her, or made her feel like she was a nobody, or even acted like she was making his life miserable, which she did. Uncle Lester went out of his way to treat Aunt Stephanie with kindness and respect, but did Aunt Stephanie appreciate that and in turn shower some of that love back on Uncle Lester, or even sprinkle a pinch of that love onto Nadirah? No. Aunt Stephanie just got uglier.

Nadirah could remember when she was fifteen and Aunt Stephanie told her she couldn't go on a weekend skiing trip with her classmates even after the trip had been paid for by Uncle Lester.

Nadirah was in her room crying when Uncle Lester got home.

"Why are you crying? I thought you were supposed to go up upstate to Frost Valley this weekend."

"Aunt Stephanie made me stay home."

"Why?"

"Because she said she needed me to go food shopping with her tomorrow."

"Food shopping? There's plenty of food in this house. If we skipped a weekend shopping trip none of us would starve. What time are you supposed to meet up with your class?"

"They already left."

Uncle Lester looked around Nadirah's room until he spotted her packed overnight bag. *"Get your bag. Meet me downstairs."*

"But, Aunt Stephanie said—"

"What did I say?"

The minute Uncle Lester walked out of her room and down the hall to Aunt Stephanie's bedroom two rooms away, Nadirah was up and changing into the clothes she had bought with money Uncle Lester had given her to wear on the ski trip. She heard the shouts and the cursing coming from both Uncle Lester and Aunt Stephanie as she hurried down the stairs to the first floor. Until Uncle Lester came out the bedroom slamming the door behind him, Nadirah wasn't sure what the outcome would be. Uncle Lester came barreling down the stairs. His nose was flaring, his eyes were blazing. From the hall table Uncle Lester snatched his car keys.

"Where's the info about the place you're supposed to go?"

"I have it." Nadirah pulled the instructions and information sheet from the side of her overnight bag.

"Lester!" Stephanie shouted from the stop of the stairs. *"You better not take her out of here!"*

Uncle Lester grabbed his coat. *"Nadirah, let's go!"* He pushed her out of the house ahead of him.

Although he said very little throughout the two hour drive, Uncle Lester drove her all the way to Frost Valley where she met up with her classmates. Before Uncle Lester left her, he said, *"You have a good time, and don't worry about your aunt."*

And for a little while, Nadirah didn't. She had a good time that

weekend and met her first boyfriend, although, because of Aunt Stephanie, their relationship was short lived.

"I see you're zoning out again," Stephanie said. "I think it's time you make an appointment to see Dr. Calhoun. I think you're about to have another nervous breakdown."

"You'd like that, wouldn't you?"

"If you think I'd enjoy you having another mental breakdown, you're wrong."

"Yeah, right." Nadirah didn't have to go to see Dr. Calhoun. She already knew what he'd say—"Get away from your aunt."

Dr. Calhoun had told Nadirah more than once to get out on her own. She started seeing Dr. Calhoun after Aunt Stephanie fell down the stairs and she couldn't stop crying. She stopped seeing Dr. Calhoun on a regular basis when she was fourteen, but every now and then she went back for an emotional tune-up. They were life-saving. She always saw those little tune-ups as maintenance to shore up her weak spine so that she could stand on her own two feet, but she always asked herself afterwards, "Am I supposed to do this the rest of my life?" She was going to be thirty soon. When was she ever going to be strong enough to stand up to Aunt Stephanie and not quake in her soul?

What was it that Uncle Lester said to me on that ski weekend so long ago? "Don't worry about your aunt." Was it as simple as that? Could I just stop worrying and walk out?

"Girl, I'm tired of your nonsense. Snap out of it and get me to the damn bathroom!"

In that instant, Nadirah realized if she took one single step toward her aunt then she'd always allow her to dictate her every move. She studied the scour look on Stephanie's face and realized, too, that was the only look her aunt had ever shown her. Not even at her high school and college graduations had her aunt been happy for her. "I hope you appreciate the money I spent on your education," was all Stephanie said at the time.

Nadirah said nothing. She knew as a fact that her education was paid for by money her parents left in trust for her. This still wasn't the time to ask questions about her trust fund, but if that was the best Aunt Stephanie could say to her on those special days, then that was as good as it would ever be between them.

Nadirah took one step back. "I have to get ready for work. Millicent will be here at nine. If you can't make it to the bathroom on your own, and you can't hold your water till Millicent gets here, then shame on you."

Stephanie gasped incredulously as Nadirah turned to leave.

"You hateful, selfish bitch!" Stephanie snapped. "You're most certainly your mother's child."

Choosing to not let her aunt's ugly words draw her into battle, Nadirah went on out of the room and quietly closed the door behind her. After all these years, Nadirah knew all too well how much her aunt hated her mother. She was thirteen when she found out why.

"Uncle Lester, why does Aunt Stephanie always talk so bad about my mother?"

Before Uncle Lester could answer, Aunt Stephanie wheeled herself into the kitchen. "Why don't you ask me that question?"

Nadirah didn't repeat the question because she had never wanted to talk about her mother with Aunt Stephanie.

"Your mother was a whore."

"Stephanie!" Lester said. "Don't say that."

"The child wants to know, Lester. She asked the question. What do you want me to do, lie?"

Lester got up from the table and left the kitchen.

Nadirah hated being left alone with her aunt, but this was one time she needed to hear what she had to say.

"Your mother wasn't worthy of my brother. Rochelle used her body to get Marcus. She tricked him. When she got pregnant, Marcus was the happiest man in the world. But what he didn't know was that Rochelle was sleeping around with a lot of other men."

What Aunt Stephanie was saying didn't sink in immediately, but once it did Nadirah felt insulted "That's not true!" Nadirah yelled. "My mother loved my father. She loved only him. She loved me."

"Yeah, she probably loved you. There was no question that you were her child. But I question whether my brother was your father."

Nadirah tried not to cry. "My ... daddy ... is ... my ...father."

"Believe what you want, but I know differently. My brother was the father of the baby your mother killed."

Nadirah gasped.

"Oh, you didn't know about that?" Stephanie asked matter-of-factly. Well, you're not the first pregnancy your mother had. You're the second. Your precious mother murdered my brother's baby, a son. When that baby was born, other than that ugly cleft lip, there was no doubt whose baby he was. He looked just like Marcus when he was a baby."

Nadirah felt sick. She knew nothing about a baby before her or about him dying.

"Your precious mama didn't tell you about any of that, did she? Well, who's surprised? Rochelle was a whore, a liar, and a murderer."

"My mother wasn't none of those things." Nadirah started to cry. "She didn't kill no baby. She loved babies. She loved me. She loved my daddy."

"All a lie," Stephanie said in an ice-cold tone. "But you know what, little girl? You keep believing what you want. I know the truth. Marcus didn't believe Rochelle killed his baby either, but I know. That baby wasn't perfect. He looked like Marcus, but he had the ugliest cleft lip I'd ever seen. That deformity didn't come from my side of the family. It came from Rochelle's line. That poor baby had a cleft lip and your momma couldn't live with that."

Nadirah didn't know what a cleft lip was, but wondered if it could have been that bad?

"Rochelle smothered that poor baby with a pillow. She snuffed out his life and stole from him any chance he had to live his life. Marcus was devastated, and it broke my mother's heart."

Tears wet Nadirah's cheeks. "But my mother wouldn't do that. She would never do that."

"Believe me, child, your mama killed that baby, but she covered her tracks well. The coroner's report listed the baby's death as crib death, but I never believed it, and neither did my mother. Mother loved that baby. After he died, Mother's health deteriorated. I hated Rochelle for that, but I'm glad Mother didn't live to see Rochelle slip you into the family. You don't look like any of us."

Nadirah couldn't stop crying. Aunt Stephanie's accusations against her mother put her back to the day she was told both her mother and father were dead. Marcus Lewis was her father. When she looked at pictures of him, she saw herself in his eyes. The rest of her face looked like her mother's, but Marcus Lewis was her father no matter what Aunt

Stephanie said. And her brother, the baby she had known nothing about her mother could have never killed. It's true neither her mother nor her father ever talked to her about him, but that was probably because they didn't want her upset. And with the two of them dead, how would she ever know the truth?

For weeks and weeks, Nadirah thought about Aunt Stephanie's accusation that her mother had killed her brother and that her father wasn't her father. Both accusations hurt, but when she convinced herself that they were lies, they began to hurt less. She looked cleft lip up in a medical book and saw what it looked like. It was different, but it wasn't something her mother would have killed her baby over. Nadirah refused to believe anything Aunt Stephanie said and when she thought about it, her father must not have believed her either. He stayed with her mother and they had her, and when they died, they were coming back from their second honeymoon. No, her mother wouldn't kill her baby nor go out with another man. It was something Nadirah's mind could never imagine her mother doing—

"Nadirah!" Stephanie shouted from her bedroom. "I want you out of my house! I don't want you here another day. I'll do much better without you!"

Back in her room feeling no less safer from her aunt's angry tirade, Nadirah let the tears she'd been holding back fall and relieve her of the tightness in her head. She'd heard those words before, but this time, she welcomed them. They were liberating. Still, she couldn't understand why her aunt's hate for her mother could weigh so heavily on her. It was definitely way past time to leave. She needed to get out on her own before she lost herself completely.

"And I got news for you, Miss Nadirah! Don't think for a minute that you're gonna get any money from me! Marcus put me in charge of his estate. I'm the executrix of his estate, and the trustee of your trust fund. I decide if and when you get a dime, and as far as I'm concerned, you'll be lucky if you get two rusty pennies to rub together!"

There, Aunt Stephanie was wrong. For one thing, Nadirah had her own money. She'd saved as much as she could over the six years from her job as a third grade teacher. When she started working, she began paying her aunt six hundred dollars a month rent. Now she was up to a thousand a month. Still, she had managed to set aside a sizeable

nest egg for the day she moved out on her own. The money her parents left in trust was due to come her way when she turned thirty in eight months, and as far as she knew, Aunt Stephanie's threats meant nothing. The money was hers legally on her thirtieth birthday.

What Aunt Stephanie didn't know was back when Nadirah turned twenty, Uncle Lester slipped her a copy of her father and mother's wills, as well as copies of her trust fund accounts and stock portfolio. From that point on, Nadirah knew at all times how much was taken from her accounts and how much interest and dividends accrued monthly. And Nadirah knew this because every month, a day or two after the financial statements came in and the envelopes had been opened by Aunt Stephanie, she would steal away into Aunt Stephanie's room on one of the three days that Aunt Stephanie came in late with Millicent from her senior citizen center outing. Closed off in her own bedroom, Nadirah made copies of everything on her all-in-one copier, scanner, fax machine. So far, Aunt Stephanie had not found her hiding place in an old suitcase down in the basement, and Nadirah didn't think Aunt Stephanie ever would—she no longer went down into the basement.

Fortunately, the one good thing Nadirah could say about Aunt Stephanie was that she had done well in managing her trust fund and had never taken anything beyond what was needed to cover the cost of raising and educating her. Then again, the fact that her trust fund was intact was because of Uncle Lester. When Nadirah was thirteen, she overheard Aunt Stephanie and Uncle Lester talking in the kitchen.

"The money is there, Lester. Why can't I use some of it to get myself a new car that's easier to get in and out of with my walker?"

"Because it's not right, Stephanie. The money doesn't belong to you."

"Some of it does. I didn't have to take Nadirah in. I could have put her in the system but—"

"Stephanie, you know damn well that would have been wrong. You promised Marcus you'd raise Nadirah if something ever happened to him and Rochelle."

"And I'm keeping my promise."

"Then keep your word regarding Nadirah's trust fund. If you don't need money to feed and clothe her, or to cover her school expenses, then don't touch it. We have plenty of money for whatever we need."

"Well, what about my fee as trustee? Don't I get something? Everyone else who manage trust funds do."

"And that's because, unlike you, most people are not related to the owners of those trust funds. You're Nadirah's blood, Stephanie. You're supposed to be taking care of her out of love for her and for your brother, not because of the money you could take from her."

Two weeks later, Aunt Stephanie had a new car. Uncle Lester bought it for her.

All those years ago, Uncle Lester set Aunt Stephanie straight about the trust fund, and to date, she had not spent anything beyond what was needed to support Nadirah, and since she finished the masters program and started teaching, Aunt Stephanie hadn't taken a dime from the trust fund.

"Nadirah! Nadirah!"

Nadirah hurried into her bathroom and turned the shower on full-force hoping to drown out the sound of her aunt's nerve grating voice.

Stephanie quieted down and listened hard for sounds of Nadirah coming back to her door. She had to go to the bathroom bad! After hearing nothing, Stephanie got up off the bed, grabbed a hold of one side of her walker, and dragged it behind her as she hurried into her private bathroom. And even while she sat doing her business, the only thing she could think of was the look of resolution in Nadirah's eyes. That look had been there when Nadirah told her she was moving out two weeks after Lester's funeral. Back then, that looked scared Stephanie to death. With Lester gone, with Lynn living in Boston, and Les living God knows where, Nadirah had to stay. Stephanie couldn't be left to live alone. Her battle with breast cancer five years ago had taken so much from her, including her left breast. The chemotherapy had taken her long, thick, black hair, and what had grown back, Stephanie never liked. Her hair was now gray, thin, and short, and time wasn't making it any prettier. Her bloated body, which she had been so proud of in her younger years, she never looked at anymore.

Stephanie touched the flatness on the left side of her chest. Even now it sickened her to know that a part of her had been cut away. The ugly scar that was left behind always served as a reminder that she wanted no one to see her naked, not even Lester if he was alive. Before

he died, they had not been intimate for years, yet she would not want him to know that she was no longer fully a woman.

Remembering Lester's words?—*"I stayed with you all these years not because of fear as you believe, but because I do love you"*— brought tears to Stephanie's eyes and shamed her for not being able to forgive him before he died. It was only after Lester died that she truly appreciated the man she married. When the lid on Lester's coffin was closed, Stephanie realized she'd never know another man like Lester and after all these years, she was so right. No man Lester's equal had even looked her way.

Stephanie wondered how had her life come to this? Her, Stephanie Denise Lewis—the girl voted most likely in her senior year of high school to become a celebrity—without a man, without her left breast, and without a life worth waking up to every morning. And now to add insult to injury, she was about to be left all alone in a splendid house she'd spent a fortune renovating. Lynn and Les were never coming back to New York City to live, and Les wasn't even going to bother calling her. No, Stephanie couldn't let Nadirah move out and leave her to die alone where no one would know. But how was she going to stop her this time?

Chapter 3

As usual, the city bus was crowded and Nadirah had to stand for her short twenty block ride to her job. She didn't once look into the eyes of a fellow passenger because she didn't want anyone to see the pain in her eyes. She focused instead on the passing storefronts and pedestrians along the route, seeing nothing and no one too clearly as she struggled to force her mind to not dwell on the ugly start to her day. She knew what she had to do—move out—and anything less would not solve her problem. Just as the bus glided to a stop a block from Intermediate School 410, Nadirah placed a call on her cell phone to her best male friend Daniel Simon and asked him to put his sister Francis, who worked with Century 21, onto tracking down a one bedroom apartment for her in Harlem so that she wouldn't have to commute to her job.

"Are you sure this time?" Daniel asked.

"I'm absolutely sure," she answered, determined that nothing and no one would stand in her way this time, especially since her sanity depended on her getting out on her own.

"Okay. So, look, why don't you come over tonight and we talk about it?"

Nadirah breathed a sigh of relief. She was grateful that although Daniel always thought she should move out and had, in fact, scolded her a few times for not being strong enough to leave, he never turned his back on her. If anything, he gritted his teeth and listened to her rant about the leech of an albatross that was sucking the very life from her, which made Daniel more her therapist than her lover. From the start, Daniel was a great listener; that is when he finally took notice of her. She'd met Daniel back in City College one afternoon when she bumped into him in the hallway. Apologies were exchanged, but that was about all, which was kind of disappointing because she'd had a school-girl crush on Daniel since her sophomore year when she sat next to him in English Lit. Of course, Daniel never

noticed her, and Nadirah didn't have to wonder why. She wasn't anywhere near as attractive as the girls she'd seen him walking around campus with. She had terrible acne on her cheeks and her chin, and to make
matters worse, her hair was a cross between braids and locks because,
although she got her hair professionally braided, she let them stay in
well over two months till the individual braids frizzed up and began to
knit into each other. That always made taking her braids out more tor-
tuous, but short of cutting off all her hair, there was no other hairstyle
to fit her busy lifestyle of school and taking care of Aunt Stephanie.

Even now, Nadirah didn't have time to worry about her hair nor
anything else that concerned the way she looked. She was no longer
going to school, but besides her full time jobs as an elementary school
teacher, and as personal handmaid and servant to Aunt Stephanie,
Nadirah worked every Saturday and Sunday with the Harlem Boys and
Girls Empowerment Center. Initially, and even now, the kids at the center were teenagers pulled off the streets by Buster "BJ" Parish, a high
school teacher and deacon up at Abyssinia Baptist Church. BJ had
grown up in Harlem and never left his roots. He started the Harlem Boys
and Girls Empowerment Center in 1997 with three of his own students,
all of whom have since gone on to graduate college. Twelve years later,
the center had a steady enrollment of at least eighty students, all of
whom were tutored in school, work, and life and communications skills.
The minute Nadirah heard about BJ's work, and that was three years
ago, she volunteered her services.

Aunt Stephanie didn't like that Nadirah was gone all day
Saturday and Sunday and tried every trick in the book to keep her from
working with the center, but Nadirah was determined that neither hell
nor high water was going to keep her locked up with Aunt Stephanie
every weekend. The center was worthwhile, but above all, for Nadirah,
it was a place to go. So all of her necessary chores for Aunt Stephanie
like food shopping, Nadirah did on Fridays after work. The home health
aide took Aunt Stephanie to her bank and to her doctors' appointments
during the week, relieving Nadirah of those chores and freeing her
weekends for the center, which is why Nadirah's clothes were so outdated and ill-fitting. They made her look closer to forty than thirty. It
had been years since she'd spent any serious money on clothes, and
what few clothing she had bought out of necessity in recent years, she'd

bought from the Indian or Korean stores along 125th Street in Harlem. Most sufficed, most were a size larger than the size twelve she actually wore in an effort to hide the broadness of her hips and the fullness of her rear end. There never was an occasion that Nadirah felt attractive, and if she took the time to examine herself in her mirror, she might never get the nerve to stand up in front of her students again, much less let Daniel or any man lay eyes on her butt naked.

No one ever said anything to Nadirah about how she looked except, of course, Aunt Stephanie, and that was usually to tell her outright, "Girl, you need help." The one time Naidrah probably did look her best, Aunt Stephanie had a problem with the cost of the dress, and that was the black dress she had worn to Uncle Lester's funeral. It was Lynn who took her to Bloomingdale's to buy the dress.

Nadirah reminded Lynn as she headed for the cashier, "Aunt Stephanie said not to spend more than sixty dollars."

Lynn made a show of looking around. "Did Mama come with us? Do you see her anywhere?"

Maybe Aunt Stephanie wasn't there in the store in person, but Nadirah certainly felt her presence in her mind. She had no real money of her own at that time as she had just started back to school for her masters, so she couldn't buy the dress herself.

"I don't know, Lynn," she'd said. "I'm not comfortable with this. Aunt Stephanie is not going to like it."

"It's not for her to like. I'm paying the difference so Mama can't say a thing."

Of course, the minute Aunt Stephanie saw the dress which cost $210.00, she knew it cost more than sixty dollars.

"That's too much money," Aunt Stephanie said, while she dressed herself in a four hundred dollar designer suit to wear to the wake.

Nadirah had left Lynn to deal with her mother while she went up to her room to hang the dress up. It was a beautiful dress, and for such a sad occasion, it was the nicest dress Nadirah had ever owned before or since. In fact, she was wearing that very same dress a year and a half ago on the rare occasion that she attended an alumni function at City College when she again bumped into Daniel Simon. This time, Nadirah's hair was freshly braided, her acne had cleared up, and her

black dress slimmed down her hips enough to make her look okay enough to encourage Daniel to ask for her phone number. Two weeks later he called. Seems Daniel had also become a teacher, but he taught math on the high school level. They became friends, then lovers, and most of the time now they were more like good friends who occasionally slept together. The truth was, there were no great romantic sparks between them, which made their friendship all the better. If anyone was pleased about that, it was Daniel's mother Mrs. Veronica Simon, whom Nadirah had to address as Mrs. Simon. They didn't hit it off too well from the first day they met, and since Daniel could never tell Nadirah specifically why his mother didn't like her, Nadirah could only surmise that Mrs. Veronica Simon didn't think she was pretty enough for her son. That didn't sit too well with Nadirah at first when she thought she and Daniel could be more than friends, but as she got to know Daniel better and saw that he cared more about what his mother thought than what she thought, she settled into her role as friend and gave up her fantasy of becoming Mr. and Mrs. As it turned out, she'd made the right decision. Mrs. Simon had a key to Daniel's apartment. One evening she barged in when Nadirah and Daniel were locked in a very intimate position in his bedroom.

Nadirah thought she'd die. She covered herself and curled up into a tight ball. Daniel, who should have been upset, simply said, "Mom, it would be nice if you knocked next time."

Knocked? The woman should not have entered the apartment without first calling or ringing the bell. Knocked? The woman never apologized, and neither did Daniel.

"She's my mother. She's going through some changes right now. She needed to talk."

It was a month before Nadirah could get over her anger at Daniel for being so uncaring of her feelings. By the end of that month she came to realize that her need for Daniel's friendship was far greater than her need for him to sleep with her.

So, after talking to Daniel about an apartment, Nadirah felt better and went on into the school to start her work day with the hope that her students wouldn't pick up on the awful mood she was in. She tried to never bring the stress and sadness of her home life into her classroom, which was the only place she felt joy or got any peace. Nadirah count-

ed herself blessed that all her twenty-six students were doing well and would be promoted out of her class. Each year, each class was just as special as the one before, but, of course, Nadirah had her favorite students and, although she tried to not show it, this year she was especially drawn to Bree Morrison.

Eight-year-old Bree Morrison was as quiet as a mouse and was as smart as a whip—on paper that is. Bree tested well, but said very little to nothing throughout the day. She reminded Nadirah so much of herself after her parents died?sullen and oh so sad. Poor little Bree looked as if she had not one great memory to fall back on. Often she looked like she would break out and cry if something was said to her that might break her little heart. Nadirah never knew Bree's story, and none of the teachers who'd had her in earlier grades could enlighten her as they'd never met Bree's parents. Neither, it seemed, were ever available to come to parent/teacher conferences, and because there were never any physical signs of abuse, and Bree wasn't talking, there was never legitimate cause to raise flags of investigative concern. But all the same, anytime Nadirah saw an opportunity to spend an extra moment with Bree, she did. Still, she was never able to get a smile out of the child who was so much like the child who lived even now inside of herself. Throughout the morning, Nadirah could not smile nor could she focus on her students and the work she assigned them.

When Nadirah heard herself ask, "Who won the Spanish-American War, the Indians or the Spanish," she couldn't help but laugh.

"Miss Lewis, Miss Lewis!" her entire class, except for Bree, called out.

With so many hands raised, Nadirah knew she was in trouble. She couldn't call on everyone so she called on Rashad, the boy seated closest to her.

Rashad spoke up immediately. "The Indians didn't go to war with the Spanish in the Spanish-American War. It was the Americans."

While Nadirah could simply argue that she had experienced a slip of the tongue, she didn't want to confuse her students. She was wrong, and anytime she was wrong in class, the student who called her on it got a reward from her goody bag full of novelty toys. This time, however, the whole class knew she was wrong and it would not be fair to reward only Rashad.

"And why was America fighting Spain?" Nadirah pointed to another student to answer the question.

"Because America wanted to free Cuba from Spain's rule," Patricia replied.

"Shane," Nadirah asked quickly, hoping to trip him up, "who declared war on whom?"

Shane answered right away. "Spain declared war first on April 24th, 1898, but Congress didn't like that, so Congress got even and declared war on Spain the next day and said it was retroactive back to April 21st. So it's like the United States declared war first."

Nadirah nodded in humility to Shane. Shane and the rest of the class got a kick out of catching her in the wrong. Sometimes Nadirah pretended to be wrong just so she could lighten the mood in her class, but this time she was totally off. Nevertheless, she was pleased. Her students were paying attention even if she wasn't.

"Fortunately for you guys, I went shopping last week. There's enough in my goody bag for everyone."

All the kids cheered—except for Bree.

Nadirah started for the closet at the back of the classroom. "Rashad, Patricia, come help me."

Just as Nadirah was taking the large bag out of the closet, Assistant Principal Hernandez knocked at the classroom door and stuck his head in.

"Miss Lewis, you're needed in Principal Crayton's office right away."

Nadirah hurried to the door. "Perhaps I can see Principal Crayton in about twenty minutes?"

"I'm afraid not. I'll stay with your class."

An odd feeling came over Nadirah. "Okay. Fine. My students are discussing the Spanish-American War. I was just about to give them all a reward from the goody bag there in the back. If you don't mind, please pass the bag around to each of the students. I'd appreciate it."

"I'll take care of it," Assistant Principal Hernandez said. He stepped back and held the door open for Nadirah to leave the classroom.

Feeling a bit anxious, Nadirah trotted down the two flights to the principal's office on the first floor. That feeling of uneasiness only intensified when she walked into Principal Florence Crayton's outer

office and her assistant Carolyn Haygood shot her the ugliest look. The look was fleeting, but there was no mistaking the look of disgust in Carolyn's eyes.

"They're waiting for you," Carolyn said dryly.

Nadirah didn't know what to think as she knocked on Principal Crayton's door. It was opened immediately by BJ Parish.

"BJ! What are you doing here?"

"Come in, Miss Lewis," Principal Crayton said, surprising Nadirah with the official tone of her voice.

Nadirah felt uneasy as she entered the office and BJ closed the door behind her. In the office also was Beverly Cotton, the school's Assistant Principal Guidance. Something was most definitely wrong. Glancing at each grave, unsmiling face, Nadirah lingered longest on Beverly's. She and Beverly lunched together most days, and although they didn't hang out much after work, she considered Beverly a friend. If Beverly knew something, why hadn't she told her about it at lunchtime? And BJ, what did he have to do with this impromptu meeting?

"Miss Lewis, please have a seat," Principal Crayton said, indicating that Nadirah should sit in the lone empty chair next to Beverly Cotton on the other side of her desk.

As Nadirah began to sit, something suddenly dawned on her. "Jasmine Polk isn't in school today. Has something happened to her?"

"Miss Lewis, this isn't about any one of our students here at 410," Principal Crayton said.

Nadirah looked over at BJ who had already taken the chair at the far side of the room. "Then what is it about?"

Principal Crayton clasped her hands together. "Miss Lewis, Mr. Parish and I both received a very disturbing call this afternoon."

Nadirah looked from one face to the other. "A call about me?"

"Someone has accused you—"

"Accused?"

BJ cleared his throat. "The caller was anonymous, but it was a man's voice. He said you were seeing one of the students—"

"Seeing?" Nadirah shot up out of her chair. "What is seeing supposed to mean?"

"Calm down, Miss Lewis," Principal Crayton said.

"Calm down?" Nadirah didn't sit, she couldn't. "BJ just accused me of, I'm assuming, improperly seeing a student, which is another way of saying child molestation."

"No, Nadirah, I'm not accusing you of any such thing. I said someone called and accused you of seeing one of our students at the Empowerment Center."

"BJ, unless you're saying 'seeing' as with my eyes, then you're intimating something improper and that's an incredible lie! I would never do such a thing!"

"I know this, Nadirah, but—"

"There is no but! Who in the world would accuse me of such an ugly thing? Who?"

"We don't know," Beverly said. "Remember, the caller was anonymous."

Nadirah smirked. "A liar always hides behind anonymity."

"Nadirah, this is a very hateful accusation that—"

"Miss Lewis," Principal Crayton said, interrupting Beverly. "I received a similar call—"

"Oh, my God! Principal Crayton?"

"The call to the school also indicated that it was with a young man at the Empowerment Center with whom you were having this affair."

"But that's an outrageous lie! I am not having an affair with any student whatsoever at the Empowerment Center or any where else on this earth. BJ, I know you don't believe this lie."

"Frankly, Nadirah, I don't. However, we have to seriourly consider the accusation and not—"

"And not take my word for it, BJ?" Nadirah asked incredulously. "Is that what this is about?"

BJ held Nadirah's angry glare. He felt sorry for her.

"Nadirah, you're not hearing us," Beverly said. "Please sit down and hear us out."

"Beverly, what more is there to hear?"

"Please, Nadirah," Beverly persuaded. "We're on your side."

With all eyes on her, Nadirah could see clearly that she wasn't getting anywhere by ranting, and then seeing how calm BJ, Beverly, and Principal Crayton were, she conceded. She sat, but not comfortably.

Every inch of Nadirah's body was taut with anxiety. She wanted to shout her innocence.

"Miss Lewis, we all sympathize with you, but we have to step back and look at the whole picture."

Nadirah wasn't stupid. She knew that Principal Crayton was going to go by the book and put her on notice that she was either suspended or that she was going to be put on administrative reassignment—meaning that she'd have to report to the Department of Education headquarters in downtown Brooklyn and sit behind a desk until an investigation was conducted.

"This is what we know," Principal Crayton began. "Mr. Parish received a call just after noon today. I received the same call a half hour later at which time I called Mr. Parish to see if he knew anything about the accusation."

"And that's when I told Principal Crayton about my call," BJ said.

"And it was definitely my name this man used?"

"Yes," Principal Crayton said. "The caller wouldn't leave a name, but he did threaten to contact the media if we didn't do something about you."

"Like fire you," Beverly volunteered.

"Oh, my God," Nadirah covered her mouth with trembling hands. She fought back the urge to cry.

"We're all baffled, Miss Lewis. We all know your character."

"Principal Crayton, BJ, this is all a lie. I am not having an affair with a student. In fact, I'm barely seeing anyone socially."

"Nadirah," Beverly said, "I believe you. I think we all believe you."

While BJ looked like he believed her, the skeptical look on Principal Crayton's face was telling Nadirah that she was reserving judgment. Principal Crayton rubbed her hands pensively. "Miss Lewis, I must remain impartial and look at this situation without bias. I've known you here at 410 for six years. You're an excellent teacher, but we all know that excellent teachers do fall by the wayside. With the notoriety of the Mary Kay LeTourneau case, and since then the Pamela Turner case in Tennessee, the Debra LaFave case in Florida, and the Nadine Nunnelee case in Kansas, I can not simply dismiss this call as a hoax

without first looking into it. However, I will admit that the allegation is quite vague. We don't have the name of an actual student. Now regarding your position here at 410, because this alleged situation is said to have taken place off of school grounds and does not involve anyone of our students, I do not have to immediately report it to OSI, the Office of Special Investigation. However, I am directing Mrs. Cotton, as AP Guidance, to look into the matter."

Beverly nodded. "I'll fill out a DOE occurrence report and hold on to it until we have something more tangible."

Nadirah's stomach was tied up in knots so tight that she was starting to cramp. She wanted desperately to crawl away and hide in her bed.

"Nadirah," BJ said, "the center does not report to the Department of Education, however I would be required to contact ACS and the police if I felt this allegations had merit. At this time, I'm not convinced. I am going to conduct my own investigation. I will be seeing all of the students up at the center on Friday night, which is, as you know, the Valentine's Day Dance and fund raiser. I plan on questioning—"

"Who will you question, BJ? Who is it that I'm supposed to be having this sordid affair with? Where did I do what I'm supposed to have done? At the center?"

"Those are really interesting questions, Miss Lewis," Principal Crayton said. "Other than to say that you might do the same thing here at 410, neither Mr. Parish nor I was given a name of the student nor any of the particulars of the affair."

"And you won't ever get a name or any of the particulars," Nadirah said with certainty. "That student doesn't exist."

"He does to someone," Beverly said. "Specifically, the caller."

"I swear before God, Beverly, there is no student who can say that he's had or is having an affair with me."

"Let's just hope so," Principal Crayton said. "In the meantime, since we don't have a name or any tangible specifics, neither OSI nor the police will be called in."

Just saying the word "police" frightened Nadirah. If they were ever called in, no matter what the outcome of the investigation, her career as a teacher would be over.

"Miss Lewis," Principal Crayton began again, "be assured, I won't simply throw you to the wolves without having solid evidence to either convict or exonerate you. We will, however, document this meeting and the call. We will hold the memo on file in the event anything should come to fruition."

"I will also document this meeting and the call," BJ said, "but I will indicate, strongly, my belief that this is either a hoax or an outright fabrication."

Nadirah hated whoever it was that was trying to destroy her life. Who could be so vindictively cruel? She had never hurt anyone. Why would anyone want to hurt her? Did the gods hate her? Nothing in her life had gone right since her parents died. Maybe she was born with a sign on her forehead that said, Destroy my life at will? Or was she really born with that proverbial black cloud over her head? It seemed so. Hadn't disaster after disaster been visited upon her life since she was eleven? Wasn't she damned when Aunt Stephanie became her...

"Oh, God. She didn't."

"Do you think you know who did this?" Beverly asked.

Nadirah sat forward in her chair. "BJ, you said the caller was a man. Could it have been a woman?"

"It really sounded like a man."

"Yeah, but suppose the caller covered her mouth with a scarf or handkerchief or something? If it was a woman, the voice might come out sounding like a man, right?"

"I don't know, Nadirah. I'd be lying if I said it was a woman."

"Could you tell anything about the voice at all? Like how the person spoke?"

Both BJ and Principal Crayton gave some thought to Nadirah's question.

"Well, I'm not quite sure," BJ said, "but it could have been a woman. I can't say for sure."

"But did the voice sound old? Did it sound haughty or pompous? Did it sound artificially proper almost to the point of pretentiousness?"

"Nadirah?" Beverly said with amazement in her voice. "Are you saying that your aunt made those calls?"

Principal Crayton's eyes widened.

"Principal Crayton, did you speak to the caller yourself?"

"Well … yes, I did. The voice was obviously mature. It wasn't a child, but I can't say for sure that it was a woman. It sounded nothing like what you're describing. It sounded more like a man."

"Well, now that I think about it," BJ said, "the voice was kind of mature, proper even. If it was your aunt, Nadirah, that was pretty low of her."

Nadirah felt sick. If Aunt Stephanie was behind this she was going to kill her.

Principal Crayton was amazed. "Miss Lewis, are you saying a relative of yours is capable of making such a heinous act against you?"

"Principal Crayton, if you knew Nadirah's aunt," Beverly said, "you'd know it was possible."

"Miss Lewis, if you believe your aunt is capable of such an act, perhaps you should question her."

"Believe me, I will."

Principal Crayton stood and everyone followed her lead. "I will write up my report before I leave this afternoon. Miss Lewis, I will get a copy to you for your file."

Nadirah nodded.

"I'll do likewise," BJ said. "Friday night I'll talk to my kids."

"I'll get there early," Nadirah said. "I want—"

"No!" BJ said quickly. "Nadirah, I don't think you should come down."

"Why not? BJ, I need to be there to talk to the kids myself."

"I disagree. You might make the kids uncomfortable."

"Uncomfortable!"

"Yes. If the kids are put on the spot they won't talk. Nadirah, let me handle this. I know what I'm doing. I can get the kids to talk to me. Trust me."

"Nadirah," Beverly said, "Mr. Parish might be right. Let him handle it."

Nadirah didn't agree, but she conceded. "I hope he can."

"It'll be all right," Beverly said.

"I must tell you, Miss Lewis," Principal Crayton began, "while no official sanctions will take place at this time, be aware that it is possible in the future if this allegation proves to have merit."

"It won't." BJ went to Nadirah and took her hand. "Don't worry. I'll do everything in my power to get to the bottom of this, and whoever is responsible will regret what they've done."

"We'll talk, Mr. Parish, after your event," Principal Crayton said. "Did you say it was a fund raiser?"

"Yes. I'm trying to raise money to keep the center open. The rent is going through the roof."

"All over Harlem," Beverly said.

"Well, we all know why—gentrification," BJ said. "Nadirah, I'll be in touch." He hugged Nadirah.

BJ's arms around her was not totally unfamiliar to Nadirah. Four months after she started working at the center, BJ asked her out. She put him off as long as she could, not because he wasn't nice because he was. BJ was a little too old for her and she wasn't especially attracted to him. At the time she was twenty-six and BJ was forty-one, and dating wasn't something Nadirah was eager to do with a man who had just separated from his wife and had two of his own children at the center. It just didn't sit right with her, but BJ never gave up. He asked her out constantly, and between them, they joked and teased, but Nadirah initially had no intention of going out with her boss.

But as life would have it, a year later, after a terrible fight with Aunt Stephanie, she did not want to go home. Nadirah stayed late at the center talking to BJ about her problems. BJ took her out to dinner and later to his apartment. She ended up in his arms and naked in his bed. She couldn't say being made love to by BJ was the worst experience she'd ever had, but being that BJ was only the second man she'd ever been with, it wasn't the best experience. Her body never craved more of him and neither did her emotional soul. But it was different for BJ, he begged for more.

"I want you so bad," he said more times than Nadirah could count. "I ache every time I see you."

BJ made Nadirah regret that she'd ever slept with him. For two weeks she dodged him whenever she was at the center until finally she had to quit, which hurt her because she really liked being around the kids. A week later, BJ met her outside the school and asked her to come back. She agreed only after BJ promised that he'd stop hounding her for sex. Two years since, BJ has kept his word and hasn't asked her out

again. In fact, he was involved, pretty seriously it seemed, with the mother of one of his students at the center, which made Nadirah breathe a whole lot easier. However, right now, with BJ's protective arms around her, Nadirah welcomed the sincerity of his comforting embrace.

"Miss Lewis, school will end in approximately forty-five minutes. You might want to leave a bit earlier. Your class is covered."

"That's all right. I'd rather be with my kids till the end of the school day." Nadirah turned to leave when Beverly took her hand.

"I'm here if you need to talk."

"So am I," BJ said. "Call me any time."

Nadirah didn't have the energy to speak. She had to save her strength for the battle that had been itching to be fought.

Chapter 4

Nadirah threw open the front door of her aunt's house with such force the door hit the wall and broke the silence with a voluminous BANG! She didn't care that the doorknob punched a hole in the hall wall big enough to mar the beauty of the peach and white wallpaper around it. It wasn't her wall after all, and she didn't care when she slammed the door closed that the glass in the windows rattled. The one thing Nadirah did care about was never spending another night under the same roof with the woman who would wish her harm and go all out to ensure it.

"Aunt Stephanie!"

Nadirah threw her briefcase and pocketbook onto the hall chair. She immediately yanked off her coat and threw it across the banister, and it was then that she noticed that the stairway seat lift was at the bottom. Uncle Lester had the lift installed on the wall along the staircase after Aunt Stephanie's fall and while she was still in the hospital. With the lift to sit on and glide on a railing up the wall to the second floor, Aunt Stephanie didn't have to lose the privacy of her upstairs bedroom and be confined to only the first floor. If the lift was downstairs, then so was Aunt Stephanie.

Nadirah headed for the kitchen. "Aunt Stephanie! I know you hear me! Where the hell are you?"

The kitchen was empty. Nadirah circled through every room on the first floor before racing up the stairs to the second floor. Aunt Stephanie's bedroom was empty.

"Aunt Stephanie!"

Nadirah tried hard to remember if Wednesday was a doctor's appointment day or a senior citizen center day, but she couldn't seem to remember. The meeting in Principal Crayton's office was the only thing that kept flashing through her mind. Never in her wildest imagination would she ever think that someone would accuse her of sleeping with a student. Why not say she was stealing school sup-

plies or even that she was screwing the school janitor? But sleeping with a student? Her of all people? It was just too crazy to comprehend. And if it was, as Nadirah suspected, Aunt Stephanie who put that lie out about her, never again in life would she lay eyes on her.

Nadirah checked her watch—3:55. If Millicent took Aunt Stephanie to one of her doctor appointments then they would have been back by now. They had to be at the senior citizen center. Nadirah almost felt like going to the center and confronting Aunt Stephanie there, but thought better of it. Why upset other people? Besides, she could use the time to calm her nerves and pack her bags. She'd go to a hotel tonight instead of to Daniel's. No need keeping him up all night because she already knew that she wasn't going to be able to sleep a wink. In fact, she … Nadirah suddenly dropped down onto the floor at the side of her bed and the dam she'd been holding back burst, flooding her face, emptying her of all the frustration and anger that overwhelmed her. She held back nothing as she wailed and sobbed so loud that she could hear her own pain. The more Nadirah cried, the more hopeless she felt. Whether Principal Crayton or BJ believed her or not, the fact that the accusation was now part of her permanent file hurt her. No matter what, Nadirah couldn't see coming through this mess unscathed. She had no hope that her life would ever get better. It wasn't worth living another day or another year if she had to live her life as she'd been living it. It just wasn't worth it.

From the pit of Nadirah's stomach rose a gut-wrenching wail that tore at her throat and deafened her ears. She concerned herself not that her cries might be heard through the brick of her building or the glass of her bedroom windows. No one would care anyway.

"Nadirah! My God!" Lynn rushed into Nadirah's room and, falling down at her side, grabbed her and held on to her as tightly as she could. "What's wrong? Why are you crying like this?"

Nadirah couldn't stop crying long enough to be surprised that her cousin was there, nor to tell her why she was in such agony. She didn't pull from Lynn's arms, nor did she stop crying. She couldn't. Her pain wouldn't let her. She felt herself free-falling deep into the depths of a dark, black, bottomless hole and saw no way to save herself.

Chapter 5

The female paramedic checked Nadirah's pupils. "Does she have a history of blackouts?"

"Not that I know of." Lynn stood back and let the two paramedics do their jobs.

Holding onto Nadirah's wrist, the paramedic checked her pulse. "Do you know if she has diabetes?"

"As far as I know, she's always been perfectly healthy."

"Did you find her like this?"

"No. She was crying when I came in. She was hysterical, but then she stopped crying and blacked out. I couldn't wake her up."

"Pass me the ammonium carbonate," the female paramedic said to her male partner who immediately passed the small bottle.

"What is her name?"

"Nadirah. Nadirah Lewis."

The female paramedic began to slowly pass the smelling salt under Nadirah's nose.

"Nadirah, can you hear me? Wake up, Nadirah."

Almost instantly repulsed by the stingingly strong ammonia smell, Nadirah squished up her nose and started moving her head from side to side. When her eyes popped open she started gagging and coughing.

The paramedic passed the bottle back to her partner to recap.

"Nadirah, are you all right?" Lynn asked.

Still coughing, Nadirah couldn't answer.

"She'll be all right," the Paramedic said. "Let me take her pressure."

Nadirah lay quietly on her bed while the paramedic took her

blood pressure from her right arm. She didn't need to be told what happened, she knew. She'd blacked out from crying so hard. And even now, as the blood pressure cup tightened around her arm, an overwhelming urge to cry again was building up inside her. She felt so unbelievably hopeless and beaten. A single tear slipped down the side of Nadirah's face. She closed her eyes to shut out the faces that were looking down at her.

"Oh, Nadirah," Lynn said, her voice cracking. "Honey, what's wrong?"

"Her blood pressure is quite elevated," the paramedic said. "150 over 100. We could take her to the hospital and she could be better evaluated there."

"No," Nadirah said, her voice hoarse. "I don't wanna go to the hospital."

"Nadirah, I think it's a good idea."

"No."

The paramedic started repacking her blood pressure cup and gage. "It's totally up to you, Miss, but do you normally have high blood pressure? Are you on any medications?"

"No high blood pressure," she answered. "No medications."

"Okay, then your pressure may have risen because you were upset. You need to rest. If you start to feel faint again, or get a terrible headache, you should put in a call to your family doctor."

Nadirah said nothing as she sat up. There was nothing any doctor could do for her.

"I'll take care of her," Lynn said, seeing that the paramedics were ready to leave. "Thank you for responding. I'll show you out."

Left alone, Nadirah again began to cry. This time she was silent. Who wouldn't cry about being accused of having an affair with a student? God, that was so not her. How someone could lie on her like that was beyond her, and if it proved to be Aunt Stephanie who told the lie— damn her to hell. It was a terrible thought, but where else did Aunt Stephanie deserve to go?

Lynn appeared in the doorway. "You scared me to death."

"I scared myself." Nadirah wiped her cheeks.

"Nadirah, you're still crying. Talk to me." Lynn sat on the bed next to Nadirah and took her hand. "Look, I know I'm not in touch as

much as I should, but I'm available to you. Whatever is going on should never have gotten to this point. Talk to me, please."

Nadirah lowered her head. She didn't even know where to begin.

"Nadirah." Lynn lifted Nadirah's chin. "I came into the house and I could hear you screaming and crying the minute I opened the front door. Tell me what's wrong."

The ugliness of the scene she had with Aunt Stephanie before she went to work and the unbelievable episode in Principal Crayton's office both flooded Nadirah's mind.

"Where's your mother?" Nadirah asked.

"That's why I'm here. Mama's in the hospital"

Nadirah was totally surprised. "Since when?"

"Since before noon. She's at Roosevelt."

"Why? What happened?"

"She took an overdose of her pain medication. She says by accident."

Nadirah stared at Lynn.

"That's what she said, but now I'm beginning to wonder."

"I would think you would. Lynn, Aunt Stephanie's medication is set up in individual dispensers. There's no way she could take an overdose."

"I'm aware of that. But Mama said she was in a great deal of pain and couldn't remember when she took the last dosage and ended up taking too much."

"You believe her?"

Lynn shrugged. "I don't know what to believe."

"Well, what was too much? How many pills did she take?"

"I have no idea. Mama wouldn't tell me."

"Even if she did tell you, Lynn, I wouldn't believe her."

"Perhaps," Lynn said, "but it's a good thing Millicent showed up for work on time. Fifteen minutes after she got here she realized that something was wrong with Mama. Millicent got her to tell her what she'd done and then she called for an ambulance. Thank goodness."

"Yeah, thank goodness," Nadirah said dryly, but she was thinking, *Too bad Millicent stopped what might have been Nadirah's salvation.*

"So is she all right?"

"They pumped her stomach. Her doctor's keeping her in the hospital overnight for observation. She should be home in the morning."

"Why wasn't I called?" Nadirah asked, although she was glad that she wasn't.

"Millicent called me. I took the first flight out and went straight to the hospital. Mama's seems to be doing okay. I decided to come here to put my bag down and wait for you. I'd just unlocked the door when I heard you crying. Why were you crying like that?"

Nadirah wasn't ready to talk about herself. "Why didn't Millicent call me at work? I'm right here in the city."

Lynn paused. "Well, Millicent said Mama told her you wouldn't care if she died."

Nadirah didn't waste her breath denying that she didn't feel that way.

"Nadirah, are you going to tell me what Mama wouldn't?"

"And what would that be?"

"What's going on between you and her?"

Without warning, Nadirah's eyes filled with tears, alarming Lynn. "Nadirah, talk to me. I'm here for you. Talk to me."

Nadirah pressed her lips tightly together as tears rolled down her cheeks.

"Nadirah, listen to me." Lynn again took Nadirah's hand and held it. "I know it's been rough for you. It's no secret that Mama was never crazy about you. Hell, she wasn't crazy about me or Les and we were her children. What has she done to make you break down like this? What happened here?"

Nadirah wiped her cheeks dry. She wanted badly to talk to Lynn, but never before had Lynn been interested in talking to her or listening to her. And the truth was she didn't know if she could trust Lynn.

"Nadirah, I know my mother. I've never been blind to her. So let me help you. What's been going on?"

At first hesitant, Nadirah looked into her cousin's eyes. They had never been especially close, but they had never been enemies. Just as she was getting to know Lynn, Lynn went off to college and never came back.

"I hate your mother." Again the tears fell. "I want so badly to not have to see her face, or hear her voice, or smell her perfume, or even speak her name again. Lynn, I don't know what to do. I have to get away from her before I curl up and die."

Chapter 6

To give voice to painful memories, to talk about her fears for a life she hated living, and to lament about dreams for a life she might never have, Nadirah exposed her soul to a cousin she thought never cared. All that she told Lynn about her life with Aunt Stephanie chilled Nadirah to the bones and brought tears to Lynn's eyes.

"Do you really believe Mama made that call?"

"With every ounce of my being."

"But why?"

"Because she's hellbent on destroying what little life I have. Lynn, my job is all I have. My kids need me. They keep me sane. They're the reason I get out of bed in the morning. If I lose my job I have nothing."

"Nadirah, you won't lose your job."

"I can lose my job, Lynn. If I let Aunt Stephanie get away with this, I will lose everything. I can't let her do this to me."

"Then don't. Stand up to her. Confront her."

"I will, but I wish to God I knew what I ever did to her to make her treat me so cruelly."

Lynn shook her head sadly. "Nothing. And you want to hear something funny? Mama, doesn't want you to leave."

"That's not true. This morning she told me to get out of her house."

"Yes, but this afternoon she said you were going to leave her and she'd be alone."

"That's too bad. I can't stay here another day. I have to get out or I'll die."

"Nadirah, I'm sorry. I never knew it was this bad."

"As long as Uncle Lester was alive, living here was tolerable. Uncle Lester made it tolerable because he was so much like my own father. He was wonderful. He never made me feel like an outsider. He treated me the same as he treated you and Les. He loved

me."

Although nine years had passed, just talking about Uncle Lester still brought tears to Nadirah's eyes, and looking at Lynn, it was the same for her. Lynn, too, had to let the moment pass before she could go on.

"Yeah. Daddy was one in a million," Lynn said, sniffling back tears. "I still miss him."

Nadirah glanced at the picture of Uncle Lester in his fireman's uniform sitting on her dresser alongside her own father and mother holding her, as a little girl, on her lap. There had never been a picture of Aunt Stephanie on that dresser.

"Nadirah, when I asked you to stay here with Mama after her accident I didn't mean for you to give up your life and stay here this long."

Nadirah chuckled sadly. "Guess what? I didn't intend to give up my life or be here this long either."

"Then why did you? I can understand the first six months or the first year, but not nine years, Nadirah. Why did you stay?"

That is a question Nadirah had asked herself more than a hundred times over the years. The answer was never quite clear or simple, and always led her back to a single question—*Where will I go?* It was a question that reminded her how alone in the world she was.

"Nadirah, if you stayed because Mama fell down the stairs all those years ago, I

told you even back then that it wasn't your fault. After Daddy died, I asked you to stay until Mama got used to strangers being in her house. But then after a while when I saw that you weren't leaving, I thought you were staying because you wanted to."

"Yeah, right," Nadirah said. "I just love being browbeaten by your mother."

"Nadirah, I didn't know what was going on."

"So why didn't you ask me?"

"I saw no reason to. Why didn't you just tell me how bad it was? I never would have guessed that anything was wrong. Whenever I'd see you, you never talked, and you definitely never complained."

"What would complaining have gotten me, Lynn? Were you going to move back in here to relieve me of the stress I was under? I

don't think so."

"No, I would not have moved back in, but, Nadirah, you could have told me something. And now that I think about it, whenever I was here you acted like you were angry with me. You didn't stay around. You'd either leave the house or hide away up here in this room. I left you alone. I thought that's what you wanted."

"You have no idea what I wanted!" Nadirah got up suddenly and went to her dresser. She picked up the picture of her parents. She was sitting on her mother's lap with the biggest smile on her face. With the size of that smile, she had to have been a happy child.

Nadirah set the picture back in its place. "No one knows what I want. Not a living soul."

"Nadirah," Lynn said softly. "When you were a little girl you were always so sad. I mean, I understood why?you had lost your parents. When I was around nineteen, I asked Daddy if you were always going to be so sad, and he said you probably would be because you'd never ever know again the love your parents had given you. I understood that also, because if both your parents loved you anywhere near close to how much my father loved me and Les, then with them gone, you'd always have a sadness in your soul. I felt sorry for you, but I didn't know how to make you happy. I didn't know how to bring joy into your life so I never tried. I never bothered you and I never demanded anything of you."

"Maybe you should have bothered me or demanded something of me, Lynn. Then maybe I would have had something to look forward to." Nadirah could still feel how sad and lonely she was growing up. "You never had time for me."

"Nadirah, there was seven years between us. Seven years is a huge gap when you were eleven and I was eighteen. Les and I were on our way to college when you came into this house. Not to mention that from the moment you got here you clung to Daddy. Les and I figured you needed him more than you needed everyone else."

"Well, what was I to do, Lynn? Uncle Lester was the only one to pay any attention to me."

"That is true, and again, I'm sorry I wasn't there for you. But my mother? Look, Mama was never easy. Believe me, I learned early how to deal with her. Mama's never been child-friendly, which is probably

why she never had any more children."

"I never saw Aunt Stephanie treat you and Les terribly bad."

"No, but you never saw her treat us terribly good either."

Nadirah thought for a moment. Aunt Stephanie was never one to hug and kiss on anyone, not even Uncle Lester. No, she couldn't say that Aunt Stephanie showered Les or Lynn with a great deal of affection.

"Nadirah, my mother doesn't even like my children, her only grandchildren. She sees them only on the occasion of the holidays, and, believe me, my children, with their spoiled little selves, would love to be the recipients of all the good things that grandmothers are supposed to be to their grandchildren. Both of Byron's parents are dead so my children lose out on both sides. It's unfortunate."

"Doesn't it bother you how cold your mother is?"

"It used to back when I was a kid. I used to think Les and I were annoying the heck out of her which made her act the way she did toward us. She didn't hit us or anything, she was just cold and not loving. So we got to a place where we just said, 'C'est mère'—that's mother."

"But, how could you be so accepting of her behavior? She was supposed to be your mother."

"We had Daddy, remember? He made up for everything that Mama wasn't."

That, Nadirah knew to be true.

"Nadirah, my father was the beacon of light in our lives. For Les and I growing up, way before you came, it was my father who, when he was home, fixed us breakfast, cooked our dinner, took me and Les shopping, read us bedtime stories, listened to our mindless chatter about our lives, and showed us how to get and give love. None of that came from my mother, and because of my father, we were able to accept her as she was."

"You're blessed to have had him."

"Yes, but you had him, too, Nadirah" Lynn said, welling up.

Nadirah looked at the strong set of Uncle Lester's jaw and the soft yet determined look in his eyes. It dawned on her that he wasn't the handsomest of men, but he had the most beautiful heart.

Riiiing!

Nadirah cut her eyes over to the nightstand where the telephone sat. She didn't make a move toward it.

Riiiing!

"Should I answer it?" Lynn asked.

"No...Yes! It might be Daniel."

Riiiing!

"Hello?" Lynn said. "No, this is Lynn, Nadirah's cousin. Who's calling?"

Nadirah closely watched Lynn's face waiting for her to say who it was.

"Daniel." Lynn held the telephone out to Nadirah.

Nadirah took the telephone. "Hi."

"I thought you were coming over tonight."

My cousin's here. Can I call you back?"

"Are you still coming over?"

Nadirah looked at Lynn. "I don't know. I'll call you back."

"Well, let me know soon."

"I will." Nadirah hung up.

"He sounds nice."

"He's a good friend." Nadirah again looked at the picture of her uncle. Why couldn't she meet a man exactly like Uncle Lester? Daniel was a good friend, but what they had together wasn't magic.

"Lynn, did you ever wonder how Uncle Lester could be with a woman like your mother?"

"I don't have to wonder, I know how. Daddy explained it to me."

That got Nadirah's attention. She went back to sit on the bed. "What did he say?"

"Well, I asked Daddy, one day after Mama had been especially cruel to him, how he could stay with her? He didn't like me asking him that, but I had to know. See, I wanted him to leave her and take me and Les with him. Isn't that terrible?"

Nadirah said, bluntly. "No."

"Well, it should be terrible when a child wishes her father would leave her mother and take her with him. Daddy thought it was terrible. He sat me down and explained his love for a beautiful young woman named Stephanie Denise Lewis."

"I met your mother the summer she was fifteen years old and moved into apartment 14J in the Saint Nicolas Housing Project. I laid

eyes on her and I was a goner. Baby, your mama was the prettiest girl in Harlem. There wasn't a boy around who didn't want to get next to her. But Stephanie was a church girl. Her mother kept a tight rein on her and her brother, and she had them in church three, four days a week. She didn't hang out on the street corners or the court yards where we all lived. Stephanie came and went, holding her little brother's hand with her head up, not talking to anyone but her sister or her mama. Boy, was she pretty. Nice legs."

"So if Mama wasn't talking to anyone, Daddy, how did you meet her?"

"Not right away, that's for sure. I was patient. Take note, baby. Patience can get you everything you want in life. That is if you wait it out and do what you need to do."

"So what did you do to meet Mama?"

"Five weeks after I first saw her, I saw her coming from the supermarket carrying two big bags of groceries. It was just after Christmas and it was real cold and there was lots of ice on the sidewalks. Well, your mama slipped and fell. She dropped her groceries all over the sidewalk. Being the gentleman that I was, I helped her up, picked up all her groceries, and, mind you, I never said anything fresh or out of the way to her. I just showed her how concerned I was that she wasn't hurt. I went with her all the way to her apartment door carrying those two bags. When her mother came to the door, I explained what happened, handed the groceries to her mother, said good night, and went on about my business. But I heard what her mother said before she closed the door. She said, 'What a nice young man.' I knew I was in and I was. Every time I saw Stephanie from that moment on, I spoke to her and she spoke to me."

"So that's it," Lynn asked, confused. "That's why you love her so much? That's how y'all got together?"

"That's how we started talking and walking home together from school. What got us together is what happened to your mother that spring."

"What happened?"

"Well, one night your mother stayed late at her church for choir practice. Her mother and brother had gone on ahead."

Lynn held her breath in anticipation of what her father was

about to tell her.

"Your mama was attacked in the elevator on her way up to her floor."

"Mama was raped?"

"It didn't get that far. Your mama fought back. She was beaten up pretty badly though. The bastard dragged her up to the roof and tried to throw her off."

Again Lynn gasped in horror. *"Daddy!"*

"Don't worry, baby. I was there."

"You saw it?"

"I came into the building and some of the other kids were talking about hearing a girl scream in the elevator a few minutes before. They thought she was taken up to the roof."

"Well, why didn't they help her?"

"Because people didn't jump into other folks' battles. That's a sure way to get hurt."

"So what did you do?"

"I took one of the elevators up to the roof. I saw what was happening and did what I had to do."

"You beat the guy up?"

"We went at it. It was him or me. I threw him off the roof."

"Oh, my God."

"Your mother was in the hospital for a week, but her testimony got me out of jail, and my parents decided to get me out of Harlem. When school ended that summer, I went to live with my grandparents down in Atlanta. I went to college down there and got into a whole other life. I was twenty-three when I came back to New York and was surprised to find your mother still living in apartment 12J. She was different. She wasn't so sweet anymore, she had an edge to her. She was sassy as heck, and I found out pretty quick that I was still crazy about her. It's been me and your mama ever since. I figured it was the attack that changed her, so I understood her. I love her, and love has no conditions attached."

Nadirah slowly absorbed Lynn's story of how Aunt Stephanie and Uncle Lester met and the tragedy that bonded them. Still Nadirah didn't see that history as an excuse for why Aunt Stephanie was so cruel to her, so cold to her own children, and so nasty to Uncle Lester.

"You know, Lynn, I'm sorry that Aunt Stephanie was hurt as a young girl. And believe it or not, I think I can understand Uncle Lester's love for her, but that's more because of who he was as a person. What I don't understand is if Uncle Lester saved Aunt Stephanie's life, why was she so mean to him?"

"I asked Daddy that, too. He said their relationship was what it was, and to accept it."

"That's it? Just accept it? That makes no sense."

"Not to us, but—"

"Lynn, other than Uncle Lester, none of us have ever seen the fifteen-year-old Stephanie he knew. I only know the woman who made my life miserable, and you know that woman as well. So how could you think that I was okay here alone with her?"

Lynn didn't know how to answer. She simply shook her head.

Nadirah wasn't letting Lynn off that easily. "You know what I think? I don't think you cared whether I was okay or not."

"Nadirah, that's not true. I did care and I care now."

"Well, Lynn, you have a funny way of showing it. I hardly ever see you, and I most definitely don't hear from you. I catch a glimpse of you when you're here visiting your mother, and when you call her, and I happen to answer the phone. You ask for her with barely a hello to me. That's how much you care, right?"

"Nadirah, that's not fair. You could have spoken to me as well."

"I don't know about that, Lynn. Looking back, I was angry with you."

"Why?"

"Because you had me stay here so that you wouldn't have to give up a minute of your life to come back here to live."

Lynn couldn't dispute a word Nadirah said. "You're right. My family means everything to me. I have nothing to give my mother just as she had nothing to give me and Les."

"But, Lynn, you and Les left me here with nothing to hold myself up with."

"Okay, you're right but I can't speak for Les, I can only speak for myself. I'm sorry. As for Les, he disowned all of us. His anger is so great at Mama that he wants nothing to do with her or me. I'm lucky if I hear from him on our birthday and Christmas. That's why my marriage

is so important to me."

"Then you are lucky because I had no one to talk to to get me through the nights after being beat down by your mother most of my waking hours." Tears fell.

Lynn started to put her arm around Nadirah.

Nadirah pushed Lynn's arm away. "Don't coddle me! Just help me get away from your mother." Again that dam overflowed.

"I will. I promise."

"God, Lynn! I can't tell you how many times I wanted to vanish into thin air and not be seen or heard by your mother. Every time I thought I could get a minute's peace, she needed me to do something for her, which is so bogus."

"Why do you say that?"

"Because I believe Aunt Stephanie is lying about not being able to walk."

Lynn drew back. "Nadirah, Mama hasn't been able to fully walk in years."

"Says who? Her doctor? When was the last time you went to see your mother's doctor or had a conversation with him about her legs?"

"What is there to discuss? Mama has nerve damage in the spine because of her fall and it affected her legs."

"That's what she says."

"Nadirah, that's what her doctors said. My father spoke to the doctors and he spoke to the physical therapists. He was with my mother every day and night till the day he died."

"Not every day, Lynn. He was a fireman, remember? There were days when he wasn't home."

"Okay, but if Mama had been faking, Daddy would have known."

"Not necessarily. What if she got better, Lynn, and told no one, not even your father? And what if she—"

"No. Nadirah, you're reaching. It's too farfetched. Mama's no angel, but she wouldn't live such a big lie all these years. What would she accomplish by pretending to be disabled? That I don't buy."

"Fine, but what if one morning Aunt Stephanie woke up and discovered that she could stand on her own without the use of a walker

or wheelchair?"

"Nadirah, that would have been a miracle and Mama would have announced it to the world. I don't believe for one minute that she enjoys not being able to walk."

No matter her argument, Nadirah saw that Lynn was closed to anything she said.

"Nadirah—"

"Listen to me. Aunt Stephanie had a great physical therapist that she let go right after Uncle Lester died. Why?"

"Because it was a waste of money. He helped her exercise her legs, but he was never going to get her to walk."

"Maybe he did, Lynn. And speaking of her legs, have you looked at them lately?"

Lynn shot Nadirah an impatient 'what a stupid thing to say' look. "Nadirah, Mama wears long skirts and pants to hide her legs. They probably don't look very good."

"They look just fine. I've seen them."

"Well, you live here, I don't."

"Lynn, your mother's legs are as big and as strong as yours and mine. In fact, they're bigger."

Lynn almost looked down at her own legs, but set her gaze on Nadirah. "She's heavier than we are, Nadirah."

"Think biology, Lynn. Think muscles. If muscles aren't used, don't they experience atrophy?"

Thinking about that, Lynn said nothing.

"Lynn, I haven't seen Aunt Stephanie's doctors in years. Millicent takes her to the doctor every two months. He gives her prescriptions for her blood pressure and Synthroid for her thyroid, that's it. Nothing is ever said about her legs."

"But that doesn't mean Mama can walk. What pills can her doctor give her that would heal her legs and enable her to walk?"

Nadirah grunted in her frustration. "Lynn, you're not here! You don't see what I see. There's carpet in most of the rooms upstairs and down. Yet, there are never wheelchair tracks in the carpet any where."

"That's because Millicent probably vacuums before you get home."

"Then what about the walker? Aunt Stephanie has a walker

upstairs and down. Why aren't there markings or indentations from her walker in the carpet in her room, the hallway, or in any of the rooms downstairs?"

Nadirah's questions struck Lynn into silence. She couldn't help but wonder if what Nadirah was saying had any validity.

"There is no question that Millicent keeps this house very clean. Even if she had noticed something odd she probably wouldn't say anything about it. She is very loyal to Mama."

"I know this. Aunt Stephanie pays her very well, and three years ago Aunt Stephanie gave Millicent the down payment to put on her house."

That surprised Lynn. "How much?"

"Oh, you didn't know about that? It was $20,000 and I know about it because I overheard Millicent thanking Aunt Stephanie. So there isn't anything Millicent won't do for Aunt Stephanie including keeping her secret."

Lynn rested her head on the ball of her hand. What if it was true? What if her mother could walk? "Okay, Nadirah, if it's true that Mama can walk, why would she lie about it all these years?"

"To keep me her slave. I wait on her hand and foot."

"That's so crazy, but Nadirah, if Mama can walk, I will personally boil her behind in hot oil."

"Well, get the pot ready because I believe she can walk."

"But since when?"

"I don't know since when, but I know when I first suspected it and that was last Thanksgiving. Millicent was off for a week. It was just me and Aunt Stephanie and she stayed downstairs in the living room during the day. I brought her meals and helped her back and forth to the stair lift morning and night. But every evening that week I spent a lot of time with Daniel to get away from here. When I'd come home in the mornings I'd find something out of place in the kitchen or something moved in my room—some little thing out of place that was in place when I left. As you can see, there's carpet on my floor, but there was never any wheelchair or walker impressions in here. However, I felt it in my bones that she had been in here."

Lynn slowly shook her head. "But that doesn't prove anything, Nadirah. I've spent enough time with Mama to know if she's faking."

"Lynn, I can't make you see or feel what I see or feel. Your mother has been living a lie. I know I'm right."

"You really believe what you're saying?"

"Lynn, I'm an educated woman. I'm a teacher! I don't believe in fairytales. I believe in tangibles. What I see and what I suspect are real. Your mother has stolen a part of my life with her lies. She made a decision as to how I should live my life without me having any say about it."

"Nadirah," Lynn took a deep breath before continuing, "...my God. If it's true—"

"I hate her," Nadirah said, welling up. "She's taken so much from me. When I look in my mirror I don't know who I am or who I'm supposed to be. And if I don't leave this house, I'll die here."

Nadirah covered her face and gave in once again to her pain. This time Lynn took her into her arms and cried with her, holding her, supporting her, showing her that she wasn't alone.

"I'm so sorry," Lynn said again. "I promise on my daddy's soul that I'll get you out of here. I won't let you down. I promise."

Chapter 7

As tired as she was last night after she and Lynn ate a late take-out dinner of Chinese wonton soup and chicken broccoli with plain fried rice, Nadirah thought she'd sleep through the night, but she didn't. On her clock radio she saw every hour that passed and feared the 6:00 o'clock hour that would come and signify to her that she had to get up and go to work. That was the one other place she did not want to show her face today, the first place being the house she lived in. Nadirah hoped that she wouldn't regret weakening and allowing Lynn to talk her into staying the night when she wanted so desperately to get from under Aunt Stephanie's roof last night. Of course, Aunt Stephanie not being in the next room lessened Nadirah's anxiety, but still she couldn't sleep. Not when she knew what awaited her in the morning at her job. As messed up as she was, what good was she going to be to her students? If anything, for the first time she felt like she'd be doing them an injustice to show up. When 6:00 o'clock did come, Nadirah knew she wasn't going to make it because she could barely lift her head off of her pillow.

Tap … tap.

"Nadirah, are you awake?"

Nadirah uncurled herself from the tight ball she lay in. "Unfortunately, yes."

Lynn opened the door. She was already dressed. "Good morning."

"That's a matter of opinion," Nadirah said, sitting up.

"Oh, we have got to get a better attitude about this beautiful new day. Have you looked outside?"

"Lynn, it's February. It's cold."

Lynn snatched open Nadirah's curtain. "Yes, but it's going to be a bright, sunny day."

Nadirah didn't bother to look toward the window. "Well, it's obvious you got plenty of sleep."

"Actually, I cat napped. I had a lot on my mind."

"Who didn't?" Nadirah said. "I didn't sleep a wink."

"Believe me, I can see how you feel. You look terrible."

Self-consciously, Nadirah touched her braids. Nothing unusual there, her hair was always frizzy. She sank back onto her pillow. That's all she needed was to be told how terrible she looked.

Seeing that Nadirah didn't see the humor in her remark, Lynn said quickly, "Byron often tells me I need to work on my sense of humor. He says my timing is off."

"Right now, Lynn, Chris Rock could be telling me the funniest joke in the world and I still wouldn't laugh."

Lynn sat on the side of the bed. "Let's start over. Are you planning to go in to work today?"

Nadirah exhaled heavily. "I really can't handle going in today."

"So don't. Call in a personal day or sick day. Play hooky with me."

Nadirah thought about it. "I could use the day to move some of my belongings out before Aunt Stephanie gets home."

"Where are you planning to move to?"

"Well, there's no hotel uptown, so I guess tonight I'll stay at a friend's. Tomorrow I'll try and find something."

"In New York City, Nadirah? It's not gonna happen that quickly."

"Well, I guess if I have to stay with Daniel for a while it'll be all right."

"Oh, is Daniel your man?"

"Daniel's a friend. A very good friend."

"Then that might not be the best place to be if you want to keep him as a very good friend."

Nadirah got Lynn's meaning right away. "True, but at such short notice, other than going downtown to a hotel, I have nowhere else to go."

"Actually, you do. Last night, I spoke to a friend of mine and Byron's who has a townhouse on West 147th Street. His name is Austin Gray and he's a sports agent out in Los Angeles."

"Which means what to me?"

"Nadirah," Lynn smiled, "Austin pretty much lives out in LA,

but he's here in the city at least twice a month. In fact, he's here now. He stays a few days then he's off to LA again. His house is empty pretty much all the time."

"So why keep the house? Why not sell it?"

"Because the house has been in his family for three generations. Austin will never sell it."

"Understandable."

"Well, Erma doesn't understand. That's his wife. She wants him to sell it."

"But it's a part of his family's history."

"Erma doesn't care about that. She figures a townhouse as grand as Austin's has to be worth at least a million and she wants her share of it."

"I guess there's no pillow talk in their bedroom at night."

"Austin and Erma haven't slept in the same house much less the same bedroom in two years. Austin's been trying to divorce her and—"

"Stop right there," Nadirah said. "Your friend's personal business is none of mine. I have my own problems. Is the townhouse available today?"

"Yes it is. I told Austin about you and explained the urgency of your need to find a place posthaste. He offered his townhouse."

"And what did you tell him about me?"

"Just that you were my cousin, a teacher, and that you couldn't stand to live in my mother's house a day longer. Very basic, nothing you have to be ashamed of."

"Good. I'll take Austin up on his offer until I find something on my own, which I hope will be real soon."

"I'm sure Austin won't be pressing you to move out. The townhouse is pretty big and he often lets friends or clients stay there when they're passing through."

"How much rent does he want?"

"Nada."

Nadirah was taken aback. "I have to pay him something."

"No, you can't pay him anything. Austin can't, technically, make money on the house, which is why he doesn't officially rent it out."

"Let me guess. The divorce?"

"Exactly. Of course, you'll buy your own food and anything else you need personally. Oh, and the utility bills will be on you, but that's about it."

"Are you sure?"

"That's what Austin said. So, cousin, you have a place to stay. Austin is headed back to LA this afternoon. He said if we miss him today then we can pick up a set of keys from the carctaker who manages his property while he's out of town."

It almost felt too good to be true, but Nadirah wasn't about to look his gift horse in thc mouth. Admittedly, she did feel better. It would have been okay to stay with Daniel, but this way she wouldn't feel like she was imposing or obliging.

"Please thank Mr. Gray for me."

"Sure, but you might have the opportunity to thank him yourself if we get a move on."

"Okay, but first I have to call in. I have to get a substitute lined up for my class."

The minute Nadirah began making her call, Lynn made herself busy in Nadirah's closet. She pulled outfits by the shoulders along the rod, inspected them, then mentally rated each less than a two.

Nadirah hung up. "This is the first time I've ever put in for a sick day."

"Wow. That's what I call dedication."

"No, that's called hating to stay home with your mother."

Lynn understood fully what Nadirah meant, but she asked anyway, "Do you really like teaching?"

"I love teaching. I love being with my students, which is why if I should lose my job because of this ugly lie I would be totally lost."

"Nadirah, you won't lose your job. We'll straighten this mess out together."

Nadirah dragged her fingers through her braids. As grateful as she was to Lynn for finding her a place to live, she was confused. Never before had Lynn been so willing to give up time for her.

"Lynn, when are you going back to Boston?"

"I don't know yet. We'll see."

"What do you mean you don't know? What about the kids? What about Byron?"

Lynn started to say something but changed her mind.

"Lynn, is something wrong?"

"Everything's fine. Byron and I talked last night. I told him I needed to be here for a while."

"He was all right with that?"

"Not exactly, but he's so involved with his job at the insurance company, he won't miss me."

Nadirah thought she heard sadness in Lynn's words. "You don't believe that."

"I do, but it's okay. Anyway, our sitter will come and stay while I'm here in the city, and Byron will overnight my laptop so I can take care of my clients online."

"Byron is a great guy, isn't he, Lynn?" Nadirah wanted badly to get Lynn to talk about her husband, her life.

Lynn lifted a black and gold trimmed skirt from the closet. "This is interesting. Where did you get it?"

"Who knows? Lynn, how long have you and Byron been married?"

"Nine years. Can we talk about this skirt? I think it's seen better days—in a circus."

"I like that skirt," Nadirah defended. She was keenly aware that Lynn did not want to talk about her marriage. The question was why?

"This is an ugly skirt, Nadirah."

"Lynn, is everything all right between you and Byron?"

"Everything's hunky-dory. You know how marriages are. Great love at the beginning, sour pill at the end."

"At the end? Lynn, are you and Byron—"

"Oh, Nadirah, don't mind me," Lynn said, not wanting to talk about her marriage at all. "Byron and I are fine. We're no different from any other couple. But, look, we have a lot to do if you wanna get out of here before Mama comes home."

Nadirah knew very little about Lynn's husband. She knew Byron worked for a large insurance company as an appraisal claims manager and, supposedly, he made good enough money to give Lynn everything she wanted. They'd been married nine years and, until this moment, Nadirah never suspected that there might be problems in their marriage, but if Lynn didn't want to talk about it, she wasn't going to

press her.

"I will be picking Mama up from the hospital as late as possible. I'd like to get you moved out before she gets home."

Nadirah looked around her room. Materialistically, everything she owned was in her room. "I need to get some boxes and I'll need to rent a U-Haul truck."

"Why do you need a truck? We can move everything in my rental car."

"Not my furniture, Lynn. Neither my bed nor my dresser will fit into your car."

Lynn looked at the old, worn bedroom furniture that her mother bought for Nadirah when she was a little girl. "Do you really need this stuff, Nadirah? Austin's place is fully furnished with the most beautiful pieces. And besides, eventually, aren't you planning to get new furniture for the new place you get? And the clothes. I have to be honest with you, all your clothes need to be dumped.'"

Nadirah's jaw dropped.

"I'm sorry, Nadirah, but your clothes are awful. You need to treat yourself to a whole new wardrobe. The clothes you have are so outdated and … and old for you."

It wasn't like Nadirah didn't know that, but were they so bad that everything had to be dumped? "Well, I can't afford a whole new wardrobe right now, and clothes are the least of my worries."

"This is true, but I think an overhaul of your entire life is called for and that includes your clothes and your hair."

Nadirah felt a tight in her chest. It was one thing for Lynn to offer to help or to use her connections to find a place for her to live, but it was another thing, altogether, for Lynn to take control of her life. That was too much like what Aunt Stephanie had done.

"Nadirah, I'm not trying to insult you. Forgive me if I did, but you should look at this as a new beginning."

Nadirah went to her closet and began taking out armfuls of clothes. She was not trashing her clothes. Maybe she should not even take Lynn up on the use of Austin Gray's townhouse.

"Nadirah, just think for a minute. You'll have a new place to live, a new wardrobe, a new hairdo, and a new life. All of these things go hand-in-hand."

Nadirah continually took clothes from the closet and threw them onto the bed.

"Nadirah, listen to me. You—"

Nadirah turned abruptly. "Must I, Lynn? Must I listen to you and do what you say? Must I let you take my hand and hold on to me like I'm a child in order to affect these wondrous changes in my life?"

"No! Nadirah, no. I'm not trying to control you. I would just like to see you look as beautiful as I know you can look. I'm not gonna lie to you, you look old. You look older than me and I'm thirty-six."

"Thanks a lot."

Lynn took hold of Nadirah's arm to keep her from going back to the closet. "You're a young woman, Nadirah, but you don't look it. I look at you and I see boring. There's no color, no joy, and no light. Your clothes give no essence of who Nadirah is."

Nadirah knew how true this was, but she was hurt all the same. "Wow, Lynn. You are your mother's daughter."

Lynn let go of Nadirah's arm.

Nadirah regretted her words the instant she saw the hurt look on Lynn's face. "I'm sorry."

Although Nadirah's words were painful, Lynn understood why she said them. "Nadirah, I'll never try to control your life. I'm not going to tell you what to buy or when to buy it. I only want to suggest what will enhance the good looks you've hidden behind the clothes you've been wearing. You deserve a better life, a nicer life, and a prettier you. And if it's about money, don't worry. Look at it as a gift from me to you."

Nadirah sat in the only chair in her room next to her dresser. "I have my own money."

"Good, but I can do this for you."

"Thank you, but money's not my problem. I've saved quite a bit, and before the year is out, I'll get the trust fund my parents set up for me. I can afford whatever I want."

"That's fine, but I feel like I need to do something for you. I feel like I owe you. If I can't—"

"Lynn, you've done enough by finding me a place to live. Thank you, but I can handle everything else."

"I have no doubt, Nadirah, that you can handle your life, but

please let me at least go shopping with you. You'll find shopping quite cathartic. A few new clothes can do wonders. There isn't a woman on earth who doesn't feel fabulous after she's bought herself a couple of new outfits. Don't you wanna feel good? Don't you wanna look good? My goodness, you should have a little fun. You deserve it."

Undecided, Nadirah took the black skirt from Lynn and fingered the material. It was some sort of polyester or something.

Lynn snatched the skirt back. "A quality skirt doesn't have top stitching on the hem and it doesn't get cleaned in the washing machine. Nadirah, you're a quality person. You should be wearing quality clothes. Putting you in this skirt is like setting a flawless white diamond in a plastic gold colored band. Yuck!"

Nadirah smiled. Was she supposed to argue against that? She couldn't.

Lynn could see that she had finally won Nadirah over. "Let's get an early start. We can pack your essentials, pack the car, find Austin's caretaker—I have his number and address—go over to the townhouse, drop off what we've packed, check out the place, get something to eat, and then hit Bloomingdales."

Nadirah was exhausted just at the thought of all that Lynn outlined. Quite ambitious, but what else was there for her to do? She wasn't going to work, and BJ wasn't going to get to speak to all the kids at the center until tomorrow night. He didn't want her there, but she was going to be there. Who could better defend her than herself? After all, it was her career, her reputation, and maybe even her freedom on the line.

Chapter 8

The ride home from the hospital was frigidly quiet. Lynn kept telling herself to say nothing for fear of starting an argument with her mother right then and there in the car. Besides buckling up, the number two rule of driving in her family was no arguing while driving. A month after she and Byron were first married, they had their first fight while she was behind the wheel. She got so involved in the argument that she forgot all about the road ahead and rear-ended a car stopped at the light. It could have been disastrous because the car she rear-ended narrowly missed a man crossing the street. Since then, Lynn never argued while driving no matter what. So keeping her mouth shut with her mother was for the best, and thinking pleasant thoughts was even better, which is why she pushed thoughts of Byron way back in the recesses of her mind. In her mind's eye she could still see Nadirah as she looked with her beautiful new hairdo and gorgeous new clothes. Yes, all had gone well and she had left Nadirah at Austin's fabulous townhouse looking like she'd always lived there.

Lynn glanced sideways at her mother's stone-faced, sour profile. If Mama thought she was mad now because she had to wait at the hospital too long then she was going to bust a gut when she found out that Nadirah moved out.

Stephanie, with her lips pressed into a thin, rigid line, was so mad she kept her arms folded high and tight across her chest the whole ride. She couldn't believe how late Lynn had been getting to the hospital. *Seven-thirty! Seven-damn-thirty! And as old and grown as I am, those damn nurses had the nerve to not let me leave unless Lynn came for me. Ridiculous! Millicent could have brought me home, but she is nowhere to be found. That's what I get for letting Millicent take the day off because Lynn, my own damn daughter, was in town and was supposed to be taking care of me, which she isn't.*

As soon as Lynn parked in front of the brownstone she retrieved

the walker from the trunk, opened the passenger side door, set the walker within Stephanie's reach, and stepped back.

Stephanie gawked at Lynn.

"Okay, Mama, get out."

"You have to help me."

"No, I don't." Lynn went to the trunk and took out a single shopping bag containing a skirt and blouse that Nadirah insisted on buying for her.

Stephanie watched Lynn close the trunk and walk toward the brownstone. "Lynn, are you going to leave me here?"

"Mama, swing your legs out, plant your two feet on the ground, put one hand on the walker, put the other on the side of the door, and pull yourself up out of the car. Simple, do it."

Stunned, Stephanie stared at Lynn. Why Lynn would speak to her in that tone when Lynn knew she couldn't do any such thing baffled her.

"Mama, the longer you sit there, the longer it'll take for you to get into the house."

"I'm your mother. Why are you treating me like this?"

"Mama, stop the drama. Get out of the car?please."

"This is the thanks I get for all the sacrifices I've made for you. Absolutely no gratitude." Stephanie grunted loudly as she made a show of straining to pull herself up out of the car. Lynn made no move to help her up to her feet. Stephanie leaned heavily on the walker as she moved slowly away from the car and left the car door wide open.

Lynn went to the car and closed and locked the door. She then hurried past Stephanie and started up the brownstone steps.

"Well," Stephanie said loudly, "aren't you gonna help me up the stairs?"

"Mama, you have your walker. Just hold onto the banister with one hand and the walker with the other."

"I can't walk up these stairs and hold onto this damn walker, too! And you stop talking to me like I'm a damn imbecile!"

"You can do it, Mama," Lynn said as evenly as she could. "Is that better?"

"Lynn—"

"Mama, how have you been going back and forth to your

appointments?"

"What do you think I have Millicent for? She helps me."

"Yes, but Millicent doesn't carry you up and down these stairs."

"I hold on to her arm, smarty."

"Well, Mama, Millicent is a whole lot bigger than me, and unfortunately, she isn't here. So take your time, one step at a time, no hurry. I'll see you inside. I have to go to the bathroom."

"Well, so do I!"

Lynn kept walking.

"Lynn!" Stephanie called out until she saw her long-time neighbor, seventy-two-year-old Joseph Vaughn, come out of his house two doors away. She immediately tried to put a smile on her face.

"Good evening, Stephanie."

"How you doing, Joseph?"

Lynn turned back.

"I'm good." Joseph locked his door and trotted down the stairs to the sidewalk. "Stephanie, you need some help?"

"Yes, I—"

"Mr. Vaughn, how are you?" Lynn started back down the stairs.

"Lynn!" Mr. Vaughn cheered. "I didn't see you there. How you doing?"

"I'm fine and so is Mama. She's moving slow, but she'll make it up the stairs all right."

"You sure?"

"Joseph, I—"

"We're sure, Mr. Vaughn," Lynn said, firmly. "Thank you. You have a good evening."

"Okay, then," Joseph said, a bit perplexed. "Y'all have a good evening." He went on down the street, leaving Stephanie fuming at Lynn.

"What the hell do you think you're doing?"

"Mama, unless you can deal with the answer, don't ask the question. Now get in this house before I lose my patience."

"Don't you dare talk to me like that! I will slap your tongue right out of your mouth!"

"With all due respect, Mama, I am not the least bit intimidated by you. I suggest you stop talking and use your energy to climb these

stairs."

Totally staggered by Lynn's coldness, Stephanie couldn't believe Lynn was going back up the stairs without her. Was she out of her mind? Had someone switched daughters on her? Sure, Lynn didn't come around all that often, but when she did she was always attentive and kind, especially if Stephanie had been sick. Why was Lynn acting like she was upset with her? Well, she wasn't putting up with that attitude.

"Lynn!"

Digging in her pocketbook, Lynn searched for the house keys.

"It's dark out here. Are you gonna leave me out here by myself?"

"Mama, first off, this is New York City. It's never dark in New York City. In fact, there's a street light right over your head. Secondly, you've lived in this house, on this block for thirty-two years. What do you have to be afraid of? Nothing. Now, if you need more light, as soon as I get this door open, I'll turn on the stoop light for you."

Stephanie began to feel afraid. "Lynn, my God! What's wrong with you? I can't believe you're leaving me out here when you know I can't walk!"

Lynn's hand finally touched the house keys at the bottom of her pocketbook. "Is that the truth, Mama?"

"And what the hell do you mean by that?"

"You figure it out." Lynn unlocked the front door.

"Lynn! Lynn!"

"Mama, people can hear you out here."

"I don't care who hears me! You get down here and help me up these damn stairs right now!"

Lynn turned away.

Appalled, Stephanie gasped as Lynn stepped through the first door and unlocked the second door of the brownstone. What did Lynn know? Did she know that she could walk on her own without her walker? If she knew, how did she find out? Millicent would never tell. She swore that she wouldn't.

Stephanie stubbornly refused to take one step up the stairs. "Why are you being so cruel to me, Lynn? I just got out of the hospital. Don't you care? Why are you so cruel to me?"

"Oh, I'm not being cruel, Mama. I'm trying to help you be more independent." Lynn reached inside and flicked on the stoop lights, illuminating the sixteen brownstone steps. "There, you have more light. I'll see you inside."

Stephanie shouted, "Where's Nadirah? Send Nadirah out here!"

Again Lynn turned back. "Nadirah's not here."

"What do you mean, she's not here? Where is she? Nadirah knows I want her here in the evening in case I need her."

Lynn stood at the top of the stairs looking down hard at her mother. How had she not seen what her mother had been doing to Nadirah? How had she been so blind? All these years, the cruelty, the demeaning comments and remarks, the demands on Nadirah's time, it was all there right in her face whenever she visited, yet she didn't realize how bad it truly was.

"Where is she?" Stephanie demanded angrily. "Where is Nadirah?"

Lynn said flatly, "Nadirah doesn't live here anymore, Mama. She moved out. She left her house keys on your dresser. She's not coming back."

It was the shocked look on her mother's face that confirmed for Lynn that she had been right. Her mother never wanted Nadirah to leave and would most likely have done anything to keep her from leaving. Maybe Nadirah was right. Maybe Mama made that call to the center and the school. If her father was alive he'd have a fit.

"So she finally did it," Stephanie said. "She moved out. Ungrateful little heifer. She couldn't move out with me here. She did it behind my back. Selfish ass. She don't care about nobody but herself. What am I supposed to do now?"

"Take care of yourself," Lynn said as she went on into the hall, leaving both front doors open for her mother to come in. She ignored the calling of her name as she rushed to the first floor bathroom at the back of the house. She really did have to go.

"Ungrateful little heifer," Stephanie said again.

Hot with anger, Stephanie took her time slowly stomping up the stairs and slamming the walker down hard on each step. The truth was that she could walk without her walker, but she did need a cane, especially on the stairs. With each year, stairs had become more difficult to

climb, but Lynn would not have known that. After all these years, why would Lynn suddenly think that she could walk? She had to know something for her to insist that she walk up the stairs by herself, but what? Gritting her teeth and swearing before God that she'd give Lynn a piece of her mind when she got inside the house, it took Stephanie a good ten minutes to get up those thirteen stone steps.

Behind her, Stephanie slammed each door loud enough to disturb any one of her neighbors on either side of her. Lynn certainly felt and heard the slamming of the door all the way upstairs where she had gone to take her shopping bag.

"Lynn Denise Wilkie! You get in here!"

Lynn moseyed out of the bedroom over to the banister and looked down at her mother. "I'm up here," she said calmly.

Leaning on her walker, Stephanie barked, "You get down here this instant and explain yourself!"

Lynn leaned over the banister. "Wow, Mama, I'm impressed. You made it up the stairs all by yourself."

"Don't you patronize me! You get down here!"

"Oh, I'll be down, Mama, you can be sure of that. But let me change out of my heels. I need to be comfortable when I come face to face with a master prevaricator."

Stephanie gasped and brought her hand to her chest. "How dare you call me a liar!"

Lynn narrowed a hard glare on Stephanie. "How dare you live a scandalous lie!"

"What are you talking about? I … I've never lied to you. I—"

"Mama, what you've done is despicable! And to keep lying about it," Lynn kicked off her heels and started down the stairs barefooted, "just makes the lie all the more horrific."

"What are you talking about? I don't know what you're talking about."

"Oh, please! Stop it!"

"What lie have I told? What lie have I lived?"

Lynn charged at Stephanie and snatched the walker from her grasp and flung it behind her, sending it crashing into the wall!

Shocked, Stephanie stumbled, but she did not fall. "Have you lost your damn mind?"

"Mama, for the past eighteen years you've lied about your condition. How long have you been able to walk?"

Stephanie locked eyes with eyes that were so clearly Lester's angry eyes. She shook in her soul from the bitter glare that damned her for the lie she had lived. Her hands began to shake.

"How could you, Mama? How could you use Nadirah like that? How could you lie to me and Les? You made us all think you were so helpless?"

Stephanie couldn't speak. Her eyes batted nervously.

Lynn's eyes watered. She sucked her teeth and walked away toward the kitchen. Her throat was so dry.

Her hands shaking, her knees weak, Stephanie went and sat in the living room and looked around. Every wall was covered with beautiful paintings and prints. Her whole comfortable twelve room house was beautiful, but now that her deception was out in the open, only she would live here and die here. It wasn't fair. Although she and Lester's marriage had been cold and unloving, it had been familiar. They were supposed to live out their lives here together. But he was gone, and now so was Nadirah. Nadirah was supposed to stay and be there for her in her twilight years. Nadirah owed her that much for taking her in.

Lynn came soundlessly back into the room. "Mama, you better tell me everything and I mean everything from A to Z, or I will walk out of this house and never speak to you again. Do you understand me?"

Stephanie closed her eyes. She had not seen the coming of this day. So to explain her deception was going to be the hardest thing she ever had to do.

Chapter 9

There was so much new, so much to take in that Nadirah's head was spinning from not only looking at herself, but at the beauty that surrounded her. She was wearing her fifth new outfit, a navy blue pantsuit with a teal scoop neck silk sweater. With her newly styled hair, Nadirah didn't recognize herself. Lynn was right, she looked different, she looked better, she looked, dare she say, beautiful. She should have looked as she do now hours before when she met Austin Gray.

She and Lynn had stopped off to pick up the keys from Paul Ramirez just in case they missed Austin at his house. As soon as Lynn unlocked the front door and stepped inside, Austin appeared at the top of the stairs and Nadirah saw right away how good looking a man he was. He was tall, not so dark, but quite handsome, and as he came down the stairs, Nadirah saw that Austin Gray's steel blue turtle neck sweater and dark creased dungarees fit him like they were custom made for him. His sweater fit his broad shoulders, hugged his well-defined muscular arms, and caressed his flat abs like a piece of Saran Wrap on a bowl. His thick, black, curly hair and 5:00 o'clock shadow made Mr. Austin Gray look like he'd be right at home in a log cabin with a hot, crackling fire. And Nadirah, with her usual drab, colorless self, was standing there looking like she'd just come off a farm somewhere.

"This must be your cousin," Austin said, extending his hand to Nadirah.

"Yes," Lynn said. "Nadirah Lewis, Austin Gray. I'm glad you two could meet."

Nadirah limply lifted her hand and felt it smothered in Austin's large hand.

"Good meeting you, Nadirah," Austin said, letting go of Nadirah's hand. "I hope you like it here. You have good neighbors next door. On the right is Miss Beulah Bradley, and on the left the

Wilsons. In an emergency, just knock at any one of their doors."

Nadirah managed to say, "Thank you," in a weak, little voice that even her own ears barely heard so she doubted that Austin Gray heard her as he turned to take Lynn into his big, strong arms.

"Hey," Austin said, "I'm glad I got to see you this time around."

"Me, too." Lynn tapped Austin on his broad chest. "You're looking well."

Nadirah wondered what it must be like to lay a hand on a chest like Austin's. Daniel's chest was nothing like this one.

"You look happy," Austin said. "Byron's doing his job, huh?"

Lynn ignored Austin's comment. "Speaking of spouses, have you been speaking to yours?"

"Only when I have to," Austin replied. "But, let's not get into that. Life's been pretty good. When are you and Byron making it out to California?"

"Who knows? Byron is … maybe you should ask Byron."

Nadirah was keenly aware that Lynn was again avoiding any discussion of Byron. Something was definitely wrong in her marriage, but until Lynn wanted to talk about it there was nothing Nadirah could do. For now, she was content to stand on the side and look at Austin who glanced her way for the second time. At least he knows I'm here, she thought. Ten minutes later a limo arrived to take Austin to the airport.

"He's such a sweetie," Lynn said once Austin had gone. "Too bad he married such a witch."

Nadirah didn't take the bait. She said nothing and asked nothing. She didn't want to know what had gone wrong in Austin's marriage, although she was curious about Lynn's. Usually, other people's drama never interested her, which is why she never watched much television. Perhaps living with Aunt Stephanie and bearing witness to and being the recipient of her cruelty did that to her. Austin Gray's life was his own and as far as Nadirah was concerned she didn't need to know the ugliness of his marriage in order to live in his house.

Riiiiig!

Nadirah hurriedly answered her cell phone. "Hello."

"Hey, it's me," Lynn said. *"Can you talk?"*

For a second, Nadirah was thrown. "Oh, I'm alone. Daniel's not here."

"I thought he was coming over?"

"He was, but I called him back and told him not to come. I wanted to be alone tonight."

"Are you all right?"

"I'm fine. I just wanted to get a sense of the house by myself."

"It's beautiful, isn't it?"

"Yes, it's really nice. Thank you for setting this up for me."

"No problem. By the way, Mama's home."

"And?"

"She's ticked," said, her voice suddenly lower. *"She's downstairs in the living room, crying."*

"About me moving out?"

"That's probably mixed up in there somewhere, but you are not going to believe the things she's told me as to why she hid that she could walk and why she took those pills."

"You got her to admit that she could walk?"

"She admitted nothing. I made her walk up the stairs by herself. She had no choice."

"I knew it! Oh, my God, I knew it! I knew it!"

"You were right. But, you won't believe how long she's been walking."

Nadirah didn't hesitate. "Five, six years?"

"More. How about sixteen years."

Nadirah gasped incredulously. "Are you kidding?"

"I was blown away. Nadirah, I could not believe what was coming out of my mother's mouth."

"Are you saying that she could walk way before Uncle Lester died? I mean, are you saying that she could walk a year after she fell down the stairs?"

"Yes."

Again Nadirah gasped. It was just too insane to comprehend that Aunt Stephanie would pretend for sixteen years that she couldn't walk when she could. Nadirah had to sit down.

"I can't believe it."

"Frankly, I'm still trying to understand how she could be so vilely deceptive."

"Lynn, your father died thinking that his wife was unable to walk.

How cruel was that?"

"Extremely."

"God!" Nadirah clinched her fist. "How vicious! How could she do something like that?"

"Are you sitting down?"

"Lynn, nothing you can tell me will shock me or justify the lie she lived."

"I agree, but do you wanna know?"

"Just tell me!"

For a tense moment, Lynn was silent. *"About a week before Mama fell down the stairs, Daddy told her he was leaving."*

Nadirah sucked her teeth disbelievingly. "She's lying. Uncle Lester would have never left her."

"Oh, she wasn't lying. Les and I were about nineteen when Mama fell down the stairs. I actually forgot about this, but about a month before that, Daddy took Les and I out to dinner. He told us he couldn't stay married to Mama and that he couldn't take it anymore. He told us because he wanted to know how we'd feel about it."

This certainly was news to Nadirah. "He was gonna leave me alone with her?"

"Nadirah, Daddy would not have abandoned you."

"Oh, no? He was going to leave me alone with that woman."

"You were only twelve years old. He would have stayed in your life."

"Not if he'd left."

"He wanted to leave, Nadirah, but he didn't."

"Why? Because Aunt Stephanie fell down the stairs and he decided to stay to take care of her?"

"No, that's when he decided to stay and take care of you."

"Me?"

"Nadirah, Daddy never liked the way Mama treated you."

"So why was he going to leave me with her?"

"Just temporarily, Nadirah. I know you know it was really hard on Daddy living with Mama, but what you don't know is Daddy had originally told us before you came that he was going to leave after Les and I went off to college, but when you came and he saw how Mama was treating you—"

"But the other day I thought you said Uncle Lester said he'd never leave Aunt Stephanie."

"No, I told you why Daddy said he loved her and why he was with her. I didn't tell you that he said he'd never leave her. That's different."

"Okay, so he stayed with Aunt Stephanie because of me? I messed up his life?"

"That's not how Daddy felt and that's not what I'm saying. Nadirah, back then Daddy was still going to leave, but he was going to seek full custody or joint custody of you because he and Mama both were your legal guardians jointly. But after Mama fell, he didn't think he'd have a chance of getting you with Mama not being able to walk. Plus, it would look like he was abandoning her."

"Lynn, I still don't get it. He was leaving or he wasn't leaving? I don't understand."

"Quite frankly, there are things I don't quite understand either, but regarding you, Daddy told me you had it pretty bad when Mama could walk. He was afraid that if he left, and Mama couldn't walk, you would have an even harder time so he stayed to watch over you."

Those same silent tears that Nadirah shed at Uncle Lester's funeral again wet her cheeks. She had known always that Uncle Lester protected her, she just didn't know that he had sacrificed his freedom to do it.

"Oh, and Mama knew. She knew Daddy was leaving. They had talked about it. In fact, they fought about it. I remember hearing Mama say if Daddy left her, she'd make him pay."

"So when she fell down the stairs she milked it for all it was worth. She got Uncle Lester to stay."

"Yes."

"But Uncle Lester died nine years ago. Why did she keep the lie going?"

*"Because she was afraid of being alone. Mama said she couldn't tell you or me or Les that she had gotten the use of her legs back, because Les and I would have stopped calling or coming around at all to see her, and you would have left if you knew she wasn't disabled.""*So she lied to keep me around and you in touch?"

"That's what it comes down to."

"For seventeen years, Lynn! She lied for seventeen years!"

"Sixteen years. Nadirah—"

"Seventeen, sixteen, one, what does it matter? The woman lied! And to make matters worse, she deceived Uncle Lester. She deceived all of us. Aunt Stephanie treated me like I was her handmaiden. It wasn't like she wanted me around because she loved me, she kept me around and humiliated me because she hated me."

"I don't know if it was hate. She—"

"It was hate, Lynn! I can't see it any other way."

The other end of the line was silent. Nadirah sensed what that silence meant.

"You feel sorry for her, don't you?"

"To some extent, maybe. I think her lie originated from a place of fear. I think she's afraid to be alone, and I also think she'll live to regret the lie, but I don't believe that she truly hates you."

"Well, whatever it is your mother feels for me."

"Nadirah, I can't blame Mama totally for how she treated you."

"So who do you blame, Lynn, me, my parents?"

"Actually, I blame myself."

"Oh, come on. Lynn, you're not the one who used me, abused me. Your mother did all that and she knew what she was doing. She's an old, manipulative woman who always demanded and got her way no matter what. We all know this about her. It's just too bad Uncle Lester had to sacrifice his own happiness for me, and for that, I feel terrible."

"But it's not your fault. If?"

"Please, let's not do ifs. The fact is Aunt Stephanie used all of us. Me? She took charge of me when I was most vulnerable. She took my fear and held it in the palm of her hands and tried to make sure that I would always be afraid. Lynn, I've lived with fear all of my life and I'm tired of living that way. If I'd had a backbone when I first suspected Aunt Stephanie of lying, of deceiving us, I would have confronted her, but…but I didn't. I wasn't strong enough."

"Well, don't blame yourself for that. Mama's a formidable being. She always had big ideas, big dreams, and a big mouth. Growing up, if it wasn't for my father, Les and I would have been afraid of her, too."

"Lucky you."

"I'm sorry you lost your parents, Nadirah."

"So am I." Her eyes still welled up whenever she saw the love

between a parent and a child and was reminded about how much she missed out on.

Nadirah and Lynn both took a pensive pause. Nadirah reflected on how funny life was. Aunt Stephanie might not have loved her, but it was Aunt Stephanie who gave her the love and protection of Uncle Lester.

"So, Nadirah, what do we do about the great deceiver?"

"Did you ask her if she made those calls to the center and my job?"

"She denied it."

"I know you don't believe her?"

"I wanna say I don't, but she came clean about being able to walk, and—"

"Probably because she figures there's no way I can prove or disprove that she made them so why admit to it?"

"Unfortunately."

Nadirah felt ill. She had been counting on Lynn to get Aunt Stephanie to admit that she'd made those calls. It would have made her life so much easier.

"Nadirah, if Mama is behind those calls—"

"If, Lynn? Who else would try to get me fired? Aunt Stephanie told you from her own mouth that she was afraid of being alone. If she got me fired, I'd have to stay in her house…well, no, I wouldn't. That's what she thinks, but I don't care if I had to live in a cardboard box under the Brooklyn Bridge, I would not have continued to live with her."

"Look, I promised you I'd find out if Mama made the calls and I will. I still have time. Tomorrow I'll be here to talk to Millicent to find out how she feels about moving in. If she can't, I have to find someone else."

"Why does anyone have to move in? Aunt Stephanie can walk. Hell, she can probably run the New York City Marathon."

"Ha! I wouldn't doubt it, but she says she's afraid to live alone, and there's no way I'm moving my family here. No way at all."

"Then don't worry about it. She'll make out okay."

"You're probably right. We'll see."

"Good. So will I see you tomorrow?"

"Of course. I'm going down to the center with you."

Beep!

A second call was coming in on Nadirah's cell phone.

"I have another call. Hold on. Hello?"

"Nadirah? Hi. Austin Gray."

Nadirah's heart thumped. "Hi. Would you hold on a minute? I'm on another call."

"Sure."

Nadirah quickly pressed the talk button. "Lynn, Austin Gray is on the other line."

"He said he was going to call. I gave him your cell phone number."

Nadirah stood. "Why is he calling?"

"To make sure everything is okay, silly. Don't worry, he's safe."

"I certainly hope so."

"Look, take the call. I'll see you tomorrow, but call me later if you want to."

"Okay." Nadirah switched over to Austin's call. "Hello?"

"Is this a bad time?"

"Actually, I was just about to call it a night."

"I won't keep you then. I—"

"Thank you for letting me stay in your home, but don't worry, I won't be here long."

"Stay as long as you like. I use the house only one week out of a month, and not even a whole week. I'm in and out when I am there. Lynn explained your situation, no problem. Oh, and by the way, I'll always ring the bell before coming in."

"Thank you. I appreciate it."

"Then I'll say good night. If you need anything, Paul Ramirez's number, as well as my own, are in the table in the front hall."

"Great. Thank you."

"So you have a good night."

"You, too."

Nadirah was left with the sound of Austin Gray's strong voice in her head. He probably seduced a lot of women with that smooth, deep, sultry voice of his. But why in the world was she even thinking about him like that? The man was married, separated or not, and she was probably not his type, but why even think about it? Looking for a man was the last thing she even had to consider. She had too much garbage to clean up in her life before she even thought seriously about

a relationship that demanded more than she was prepared to give. That's why Daniel was so right for her. He demanded nothing and expected even less from her. If anything happened between them, it happened and neither one of them missed a step. The friendship they shared was what it was and neither questioned it.

Nadirah went about hanging up her new clothes in her temporary closet. She had a long day ahead of her and needed to get some sleep. At least she hoped she was going to be able to sleep without thinking about Aunt Stephanie and her incredulous lie. How could the woman let Uncle Lester leave this earth thinking that she couldn't walk? Unforgivable. No, she never wanted to see Aunt Stephanie or ever be in the same room with her again. In fact, when it was time to transfer her trust fund into her name, she was going to hire an attorney just so she wouldn't have to personally deal with her aunt.

Nadirah exhaled the last thoughts of Aunt Stephanie for the night. She was looking forward to going to bed knowing that no one would tap on the adjourning wall, bang on the floor with a cane, or ring a bell to get her attention. Yes, this was indeed a new beginning.

Chapter 10

Nadirah hated that the cold, icy rain and chilly winds of February forced her to wear her long, overstuffed down coat along with a wool hat pulled down over her newly relaxed hairdo, and a long, wool scarf wrapped twice around her neck. For the first time in her life, underneath her coat, Nadirah felt stylishly put together, and although she knew it was egotistical on her part, she wanted everyone who set eyes on her to see how great she looked. And that was just it, she looked great, and she felt great, which didn't make sense, not when she had a black cloud of child molestation looming over her head. Until her name was cleared, Nadirah most definitely had something to worry about.

"That won't happen," Lynn had said yesterday while they were shopping. "You're innocent, and you will be proven so."

Nadirah certainly hoped so, but she wasn't naive. She knew how a single vicious lie could take on a life of its own and bury the truth so deep it would take an oil-dredging machine to unearth it. Nadirah glanced up at the wall clock at the back of her classroom. It was just eight-fifteen. She had been in her classroom sitting behind her desk since six forty-five. That was the earliest she'd ever entered the building, but she had to put together her lesson plan for her class since she hadn't done so the day before. In fifteen minutes her students will walk in, some bright-eyed, eager to learn; some grinning, looking to have fun; and that challenging few who wear their ho-hum attitudes on their sleeves will bring up the rear and ignite the fire within Nadirah to show them that their world can only be broadened by the knowledge they gained. With her lesson plan now complete, Nadirah began passing out the morning's math worksheet just

as the sound of chattering students entering the halls reached her.

"Hey, I missed you yesterday."

Nadirah turned to see Marilyn Gaines at her classroom door.

"Wow! You look great."

"Thank you."

"I was going to ask if you were sick yesterday, but I think I should be asking who is your stylist?"

"My cousin Lynn," Nadirah said, smiling.

"Well, she certainly did a wonderful job. I almost didn't know you."

"I'd be insulted if it wasn't for the fact that I almost didn't know myself this morning."

"You look great. You look fifteen years younger. Actually, you look your age now."

Now that remark only confirmed what Lynn had said about her looking like an old lady when she was only twenty-nine. Wow, she must have looked really bad.

"Well, I hope I don't shock too many people around here," Nadirah said, no longer wanting to hear about how differently she looked. "So did I miss anything yesterday?"

"Same old craziness. I tried to call you last night to talk to you about the class party this afternoon, but I got a disconnect message."

Nadirah gasped in surprise. She had totally forgotten about the Valentine's day party for her and Marilyn's class.

"You forgot?" Marilyn asked.

"I sure did, but I have everything I need stored in my closet. My kids?"

"Miss Lewis!" Patricia said, entering the classroom. She stopped, looked hard at Nadirah, then she rushed to her and hugged her. "You look beautiful."

Smiling from the warmth of Patricia's hug, Nadirah hugged her back. "Well, thank you, sweetie. Did the class behave for the substitute yesterday?"

"I did, but Shane and Michael didn't. They kept talking and getting out of their seats."

"I'll have to have a talk with Mr. Shane and Mr. Michael," Nadirah said. "Go take off your coat and get started on the math sheet."

"Okay," Patricia said, still smiling at Nadirah as she walked away.

"Marilyn, I'm using my cell phone for now."

"Miss Lewis!" two more students exclaimed excitedly as they entered the classroom. "You look different!"

Marilyn laughed. "I think I'll leave you with your admirers. I'll see you at lunch." Marilyn hurried off down the hall to her own fourth grade classroom.

Within minutes, Nadirah's students filled her classroom and each and every child had something to say about how good or how different she looked. At the ringing of the eight-thirty start of class bell, Nadirah directed her students to sit down. It wasn't until she took attendance that she realized that two of her students, Bobby Harris and Bree Morrison, were absent. It disturbed Nadirah that she had not noticed Bree's absence sooner. She felt badly because, perhaps, part of Bree's problem was that no one noticed her. Nadirah vowed that she'd be more attentive to Bree when she returned to school.

Throughout the day, Nadirah expected to be called to Principal Crayton's office, but never was. Nothing had been placed in her mailbox yesterday nor today which gave Nadirah concern. Still, she felt Principal Crayton should tell her something good or bad about how her investigation was going, or was it too soon for that? Nadirah's anxiousness to find out if anymore was said about the accusations against her kept her glancing at the clock. By the end of the day she figured no news was good news.

"Nadirah, I was hoping to catch up with you before you left today," Beverly Cotton said, coming up behind her at the time clock about to punch out.

"I was looking for you at lunch time."

Beverly stepped back and gave Nadirah the once over. "I've been incredibly busy, but look at you. I heard about how different you looked. You look really good."

"Thanks. Have you heard anything…you know about—"

Beverly pulled Nadirah aside to let other teachers get to the time clock. She said in a low voice, "Come to my office."

Nadirah's heart thumped. "Was there another call?" Nadirah asked as soon as Marilyn closed her office door.

"No, and I don't expect there will be another call. This is about your student Bree Morrison."

"Bree wasn't in school today. Did something happen to her?"

"She's in the hospital. Columbia Presbyterian."

Nadirah set her briefcase on a chair. "Oh, no. What happened?"

Marilyn slipped around her desk and took a folder from the side drawer and handed it to Nadirah.

As Nadirah began to read, the fine hairs on her arm bristled. "This can't be right."

Beverly sat behind her desk. "According to the social worker who called about twenty minutes ago from Administration for Children's Services, it is. They wanted to know if I had been counseling Bree, or if you, her teacher—"

"Why didn't you send for me?"

"I did, but you weren't in your classroom."

"Oh. I was down in the cafeteria with my class. We had a party with Marilyn's class. I dismissed them from there."

"Well, ACS wanted to know if we had any knowledge of Bree's situation."

"What situation? I've talked to Bree and could never get any-thing out of her. Bree's very withdrawn. Her parents have never responded to letters I've sent asking them to meet with me. They have never come in for parent/teacher conferences, and the one time I called Bree's house and actually got her mother on the phone, Mrs. Morrison told me, in no uncertain terms, that my job was to teach her daughter in school, and that once the 3:00 o'clock bell rang I had no say about her daughter's life. Then she hung up on me. That's the only contact I've ever had with a parent of Bree's. I've checked, but there have never been any physical signs of abuse, and I've tried to—"

"Were there ever any problems between Bree and other children in the class?"

Nadirah began shaking her head. "No."

"Did any of your students ever make fun of Bree or pick at her?"

Nadirah thought about it. "Maybe once back at the start of the term, which I put a stop to immediately. Another student called Bree a baby because she spoke so softly when she answered during roll call.

Beyond that, I've never heard of or seen anyone picking at Bree. If I had, I would have stopped it."

"Evidently this is no fault of the school," Beverly said, taking the file back from Nadirah. "The answer to why Bree tried to kill herself is definitely in her home."

It hurt Nadirah's heart to know that Bree, only eight years old, was in such pain that she saw no way out but to try and take her own life. It was too awful for Nadirah to comprehend.

"Beverly, are they sure Bree tried to kill herself? She's a baby. Baby's don't kill themselves!"

"Mrs. Hamilton, the social worker who called, said that Bree drank almost a half bottle of pine disinfectant, which was kept under the sink in the bathroom."

"Maybe the bottle was on the counter in the kitchen, may—"

"Nadirah, I've already done the maybes. Bree isn't blind, she can read. We all know that, her test scores verify that she can read. Plus, with the first taste of the disinfectant, if it was a mistake, Bree should have spit it out. She didn't. She drank it down."

"Beverly, I simply can't imagine that poor baby doing that to herself."

"Well, it seems she did. Mrs. Hamilton said that Bree's mother stated that the disinfectant was kept in the bathroom under the sink and nowhere else. She said that Miss Morrison?there is no mister?was awakened this morning by Bree's moaning and found her in the bathroom on the floor throwing up. The bottle was open on the floor next to her."

"Poor baby."

"The police, the doctors, Mrs. Hamilton, everyone is concluding that Bree drank the disinfectant on her own and that she had to have been trying to kill herself."

"Is she going to be all right?"

"Her doctor thinks so, physically. She'll be in the hospital a week at least. They pumped her stomach and have her on medication. When Bree gets out of the hospital, however, Mrs. Hamilton wants to put her in counseling. And, more significantly, ACS is seriously thinking about not releasing her to her mother, but instead, are considering putting Bree in foster care."

"Is the agency thinking that Miss Morrison is negligent or maybe that she's an unfit mother?"

"That I have no information on, but it was the mother who called 911 and got help for Bree. Still, ACS wants to take a look at Miss Morrison before they place Bree back with her. It's probably procedural."

"Beverly, you said there is no Mister Morrison. Are you there any other relatives?"

"Single mother. That's all Mrs. Hamilton said on the subject."

"So what can we do to help Bree? If she goes into foster care will she still come to this school?"

"Not necessarily. Bree could end up anywhere in the five boroughs. We may well lose her here at 410.

The thought of losing another one of her students to the system didn't sit well with Nadirah. Already there were six students in her class in foster care and had been for a varying number of years. Luckily, two of her students were about to be adopted by their foster parents, while at least one was scheduled to be moved to another foster home in the area. It wasn't the foster care system Nadirah was against, they certainly filled a very essential need, it was the handful of individuals in the system who used the children to line their pockets. Those foster parents were the ones who, at times, did more harm to the children than the parents from whom the children were taken. She didn't want that for Bree.

"Beverly, what if I take Bree when she's released?"

Beverly raised her brow. "You?"

"I'm already Bree's teacher. If I were also her foster parent, I'd be with her, literally, around the clock. I could do so much to help her. You're the Assistant Principal of Guidance here at the school. You would see that Bree receives counseling, either from yourself or from whomever the city appoints, and Bree won't be taken completely out of familiar surroundings."

"Well, I see your point, Nadirah, but I don't know if?"

"Bree won't have to deal with the emotional estrangement from her mother and her school. Yes, she's quiet here, but this school is familiar to her. I could help her with whatever her problems are."

"Of course, you could, but, Nadirah, you don't have a place of your own. You live, very unhappily, I might add, with your aunt who

isn't a very nice person."

"I used to live with my aunt, who isn't a very nice person. Yesterday, I moved. That's why I didn't come in."

Beverly sat forward. "You have your own apartment?"

"I'm staying in a townhouse on West 147th Street. I have the use of a good percentage of the house. I'm looking for my own place, but the owner has assured me that I can stay there as long as I wish."

"But that doesn't qualify as a permanent residence."

"It could if I ask the owner, who is very close to my cousin, for a lease. If we explain the reason, I'm sure I can get one."

Beverly flipped through Bree's file. "I don't know."

"Think about it, Beverly, please. I really wanna help Bree."

"Suppose the agency says you're a single woman under thirty who has never lived with a child who may well be too close to the situation?"

"Yes, I am single with a very inactive active social life, and, no, I've never had children of my own, but I've had, for the past six years, many children under my care, entrusted to me by the New York City Department of Education. My closeness to Bree I would think is a plus. Beverly, I am willing to give Bree all of my time to get her through whatever it is that made her want to kill herself. You know me. You know how much I care about children."

Beverly had to agree. "You have my support. The question is if Bree ends up in foster care, will ACS permit you to foster her? And what about Bree's mother? She may fight the placement, and, more importantly, you'd have to be approved for the foster care program."

"Fine. I do hope Bree's mother fights for her, then we'd know that she cares. And as for me being approved, why shouldn't I be? I'll do whatever I need to do to be ready just in case. Bree may be in the hospital one or two weeks, right? I have a little time. Maybe I can get some kind of emergency accreditation. I'll do whatever I need to do. If you help me, we can do whatever it takes to get ACS to consider me for temporary foster parenting. I'll get my cousin to talk to her friend about giving me a lease, and you can contact Mrs. Hamilton to see what she thinks. We can only try, but I really want to do this."

"Obviously," Beverly said, impressed. "But, and there is a but, Nadirah. Let's say we get the ball rolling and everything is going your

way, but then that call Principal Crayton got the other day rears its ugly head?"

That quickly, the feeling of elation Nadirah had begun to feel at the possibility of helping Bree dropped to the pit of her stomach. How could she have so quickly forgotten about the call?

"How do we explain it, Nadirah? What if that call stands in your way?"

Nadirah could not allow that. "Tonight, I'm going to the center."

"But didn't Mr. Parish ask you not to come? He said he would speak to the students?"

"Yes, but I wanna be front and center when he does. Beverly, if I'm there, there isn't one student who can look me in the eye and tell that lie about me."

"I should hope not, but you know as well as I that a liar will hold on to a lie like it's his last breath."

Aunt Stephanie and her seventeen-year lie came to Nadirah's mind. "Let's just hope that none of the boys at the center are hardcore liars."

"I tell you what," Beverly said, coming around her desk to Nadirah. "Let's see what happens tonight. If all goes well, Monday morning, I'm on the phone. Personally, I like your idea of taking in Bree. You're good with children and your students love you. So if anyone can help Bree, you can."

Nadirah embraced Beverly. "I hope I get the chance."

"We'll see. I'll try to speak with Principal Crayton before she leaves today. You take care of that business at the center tonight and give me a call tomorrow."

"Done."

"Well," Beverly said, feeling relieved, "I'm glad I caught up with you."

Nadirah picked up her briefcase. "Do you think I can get in to see Bree at the hospital?"

"Maybe you should wait until I speak with the social worker."

Feeling like she was near tears, Nadirah barely mouthed, "Okay."

Again, Nadirah and Beverly embraced. For the first time in her life, Nadirah felt like she had a purpose. She left work determined to see

that purpose through. BJ wanted her to stay away from the center tonight, but that wasn't happening. Whoever it was that tried to besmirch her name had better take cover. She was armed with purpose, anger, and determination, and as God was her witness, she intended to annihilate anyone, Aunt Stephanie in particular, who tried to hurt her.

Chapter 11

Dress down, dress up, show her legs, cover her legs, turtle neck, v-neck, loose-fitting, tight-fitting, Nadirah was overwhelmed and definitely undecided. It took her every minute of the two hours she had to get ready to find something to wear that wouldn't show too much of her body and make people think it was possible that she would seduce a teenager. She ended up putting back on the suit she'd worn to work, and by the time she walked into the noisy center packed with dancing kids with Lynn at her side, her heart was pulsing, her breathing was shallow, her jaw was tight, her shoulders were squared, and her eyes were angry. Nadirah felt like a hyped-up boxer entering the ring. She set her sights on every male student in the room, looking from one to the other wondering which one told the lie about her. Searching for the truth blinded Nadirah's eyes and deafened her ears to anything frivolous. She didn't hear the finger-popping, foot-tapping hip-hop music that had all the teenagers on the floor dancing, neither did she pay particular attention to the numerous red balloons and heart-shaped figures that decorated the large storefront center.

Lynn observed the entire room. "There are a lot of kids here."

Nadirah began unbuttoning her coat. "There are always a lot of kids here. The question is, which one hates me enough to lie on me?" She took off her coat.

Lynn began taking off her own coat. "So how are we going to find out?"

In that instant, Nadirah locked eyes with sixteen-year-old, curly-haired Felipe who had just realized who she was.

Felipe rushed at Nadirah. "Oh, snap! That's you?" he asked, standing in front of Nadirah with a wide, toothy grin on his face. "Man, you look fine!"

Under any other circumstances, Nadirah would have been

secretly thrilled that a sixteen-year-old student thought she was fine. No one had ever in her entire life called her fine, and unfortunately, now wasn't the time for Felipe to make that declaration.

"Felipe," Nadirah said, starchily, "I need to speak with you."

Felipe boldly looked Nadirah over as he walked around her and Lynn. "You got you one of them makeovers, didn't you?"

Nadirah wondered if Felipe, one of her more talkative students, was capable of spreading lies about her.

"Yo! Drew! Brian! Melvin! Hey, man, look at Miss Lewis!"

Nadirah had not wanted to draw too much attention to herself, but Felipe was making sure that everyone noticed her.

"Here they come," Lynn said, backing away from Nadirah.

Nadirah reached back for Lynn, but Lynn quickly whispered, "Go ahead, talk to them." Lynn quickly stepped back as more students approached Nadirah.

"Miss Lewis! You the bomb!" sixteen-year-old Drew said, smiling at Nadirah.

"Yeah," agreed seventeen-year-old Melvin. "You look better than the chicks in here."

Nadirah saw that more students, boys and girls alike, were coming her way. "Melvin, let's not do comparisons. Remember, most people don't like that."

"Yeah, you right…you right. You taught us that."

"Hey, Miss Lewis, you wanna dance?" Drew took hold of Nadirah's hand, but she immediately pulled it back.

"I'm your instructor, Drew. I don't ever fraternize with my students."

Drew's eyes widened. "Does that mean you can't dance with me?"

Melvin popped Drew upside the head. "Yeah, stupid! Ain't you got no edgemacation?"

A roar of laugher went up.

"You look good, Miss Lewis," Kia shouted over Felipe's shoulder.

Nadirah didn't hear Kia. She was focused on all the male students encircling her as more students, out of curiosity, stopped dancing to see what was going on in the cluster of students near the door.

Nadirah studied excited, curious faces; searched bright, inquisitive eyes; and listened for any words that hinted at an imagined or an illusionary personal relationship with her.

Suddenly the music stopped and a chorus of excited chatter filled the center.

BJ Parish made his way through the crowd, easily nudging aside any one in his way. "What's going on over here?"

"Look at Miss Lewis," Kia said, pointing Nadirah out to BJ. "Ain't she tight?"

Like everyone else, BJ was at once surprised at how different Nadirah looked and was momentarily hushed of words, but he knew her immediately. He had always thought her attractive, the change only made it more evident to everyone else.

"So this is what the excitement is about," BJ said, good—naturedly, although he was not especially thrilled to see Nadirah. "Miss Lewis, undoubtedly, you have the ability to stop a party just by showing up."

"No, I think the kids think I have a bagful of free iPods to hand out," Nadirah said, raising her hands to show that she had nothing. "Sorry."

BJ pulled Nadirah aside and said in a low voice, "I thought we agreed you wouldn't come down tonight."

"BJ, I couldn't stay away. I have to know who's accusing me."

"This might not be the venue to find out."

"Oh, I think it is. Have you spoken to any of the kids yet?"

"No."

"When will you?"

"Nadirah, I don't think tonight is ideal."

Nadirah was taken aback. "But, BJ, all the kids are here. We can talk to them one at a time back in your office without disrupting the party."

"I don't wanna handle it that way."

"Then how do you wanna handle it?"

"Maybe we should just let it go. I think the call was a hoax."

Nadirah wasn't comfortable with just letting it go. "But shouldn't we question the kids just to make sure?"

"No. Let it go."

Nadirah glanced uncertainly at Lynn. "Just like that?"

"Let it go, Nadirah." BJ turned away from Nadirah. He said loudly, "Okay. Let's get back to doing what you kids do best—partying."

"No! Wait!" Lynn grabbed a chair and quickly stepped up on it. "Hey, everyone! Can I get your attention before you turn the music back on?"

"Get down!" BJ ordered.

"Who's she?" Drew asked.

"Lady, what do you think you're doing?" BJ asked, moving toward Lynn. "Who are you?"

"She's my cousin, BJ. Lynn Wilkie," Nadirah said, wondering what Lynn was up to.

"I don't care who she—"

"Mr. BJ Parish, how are you?" Lynn asked pleasantly. "I'm sure you don't mind if I speak to your students for the briefest moment."

"Yes, the hell I do! Get down. Now!"

The gruffness in BJ's voice and the ugly scowl on his face floored Nadirah. This wasn't the same caring BJ who mentored to troubled students and gave them direction.

"Mr. Parish," Lynn said, sweetly, "I promise, I'll let the kids get back to their partying in just a moment."

"Lady, I'm the director of this center. Any announcement you have to make to my students goes through me first."

The students grew quieter as they watched the scene in front of them play out.

"I understand that, Mr. Parish," Lynn said, "and I don't have a problem with it. But since you're standing right here, I thought perhaps I could ask your students a question or two in your presence."

Nadirah looked from Lynn to BJ.

"Lady, I'm in charge here! You will not question my students."

"Nadirah!" Lynn shouted, "Do I question or not?"

Everyone looked to Nadirah, who was looking at Lynn.

"It's your life," Lynn concluded.

"I want you out of here!" BJ suddenly snatched Lynn down off the chair, making her shriek when she came down hard on the floor while the chair she'd just stood on crashed down on its side.

Grimacing, Lynn swatted BJ's hand off of her. "Don't touch me!" Lynn held her arm as if she were in pain.

Nadirah rushed to Lynn and put her arm around her waist. "Lynn, are you all right? Did he hurt you?"

"I didn't hurt her!"

BJ's uncharacteristic brashness surprised everyone including Nadirah. "BJ, what's wrong with you?"

Lynn glared at BJ. "Don't you ever put your hands on me again!"

BJ scowled menacingly at Lynn. "Get out or I will call the police."

"BJ, would you please calm down?" Nadirah said. "You told me you'd talk to the kids—"

"I said I would talk to the kids! Not your damn cousin. Now get out!"

"No, we are not leaving," Lynn said. "Unless you question your students, we have every right to question them ourselves."

"Question us about what?" several of the students asked.

"You have no rights in my center! Get the hell out!"

"What she wanna ask us questions for?" Felipe asked.

"Yeah, what we do?"

BJ turned on his students. "Y'all get back to your party or I'll end it right now!"

"Man, BJ, you buggin'," Debra said.

"BJ, man, you close down the party, we ain't gonna make no money."

"BJ, let the kids have their party," Nadirah said.

"You leave and I will."

"BJ, I don't understand. Why are you so upset? We only wanted to ask the kids if any of them—"

"Miss Lewis, you're fired! Get off the premises."

"Are you kidding?"

"Why you firing Miss Lewis?" Brian asked.

"What she do?" Felipe asked.

"I'm ordering you off the premises or—"

"Or what, Mr. Parish?" Lynn asked, her hands on her hips. "Why is it that you don't want us to question your students?"

Nadirah could not believe what was happening.

"Get out of here!"

"Dag. Why y'all freaking out?" Kia asked. "Y'all must be on something."

"I know that's right!" Several of the kids high-fived each other.

"Justin! Turn that damn music back on!" BJ ordered.

Nadirah grabbed the same chair Lynn had stood on and got up on it herself. BJ went to grab her, but Lynn grabbed his arm and pulled him back.

"If you touch her, I'll call the police myself, and I don't think that's something you want."

"Your threat don't mean a damn thing." BJ pulled his cell phone from his pocket and flipped it open.

Nadirah raised her arms to settle the students down. She watched BJ press a single button on his cell phone knowing full well it was the emergency 911 button.

"Listen to me!" Nadirah shouted.

"Turn on the damn music!" BJ again ordered, his ear to the small cell phone.

"This is messed up!" Melvin said.

"Kids! Please listen to me!" Nadirah shouted. "You all know me!"

"Don't listen to her!" BJ ordered. "Hello, hello!"

"Y'all got some def drama up in here," Debra said, slapping hands with Kia.

Her hands shaking, Nadirah pushed on. "I've been here for all of you, and you all know this."

With one finger in his left ear to shut out the noise, BJ spoke into this cell phone. "I have a disturbance at the Harlem Boys and Girls Empowerment Center…"

"What you gotta ask us, Miss Lewis?" Kia asked.

"Yeah. Go ahead and ask us."

BJ continued on his call. "… on West 135th Street between Frederick Douglas Boulevard and St. Nicolas …"

"Okay," Nadirah said, watching BJ. "Mr. Parish informed me that one of you kids called him and my principal at my job…"

"Shut the hell up!" BJ suddenly snapped his cell phone shut.

"...and told him I was having—"

"Shut up!" BJ went to grab Nadirah, but Melvin and Felipe quickly jumped in front of him, blocking him and keeping him away from Nadirah.

"Don't put your hands on her, man!" Melvin said, threateningly.

"Get out my way, Melvin. This isn't your business."

"It's my business if you 'bout to put your hands on her, man. You know I ain't down with that."

"Me neither," Felipe said. He and Melvin stared down BJ.

"It's like that, huh? You boys gonna gang up on me? After all I did for you."

"What's right's right, man. You don't put your hands on a woman. Ain't that what you and Miss Lewis been tryin' to teach us?"

"Yeah, BJ," Brian said, sidling up next to Melvin. "What's up? How come Miss Lewis can't ask us a question?"

Nadirah swelled with pride.

"Yeah, BJ," Debra said. "You always said we should listen to her. Why can't we listen to her now?"

"Yeah!" a chorus of kids shouted.

"I wanna know what's up?" Kia asked.

"Me, too," Debra added.

"Y'all just nosey," Brian chimed in.

"Aw, shut up. You wanna know, too."

BJ glared up at Nadirah. "You see the dissension you've caused here? You trying to undermine everything I done with these kids?"

"Of course not. But, BJ, I thought we were after the same truth."

"This is not the way to handle it."

"Handle what?" Melvin asked.

BJ grumbled angrily while glaring at Nadirah. "You kids get back."

"Go ahead, Nadirah," Lynn prompted. "Get this over with."

Nadirah looked at BJ who was glaring bullets at her. "First, I want to apologize to all of you for bringing this mess into your party, but I had no other choice."

BJ grumbled. "You had a choice."

Nadirah ignored him. "A few days ago, Mr. Parish informed me that someone called him and told him that I was having an affair."

"Sex?" Debra asked.

"Yes, an affair with one of the students here."

"Oh, snap!" several of the boys said, laughing while slapping high fives.

"This is serious!" Lynn shouted, getting everyone's attention. "This accusation can end Miss Lewis' teaching career unless the truth comes out. You all know her, and if you kids care about her, you will help her expose the lie and the liar."

"This is ridiculous!" BJ said gruffly. "Miss Lewis, I'm disappointed in you. I don't approve of your methods. You bogarted your way in here and disrupted the activities without first consulting me, without regard for the students, and without respect for my program. This is my damn center! You should have respected me and the center. You owe me that."

"BJ, I've always respected you and the center. Your work here is just as important to me as—"

"This center is me! It's because of me this center exists at all!"

"Man, he's really buggin'," Debra said.

"BJ," Nadirah said, "I'm quite aware of all that you've done for the kids and the community, but?"

"Your behavior tonight is a slap in the face to all I've done here. Where do you get off usurping my authority?"

"BJ—"

"Your services," BJ boomed, "are no longer needed here!"

Nadirah felt like she was the one slapped in the face. She stared at BJ.

"Aw, man," Felipe said. "That's cold."

"You kids get back to partying or I will shut it down quick, fast, and in a hurry!" BJ turned and pushed his way through the throng of kids toward the back of the center where his office was, totally confusing the kids and Nadirah.

"Forget him," Felipe said, flipping off BJ behind his back. "Miss Lewis, you wanna know if one of us told BJ we was doing the thang with you?"

"Yes, I do," Nadirah said, struggling to stay calm, although her

heart was pounding. "I need to know if any one of you ever told anyone that I was having… an affair with any student in this center?"

"You fine, Miss Lewis, and I'd love to hit—"

Slap! Kia smacked Felipe upside his head. "Shut up, stupid! This is serious."

"Felipe, please," Nadirah said. "This is my life I'm talking about. It is really important."

"Okay, okay," Felipe said, rubbing his head. "It wasn't me."

"Who was it?" Nadirah asked, looking out over the room at all of the students. "Was it any one of you?"

"No."

"Not me."

"I never heard anything like that."

It went around the room like that, every student, male and female, denying saying anything about Nadirah having an affair with one of them.

"That's dope," Brian said. "If I ever find out who said it, I'ma bust his ass."

"Me, too," Felipe agreed.

"You believe us, don't you, Miss Lewis?" Kia asked.

"Yes, I do, and I wanna thank you guys for listening to me. I hope you'll forgive me for busting up your party."

"Hey, it's still early," Lynn said. "Why don't someone turn the music back on, and you kids get back to doing your thing?"

"Yeah!" Drew said. "Let's do this!"

Loud, pulse-thumping music abruptly filled the large storefront center. The kids went back to dancing, forgetting all about the drama that interrupted their night.

Lynn helped Nadirah down off the chair. "Your Mr. BJ Parish has got some serious issues with him."

Nadirah didn't know what to think. BJ was supposed to be on her side. He was supposed to be her friend. Nadirah slowly pulled her coat back on and started toward the door.

"He's a real bastard," Lynn said. She grimaced as she pulled on her coat from the pain in her arm."

"Lynn, you are hurt."

"Nadirah, I'm fine. It's your so-called friend who has a prob-

lem."

"Undoubedly. Lynn, I don't understand. BJ told me he'd get to the bottom of the lie tonight, and then I get here and he's changed his mind. I thought BJ would call the students into his office one by one and question them."

"One would think, but why didn't he?"

"I don't have a clue. BJ knows how important this is. How could he do this to me?"

Lynn had no answer for Nadirah.

"I just don't get it. Lynn, when he went after you, everything got out of control. He even called the police!"

"Nadirah. If that man called the police, they would have been here by now. He was bluffing. He was trying to scare us into shutting up. I don't think he wants you to find out the truth."

"Isn't that the way he came off?" Nadirah looked back into the center. "Maybe I should go back in there and confront him."

"Not on your life." Lynn gently pulled Nadirah away from the door. "Nadirah, that man is not your friend, and I guarantee you, he does not want to speak to you."

"But I work with him, Lynn."

"Not any more."

Nadirah didn't believe BJ meant to fire her. "BJ needs me here at the center."

"You want him to need you, Nadirah, but he doesn't. And if you think about it, do you really wanna work for someone who goes ballistic over you trying to clear your name?"

Nadirah didn't have to think about that. "I guess not, but this is so strange. A few days ago, BJ was behind me in wanting to get to the truth."

"No. BJ was in front of you showing you his tail. If he had been behind you, he would have pushed you up on that chair so that you could have questioned those kids outright."

With her silence, Nadirah agreed. She looked back through the glass door of the center at the students dancing and having the fun they had come there for. Something wasn't right.

Lynn began to lightly massage her arm, which drew Nadirah's attention.

"Lynn, he did hurt you."

"No. I … I fell off a ladder the other day when I was trying to hang curtains in my bedroom."

"Let me look at it." Nadirah reached for Lynn's arm.

"No. I'm okay." She stopped massaging her arm. "Don't worry about it."

"Are you sure? Maybe we should go to my doctor. Dr. Pinckney's really good."

"Nadirah, I'm fine. Really. What we should be doing is trying to figure out what game Mr. BJ Parish is playing."

"Yeah. He certainly wasn't acting right in there. I wonder why?"

Chapter 12

With no special plans and no need to rush out, Nadirah sat in her nightgown curled up on the living room sofa, sipping a cup of cinnamon tea. The television was on, but she was only half listening to the late morning news. Her mind kept seamlessly replaying over and over the drama from the center. Her night had been one long sleepless nightmare of BJ, frothing at the mouth, pounding his chest, shouting incessantly about who he was and how the center was nothing without him. She'd always known about BJ's machismo attitude, but she had no idea that he was so irrational to boot. No matter how many ways Nadirah tried to look at what happened at the center, no angle made sense. She could not pinpoint anything, singularly or cumulatively, egregious enough to qualify as the culprit that might have set BJ off other than her putting BJ himself on the spot.

Maybe the liar Nadirah was trying to expose unwittingly exposed himself. Could it be possible that BJ made up the lie about her? That simple yet complicated probability alone might explain his irrational behavior, but it wouldn't explain why he would do such a horrific thing to her.

Buzzzzzz!

Nadirah went immediately to the door and peeked out—it was Lynn.

"You look right at home," Lynn said, taking off her coat.

"Well, for now," Nadirah said, sitting again on the sofa. "This is home."

"Speaking of home, I was thinking. Nadirah, instead of you looking for an apartment, you should start looking around for a house. It would be a great investment."

Nadirah took a quick sip of her very cool tea. "That's a bit ambitious for me right now, especially with so much going on."

"You could hire a good real estate broker. Let him or her do the work. All you'd have to do is look at what they come up with."

"Lynn, I'm sure there's a little more to it than that, not to mention the cost of houses in Manhattan, which I can't afford."

"I don't see why not. You'll soon get your trust fund so money won't hinder you. Plus, you don't have to stay in Manhattan. You'll be able to afford to move anywhere you want."

Lynn mentioning her trust fund made Nadirah wonder aloud, "Do you know how much is in my trust fund?"

"The exact amount? No. But I figure by now there has to be at least four million on account."

Although Lynn was under by one and a half million dollars, Nadirah was surprised that she knew there was that much. No doubt Aunt Stephanie discussed it with Lynn when she really had no business doing so.

"Am I right?" Lynn asked.

"I'm not sure," Nadirah lied. "Your mother has always refused to give me any information about my trust fund."

"That's ridiculous. I'll talk to her. I'll find out how much you have."

"No, that's okay, don't worry about it. I'll find out soon enough."

A long time ago, Uncle Lester had told Nadirah to never discuss with anyone her trust fund. He said, "Greed has no compassion and no friends." So taking his advice, Nadirah had never spoken about the money she'd soon inherit.

"The fund will be turned over to you when you turn thirty, right?"

"That's what I was told," Nadirah said, feeling uneasy. "So, are you excited to be going home to your children?"

"I can't wait to see my babies. I really miss them."

"Erin's the oldest, right?"

"Yes, she's eight and as grown as she can be. I talked to all three of them this morning. They're okay. They're in good hands. My sitter is really good."

"It must be wonderful to have a devoted husband and three beautiful children."

"Yeah," Lynn said, dryly. "Nadirah, when is your birthday?"

That question surprised Nadirah. "October 16th. Why?"

"Well, it just dawned on me that we've never celebrated any of

your birthdays. Not even when you were a child."

Whether Lynn knew it or not, the fact that Uncle Lester was the only one who ever remembered her birthday was part of a painful memory for Nadirah. After he died, her birthday came and went like the seconds on a clock.

"I have an idea," Lynn said.

Nadirah could almost see in Lynn's eyes what she was about to say.

"I think we should have a party for your next birthday! A big party!"

Nadirah began shaking her head. "No... no, I'm not comfortable with throwing a party for myself."

"You won't be throwing the party, I will."

Again Nadirah shook her head. "That's all right. I don't want a party."

"Nadirah, you'll be turning the big three-o. You have to celebrate! It'll be like a coming out party. You'll be financially independent; this mess from the center will be behind you because I believe Mr. BJ, for whatever reason, lied; and you'll be totally on your own in your own place. You have to celebrate."

Still shaking her head, Nadirah definitely wasn't comfortable with the idea of throwing a party of any kind. Besides, who would be there? Three people from her job, Lynn and her husband, and Daniel? She never had a lot of friends mainly because she had to always stay close to home because of Aunt Stephanie. And now, although she was out from under Aunt Stephanie's roof, she didn't see herself becoming a social butterfly.

"Don't say no, Nadirah, at least not right now. In six months you might feel differently."

"I doubt it."

"Oh, you're such a party pooper," Lynn said, pretending to pout. "Okay, even if you don't let me throw you a party, I will most definitely be celebrating with you. Turning thirty is a milestone in every woman's life."

"That's what I hear," Nadirah said, not too thrilled at the thought of turning thirty. It scared her. She had no doubt that she could handle her money, her fear wasn't about that. What she feared was not

having someone who truly loved her in her life. If she never found that kind of love then she might never have children, which means she might never know what it is to truly give or get love.

"Obviously," Lynn said, "you're not too thrilled about turning thirty. Let's get back to talking about where you might want to live."

Nadirah hadn't given much thought to where she might want to live outside of the Upper West Side and Harlem. Since arriving in New York City, those were the areas of the city she knew best. She looked around the large, beautifully molded living room.

"If I could find something like this in this neighborhood, I wouldn't complain."

"I bet you wouldn't. Do you want me to get a broker to start looking for you?"

"Thanks, but Daniel's sister is in the real estate business. I'll talk to her Monday. I just don't want to think about anything heavy the rest of the weekend."

"After last night, I don't blame you. So, have you spoken to your Daniel?"

"No, why?"

"Mama said he called the house twice last night while I was out with you. Doesn't he have your cell phone number?"

"He's called, but I wasn't up to speaking to him. He left a couple of messages. I'll call him tomorrow."

"Are you avoiding him?"

"No… well…I guess I am. I just need to be totally alone for a minute."

"I thought you said Daniel didn't demand anything of you?"

"He doesn't. Daniel's been a great friend, but for the first time in my life I'm living alone, and I want to totally experience it alone. I wanna discover who I am without anyone asking me anything as simple as the time of day."

"Aren't you forgetting something?"

Nadirah didn't get Lynn's meaning. She looked at her questioningly.

"Your student. Didn't you tell me you'd like to be her foster mother?"

"Oh, Bree? Sure. I'd still like to be her foster mother if she's

placed in the system, but I won't know about that for a few days. But until then, this weekend, I'll rest and I'll get my head together. I'll simply enjoy being alone."

Lynn started to stand. "Then I guess I better leave."

"No!" Nadirah reached out and pulled Lynn back down. "You stay. It's other people I don't want around me. You're my family. I need you in my life."

Lynn chuckled. "My feelings were about to be hurt."

"They need not be. You've been a great help to me these last few days, and I appreciate it."

Lynn smiled. "I only wish I'd been around more for you."

"Well, you made up for it last night at the center. Just your being with me was great."

"I hope so. I think by Monday you'll know if Mr. BJ Parish intends to make trouble for you."

"Well, I'll check in with Beverly Cotton when I get to school on Monday. The worst that could happen is that another call will come in and a student will be identified. If that happens, an official investigation will get underway."

"I don't think you have to worry about that. Those kids seem to be solidly behind you. I think your problem is Mr. BJ Parish. I think he's lying."

"I'm thinking that myself, but let's not talk about that either." Nadirah sighed and then stretched. "I think I can eat something now."

"That's a good sign," Lynn said, as Nadirah stood. "Look, I put in a call to Austin and left him a message about the lease you asked for."

"It has to be legitimate, and I will pay Austin rent."

"I'll explain everything when I talk to Austin. He has a good heart. He'll understand what you're trying to do for your student."

"I hope so. You'll still be here Monday, won't you?"

"Actually, I'm leaving Sunday morning."

Nadirah was at once saddened to hear that Lynn was going home. "Oh, I'll miss you."

"I'll miss you, too."

Aunt Stephanie, whom Nadirah hadn't given a thought to, suddenly popped in her mind. Her jaw suddenly tightened.

"What you're thinking, Nadirah, is all over your face. Don't

worry. Mama doesn't know where you are so she won't be bothering you."

"Did you get someone to stay with her?"

"Well, Millicent will be there during days as she always is, but her sister Barbette Haygood will be with Mama in the evenings until midnight. After that she'll be on her own, but by then Mama should be asleep."

The tenseness in Nadirah's jaw eased up.

"You don't have to worry about her," Lynn said.

Nadirah picked up her cup. "I could use some fresh tea. Want some?"

"I'll pass." Lynn stood also. "I have a lot of errands to run before I leave."

"Do you want me to go with you?"

"No… no, its mommy shopping for the kids. You just keep enjoying being alone."

"Will you call me in the morning before you leave?"

"I'll call you tonight and tomorrow." Lynn retrieved her own coat and began pulling it on. "I wasn't going to mention this, Nadirah, but Mama asked me to tell you to come by to see her."

Nadirah stopped dead in her tracks. She gave Lynn a "are you serious" look.

"I know. I told her you were really busy settling into your new place and that it might be a while before she saw you."

"Lynn, why soft-soap it? Why not tell her outright I don't wanna ever see her again. I'm sure she won't have any difficulty figuring out why. And after living the lie she lived all these years, Lynn, I don't know how you can stand to be around her yourself."

Lynn considered first the words she'd use. "You and I both agree, Mama's a bitch for what she did."

"Supreme bitch," Nadirah said, setting her cup back on the table.

"But the problem is, that bitch happens to be my mother. I think God would frown down upon me if I turn my back on her completely. But don't get me wrong. I'm not at Mama's beck and call, but I will make sure that she's all right. I'll do my daughterly duties, I'll call to check on her, I'll come if she needs me, but I will always wear very clear glasses

around her. My mother can't be trusted. I know this quite well."

Lesson one, Nadirah thought. *I have to learn to be bigger than the problem and not let the problem make me ugly.* "Well, Lynn, maybe one day I'll grow up to be just like you."

"I hope not." Lynn started for the door. "I hope you're a whole lot stronger than me. A whole lot more unafraid."

Lynn's remark struck Nadirah as strange. She looked at Lynn questioningly.

"Oh, don't mind me. I say stupid things sometimes. Come here. I gotta go."

Lynn hugged Nadirah and Nadirah hugged Lynn back, but she felt Lynn holding onto her as if she were desperate for her embrace. When Lynn let go, Nadirah saw fleetingly a woeful look in Lynn's eyes.

"Lynn is?"

"I gotta go." Lynn abruptly tore herself away.

Nadirah watched Lynn hurry down the steps wet with fresh falling rain to the street. There was something disturbingly wrong in Lynn's life, but it was clear that Lynn had no intension of letting on what that might be. Until Lynn talked, there was nothing Nadirah could do. She closed the door on the cold, overcast day. She yawned wide and big, bringing water to her tired eyes. If she went back to bed, who would know, and more importantly, who would care? She lived alone now and her time was hers to do with what she wanted, and what she wanted this instant was to feel that big comfortable bed under her body. She was a little hungry, but food would have to wait. She was going back to sleep. Almost as soon as her head lay on the pillow, all troubles that weighed on her mind no longer remained as she closed her eyes. Thoughts of Lynn's last remark lingered, but didn't keep the sweetness of sleep from wrapping her up in a cocoon of darkness.

Chapter 13

In the seven weeks since leaving Aunt Stephanie's house, and in the same time since experiencing the ugly scene down at the Empowerment Center, every day Nardirah found herself thinking what a difference a day really made. The day Bree Morrison came to live with her was no different. Although she had asked for Bree, and although she had prepared for Bree, when the doorbell rang five weeks ago and she opened the door to Mrs. Hamilton standing with Bree at her side, Nadirah was suddenly conflicted. While she was glad to see Bree and was eager to help her, it was at that precise moment that it hit Nadirah that she was going to be singularly and solely in charge of a child outside of her classroom. It was then that an old familiar feeling—fear—crept up on Nadirah and filled her with doubt as to whether or not she was capable of parenting a child who was not a baby, but an eight-year-old with grownup-size problems. When Mrs. Hamilton left Bree behind and Bree still hadn't raised her big, sad eyes to look at Nadirah, Nadirah couldn't help wondering if she had taken on more than she was capable of handling.

That was five weeks ago, and now Nadirah was certain she had no idea how to get Bree to open up. Bree didn't talk in class and she didn't talk at home so Nadirah never knew what Bree was thinking. She had tried everything—patience, roll-playing, coaxing, and even bribery. Nothing worked. Bree remained nestled in her world of silence, speaking to no one, asking for nothing, not even food. Nadirah fed Bree when she fed herself, but Bree ate very little and threw up if Nadirah force fed her when she didn't want more. Bree was a frail little child and looked more like a six-year-old than a child who was supposed to be going on to fourth grade. Up until Bree landed in the hospital, Nadirah had planned on passing her on to the fourth grade, but since coming out of the hospital, Bree did very little in school beyond sitting and reading to herself at her desk.

If Bree was absorbing any of the lessons, Nadirah had no way of knowing because Bree wouldn't take the weekly quizzes. Nadirah knew only that she had a little girl to take care of who was hiding somewhere deep inside herself, too timid, too afraid to come out and join the rest of the world.

In school, not that she was getting anywhere, Beverly personally counseled Bree, while outside of school, Mrs. Hamilton worked to find Bree's mother, who had up and walked out of her apartment, leaving everything behind and no clue as to where she had gone or why Bree had attempted to take her own life. Nadirah couldn't understand how a mother could just walk away from her child and not look back.

With Bree's fifth week living with Nadirah coming to a close, Nadirah decided to ease up on trying to get her to talk. Instead she decided to give her space to find her way at her own pace to peek her head out from inside her shell. Since they'd been home from school, Nadirah said nothing to Bree and took her barely touched plate of food away without a word said. Tonight she wouldn't do her usual—she wouldn't sit with Bree trying to draw her out until it was her bedtime. It was only 6:15, too early to put Bree to bed. She took her into the living room and turned the television on to the Nickelodeon channel. Whether Bree wanted to watch Nickelodeon or not, Nadirah didn't know and figured if Bree wanted to watch anything else she would change the channel herself. She wasn't giving up on Bree, she was just giving her some space.

While she kept Bree in her direct line of sight in the living room, Nadirah sat at the dining room table preparing lesson plans, marking test papers, and keeping her daily journal of her day with Bree. It disturbed her that Bree sat as still as a statuette not reacting to anything she saw on television. Bree never cracked a smile, laughed out loud, or raised a brow. Nadirah wondered what was on Bree's mind? What was she thinking? How was she feeling? Not knowing any of the answers was bothersome, and Nadirah was again reminded of how tough her job of parenting Bree was turning out to be. Somehow she had to find a way to knock down that indelible wall of silence Bree surrounded herself with.

After working about forty-five minutes, a strange feeling came over Nadirah. She felt like she was being watched. She looked up, and

surprise, Bree was looking at her. They locked eyes and Nadirah felt herself drawn into the saddest most soulful brown eyes she'd ever seen.

"What's wrong, sweetie?" Nadirah stood. "Do you wanna talk to me?"

Bree said nothing, yet she didn't look away, which for Nadirah was a good sign. Maybe Bree was ready to talk, and hoping that she was, Nadirah started into the living room.

Buzzzzz!

Annoyed at the bad timing of the interruption, Nadirah checked her watch. "Oh, no," she said, realizing that it was most likely Daniel who was supposed to stop by later to bring her the third group of apartment listings his sister Chandra prepared for her. Nadirah threw Bree an apologetic glance as she went to open the door.

"Hey," Daniel said, pecking Nadirah on the cheek as he came inside.

"You're early," Nadirah said, closing the door.

"I know, but I was near by and I figured I'd come on ahead."

Nadirah said in a hushed voice, "But you were supposed to come by after Bree went to bed, Daniel, not before."

"I know, but it was either come on ahead or go all the way across town in all that traffic just to turn around and come back again through all that traffic. It's Friday. You know it's crazy out there. Besides, I think it's time Bree and I met."

"Daniel, have you given a thought to what I might think?"

"I am thinking about you. I would like to help you with Bree."

"But, Daniel, I don't want Bree to feel that she has to compete for my attention."

Daniel looked at Bree who wasn't looking at either one of them. "I don't think you have to worry about that."

"Daniel—"

"Here, look at this." Daniel handed a medium size yellow manila envelope along with a medium size gold gift bag he carried to Nadirah.

"What's this?" Nadirah asked, looking at the gift bag.

"Something special?not for you."

"Daniel, what are you doing?"

"Helping. Which reminds me—besides me, how many

strangers have you had around Bree?"

Nadirah didn't try to hide the fact that she was insulted. She'd had no one around Bree nor herself, that is except for Daniel once Bree was asleep, since she moved into Austin Gray's house.

"Come on, Nadirah. Don't be so sensitive. I'm agreeing with you. Bree shouldn't be around too many strangers. I'm willing to do whatever I can to help bring her around."

"Well, you're not helping when you disregard what I say, and I say it's too soon to introduce Bree to other people. She's still pretty troubled."

Daniel looked around Nadirah into the living room at Bree, who was now looking down at her hands in her lap.

"She's a little thing, isn't she?" Daniel said in a low voice. He took off his heavy wool jacket.

"She's very fragile, physically and emotionally, Daniel. Which is why this is not the best time."

"I don't agree. Didn't you tell me last night that you were stumped, that you didn't know what else to do?"

"Yes, but I—"

"Look, I have an idea." Daniel thrust his jacket at Nadirah and simultaneously took the gift bag from her hand. He quickly slipped around her and went into the living room before Nadirah could stop him.

"Hey, Bree!" Daniel said, cheerfully. "Can I sit with you and watch television?"

Bree didn't raise her head as Daniel sat on the sofa next to her.

"Do you know who I am?" Daniel asked.

It was obvious to Nadirah that Bree wasn't the least bit curious about who Daniel was—Bree didn't look his way. Nadirah tossed Daniel's jacket onto the back of one of the living room chairs.

"Daniel, I need to speak to you back in the kitchen."

"Give me a minute." Daniel looked to Bree. "Bree, I'm Daniel. I am a really good friend of Nadirah's and I want to be a really good friend of yours."

From Bree came not a peep.

"Daniel," Nadirah said, her teeth tight. "We need to talk—now."

"Just a sec." Daniel set the gift bag on Bree's lap. "Inside this bag, Bree, is something special just for you."

"Daniel?"

"Shh!" Daniel said, shushing Nadirah which made her all the madder. She wanted to snatch the gift bag off of Bree's lap but didn't. She didn't like that Daniel took it upon himself to introduce himself to Bree and now to give her a present without first consulting her, she wasn't liking him one bit.

"Bree, why don't you take it out and show Nadirah?" Daniel opened the bag and held it up to Bree for her to look inside, which she did very shyly.

Bree looked at Nadirah and Nadirah saw for the first time that Bree was asking her for to do. She crouched in front of Bree.

"Sweetie, do you want me to take it out for you?"

Bree nodded once. From the gift bag, Nadirah took a square pink zippered case with a long string. Nadirah put the case in Bree's hands.

Daniel urged, "Unzip it."

Having no choice but to go along with Daniel, Nadirah prompted, "Go ahead, sweetie. Unzip it."

Saying nothing, Bree slowly unzipped the case and revealed a Game Boy Advance SP.

"It opens like this," Daniel said, easily flipping open the electronic game. "And it turns on like this." He slid a lever on the right side to the on position. A soft musical tone sounded and a colorful Game Boy Nintendo logo leaped onto the small two by three inch screen.

"Wow, Bree," Daniel said as the Wild Kingdom animation title appeared on the small screen. "Look at that! It's Wild Kingdom. It's a game cartridge. Let me show you how it works."

Daniel began to manipulate the directional arrows and buttons on the Game Boy system, sending the jungle animals into action. Nadirah studied Bree's face and saw Bree's eyes brighten as she watched the adventurous scenes on the screen.

"Would you like to try it yourself?" Nadirah asked.

Bree shrugged slightly.

"Sure she would," Daniel said, giving the Game Boy to Bree. He placed her fingers on the buttons. "Try it."

Her movements were hesitant, but Bree, on her own, moved the

animals along at a much slower pace. Nadirah was relieved that something as simple as an electronic game peaked Bree's interest. Why had she not thought of it? She'd given Bree stuffed animals, board games, and dolls, but none had brightened her eyes or made her smile.

Daniel stood. "You said you wanted to speak with me?"

The smirk on Daniel's lips, the self-confident twinkle in his eyes, the haughty tone of his voice set Nadirah's teeth on edge and stiffened her spine. She walked off toward the kitchen. Daniel followed with a smile on his face.

As soon as she was out of Bree's earshot, Nadirah turned on Daniel. "You had no right—"

"Did you see her face?"

"You still had no right to come when I asked you not to."

"But did it work?"

"That's not the point, Daniel," Nadirah said, frustrated by Daniel's dismissal of what she was trying to get across to him. "You will not take charge of my life like this."

"How am I taking charge of your life? I just bought the kid something I figured might bring her out of her shell."

A child's playful giggle made Nadirah and Daniel both look back toward the living room. They couldn't see Bree, but the sound of her giggling told them both that she was enjoying playing with the Game Boy.

Daniel's arrogant look of "I was right" really irritated Nadirah and annoyed her even more when she could visibly see his chest rise.

"You should have spoken to me before you purchased anything for Bree."

"I didn't, I'm sorry. Get over it."

"Aaaa! Daniel, this isn't a game! You should have told me what you were going to do or you should have suggested to me so that I could have bought the Game Boy for her."

Daniel leaned back against the counter. "Nadirah, whether you made the purchase or I made the purchase, the result would have been the same. I just happen to be the one, not surprisingly…"

Nadirah's eyes widened.

"…to think of it. And besides, I didn't think I needed your permission to spend my money."

Thinking about Bree, Nadirah reminded herself to speak softly. "Am I supposed to be an idiot, Daniel? Not surprisingly? Whether you think so or not, I'm just as intelligent as you. You're not the only one who could have come up with the idea of giving Bree an electronic game, and as for you spending your money, big deal. You have it to spend so spend all you want."

Unruffled, Daniel chuckled. "You know, I just realized what this is about. Your feelings are hurt."

Nadirah began shaking her head.

"Don't deny it. Your feelings are hurt because you didn't think of it and you're having a hard time telling me that I was right."

If she could burn a hole in Daniel's face with a simple glare, Nadirah would have.

"Well it's true," he said.

"Daniel, you've always been arrogant, but your supercilious attitude is making me sick. So what you thought of getting Bree an electronic toy. Big deal. That isn't the point. The point is, you should have spoken to me first. That's what makes you wrong."

"I don't think I was wrong. I was only trying to help."

Was he dense? Why wasn't he getting it? Nadirah wanted to punch Daniel's over-confident smirk right off his face. Besides his meddlesome mother, Daniel's arrogance and the habit he had of always putting the onus on her about anything she called him on or questioned him about always irked her. What if his toy hadn't worked? He wouldn't be so smug, would he?

"Daniel, here's a new concept. You are wrong today, you have been wrong before, and you will be wrong in the future about a whole lot of things."

"I doubt it. Unlike you, I would never tell you that I was incapable of solving such an elementary problem ..."

Nadirah could feel blood rushing to her face. At that moment she felt nothing but loathing for Daniel.

"... I would have figured it out myself."

"Or your mother would have figured it out for you." Nadirah knew she had hit home when that self-satisfied smirk instantaneously vanished from Daniel's face. He stepped away from the counter.

"What is that supposed to mean?"

"What do you think it means? But you know what, Daniel? Forget it. Go home." Nadirah started to leave the kitchen, but Daniel stopped her.

"If you can say something as contemptuously insulting as that, then you should be able to aggressively defend it."

Nadirah boldly faced Daniel knowing that she could easily back up her words with fact. Getting a good look at Daniel, she saw how weak he really was. He seemed to have no clue how much control his mother had over him. Nadirah could remember the time his mother told him to turn down the offer he received from City College to travel abroad to teach in Africa for a year. Daniel was excited about the prospect of living and teaching in Africa, but his mother wasn't. How his mother felt took precedence over what both Nadirah and Daniel's father had to say about the advantages of such a prestigious, all expense paid offer, especially when his mother's blood pressure shot up from crying about losing her baby.

"I can't go," Daniel had said. "My mother can't handle it."

"Your mother is like my aunt," Nadirah countered. "She's very manipulative."

Daniel was insulted that she had the gall to compare his mother to her aunt. He sulked for about a week and wouldn't answer her calls until she sent him a card apologizing for what she really wasn't sorry for. Unfortunately, she needed Daniel, he didn't need her, or else she would have left him alone the same night they started speaking again.

"You're weak, Nadirah," Daniel had said. "Your aunt treats you the way she does because you can't stand up for yourself."

How ironic that Daniel would say that to her when he himself wasn't allowing her to stand by what she asked him to do? And that was just it, if she wanted to keep Daniel in her life she'd have to stand down and let him do as he wanted in her life, but she was through letting someone else control her life.

"Daniel, I suggest you go home before either one of us say something we'll regret."

"In that case, perhaps we don't have the relationship I thought we had."

Nadirah considered Daniel's meaning. "Perhaps not."

In Daniel's eyes, Nadirah saw uncertainty. For once he wasn't as

sure as he thought he was about who she was. As much as she loved having Daniel as a friend and part-time lover, she was no longer willing to validate his ego by suppressing her own. She looked challengingly at Daniel and held his perplexed gaze. In the end, it was Daniel who looked away and walked away.

When her day began, no way would Nadirah have predicted that it would end with the loss of a friend.

A long time ago, Nadirah taught herself, in spite of what emotional upheaval she was going through, to focus on the task at hand and get it done. That's how she got through school and how she was able to work on her job as a teacher. Long after she put Bree to bed with her Game Boy charging on the dresser in her room, Nadirah sat at the dining room table finishing up her school work. For an hour after Daniel left, she had sat with Bree in the living room and watched her entertain herself with the Game Boy. Clearly, Daniel's gift engaged Bree and got her to react when she herself had been unable to. Still, Daniel was wrong for the way he went about it, and Nadirah wasn't backing down.

Chapter 14

Buzzzz! Buzzzz! Buzzzz! Buzzzz!
Nadirah's eyes shot open!
Buzzzz! Buzzzz! Buzzzz! Buzzzz! Buzzzz! Buzzzz! Buzzzz!
"What in the world!" Nadirah bolted from the bed.
Buzzzz! Buzzzz! Buzzzz! Buzzzz! Buzzzz! Buzzzz! Buzzzz!
"Make it stop! Make it stop!" Bree screamed.
Nadirah rushed into Bree's room. She flipped on the light. Bree was sitting up in bed with her hands covering her ears. Her eyes were squeezed shut.
Buzzzz! Buzzzz! Buzzzz! Buzzzz! Buzzzz! Buzzzz! Buzzzz!
"Make it stop, Miss Lewis! Make it stop!"
"I will! You stay here."
Buzzzz! Buzzzz! Buzzzz! Buzzzz! Buzzzz! Buzzzz! Buzzzz!
Nadirah hurried from the room, flicked on the hall light, and rushed headlong down the stairs straight to the front door. She couldn't imagine who it could be besides Daniel, although it had been two weeks since she heard from him. If it was Daniel, she was going to kill him. Nadirah snatched open the door without first looking!
"Dan—"
Nadirah was stopped cold by the blisteringly angry woman that stood before her who was just as surprised to see her.
"Who the hell are you?" the woman slurred.
Nadirah's mouth opened, but that was all it did.
"That bastard!" The woman barreled into Nadirah, shoving her aside as she stormed inside the house.
"Hey! Wait a minute!"
"Austin! Austin!"
Nadirah reluctantly closed the door. "Miss! Miss, Austin isn't here."
"Where is he?" The woman started for the living room, but seeing that it was dark, started for the back of the house, but turned

back so fast she teetered.

Nadirah was careful to keep her distance from the woman. She didn't know what to expect, but it was clear the woman was drunk. "Miss, he's not here!"

"Do I look like I believe you?" The woman looked up the stairs. "Austin, you get your ass down here this instant or I swear before God I will burn this son of a bitch down!"

"Mr. Gray isn't here! He's in California!"

The woman turned on Nadirah. "Mr. Gray. Yeah, right. Who the hell are you and what're you doing in my damn house in your ugly-ass nightgown?"

Nadirah glanced down at her flannel nightgown. It might not be pretty, but it was warm. "I live here," she said.

"Like hell you do! You screwing my husband?"

"Your husband? Are you Mrs. Gray?"

"Mrs. Austin Gray, honey, and I don't mean his mother. What you doing in my damn house?"

"I'm living here—temporarily. Mr. Gray is renting the house to me."

"So he's renting, huh? The sneaky bastard. How much you pay-ing him?"

Lynn's explanation about why Austin couldn't officially rent out his house flashed in Nadirah's mind. "I pay one hundred dollars a month to cover utilities."

"One hun…you lying. You're covering for him."

"No! That's what I pay. Do you need to see a cancelled check?" Nadirah was glad that she had thought fast about the amount of money she said she paid.

"Bitch, you better not be screwing my husband."

Nadirah bristled from the caustic assault, but she said calmly, "Mrs. Gray, my cousin and her husband are good friends of your hus-band's, which—"

"Don't tell me. You're that bitch Lynn Wilkie's cousin?" Erma went into the living room and switched on the light and flopped down on the sofa. "I never liked that bitch so I sure as hell don't like you. Get the hell outta my house."

Still standing in the entrance foyer, Nadirah glanced up the

stairs. She needed to go up to Bree to reassure her that everything was okay, but she had to first deal with Austin's crazy wife. How in the world did he marry a woman like this? They didn't resemble each other in any way. This woman was ghastly overdone with blood red lipstick, extra long, fake, jet black eyelashes, lots of deep, dark gray smoky eye shadow, and enough horse hair extensions down her back to pin the tail on a whole coral of horses. Nothing about Erma Gray said class.

"Mrs. Gray," Nadirah said, aware that she was calling a woman in her mid thirties Mrs., "I don't want any trouble."

"Then get the hell out and you won't have any," Erma said, taking off her coat.

Going all the way into the living room, Nadirah glanced at the clock on the DVD player. "Look, it's two-ten in the morning, and—"

"I don't give a damn what time it is. I wanna talk to Austin and if he doesn't get his narrow ass in here quick, fast, and in a hurry, I'm gonna go upstairs and drag his ass out of bed." Erma started digging down inside her pocketbook. "So tell him to get down here."

"But he's not here, Mrs. Gray. He's in California."

"Liar! Austin is right here in this damn house hiding from me! I called out to California. They told me he was in New York." Erma took from her pocketbook a pack of cigarettes. "When he's in New York, he stays here. I came by this afternoon and nobody answered the damn door, but I wasn't leaving tonight until that damn door opened and it did." Erma went back to digging inside her pocketbook.

"Mrs. Gray, if you were here earlier in the day, I was at work. But Mr. Gray is not here and hasn't been here. I'm here, and I'm here legally, and from what I understand, you're the one who isn't supposed to be here."

"Like hell I ain't!" Erma shouted. "I'm still Mrs. Austin Gray, and I have every damn right in the world to be in this old-ass house."

Nadirah felt like she was talking to a raving maniac. "Mrs. Gray, there is a child upstairs trying to sleep. Would you please hold your voice down?"

"Bitch, don't tell me what to do! I'll talk as loud as I damn well please!" And she did, speaking as loud as she could. "Where the hell is my lighter?" At that moment, Erma found it and lit her cigarette.

Nadirah watched helplessly as Erma Gray began puffing a

cloud of white smoke in the air. She hated cigarette smoke and definitely didn't want anyone smoking around her. "Mrs. Gray—"

"Bree?" Erma blurted as she, looking past Nadirah, tried to focus her drunken eyes. "I be-damn! That is you. Girl, what you doing here?"

Bewildered, Nadirah did a double take at Bree who had come quietly up behind her and was staring frighteningly wide-eyed at Mrs. Gray.

"How do you know Bree?" Nadirah asked.

Erma ignored Nadirah. She tried to stand, but wobbled. She plunked back down on the sofa with a grunt. She started to take a drag on her cigarette, but her hand shook so hard she couldn't get the cigarette to her lips. She dropped her hand to her lap and looked past Nadirah.

"Bree, where's your mother? Is Dottie here, too?"

Nadirah kept looking from Erma Gray to Bree and was surprised when Bree hurried to her side and threw her arms around her waist, holding onto her. Nadirah put her arms protectively around Bree.

"What're you doing with my sister's kid? Where's Dotty?"

Nadirah was dumbfounded. "Bree is your niece?"

"Did I speak Russian? Bree, get your little ass over here."

Clinging tighter to Nadirah, Bree began to whimper softly.

"Bree, did you hear what I said? Get over here!"

Bree hid her face in Nadirah's side and began to cry. Nadirah could understand Bree's tears. If she had such a witch of an aunt, she'd—wait a minute. Nadirah did have such a witch of an aunt and had cried many a days because of it. But the odds of Austin Gray's drunken wife being Bree's aunt was too unreal to be believed.

Nadirah wrapped Bree up in a protective embrace.

"Ain't this a bitch?" Erma said. "You trying to keep my niece from me. Ain't this a bitch?"

"Mrs. Gray, I'm Nadirah Lewis. I'm Bree's teacher and foster parent."

Erma angrily stubbed out her cigarette on the glass top coffee table. "What the hell kind of mess is this? My niece got a mother. You ain't her goddamn mother!"

"For the time being, Mrs. Gray, in the absence of Bree's moth-

er, I am Bree's foster mother."

"This isn't high school. My sister isn't absent! You just don't know where the hell she is."

"Do you know where Miss Morrison is?"

"If my sister wanted you to know her damn business, she'd tell you herself. And you are most definitely not keeping her kid. Bree, get your tail over here, now!"

Cryign, Bree tried to hide behind Nadirah.

"Mrs. Gray, Bree stays with me until I hear otherwise from ACS. And—"

"Wanna bet?"

Nadirah's stomach quivered. Did she and Bree have something to fear from this woman?

"Mrs. Gray, if you know where Bree's mother is, I suggest you tell her to contact Mrs. Belinda Hamilton at ACS as soon as possible. The matter of where Bree will live has to be determined between your sister and ACS. But for now, Bree will remain here with me."

"You have the nerve to not only try and steal my husband, but you're trying to take my blood. What's wrong, bitch, can't you have your own kid and get your own man?"

A street fighter Nadirah never was. She cringed every time Erma Gray called her a bitch. "Mrs. Gray, if you must keep insulting me, I'd appreciate it if you would do it on the other side of the front door."

"Bitch, don't even think you can put me out of my own damn house!"

Bree cried louder.

Nadirah looked around the room. She didn't know what she was looking for until she saw a cordless telephone standing up in its cradle on the table. But what good was it? The house phone was turned off and her cell phone was upstairs.

"You don't know who you messing with," Erma said, standing, this time unfailingly. "I'm not like Austin. I'll kick your ass. Austin is a punk who pretends to be so refined and professional. The real deal is, Austin is a nobody. He's a fake. Me? What you see is what you get. I'm Harlem born and bred, baby. Get up in my face, I'll kick your ass every which way but loose. You don't mess with me or my family. No matter

how that kid got here, she's still my blood, and this is my damn house, and Austin is my husband. If anybody's getting the hell out of here, it's you."

Nadirah started trying to peel Bree off of her. "Go upstairs to your room, Bree."

"Yeah, Bree. Get your ass upstairs and get dressed—now!" Erma started toward Nadirah, forcing Nadirah to step back with Bree crying and clinging to her.

"You're scaring her."

"Oh, no you didn't say that! Bree, I know you're not calling yourself scared of me. Girl, you just don't know."

To Nadirah, that was an odd thing for Erma Gray to say. "Go on, Bree," Nadirah said, pushing Bree toward the stairs. "I won't let her hurt you."

Erma stood menacingly in front of Nadirah. "Like what are you gonna do? You can't beat my behind."

Nadirah almost wretched from the foul smell of Erma Gray's alcoholic breath. In all her life, Nadirah had never had a single fight and no idea how to protect herself. While her heart quivered and her stomach flopped, she had to somehow not let on that she was afraid.

"If you don't leave, I'll call the police."

"Call the police, and it'll be the last call you ever make," Erma threatened, but then she started to laugh, unnerving Nadirah. "What am I talking about?" Erma asked rhetorically. "Bitch, you won't get a chance to get to the phone." Erma suddenly jabbed Nadirah in the shoulder. "You ever been on the street half naked?"

Nadirah's stomach dropped to her knees and she started backing up. "Don't touch me!"

Erma shoved Nadirah harder, forcing her out into the foyer. "What're you gonna do?"

"Don't touch me!"

"I'm so scared." Erma again shoved Nadirah. This time even harder, slamming her into the front door.

Scared is what Nadirah was. She screamed, "Stop it!"

At the top of the stairs, Bree wailed at what she'd just seen her aunt do to Nadirah.

"Bree, shut up!" Erma shouted. "And you, bitch. Leave. Or I'll

throw you outside on your naked ass."

Bree cried harder.

"I'm not going anywhere!" Nadirah said defiantly.

"Wanna bet?" Erma grabbed a fistful of Nadirah's nightgown and while they strugged, Erma tried to unlock the door.

As hard as she tried, Nadirah could not pull her gown free of Erma's grasp, nor could she stop Erma from dragging her closer to the front door. Erma overpowered Nadirah. She grabbed her around the waist from the back and pushed her within a foot of the door when the door suddenly opened, surprising them both.

Bree's crying had become fits of coughing.

Austin was aghast at the scene before him. "What the?"

Nadirah back-elbowed Erma in the stomach, knocking the air out of her, doubling her over. Nadirah broke free.

"Bitch, I'ma—" Erma went to punch Nadirah, but Austin grabbed her arm in midair, squeezing it hard enough to shoot pain into her arm.

"Erma! What are you doing?"

"Get the hell off me!" Erma tried to hit Austin with her free hand, but he grabbed that arm and twisted it also. "Oww!"

Austin caught a whiff of Erma's breath. "You're drunk! Erma, how can you be drinking? You're supposed to be on medication."

"Get her out of here!" Nadirah said.

"Look, I'm sorry about this," Austin said, glimpsing Nadirah from the back in her nightgown as she fled up the stairs.

"What you mean you sorry?" Erma spat. "I got every right to be here! You—"

Austin snatched Erma so hard he thought he'd broken her arm and quickly eased up.

"Aaaaargh!"

Nadirah took Bree back into her bedroom, closing the door behind them.

"Erma, shut up! If Miss Beulah calls the police on you again, they'll arrest you this time because I will press charges."

"Screw you, Austin, and that fat ass old bitch, too. You just try and press charges against me. I will—"

Austin dug his fingers into Erma's arm, shutting her up. "You

won't do a thing."

"Ouch! Get off me!"

Austin gritted his teeth. "You disgust me."

Back out in the hall, Nadirah called down, "Get her out of here!"

"Bitch, you don't—"

Austin again snatched Erma. "Shut up!" He started pulling Erma out onto the stoop.

"My coat! I want my coat and my pocketbook."

"Her things are in the living room," Nadirah said. "I'll get them." She started back down the stairs.

"Don't you touch my stuff!" Erma growled.

"I got it," Austin yelled up to Nadirah. "I'm really sorry about this."

"Don't be apologizing for me!"

Austin snatched Erma toward the living room. He didn't let up on his painful hold on her arm even when she picked up her coat and pocketbook.

"You're hurting me!"

Austin pulled Erma toward the front door and called out to Nadirah, "Come down and lock the door."

Erma was infuriated. "You banging that bitch, aren't you? That's why you won't talk to me?"

"Move!" Austin snatched Erma closer to the door and opened it.

"Austin, please give me another chance. Don't divorce me. I'll stay on my medication. I won't go off on you no more."

"Go!"

"Austin, I won't lie to you anymore. I'll be a better wife. I promise. Please, I promise. Please Austin, please. Don't divorce me. I need you."

"Go! Go!" Embarrassed and disgusted, Austin pushed Erma out of the house.

"I know what you want, Austin. I know you want a baby. I'll give you a baby. If you give me a chance, I'll get pregnant again. Just give me a chance."

Austin slammed the door behind them.

Hurrying down the stairs, Nadirah quickly double-bolted the door and ran to the living room window. She lifted one of the slats in the closed blinds just in time to see Austin push Erma into the passenger side of a dark car and apparently threaten her because Erma didn't get back out of the car. How Austin had married a woman like that Nadirah couldn't begin to figure out. It was obvious their marriage hadn't been a walk in the park. Medication? What did Erma Gray need medication for? Nadirah watched until the car drove off the block. She then let go of the breath she had been holding since Erma Gray bullied her way into the house. The fact that she was Bree's aunt was disturbing. Was Bree's mother anything like her sister? Chances were she was. Why else would she desert her child? If Bree had to go back to living with her mother or, perhaps, her aunt, it would be a crime. No, Nadirah could never let that happen. She'd keep Bree herself rather than hand her over to any one of her family members who would most definitely do more harm than good.

Chapter 15

"Miss Lewis."

Bree's soft little voice instantly awakened Nadirah. In the lamp-lit bedroom, she raised her head and looked at Bree. Bree was still in bed next to her, but she was sitting up. After Austin hastily escorted his wife out of the house, Nadirah had gotten Bree to lie down again by promising to sleep with her in her bed. Bree had slept but Nadirah had not, at least not until after four A.M.

"What's wrong, sweetie?" Nadirah asked, sitting up.

"I'm hungry."

"Sure you are." As sleepy as she was, Nadirah remembered that Bree had not eaten dinner, yet she was quite pleased. This was the first time Bree had strung two words together since she was released into her care. Oh, Bree had said yes or no, but that was about all. And now to say that she had a need for something—food—was a milestone. Nadirah glanced over at the window at the early Saturday morning light seeping through the blinds. It was probably no later than 7:00 or 8:00 o'clock.

"I'm hungry, too," Nadirah said, yawning, although the truth was she was more sleepy than hungry. "I want pancakes, and eggs, and bacon. How about you, Bree? What do you want?"

Bree shrugged her shoulders.

"Oh, I know. You look like a spinach and rice kind of girl to me."

Bree screwed up her face.

Feigning surprise, Nadirah asked, "You don't like spinach?"

Bree shook her head no.

"H'mm, baked beans?"

Bree frowned.

Nadirah laughed. "Not for breakfast, huh?" Nadirah gently touched Bree's cheek. "I know. I think you might like pancakes with lots of syrup and crispy bacon. Maybe even some milk. What do you

think?"

Bree nodded.

"Good. First order of business, let's get ourselves washed and dressed." Nadarah gently brushed back the stray strands of hair on the side of Bree's head. "Do you need me to help you?"

Bree shook her head.

"Oh, that's right, you're a big girl, and big girls dress themselves. Let's see who gets dressed first. The winner gets a special surprise."

Bree's eyes lit up. She sprang up off the bed and hurried to the closet.

"Bathroom first, Bree," Nadirah said. "Brush your teeth, wash your face, and take a shower."

Bree ran out of the room heading for the bathroom.

Whatever it was, the Game Boy or the unexpected nightmare of a visit from Erma Gray, Nadirah was grateful for what little Bree said. While she made Bree's bed she said a silent prayer of thanks. Maybe now that Bree was beginning to talk she could get her to tell her why she tried to take her own life.

Austin's renovated townhouse had the luxury of two bathrooms upstairs and one half bath on the first floor. In twenty minutes, Nadirah and Bree both had showered and dressed. Although Nadirah had finished first, she stayed in her room until she heard Bree out in the hall. Then, carrying her shoulder bag and jacket, Nadirah pretended to rush from her bedroom out into the hall.

"You beat me!"

Bree smiled broadly.

Nadirah looked Bree over. She wasn't too crazy about the lightweight yellow blouse Bree had chosen to wear with her jeans as it was going to be a chilly April day, but she would let her wear it.

"Bree, how about you go and get that pretty, blue jacket I bought last week and wear it over your blouse? I think it would look really nice."

"Okay," Bree hurried back into her room.

"And put on your new sneakers," Nadirah said, starting down the stairs. "We're going out for breakfast."

"My treat, if you wait for me," a man's voice said, startling

Nadirah and stopping her on the stairs. She looked back and was surprised to see Austin Gray standing in the doorway of his bedroom in his
bathrobe and pajamas.

Nadirah stood like a deer caught in headlights of a car.

"After last night, I owe you," Austin said.

Still, Nadirah said nothing.

"I got back around four-thirty this morning and you were
asleep. I didn't want to wake you by ringing the bell."

"Thank you. I had only just fallen sleeping."

Austin studied Nadirah's face. "Nadirah, right?"

"Not an easy name to remember, huh?"

"Oh, I remember your name. It's you I don't quite remember.
You look …" Austin didn't want to say prettier or better, so he said, "different."

Was different a good thing or a bad thing? Nadirah suddenly felt
self-conscious, although she knew she had nothing to feel self-conscious about. Under Austin's gaze, she didn't know what to do with her
hands so she took hold of the banister with both. For an awkward
moment, neither said anything.

"Breakfast?" Austin finally asked.

"Well, sure, but—"

Bree came out of her room.

Austin recognized her right away. "Bree!"

Bree beamed. "Uncle Austin!" Bree ran to him and jumped up
into his arms. She hugged him tightly around the neck. He kissed her.
She kissed him.

Nadirah watched at the reunion scene fold in front of her. Of
course, Austin would know Bree if his wife was Bree's aunt, but the way
Bree ran to him astounded Nadirah when Bree had not reacted that way
to Mrs. Gray.

"Hey, baby," Austin said, still holding Bree in his arms. "What
are you doing here?" He looked to Nadirah for answers before he turned
and carried Bree, now crying, into his bedroom.

Not knowing what else to do, Nadirah crept almost on tiptoes
up the stairs to Austin's room. He was sitting with Bree on his lap on the
side of his large king size bed. He was holding her, rocking her, and
comforting her like he had done it before.

"Come on, baby, stop crying. Talk to me. What happened? Where's your mother?"

Bree wouldn't stop crying. Austin again looked to Nadirah for answers.

"What's going on? Is Dorothy here?"

"No," Nadirah said, shaking her head. "She's not here. I'm Bree's foster mother."

"Her foster mother? Where's Dorothy?"

"We don't know, but I'm also Bree's teacher. Your wife didn't tell you?"

"She didn't mention Bree. I didn't know Bree was in foster care. Why? Why didn't Erma take her if there was a problem with Dorothy? But Erma should know where Dorothy is. Didn't she tell you?"

Bree's crying started subsiding.

"Your wife told me nothing. And, as I said, no one knows where Bree's mother is." Nadirah took a few steps into the room. "When your wife showed up it was the first I'd ever seen her and I definitely didn't know she was related to Bree. I've never even met Bree's mother, she's never come to the school. I have Bree because she was in the hospital and her mother abandoned her. No one's heard from her."

"Dorothy had some problems, but she cares a lot about Bree. She wouldn't abandon her. And you said Bree was in the hospital? Why? What for?"

"Well … she—"

"Mommy made me drink nasty poison stuff," Bree blurted.

"What's she talking about?" Austin asked.

Nadirah quickly sat on the bed next to Austin. "Bree, are you saying your mother made you drink that disinfectant?"

Bree nodded definitively.

"Disinfectant!" Austin was thunderstruck. "Dorothy made you drink disinfectant? Bree, are you sure?"

Again Bree nodded. "Mommy, holded my face and made me drink it. It was nasty. It burned my tongue and my throat."

"Oh, man. I don't believe this."

But Nadirah did. "That's why Bree was in the hospital," she explained. "She could have died."

"Damn!" Austin completely enclosed Bree in his arms. "Erma

never said a thing. This is—"

"ACS couldn't locate any family members. When they said they were putting Bree in the system, I asked if I could take her. My principal and the guidance counselor both backed me and I was given Bree until a determination could be made."

"I'm so glad you were looking out for her. When Lynn told me you needed a lease because you wanted to help a kid in your class, I had no idea—" Words failed Austin as he choked up. He went back to rocking Bree.

Nadirah pushed her urge to cry way down. "It's been tough. Bree's been in counseling since this all happened about two months ago, but we haven't learned anything. She's been holding a lot in."

"I bet." Austin pulled Bree back a bit so that he could see her face. "Bree, baby, can you tell me why your mother made you drink that stuff?"

Bree nodded meekly.

Nadirah anxiously waited for Bree to speak. She gently rubbed Bree's back.

Bree said softly, "Mommy said it was hard taking care of me by herself. She said she wasn't supposed to keep me. She said I wasn't supposed to be her baby."

Baffled, Nadirah asked, "What does that mean?"

"Bree, maybe your mother meant that you were no longer a baby and that you were growing up."

Bree shrugged her uncertainty. "Mommy said God could take care of me better. She said she want me to go live with God."

Nadirah gasped softly to herself.

"I can't go live with God, can I? He's in heaven, right?"

Tears leaped into Nadirah's eyes.

Austin dug down deep to keep from showing how upset he was. For the longest seconds, neither he nor Nadirah could speak, but Bree could.

"Mommy said she really loved me. She said she had to protect me from Aunt Erma."

That Nadirah could believe.

"Did your Aunt Erma ever hurt you?" Austin asked.

"Uh-huh. A lot of time she pinch me. She pinch me hard on my

arm. It hurt a lot. Mommy said God won't let Aunt Erma pinch me if I go to heaven."

Austin cleared his throat. "Bree, I won't let your Aunt Erma pinch you ever again, okay?"

"Okay."

"Neither will I," Nadirah said.

"Okay, 'cause her pinches hurt, and you know what else? Aunt Erma said she gonna take me from my mommy."

"Really?" Austin asked, surprised. "When was this?"

"Before I got sick."

"None of this makes any sense," Austin said.

"Bree," Nadirah said, "do you know where your mother is?"

Bree shook her head.

Again neither Nadirah nor Austin spoke. There were so many questions, but both knew that many of the answers were not going to come from Bree.

"Uncle Austin?"

"Yeah, baby."

"I'm hungry."

"I tell you what, Bree," Austin said. "Give me five minutes to take my shower and get dressed and I'll take you to get the best breakfast you ever had."

"Five minutes, Uncle Austin? You always take a long shower. You take more than five minutes."

Nadirah smiled. There was no doubt that Bree was familiar with Austin. Yet, Bree had never given the slightest hint that she had ever been in his house.

"I'll take a short shower this time." Austin kissed Bree on the head and lifted her off his lap. "Six minutes, okay?"

"Okay," Bree smiled.

Nadirah took Bree's hand. "We'll wait downstairs for you."

"I'll hurry it up, but wait a minute. Bree, why don't you go down to the kitchen and see if you can find some crackers. You still like crackers, right?"

"Uh-huh."

"Bree," Nadirah said, "the crackers are on the counter next to the refrigerator."

"Okay." Bree ran from the room and could be heard running down the stairs.

"I don't understand any of this," Austin said. "Why would Erma wanna take Bree from Dorothy, and Dorothy be so desperate that she'd try to kill Bree?"

That wasn't a question Nadirah could answer. "I don't know, but Bree definitely wasn't happy to see your wife."

"I guess not." Unexpectedly, Austin took Nadirah's hand, surprising her. "Look," he said, "I'm glad you brought Bree here. She's a great kid. Thank you for helping her."

Nadirah simply nodded, but she was just as grateful to Austin for letting her stay in his house. Coyly, slipping her hand out of his, she asked, "So Bree's been here before?"

"She used to live here. Didn't she tell you?"

"No. When Bree was brought here she never said a word. In fact, Bree hasn't been speaking at all. Today is the most she's spoken, period. Even before that incident with the disinfectant, she didn't talk much. This is the first time Bree has told anyone that her mother forced her to drink that stuff."

"Man. I just can't grasp the concept of Dorothy making Bree do something like that."

"Well, I always had a problem believing Bree drank that stuff on her own. Please, tell me something about Bree's mother so I can understand this."

Austin went to his dresser. "Bree was about five when she lived here for about a year with Dorothy. Erma asked me to let Dorothy stay here until she got on her feet. Seems she'd lost her apartment." Austin took a pair of black briefs from the second drawer.

Seeing the briefs in his hand, Nadirah looked away. She looked around the room that she had been told was off limits.

"After a year, Dorothy left so I figured she'd gotten on her feet, but now that I think about it, I don't know why she left. The last few months she was here I started spending more time out on the coast so I can't say what was going on back here. But to be honest, my life was pretty messed up so I may have missed some signs that things weren't okay with Dorothy. At the first opportunity I got away."

As curious as she was about Austin's marriage to Erma, espe-

cially after her unfortunate encounter with her, Nadirah wasn't about to ask questions.

"What about Bree?" she asked. "How was she when she lived here?"

"She seemed fine. She was a talker. An inquisitive kid. Nosy as heck. Sometimes she asked too many questions, but I had a pretty good rapport with her. She liked for me to read to her a lot, which I did almost every other day. Oh, and she loved orange Jell-O. She was crazy about the stuff." Austin began smiling as he reminisced and chuckled. "I learned how to make Jell-O because of Bree."

Nadirah smiled.

"She was a good kid. I tried to make time for her because I figured she was lonely. There were no other kids around and Dorothy never really played with her. In fact, it seemed she was always pushing Bree off on me to look after. Erma wouldn't do it so I guess it was on me."

"She probably wanted Bree to see you as a father figure."

"That crossed my mind."

Austin took a black t-shirt from another drawer. "Was Dorothy nice to Bree? I mean, did she show her love or give her much affection?"

"I wanna say yes because I've seen Bree sitting in Dorothy's lap, but I've also seen her push Bree away when Bree wanted to be near her. I don't know. I haven't seen Dorothy in at least two years. After Erma and I separated, I had no contact with Dorothy after she left here. But when she was here, Dorothy was terribly moody. She was a nice enough person, but she could swing from being very quiet and laid back to being a party girl. Every now and then she would hang out with Erma and Erma, who wasn't a hardcore party girl when I met her, within a year into our marriage did a one-eighty. She used to get Dorothy to hang with her when I wouldn't, which was most of the time. That's how I got to spend so much time with Bree. So as for Dorothy showing Bree love, I guess she loved her kid. She never showed me that she didn't. She was raising Bree alone which carried its own problems, but I never saw Dorothy mistreat or abuse Bree."

Nadirah pondered Austin's profile of Bree's mother. She wondered aloud, "Then what would make her force Bree to drink disinfec-

tant?"

"Don't know. Can't even begin to guess."

"It's beyond me," Nadirah said. "By the time Bree came into my class she was nothing like the child you describe. She definitely wasn't a talker and was by no means inquisitive. Whatever happened after she and her mother left your house changed her."

"They probably had a very difficult time out on their own."

"So what happens if Bree is placed back with her mother? Who's to say something bad won't happen again?"

"Yeah," Austin said, pensively.

"And the fact that everyone thinks that Bree tried to take her own life when it was her mother who made her drink that stuff, is serious."

"Well, we can't let ACS continue to believe that."

"No," Nadirah agreed, keenly aware that Austin had said we.

"Uncle Austin," Bree called. "Are you ready yet?"

"I will be in a minute!" Austin began untying his robe.

"Oh," Nadirah said, looking away. "Why don't I go down and keep her company?" She started toward the door.

"I'll be down in about five minutes. Oh, Nadirah," Austin said, stopping her at the door. "By the way, I like your new look."

"Oh… ah…thank you." Nadirah quickly left the room and pulled the door shut behind her. She wondered how Austin happened to show when he did. Then, too, she couldn't help but think how coincidental it was that Bree, her student by way of her mother's relationship to her sister Erma, who was married to Austin Gray, was related to Austin Gray; who Nadirah had never heard of before until she decided to move out of her aunt's house; and that it was her cousin Lynn who suggested she move into her friend Austin's house. Nadirah was reminded of six degrees of separation where one person knows one person that leads to the next and back around to the first person in the circle. In the long run, what would her association with Bree's family come to? What would it mean to her life?

Chapter 16

It was one thing for Nadirah to have always known the meaning of that old adage "feel like the third wheel," but for her to actually feel like that third wheel unexpectedly awakened an emotion in her she had never known—jealousy. It was a strange, tense, uncomfortable feeling that, although it shamed her, made her almost dislike Austin Gray. Throughout their long late morning breakfast of pancakes, bacon, and eggs, Nadirah had sat across from Austin and Bree quietly watching them teasingly play with each other, telling silly jokes, and, for the first time, hearing Bree giggle and laugh like the happy, carefree, little girl she was supposed to be. As hard as Nadirah had tried she had never gotten Bree to laugh nor smile, and, in a matter of moments, Austin had succeeded. Logically, Nadirah knew that Bree let down her guard and opened up to Austin because she knew him, but still silly little pangs of jealousy overshadowed he good sense when Bree put her hand in Austin's, and not hers, as they left the restaurant. She had to take a deep breath and remind herself she had no reason to feel ignored by Bree or left out by Austin, and she also had no reason to be jealous of Austin when he was actually good for Bree.

"It's turned out to be a pretty nice day," Austin said. "It's warming up."

"Yes, it is," Nadirah said, indeed feeling the frigid chill of early April easing up as the late morning sun brightened the earlier overcast sky.

"Uncle Austin, can we go to the park?"

"Bree," Nadirah chimed in, "I'm sure your uncle has appointments to get to. I'll take you to the park."

Poking out her bottom lip, Bree hung her head.

"Actually," Austin said, "my appointments were yesterday. Today I'm free. Bree, I'd love to go to the park."

Bree snapped her head up, flashed the brightest smile, and

gave Austin the biggest hug around his waist.

Austin winked at Nadirah. "Don't take much to please you, huh, Bree?"

"Uh-uh. Uncle Austin, when you divorce Aunt Erma I'm gonna marry you, okay?"

"Okay."

Nadirah enjoyed the twinkle in Austin's eyes.

"Uncle Austin, we gotta get engaged before we get married because that's the law. You know that, right?"

"We sure don't wanna break the law," Austin said. "I guess we better get engaged right away after I get my divorce, but we have to wait till you turn forty before we can get married. That's the law, too."

Both Nadirah and Austin could almost see the wheels turning in Bree head. Austin winked at Nadirah, and almost burst out laughing when Bree's eyes widened.

"Forty is old, Uncle Austin."

"I certainly hope not," Austin said, knowing in a few years he'd be knocking at forty's door.

"No, Bree. Forty isn't old. Forty is like being twenty?twice. Twenty isn't old is it?"

"No, but twenty, twice is." Bree skipped away as happy as she could be.

Holding his laughter inside, Austin belly laughed until Bree was a distance away. Nadirah let herself go, too. She was truly enjoying the Bree that Austin had awakened.

"That kid is hysterical," Austin said, when he was finally able to stop laughing.

"She is such a different child." Nadirah kept her eyes on Bree who had stopped at the corner to wait for them.

"She's a great kid. I always had fun with her."

"Well, she's totally smitten with you."

"A little girl's crush. If her father was in her life he'd be her first love, not me."

"Hurry up!" Bree called.

"We're coming!" Austin said, picking up his pace and forcing Nadirah to do the same. "Hey," he said to Nadirah, "we could either walk over to Riverbank State Park on the Hudson or over to St. Nicholas

Park. We're about the same distance from both. You choose."

"Riverbank. I like the water, but are you sure you don't have some place you have to be? I thought you only came into town on business."

"I took care of business yesterday. Today I was supposed to leave town…" Austin checked his watch, "…thirty minutes ago."

"You missed your flight?"

"I rescheduled it. I decided to book a later flight so I could be here to make sure there was no repeat of last night, but then when I saw Bree this morning I changed my flight to tomorrow morning."

H'm, good-looking and considerate, Nadirah thought.

Austin went to Bree and took her hand. "I see you remembered not to stand too close to the curb."

"You taught me that," Bree said.

Nadirah stood on the other side of Bree. This time she reached down and took Bree's hand and was relieved when Bree didn't pull away. Together, at the change of the light, she, Bree, and Austin crossed big, wide Broadway heading toward the Hudson River. It wasn't the day Nadirah had planned, but the day was proving to be especially rewarding. Bree was talking, she was happy, and that's all that mattered. With Bree skipping off again toward Riverside Drive, Nadirah was anxious to talk to Austin.

"I thought you stayed at the house whenever you were in town?"

"I usually do, but I stayed with a client up in Mount Vernon."

"Someone famous?"

"Nearly famous. Shane Archer. He's a wide receiver for the New York Jets. I came in to meet with the Jets' management about him."

"Did it go well?"

"We got what we wanted—a bit more money, but more importantly, more time on the field."

They caught up with Bree and crossed quickly over the vast Westside Highway into Riverbank State Park. Bree took off running again, excited to be in the park, which was already teeming with a horde of gleeful, playful children. Bree joined right in, never once looking back to see if Nadirah or Austin were close by.

"I am totally baffled," Nadirah said.

"Why?"

"Because I can't believe that's the same joyless, doe-eyed little girl who sat in my classroom for months and never smiled or talked, running off eager to play. It's like someone flipped a switch and she changed."

"Hey, I'm glad she did because I don't know the kid you just described." He looked around for an empty bench. "Let's sit over there."

"Shouldn't we follow Bree?"

"Nah, she's all right. We can see her from here." Austin went and sat on the bench.

Hesitant, Nadirah kept looking back at Bree as she went to join Austin.

"Relax," Austin said. "Look, she's already made a friend."

Nadirah saw that Bree was running behind another little girl who was running over to the slide. Bree began climbing the ladder right on the girl's heels.

"Shouldn't we tell her to slow down? She's going to fall."

"Nadirah, scraped knees and elbows are all part of childhood. I had my share. How about you?"

"Yeah," Nadirah said, remembering how much fun she used to have going to the park with her parents. And, yes, she did scrape her knees a few times.

Austin sat back with his arms stretched out across the back of the bench. "Man, this feels good. This is the first time I've been able to cool out like this in a long time."

Aware of Austin's arm behind her, Nadirah didn't sit back. "Busy life, huh?"

"Pretty much."

Nadirah focused on Bree, who was stretching her arms up trying to reach the swinging rings above.

"Listen," Austin began, "I'd like to apologize for last night. Erma had no business in my house."

"Well, I'm glad you arrived when you did."

Bree's new friend was trying to heft Bree up to catch hold of the rings, putting Nadirah on edge.

"I hadn't planned on coming to the house, especially at that hour, but I checked my messages and heard how drunk Erma was. I fig-

ured she'd go looking for me."

"That she did," Nadirah said, watching as Bree grabbed hold of the rings, swing once, and then fall to the ground. Nadirah stood.

Austin had also never taken his eye off of Bree. "She'll get up," he said. "You're probably more hurt than she is."

Chuckling, Nadirah sat. "Yeah, and being a teacher you'd think I would be use to children falling on the playground. Do you have any children?"

Austin brushed invisible dirt from his pants leg. "Not a one, which is probably for the best."

That, Nadirah had no doubt.

"Look. Now that I know Bree's situation, I'll do all I can to help out. I'll stay in touch."

"I'm sure Bree would love that." Nadirah would like that herself.

From the moment Austin realized who it was that Nadirah had taken in, he knew that he liked her for her kindness, but now he found himself liking her for herself. It was easy sitting with her and talking with her. It had been a long time since he felt this at ease with a woman. The last time he had been this at ease with Erma was the year they went together before she talked him into marrying her, and the truth was Erma didn't do much talking. Looking back, that whole year from the time they met, to the time they got married, was a blur of sex and more sex to the point of exhaustion. Every night Erma exhausted him. Relaxed? He was almost dead by the time he and Erma went to sleep every night. He could never say Erma wasn't the best he'd ever had because she was. She did things to him that most men could only fantasize about. If anyone had told him that Erma had him p-whipped he would not have been able to deny it. Under Erma's spell he was fooled into thinking that she was worth spending the rest of his life with. How wrong she was, and so was he for not using the head on his shoulders.

"Earlier," Nadirah began, "you mentioned Bree not having her father in her life. Do you know her father?"

"Can't say I do. I met one guy who Erma said was Bree's father, but I saw him maybe twice the whole time Dorothy and Bree were in my house. That's all."

"Well, his loss."

"Yeah," Austin said. "I wish Bree were my kid."

"Too bad you aren't. Bree's crazy about you and you're great with her."

Austin said nothing. He was remembering how good Bree's arms felt around his neck when he first saw her.

After a minute, Nadirah asked, "Are you all right?"

Austin clasped his hands together. "Just thinking."

Austin again slipped into silence leaving Nadirah to regret her comment about him not being Bree's father. It obviously opened old wounds. He looked so much like a little boy who didn't get what he wanted most for Christmas.

"I think I'll go check on Bree." Nadirah started to stand.

"Erma and I almost had a kid," Austin suddenly revealed. "Actually, we could have had several kids."

Nadirah stayed put.

"Until Erma got pregnant, we weren't all that serious. The long and short of it, we got married because Erma was four months pregnant, but a few weeks after we were married, she miscarried."

"Oh. I'm sorry."

"Yeah, it was a bad time. Erma must have cried for a week. For months, she had terrible episodes of depression that strained our marriage, but she was convinced if she got pregnant again that everything would be all right. In two years she got pregnant three more times and each time the pregnancy lasted less than three months. Erma was a mess, and I was pretty bad off myself. It was rough. I wanted to adopt, but Erma didn't. She was determined to give me our baby. So finally she listened to me and went to see a doctor. She had fertility screening, internal sonograms, everything, but there was never a clear explanation for why she kept miscarrying."

"Her doctors couldn't find anything?"

"Fibroids. Erma had several fibroids, but it seems they weren't significant enough to interfere with her carrying a baby to term."

"Austin, you said, finally she went to see a doctor. Wasn't she seeing a doctor, a gyn, a specialist, or somebody all along?"

"Erma hates doctors. She calls them all quacks. She never went to see a gyn until after the fourth miscarriage, and even then she didn't believe what she was being told, and that was to stay off her feet until

her pregnancy was more advanced and stable. Erma was convinced there was nothing wrong with her. I got her to go to another doctor who wanted to remove the fibroids, which he said was the problem."

"Was he talking about giving her a hysterectomy?"

"I don't think so. He was talking laser removal of the fibroids, but Erma wouldn't hear of it. She wanted to try one last time to get pregnant before her insides were messed with. I guess I went along with her to appease her. Privately, I was hoping that this last time would be the charm. It almost was. Erma got pregnant. She was put on complete bed rest. The pregnancy was rough from the beginning—Erma hated staying in bed."

"It had to be really difficult for her."

"It was for both of us, but I pulled out all the stops. I stayed out of the office as much as I could to be with her. Back then I worked for ABC Sports as a producer. I had a housekeeper five days a week. Erma didn't have to wipe her own ass if she didn't want to."

"So what went wrong? How far along did she get?"

"Seven months."

"Oh, no."

"Yeah, it was rough."

"Were you with her?"

Austin chuckled sadly. "As life would have it, I wasn't. I was out of town. That weekend, my mother was staying with Erma. By the time I got back, my mother was dead, my baby was dead, and Erma was in worse shape than I'd ever seen her. She—"

"Your mother was dead?"

"She had a heart attack. It was her second one."

"Oh, my God."

"Yeah." Austin's eyes glistened. "Erma blamed the doctors, she blamed me, she even blamed by mother. She said my mother stressed her out and made her miscarry."

"What did she mean by that?"

"She said she started having premature contractions and my mother refused to take her to the hospital."

"Refused? But EMS would have come for her."

"Erma said my mother wouldn't call EMS."

"Really?"

"That's what Erma said. She said they argued about it."

"Do you believe her?"

"The truth? I don't know. I know she wanted the baby, and my mother wanted us to have the baby as well, which is why she agreed to stay with Erma. What happened? I only know what Erma told me. In the end, my mother's death and the aftermath of the miscarriage slammed the door shut on the marriage. Erma became more erratic. Everything was unfair to her. Oh, did I mention that Erma's sister was pregnant at the same time Erma was?"

"No."

"Well, she was, and Erma hated her for it. She started treating her really badly. She thought it was unfair that Dorothy was having a healthy pregnancy and she wasn't even married, whereas she was married and couldn't carry a baby to term."

"That's selfish."

"Not to Erma. Erma goes after what she wants. If anything or anyone gets in her way, she barrels right through. When Dorothy had Bree, Erma couldn't handle it. As close as they were, she stopped speaking to Dorothy and, eventually, Dorothy stopped coming around except for later when she and Bree had to stay at the house."

"I guess it was too painful for your wife to see her sister with a baby," Nadirah said, sympathetically. "She was hurt. She had lost all her babies, and she was possibly never going to ever have children."

"Yeah, I understood that, but the funny thing was, although Erma and Dorothy fell out, Erma was sending money to Dorothy to help her out."

"That was nice of her."

"Yeah, but if you know Erma, giving isn't who she is. She's a very selfish woman. I asked her about sending money to Dorothy and she said no matter what, Dorothy was still her sister and she had to help her. I left it alone. It wasn't for me to question further."

"Did she tell you how Dorothy was living?"

"During that period, it seems Dorothy was raising Bree on public assistance. Erma always said Dorothy was slow. I think she was getting some sort of public assistance or SSI for being slow."

Nadirah listened intently.

"At some point, when Bree was about seven, Erma told me that

Dorothy got herself a job, a better apartment for her and Bree, and seemed to be holding strong, but somewhere along the way something went wrong. By that time, Erma and I weren't talking much so I have no idea what happened."

"Poor, baby," Nadirah said, looking at Bree. "No telling all she's gone through. Do you think you can find Dorothy?"

"I doubt it. Dorothy and I never connected. We didn't talk or hang out so I don't know how to locate her. But Erma, with a little persuasion, might be able to. As much as I don't want to, I'll talk to her and see if she'll tell me where Dorothy might be."

"Thanks, but if it's going to cause—"

"Problems? Oh, it will cause major problems, but if it'll help Bree then … wait…" Austin said, removing his arms from the back of the bench and allowing Nadirah to finally sit back. "Let's think this thing through. Will it really help Bree if I find her mother?"

"I would hope so, but I see what you mean. It could be a double-edged sword."

"Exactly. Suppose we get Bree back with her mother and her mother again tries to kill her, but this time succeeds? Do we want Bree's blood on our hands?"

"No, but in light of what Bree told us, ACS needs to know where Bree's mother is and so do the police."

"Granted, but if Dorothy is never found, Bree won't have to go through the heartache of having to be dragged through the system and the courts. Unless it can be proven that Dorothy made Bree drink disinfectant, and it is Bree's word against Dorothy's, Dorothy may not go to jail or lose parental custody of Bree. Have you thought about that? Bree may well benefit by being placed with an adoptive family that really wants her."

Letting Austin's meaning sink in, Nadirah pondered the *what ifs*. "But what if Bree is placed with a family that is only in it for the money paid by the city? And what if, in the hands of the wrong family, Bree is hurt just as badly, if not worse, than she has been by her own mother?"

"That's negative thinking."

"No, it's realistic thinking. Austin, almost every day there's something on the news somewhere in this country about kids being

harmed by foster parents, adoptive parents, as well as their own parents."

"This is true, but we can't go into this thinking that Bree is going to get the wrong family. But if that bothers you, Dorothy has other family members who might be better for Bree than Dorothy."

"Certainly not your wife?"

"No, no, not Erma. There are some cousins out on Long Island, but I don't really know any of them."

"Okay, but suppose your wife seeks custody of Bree? Austin, Bree's afraid of her. I know you wanted to have your own children with your wife, but, no offense, I personally don't think a porcupine with razors for quills would be safe with Erma."

"Well, I for one wouldn't recommend Bree be placed with Erma, especially knowing that Erma never liked Bree. She always said Bree was a clingy, little brat."

"Nice."

"It didn't matter to Erma that Bree was a baby, Erma resented her as if she was a problem for her."

"Maybe she was. Maybe she didn't like having to support her."

"Maybe, but I think it was more like she hated that Bree was born."

"Could be. She is jealous hearted, which is why I don't see her seeking custody of Bree unless there is something in it for her. When we accepted that Erma could never carry a baby to term, talk of babies became taboo. Before we were married, Erma wanted two children. After she couldn't have her own biological children, she wouldn't discuss adoption and never wanted children around her—especially Bree.

"Believe me, Bree is quite aware of this. She wouldn't go to your wife last night."

"No surprise." Austin began to wring his hands.

Again an uneasy silence fell between them, and again Nadirah focused on Bree. After a few minutes, Austin asked, "Did Lynn tell you anything about me and my wife?"

Nadirah remembered Lynn starting to tell her something about Austin's marriage, but she had stopped her. "No, she didn't."

"That's surprising. When did you speak to her last?"

After a second's thought, Nadirah answered, "It's been about

two weeks. We don't speak that often, but I'll probably see her tonight. She and Byron are supposed to be here this weekend for some insurance industry event. Since you're here, they'll probably want to get together with you."

"Maybe." Austin suddenly stood. He searched the mob of kids in the park looking for Bree. "I don't see her."

Nadirah had never taken her eyes off of Bree. "She's right there." She pointed across the park to the swings. "See her there at the swings? The blue jacket. See her?"

"Oh, yeah. I see her." Austin sat.

Again that uneasy silence. Nadirah started standing. "Maybe we should start back. I'll go get Bree."

"Wait a minute," Austin said, stopping Nadirah. "I'm sorry about last night."

"Oh, don't worry about it. I'm fine. You're the one who has to still deal with your wife. It must be rough."

"It's pretty bad, but you know what? I see the light at the end of the tunnel."

"Good." Nadirah had her fill of talk about Erma Gray. She stretched out her legs.

Austin got the message but he had one last thing to say. "Nadirah, let me give you a bit of advice. I don't know if you're with someone or not, but before you make a lifetime commitment, make sure you know who you're dealing with. Don't be fooled by the lies because after the lovin' diminishes it could get ugly."

Although Nadirah hadn't experienced marriage herself, she'd been an eyewitness to her Aunt Stephanie's and Uncle Lester's marriage and theirs was far from pretty. Still, she couldn't say that she had ruled out marriage for herself because her own parent's marriage, if she recalled correctly, was pretty good. Still, she wasn't naive. She knew there were just as many bad marriages as good marriages in the world. Secretly, she had hoped that one day she'd be lucky enough to meet the right person to have a family with. Living out her life alone wasn't what she wanted for herself. As for Austin, seeing as how

he was clinching his jaw, it was obvious that the bitter taste left in his mouth from his marriage to Erma had spoiled his taste buds for any flavor of marriage. Erma had ruined him for all the other women he'd

ever meet. What a loss.

"Let's go get Bree," Nadirah said. "I promised her a special surprise if she got herself dressed before me this morning."

Before standing, Austin rolled his head from shoulder to shoulder to relieve the stress in his neck he'd brought on himself by thinking about his marriage to Erma.

"What's the surprise?" he asked.

"Come with us and find out."

Nadirah walked off leaving Austin where he stood. He was undecided and unsure, but definitely intrigued. He watched Nadirah walk away. He liked her view from behind as much as he liked what she had to offer in the front. Nadirah was a good looking woman with a big heart. He liked her, but all women were great in the beginning. Only a few ever turned out to be genuine. Byron had lucked up because Lynn was genuine. He wondered if Nadirah was one of the rare few who would not change after marriage.

From where he stood, Austin could see Nadirah closing in on Bree. He was glad Nadirah had Bree because she would protect her. If he could he'd do the same, but he had to get back to California. His life was there, not in New York.

Chapter 17

After so many years of hiding behind her wheelchair, something as simple as standing in the kitchen making her own tea and cutting a slice of her own homemade lemon cake, was like experiencing life after awaking from a long, deep coma. Stephanie could admit to herself that maybe she was wrong for living a lie, but she would never admit to any living soul that she had cut off her nose to spite her face. She had missed out on so much in her defiant determination to at first hold on to Lester, and after he died, Nadirah. She had missed out on something as small as walking down the street to the corner, and something as big as being able to travel around the country and around the world to places she'd seen only on her television. In the end, who did she hurt? Certainly not Nadirah. She was off somewhere living her life without a care about her or how she was getting on, while she was left all alone to grow older without a word of thanks for taking in an ungrateful child.

Now as she carried her tea and cake into the living room and sat in the chair that Lester once claimed as his favorite, Stephanie recalled the day she decided to say she could no longer walk. It was the day after she fell down the stairs and Lester walked into her hospital room. Seeing his face reminded her of what he'd told her just days before her fall.

"I can't do this anymore," he said. "I can't stand who you've become and I hate who I've become because of you."

"You can't leave. So what are you saying?"

"I am leaving, and before you say it, you do what you have to do. If I have to go to jail then so be it."

Lester had said no more to her until she fell. She lay in her hospital bed while Lester got after the doctors and nurses about her care gave birth to the idea that Lester would never leave if she was disabled. He wasn't the type of man to run out on his responsibility nor his family, he was morally too righteous for that, not to mention

that he always took her at her word and would never second-guess her nor question her about not being about to walk when the doctors said she could. And he didn't disappoint her. Lester stayed, her marriage was intact, her lifestyle remained the same, and she became the greatest actress in the world while imprisoning herself behind a wall of lies. She had no idea she'd end up wasting invaluable years of good health. On top of being fat and suffering with hypothyroidism, she had developed diabetes.

"Mama," Lynn said, entering the living room, "should you be eating cake?"

"I'm taking my pills." Stephanie closed her mouth around a big chunk of moist, sweet cake. At this point in her life she wasn't thinking of depriving herself of anything enjoyed.

"But, Mama, you still have to watch what you eat. You're lucky you're just on pills and not insulin injections."

Stephanie moved her cake from side to side in front of her face while she followed it with her eyes. "You satisfied? Did I watch it close enough for you?"

"Okay, Mama, be cute, but don't say I didn't try to stop you."

"I won't."

"Fine, but look, I need to talk to you."

"Isn't that what you're doing?" Stephanie forked off another piece of cake.

"Mama—"

"So where's this event you're going to?"

"At The Carlyle, downtown. How do I look?"

Stephanie looked Lynn over as she turned slowly in front of her in her burgundy gown. "H'mm…that looks like one of my old gowns. You been in my closet?"

Lynn almost laughed. "This is my gown." Lynn sat on the sofa. "So what are you gonna do tonight?"

"Something really exciting."

"Really?"

"I'm watching television," Stephanie said, flatly. "Whoopee for me."

Not appreciating her mother's insipid attitude, Lynn said straight out, "Mama, your life is what you make it. You don't have to be

alone. Isn't Barbette coming tonight?"

"Barbette wasn't my friend. She was my employee who, by the way, I fired."

Surprised, Lynn asked, "When?"

"Two weeks ago. She was stealing from me."

"Mama, you never said a thing about that."

"If I had told you, were you gonna come and take her place?"

Lynn counted to ten in her head. Her mother was pricking her nerves. "Mama, if I had known I would have tried to get someone else in here."

"Obviously, I don't want anyone else in here. I'm fine by myself."

"Fine, if that's the way you want it, but, you don't have to stay in the house all the time. You should get out more. You're not crippled." Only when Stephanie didn't say anything did Lynn realize what she'd said. "Well, not anymore anyway."

Stephanie smirked at Lynn then ate another forkful of cake. She flicked off Lynn's remark like she'd flick a lady bug off her shoulder.

"What about your church, Mama? They have something going on tonight, don't they?"

"Choir practice, and I'm not about to join a bunch of shrieking, sexually frustrated women so don't waste your breath trying to tell me to give it a chance. I won't."

"Suit yourself," Lynn said, glancing over the coffee table. "Where's the remote?"

"Where it belongs," Stephanie said, not making a move to pass it to Lynn. She left it stuck down in the side of the seat cushion of her chair. "Why is your husband taking so long?"

"We have time, Mama. I took my shower first so I'm ready first. It gives me a chance to talk to you. I have a problem to discuss with you."

"Now that's something I don't think I've ever heard you say to me. H'mm…I guess you wish your father were alive, huh? Then you would not have had to say it at all."

No truer words were ever spoken, but Lynn couldn't say that out loud. Hell, she couldn't even look her mother in the eye, for what she had to talk to her about was humiliating. She wished she didn't have to

talk about it at all.

"I thought so," Stephanie said. "Sorry I'm not your father, but those are the breaks. Look, my show's about to come on and I'm used to watching it by myself." Stephanie munched on another forkful of cake. She ignored the quizzical lift of Lynn's brow as she dug the television remote out from the side of the seat cushion and changed the channel.

Lynn chuckled under her breath as she crossed her leg. "I would think, Mama, that you'd be glad to have company for a change."

"What makes you think it's your company I want?"

That insult hit Lynn between the eyes. "I guess I should just keep my mouth shut." She picked up a two-month-old issue of Ebony Magazine and began to flip through it.

"Oh, don't act like I hurt your feelings. I know you don't give a damn about me. When I die I'm sure I'll just make your day."

Lynn could feel the acid from her empty stomach backing up in her throat. "Mama, if you just have to be bitter, please keep it to yourself."

"So that's what I am—bitter? If that's the case, why do you even bother to come here?"

Damn you, Byron. This is your fault! Lynn flipped angrily through the magazine.

Stephanie went back to channel surfing. Her show wasn't on yet and there wasn't a thing that interested her. Just as irritable as Lynn, Stephanie dug into the remainder of her cake. She set the empty plate down hard on the table. Lynn didn't look up, which annoyed Stephanie even more.

"You don't come here all that often, Lynn, but when you do, clearly you don't wanna be here. I know you don't like me. You sided with your brother and Nadirah against me. None of you understand why I had to do what I did and none of you wanna hear what I have to say about it."

Huffing loudly, Lynn slapped the magazine closed and tossed it back onto the table. "Let it go!" Lynn went to shaking her foot. She definitely wasn't in the mood for this.

"Your brother acts like I killed somebody. He won't return my calls, and Nadirah, with her ungrateful behind self, hasn't even called or come by here one time to check on me. I could be dead for all she care."

Lynn couldn't take it anymore. "Are you asking for pity, Mama?"

"I'm asking for respect, dammit! I deserve respect."

"Are you serious? What about Daddy? Didn't he deserve respect? You didn't show him any respect by lying to him and making him stay with you out of pity."

"Your father didn't stay with me out of pity. He stayed with me because he loved me."

"Mama, I know the truth! Daddy was going to leave you."

"That's not true."

"Daddy told me and Les he wanted out, but he stayed because of Nadirah. And what about Nadirah, Mama? You didn't show her respect by making her stay here and kowtow to your every command." Lynn snatched up another magazine, opened it quickly, but then slapped it closed. "Mama, you did Nadirah wrong. You have no right to expect respect from her."

Musingly studying the buttons on the remote, Stephanie thought about the promise she made to her brother soon after Nadirah was born. "I'll take care of Nadirah if something ever happens to you," she assured him. "I'll treat her like she's my own." As far as Stephanie was concerned, she kept her promise.

"I did the best I—"

"Mama, please don't tell another lie, and don't try to justify what you did."

Stephanie got mad all over again. "I shouldn't have to, dammit! I'm the one who had everything to lose."

"See, this is why I've avoided talking to you about this. I can't stomach you thinking that you were the victim."

"Well, I am the one who was pushed down the stairs and almost killed!"

"You weren't pushed down those stairs! You slipped. You fell. You lived!"

"I was crippled!" Stephanie said through her teeth.

Byron quietly entered the living room.

"For how long, Mama? A day? A month? I don't know. You lied, not for one month or one year, but you lied for almost *seventeen* years. Come on. How can you expect any of us to understand that or embrace

you with forgiveness?"

"Lynn," Byron said, his voice calm, "don't be so hard on your mother. It could not have been easy for her."

"Yeah, I bet."

"The hell with you!" Stephanie shot up from her chair, knocking the remote to the floor and spilling her tea onto the table. "I don't expect anything from you or anyone. I'm on my own. I've been doing fine and dandy without any of you."

"That's great, Mrs. Richards, but we're here for you," Byron said, solicitously, although with his eyes he was admonishing Lynn to stop antagonizing her mother. "We're family. We have to be here for each other. Right, Lynn?"

Lynn got Byron's meaning and realized what he was trying to do, although in the heat of argument with her mother, she had forgotten what she was supposed to do.

"Humph!" Stephanie said. "She doesn't care a thing about me. She blames me for how I went about trying to hold on to my family."

Lowering her eyes, Lynn shook her head in disgust.

"Lynn," Byron said, his voice steady yet stern, "you've upset your mother. You should apologize to her."

Lynn wished her mother and Byron would both drop dead. They both made her sick.

Feeling finally like someone was on her side, Stephanie sat back down. "Don't make her do something she don't want to. Not on my account."

Byron went over to Stephanie and picked her television remote from the floor. "She cares, don't you, Lynn?" He handed the remote to Stephanie.

"Byron, I want my mother to understand that Les, Nadirah, and I have a right to be upset. She should have told us the truth."

"And she understands that, don't you, Mrs. Richards?"

Stephanie folded her fleshy arms high across her broad chest. "Don't put words in my mouth."

"I'm sorry. I didn't mean to do that. I just want you to know we all want the same thing, peace in the family. Right, Lynn?"

"Doesn't everyone?" Lynn stood. "We should go, Byron."

Byron checked his watch. "Yes, look at the time. Mrs. Richards,

can we bring something back for you?"

With her eyes on Lynn, Stephanie said, "I don't need a thing."

"Are you sure? We don't mind."

"She said she doesn't need anything, Byron. Mama, I have my keys. Don't wait up."

"I hadn't planned to."

Byron took Lynn's coat and held it out for her to slip into. "Then we'll say goodnight," he said with a charmingly seductive smile, leaving Stephanie in his wake to wonder why she hadn't noticed before that he looked so much like Lester, especially when he smiled.

Safe inside their car, Byron hit the steering wheel with his fist. "Why in the world would you antagonize her like that when we need her help?"

"I didn't start it, she did."

"This is not a child's game, Lynn. We could lose our house. We could lose everything. We need money and your mother is the only one who can give it to us."

"I know that."

"Then act like you know it, dammit! Go easy on her. Kiss her ass every which way but the wrong way until you get the damn money."

"Fine! But thank you very much, Byron, for putting us in this God awful situation."

Byron grabbed Lynn's wrist and squeezed it, pressing her flesh into her bones and making her grimace from the pain.

"How many times do I need to hear you remind me about what I did?"

Gasping from the pain, Lynn cut her eyes at Byron, but she quickly rolled them away. She hated him. She looked out the window into the drizzly night. Although they sat in their car in the dark behind foggy windows, Lynn fought to keep from crying in public.

With his voice tensed, Byron said, "When we get our heads above water, I told you, I'll never day trade again. I'm done with the stock market, but you better do your part and get us the money to get out of this damn hole." He thrust Lynn's wrist into her lap, releasing her.

Lynn began massaging her wrist. "Hurting me won't change the facts, Byron. You got us into this mess, not me. You should get us out of it."

With the ball of his hand, Byron hit the steering wheel. "Don't you think I would if I could? I have no way to get my hands on that kind of money. You do. So shut your mouth and get the damn money!"

Byron's insistence that she "get the damn money" made Lynn all the angrier.

"If you think it's so easy to 'get the damn money' then you go ask my mother for the money. You don't need me. You know how to sweet talk her."

"I swear to God, Lynn. If you keep messing with me, I'll—"

"What, Byron?" Lynn still massaged her wrist. "Beat me up? How many times can you beat me up before you kill me? Then what good will I be to you?"

Clutching the steering wheel, Byron snarled. "Dammit! I didn't hit you."

The tears came. "Byron, I can't do this anymore."

Byron pushed against the steering wheel. For a minute he wrestled with the demon inside his head that told him to knock the hell out of Lynn.

"Byron, what if I can't help you."

"You will help me," he said calmly.

"But suppose Mama doesn't have as much as we need? What if she doesn't have much left over from Daddy's money or the money she made from selling her business?"

"Your mother isn't broke, Lynn. Look at the way she lives."

"Yeah, but Mama didn't just wake up yesterday and set herself up like this. She established her lifestyle years ago. She was always smart with her money. Mama *intelligently* invested the money Daddy left her."

Byron shot a smothering glare at Lynn.

"Byron, what if Mama doesn't have a spare quarter of a million dollars to give to us and still have something for herself to live on? Let's be real. Mama's not Oprah. She can't gift you with hundreds of thousands of dollars."

Byron wiped away the fog on a section of the windshield and peered through it up at the brownstone. He studied its great condition.

"This house alone has to be worth about a million."

Lynn began shaking her head.

"You own part of that house."

"No, that's my mother's house."

"And yours."

"No! My father had my name and Les' name put on the deed to keep it in the family, but the house belongs to my mother. It's not up for discussion, Byron. I won't manipulate Mama or Les into selling it to settle your debt."

"Our debt, baby. What's mine is yours, for better or worse."

Tears rolled down Lynn's cheeks. Ever since she discovered Byron's obsession with day trading seven months ago, and started getting phone calls two months ago from collection agencies, she hadn't been able to sleep. She had no idea that Byron had gotten them so deep into debt that his wages were being garnisheed or that a lien had been placed on their house. How Byron had hidden that from her so long when she was home all day and got the mail, she couldn't imagine at first, until she learned that he had set up a post office box and had redirected all of his mail there, and she hadn't even noticed. Of course, it didn't help that Byron handled all of their personal finances. How big a mistake was that?

Byron put his arm around Lynn. "I'm sorry I let it get this bad."

Lynn was tired of hearing how sorry Byron was. She pulled away from him. Having his hands on her soon after he hurt her had always made her skin crawl.

"I don't know what we're gonna do if Mama can't or won't help us. Honestly, Byron, she might not have that kind of money."

Taking a breath, Byron turned the key in the ignition, starting the car. "Your cousin does. What about her trust fund?"

"I already told you. That's Nadirah's money."

"Your mother is the trustee of the fund, Lynn. She has access. Your cousin can't get the money until she's thirty. So—"

"No."

Byron again grabbed Lynn's wrist and leaned in close. "You will."

Tearing, Lynn shook her head.

Byron squeezed. "Yes, you will. Your cousin has the money. You said yourself she doesn't know the true value of her fund. She and your mother don't communicate so you should be able to talk to your

mother about letting me look into the account and—"

Lynn tried to pull her sore wrist free. "And what, Byron? Let you invest Nadirah's money?"

"No, I wouldn't invest it. I'd use it and say I invested in the wrong stock."

Lynn was incredulous. "You're talking about outright stealing Nadirah's money. I can't let you do that."

Byron's grip tightened even more on Lynn's wrist. "Don't you ever tell me what you can't let me do. You're gonna get me that money. Unless you have a better way out of this problem, which you don't, you're gonna do exactly what I tell you."

Although in agony, Lynn couldn't back down. "Byron, can you hear yourself? You're plotting to steal Nadirah's money."

Byron squeezed Lynn's wrist so hard that he could feel every bone under her flesh move.

Lynn's fingers tingled from the lack of circulation while pain shot up her arm. "Let go of me," she cried.

"Lynn, I'm trying hard to not put your head through that window! If I lose it, it's gonna be your fault! Now shut your mouth and do what I told you to do. Get me the damn money!"

Lynn was close to throwing up. The queasiness which had assaulted her stomach since she found out the truth about their finances had never let up and was now more intense, but she had always thrown up after Byron's beatings. Two years ago after he had almost beat her to death, he had promised to never hit her again. He had taken an anger management course and had stopped drinking in exchange for her not telling the police the truth about who it was that had beaten her. She had lied and said she was mugged on the street, but she knew by the way they looked at her that they didn't really believe her. But they could do nothing without her confessing to the truth. Byron was a woman beater, and had been almost from the start of their marriage. No one else knew, and as many times as Byron had convinced her that he was sorry and would never touch her again, whenever something went wrong it was her he took it out on.

"You're pathetic," Byron said, letting go of Lynn's wrist.

"I sure am if I let you steal from my family." Lynn's stomach was cramping painfully.

"Lynn, you're not worth the dirt under my shoes. I hate that I even married you."

For Lynn, she had no greater regret than marrying Byron. He fooled her good. He was nothing like the man she fell in love with.

"Get the money, Lynn. Is that so much to ask? I've never asked you for much of anything before, but I've given you everything. Now I'm asking you, begging you, to do something for me. Dammit, just ask your mother for the money. If it's your cousin's money, she won't miss it if she doesn't know what's there. And actually, since your cousin won't get the money till October, if we borrowed a little more than what we need for the bills now and invested what's left in the account, her fund could recoup what we took and then we wouldn't even have to pay her back."

Oh, God. Why did I tell him about Nadirah's trust fund? Lynn held onto her aching wrist. She couldn't believe how far gone Byron was and she saw no way to redirect his focus.

Byron saw the horrified look on Lynn's face. He looked at her holding her wrist. "Cut it out. I didn't hurt you." He went to take hold of Lynn's wrist, but she pulled away. She pressed herself against the door.

"Lynn, I swear, I won't play the stock market again. Just help me help us get out of this mess. Please."

"Byron, why don't we wait till October and sit down with Nadirah and, respectfully, ask her for the money."

Byron exhaled loudly. "October is too damn far away! We need the money now. If your mother doesn't have the money, we need to get her to lend us the money from your cousin's account now."

"And how am I supposed to get my mother to do that, Byron? She's not gonna just hand Nadirah's money over to us because we ask. And you keep saying lend. How would we ever pay that money back?"

"You're her daughter, dammit!" Byron punched Lynn on the thigh, making her recoil and shriek. "She'll give it to you if you would just be civil to her. If she doesn't give it to you, it's your own damn fault for being so nasty to her."

Lynn started to cry.

Byron looked coldly at her. "Shut up! Crying never solved a damn thing."

Lynn instantly dried up. "Neither does hitting me!"

"Don't you raise your voice at me!" Byron reared his fist as if to strike Lynn. She flinched, and for an uneasy, fearful minute Byron's fist hovered near the side of her face.

"See, Lynn, this is your fault. You're making me crazy." He lowered his fist. "Come on, baby. I'm just asking you to be nice to your mother. How hard can that be?"

Lynn cautiously sat up straight, but she stayed close to the door. "I can't do it."

Byron suddenly slammed the side of Lynn's head into the side window, startling her and forcing an animalistic howl from her throat. Thinking that he had cracked the window, Byron snatched Lynn back toward him and held her close while he glanced around furtively to see if anyone had seen what he had done. He checked the window. It was intact.

Trying to raise her hand up to her head, Lynn cried harder when Byron held her hand down in her lap.

He hissed, "Shut up!" He buried Lynn's face against the side of his chest. "Do you want the kids to be put out on the street? Do you want us to lose our house? Do you?"

Lynn's muffled cries could not be heard outside the car. She tried to scream, but Byron pressed her face into his body, cutting off her air and making it hard for her to breathe.

"Lynn, listen to me. I can't go back and change what I've done. I can go forward, Lynn, and you have a resource to smooth the way. I don't. My parents don't have a dime, your mother does. Your cousin does. Either you get it from them or we go under. It's up to you. You decide where you want our kids to lay their heads thirty days from now."

Byron shoved Lynn into the door, hurting her shoulder. Tears poured from her, blinding her as she tried to get a good look at the man she once adored. Gingerly touching the side of her head, she realized for the hundredth time that Byron had broken every promise he'd ever made to her. He'd promised to love her forever, to protect her from harm, to provide for her, to give her the best for the rest of her life, and most importantly of all, he'd promised to not hit her again. Everything he said had been a lie. He never loved her, not in his soul.

"I hate you," she said.

"Big deal. I hate myself."

"That doesn't bother you, Byron. You don't care about what other people think."

Byron yanked the car in gear. He jerkily maneuvered the car out of its tight parking space and shot out in front of an oncoming car whose driver jammed his brakes and blasted his horn. Byron never gave the driver behind him a thought and neither did Lynn. Her mind was on getting away from Byron and keeping him from getting his hands on Nadirah's money.

Chapter 18

Carrying with her a glass filled with ice cubes and an unopened bottle of spring water, Nadirah stopped to turn out the kitchen light. She had tarried as long as she could waiting for Austin to come back downstairs, but he never did. She hadn't heard a sound from him since he took Bree up to bed more than forty-five minutes ago. By now Bree had to be asleep. By the time they got back, Bree was exhausted from her morning playing in the park and then from her long trek from Harlem into Brooklyn, by train, to the newly renovated Brooklyn Children's Museum. Bree's head was spinning from all the activity she participated in at the Museum. She fell asleep on the train coming back, but still, she was cognizant enough to know that it was Austin she wanted to put her to bed. On their way up the stairs, Nadirah overheard Bree asking Austin to read her a bedtime story, which was something Nadirah had been doing since Bree came to live with her. This time, however, she didn't feel hurt nor left out and didn't mind sharing Bree with Austin. She had gone back into the kitchen with the hope that Austin would want to come back down and talk to her.

Maybe Austin had gone to bed himself? He did have an early flight back to LA in the morning. It was only eight thirty-seven, but it had been a long day and a short night the night before. Nadirah should be tired herself, but she wasn't. She felt restless. She felt anxious, and she was pretty sure why. As she went from room to room on the first floor turning out the lights on her way up to her bedroom, Nadirah couldn't get Austin off of her mind.

Throughout the day, she got to see first hand how and why Bree was so enamored of Austin. He treated Bree like she was a little princess. He wiped her mouth after she'd eaten, he lifted her up when she couldn't reach a button at the museum, and he carried her from the subway to the house to keep from waking her. He really cared about Bree and Bree knew this. She responded to Austin like

she had not responded to anyone else. Austin's genuine affection for Bree so impressed Nadirah that she found herself more than a little bit attracted to him, which is why she was a little hurt that Austin hadn't said goodnight to her. Especially after the day they'd had together with Bree. It was only a feeling, a strong feeling at that, but she thought she'd made a connection with Austin. Something special passed between them on the way home on the train.

The A train was crowded. The only seat they got was between two rather large women whose wide hips left the seat between them rather tight for either Austin or Nadirah to sit in. So they sat Bree in the seat to keep her from falling from the motion of the train. Together, she and Austin stood side-by-side holding on to the overhead bar. They didn't talk?the voluminous rumble of the train decided that for them. But they swayed stiffly back and forth, side to side, often in unison, and sometimes against each other, most times against their will. Nadirah didn't mind feeling Austin's body bump against hers because it felt good. It stimulated her in the most unexpected places and made her wonder what it might be like to bump against Austin with absolutely nothing on. She flushed at the thought, and after the initial words of pardon, she and Austin both stopped saying anything at all and simply smiled at what they had no control over—the motion of the train. They eased closer together, touching from shoulders down, slightly pressed against each other, neither acknowledging the use of the other's body to steady themselves. For sure, Nadirah felt they'd made a connection on the early evening northbound A train.

At the top of the stairs, Nadirah looked down toward Austin's closed bedroom door. No light shone underneath. "Goodnight to you, too," she said to herself. She took her glass of ice cubes and bottle of water into her room, set them down, and came right back out to check on Bree. She eased Bree's bedroom door open expecting to see Bree's room lit only by a nightlight and Bree asleep in her bed. Instead, the bedside lamp was on and Bree, although she was asleep, lay in the crook of Austin's arm against his side while he half lay on his back against the headboard with the book he had been reading on his stomach. He, too, was asleep. For a minute, Nadirah stood at the door watching them both sleep the sleep of the tired, but it was Austin who interested Nadirah most. Even in sleep, with his arm around Bree, he looked like he could

protect her from anyone who might try to harm her. Nadirah wouldn't mind having one of Austin's strong arms around her shoulder as well. Bree was a lucky little girl.

Nadirah decided to leave them as they were. She went carefully over to the lamp and clicked it off, instantly plunging the room into darkness until seconds later the nightlight's automatic sensor switched the nightlight on and a ray of soft, white light splashed the wall near the window. As soon as her eyes adjusted, Nadirah turned to leave.

"What time is it?" Austin asked softly.

Nadirah quickly turned back and answered just as softly. "It's almost nine."

Austin looked down at Bree. He tried to move his arm, but when Bree's head moved, he stopped.

"Let me help you." Nadirah leaned over Austin, slipped her hand under Bree's head, and gently lifted her just enough for Austin to slip his arm from under her. They left Bree tucked in her bed, sound asleep, unaware that Austin was no longer her pillow.

"I'm sorry I woke you," Nadirah said once she and Austin were outside Bree's room. They stood at the railing in the narrow hallway in front of Nadirah's room.

"I'm glad you did." Austin leaned back lightly against the railing. "The Children's Museum was a nice surprise for her. She had a good time."

"Thanks to you," Nadirah said, as she stepped across the hall and leaned back against her door. "Thank you for coming with us."

They stood with only a foot of air space between them.

"It was my pleasure," Austin said, sincerely meaning it. He liked Nadirah. It was a turn-on just talking to her. When this weekend started out, he had no clue that it would end with him wanting to make love to her. With all that was going on with Erma and their divorce, the last thing on his mind was getting involved with anyone, especially long term. From what he could see, Nadirah was a wake up in the morning and go to sleep with kind of woman, not a one-night stand, heat of the moment kind of woman. The problem was, long term isn't what he was looking for, but, man, he sure as hell wanted to make love to her.

There was no mistaking what Nadirah saw in Austin's eyes—desire, the same thing she was feeling in her belly. That sweet, tingly

feeling that tightened her belly and pulsed in her most passionate of places while yearning to be sated could not be denied. She'd felt it before with Daniel, but not this intensely. Would she be wrong to let Austin know that she wanted to give him what his smotheringly seductive eyes said he wanted?

"What are you thinking?" Austin asked.

Nadirah dared not say. She wasn't that brave. "Maybe it's time to say goodnight."

Austin stepped away from the railing. He was a breath away from Nadirah and could feel the pull of her body. "It's still early."

"You have an early flight."

Standing so close to her, Austin could smell the heat, intoxicatingly sweet, rising up from Nadirah's breasts. He wanted to take her into his arms, close his eyes, and inhale her scent completely, but if he did, he might end up regretting it. Nadirah was technically his tenant, and he shouldn't mix business with pleasure. Not to mention that she was taking care of his soon to be ex-wife's niece. He shouldn't want to kiss Nadirah so bad that he'd step over the line and compromise her as well as himself, but damn if he didn't want her.

"I can sleep on the plane," he said.

Nadirah was feeling weak in the knees. "Yes, but you have to first get up to make it to the plane."

"True." He touched her arm and slowly let his finger glide gently down to her hand. "Maybe I just won't go to sleep at all. That way I'll already be up."

It was suddenly downright hot in that hallway. Every nerve in Nadirah's body responded to Austin's touch—she literally tingled all over. With him holding her hand, she struggled to appear unfazed on the outside, while on the inside she was throbbing with desire.

Her throat was dry. "So what will you do to stay awake?"

"I don't know," Austin said, steadily holding Nadirah's gaze while he gently rubbed the back of her hand with his thumb. "You have any suggestions?"

Nadirah asked innocently, "You mean besides playing cards?"

Austin leaned in inches closer to Nadirah which instantly ignited an amorous fire in his groin. He whispered huskily, "Yes."

Nadirah was almost afraid to breathe. If she inhaled deeply

enough her lips would touch Austin's. If she wanted to move away she couldn't, not with the door at her back. If she wanted to kiss him she could, and as much as she wanted to she wasn't going to. She never wanted it said that she made the first move.

"Scrabble," she whispered. "We could play—"

Austin's lips lightly brushed Nadirah's, silencing her words, numbing her mind to anything but the feel of his lips as his lips parted in unison with hers and they began to explore what each had been wondering about on the train ride home. The kiss was as sweet and tender as Austin imagined, and as powerful and as gentle as Nadirah had hoped. As his arms slipped around her body and he drew her tight against—

Buzzzz!

Nadirah gasped and started to pull away, but Austin enveloped her tighter in his embrace, pulling her back into the wonderment of their kiss. Neither were expecting company, both were hoping whomever it was would go away.

Buzzzz!

This time, Nadirah did end the kiss. "We better see who it is before the bell wakes Bree."

"Yeah," Austin said, realizing that it could be Erma, wild and angry, at the door. Reluctantly, he let go of Nadirah and raced down the stairs to the front door armed with his own anger to stop Erma in her tracks.

Somewhat embarrassed that she had fallen so easily into Austin's arms, Nadirah slipped away into her room and closed the door.

Austin opened the door and was surprised to see Lynn and Byron just as they were surprised to see him.

"Hey, man!" Byron said. "I didn't know you were in town."

Although disappointed that what rapture he and Nadirah might have gotten into was interrupted, Austin was relieved that their uninvited guests were friends and not an enemy. He opened the door wider.

"I knew you were in town," he said, shaking hands with Byron. "Good to see you, brother."

Following Lynn inside, Byron pasted a slight smile on his face. "It's been a while," he said. "How's it going?"

"Everything's good." Austin turned on the light in the foyer and

lead Byron and Lynn into the living room.

"The house is so quiet," Lynn observed as she took off her jacket. "Is Nadirah here?"

"Yeah, she's … " Austin clasped his hands together. "I think she's upstairs in her room. Want me to call her down?"

"No!" Byron said quickly. "Baby, why don't you go up and see her?"

Lynn knew Byron wanted her to feel out Nadirah to see if she had any idea how much she had in her trust fund.

"Yeah, go on up," Austin said. "When you get back, I'll have a glass of white wine waiting for you with your name on it."

"Not my name." Lynn walked off leaving Austin puzzled.

"Ignore her. It's that time of the month," Byron said. "But look, I'll take a brandy."

"Since when do you drink brandy?"

"Since I decided it was a better drink to order at dinner than rum, and since I don't wanna mix my drinks."

"Yeah, you're right about that," Austin said. "So what's going on with you and Lynn?"

"Lynn and I are fine."

Hoping that he wasn't reading Byron wrong, Austin forgot about the brandy he was supposed to get from the kitchen. "Okay, I've heard the lie. What's really going on?"

"I told you. Everything's fine." Byron moved away from Austin. "Where you keep the liquor these days?"

Austin led Byron into the kitchen. Right away he looked through an upper cabinet looking for a bottle of brandy. What he found was an unopened bottle of white wine and a half empty bottle of scotch.

"Damn," Byron said. "There's not a drop of brandy in this place."

"Hey, I'm not here much. We can always take a walk."

"Pass me the JW," Byron said, indicating the bottle of Johnny Walker Gold at the front of the cabinet.

Austin took down the bottle. "I thought you weren't mixing your drinks."

"Man, just give me the damn bottle."

Austin stepped aside and let Byron get the bottle for himself.

He watched Byron take a glass to the refrigerator door to get ice from the dispenser. And while Byron poured himself a drink and gulped it down in a single breath, Austin, tight-lipped, wondered what troubles Byron was trying to drown.

Byron poured himself another drink, and like the first, he downed in one thirsty gulp, and when he poured the third shot he turned his back to Austin's bewildered eyes.

"New problem, old solution," Austin said.

"Am I supposed to know what you're talking about?"

"When we were in college, our third year, you up and started hitting the bottle like there was no tomorrow. Even back then, you wouldn't come straight out and tell me what was wrong."

Byron fixed his eyes on his glass. He couldn't deny what Austin was recounting.

"I had to hound you to death until you finally spilled, but that was just days before you were due to get kicked out of school for not paying your tuition. This time around, I don't have time to prod you into opening up, nor do I have the patience. I'm guessing, if you're hitting the bottle, it's financial. How bad is it?"

Byron raised his eyes. "I'm about to lose everything."

Chapter 19

Lynn marveled at the change she sensed in Nadirah. "You look …different…more … more womanly, more vivacious, and it's not the clothes. It's you. You're glowing from within. Please do share your joy."

Smiling, Nadirah wasn't ready to tell Lynn about her feelings for Austin. "Not much to share other than I'm beginning to enjoy parenting the little girl sleeping in the next room."

"Well, being a mother certainly agrees with you. You should think about having your own."

"Oh. I think I'll wait on that."

"Maybe you won't have to wait too long. Anything magical going on around here?"

Of course, Nadirah knew what Lynn was hinting at. "Actually, there is. Bree has been opening up like a little flower."

Lynn pursed her lips. "You know what I mean."

"I do and the answer is, not a thing. Anything else you want to know?"

"What about that mess at the center? You hear anything more about the calls?"

"It's like it never happened."

"Although that is strange, it is a good thing. Maybe it's over."

"Hopefully, but I still would like to know who the caller was."

"Well, Mama says it wasn't her, and a part of me believes her."

"No disrespect, Lynn, but your mother is a liar and liars don't change overnight."

"True," Lynn said, looking at Nadirah, but it was Byron she was thinking about. He was the consummate liar and he was never going to change.

"What?" Nadirah asked. "Do I have a wart on my nose?"

"You just look so different since you left Mama's house. You don't look so stressed. You look relaxed."

"For the most part, I am, but what about you, Lynn? What's at the root of your stress?"

"What stress?"

"Lynn, you can't hide what I see all over your face. You look like you're in incredible pain."

Lynn fell silent. Her eyes instantly welled up.

"Lynn, talk to me."

Lynn got up and hastily wiped at her eyes. "You've been away from Mama a little while now, do you think you'll ever speak to her again?"

Nadirah reached out for Lynn's arm, but Lynn turned away, although not before Nadirah saw her face.

"Lynn, why can't you talk to me? I know there's something wrong."

Lynn pulled herself together like she'd done so many times before. "Can we please not talk about me? I'm fine. My goodness, I had a little headache earlier. I took something for it, but now it's back."

Nadirah didn't believe her. "Lynn?"

"So Nadirah, I know you and Mama won't be sitting and schmoozing over afternoon tea anytime soon, but do you think you'll ever talk to her again? She's been asking about you. Maybe—"

"Save your breath." Nadirah changed her position on the bed, sitting now on her other leg. "It's not happening. Lynn, I respect that Aunt Stephanie is your mother, and I respect that Uncle Lester, at one time, loved her with all of his heart. But I am not you, nor am I Uncle Lester."

"Of course, you aren't, but—"

"I don't like your mother, Lynn, and I most definitely don't love her. Therefore, talking to her or seeing her is not something I have to do."

Nadirah's sentiments didn't surprise Lynn, but she needed to know if Nadirah planned on talking to her mother about her trust fund. But to broach the subject of the trust fund without setting off Nadirah's alarms was a bit of a quandary.

"Nadirah, I understand how you feel," Lynn said, "but do you think you'll ever forgive her?"

"Who knows? Right now, I just know I don't want anything to do with her."

"That's understandable," Lynn said, although she still wasn't sure if Nadirah meant she wouldn't discuss her trust fund with her mother.

"So how was the dinner?" Nadirah asked. "It ended pretty early, didn't it?"

"We left early," Lynn said quickly. "Nadirah, you know I understand, especially after the way Mama's treated you, that you'd want nothing to do with her, but—"

"Lynn, didn't you and Byron enjoy the dinner? It had to be a great networking opportunity for Byron."

Nadirah's insistence on talking about her and Byron irritated Lynn. "Byron had no business being there. He's a fraud."

That, Nadirah didn't expect. "In what way, Lynn?"

"Look, I don't wanna talk about Byron or about the dinner. I need to know if you are ever going to speak to Mama again? She is family."

"Your family, Lynn, but speaking of family, what's going on with you? What is it about Byron you don't wanna talk about and why are you pressing me to talk to your mother?"

"Nadirah, I'm only thinking about you. I don't want you to carry the burden of hating Mama on your soul. She feels badly about what she did. Of course, you and I both think she's out of her mind to think that you'll stop by for Sunday dinner."

"Not even if I was starving to death."

"Well, stranger things have happened, especially if forgiveness—"

"Lynn!" Nadirah couldn't stomach talking about Aunt Stephanie and forgiveness a second longer. "I am not going anywhere near your mother ever again in life. Accept that. Leave it alone."

"Okay. I will." Lynn had her answer.

"Thank you. Now what about you, Lynn? You can't keep covering up what I see in your face. You—"

"Nadirah, you see nothing. I said I'm all right and I am."

Nadirah put up her hands in resignation. "Fine. If you say you're all right then you're all right. I won't bring up your marriage again."

"Thank you."

Nadirah got off the bed.

"Why don't we go downstairs and join the guys?" Nadirah started from the room before Lynn could say otherwise.

Lynn didn't want to leave the seclusion of Nadirah's room but did anyway. No where on the first floor did they find Austin or Byron.

"They must have gone out to the store," Nadirah said.

"It would have been nice if they said something to us."

"It's no big deal." From the cabinet, Nadirah took a box of Wheat Thins. "They probably thought we'd figure it out. After all we are women."

Lynn said flatly. "Yeah, we are smarter than the average bear, aren't we?" Lynn sat at the table. Again she took a visual appraisal of Nadirah. "You seem right at home.

"This is where I live for now. So I am at home."

"Have you been looking for a place?"

"Of course, but Austin said I could stay as long as I want."

Lynn remembered what Nadirah had said about not staying long in Austin's house. "That's great, but you were adamant about not staying here long. What's changed?"

"Specifically, the little girl asleep upstairs."

"What about her?"

"She's Austin's wife's niece?"

Lynn's eyes widened. "Run that by me again."

"Bree is Austin's niece by marriage."

"You're kidding."

"Oh, and I met Austin's wife yesterday. Real nice lady."

"Erma is a blood sucking leech," Lynn said. "Austin should have never married her, but that's another subject. Right now I wanna hear every sordid detail of little Bree's connection to Austin, Erma, and now you."

Sitting and sliding the box of Wheat Thins toward Lynn, Nadirah began her story of six degrees of separation with the hope that Lynn might let down her guard and do some talking herself.

Chapter 20

When the doorbell rang, it wasn't the lateness of the hour that irritated Stephanie, nor the fact that she had just gotten out of the shower and was dressed only in a long lounging gown with nothing underneath, it was the who at the door that upset her. There was no smile on her face nor warm words of welcome when she opened the door.

"I told you not to come here again."

BJ pushed past Stephanie. "I wouldn't be here if you paid me my money. You've been giving me the run around for weeks."

Stephanie used her cane to close the door. "We've settled our business."

"Not quite," BJ said, realizing that Stephanie wasn't in a wheelchair. "I see you've been blessed with a miracle. When did you give up your wheels?"

"That's none of your business." Stephanie went on into the living room and sat while BJ eyed her suspiciously.

"It truly is a miracle," BJ said flatly. "From wheelchair to track star. What's your secret?"

Not seeing the humor, Stephanie said, brusquely, "Cut the crap! I have no patience for nonsensical banter."

"I'm sure you don't, Mrs. Richards." BJ sat across from Stephanie. "At least not at your expense."

Stephanie flipped her hand in disgust at BJ. "I'm not about games, Mr. Parish, and you're playing with me. I don't like it."

"Mrs. Richards, if you weren't about games then you should have never called me. You should have never propositioned me."

"Obviously, that was my mistake, but you didn't have to play, Mr. Parish. You're a grown man, you could have said no."

Knowing that he couldn't dispute this, BJ said nothing.

"You made a commitment, but, Mr. Parish, you didn't fulfill that commitment. You didn't get Nadirah fired from her job. That

was our deal. You were to get her fired."

"I was supposed to report improper behavior to her principal, which I did. I told your lie. What the fallout would be, I had no control over."

"You had all the control, Mr. Parish! You should have gotten one of your delinquents to back you up."

"You listen to me, old woman." BJ jabbed his finger toward Stephanie. "I let you talk me into this scheme because I needed the money for my center. But I told you I wouldn't involve my kids and I still won't."

"Is that why you lost it when Nadirah and Lynn tried to question your kids?"

"Damn right. I told you from the start, and I told you the night of the dance, my kids were never to be brought into this mess."

Stephanie again flipped her hand at BJ. "You certainly are a contradiction, Mr. Parish. It was your idea to say that Nadirah had slept with one of your delinquents in the first place. You involved your kids when you said that."

"Well, that's as far as it goes. I might break the rules for the good of the center—"

"So it was for the good of the center that you said Nadirah was sleeping with one of your students?"

"Old woman, you didn't come up with anything better. Other than drugs, what else was there? Everyone knows Nadirah doesn't use drugs. No one would have been convinced of that. I said she was sleeping with one of my kids, but—"

"But you never expected for Nadirah and Lynn to show up and go after your delinquents."

"Stop calling them delinquents!" BJ roared. "Those kids just need a break. I'll never sell out any one of them. What I do and how I do it is for them. I'm all most of them will ever have. They count on me."

Stephanie applauded. "How noble, Mr. Parish, but it seems to me you dragged your cape through the mud."

BJ slowly got to his feet.

"H'mm," Stephanie said. "I wonder who's in charge of defrocking super heroes. Who can I report you to?"

"You expose me, old woman, and—"

"Stop calling me 'old woman'!"

"If you try to expose me, I'm sure Nadirah and your daughter will have plenty to say when I tell them you paid me to destroy Nadirah's life just so you could keep her your personal slave?"

The smirk on Stephanie's face deepened.

"You think, old woman, they'll show you love or contempt?"

Although her face didn't show it, Stephanie was scared. If Lynn found out she did one more thing to hurt Nadirah, she'd disown her for good. As for Nadirah, Stephanie wasn't concerned. How much more could Nadirah hate her? And Les, he was no longer speaking to her anyway, so she had nothing to lose.

"Yeah, you better think about it," BJ said, feeling more in control although he couldn't stand still. He moved anxiously about.

"I want my money tonight. Five thousand, tonight."

"My, you must be desperate, Mr. Parish. You broke? You need my help?" Stephanie asked, feigning concern.

"Cut the bull, goddammit! You know damn well I'm broke. My center is broke. The lease went up. I got to keep paying the rent. You promised me ten thousand. I need the balance."

"You should have gotten Nadirah fired then."

"No, I should have never agreed to mess with Nadirah. You destroyed my relationship with her. She was one of the best volunteers I had. She'll never work with me again."

"That's your fault. You should have come up with a better plan to get Nadirah fired that would not have brought her into your center questioning your delinquents. You don't bring the enemy to your front door. You meet the enemy on neutral territory."

"Old woman, just pay me my damn money so I can get the hell out of here."

Stephanie wished that she had a gun because she'd shoot BJ as sure as she'd shoot a grizzly snarling down on her with his teeth bared. She hated stupid, arrogant men who would do anything for money, but when things don't work out like they want they run like babies back to their mama's breasts.

"So what you gonna do?" BJ asked. He stood more than a yard away from Stephanie and was itching to smash something in her sneer-

ing face.

Trying to not show BJ that he had the upper hand, Stephanie cooly crossed her big legs, which exposed a good portion of her fleshy upper thigh through the side slit. It was but a fleeting second, but she saw BJ look at her thigh, prompting her to look at the slight bulge in the front of his pants. She didn't even try to hide her blatant observation of his crotch. There was definitely something lurking under there, just how big she wondered. She almost wanted to ask BJ to unzip his pants. Suddenly, she was tickled. It had been a very long time since she thought about being with a man."

"You better tell me something," BJ said, "before I have a talk with Nadirah."

Stephanie wasn't thinking about Nadirah. After Lester died, her vibrator had become her trusty nighttime companion. But electric currents and a rubberized head have never been able to do what a living, breathing man could. Until now, looking at BJ Parish's crotch, it had not entered Stephanie's mind that she might want to lie down with a man again. Now that she was thinking like that, even a weak man like BJ Parish might do. Sure, he was at least two decades younger than she, and maybe he had never entertained the thought of sleeping with a woman darn near as old as his own mother, his fat mother at that, but if she put a couple of hundred dollar bills between her thighs, there's no telling what he might do to claim them.

"Are you listening to me? I want my damn money!"

"Would you please calm down! My goodness. I heard you the first time."

"Then pay me or I tell Nadirah everything."

"Do you think you can tell her without implicating yourself?"

"Ever hear of email? My email address gives me complete anonymity. The lie I make up to point the finger at you will in no way touch me."

"Don't be too sure of that, Mr. Parish. Lies have a way of worming their way to the surface and exposing themselves for all to see." Stephanie's own words weren't lost on her.

"I guess you know about that, huh?"

Stephanie chuckled sadly. Yeah, she could speak from experience, but she wasn't so old she didn't know the damage an email could

do to her fragile relationship with Lynn. Well, here's where brain meets brawn.

"Have you considered, Mr. Parish, that an impropriety on your part could lose you your center?"

Feeling unusually warm, BJ loosened his tie. "This is all a game to you, isn't it?"

"Actually, no," Stephanie said, softening the tone of her voice, "but I figure unless we take care of each other, we could both lose."

"And how do you propose we take care of each other?"

"Sit down, Mr. Parish, or I won't tell you what's on my mind."

While Stephanie softened her gaze, BJ glared daggers at her. Huffing loudly, he turned to go back to the chair and didn't notice that Stephanie had opened the slit in her gown a few inches more. She thought of unzipping her gown from the top, but with only one breast, she had no cleavage to show off and she certainly didn't want to turn BJ off. If he noticed at all that there was more thigh to look at when he faced her again, he didn't show it.

"Say what you gotta say," he said.

"As an aside, Mr. Parish. Did you ever sleep with my niece?"

"Hell no! What you ask me that for?"

"Just curious. So how would you like to double what you say I owe you?"

Immediately suspicious, BJ paused.

"Ten thousand," Stephanie said, carefully watching BJ's eyes glaze over. "I'm sure your center would appreciate my magnanimous gift. Don't you think?"

In his head, BJ calculated how far ten thousand dollars would take his center. "I won't go after Nadirah again."

"I didn't ask you to," Stephanie said. "Besides, I don't need her anymore."

"Now that you can walk you shouldn't need anyone," BJ said. "By the way, how is it that you can walk at all? Nadirah told me—"

"Do you wanna hear what I propose or not?"

BJ pondered the pros and cons of getting in cahoots with Stephanie again. Yeah, he needed the money. The first five thousand was gone. He'd used it to pay the back rent for the center, but if he could get his hands on the additional five, the center would be set because he'd

be back on track. Stephanie's offer was tempting, but at what price?

"The clock is ticking," Stephanie said. "In another minute, I will take my offer off the table, but before I do that, let's speak of fairness. I didn't get the results I paid for. Therefore, I believe I'm entitled to some satisfaction."

"Like what?"

"Ten thousand dollars is a lot of money to simply give away, Mr. Parish, especially when I'm not guaranteed to get anything in return."

"So what do you want?"

"Well, we both have needs. You need to keep your center up and running. Have you asked yourself where your delinq...excuse me, your students will go if the center is closed down? Or have you considered how long it will take for most of them to drop out of school and give Rikers Island as their legal address?"

It sickened BJ to think of his kids ending up back on the street. "What do I have to do?"

Stephanie softly drummed her fingers on the top of her thigh, prolonging the suspense. This was no time to be shy. Unless she asked for what she truly needed she wasn't ever going to get it.

"Goddammit, woman—"

"Sex," Stephanie said as calmly as she'd say, 'good morning.' She watched the color drain from BJ's face. He didn't get up, he didn't flinch, he didn't laugh. He gaped at her in stunned silence. What his answer would be, Stephanie could not read in his startled eyes.

"Five thousand tomorrow morning after the bank opens; five thousand, four weeks from now."

BJ's mouth closed, but he didn't know what to say.

"I guess you wanna know why four weeks? Well, I figure it'll take four weeks for you to earn the balance."

BJ's mouth dropped open.

Daring to be risqué, Stephanie, her eyes fixed on BJ, uncrossed her legs and when she saw him lower his eyes, she began to slowly ease her gown up her legs and even further up on her thighs exposing their fullness. It was too late to be ashamed of their fleshiness, they were all she had to work with. She didn't know what she'd do if he rejected her, but what other way to find out than to show him what she needed from

him. Naughtily, Stephanie opened her thighs showing BJ what she need-ed him to take care of.

"How good are you, Mr. Parish?"

BJ stared, transfixed at what lay before him uncovered.

"Can you rise to the occasion, Mr. Parish? Can you give an old woman, who's probably as tight as a thirteen-year-old virgin, more orgasms than an electric vibrator?"

Stephanie gently touched herself, while BJ, unable to pull his eyes away, lay his hand atop his crotch and lightly squeezed what was rising there.

Still with her eyes on BJ, Stephanie began rubbing herself, and when she saw BJ breathing a little deeper, she knew he would put a bit more muscle in his engine. She wasn't stupid so she wasn't about to fool herself. BJ's prime motivation was money, but it wouldn't hurt if she imagined, just for a little while, that he wanted to be with her.

Chapter 21

Lynn and Byron entered Stephanie's house to the soft smooth, sultry sound of Nancy Wilson streaming down the stairs from Stephanie's bedroom. Lynn wasn't altogether surprised to hear the music. When she was living at home, her mother used to often play her music late into the night until she fell asleep.

Byron looked hopefully up the stairs towards Stephanie's bedroom. "Go up and talk to her."

"Byron, it's late. Can't we wait till morning?"

"Are you trying to back out?"

"I said I'll talk to her and I will. But it's best to do it in the morning."

"You get me sick." Byron peeled off his jacket and tossed it over the banister.

"I'll talk to her in the morning. I promise."

Byron shot Lynn a contentiously disgusted look. "I need a drink." He went off into the kitchen with Lynn on his heels.

"Byron, you've already had too much to drink."

"Get the hell outta my face."

Lynn closed the kitchen door. "Byron, please don't add more alcohol to our problems. I can't handle both. It's too much."

Byron sneered down at Lynn. "What are you gonna do? Walk out on me?"

Lynn saw clearly the threat in Byron's eyes. She'd made the mistake once before of threatening to leave. That's when he tried to choke the life from her. She stepped back from him.

"Byron, you have to stop drinking."

"I had one drink. Do I look drunk to you?"

To keep from lying, Lynn looked away.

"C'mon, Lynn. We'll get through this." Byron put his arm around Lynn, but she pushed him off.

"The hell with you." Byron snatched a glass out of the dish

drain on the counter.

"Byron," Lynn said as calmly as she could. "What if Mama doesn't give us the money? What then?"

Unable to answer that question, Byron said irritably, "You're always so damn negative! Goddamn! Think positive for once."

"If I could see something positive about our situation, I would. Byron, we're in serious trouble. You have to face the reality of what you've done to us."

"I know what I've done. You just do what I told you to do and we'll be fine."

Lynn's head began to throb. It was all on her shoulders to fix Byron's mess. "Maybe you should have taken the money Austin offered."

"How many times do I have to tell you it wasn't enough?"

"Shhh! You're gonna wake my mother."

"And you're gonna make me knock you the hell out if you don't get off my back!"

"But, Byron, $25,000.00 is more than we have. It would have paid off one of the credit cards."

"What about the other five, Lynn? Paying off one card would not have made a dent in what we owe. That little bit of money is like teasing a drunk with an eye dropper of alcohol. I need real money, dammit. I need half a million dollars."

Lynn's stomach fell to her knees. "We owe $250.000.00, Byron. Why do you need twice that much?"

"To put in the bank, to replenish the kids' college fund, and to set us right. That's why I need real money, Lynn, not pennies." At the refrigerator, Byron jammed his glass under the water dispenser, half filling it.

"Austin's pennies would have reduced what we have to ask Mama for by twenty-five thousand dollars."

Byron slammed his glass on the counter and spun around. "What is it, Lynn? You don't want me to ask your mother for the money? Is that it? You don't want her to know that you married a screw-up? Will that embarrass you? Will it make you less successful in your mother's eyes?"

"This isn't about me!" Lynn said, remembering to keep her

voice low. "This is your mess, Byron. Unfortunately, I'm married to you and have to bear an equal share of your liability, but you remember this. Without me, you will never get your head above water. If I walk, I'll be okay. So if I were you, I'd be real nice to me."

Byron balled up his fists, clinched his jaw tight, and drew back to ram his fist into Lynn's face. She shrieked and cowered, covering her head. Byron stood over her, his teeth bared, his fist menacingly tight. Like a prize fighter who'd just knocked down an opponent, he sneered down on Lynn's quivering body.

"Why you always bring me to this?" He abruptly turned and rammed his fist into the side of the refrigerator door with a loud thud, denting it.

Again Lynn shrieked.

Byron snarled. "I hate your dumb ass!"

Lynn didn't stand, her legs were too weak. Byron grabbed her by the shoulders and pulled her to her feet.

"I wasn't gonna hit you," he said, looking at how shaken she was. He hugged her to him. "Baby, you gotta do this for me. Please. Just help me this one time."

Lynn timidly pulled out of Byron's hold on her. "I'm scared, Byron. You're out of control. You're drinking again, you're threatening me, you scare the kids, and tonight you walked out on Austin because he couldn't lend you more than $25,000.00."

"That's peanuts to him!"

"But it's his money, Byron! Whatever he chooses to give to us, we ought to appreciate. You—"

"Do you know how far back Austin and I go?"

"But that doesn't matter. Byron, you're not Austin's responsibility. You can't bank on your friendship with him to bleed him dry."

"I wasn't trying to bleed him dry. I needed more. Austin has money, he's not broke."

"He would be if he gave it all to you."

"That's bullshit. He got the money."

"Okay, but don't you get it? It's his money, not yours."

Byron narrowed a cold, hard glower on Lynn. "If you'd gotten with Austin you wouldn't be having this problem, would you?"

"Don't go there," she said, although secretly she wished she had

married Austin, but she and Austin had never clicked the way she and Byron had. It was truly love at first sight for them, but too bad she couldn't see what her life with him would become.

"You wanna get with him now, don't you? He's getting a divorce. His marriage is bogus just like mine is. Go on, go to Austin." Byron shoved Lynn.

"Stop it."

"Go on." He shoved Lynn again, harder. "You never believed in me. You never supported me."

"Don't do this."

"Austin didn't mess up like me. He has plenty of money. You think he's more man than me, don't you?"

Moving further back from Byron, Lynn refused to let him draw her into his petty jealousy of Austin.

"What am I talking about?" Byron said. "Austin doesn't want you. You're used up. You don't look no where as good as you used to. Austin would be a fool if he looked at you twice. You're nothing. You have nothing going for you. You're not even a good wife or mother."

Lynn fought back tears. "Your insults don't affect me," she lied. You can try and tear me down all you want, I don't care. If it makes me a bad wife because I won't support you in your quest to put us out on the street begging for handouts, then so be it. And believe me, Byron, if I had known a long time ago how you were managing the money, I would have said something way before you got us to this point."

"I'm not the only one who spent money—"

"No! Don't even try it," Lynn said. She pointed an accusatory finger at Byron. "This is all, Byron. You gambled away on stocks, in one day, ten times what I spent in any given year on shoes, on knick-knacks, or on a truckload of toys. So don't twist your mouth to say I contributed in any way to our financial annihilation."

"Okay, so maybe you didn't spend like crazy, but if you had a real job—"

"My job is real. Whether you accept it or not. Because I work from home doesn't make what I do any less real. I earn my own money. You've never had to buy a single tampon for me or a pamper for our children. But now that I think about it, considering that you made a hell of a lot more than me, you did ask me for money once too often. Oh,

but dumb, stupid me gave you what little money I had without realizing that there was a problem. How dumb I was? I must be a joke to you."

Byron leaned back against the refrigerator door. "For once you got something right. You are a joke."

Lynn didn't think she could hurt any more than she already did.

"Oh, but wait a minute," Byron said. "I'm a fool for wanting to give you and the kids the best life I possibly could."

"Don't use me and the kids as your excuse for gambling. Byron, you thought you could spin the wheel and get lucky, but you were like every other fool feeding all of your money into a bottomless slot machine. Behind my back, you stole our children's college funds, charged all of our credit cards into the ozone, took out a second mortgage on our house, and at the end, you squandered all of our savings in the stock market. You're right, Byron, you are a fool."

Mute of words to defend himself or to further insult Lynn, Byron slipped his hand inside his jacket pocket and blatantly pulled out a pint of scotch and opened it in Lynn's face. He contemptuously toasted her before turning it up to his mouth. Lynn watched helplessly as Byron drank half the bottle before he lowered it. For the longest seconds they locked eyes, saying nothing from their lips, but shouting with their eyes their intense anger and disappointment with each other. When the tears came, Lynn turned and walked out of the kitchen.

"Yeah, go ahead," Byron said. "Walk out on me. I knew you would."

Out in the foyer, Lynn started up the stairs and collided with BJ Parish. She couldn't believe her eyes. Gaping at him, she forgot all about her tears and the pain in her heart.

"What are you doing here?"

BJ glanced back up the stairs at Stephanie, wearing just a nightgown, standing at the railing. Seeing the shocked expression on Lynn's face almost made Stephanie burst out laughing, but she simply smiled. She didn't know who was more startled, Lynn or BJ.

"Mr. Parish, you do know my daughter Lynn Wilkie, don't you?"

Lynn and BJ both look incredulously up at Stephanie, but Lynn quickly returned her attention back to BJ and his lopsidedly-buttoned shirt. Her gaze immediately dropped down to BJ's unzipped pants which

he hastily zipped with his back to Lynn.

"Mama!"

"Oh, get real!" Stephanie said.

"Damn," BJ muttered as he went on down the stairs to the front door.

From the back, Byron strolled into the foyer. "What's going on out here?"

"Thank you for stopping by, Mr. Parish," Stephanie said. "You'll be hearing from me."

"Mama," Lynn said as BJ pulled the door up hard at his back, "you didn't!"

"Who the hell was that?" Byron asked.

Stephanie went back into her bedroom and closed the door, leaving Lynn confused.

"Lynn, who was that?" Byron asked.

Any other time, Lynn would not have hesitated to talk to Byron about what she suspected, but since she was angry with him, she had nowhere else to go but up the stairs to her mother's bedroom where she, unceremoniously, barged into the room and slammed the door behind her.

"Mama, have you lost your damn mind?"

Stephanie tossed her robe onto the bed. "Are you ever going to learn how to talk to me?"

"What in the world is that lowlife doing in this house at midnight looking like he'd been doing something I don't even want to begin to think about."

"Then don't."

"Mama, what have you done?"

Stephanie sat on the side of her bed. "None of your business."

"Mama!"

Ignoring Lynn, Stephanie leaned her cane against the wall between her bed and the nightstand.

"Oh, my God!" Lynn clutched her head.

"Child, grow up. This is the real world. Men and women—"

"Don't patronize me! Mama, I know what you did. You and that lowlife, BJ Parish, schemed to get Nadirah fired. Why did you do that?"

Stephanie let out an agitated breath of annoyance. "You have all

the answers, you tell me."

"You're despicable. I wish Daddy were here to deal with you."

"You poor, deluded child. You still think your daddy can walk on water, don't you?"

"Compared to you, Mama, Daddy?"

"Saint Lester. Humph! What a hero. Do you think he'd applaud me getting laid after all these years?"

"Don't talk about my father like that. Daddy was a good man. He?"

"When the hell are you gonna open your eyes and see what kind of man your father really was?"

"He was a man you obviously didn't appreciate."

"You're right. I don't appreciate a liar and a cheat."

"Daddy wasn't—"

"Your daddy lived a lie every day of his life. He fooled you kids into thinking that he was a saint and I was the devil's own. Your daddy—"

"I won't have you blaspheming my father in an attempt to make what you've done look good."

"Child, I'm not ashamed of anything I've ever done. I hold my head up everyday."

"You're disgusting, Mama. I'm ashamed to be your daughter."

If that was supposed to bother Stephanie, it didn't. "There are worse mothers out there than me, but if you see me as intolerably cruel or as a straight up bitch, you have your father to thank."

"I don't think so, Mama. That honor is all yours."

"Are you sure about that, Lynn? Are you sure Saint Lester had nothing to do with shaping who I am?"

"Daddy told me—"

"Your daddy told you lies. He fooled you and your brother. You all thought the sun rose and set on Saint Lester's head, but I know who Saint Lester really was. He was a fraud."

Considering the source of those ugly words, Lynn told herself to not let them hurt her, but they did. They wouldn't roll off her back.

"What about you, Mama? What are you?"

"Patient."

"Ha! You're a liar. You're a master manipulator. You keep call-

ing Daddy Saint Lester. The truth is, he was a saint to stay married to you."

"Your daddy was more like me than you think."

Lynn's throat was so tight she couldn't swallow. "He was nothing like you. He was unlike any man I've ever known."

"My. What a statement, Lynn. Isn't your precious husband as good as your father?"

Lynn ignored the question. "You're the one who cheated, Mama. I can remember you seeing other men. Not one, not two, many, many men. It wasn't like you tried to be descret. Your men called here, they picked you up from here. Les and I weren't blind, deaf, or dumb. I remember all of this. And Daddy? He knew. He saw what we saw, and I never could understand why he didn't put a stop to it. He would never talk about it, he just kept hushing me up. So if anyone was a liar and a cheat, Mama, it was you."

For the first time in a long time, Stephanie had no quick come back. Everything Lynn said was true. What was there to deny or defend? She had never tried to hide her extramarital activities, she saw no need to. Her goal was to hurt Lester and at every opportunity, she threw her lovers in his face. He couldn't do anything about it, he had drawn first blood, but Lynn didn't know that. She had been blissfully unaware of her father's wrongdoings and saw only the demon who made him unhappy. Maybe it was time Lynn knew the truth.

Stephanie started to laugh. She laughed that bitter laugh that soured Lynn's stomach and troubled her mind. Stephanie laughed at the confused look on Lynn's face and thought about the look Lester would have on his face if he knew she was about to strip him of his self-acquired halo. After all these years, it was pathetically funny, and Stephanie couldn't stop laughing.

Chapter 22

No matter how many times Austin asked aloud, "What did he expect me to do, write a check?" he didn't expect Nadirah to answer the question since she had no idea Byron and Lynn were having financial trouble until she heard him and Byron arguing on the stoop outside the house. He and Byron had argued all the way back from the bar, neither getting his point across, both not understanding why the other was being selfish.

"Man, I told you, I don't have that kind of money!"

"You have it," Byron said, "you just don't have it for me! I wouldn't do that to you, Austin. If I had it, man, I'd give it to you."

"That's just it, Byron, but I don't have that kind of cash."

"But you can get it! I said I'd pay you back with interest."

"Byron, you're not hearing me. I don't have a quarter of a million dollars! Damn! Do you know how much money that is?"

"Hell yeah, I know! Man, I could lose everything! Doesn't that mean anything to you?"

"Me? Man, this is your debt! I didn't spend a dime of your money, but I sure as hell would like to know how you could let your-self get that far behind the eight ball?"

Byron refused to explain himself again.

"Byron, you have a family. Gambling, no matter what form, and family don't go together."

"Man, save the lecture! I know what I did. I don't need you to beat me over the head. Right now I need money. Either you're gonna give it to me or you're not."

The audacity of Byron's demand and attitude confounded Austin. "Man, you need to—"

"Don't tell me what I need to do! I already know," Byron said, angrily. "Look, I can't explain how I let it get this bad, but I need your help. Austin, if you had the need and I had the money, I'd give it to you. No questions asked. That's what our friendship means

to me. I'd have your back no matter what. I wouldn't punk out on you."

For the second time, Austin felt like punching Byron. Earlier while they were at the bar, Byron had drunk a little too much and had gotten a bit too loud. The bartender had asked them to take it outside, and once they were outside, Byron, in all his frustration, pushed him. Austin had come dangerously close to throwing a punch when he remembered who it was he was about to fight—a longtime friend. Even after Byron cursed him, Austin held back, but he sure as hell felt like knocking Byron out.

"Come inside," Austin said at his front door. "We need to sit down and talk calmly about this."

"The hell with that. Send my wife out."

In Byron's tumultuous wake, from where she sat in the living room across from Austin, Nadirah had listened to Austin vent his anger and disappointment at Byron, but she suspected that most of Austin's angst and torment came from not being able to give Byron the money he asked for. Personally, if she were Austin, she wouldn't torture herself like that. This problem was of Byron's making, he should be the one to suffer the consequences and the headaches, but, of course, Lynn and the children would suffer, too. And what about Lynn? As many times as they had spoken, Lynn had never mentioned the trouble they were in. Two hundred and fifty thousand dollars was a lot of money to owe. Like Austin, she couldn't fathom how Byron could ask to borrow that kind of money from anyone but a bank.

Austin brought his fist down on the arm of his chair, startling Nadirah. He couldn't sit a minute longer. He went to the window and looked out just as several teenage boys walked past the house talking too loud for the lateness of the hour. He turned back to Nadirah.

"How could Byron form his lips to ask me for a quarter of a million dollars as easily as if he were asking for a five dollar handout?" Again, Austin wasn't so much asking the question to get an answer as he was asking it to himself out of sheer disbelief.

"You know," Nadirah began, "I was—"

"He must be on something besides alcohol," Austin said, not hearing Nadirah. "Back in college, Byron always pretended to be more than what he was—a kid on welfare from one hundred and twenty-third street getting by on financial aid grants and loans. Byron was always

scheming, always trying to figure out how to make the big bucks with as little effort as possible. For a while there, he even sold crack, but stopped after he almost got caught selling on campus. He was lucky as heck that he was near the bathroom."

"He flushed the drugs?"

"And not a minute too soon. Campus security was right on him, but because he had nothing on him, they had to let him go."

Nadirah hadn't known much of anything about Byron's past and, actually, she knew nothing about who he was now, but still, she was surprised by Austin's revelations. Surely, if Lynn didn't know before she married Byron the kind of man he was, then she must know now who he is. She must be devastated about the financial stranglehold he put them in.

Fuming, Austin went back to looking out the window.

Nadirah didn't know how to make him feel better. "You must really care about Byron."

"Not enough to give him $250,000! Hell, I'd be stupid if I put myself out to save his dumb ass. The man … no, the boy, is stupid. I just can't believe he couldn't stop himself from trading when he lost the first ten thousand, and I'm being generous. I would have stopped after the first five. But not Byron. He can't be beat."

"I think, now, he knows that he can be beat."

"I doubt it. The man is stupid."

Nadirah couldn't agree more. "Now I know what's been bothering Lynn."

"She never said anything to you about this situation?"

"Not a word," Nadirah said. "And I'm worried for her and the kids."

"Unfortunately, Lynn's in this mess by default, but helping Lynn, is helping Byron, and I'll be damned if I help Byron. Hell, I was stupid when I offered him $25,000.00 that he had the nerve to throw back in my face."

"Wow," was all Nadirah could say.

"It was a pittance. I insulted him. So unless you have a quarter of a million dollars to throw away, Nadirah, don't bother. You'd only insult Byron, which is an insult in itself when he doesn't have a pot to piss in."

Nadirah's mind was on her trust fund. She had the money, but

besides trying to figure out how to tap into the fund before October, she had to decide if she wanted to give a quarter of a million dollars to a man who might well turn around and selfishly put his family at financial risk again by playing the stock market or wherever else he might be so inclinded to gamble on. Austin was right. Helping Lynn would be helping Byron, but how could she not help Lynn? Lynn had helped her.

Nadirah turned away from the quiet of the street and went back to sit in her chair. "How nice it would be to win Lotto."

"Every poor man's dream, every state's windfall. Byron needs something more concrete than a lottery ticket."

Nadirah was a touch sensitive that Austin was thinking she saw the lottery as the answer to Byron and Lynn's problem, but she kept her feelings to herself, just as she was keeping thoughts about her trust fund to herself.

"I'm going to bed. I have an early flight."

Riiiiiing!

Austin immediately reached for his cell phone. "Yeah!"

"It's about time you put your damn phone back on? Don't you check your messages?"

"Erma, what do you want?"

"We have to talk."

Austin glanced at Nadirah before walking out of the living room. "We're done talking. Talk to my lawyer."

Austin left Nadirah without so much as a goodnight, but Nadirah understood. A call from someone as vicious as Erma would distract her, too. Not to mention on top of already being angry at a friend who had done something as destructively insane as Byron.

"You don't give a damn about Bree," Austin said as he climbed the stairs. "Stay out of her life."

From the bottom of the stairs, Nadirah caught sight of Austin as he disappeared into his room. She couldn't hear anymore of what he was saying, but it bothered her that Erma Gray might be planning to lay claim to Bree. Whatever it took, she couldn't let that happen. Come Monday, she'd contact Mrs. Hamilton and tell her about her encounter with Erma Gray. Surely ACS had a policy against placing children with deranged relatives.

Chapter 23

Stephanie's phony laugh grated on Lynn's nerves. There wasn't a damn thing funny about what she'd said.

Breathless from laughing, Stephanie wiped at the tears that came not from joy, but from pain. Her own pain. Lynn would never understand how it hurt to be demonized when, throughout all those years, she had only been determined to get even.

"Tell me, Lynn. Can you say with certainty that your daddy never cheated on me?"

"As nasty as you were to him, I would not have blamed him if he did."

"Oh, I see."

"Why are we still talking about this? Whatever Daddy may have done—"

"What he did was sleep with Fiona Brown."

"You're delusional. Fiona Brown was Daddy's cousin!"

"Fiona Brown was his whore."

Lynn gasped. "That's a lie!"

"No, your daddy was the lie. He was a living, breathing lie. Oh, I'm not gonna say Lester wasn't a good man, or that he wasn't a great father, he was, and in the beginning he was a good husband. Our marriage was wonderful, it was a dream. Lester was a dream. How we met and how he courted me, most women only dream about, but after we were married, after I got pregnant, after I put all my faith and all my trust in him, Lester gave me his ass to kiss. Your father killed every ounce of love I ever had for him."

"Who do you think you're talking to, Mama? I was here. I saw the dynamics between you and Daddy. You didn't love him, and you never wanted me or Les. If it wasn't for Daddy, in this house, Les and I would have never known love. Daddy took care of us, Mama, not you. Daddy loved us because you wouldn't."

"Yeah, I guess you were lucky to have such a great father,

but did you ever ask yourself why your daddy gave you what I would-n't?"

Lynn couldn't imagine there would be a plausible answer to that question. "I didn't have to. I already knew you were simply incapable of loving anyone but yourself."

A low, slow rumble started way down deep in Stephanie's throat as she thought about getting the last laugh on Lester. Lester never want-ed Lynn and Les to know the truth about their relationship. He enjoyed having their love all to himself. He was the selfish one.

"Sit down," Stephanie said. "Let your negligent mother school you."

"You can't tell me?"

"Oh, darling, I can tell you plenty. Especially if you think Fiona Brown was your daddy's cousin."

"She was. Daddy told us she was. She told us she was. You're lying about her because you never liked her just like you didn't like any-one in Daddy's family."

"Lester's family didn't like me. They hated that he married me. I wasn't good enough."

"That's not true. Daddy said you cursed out his mother over some trivial, insignificant incident at her house."

Stephanie chuckled low and deep in her throat. "I like those words, Lynn. Trivial. Insignificant. I even like the way they sound."

"I'm done talking to you." Lynn put her hand on the door knob.

"Oh, don't leave now, sister. This little talk is long overdue."

"I don't need to hear you trash my father's memory."

"But don't you wanna know about that *trivial, insignificant* incident, Lynn? Don't you wanna know what it was like for me to find my husband in bed with his Cousin Fiona in his own mother's house?"

There was that queasy, nauseating feeling again. Lynn had to breathe deep to keep from tasting the nastiness of the words spewed from her mother's mouth.

"My," Stephanie said, "I would wanna know about the triviali-ty and the insignificance of such an incident. Especially if my father dis-respected my pregnant mother in such a shameless manner."

Lynn shook her head. "It's not true."

"Lynn, you should have been there. Oh, but you were there, you

just didn't see anything. You were still in my belly."

"Mama, what are you saying?"

"Oh, just that I was eight and a half months pregnant with you and your brother. Needless to say, dumb, ignorant me, lost her cool and cursed out Big Mama Ruth, all two hundred and fifty pounds of her, because she was home at the time and, in fact—oh, and you'll like this, Lynn—Big Mama Ruth set your daddy up with his whore in the first place. Wasn't that sweet of her?"

Lynn was chilled by the cold, dark look in her mother's eyes, which belied the false sweetness in her voice. "Mama, none of this is true."

"As God is my witness," Stephanie said, raising a single finger. "Oh, and I forgot! There was the little matter of your daddy's bitch of a mama saying that I wasn't pregnant with her son's babies…"

"Stop it."

"… Imagine that, Lynn. Lester wasn't your father according to his fat-ass mother. And me? I was a piece of project trash who probably didn't know who my babies' daddy was. Your grandmother tried to get your daddy to leave me for his whore, which happened to be her best friend's daughter. She said I wasn't good enough?"

"None of this is true."

"It's all true. With his mama bitching in his ears, I'm amazed Lester had the balls to up and marry me in spite of her."

Lynn couldn't and wouldn't accept what her mother was saying about the father she loved and the grandmother she never was allowed to see. There is no way she could believe her mother over her father.

"Daddy never, ever said anything about what you're talking about."

"I guess he forgot all of the insignificant details when he was telling his side of this trivial story. The bastard." Stephanie could feel her pressure rising. "I should have killed him, killed his whore, and killed his no good mama on the spot! But when all hell broke loose, I went into labor and all I could do was damn them all to hell while I writhed and screamed on the floor of that bedroom, humiliating myself and praying for God to kill Lester's babies and tear them from my body."

Lynn cringed at the hate she heard in her mother's voice.

"Your father betrayed me. He lied to me."

"Daddy?"

"Don't you dare defend him! I was his wife. I was the one he cheated on, not you. You've gone your whole life believing your father's lie and I allowed it because as long as you believed him, I could continue to hate him and distance myself from you and your brother. From the time you were born, I wanted nothing to do with you."

Flashes of Byron's disdain for her and now her mother's outright confession of her hate for her, filled Lynn with loathing for them both.

"I hated your father."

Lynn wiped at a single tear that eased down her cheek which in no stopped Stephanie from telling her story.

"Lynn, I'm going to be blatantly honest with."

"Isn't that what you've supposedly been doing?"

"Don't get smart. I've been telling you the truth. And part of that truth is, I blamed God for letting you live. You see, if you and Les had died like I wanted you to, then I could blame Lester and he'd have to live with the guilt of your deaths to his soul. But God didn't see it my way. He let you live so I washed my hands of raising you. I told Lester if he wanted his children to eat then he'd better put the food in your mouths himself and he did. Ironically, because of me, he became a great father."

"If this is all true and you hated Daddy so much, why didn't you leave? Why didn't you go and forget all about us? It would have solved all of our problems."

Stephanie thought about the day her mother died. Her mother looked her in the eye and said, *"Promise me, Stephanie, you won't end up like me?alone, without someone to love. No matter what, you stay with Lester. He loves you."* She kept those words close to her heart because she didn't want to end up alone and on welfare.

"Mama," Lynn said, "why didn't you leave?"

Stephanie chuckled sadly. "Maybe it was something my mother said, or maybe I stayed because I loved your daddy."

"Oh, please! You just said—"

"I loved Lester! Even in all my anger, I loved him, but I could never forgive him."

"That's where you're different. Daddy would have forgiven you for anything. He had a soul. He had a conscious, which is why I don't believe he cheated on you. Why would he?"

"Why does any man cheat? Do they really need a reason?"

"Daddy wasn't any man. He—"

"Your daddy was every man. Open your eyes, Lynn. I was pregnant. Your father wanted me to continue on as if nothing was different in our lives. He wanted sex, he wanted my attention. I couldn't baby him when I was carrying, not one baby, but two. Lester and I argued a lot. He couldn't handle my mood swings, he couldn't handle having to take care of my every need. Lester ran to his mother's whenever we fought and whined to her like a little girl. It was at her house, he found what he wanted—Cousin Fiona. I wonder if that bitch is still alive?"

Lynn's tears had dried up, but she was emotionally exhausted. She wearily sank into the chair near the door.

"Sorry to disillusion you about the great man, but Lester did me wrong."

Lynn wasn't about to let her mother have the last word. "I don't believe your lies because if Daddy hurt you so badly, you would have left."

"Have you left your husband? Doesn't he hurt you?"

Stunned into silence, Lynn stared at her mother. The look in her mother's eyes said she knew Byron was abusing her, but how could she know? She had never told a living soul.

"Why don't you leave the bastard?" Stephanie asked. "Is it too hard?"

"You don't know what you're talking about. Byron and I are fine, and this is about you, not me. I've never caught my husband with another woman."

"Oh. So women only leave their husbands if they catch them in an act of infidelity? H'mm," Stephanie said with a little smirk, "there are worse things that men do. But as for me, I had nowhere to go. Unlike you, my mother was dead and my brother, Marcus, was finishing college and moving on with his life. Back then, I wasn't making any money, your daddy made it all. He'd already bought this house and I wasn't leaving it. I bedamned if I let him bring his whore inside my house. I stopped sleeping with your daddy and got myself a lover. Oh,

but your daddy wasn't missing out on anything, he kept Fiona on the side for years. If she's dead, I guess she died with him inside her. Who knows?"

"You don't have to be so vulgar, and you can't make me hate my father."

"I wouldn't waste my time."

"I know who Daddy was …"

"You think you do."

"… I know his soul, which is why I still don't understand why he wouldn't he leave you. What you're saying doesn't make sense. Daddy was planning to leave you when we were older but Nadirah came into our lives. Daddy could have just as well left you when we were born. He could have taken us with him, you would not have stopped him. There's something still that you're not saying."

Again Stephanie chuckled low and dry. "I never said you were stupid. Take note, child. Guilt, money, and fear will keep any man with his wife, no matter how badly he wants to walk."

If what her mother said about her daddy having an affair was true, Lynn understood the guilt, but she didn't understand the fear. "What was he afraid of?"

"Me."

"Why?"

"Because I told Lester I'd fight him tooth and nail for sole custody of you and Les, that I'd present myself as mother of the year and tell the court how I went into labor and where. No sane judge in his right mind world would give custody of two innocent babies over to an adulterer who'd disrespect his pregnant wife in such a manner. You see, I knew how much Lester wanted you and Les. Oh, and there's one other very important thing. I also knew there was no statue of limitation on murder."

Lynn knew immediately what her mother was talking about. "He was defending you! You were being raped!"

"Oh, so he told you about that? See, that's what I told the police at the time, but if your father had walked out on me, I would have told them he threatened me into lying."

"They would not have believed you. Daddy married you."

"To keep me quiet."

"That's a lie!"

"Were you there?"

"Mama, Daddy was protecting you! He didn't kill that boy on purpose. How could you hold that over his head? No matter what Daddy did, he—"

"He broke his promise. He cheated on me while I was pregnant. Don't you understand that, Lynn? Your saint of a father was sleeping with another woman and for all I know, there were a lot of other women."

"Daddy wasn't like that!"

"Unblock your ears, Lynn! Lester was exactly like that. This isn't hearsay. I saw what I saw. Your daddy was caught in the act by me! You hear me? I saw him ass high, humping hard on top of his whore." A tear slipped from Stephanie's eye. She quickly wiped it away. "I trusted no one in the world more than I trusted Lester, and he let me down. He proved to be no more different than any other man who has a hard time keeping his zipper up."

Lynn leveled a cold, hateful look on Stephanie. "You know about that, don't you?"

"Lynn, I'm confused here. How is it that you don't see your father's wrongs, when you see mine so clearly?"

Lynn ignored the stinging in her nose. "Because you were incapable of loving your own children despite what your husband did to you. You gave birth to Les and I, Mama, and before we were even born, you were the one we knew, the one we craved to be held by. I know this, Mama. I have my own children. Don't you see? You let us down. Daddy didn't ignore us. He didn't turn his back on us. You did. If he cheated on you, I'm inclined to believe he had just cause."

Stephanie smirked. "This was a waste of time." She lay back stiffly on her bed with her hands, fingers entwined, atop her stomach.

"No, Mama, definitely not a waste of time. We've been long overdue for this talk for a very long time. I want you to have the guilt on your soul that you never kissed your children. We saw you every day, but we knew the babysitter better than we knew you. We called you 'Mama' because Daddy told us to, but you were never a mother to us."

Stephanie smiled to herself. Yeah, it was a waste of time talking to Lynn. She would never understand why she couldn't love them. She

would never accept her father's wrongdoing, but that was all right. Those years were gone and could never be gotten back, and Stephanie wasn't about to let herself wallow in shame nor sorrow. Unwittingly, because she had lied about not being able to walk, she had already imprisoned herself for too many years to count. She was free now and wanted to do everything she'd deprived herself of. She closed her eyes and tried to take herself back to that place BJ had taken her before Lynn came into her room and opened up the hurt of all those years ago.

"No matter what Daddy did, I'll always love him. I'll always stand by him."

Stephanie couldn't care less. The Lester she once knew and loved was so far removed from her mind that she had long ago forgotten about him. She'd had many lovers over the years, but had become celibate after she fell down the stairs. No man had touched her in seventeen years until tonight and that memory was more on her mind than Lester or Lynn. She shut the sound of Lynn's voice out of her ears and closed her eyes, allowing the vision of BJ mounting her to not only take shape in her mind, but in her body as well.

"Mama, are you listening to me?"

Stephanie could almost feel BJ entering her. She began to gently move her hips.

"Mama, Daddy isn't here to defend himself, but Nadirah is. When I tell her about BJ, I hope she comes here and tells you off."

"Leave," Stephanie said, feeling her body warm. The hell with Nadirah.

"No. I'm not through—" Lynn couldn't believe what she was looking at. Her mother was gyrating her hips right in front of her. "Mama!" Lynn stood. "Mama, what are you doing?" For the first time, Lynn noticed the disheveled condition of the bed and considered what had happened there.

"Mama, how could you?"

"How could I not?" Stephanie smiled to herself. Yeah, BJ might be a bastard, but he was a hard humping, hit the right spot son-of-a-gun. His age, if anything, was to her advantage. For two straight hours, BJ rocked her world! He might not have wanted to sleep with her in the beginning, but once he got started, no one could have told her that he didn't want to. Goodness, goodness, goodness, that man was on fire.

What he put on her and what he did to her made Stephanie question how in the world had she gone so long without a man? Her vibrator was certainly no match for the real thing. And to know that everything still works, wow! Stephanie smiled at the memory of the moves she herself put on BJ. She wasn't so old that she forgot how to get up in the saddle and ride with the wind in her hair. Whoa, boy! Her body was still feeling the hard, deep thrusts BJ put on her.

Oh, my! Stephanie crossed her legs at the ankle and squeezed her thighs as tight as she could to keep from outright moaning. The orgasmic sensations grew stronger. Stephanie couldn't stop them and she didn't want to.

Lynn couldn't believe what her eyes were telling her she was witnessing. "Mama! Oh, my God!"

Stephanie was almost there, but she needed help. She reached down along side her bed and picked up her well used, long-handled vibrator.

"What're you gonna do with that?"

"Use it."

"Mama!"

"I suggest you leave."

"Mama, are you—"

"Damn right! I'm about to do me. I'm not so old I can't enjoy what you enjoy. And from now on, whether it's BJ Parish or the man in the moon, I'm going to have a living, breathing being taking care of my needs. Now get out of my room, and don't ever mention your father's name to me again."

"Mama?"

Stephanie turned on the vibrator and its motor instantly began to hum. She opened her thighs.

Gasping incredulously, Lynn dashed out of the room and bumped right into Byron. Her voice hushed, she quickly pulled the door closed. "You are not gonna believe—"

"I heard everything."

"Ahhh!" came Stephanie's moan through the door.

"Oh, God!" Lynn grabbed Byron by the arm and rushed him down the hall into her old bedroom.

"We can definitely get the money from her," Byron said excit-

edly as soon as Lynn shut the door.

Lynn kicked off her heels. "And how do you figure that, Byron?"

"We tell your cousin about your mother and her lover."

"Do you really think my mother is afraid of what Nadirah might say to her?"

"Maybe not right now, but if we can get our hands on the trust account information and siphon—"

"Byron." Lynn lowered her voice even more. "You're still talking about stealing from my family."

"Lynn, we have one chance and this is it. We take the money under your mother's name, and before you say anything, I know you can sign her name, I've seen you do it."

"When she's in the hospital, Byron, not when she's home. She?"

"Shut up! We are going to do this. We have no choice. By the time the debit comes to your cousin's attention five months from now, your mother will have to explain it. The worse case scenario, your cousin might press criminal charges against your mother."

"And I'm supposed to stand around and let that happen to my mother and my cousin?"

"Do you care, Lynn, what happens to your mother? After everything she just disclosed to you, do you love her anymore than you did this morning?"

Stumped by Byron's questions, Lynn didn't know what to say. The sad truth was, she felt nothing, not even hate, for the woman who gave birth to her.

"First thing," Byron said, "we have to get the trust fund documentation. Your mother keeps it in her room, right? Well, tomorrow morning after she goes to church, we get everything we need."

"Byron, we can't do this."

"Your mother will be gone at least two hours. We'll have time to go somewhere to copy the papers and put the originals back before she returns."

Lynn's hands began to shake. "Copy them?"

"We need a full copy so that we understand all the terms of the fund. If I'm correct, with your mother's signature, or should I say with you signing as your mother, we should be able to take out as much as

we want."

Starting to wring her hands, Lynn sat on the side of the bed. "I can't do it."

"You can and you will."

"But I don't feel good about this."

Byron grabbed Lynn's wrist and twisted it as he bent down and got close in her face. She smelled his sour, alcoholic breath. She tried to lean away from him, but he yanked her back. "Do you feel good about losing everything we own?"

Despite the pain, Lynn said, "You should be asking yourself that, Byron. You're trying to make me steal from my family for you."

"For us, dammit!" Byron hissed. "And I'm telling you now, you either get the money or kiss me and the kids goodbye."

Again the tears. Byron's threat wasn't new. He'd told her many times before he'd take her kids and she'd never see them again. She believed him.

"Look." Byron let go of Lynn's wrist. "Let's just do what we have to do. Let's get the money and put this behind us. Can we do that, Lynn, and start over? Please."

Lynn rubbed her sore wrist. "Suppose it's not as easy to get the money as you think?"

Byron smirked. "Believe me. It's a lot easier than you think."

Lynn sat in awe of her own blindness. She wondered how was it that she didn't see this greedy, manipulatively, cruel, abusive man before she married him? He looked so much like the man she fell in love with. His voice sounded like that of the man she fell in love with, but the soul of the man she was looking at didn't belong to the man she married. This man's soul was larcenously selfish and ugly. He beat her, he cursed her, things he never did when they were going together. In all these years, she had closed her eyes to what he had become because she couldn't accept that she'd made the wrong choice.

Byron sat down next to Lynn and put his arm around her. Although she let his arm stay, Lynn was repulsed by his touch.

"Baby, just do this for us. I'll make it up to you, I promise." He kissed Lynn on the side of her head. "I know you're disappointed in me, but everything I did, I did to make life better for you and the kids."

"You need help, Byron. You have to get help."

"After everything is taken care of, I'll get help. I promise."

Lynn bowed her head to keep from looking into the lying eyes of the man who would say anything to get her to do what he wanted. He would never seek help, he was too proud for that. But where did that leave her? What was she going to do? If she went along with him in stealing Nadirah's money she'd be just as larcenous as him. Could she live with that? Could she look Nadirah in the eye and not feel shame?

Byron began rubbing Lynn's back. She stiffened, but he kept rubbing her anyway. "Baby, everything is gonna be all right," he said as he let his hand slide down to her behind. "I promise."

Lynn tightened her thighs. She knew Byron's routine. She knew what was coming next—his seductive lips on her neck, his masterful hand on her breast, and then ever so slowly moving down her body to her thighs and what lay in wait for him to arouse and stimulate.

"No. Don't." She tried to push his hand away, but each time Byron returned to the spot he knew so well, massaging it, electrifying it, making it pulse at his touch. She started to get up, but he pulled her back down, and in one quick move, laid her back on the bed while he himself got down on his knees in-between her thighs.

Lynn tried to sit up. "Byron, I don't want this."

"Baby, yes, you do."

"No, Byron. And my mother…my mother might hear us."

"I think your mother's busy." Byron pushed Lynn back down. He slipped his fingers under her panties and eased them aside in anticipation of his moist tongue touching her. Still, he teased her with his fingers, making her weak and more angry at the same time.

"Byron, I don't wanna do this."

"You love it," he teased.

Lynn tried to again sit up. "No."

Byron shoved Lynn back down, and with the ball of his hand, pressed down on her chest holding her down.

"Shut up," he whispered harshly. "What the hell's wrong with you?"

"I don't want this."

"Shut up. I'm trying to make love to you. Shut the hell up and let me."

Seeing the anger in Byron's eyes and knowing what would hap-

pen if she kept pissing him off, Lynn inhaled her resistance and urge to rise up against him. As Byron buried his face in-between her thighs and went about his business of using his tongue like an anteater, tears rolled down the sides of Lynn's face. She closed her eyes, she closed her mind, and she closed off her emotions to what he was doing to her and to what she was beginning to feel. Although she didn't want it to come, that old familiar sweetness between her thighs intensified. And as her troubled mind struggled to resist, with each stroke of Byron's tongue, her body weakened and it craved even more of what Byron had to offer. She didn't resist when Byron opened her thighs wider and with his tongue drew a plaintive groan of conflicting feelings from her. Unwillingly, she let go of the anger that brought tears to her eyes. Byron was working his magic, subduing her, making her, once again, his puppet. After all these years, he still knew how to satisfy her sexually, but what he didn't know was how to respect her, how to control his temper, nor how to stop himself from going after that elusive financial windfall.

Lynn could feel herself about to climax. This wasn't right. Not when she was about to betray Nadirah who didn't deserve to be hurt by everyone in her life. This was wrong! How could her own body betray her like this?

"Stop it!" Lynn tried to again sit up.

Byron suddenly grabbed Lynn around the throat, shutting her up. She grabbed his hand, but the more she tried to pull him off of her, the tighter his grip became.

Lynn gasped for every breath.

With his free hand, Byron hurriedly unbuckled himself. Then, roughly spreading Lynn's legs again, he threw himself atop her and thrust himself inside her like a conquering warrior. He began grunting as he began his brutal rough ride inside the woman he pledged to love, honor, and protect.

Clawing at Byron's hand around her neck, Lynn took the pounding of her body just as she'd done so many times before until she reminded herself that, as hard as it was, she had to stop fighting and relax. For the more she fought, the harder Byron would choke her and the harder he'd screw her. Telling herself to relax, Lynn stopped clawing. She instead reached down and touched Byron's behind, stroking him, sending Byron the message that he had won.

Byron let go of Lynn's throat. "Why you always make me hurt you?" he asked, kissing her hard on the lips. "I love you, Lynn. Just stop fighting me." He then braced himself on the bed with both elbows and continued getting his pleasure while Lynn stared up at the ceiling with hate in her heart. There had to be a way out. There had to be a way to end her marriage.

Chapter 24

Before leaving her students to the teacher's aid, Nadirah glanced back at Bree and nodded to assure her that she'd be back. Bree got the message and went back to doing her multiplication problems. Since talking to Austin before he left out Sunday morning, Nadirah couldn't help but worry that Bree would be taken from her and handed over to Erma Gray. Nadirah had spoken to Mrs. Hamilton first thing that morning and confirmed that Erma had contacted ACS and applied for guardianship, and despite what Nadirah told Mrs. Hamilton about Erma, Mrs. Hamilton said, as a blood relative, Erma would be considered.

"Good news/bad news," Beverly said as Nadirah entered her office, "which one first?"

Nadirah sat. "One always cancels out the other so my choice would be neither."

"Chicken."

"That I am, but tell me anyway."

"Mrs. Hamilton called. ACS found Bree's mother."

"Where is she?"

"Bellevue. Psychiatric admission. Two weeks ago."

"Oh, my God," was all Nadirah could say.

"She was brought in off the street, ranting incoherently. The only thing anyone could figure out was that she was saying that her baby wasn't her baby or that her baby was dead. Something like that."

"She thinks Bree is dead?"

"Seems so. Mrs. Hamilton says Miss Morrison is pretty bad off. In fact, the short-term prognosis isn't very good. Bree definitely won't be going home to her mother anytime soon, if ever."

"That may be best for Bree, but unfortunately for Bree, at the same time she'll remember her mother in the worst light for the rest of her life. She'll always have questions."

"I expect she will, which is why continued therapy and the best placement is essential."

"Which is why, Beverly, I told Mrs. Hamilton I wanted to file for permanent custody. She said she'd get back to me, but that Dorothy Morrison's parental rights had to be severed, which could take a year before anything permanent can be discussed, and that's only if no family comes forward."

"Nadirah, you know I will support you in getting Bree, but in case you didn't know, Bree's aunt, Mrs. Gray, plans to file for custody."

Nadirah stood. "Beverly, Bree can't possibly go to live with that woman. I told you Erma Gray is pretty far out there herself. She's definitely not a viable choice for parenting Bree. She's—"

"Mrs. Hamilton and I discussed Mrs. Gray and she mentioned that she'll look into her background. However, Nadirah, just so you know, Mrs. Gray is the one who tracked down her sister at Bellevue."

"Well, kudos to her, but I hope Mrs. Hamilton keeps in mind that Bree is afraid of Mrs. Gray and would not go to her when she called her. And I would think Mrs. Gray's home, with her being in the middle of a divorce, would not make for an ideal environment for Bree."

"Point well taken, but Mrs. Gray is family-related so she will be considered. She's very adamant about becoming Bree's legal guardian."

"Which I don't understand." Nadirah went and stood behind her chair. "I spoke to Mr. Gray and he does not want his wife to get custody of Bree. He said she never liked Bree and he said he'd write a letter to Mrs. Hamilton at ACS, which I hope will work in Bree's favor for the best placement for her."

"The letter might help, but be careful, Nadirah. On a personal level, you do not want to get in the middle of the fight between Mr. and Mrs. Gray. It's not a good place to be."

"Beverly, my relationship with Mr. Gray is strictly business. I rent from him. I didn't know about his connection to Bree when I moved into his house and even then, it wasn't until he actually saw Bree that their family relationship by marriage was revealed."

"It certainly is strange," Beverly said, "but stranger things have happened."

"Yes, but, Beverly, you should see how Bree is around Mr. Gray. She's a different little girl. Mr. Gray has a way with her that's won-

derful to observe. I have never seen Bree laugh and smile the way she does when she's with him. It's a beautiful thing to see. She's really a wonderful child."

Beverly smiled. "I know."

"Beverly, I want Bree to know that she's safe and that she's loved."

"Nadirah, with you she'll know this. So what do you have planned for the weekend?"

Nadirah stopped at the door. "Who knows. Maybe The Bronx Zoo. We'll see if the weather holds."

"What about early dinner at my house this evening? My sister is coming over and bringing my niece, who's the same age as Bree. I think they'll get along."

"Oh, we'd love to come, but I have an appointment with a lawyer after work."

"Come after the meeting."

"Okay. Six o'clock? Is that all right?"

"Six is fine, and if you like, I'll take Bree home with me so you can take care of your business."

"Are you sure, Beverly? What about William? Two little girls equal noise. Won't he mind?"

"William falls asleep after dinner. He won't hear a thing. Drop her here on your way out."

"Thank you, I will."

With so much on her mind—Bree's mother, Erma Gray, Lynn and Byron, and her own trust fund—Nadirah hurried back to her class-room feeling the weight of the world on her shoulders lighten a tiny bit because of Beverly's helping hand. It was a great feeling to know that Beverly was in her corner. After twelve years of marriage, Beverly and William had no children. Beverly had wanted to adopt, but William was never for it. He said he wasn't raising a kid he didn't know where it came from. Beverly didn't push him, but Nadirah knew all the love Beverly had to give was heaped upon her nieces and nephews. She often wondered if that was enough for Beverly?

For Nadirah, there was so much to deal with and work through. While she had conflicting feelings for Bree's mother, she outright detested Erma Gray and hoped to never cross paths with her again. For

some reason, that woman reminded her so much of Aunt Stephanie—
her attitude, her marriage. Nadirah shuttered at the comparison. How is
it that good men always marry selfish, conniving women? Dumb question. Selfish, conniving women know how to go after and get good men.
Maybe that's why she didn't have a man. She never was selfish and
wouldn't know how to be conniving. Oh, well. Maybe one day the good
girls will luck up and that goes for Lynn, too. Her husband Byron turned
out to be less prince and more frog. She hadn't spoken to Lynn about her
money woes and planned not to until she knew whether or not she could
take a loan against her trust fund. No use getting Lynn's hopes up just
to let her down. But if she is allowed to borrow against her trust fund,
she may as well get enough money to buy herself a house. For Bree's
sake, she wanted to give her a place to call home where Erma Gray
won't walk in on them and turn their world upside down.

❧❧❧

Bree fell asleep before Nadirah finished reading "The Daughter of
the Sun and the Moon" from the African Folktales anthology. Nadirah
was kind of disappointed, although she knew how tired Bree was after
her long day at school and then playing with Beverly's niece after dinner, but she wanted to know herself how the frog was going to get the
maiden to leave her home in heaven to come to earth to meet her future
husband. As much as she wanted to know, Nadirah wouldn't cheat and
read ahead, she'd wait until Bree's bedtime tomorrow night to finish the
tale. She was enjoying her and Bree's little bedtime ritual of prayer and
reading tales, and could see herself doing it for a long time to come.

Nadirah gently kissed Bree on the cheek and slipped out of her
room without a sound. She was tired herself, but wasn't going to have
the luxury of going to bed early, she had a lesson plan to prepare.

Buzzzzz!

"What now?" Nadirah trotted down the stairs to the first floor.
This time she took the precaution of peeking though the peephole and
immediately she exhaled her annoyance that Daniel had, again, taken it
upon himself to come over without first calling. They hadn't spoken in
weeks and really she had nothing to say to him now.

Buzzzzz!

Nadirah glanced back up the stairs, before opening the door and quickly stepped out onto the stoop, pulling the door up behind her and was caught off guard when Daniel slipped his arms around her waist and drew her close, kissing her on the mouth. Nadirah immediately pulled away and glanced up and down the block to see if anyone was outside watching them. She saw no one. The block was quiet. The street lights hovered high above spotlighting the wetness of the streets below. It had rained briefly, and she didn't even know it.

"Hey. Aren't you glad to see me?"

Nadirah hugged herself against the damp night chill. "What do you want, Daniel?"

"I'm fine, Nadirah, thank you for asking. Aren't you going to invite me inside?"

"Bree is asleep. I don't wanna wake her."

Daniel made a show of looking around him and back down the stairs to the street. "Do you see any revelers with me?"

"Daniel, I have work to do. I'd like to get back to it so that I can get to bed."

"I've lived this scenario with you many times, Nadirah. You've always gotten your work done, and you didn't mind sleeping with me."

"Things are different now, Daniel. I live with a little girl who does not need confusion in her life."

"That would me—Mr. Confusion?"

Oh, God. "Daniel, what are we doing? We're better friends than this."

"That's what I thought. So why have I been ostracized?"

"You have not!" Nadirah said, careful to lower her voice.

"We're not speaking. You haven't called."

"Daniel, I've been very busy with work and Bree. I have not ostracized you. This is just not a good time for me to be distracted by anything or anyone."

"Wow. I never thought you saw me as a distraction. Oh, but maybe I'm wrong. All the other times I've been there for you, was I a distraction or your escape from your aunt's abuse?"

Blowing out a full breath of frustration, Nadirah looked away from Daniel and in her mind counted to ten. He was really messing with her head.

"What was I, Nadirah? A distraction or a savior?"

"Okay, Daniel. Yes, in my time of emotional need, you were always there for me and I appreciated it then, and I still do now. However, at this point in time, Bree needs my undivided attention. Her well-being is very important to me. She—"

"Do you consider me not good for Bree?"

Nadirah huffed softly. "Daniel, I told you before, Bree is very fragile. I don't think having a lot of people around her—"

"Last time I added one plus one, the sum was two. Since when is two considered a lot, Nadirah? Enlighten me."

Nadirah scratched her head. She wasn't getting anywhere with Daniel. She glanced at a car passing by, and then across the street at a man leaving his house and hurrying down the block. To tell Daniel outright that she didn't need him around second guessing her, one-upsmanshipping her, or doing whatever he damn well pleased without consulting her, would spark an argument that she wasn't up to.

"Daniel, I—"

"Are you seeing someone?"

That question threw Nadirah. "Do I look like I've had time for romance?"

"So the guy I saw you with over in Riverbank Park was a stranger who happened to leave the park with you holding hands with Bree?"

Nadirah forgot that she was cold. She dropped her arms to her sides and raised her chin. "Am I supposed to infer from your question that you were spying on me?"

"I just happened to be in the park. Was there something to spy on?"

"Stop playing with me, Daniel! I'm not too comfortable with the way you're coming across. What's going on?"

"What's going on with you, Nadirah? As long as you were in your aunt's house you needed me. I was your closest friend. You get out on your own, get yourself a kid, I see you with another guy, you got a ready-made family, and you suddenly don't need me anymore. I'm thrown out like last night's trash. What's up with that?"

Nadirah took a step back. She was slow in getting it, but she finally got it. Daniel was acting like a little boy whose best friend had

gone across the street to play with the new kid on the block. Daniel was jealous of Bree and Austin.

"So are you gonna tell me who the guy in the park is or is that none of my business?"

"The guy in the park happens to be the owner of this house and, as well, Bree's uncle." Nadirah saw the stunned look on Daniel's face. "Do you have a problem with that?"

"Cozy coincidence. Does he sleep here, too?"

"You need to stop this."

"Does he sleep with you?"

Just as Nadirah expected, Daniel put his foot in his mouth, but she wasn't going to strain herself trying to defend herself. Daniel's pettiness wasn't her problem.

"Go home, Daniel."

"You can't blame me for asking, Nadirah. You two looked like lovers in the park. If someone had asked me, I'd swear you were husband and wife, and everyone knows what husbands and wives do?"

Nadirah pushed open the door to go back inside. "Goodnight, Daniel."

"Wait a minute." Daniel reached out for Nadirah's arm, but she pulled back. "You're sleeping with him, aren't you?"

Nadirah wondered what she'd ever seen in Daniel. In the worse way, she wanted him gone. If she ever saw him again it would be too soon. She slowly backed into the house and started to close the door as soon as her breasts cleared the door frame, but Daniel thrust his arm against the door stopping Nadirah from shutting him out.

"That's it? You're done? We're over?"

Nadirah pushed back against the door. "I said goodnight, Daniel. Leave it at that. Let's not make it any worse."

"Worse than what, Nadirah? We don't see each other anymore. You broke up with me without giving me notice. You—"

"Wait a minute!" Nadirah again stepped out onto the stoop. "Were we ever really a couple? Did we ever make a real commitment to each other? Clue me in because I don't know anything about it."

"You don't know about us sleeping together or about you staying at my house?"

"But Daniel, did you ever ask me to be exclusive, although I

was anyway? Were you ever exclusive with me, Daniel? Of course not. I know about all the other women you were with and when you were with them."

"If you knew, why did you keep coming around?"

"Like I said, you were a good friend. Sure, in the beginning, I wanted more and, in fact, I hoped for more, but that's not what you wanted. I admit I was hurt, at first, but then what the heck. I was seeing no one else but you. I was comfortable, you were nice, we got along, so why not? You made no demands on me, I made no demands on you."

"That's the way I thought you wanted it."

"That's the way it ended up."

"You never said a thing, Nadirah. I looked at you like you were my woman. You let me think you were. So now you don't need me, you got somebody else. You used me."

Nadirah laughed softly. "You would turn it around, wouldn't you? Daniel, I allowed you to use me. Anytime you wanted to be with another woman you canceled on me, and a couple of times you even left me at your house while you went to meet up with the woman of the hour. So don't start making noises like you're jealous or like I threw you out, as you said, like last night's trash. You were never serious about me. I knew it and so did you. So let's stop being ugly."

"So this is it?" Daniel asked. "We're never gonna be together again?"

Nadirah almost laughed out loud. She couldn't believe he didn't get it. "I'd like to think that we're still friends."

"I don't need anymore friends."

If Daniel thought he was hurting her, he wasn't. "That's on you," she said.

For a few seconds, they looked at each other knowing full well that they could never be friends again.

"That little girl isn't yours," he said. "You're playing house. You're playing mommy, but you'll never be a good mother, you ..."

Nadirah's face dropped. Daniel had finally succeeded in hurting her.

"...and you have too much baggage. Your aunt did a job on you, you're messed up. What man is gonna want you for anything other than his whore?"

The ugliness of Daniel's words and the hateful look in his eyes gripped Nadirah's heart and squeezed out any and all affection she might have had for him. While her eyes became tearful, her hand itched. She slapped him, shutting his mouth. She then went abruptly back into the house and slammed the door, double bolting it. She lay back against it as if to make sure it stayed closed.

"Nadirah. I'm sorry. I didn't mean it."

When she no longer heard Daniel's voice, Nadirah didn't peek out to see if he was still on the stoop or if he was on his way down the stairs. She didn't care. If the earth swallowed him up, she wouldn't give a damn. Having Daniel in her life had served its purpose, he'd gotten her through many a hard time, but she didn't need him anymore. The tears that emptied from her were for the loss of a friend. She understood his anger, but not his attempt to demoralize her. If she learned anything from her relationship with Daniel, it was never tell everything about herself to any man. He'd only throw it back in her face the moment he got angry with her, but Nadirah wasn't going to allow herself to wallow in self-pity because she had too much to do. Where her life was headed, there was no room for friends or family who took her for granted or hurt her when they could no longer use her. Aunt Stephanie and Daniel could both kiss her ass, she didn't need them. Beverly and Lynn were all she needed, she could trust them both, and as soon as her attorney cleared the way for her to take an advance against her trust fund, she was going to get the money she needed to help Lynn, Bree, and herself. There was no room in her life for users or abusers.

Chapter 25

Stephanie caught her cane before it fell to the floor. She leaned it back against the kitchen counter. The cane had become a nuisance. It was always falling when she wasn't using it. And that was just it, she hated that she still had to use it. All those years she pretended that she couldn't walk when she could, she had not been diligent about keeping up her physical therapy or exercise to keep her joints limber and strong. She had sat in her wheelchair and weakened her muscles and bones and stiffened her joints. Now that she was up on her feet, she needed her cane to hobble around on. She was too old and too fat to get down on the floor to stretch and limber up so she didn't even try. She hated that her blubbery body was a far cry from the tight, hour shape figure she had in her early years, but she couldn't let herself dwell on it. If she did, she would not have had the nerve to open her thighs and take BJ inside her body the way she'd done Saturday night. He must have liked it because he was sitting out there in the living room waiting for her to bring him a drink when he had already been paid and was free to go on his way.

"You need help?" BJ asked from the kitchen door.

Stephanie poured orange juice into the second glass of volka. "Sure. You can carry the drinks for me."

BJ walked up close behind Stephanie and, to her surprise, stayed behind her as he reached around her to get the drinks. With a drink in each hand, BJ didn't back away. He lightly pressed himself into her full, soft behind. Stephanie didn't protest, she stood with her stomach pressed into the counter enjoying the feel of the hardness behind her. Seeing no need to talk, and no need to second guess what the other had in mind, Stephanie and BJ stood pressing and pushing against each other, feeling the sparks that flew between them—that is until Stephanie took the drinks from BJ's hands and set them back on the counter. She then took his hands and placed them on her right breast, giving him permission to stimulate her by sliding them across

her budding nipple. When he went to touch her left breast, she stiffened, but she didn't stop him. It was better he found out now. He had been too busy in their first encounter to get into foreplay where he might have discovered that she had only one breast.

BJ touched that flat scar-marred skin that for so long Stephanie had been ashamed of. His hand stopped moving. Stephanie held her breath. She couldn't see his face, but she could feel him breathing on her neck. BJ said nothing as he gingerly touched her again. His hand moved slowly across her chest, from the flatness of her left side, to the fullness of her right side, then back again. Still saying nothing, he began grinding himself into Stephanie, at first lightly, and then with such intensity he pushed her forward onto the counter where she braced herself with her arms to keep from falling onto her face. BJ's hands freely roamed where they pleased until he directed them to take hold of Stephanie's long, flouncy lounging gown. He gathered it up little by little until it was pulled all the way up in the back exposing her broad, black-pantied behind. BJ then stuck his left hand up the side of Stephanie's panties and his right hand up the other side. Still, Stephanie didn't move or squirm uncomfortably as BJ fondled and kneaded her rolls of soft flesh. She liked the feeling of BJ's hands on her and liked it even more when he slipped both hands around her body to her garden of delight and began exploring and tantalizing her while he continued to grind himself into her behind. Stephanie forgot about her missing breast. Her heart pounded as the pulsing between her thighs grew more intense. She spread her legs farther apart to give BJ's hands easier access to her center of pleasure.

BJ's breathing grew heavier as he quickly unbuckled his pants with one hand and freed himself against Stephanie's backside. With that same hand, he grabbed her panties at the waist and tried unsuccessfully to yank them down off of her rump. Stephanie, still bent over, reached back and pulled her panties down to the middle of her thighs and let BJ pull them the rest of the way down. She paid no mind to her cane when she heard it hit the floor next to her. She was busy and right now she didn't need it.

Neither she nor BJ had to say what the other wanted. They worked together in getting back in position for BJ to do what they were both hot for. In the kitchen that had only known the preparation of food

and the chatter of voices, Stephanie panted, moaned, and screamed into her damp dishrag smelling faintly of lemon dish detergent. She pushed her behind back into BJ and literally cheered him on as he rode her hard and masterfully while simultaneously pleasuring her and hurting her. Damn the pain! Stephanie took the pain and chalked it up to a minor inconvenience that was overshadowed by the absolute pleasure she was getting, but then just when she sensed that BJ was about to reach his point of no return, she straightened up and whipped herself around to face him. Before BJ could react to being abruptly detached from her at such a pivotal moment, Stephanie just as abruptly pulled him down onto the hard ceramic tile floor and agilely straddled him, sitting herself down right on top of him, and within seconds, she was riding him just as hard as he had been humping her.

Panting breathlessly, BJ's eyes rolled back in his head as his body stiffened and Stephanie drew from him a spasmodic eruption of passion so forceful, she could feel it in her belly. When they were both sated, neither could believe how good they each felt. BJ gently turned Stephanie over onto her back and, again surprising her, he lay high atop her and stuck his tongue in her mouth and kissed her passionately long and deep. She didn't think, *What's he doing?* she just went on with the kiss. Yet, she wondered when he'd be ready to ride her again? She was breathing hard, but the hunger in her body gave her energy she thought she had long since lost.

BJ flopped over onto his sweaty back. "Goddamn! Woman, you about killed me!"

Pleased with herself, Stephanie let her hand wander purposely down BJ's thigh. By the way he was breathing, she hoped he didn't croak before he got it up again for her.

BJ looked quizzically at Stephanie. "How old are you again?"

Smiling pridefully, Stephanie said, "Sixty-six my next birthday." She had nothing to be ashamed of. "Too young for you?"

Laughing, BJ asked, "Did you kill your husband?"

"I beg your pardon."

"Joke. I was joking, but you about killed me. Lady, you're hot!"

Stephanie laughed. Yeah, she was hot. For the first time in years, she was a woman full of scorching desire that needed a man who could outlast her and satisfy her. She wasn't looking for a husband, she'd

been that route before and got hurt. What she needed and what she wanted was a lover, a man who didn't live with her yet slept in her bed only when she wanted him to.

BJ wiped his sweaty forehead. "If I wasn't the one doing you, I wouldn't believe this in a million years. I'm forty-four years old, and I thought I'd seen it all. No one could have told me a woman your age and your size could lay me out like this. Damn, that was good!"

Stephanie said seriously, "I'll take that as a compliment, but you did a pretty bang up job yourself. You made my day, or should I say, my night?"

"It's early, baby. I'm not sleepy yet." BJ tucked himself away and closed his pants.

Smiling to herself, Stephanie pulled herself up into a sitting position and pulled her gown down around her knees.

"Let me help you up."

BJ sprang up off the floor. He locked hands with Stephanie and, grunting, pulled her sore body up off the floor. Embarrassed, she couldn't look BJ in the eye. He had to be thinking how fat she was. She went to bend down for her cane, but BJ beat her to it and retrieved the cane from the floor.

"I see chivalry isn't quite dead," she said, taking the cane.

BJ nodded and watched Stephanie hobble out of the kitchen before taking his drink and gulping it down.

Outside the kitchen, Stephanie put her hands on her hip and tried to stretch the kinks out of her lower back and then out of her hip joints. Her hip joints screamed in pain and contributed to her not being able to straighten her back. Her knees, stiff and swollen, hurt like hell. If she could sit in her wheelchair right then and there she would do so gladly.

"Are you all right?" BJ asked behind Stephanie.

"Oh, I'm fine." She hoped her pain didn't show on her face. "My back goes out every now and then."

"Mine, too. I blew out my L5 disk trying to lift a treadmill down at the center. You need help getting up the stairs?"

Pleasantly, but curiously surprised, Stephanie looked at BJ. He was being too nice. Why? He had half his money. She'd blackmailed him into screwing her in the first place, which he was doing a mighty

fine job of, but he didn't have to go out of his way to be nice to her.

"You need my help or not?"

"Sure. If you don't mind."

BJ took Stephanie's arm and put it through his own. Together they began their slow, steady climb up to the second floor.

"Your daughter knows about us, doesn't she?"

"Yep."

"Does Nadirah?"

"Don't know. Nadirah doesn't come around. You worried about her knowing?"

BJ stepped up another step. "That phone call might cause a little problem for me."

"Maybe not. It was only one call. No one suspects you, but—"

"Doesn't your daughter? She saw me here, she was with Nadirah at the center. I'm sure she can connect the dots."

"Well, Lynn was never a tattletale. I think she'll keep quiet, if anything, to keep from hurting Nadirah. Now if it was my son Les who'd seen us, he'd be all over it. Let's just hope Lynn doesn't tell Les about any of this." Straining, Stephanie pulled herself up the last step with a grunt. Her knees and legs hurt so bad she could hardly stand it.

"You know what you need?" BJ asked.

"A thousand gram pain killer?"

Laughing, BJ led Stephanie into her bedroom. "A pain killer for sure, but a nice, hot bath, too. I'll run the water for you."

Again stunned, Stephanie drew back. "You'd do that for me?"

"Hey, you did a whole lot more for me tonight."

"Oh? You mean the money?"

"Well, that'll keep my center open, but damn! I'm talking about the sex." BJ touched himself. "I'm getting on the bone just thinking about it."

Stephanie's eyes dropped to BJ's crotch and a smile tickled her lips. She moved BJ's hand aside and felt for herself what he was talking about. She palmed his heaviness and forgot about the pain in her knees and hips, and ignored the stubborn kink in her back. If she lay on her bed she could take whatever BJ was ready to give her. She unzipped him and felt his flesh.

"Do you think the doctor would approve of this painkiller?" she

asked.

"I don't see why not, it's legal." BJ began easing Stephanie toward her bed.

This time, BJ stripped Stephanie of her gown and himself of his clothes. Neither gave another thought to Lynn, Les, or Nadirah. Only the pleasure they were getting and giving consumed them.

Chapter 26

No matter how many times Nadirah looked at her financial statement, it didn't change the fact that $500,000.00 had been debited from her trust fund just three days earlier. Half a million dollars? Where did Aunt Stephanie get the nerve to raid her trust fund of half a million dollars? How did she expect to get away with it? What reason could she possibly have? Certainly Aunt Stephanie couldn't say she took the money for her because she was good and grown and no longer needed support disbursements. This was outright stealing?

Nadirah's hand came down hard on her attorney's desk. "Mr. Ward, my aunt hates me. She hates me because I left her. She stole my money to get back at me." Nadirah slid to the edge of her chair closer to the desk. "I wanna sue her for every penny she stole from me! In fact, I want her arrested. I want her thrown in jail and hung from her toenails until blood oozes from her ears!"

Mr. Ward laid down his pen. "Rather graphic, Miss Lewis. This is New York City, not Iraq under Hussain."

Nadirah slid back in her chair. "Mr. Ward, my aunt has no right to contemptuously steal from me. Did she think I wouldn't notice a half a million dollar withdrawal?"

"It is a rather large, conspicuous sum," Mr. Ward agreed. He again studied the trust fund documentation. "As the sole trustee, your aunt—"

"Sole trusteeship does not give my aunt the right to raid my trust fund. She was not supposed to touch my trust unless it was for my personal support or education. Aunt Stephanie has not had to tap into my account in well over six years. I have been totally supporting myself with my own income as a teacher for six whole years. For my aunt to take half a million dollars from me is criminal and she should be held accountable. But what I don't understand is why is it that no bells or whistles went off when she withdrew that much money? It was half a million dollars for God's sake! Why didn't the

bank question her?"

"The bank can't be held accountable for that."

"Well, they should be, Mr. Ward. $500,000.00 isn't exactly pocket change. My bank questions me whenever I want to withdraw even a hundred dollars from my savings account. They want my driver's license, I have to sign in front of them, and they check my signature. I would think a bank would do a whole lot more for a half a million dollar withdrawal. That money my aunt took wasn't for me. I no longer live with her."

Again picking up his pen, Mr. Ward jotted a quick note to himself. "Miss Lewis, if your parents had set up a mandatory trust for you, which would have limited how much could be withdrawn at any given time, we could demand answers to your questions. However, the type of trust you have is a discretionary trust."

"I know that."

"Then you know that a discretionary trust leaves a fair amount of discretion with the trustee as to how the beneficiary, which is you in this case, is to receive the benefits of the trust."

"Fine, but the money wasn't for me."

"Your aunt's discretion could be as narrow as she deems necessary or as extremely broad as she might determine."

"Are you serious?"

"Very. With that in mind, the bank would not question the amount of money your aunt withdrew. It is not their place to question why she wants the money or why she needs as much as she took."

"So she has carte blanche on my money until I'm thirty and I have no say? Mr. Ward, my aunt could wipe me out over the next five months and leave me with nothing!"

"Well, we can stop that," Mr. Ward said. "We will file suit seeking enforcement of the trust, citing that you are no longer a minor under your aunt's roof and, therefore, no longer need support disbursements from the trust. This should nullify her from further withdrawing funds from the account."

"Please file the suit. We have to stop my aunt."

"Well, it will take some time."

"How much time?"

"It depends on the court docket, but in the meantime, I would

file for an injunction against your aunt, staying her from any further improper action against the trust, which she'd have to abide by until the court makes its final ruling."

"I don't want her to have any access whatsoever to my account."

"We'll ask the court to remove your aunt as trustee, and request that an impartial party be appointed to hold legal title and manage your trust until it is to be turned over to you in five months."

"I want her removed immediately."

Mr. Ward again jotted on his legal pad.

Nadirah couldn't remember when she had last been this upset. Then again, yes, she could.

"What about the money already taken—the $500,000.00? How do I get that back?"

"If the funds were taken illegally—"

"Which they were."

"Then the court will order your aunt to pay monetary restitution."

"It better be every last dime." Nadirah grabbed her tote bag off the floor and stood. "Is there anything I need to sign before I leave?"

Mr. Ward stood also. "No. My assistant will keep you apprised of the proceedings, but you call me whenever you need to. I'll have the advance against your trust tomorrow afternoon. If you like, I'll have it messengered to you at your home."

"I'll be home by three-thirty."

Out in the waiting room, Bree was still sitting in the chair Nadirah had left her in.

"Thank you," Nadirah said to Mr. Ward's assistant Arlene. "She wasn't a problem, was she?"

"Not at all," Arlene said. "That game she's playing kept her pretty occupied."

Bree's Game Boy was another reminder to Nadirah that Daniel had given it to Bree without first consulting her. She'd had enough of other people controlling her life. She was done with that, which is why she felt no better leaving her attorney's office than she did when she arrived. The muscles in her shoulders and neck were still tight and she was tempted to march straight to Aunt Stephanie's and confront her, but

it was Bree at her side walking the nine blocks to the townhouse that kept Nadirah from going off on a major screaming fit and telling the woman who stole from her in no uncertain terms how much she hated her, but she realized Aunt Stephanie wouldn't give a damn about how she felt. She never did before and obviously didn't care now, stealing her money the way she did. Why?

Nadirah stopped dead in her tracks. "Byron!" she said, aloud to no one, but the man coming toward her gave her a strange "You crazy?" glare.

Bree asked, "What you say?"

"Come on!" Nadirah took off walking briskly down 147th Street. Aunt Stephanie had to have taken the money for Lynn and Byron! They were all in on it! How could Lynn do her like that?

"Miss Lewis," Bree said. "Miss Lewis, you're walking too fast."

"Oh! I'm sorry." Nadirah slowed down and was surprised to see that they were only three doors from the townhouse. She had been holding Bree's hand, but with thoughts of Aunt Stephanie and Lynn driving her, she had been practically dragging Bree along. The poor child was terribly winded.

"Hey, Bree!"

Nadirah stopped at the foot of the stairs to the townhouse. She and Bree both looked at the car sitting at the curb. Erma Gray was sitting in her car with the window rolled down.

"Bree, come," Erma ordered.

Bree lay her head against Nadirah's side and, like before, Nadirah put her arm protectively around her.

"Mrs. Gray, I'd appreciate it if you would go through ACS if you wanna see Bree."

"Bitch, I can see my damn niece anytime I feel like it."

The woman didn't look drunk or sound drunk, but the fact that she called Nadirah a bitch meant she didn't need alcohol to act like a fool.

Erma got out of her car and left the door open. "Get over here, Bree! You're going home with me."

Bree's face instantly scrunched up. Tears popped into her eyes.

Nadirah reached inside her tote bag and took out her retractable

umbrella. This time, if Erma got physical with her, she'd beat her off if she had to.

Erma put her hand on her hip. "And what do you think you're gonna do with that?"

"Bree, take this." Nadirah put her tote bag in Bree's hand and pushed her up onto the first step. "Go up to the door."

"Bree, you get over here!"

"Go, Bree!" Nadirah pushed Bree up onto the second step. "Go!"

Bree ran up the stairs, straight for the door.

Erma stepped a foot closer to Nadirah. "You can't stop me from taking my niece."

Nadirah adjusted the compact umbrella in her right hand, gripping it tighter. Her heart was thumping, but she wasn't afraid. She centered herself in front of the steps to block Erma just in case she tried to go up the stairs after Bree.

"Bitch, I will shove that umbrella up your ass and take my niece before you can bat an eye!"

Nadirah balled up her fist.

Erma Gray stepped another foot closer, but she didn't attack. She looked Nadirah up and down. "You think you bad enough to fight me?"

Nadirah held her jaw so tight, she couldn't open her mouth to say anything. She just knew she had to hit hard and fast if Erma made a move to go toward Bree or even herself.

"Miss Lewis," Bree said, "the police lady wanna talk to you."

"What?" Nadirah couldn't take her eyes off of Erma so she couldn't look back at Bree, but she saw shock register on Erma's face.

"You little bitch!"

"Don't you talk to her like that!"

"Bitch, if you think you're gonna keep that little brat away from me, think again. I'll get her, bet on it." Erma abruptly walked off. She got back into her car and drove away.

For the life of her, Nadirah couldn't figure out what happened until she looked up at Bree. Bree was holding her cell phone out to her. Nadirah couldn't believe it. On her own, Bree had gotten her cell phone from her tote bag and dialed 911. More and more, she was seeing the

potential of this little girl. No way could she ever allow Erma Gray to get her hands on Bree.

"I called the police, Miss Lewis. Was that all right?"

"Honey, it was more than all right." She took the cell phone. "You did a good thing. Thank you."

Nadirah held onto Bree, kept her eyes on the street, and took her time explaining to the police dispatcher why Bree had made the call. It didn't make sense that Erma Gray would come after Bree when it was obvious she hated her. Something wasn't right. What it was, Nadirah had no idea, but she had better find out if she was going to protect Bree. But first things first, she had to protect herself and her money.

Chapter 27

Nadirah was tired and she was running late. At seven-thirty in the morning, cold cereal, cold milk, and a feeble smile was the best she could offer Bree without exposing how upset she really was. Exactly at what hour of the morning she finally fell asleep she couldn't say. Throughout the night she had repeatedly turned her television on because she couldn't sleep, but then she'd turn it off when she felt like she could. The last time she glanced at the clock on the DVD player it was three forty-seven in the morning, and even at that hour she dialed Lynn's number, and like all the many, many times since late yesterday afternoon, she got no answer. She had tried both of Lynn's numbers—house and cell—to no avail. It was obvious since Lynn could see who was calling that Lynn was hiding from her, why else would she not answer her calls? There's no way Lynn didn't get her messages or not know why she was calling. She was hiding, but she couldn't hide forever.

"Let's go, Bree. We don't wanna be late for school."

Bree pulled the straps of her red backpack onto her shoulders. "I can't find my jacket."

"It's there on the chair in the dining room." Nadirah went on to the door and unlocked it. "Hurry, sweetie."

Together Nadirah and Bree stepped out onto the stoop. Nadirah reached back to pull the door shut.

Riiiiing!

Nadirah knew right away that it wasn't the ring of her cell phone inside her pocketbook.

Riiiiing!

"Wait here." She hurried back inside, leaving Bree out on the stoop.

Riiiiing!

It was indeed the telephone ringing inside the living room. "Hello?"

"Hey, it's me," Austin said. *"I got your message, but I was in meet-ings till late last night."*

"Oh, no problem, but when did you turn the phone on?"

"Yesterday. I thought it would be more convenient. How's every-thing going?"

"Not too well. Your wife swooped down on Bree and I yesterday afternoon outside the house."

"Damn. I'm sorry about that. Did you call the police?"

"Bree did."

"Good for her. Did Erma touch you or Bree? Did the police come?"

"No to both questions. She left when Bree said she had the police on the phone."

"Smart little girl. Is Bree all right?"

"She was a little shaken up, but she's okay now."

"Good. Look, don't worry about Erma, I think I know how to cool her out."

"Just make her stay away from us. Did you send off the letter you said you'd write?"

"Two days ago. The social worker should have it. I sent it overnight express."

"Thank you, because your wife is pushing to get Bree."

"Miss Lewis!" Bree called from the front stoop.

"I have to tell you, I don't understand it. Erma has never put this much energy into seeing Bree."

Nadirah glanced toward the front door. "So why now?" She could-n't see Bree, but knew from her voice that she was just outside the door. Nadirah checked her watch. "Austin, Bree and I were on our way out to school. Can—"

"Miss Lewis!"

"I'm coming, Bree!"

"Look, you go ahead. I just wanted to catch up with you before you left out."

"May I call you later today? I need to talk to you about Byron and Lynn."

"Anytime after eight your time. Have you spoken to Lynn?"

"No, but I better speak to her before the day's out. I believe she and my aunt—"

"Aaaaaaaaaargh!" Bree screamed, startling Nadirah.

"Bree!" Nadirah slammed the cordless telephone on the table. She ran out the front door just as Erma was pulling Bree off the bottom step.

"Miss Lewis!"

Nadirah dashed down the stairs. "Let her go!" She grabbed Bree around the waist and tried to pull her away from Erma. "Let her go!"

"You let her go! She isn't your kid! I told you—"

Bree screamed louder.

Nadirah tugged harder. "I told you yesterday to stay away from her."

"Bitch, I done told you, you don't tell me what to do!"

Two teenage boys, laughing at the tug-of-war blocking their way, stepped off the sidewalk into the street and went around them.

Screaming, Bree began digging her nails into Erma's hand.

"You little brat!" Erma twisted Bree's left arm to stop her from scratching her, which made Bree scream piercingly loud.

"You're hurting her! Let her go!" Nadirah yanked with all her might and snatched Bree out of Erma's grasp just as she let up to get a better hold on Bree. Erma tried again to catch hold of Bree, but Nadirah knocked her hand away and pulled Bree behind her own body.

"Give her to me!" Erma shouted.

"Until ACS tells me otherwise, you are not getting her. You scare her! She's afraid of you!"

"That's because you turned her against me!"

"I have never said anything about you or against you!"

"You're a liar!"

"Erma!" An old, gray-haired woman shouted from her first floor window next door. "What you doing to that poor child?"

"Mind your business!"

"You leave that child alone or I'll call the police on you again."

"Beulah, you go to hell, you nosey old bitch!"

Miss Beulah gasped with her hand over her heart.

Clutching Bree to her, Nadirah quickly pulled her back to the townhouse stairs. "Leave us alone. Are you crazy?"

"That's what she is," Miss Beulah said. "She's crazy. She ain't

never been nothing but trouble."

"Old woman, you better stay the hell outta this!" Erma warned. "And you, bitch…"

"She keep saying bad words, Miss Lewis. Make her stop."

"…you think by keeping my niece, you can get my husband. Well, think again. You'll never get him!"

Nadirah caught hold of the stoop railing and held fast to Bree. "Lady, I don't want your husband."

"Yes, you do! That's why you want my niece so he'll come around you more."

"She's talking about herself," Miss Beulah said. "She want Austin back herself."

"You give me my damn niece!" Erma again tried to grab Bree, but Nadirah pulled away.

"Get away from us!"

"Give me my damn niece!"

"You should be ashamed of yourself, Erma. You trying to use that poor child to get Austin back when he don't want you."

"Shut up!"

Miss Beulah wouldn't. "Austin's crazy about that little girl, but he don't want you."

"Shut up, you old bitch!"

"Austin know you ain't worth spit," Miss Beulah said, dead set on speaking her mind. "That's why he left you. You just trouble. The minute I laid eyes on you, I told Austin you was nothing but trouble."

"Keep talking. You just keep talking!" Erma threatened. "You fat, old bitch."

"You ain't never had no respect, Erma. I don't know how you got a good man like Austin to marry you. He musta been drunk outta his mind to marry something sorry like you."

"Shut up!" Erma screamed. She started looking around like she was looking for something.

Still holding on to Bree, Nadirah began backing up the stairs.

Miss Beulah wasn't finished. "I know Gladys is turning over in her grave knowing that she left her son with a gutter rat like you. Thank God y'all didn't have no babies. God knows what he was doing."

"Screw you, you old bitch!" Erma kept looking around on the

ground.

"Shame on you, girl!" Miss Beulah said. "No respect for nobody."

In the gutter, Erma spotted an empty aluminum soda can. She snatched it up and hurled it toward Miss Beulah's window, but Miss Beulah had already ducked out of the way. The can sailed through the open window.

"You old, nosey bitch!"

"I'm calling the police on you!" Miss Beulah yelled.

Nadirah scurried with Bree back into the house. She slammed and locked the door. She could hear Erma outside ranting a string of curse words at Miss Beulah next door. The woman was crazy.

"Call the police, Miss Lewis. Call them," Bree said excitedly.

Nadirah started to pick up her pocketbook from the floor near the door, but then she remembered that the house telephone was on, and that's when she remembered she had been talking to Austin. With her arm still around Bree, Nadirah picked up the phone. "Hello … hello?"

"I'm here!" Austin said anxiously. . *"What's going on there?"*

"Your wife is outside!"

"What?"

"She tried to take Bree again! Austin, she's hellbent on getting Bree. She won't leave us alone!"

"What the hell's wrong with her? She can't be that desperate for money. She has a job."

"It's not the money, Austin. It's you," Nadirah looked down at Bree who was attentively looking up at her. "Hold on a minute. Bree, sweetie, why don't you go upstairs to your room and turn on the television? I'll be up in a little bit."

"But what about school?"

"I'll call the school in a minute. We'll go in late. You go on, I'll be up. And close your door, okay?"

"Okay." Bree slowly walked out into the foyer where she stopped. "Miss Lewis."

"Yes, Bree."

"You won't let her get me, will you?"

"Of course not." Nadirah went to Bree, hugged her, and kissed her on the forehead.

"I'll be up soon."

"Okay."

Nadirah waited and watched Bree go up to her room and close the door. "Austin, did you hear Bree? She's scared your wife will get her."

"She won't. I promise."

"How can you promise that? You're thousands of miles away. Your wife is here acting a fool outside the door. I think she believes if she had Bree then you'd come back to her."

"Why would I go back to her if she had Bree?"

"Because she knows how you feel about Bree, Austin. Didn't you tell me yourself that you were the only one to care for Bree when she and her mother stayed with you? If your wife had Bree, you'd probably come around to make sure she was all right."

"Of course, or I'd worry about Bree, but that's the extent of it. If anything, I'd try to stop Erma from getting Bree in the first place. I'd never go back to Erma because she had custody of Bree. Nno way! Not after all her craziness and lies."

"Well, I don't think she knows that, Austin, and even if she knew, she probably won't accept it. Right now the problem is if your wife—"

"My soon to be ex-wife."

"Whatever. Austin, if she keeps coming after Bree, she'll hurt her. I don't think she sees any other way to get you back but through Bree. What about her sister? Do you think she'd want your wife to have Brec?"

"Nadirah, I have no idea. Look, call the police, file a report. Then call that social worker on Bree's case and tell her what's going on. She can probably do something to stop Erma. Tell her that Erma is sick, she's bipolar. She's supposed to be on medications, an antimanic and an antidepressant. When she drinks she doesn't take her medication, and it appears she's been drinking a lot, which makes her act out worse."

"That's an understatement."

"And from what you told me she did yesterday and just minutes ago, she's really manic. I told the social worker that in the letter."

"I wish you had told me! Then I would have known what I was dealing with. Austin, your wife is on a very destructive path with only you in her line of sight. Bree is a means to an end for her. Bree will end

up hurt and so will I because I'm in her way. You have to do something."

"Okay, look, I'll call the police from here. I can give them more information about her and have them call you to get the particulars of what's going on there. You call that social worker and then call me when you're done talking to her and the police."

As soon as she got a dial tone, Nadirah first called her job. Her second call was to Mrs. Hamilton. She was taking Bree to school, but she had business elsewhere to take care of in person.

Chapter 28

Nadirah didn't know what to expect. It had seemed like a good idea when she left Bree with Beverly at school that a visit to Dorothy Morrison was in order, but as she stepped off the elevator onto glistening white tiled floors and passed through halls of flat, pasty white walls into a locked ward of men and women in distress and mental agony, she wondered if it was a good idea after all. Nurses in white, doctors in white, patients roaming about dressed in mismatched, wrinkled street clothes, ill-fitting cotton hospital gowns and blue striped robes all unnerved Nadirah. While the nurses and doctors moved about with purpose, the patients, most older than thirty, seemed lost. Some in their silence, others speaking aloud in a jumble of words that fell on disinterested ears as they moved about aimlessly with no escape from the white walls and locked doors that imprisoned them.

There were patients sitting around as if they sat on a beach staring out to sea lost in thought with nothing particular to focus on, and patients, too, who rocked back and forth in a world that only they knew. If their haggard, lifeless faces and blank eyes were any indication of their emotional agony, Nadirah wished she could close her own eyes to protect herself from their pain. The rooms she glanced in that had patients in them, she wondered what horrible things happened to them to make them curl up as they once did as babies and withdraw from the world. She wondered that about all the patients she saw, and in particular about Dorothy Morrison, who lay atop her bed in her room far from the nurse's station where Nadirah had signed in.

Timidly, Nadirah entered the room. She didn't know if she should sit or stand. Dorothy didn't stir and she didn't open her eyes, but Nadirah knew she was awake—she nibbled steadily on her very cracked, very bloated, peeling bottom lip. Small patches of dried blood and fresh raw skin dotted her lip. In profile, Dorothy looked

very much like her older sister Erma except she was obviously much thinner and perhaps prettier if it were not for her badly gnawed lip. Her long, uncombed hair looked like a tangled bird's nest and was in desperate need of braids or a strong rubber band. Dorothy was the same age as Nadirah, but Dorothy looked years older.

"Miss Morrison, I'm Nadirah Lewis. If it's all right with you, I'd like to speak to you."

Other than continually nibbling on her lip, Dorothy didn't move.

Although uncertain, Nadirah lifted the chair from against the wall and quietly set it closer to the bed, yet far enough away that Dorothy couldn't reach her if she got violent.

Nadirah sat. She folded her hands in her lap atop her bag and waited in the silence of the room. There was a second unmade bed, but no one was in it. Nothing about the room was personal, nothing about the white walls was warm or inviting. It was a hospital room after all, but Nadirah knew for many of the patients, their stay was long and rooms like this were more home than not. Nadirah prayed that she never had to experience a stay in a psychiatric ward.

"What do you want?" Dorothy asked in a very low, soft voice that was loud enough to snap Nadirah's attention back on her, although Dorothy didn't lift her eyes to look at Nadirah.

"I need to talk to you about your daughter Bree."

Still not looking at Nadirah, Dorothy went back to nibbling on her lip.

"I don't know if you know this, but Bree is all right. She's been out of the hospital for several weeks now. She's doing well."

Dorothy gnawed a small, scaly patch of skin off her lip, drawing blood, turning Nadirah's stomach when she sucked the blood in and chewed the skin.

"Miss Morrison, Bree is very happy where she is. She's well taken care of and she's thriving in school."

"You her social worker?"

"No. I'm Bree's teacher and foster mother."

The nibbling stopped. Dorothy looked fully at Nadirah. "She lives with you?"

"Yes. Miss Morrison, Bree is a wonderful little girl. She's smart,

she's pleasant, and she's starting to open up and talk to the other kids. She has great potential and—"

"Does she ask for me?"

Nadirah didn't expect that question. If anything, she had hoped that Dorothy would ask about Bree's health. "No. I'm sorry, she hasn't, but she really hasn't been talking very much."

Nibbling again, Dorothy averted her eyes.

"Miss Morrison, I don't know exactly how it came to be that Bree drank disinfectant and ended up in the hospital."

Frowning and tensing her brow, Dorothy bit down on her lip, digging her teeth deep.

"I won't make you uncomfortable by questioning you about it, but I wanna thank you for getting medical help for Bree as quickly as you did, because if it wasn't for you, Bree might have died. You saved her life."

Dorothy turned her face into her pillow completely away from Nadirah, but Nadirah knew by Dorothy's sudden deep breathing that she was in distress. Perhaps that was a good sign that she did feel something for what she'd done to Bree, but what could have been so bad that she'd rather see her child dead than waking each day to fulfill the promise of her potential?

"Miss Morrison, your sister Erma has filed for custody of your daughter. I know she's Bree's aunt, and I know you might want family to look out for Bree, but I don't believe your sister is the best person to take care of her. I think we all want the best for Bree, she is a special little girl, but your sister seems to … to not want the best for her. Now, I'm sure you love your daughter, Miss Morrison, and … and she loves you—"

"No she doesn't!" Dorothy blurted, abruptly sitting up and startling Nadirah. She almost bolted out of her chair. Dorothy clutched her pillow to her chest. "Bree doesn't love me. She never loved me, not even when she was a baby."

"Of course Bree loves you. When she was a baby, you had to be her whole world."

"No. No." Dorothy went to rocking. "I didn't love her either. I didn't want her. She wasn't my world."

"You don't mean that. Bree's your child, your baby. You must

love her."

Dorothy dug her teeth deep into her lip, making it red and bloody.

"Miss Morrison, please stop hurting yourself." Nadirah glanced anxiously out into the hall hoping that a nurse or doctor would appear. None did. Nadirah dug down in her bag for tissues. She found them and handed them out to Dorothy. "You're bleeding. You're hurting yourself."

Dorothy ignored the tissue and Nadirah. She bit down even harder scaring Nadirah into feeling bad that she'd upset her. Cautiously, Nadirah dabbed at the blood on Dorothy's lips until Dorothy began whipping her head from side to side making it difficult for Nadirah to touch her lip.

Nadirah hurried out into the hall. She looked searchingly toward the nurse's station and saw no one. She rushed back into the room. She didn't know what to do. For sure the staff will blame her for upsetting a patient.

"Miss Morrison, it's okay. Forget what I said about Bree. In fact, let's not talk about Bree. Can I get you some water?"

The painful biting, the steady rocking, and finally sorrowful tears rolling down Dorothy's cheeks, tore at Nadirah. "I didn't mean to upset you. I'm going now. I'm sorry." Nadirah turned to leave.

"I wasn't supposed to be Bree's mother," Dorothy said. "I never wanted to be anybody's mother. I never wanted children. I don't like children. I don't like them all over me, needing me, wanting me to pick them up. Nobody picked me up when I was a baby. My mother had other things to do. She was a crack addict. She was never home. I'm not … I'm not … I was never spoiled. Not me, Erma. Erma was spoiled. She got everything. My grandmother gave her everything. I don't like Erma. She's not my real sister. I don't want her to be my real sister. She's mean. She always hurt me. She always makes me cry."

Watching Dorothy rapidly rock back and forth, Nadirah listened intently.

"I don't like Erma. I hate her. I hate her. She made me take Bree. I didn't want to. Bree's not my baby. I wasn't supposed to have no baby. Erma acted like she wanted a baby, but she really didn't. Not me. Not me. I didn't want no baby. Erma lied. She tricked me. She made me have that baby. That baby ain't mine. Erma was supposed to take her. She was

... she was supposed to change her diapers and feed her. Not me. Not me. That baby ain't mine. She wasn't supposed to be mine. It's not my fault. She died. It's not my fault."

While the rocking continued and the lip biting resumed, Dorothy said nothing more. Nadirah stood at her bedside floored by what she'd heard. What it all meant she didn't know, but there was no doubt in her mind that Dorothy Morrison was confused, but not confused about her feelings for her sister.

"Miss Morrison?"

"She went out on you, huh?" A woman's scratchy voice asked.

Nadirah turned to see a plump, red-headed, middle-aged white woman dressed in a dirty hospital gown behind her. In one hand the woman had an orange and a banana. In the other she carried a plastic water pitcher.

The woman went to the other bed in the room. On the bed she placed her fruit in the center. "She do that a lot," the woman said.

"Should I get a doctor or a nurse?"

"She had her pills already." The woman began pouring water over her fruit, wetting the bed, soaking it.

Nadirah started to say something, but she remembered where she was. "I have to go."

The woman smiled. "Bye." She continued washing her fruit.

Nadirah hurried from the room and rushed out of the ward. On her way down on the elevator she thanked God for her emotional health. She'd never take it for granted again. Dorothy Morrison was seriously ill, and it seemed her baby and her sister were the cause.

✂︎∞✂︎∞✂︎

Heavy noontime traffic prolonged Nadirah's angst and her cab ride back uptown to Harlem. She couldn't erase the vision of Dorothy Morrison biting down on her lip from her mind nor could she make sense of anything she ranted on about. Nadirah shuttered at the thought of ever having to be put away because her mind deserted her. Still, with so much on her mind, she couldn't dwell solely on Bree's mother. She had to reach Lynn. Twice since getting into the cab, she had dialed Lynn's number and kept getting her voice mail. She had even tried to

reach Austin again to tell him about her visit with Dorothy Morrison and to ask him what her babbling might have meant. And just as importantly, Nadirah needed to talk to Austin about Byron and Lynn, but, Austin, too, she couldn't reach.

God, where was everyone? Why was she slouching around all alone in a tub of troubles that she had nothing to do with creating? Was this her fate? Was she always to be alone in the world? Feeling all alone with no one to turn to was not new to Nadirah, it had been part of her existence since her parents died and had settled in her soul the day Uncle Lester died. His death filled her with an emptiness and aloneness that she had never been able to rid herself of until Bree. Taking Bree into her life filled that empty space in her heart and gave her a reason to look toward the future. She didn't want to lose Bree nor did she want to lose the money her parents left to her that she could use to give Bree an even better life.

A quick glance at her watch, Nadirah saw that she had four hours before she had to get back home to meet up with Mrs. Hamilton. Bree she didn't have to worry about—Beverly was taking her home after school and now, with no other choice, Nadirah knew she had to go back to face the woman who gave her a bed to lie in, but never a shoulder to cry on. Aunt Stephanie's house was where she had to go to get her money back.

Chapter 29

As Nadirah climbed those old, brown, concrete stairs, she was reminded that she wasn't supposed to have to come back to this house so soon after escaping its treacherous hold on her. She hadn't planned to come back at all, not even for a funeral, but as life would have it, here she stood ringing the bell in anticipation of coming face to face with the woman who never liked or loved her. Twice she had rang, but the door had not yet been opened to her.

"If you had kept your keys ..."

Nadirah turned and looked back down the stairs at Stephanie.

"... you wouldn't have to ring the bell."

If it had been anyone else, Nadirah would have said, "Wow!" Aunt Stephanie looked that different. A new hairdo, make-up, and standing upright with only the assistance of her cane. That alone was a sight, but Nadirah wasn't surprised. She knew Aunt Stephanie could walk, but seeing her all dressed up in a sharp, navy blue pants suit was like looking back in time when Aunt Stephanie was fussy about her looks and particular about her clothes.

Carrying a shopping bag of groceries, Stephanie slowly climbed the steps. "I was wondering if you'd ever come this way again."

Nadirah intentionally squared her shoulders, readying herself for battle. "I hadn't planned to."

"Humph. Must be really important then." Stephanie stepped up next to Nadirah. She set her shopping bag down and didn't bother to pretend that she wasn't looking Nadirah over. "Suits you," she said of Nadirah's new look.

"Likewise," Nadirah said, somewhat taken aback by her aunt's calm demeanor.

"They say change is good for the soul. We seem to both agree." Stephanie unlocked the door and went on into the house

leaving her groceries on the stoop.

As she watched her aunt walk into the house, for the briefest moment, Nadirah thought about leaving the bag on the stoop. The truth is she was thinking about staying on the stoop herself. She didn't need to go inside to ask about her money.

"You coming in or you gonna stay out there and adorn my stoop like a statue?"

Nadirah snatched up the bag of groceries and went into the house. She closed the door because she had to, but she really didn't want to. So many memories, most of them sad, flooded her mind and weighed her down. As beautiful and as bright as the house was, Nadirah's years of unhappiness within those walls dulled the colors and dimmed the brilliance of the sunlight streaming through the windows. Standing in the foyer she remembered the first time she stepped foot in the house as a little girl. Back then, it was all so big, so new, so not like home. Now, it didn't feel so big, and it definitely wasn't new, yet it still didn't feel like home.

"How long you gonna hold that bag?" Stephanie asked from halfway down the hall. "I have some perishables in there."

Snapping out of it, Nadirah took the bag to the kitchen. She set it on the counter and automatically began emptying the bag.

Stephanie pulled out a chair from the table. "Old habits, huh?"

Nadirah looked at the container of cream cheese in her hand. Yeah, old habits were hard to break. She went ahead and put the cream cheese, cold cuts, and ice cream in the refrigerator. The rest of the food that belonged in the cabinet, she left on the counter. She wasn't there to reclaim her old role as handmaiden; she was there to get answers. She faced Stephanie.

"Why did you—"

"Haven't you learned to smile yet?"

"Give me something to smile about, and I will. I need—"

"You don't live here anymore. You don't have to look at my face everyday. Aren't you happy?"

"Ecstatically. Aunt Stephanie, I—"

"You don't call, you don't come around. Do you intend to forget everything I've done for you?"

As frustrated as she was that Stephanie kept cutting her off,

Nadirah couldn't let that question go unchallenged. "Tell me, Aunt Stephanie, what exactly did you do for me besides use me as your hand-maiden, saddle me with poor self-esteem and an unquenchable thirst for affection?"

Not that she could deny that she was never affectionate toward Nadirah or especially nice to her, but Stephanie was offended all the same. "So in all these years, you don't think I've done anything right by you?"

Nadirah looked away. This isn't what she came here for. She wasn't up to trying to get Aunt Stephanie to see, with her cloudy vision, what her life had been like under her roof.

"You hate me, don't you?" Stephanie asked.

Nadirah answered cooly, "Yes," and it felt good saying it.

Stephanie didn't blink an eye. "I guess I didn't treat you the best over the years, and..."

"The best?"

"... I can't turn back the clock. If it helps you to hear me say I'm sorry, then so be it. I'm sorry. Can you ever forgive me?"

Nadirah stood stone cold still in disbelief. An apology and for-giveness were the last things she expected to hear from her aunt's mouth. She searched her face to see if she was joking, but there wasn't a smirk nor an April fool glint in Stephanie's eyes.

"Is forgiveness so farfetched, Nadirah? I know you never went to church much."

"Neither did you."

"I do now, and I've learned to forgive. God forgives us all of our sins. He doesn't hold grudges and neither should we. We can forgive each other, Nadirah, in the name of Jesus Christ."

Not believing what she was hearing, Nadirah stared at Stephanie. Never would she have guessed that Stephanie would get reli-gion, but then again, what kind of religion did she have? The perpetrat-ing a fraud kind of religion or the real to the soul kind? It was no secret that some of the biggest hypocrites were the men and women behind the pulpit, and as well, the sanctified sisters sitting at the foot of the altar.

"You know what, Aunt Stephanie? I'm really not here for this. How you treated me all of my life, and how I feel about it now, I'll deal with on my own. I'm glad you found God and you have obviously found

some balance in your life, but, truthfully, I'm sure you could care less about my opinion of you. You'll go on living and breathing without a thought about me, and I'll do the same regarding you."

"Life goes on, they say, but you forget one thing, Nadirah. I'm all the family you have. Good or bad, you and I are family."

"My, is this a new revelation? Are you now saying that I am my father's child? For years you said your brother Marcus was not my biological father."

"Well, I wasn't in the bedroom with your mother when she got pregnant so I can't say who exactly got her pregnant, but Marcus always claimed you. I can only go by what he said."

"How magnanimous of you. Is this miraculous change due to your profound religious enlightenment?"

Smiling musingly to herself, Stephanie couldn't exactly blurt out that it was more than religion that freed her mind and soul and gave her peace. It was the gospel according to BJ's divine lovemaking that washed the hate out of her heart for Lester and opened her eyes to what she had done to Nadirah, and as well to Lynn and Les. Why is it that none of her previous lovers, all those years ago, had the power in them to inject her with the milk of human kindness? How different her life could have been.

"Aunt Stephanie?"

"I was pretty bad, huh?"

"Aunt Stephanie, stop patronizing me. I came here—"

"I never beat you!"

"No, but you abused me, you tore me me down emotionally…"

"I never—"

"… What you fail to understand, Aunt Stephanie, is that abuse comes in many forms. Psychological and emotional abuse are just as bad. I bare the scars not on my back but on my mind. You never gave me love or made me feel like this was my home. You made me feel like a street urchin you were forced to feed, forced to put up with. My God, you made me clean this house like I was a slave and wait on you like I was your handmaiden. Aunt Stephanie, you lied about your inability to walk in order to keep me indentured to you. You made me carry the guilt of your falling down the stairs just to keep me under your thumb."

Although Stephanie didn't look away from Nadirah's accusato-

ry glare, she didn't challenge her.

"Aunt Stephanie, if I had to recount everything you did to hurt me, I'd need a spreadsheet to lay it out. And the sad thing is I don't know why you treated me that way."

"Haven't you spoken to Lynn?"

"No, I haven't, which is why I'm here. I—"

"Lynn and I had a long talk. Maybe it's time I tell you as well why, for so many years, I was so spiteful."

"No!" Nadirah put up her hand. "I don't wanna know. Whatever you have to say can't and won't change a single day of the past eighteen years. So please do me a huge favor—don't tell me anything about your past because, personally, I don't care because it changes nothing."

Stephanie pushed her hurt way down. "Well, can't blame you for that," she said. "I know how badly I treated you. That's why I asked if you could ever forgive me."

"I don't wanna talk about forgiveness."

"Okay, but let me say this. Life is about change. Maybe you think it's a bit late in coming for me, but I think it's right on time. I'm trying to be better, that's all I can do."

"You have to live with you, Aunt Stephanie, not me."

"Maybe having to live with myself is just as good a reason as any to change. Don't get me wrong, I'm no angel. I haven't changed that much. I know I can't go back thirty-six years and welcome my babies into the world with open, loving arms, nor can I go back and hold you in your time of grief, but I can go forward and try to make amends for the wrongs I've done."

Dumbfounded, Nadirah wondered what alien being had crawled into her aunt's ears and worked some miraculous surgery on her brain, or was Aunt Stephanie gaming her?

"You must think I'm stupid."

"Not really, but you don't think I'm sincere about making amends to you, then—"

"Make amends to me by giving me back every penny of the $500,000.00 you stole from me."

Stephanie drew back. "I stole what!"

"So much for your newfound religion."

"Girl, what are you talking about? What $500,000.00?"

"Aunt Stephanie, my trust fund is minus $500,000.00 as of two days ago. You're the sole trustee."

Stephanie gaped at Nadirah.

"Either you're a great actress or you—"

"Or I don't know what the hell you're talking about! Five…hundred…thousand…dollars! Are you kidding me?"

"Did you take the money or not?"

Stephanie grabbed her cane and rushed from the kitchen. "I'll get to the bottom of this!"

After a heartbeat of a hesitation, Nadirah took off behind Stephanie and followed her up the stairs to her bedroom. Stephanie went straight to her closet and retrieved the trust fund statements. She found the most recent one and opened it.

"All the money's here."

"The money was taken Monday. That statement is two weeks old."

Stephanie looked at the date in the upper right hand corner. "Nadirah, until you turn thirty, your account can't be touched by anyone but me and I haven't taken a dime."

"According to the bank you have."

Stephanie went to her telephone and dialed the number on the statement. Nadirah listened while Stephanie gave the fund account number and answered all the bank's questions identifying herself to be who she claimed to be.

"When was the last withdrawal from this account and how much?" Stephanie demanded.

When Stephanie's eyes widened and her mouth opened, Nadirah's heart sank. It was then she knew it could only be Lynn who had stolen from her.

"Who signed for the money?" Stephanie asked.

Nadirah waited.

"No, the hell I didn't! I haven't taken money from that account in years!"

"Aunt Stephanie."

"Don't ma'am me! Somebody better tell me what happened to that damn money."

"Aunt Stephanie!" Nadirah said louder.

Stephanie held her hand up to tell Nadirah to wait a minute. "How in the world do y'all let just anyone walk into your bank and take $500,000.00 from an account without making sure it's the right person? My personal accounts are at Republic! I haven't been to your bank, nor have I withdrawn any money through any other means from your bank."

"Aunt Stephanie, hang up."

"You get me somebody on this damn phone who can straighten this mess out immediately! You get me the damn bank president, you hear me?"

"Aunt Stephanie. Aunt Stephanie, hang up."

"Hang up? Nadirah, somebody stole your money and I aim to sue the bank if they don't put every damn penny back into your account this day!"

Nadirah took the phone from Stephanie.

"Girl! What—"

"It was Lynn." Nadirah hung up the phone.

"What was Lynn?"

"Lynn and Byron took my money."

Not fully comprehending what Nadirah was saying, Stephanie looked at Nadirah.

"I've been trying to reach Lynn since yesterday. She's not answering her phone."

"What does Lynn not answering her phone have to do with your money?"

"Byron gambled a quarter of a million dollars away on the stock market."

Stephanie didn't like a bit what she was hearing. "He did what?"

"He and Lynn were going to lose everything. They asked a friend for the money, but he didn't have it. Lynn obviously remembered my trust fund, but you know what's funny? I went to the bank to take an advance against my fund to get the money to bail them out."

Sinking down on the side of her bed, Stephanie said, "I don't believe this."

"Lynn had to be the one who forged your name."

"But she would have needed my ID, my picture ID. She can't pass for me."

"Sure she can. She looks like you, she's just not as heavy as

you."

"Or as old."

"Well, she did it somehow. The money's gone."

"Yes. But you don't know that it was really Lynn."

"Aunt Stephanie, Lynn was here this past weekend. She stayed here in your house. She knows where you keep everything, including my trust fund information, your bank information, and your personal ID. No one else had access to information about my trust fund but you and Lynn. This past weekend, were you always here at the house with Lynn and Byron? Can you say in fact that they had no access to your room alone?"

Stephanie didn't bother mulling over in her mind whether Lynn came into her room or not. She knew Lynn had been there because when she got home Sunday afternoon she found her closet door closed on the sleeve of her bathrobe hanging on the inside of the door. She had always made it a point to push the sleeve inside before she closed the door, but she had not given it a second thought because Lynn was no stranger to her room or closet. For years, Lynn took care of some of her banking and house concerns.

"I went to church Sunday morning," Stephanie admitted. "Lynn and Byron stayed here."

"And that's when they got my trust fund information. Aunt Stephanie, Byron and Lynn are both desperate."

"Owing that much money, they oughta be. But I bet you that bowlegged, lowlife son of a bitch talked Lynn into stealing that money. I told Lynn that boy was no good, but did she listen to me? Hell no! She listened to her father who thought Byron was a good man, a man with potential, a man with a big, bright-ass future. Ha! He has a future in Ossining State Prison!"

Nadirah stood back and watched Stephanie punch Lynn's telephone number into the phone. If breathing was smoke, Stephanie would be puffing it out.

"Answer the phone, dammit!" Stephanie was gripping the phone so tight, her hand hurt.

"Lynn! What the hell have you done?"

Nadirah couldn't believe Lynn answered the phone.

"You know what I'm talking about! Nadirah's money!"

"Oh, don't tell me she's going to deny it!" Nadirah said.

"Lynn, don't mama me and don't you dare deny it! You let that bastard talk you into stealing half a million dollars from Nadirah's trust fund. What's wrong with you?"

Nadirah wished she could hear what Lynn was saying.

"I don't wanna hear that, Lynn! Your husband is a thief. You're both thieves!"

Nadirah watched her aunt in awe. Aunt Stephanie was actually fighting for her and it was a strange sight to behold. Still, Nadirah wasn't convinced she could trust her. For all she knew, this blustering was all just an act.

"Lynn, as long as life lasts, and death passes, if I get my hands on that scheming son of a bitch I will castrate him and throw his balls to the buzzards! You tell that lowlife I want that money back."

Stephanie listened.

"What is she saying?" Nadirah asked anxiously.

"Well, he better go get it back. If he doesn't return all of it, I will call the police and have his ass locked up for grand larceny. Do you hear me, Lynn?"

The scowl on Stephanie's face deepened, she began shaking her head.

"Lynn, you could go to jail your damn self! Why would you let a man turn you into a criminal?"

Nadirah reached for the telephone. "Let me speak to her." Stephanie gave it to her.

"Lynn, how could you do this to me?"

Lynn didn't answer.

"Lynn, you didn't have to go behind my back. I would have given you the money." A hollow silence echoed in Nadirah's ear. "Lynn, I thought you were someone I could trust."

Dead silence.

"Hello? Lynn?" Nadirah looked at the phone. "She hung up!"

"Well, I'm calling her back!"

"She won't answer." Nadirah hung up the telephone. "She probably needs time."

"To do what? Leave the country? They could with half a million dollars."

"Oh, they're not going anywhere. It would cost too much to start over."

"Stupid people don't know that," Stephanie said. "Lynn should have come to me. I might have cursed that bastard of a husband of hers out, and I probably would have told her to leave his ass, but I would have helped her out. The hell with him, he could hang by his balls from a flag pole for all I care. And by the way, they don't have all the money. Lynn said Byron's already paid off some of their debt."

"Oh, no."

"That money's gone, Nadirah. I think we should bring Byron up on charges."

"But what about Lynn? She was the one who impersonated you. I think she'd be in more trouble than Byron. He could walk. He could say it was all Lynn's doing."

"We'll see about that!" Stephanie began flipping through her personal telephone book. "That bastard isn't getting away with this. What time is it?"

Nadirah checked her watch. "Oh! I have to go!"

"Don't you wanna straighten this out?"

"Of course, I do, but I have a meeting I can't miss. I'll call you."

As strange as those words sounded to her own ears, and as sour a taste they left in her mouth, Nadirah knew she had no other choice but be in touch with her aunt if she wanted her money back. Byron had already spent some of it so they had to work fast to get the rest before it was all gone. And what about Aunt Stephanie? Lynn was her daughter for better or worse. They weren't close, but Lynn was still her daughter. With her new attitude, Aunt Stephanie was definitely not going to want to hurt Lynn anymore than she'd already hurt her in her lifetime. How was she going to go after Byron and not hurt Lynn?

Chapter 30

Beverly brought Bree home with barely ten minutes to spare before Mrs. Hamilton rang the bell. If she'd had a whole hour to spare, Nadirah would have lay out across her bed and taken a nap. She was mentally depleted from her encounters with her aunt and Bree's mother. At least she wasn't going to have to do battle with Mrs. Hamilton?Mrs. Hamilton was there to help her keep Erma Gray away.

As was her routine, Mrs. Hamilton first talked with Bree with Nadirah in the room and then alone without Nadirah. Although Nadirah was used to the process and understood what Mrs. Hamilton was doing, she still didn't like it. She always felt like Mrs. Hamilton didn't trust that she was treating Bree right. As a teacher, Nadirah knew that kids didn't speak their minds with their parents in the room, but she was offended just the same that she couldn't be with Bree when she was being questioned. For the past twenty-five minutes, Mrs. Hamilton had been sitting out on the stoop talking with Bree. That was fifteen minutes longer than she usually spent alone with her and Nadirah was beside herself. What could she possibly be talking to her about that long?

Riiiiing!

Nadirah hurriedly answered, "Hello!"

"Hey," Austin said. *"Sorry it took so long to get back to you. I was in meetings all day."*

"No problem," she lied.

"Is Erma still harassing you?"

"Not since this morning, but the social worker is here. She's outside with Bree. I'll be speaking to her about your wife in a little while, but I wanted to speak to you about Byron and Lynn."

"What are they up to? They rob a bank yet?"

"Well, close to it." Nadirah decided to tell Austin about her trust fund. "They stole half a million dollars from me."

Austin paused. *"You had ... how did they do that?"*

"Lynn forged my aunt's signature to debit my trust fund."

"Damn! That's low."

"And very desperate."

"I should have put my foot up Byron's ass. Have you spoken to Lynn yet?"

"She's been avoiding me. I found out because I was trying to take an advance against my trust fund to help them out and to start house hunting for myself and Bree."

"So being underhanded, they blew it. I'd have their behinds arrested."

"I spoke to my aunt since she's the trustee over my trust fund, and she's planning to do something to get the money back. But I don't think she can."

"If you're talking about Lynn's mother, if she's on it, then she just might get your money back. As for Byron, I can't believe he got Lynn to steal for him."

"He's her husband. She loves him."

"Yeah, well, love only goes so far. Lynn should have drawn the line. I'm sorry they ripped you off like that."

"So am I, but, look, there's something else. I went to see Bree's mother this morning at the hospital."

"How is she?"

"Not good. She's out of it. She rants about your wife and Bree. I couldn't really make sense of everything she said, but I got that she never wanted a baby. She said it was your wife who wanted a baby."

"Ttha's true."

"Yes, but why would Dorothy, in her condition, lament about not wanting a baby while her sister did? Bree is eight years old, yet, her being born weighs on Dorothy's mind. Like that's what pulled her into the abyss of mental illness. She said she never loved Bree and that she wasn't a good mother. How could she never love her own child?"

Again Austin paused. *"I don't know, but I bet Erma does. Do you know if Erma's gone to visit her?"*

"I don't know, but I would like to visit Dorothy again to see if she'll talk more coherently about Bree."

"Does she know who you are?"

"I told her, but I don't know if she understood."

"Maybe I'll try to visit her next time I'm in town."

This time, Nadirah paused. When was that going to be?

"Anyway, Nadirah, aside from the stress of this day, how are you?"

Nadirah didn't smile, but she was flattered that Austin asked about her. "I'm good."

"That's not what I'm hearing in your voice. Look, I'll be coming to town next week Friday. I'd like to take you and Bree to dinner if you're available."

"I think Bree would love that."

"I hope you will, too."

The front door suddenly opened.

"I have to go," Nadirah said. "I'll let you know what happens." Before Austin could say goodbyc, Nadirah hung up. "I was just about to check on you guys," she said.

"We had ourselves a good little talk," Mrs. Hamilton said. "Right, Bree?"

Bree said nothing as she went straight to Nadirah and turned her face into Nadirah's side away from Mrs. Hamilton.

Nadirah began to slowly rub Bree's back. "Is everything all right?"

"Everything's just fine," Mrs. Hamilton said. "Bree, why don't you go up to your room while Miss Lewis and I talk?"

Bree looked up at Nadirah for her okay. With a nod, Nadirah sent Bree on her way. She then led Mrs. Hamilton into the living room.

"I appreciate you coming at such short notice," Nadirah said as they both sat.

"I was planning to meet with you in a few days anyway. Today is as good a day as any to talk about this situation with Mrs. Gray."

"Well, Mrs. Gray has twice tried to take Bree. Bree is terrified of her. Mrs. Gray won't is very persistent and quite violent. Mrs. Hamilton, Bree feels safe here, she's been opening up. She talks more, she's eating more, but whenever Mrs. Gray comes around, afterwards, Bree clings to me because she's afraid she's going to be taken away."

"It's obvious Bree has grown close to you," Mrs. Hamilton said, opening her leather notebook, "and that's expected. Bree tells me she likes living with you, and that's good. However, there is the issue of her

aunt, Mrs. Gray, who has informed ACS that you won't allow her to see Bree."

"Am I supposed to let her see Bree? Mrs. Hamilton, you've never given me any directives on that. Aside from which, Mrs. Gray hasn't once approached me civilly asking to see Bree. She keeps swooping down on us on the street, grabbing Bree before we even realize what's happening. This morning she caused such a disturbance outside that the neighbors called the police. It was awful for Bree."

"I'm sure it was."

"So what do we do about Mrs. Gray coming around here unannounced?"

Mrs. Hamilton coughed lightly into her hand. "Miss Lewis, let me first say this, the complication here is that you're living in Mrs. Gray's husband's house, which I wasn't originally aware of."

"Neither was I, Mrs. Hamilton, until a few weeks after Bree was living with me. Mr. Gray is a close friend of my cousin. I didn't meet Mr. Gray until I rented this place from him, and even then, our meeting was very brief. I found out about Mrs. Gray and her relationship to Bree around the same time I found out about Mr. Gray's relationship to Bree. If Mrs. Gray has inferred an illicit relationship between myself and Mr. Gray, she's wrong. Mr. Gray is my landlord. He does not live here, and in fact, does not live in New York City. He lives in Los Angeles. And from my understanding, after speaking with Mr. Gray, when Mrs. Gray came here the first time and assaulted me, I learned that he and Mrs. Gray are in the middle of a very contentious divorce."

Mrs. Hamilton jotted quickly in her notebook. "Mrs. Gray said you hit her, and—"

"That's incorrect!" Nadirah didn't like having to defend herself. "Mrs. Gray put her hands on me and all I did was push her away. You need verification of this, go next door and speak to Mrs. Bradley. She can tell you all you need to know about Mrs. Gray."

Again writing, Mrs. Hamilton finished her thought before looking up. "Here's the situation. In the placement of children, if a biological parent is deemed unsuitable to parent a child, ACS ..."

"I know this."

"... will seek to place that child with a family member ..."

"But is that the right choice?"

"… and if that placement is not available to the agency or deemed unsuitable, the agency will seek non-family placement. Bree does have family."

Nadirah felt like she was punched in the stomach. "You can't put Bree with Mrs. Gray."

"Miss Lewis, our first concern is Bree. Mrs. Gray says all she wants to do is give her niece a loving home."

"Isn't that what I'm giving her?"

"The decision to place Bree with Mrs. Gray is in no way a reflection of your care. This is solely a decision based on family relationship."

Nadirah was close to screaming, "How stupid are you?" but she refrained. "But, Mrs. Hamilton, you're putting Bree back in a dangerous situation. I told you, Bree said her mother made her drink that disinfectant, and lo and behold, Miss Morrison is in a psyche ward in Bellevue."

"That has nothing to do with Mrs. Gray."

"Yes, it does! Mrs. Gray is very volatile. According to Mr. Gray, she's bi-polar. She's supposed to be on medication, which she probably isn't taking because she's been drinking. She showed up here drunk."

Writing quickly, Mrs. Hamilton for the first time seemed concerned. "Are you sure she was drunk?"

"Yes, I am. Ask Mr. Gray, I'm sure he can tell you more."

"We'll investigate further, but for now, Mrs. Gray reported that she came here to see the child and was stopped by you."

"Mrs. Gray didn't even know Bree was here when she initially pushed her way in. She came looking for her husband. When she showed up she was drunk, she was loud, and she was violent."

"That's not what Mrs. Gray says."

Nadirah was losing patience. "Mrs. Hamilton, of course, Mrs. Gray is not going to tell you the truth about her behavior or inebriated condition. She wants to get custody of Bree, why would she paint an ugly picture of herself?"

"Miss Lewis, I've met with Mrs. Gray. She's a long-time office manager for a city agency. She's very professional, very presentable—"

"Mrs. Hamilton, you and I have met two different women. The woman I met is desperate to get back with her husband. She's nothing like you describe. She's an emotional wreck. She comes here screaming

for her husband and accuses me of sleeping with him."

Mrs. Hamilton looked questioningly at Nadirah which piqued her.

"No, I am not sleeping with Mr. Gray!"

Mrs. Hamilton wrote again in her notebook.

"Mrs. Hamilton, why am I the one under scrutiny?"

"You're not, Miss Lewis. You've been very good for Bree."

"Then why are you taking Bree from me?" Nadirah stood. "Mrs. Gray is not the right person to take care of Bree. Bree will get caught up in this mess between Mrs. Gray and her husband."

"Hopefully not, but why would Mrs. Gray try to use Bree to get her husband back? Bree's not his child."

"No, but Mr. Gray is very good with Bree. I understand they both want children, but couldn't. This is another reason she intends to use Bree to pull Mr. Gray back to her. He cares a lot for Bree. She intends to use Bree as a pawn."

"Did she tell you this herself?"

"Not in so many words, but that's why she wants Bree. Mrs. Gray thinks this is why I want Bree—to get her husband. In her mind, I'm a threat."

Mrs. Hamilton began shaking her head. "If you can't prove this, I can't question Mrs. Gray's motives. She is family."

An intense ache tightened the muscles in Nadirah's shoulders. "Mrs. Hamilton, Mrs. Gray doesn't even like Bree. Didn't you get Mr. Gray's letter?"

"Mr. Gray's letter carries very little weight considering that he and Mrs. Gray are going through a divorce. His views are biased."

Nadirah began pacing to keep from screaming. "So nothing any of us have to say will stop you from placing Bree with Mrs. Gray?"

"Miss Lewis, that's not the case. Everything is taken into consideration."

"But what if Bree gets hurt again?"

"I will closely monitor Mrs. Gray's home and see Bree as often as bi-weekly."

"Harm can come to Bree in ten minutes, Mrs. Hamilton. By the time you find out about it two weeks down the road, it might be too late."

"Let's think positive, Miss Lewis. Mrs. Gray appears sincere in her application to take custody of her niece."

"Of course, she—"

"Miss Lewis, before Bree is taken out of your care and placed anywhere, I will thoroughly investigate any questionable concerns that may prove detrimental to her."

"Will you check Mr. Gray's claims about Mrs. Gray being bipolar?"

"I'll find out who her doctors are and whether she's being treated. As well, I'll ask Mrs. Gray directly how Bree will fit into her life."

"Oh, I'm sure she'll be real forthright with you."

"I'm sure she will be," Mrs. Hamilton said, choosing to ignore Nadirah's sarcasm. She put her notebook away. "She's the closest relative to Bree's biological mother."

"Speaking of Dorothy Morrison, I went to see her this morning."

Mrs. Hamilton raised her brow. "You went to Bellevue?"

"I did, and I don't think Dorothy Morrison wants her daughter to be with her sister. I think she feels that her sister has always tried to take Bree from her."

"She was lucid enough to express that to you?"

That question gave Nadirah pause. Lucid, Dorothy Morrison wasn't, but somewhere in her chattering incoherence there had to be some truth.

"Miss Lewis," Mrs. Hamilton said, standing, "you obviously care a lot for Bree, and that's commendable. The agency is more than pleased with all you've done for her, and again I assure you, we will not put Bree in harm's way. I will recommend to my director that we investigate Mrs. Gray further. In the meantime, I'm scheduled to visit Miss Morrison at Bellevue Hospital Friday morning. Please Miss Lewis, do not go back to visit Miss Morrison. You don't want it said that you were bothering her, and regarding Mrs. Gray, I will ask her to stay away from you and Bree until a final decision is made. Will that do?"

Nadirah said, "I guess so," because there was nothing else she could say. As far as she could tell, unless something real ugly popped up about Erma Gray, ACS had already made its decision to place Bree with her. Bree was going to be lost to her, and if Nadirah's gut feeling

was right, Bree could lose her life.

Chapter 31

In the shadowy darkness of her kitchen, the souring fruity smell of the pared apple she had tried to eat two hours before filled Lynn's nostrils. Although she couldn't see the apple clearly, she knew by the strong fruity smell that the white of the apple had turned brown and was rotting just like her marriage. Picking up the small paring knife and the apple, she took it to the garbage pail near the sink and dropped it in. The knife, she set in the bottom of the sink. She then went back to the table and again glanced at the digital clocks on her stove and microwave oven. The stove clock was one minute slower, but it made no difference, Byron still wasn't home. For two hours, Lynn had been sitting at the kitchen table across from the window through which she had a prime view of the garage on the side of the house. She kept waiting for the motion sensor light over the garage door to flash on as it always did when Byron drove in after dusk. The light hadn't flashed on once and Lynn was itching with anxiety. Byron had called at four forty-five to say that he was on his way and had a surprise for her. That was more than four and a half hours ago. Since then she had called his office and his cell phone, but he wasn't answering. Wherever Byron was, Lynn hoped to God he wasn't foolishly spending the money they had stolen.

Stolen. That was the operative word. They hadn't borrowed, they hadn't been gifted, they had actually outright stolen Nadirah's money, and although Lynn had anticipated how badly she'd feel about stealing from her own cousin, she didn't expect to what depths her shame would sink her. Since hearing Nadirah's voice on the telephone, she had been miserably depressed. She couldn't sleep, she couldn't eat, and she was functioning minimally as a mother. Ignoring her children and sitting off by herself in the dark was not a good thing, but she couldn't look at herself in the mirror and, worst of all, she couldn't look her children in the eye while trying to teach them that lying and stealing was bad. How had she become so weak

that she had been unable to stand up to Byron for what she knew to be wrong? She had stood up to BJ Parish for Nadirah, and she had confronted her mother about her incredible lie. So why couldn't she stand up to Byron as well? How had he gained such power over her to the point that he suppressed who she was, who her father taught her that she was? God, her father would be so ashamed of her, especially for what she had done to Nadirah.

Beginning to tear, Lynn said, "I'm sorry, Daddy." She lay her head down in the crook of her arm and wept.

"Mommy!"

Lynn wearily raised her head.

"Mommy!"

"Erin, you're supposed to be sleeping."

"When are you coming upstairs?"

Pausing a moment to pull herself together, Lynn told herself to not yell at her child. Erin, the oldest, was only seven and wouldn't understand her anger.

"Erin, I'll be up soon. Just go back to bed, please."

"Mommy, you keep saying that, but you never come."

"Erin, I was up there. I kissed you good night. I said prayers with you. Please lay back down and don't wake Byron or Liz. I'll be up. I'm waiting for Daddy."

"Okay," Erin said in the saddest little voice, which Lynn barely heard because, just then, she heard a car door close. Her eyes shot to the window. The light was on over the garage. She rushed to the window. Her heart sank. Byron had not parked his blue Camry, he had parked a brand new, white-on-white Mercedes that sparkled like a new diamond under the spotlight over the garage.

Lynn felt weak in the knees. She made it back to the table just in time to fall into her chair. Covering her mouth, she muffled herself to keep from scaring Erin with her screams of anger and rage. In the darkness she listened to the single click that unlocked the front door. She listened to Byron's footfalls as he walked on the hardwood floor leading to the kitchen. She watched him as he dropped his keys onto the kitchen counter and flicked on the kitchen light. She didn't bother pasting a fake smile on her lips.

She asked right away, "How could you?"

"Damn!" Byron said, startled. "What are you doing sitting in the dark?"

Just hearing Byron's voice ignited a rage inside Lynn so intense, she grit her teeth and shook her fists as hard as she could to keep from screaming and lashing out at him.

"What the hell's wrong with you?" Byron asked with a petulant edge to his voice.

Lynn couldn't look at Byron. She covered her face with her hands and cried.

"Woman, I'm not in the mood for your hysterics. I had a hard day." Byron went to the refrigerator and looked inside for his prepared dinner plate, which he saw immediately. He took the covered plate to the microwave and set the timer for three minutes. He then shed his jacket, hanging it on the back of one of the chairs at the table onto which he also sat. He reached across to Lynn and yanked her hands away from her face.

"What's wrong with you?"

"Did you buy that car?"

"Oh, you saw it?" Byron smiled. "Nice, huh?"

"Byron, you didn't need a new car. You were supposed to use that money to pay off all of our debt."

"And I will."

"But, Byron, that car—"

"Damn, Lynn! I spent a little money on something I wanted. So what? Damn. The bills will be paid."

"But that car cost at least $80,000, Byron. We can't afford that."

"Obviously, we can, I bought it."

"But, Byron, that's $80,000 that was supposed to pay off bills!"

"Wrong. We took a little extra, remember? I bought the car with that. The bills will be taken care of, so drop it."

"But, Byron, you—"

"Goddammit, Lynn! Shut the hell up! I got the car. That's all there is to it."

Beep...beep-beep...beep!

Byron angrily pushed the chair back as he got up and went to the microwave.

Lynn couldn't silence her tongue. "Byron, we stole my cousin's

money to get ourselves out of debt. That in itself was wrong and I can only imagine what Nadirah thinks about me."

"Screw your cousin!"

"Byron, Nadirah's never done anything to you. We should not've done this to her, and then for you to turn around and spend $80,000 so frivolously is blatantly indulgent. It's like you're thumbing your nose at her!"

"I didn't come home to hear this mess. I could have stayed where I was." Byron grabbed his plate from the microware.

"And where was that, Byron? Who were you with?"

Byron uncovered his plate and seeing what his dinner was, tossed the plate onto the counter, splattering the cream sauce and noodles over the side. "What the hell you feeding me? I ain't eating this sludge."

Lynn suddenly got up from the table. She started out of the kitchen.

"Where are you going?"

Lynn kept walking.

Byron raced behind her. He grabbed her by the arm, stopping her. "Get back in here."

"Let go of me."

He slapped Lynn on the head. "What did I say?"

"Let me go, Byron." Lynn tried to pull her arm free, but Byron gripped her harder, numbing her arm.

"You don't walk away from me, dismissing me like I'm a nobody."

"I'm done with you, Byron. I'm leaving. Let me go."

Byron pulled Lynn back into the kitchen and shoved her hard into the kitchen table. With his finger, he began jabbing her on the forehead. "You're not going any where. You get that, dumb ass? No where."

Cringing away from the assault of Byron's finger, Lynn kept moving backwards away from him, but he moved steadily forward like a lion on the scent of its prey.

"We were wrong, Byron. We should have never taken Nadirah's money."

"Well, we did, and now suddenly you got religion?"

"I never wanted to steal that money. You made me. You—"

Slap!

Lynn's head snapped back so hard, she stumbled backwards into the kitchen sink. She cried out from the pain that shot through her jaw.

"Hitting me won't change anything. You—"

"Oh, no?"

Slap! Slap! Slap! Slap! Slap! Slap!

Cowering under the brutal assault against her face and head, Lynn fell to the floor. From deep in her gut she cried, "Stop it! Stop it! Stop it!"

Walking softly on bare feet, her face wet with tears, Erin walked timidly to the doorway of the kitchen and stood in stunned silence looking at what she had been listening to upstairs in her bedroom.

"Shut up! I'm tired of you bitching! You got your men mixed up, Lynn. I'm not your spineless father."

"No, you're not my father! You're nothing like him."

"Damn right! Your father was a weak, punk-ass belly crawler. He didn't have the backbone to stand up to your loud mouth, castrating, witch of a mother. Don't even think I'm going to let you bitch at me like she did him. And your stupid cousin? I don't give a damn about her dumb ass. When I need more money, you're gonna take more from her. What's she gonna do? She can't do a damn thing to me. My signature isn't on her papers. Your mother's is. Now get your ass up and make me something I can eat. I ain't eating that slop!"

Cowering still, Lynn continued to cry. She didn't know, behind Byron standing in the doorway, Erin was also crying.

"Get up!" Byron kicked Lynn hard on the leg.

Lynn screamed in pain, and so did Erin. "Don't hurt Mommy!"

Lynn and Byron both were startled to see Erin looking at them.

"Oh, God." Lynn started trying to get up off the floor. She never wanted any one of her children to see her again beaten down by their father.

"Hey, baby," Byron said sweetly. He went and picked Erin up. "Aren't you supposed to be sleeping?"

Erin leaned back away from Byron.

Lynn limped across the kitchen. "Give her to me!"

Byron turned with Erin away from Lynn. "Where's my kiss?"

Byron turned his face so Erin could kiss his cheek, which she did ever so meekly. He then kissed her. "You miss your daddy?"

Wide-eyed, Erin looked directly into Byron's eyes. "How come you kicked Mommy? That was mean."

Byron put Erin down. "I was just playing with Mommy."

"But she's crying. You hurt her. You're not supposed to hurt her."

"Mommy, did I hurt you?" Byron sweetly asked Lynn.

Lynn refused to tell another lie. "Erin, I want you to go back upstairs."

"But I wanna stay with you."

Byron turned Erin toward the doorway. "Erin, you do like your mother said. Go back upstairs to bed. Mommy and I have something to talk about."

"Mommy."

"I'll take you back upstairs," Lynn said, although she was almost blind with pain. She reached out for Erin's hand, but Byron took Lynn's hand and squeezed it, crushing her fingers into each other. Lynn couldn't help gasping in pain, but she tried to put on a face of calm for Erin.

Lynn strained to keep her composure. "Erin, you go on up by yourself. I'll be right behind you."

"But I want you to come with me."

Byron squeezed Lynn's bones in her hand harder. "Go on, Erin, before I spank you for not doing what I told you to do."

"She's going!" Lynn said anxiously. "Erin, go on, baby. I'll be up in a minute."

"You promise, Mommy?"

"I promise. Now, go on. Hurry up. Run."

"You told me not to run in the house."

"You're right. Walk fast, okay?"

The uncertainty, the confusion in Erin's face was clear to Lynn as Erin walked away. This was not the first time or the second time Erin bore witness to Byron hitting her, but this time she wasn't going to lie to her daughter to make Byron not look so bad. This time, she was going to tell Erin the truth about her father's abuse.

Gathering her strength, Lynn punched Byron as hard as she

could in the side with her right hand and quickly, when he recoiled, snatched her left hand from him. She then skittered back out of arm's reach.

Byron chuckled. "You never give up, do you?"

"You're not gonna ever touch me again."

"Are you sure about that? You think you can stop me?"

"I'm leaving you, Byron. I'm taking the kids and I'm leaving."

"Let's get this straight." Byron began moving threateningly closer to Lynn as she continued backing away. "You'll never take my kids from me."

"I won't let you hurt them the way you've hurt me."

"If you didn't aggravate me, I wouldn't have to put my hands on you."

"No, it's not me that makes you hit me, Byron, it's you. You're the abuser, you're the woman beater. I'm going to tell everyone how you've hurt me. I won't live your lie anymore. I'm telling Nadirah you forced me to steal her money. I was a fool. You're not gonna pay off your debt, you're gonna keep spending and spending and spending. You won't be satisfied until you put us out on the street. Well, I won't keep living like this, Byron. I'm finished. I won't steal another dime for you. I'm going to the police; I'm going to my mother. I'd rather deal with her than keep living with you. I want a—"

Byron lunged at Lynn, slamming her against the counter near the sink. Although Lynn flailed her arms trying to ward him off, Byron was still able to grab her around the neck, choking her, cutting off her life's breath as he painfully bent her spine back. With her mouth wide, her tongue hanging out, Lynn panted desperately as she clawed at Byron's face, scratching him, drawing blood as her throat was being crushed.

"I could snap your neck in seconds and not even blink an eye."

Gagging for the air that lay in wait all around her to be gulped, Lynn was close to blacking out.

"Bitch, you threaten me again I'll kill you as sure as I'm standing here."

Her heart racing, her head and lungs about to burst, Lynn had no doubt that Byron was already killing her. How long did it take to die? She didn't want to die. She didn't want her children to be without her.

She had to save herself. Lynn began frantically searching the counter, the dish drain, the sink, for whatever her hand could gain hold of?the paring knife.

"Bitch, you don't run this show. This is my damn house. Everything in it belongs to me, including you and my damn kids. I will kill all of you before I—"

The paring knife found its mark in the side of Byron's neck. The ugly words that spewed from his mouth instantly stopped. His eyes popped, his hands jerked and snapped Lynn's neck. Almost in slow motion, Lynn began slumping to the floor even while Byron tried to hold her up with one arm while reaching up and slowly pulling the paring knife out of his neck, unblocking the flow of blood that pumped from his jugular.

In disbelief, Byron clutched his own throat. He dropped hard to the floor atop Lynn's crumpled body. While Lynn breathed no more, Byron took his last spastic breaths not believing that Lynn had killed him.

Sitting at the top of the stairs, Erin called softly, "Mommy. Mommy."

Chapter 32

Nadirah didn't bother dressing Bree in street clothes before hastily leaving the house. It was cruel enough to waken her from a deep sleep to put a jacket on her and hustle her into a cab to take her to Beverly's. She didn't know what she'd do if Beverly wasn't there at every turn. When Nadirah's cell phone rang at 11:23 P.M. and she saw that it was her aunt calling, she knew immediately that something was wrong. It was the first time Aunt Stephanie had called her since she left her house five months ago.

"Lynn's dead," Aunt Stephanie had said in the shakiest, most pitiful voice Nadirah had ever heard. Those words chilled Nadirah's body and popped her eyes wide open. Aunt Stephanie had broken down and cried then and Nadirah had not been able to find out anything more. Leaving Bree with Beverly, she grabbed the same cab back uptown to Aunt Stephanie's. If Lynn was dead, she needed to know how and most definitely why.

At Aunt Stephanie's house, Nadirah hurried up the stairs and was met by the opening door before she reached the top step. The face that greeted her gave her startled pause. She pulled up short.

"I would have lost the bet," BJ said. "I didn't think you'd come."

"What are you doing here?"

"Oh, you don't know? Well, Stephanie and I—"

"Stephanie and I? Is that supposed to mean something?"

"You coming in?"

Nadirah watched BJ open the door wider. She didn't forget why she was there, but she sure as hell wanted to know why he was. After a second's hesitancy, she sidled past BJ into the house that he obviously felt at home enough in to take it upon himself to open the front door. She had introduced BJ to Aunt Stephanie a while back when she first started working at the center, but that introduction had not made them friends. The few times BJ picked her up from the

house he had respectfully spoken to Aunt Stephanie although, because of the way Aunt Stephanie treated her, he didn't like her. So how is it now that he was opening her front door?

"I'm confused, BJ. You and Lynn were not friends."

"I'm a friend of the family."

"Since when, this morning?"

BJ smirked smugly. "Since your aunt needed someone to talk to and you weren't around."

"Of all people, how would she know to call you? Or did you just happen by out of your way to the center?"

"Stephanie is upstairs."

Nadirah cut her eyes at BJ. Stephanie? Again he called her by her first name. No, BJ wasn't acting like any stranger who just happened by. His shirt was open at the collar, his shirttail was out of his pants, and he was barefooted.

"BJ, am I supposed to pretend that I'm stupid and don't have a clue as to what's going on, or should I believe my eyes and use the good sense God gave me?"

"Believe what you want." BJ started for the living room.

"You snake."

BJ turned back. "Why do I have to be all that? Why can't I just be what I say I am—a good friend?"

"Oh, like you were to me, BJ? The kind of *good friend* who accused me of sleeping with a student?"

"That's behind us."

Nadirah got it completely. "You bastard. It was you and that heartlessly decrepit woman upstairs who tried to get me fired."

"You better go talk to your aunt."

"You always said you'd do anything to keep the center open, even if it meant selling your soul or," Nadirah's eyes dropped to BJ's crotch. "I see you meant it. There is no shame in your game, is there, BJ? I guess I'm lucky you didn't get any of the kids to lie for you or I'd really be in trouble."

"I'd never involve the kids, which is why you would have been all right."

"You're slime. You did involve the kids the minute you said I slept with one of them. Tell me, BJ, how many pieces of silver did you

get? Was it enough to keep your center open?"

BJ didn't bother to answer. Turning his back on Nadirah, he went on into the living room.

Nadirah wasn't finished. She went after BJ. "I see who you are, BJ. Your so-called dedication to education and the kids on the street is a lie. I should have seen it. When you started getting more and more recognition from the media, you reveled a little too much in it. It wasn't for the kids you kept the center up and running, it was for you, for your ego. You used the center to inject yourself with a heavy dose of the testosterone you were sorely lacking."

BJ grabbed the remote control and switched on the television, turning up the volume.

Nadirah raised her voice. "You were never the big man on campus, BJ. You had big dreams, but you never had followed through. The Empowerment Center is the only thing you've ever succeeded at, and losing it would remind you that you are a nobody. Your wife knew it, and so do I. Well, thumbs down to you, little man, for selling me out to make yourself look big."

Continuing to ignore Nadirah, BJ remained focused on the television.

"Nadirah!" Stephanie called from the top of the stairs.

Nadirah shot a hateful, intense glower up at Stephanie. Seeing her dressed in her nightgown did nothing to dissuade Nadirah from what she had only at first blush surmised—that her aunt and BJ were sleeping together.

"It's me you need to talk to," Stephanie said.

Nadirah looked back at BJ just as he turned the sound down on the television.

"Come upstairs, Nadirah."

"I'd rather sleep with scorpions. I know what they're capable of."

"But I can explain everything."

"I don't need to know." Nadirah started for the door.

"What about Lynn? Do you care about her? Don't you wanna know what happened?"

Nadirah spun around. "Don't use Lynn! If it's true that she's dead, that would be the only truth that's told in this house tonight!"

"Lynn is dead!" Stephanie croaked. "Don't you care?"

"Do you? You're the one who never gave Lynn any love, the one who never appreciated her. You let Lynn leave this earth without ever knowing a mother's love when you're the one who gave birth to her. The only person you ever cared about was yourself. Oh, let's not leave out your lover."

Nadirah glanced into the living room at BJ settled back on the sofa, right at home, watching television. She felt like charging at him and beating him over the head with her fists. How had she ever worked alongside him and called him her friend and not know the depths to which he'd sink to get what he wanted?

"You don't have to believe me," Stephanie said, "but in my own way, I loved Lynn and—"

Nadirah's eyes watered. "Save it for someone who gives a damn. Right now, I don't even care about what you and BJ have going on in here. I care about Lynn. I care about her children. Other than Uncle Lester, Lynn was the only family who cared about me. For me, she stood up to that bastard," Nadirah said, pointing at BJ, "while you laid in bed with him to plot against me, to keep me tied to you. You're despicable." Nadirah grabbed the doorknob.

"But Lynn stole from you! I didn't. I never—"

"Yeah, Lynn stole from me! But I bet she was forced to. She's dead now, isn't she?"

"She was murdered! Lynn was murdered!" Stephanie shouted, freezing Nadirah in her tracks. "That bastard, her husband killed her. But he's dead, too. She got him, and she got him good."

With her hand still on the doorknob, Nadirah couldn't let go and couldn't turn around. She could hear her aunt crying high above her head, but that was all she could hear. She was remembering those eerie moments in time when she felt Lynn's sadness and questioned whether everything was all right. Lynn always adeptly skimmed over the questions, preferring to keep the troubles of her married life to herself.

Nadirah wouldn't let herself cry. "I don't know why you're so upset," she said to Stephanie. "It's your fault Lynn's dead."

Stephanie gripped the banister. "How is it my fault? I wasn't there!"

"That's just it. If you had been there for Lynn, she might have

been able to turn to you for help. She might have been able to talk to you about her marriage."

"She was talking to you, Nadirah. Did she ask you for help?"

Nadirah wiped away her tears. "No. She didn't ask me for help. She probably didn't know how. You see, Aunt Stephanie, Lynn and I were just getting to know each other. We never had that opportunity before she and Les left home to get away from you. Again, it all comes back to you and the love you didn't give your children."

"That's enough, Nadirah!" BJ said. He came to within a foot of Nadirah. "Stephanie gets the point. You don't have to crucify her."

Nadirah looked BJ squarely in the eye. "Get out."

BJ looked up at Stephanie and then back at Nadirah. He smiled smugly. "This isn't your house."

"And neither is it yours." Nadirah opened the front door. "Get out."

BJ crossed his arms over his chest. He wasn't going anywhere.

Nadirah didn't bother to look at Stephanie. "It's either him or me."

"Then it's you," BJ said. "Stephanie don't need you. I'm here. Right, Stephanie?"

Stephanie looked down upon BJ and Nadirah. The truth was BJ could do more for her than Nadirah could ever dream of. Now that Lynn was dead, she'd probably never hear from Nadirah again.

"Stephanie, I'll help you with your daughter's children," BJ said. "I could—"

"Over my dead body!" Nadirah said. She suddenly grabbed BJ and tried to pull him to the door.

"Have you lost your mind?" BJ swatted Nadirah's hand off of his arm.

"Get out!"

"Stephanie, you better talk to this girl!"

The angry, determined look in Nadirah's eyes reminded Stephanie so much of Lester the day he came to her rescue on the roof of her building. He fought hard to save her that day, and despite how badly she treated him throughout their marriage, he was just as determined to save his children. Maybe that's what Nadirah was set on doing for Lynn's children.

"You better tell him to get out," Nadirah said.

"You're not in charge here. Stephanie, tell her I'm staying."

Stephanie sighed in resignation. "For the time being, BJ, maybe it's for the best that you leave."

Not expecting to hear those words, BJ stared up at Stephanie. Nadirah opened the door wider.

"BJ," Stephanie said, "I'll call you tomorrow."

Confused, BJ kept looking at Stephanie.

"Are your feelings hurt, BJ, or is that desperation I see in your eyes?" Nadirah asked.

"Go to hell."

"Actually, if you go there, I'm sure you'll find some lonely old lady to work your magic on."

BJ looked hatefully at Nadirah. "You were never worth my time."

"Wow, BJ. I don't remember you saying that when your eyes were rolling back in your head and you were calling out my name and telling me how much you loved me."

Stephanie gasped, drawing BJ's attention to her.

"She's lying. I never slept with her."

"He's right, Aunt Stephanie. He didn't sleep with me. He was wide awake screwing me all night."

Again Stephanie gasped.

"That's a damn lie! Stephanie, I swear, I never touched her!"

"Aunt Stephanie, does he still work his mouth like a fish when he's about to come?"

"Dammit, BJ! You told me you never slept with her!"

"I didn't! She's lying."

Stephanie closed her eyes.

"Stephanie, don't listen to her! She's lying. She's trying to drive a wedge between us."

"My, BJ," Nadirah said, feigning innocence. "Why would I do such a terrible thing?"

"Stephanie, I never slept with her. She worked for me at the center. That's all."

Stephanie shook her head. She'd be lying if she said she didn't believe Nadirah when she did, but God forgive her, she still wanted BJ. But if she allowed him to stay, Nadirah would know how desperate she

was for a man.

"Goodness, BJ," Nadirah said, "Don't you ever tell the truth?"

"Stephanie. Stephanie, she's trying to get to you. She's trying to upset you. She's—"

"That he's right about," Nadirah said. "I do wanna upset you. Both of you."

"See! She admits it. She's lying."

"Get it right, BJ. You're the liar. In fact, whatever you two got going here is built upon nothing but a bed of lies."

"Shut up, Nadirah! I—"

"BJ!" Stephanie said. "There were to be no lies between us."

"Stephanie—"

"Aunt Stephanie, I think he's about to tell another lie or maybe he's about to start begging. BJ, remember how you got down on your knees to beg me to sleep with you a second time, which, thank God I didn't."

BJ started buttoning his shirt. "It was the biggest mistake of my life."

"Ditto," Nadirah said.

BJ busily tucked in his shirttail. "The hell with it."

Nadirah would have laughed at BJ's humiliation if the whole thing wasn't so sad.

From the living room, BJ quickly retrieved his shoes. At the front door he turned back to Nadirah.

"You—"

SLAP!

Totally taken aback by the slap, BJ stumbled backwards out the door. Before he could get his footing and react, Nadirah slammed the door in his face, but BJ tried to have the last word. He slammed his fist into the locked door. He banged on it several times, calling her names that men with no scruples called women they have no respect for. Nadirah didn't care. BJ was a man she'd never respect again. She looked up at Stephanie.

"Nadirah?"

"No, I don't want to know. I'm here for Lynn and nothing more. Where are her children?"

Chapter 33

There is something not right about the sun shining so bright on a day so sad as the day Lynn was laid to rest deep in her grave of dirt and darkness. It should have been a dreary, rainy, overcast day, then Nadirah would not have wondered if Lynn would have been playing in the park with her children or at the beach splashing them with water. Lynn lay alone in her grave, no coffin above her or below her. Byron was buried elsewhere by his family on a day that neither Nadirah nor Stephanie cared about. While they had no say whether Lynn and Byron's spirits found their way into eternity together, in the real world, they could make sure that Lynn and Byron's earthly bodies were not buried within a mile of each other. As it was, they took with them into their graves the secrets of their marriage. What went on within their marital walls they shared with no one outside. What was known for sure was that Byron had been hurting Lynn for years. Her body was a road map of scars that the coroner classified as evidence of abuse. Lynn had died by Byron's hands just as he had died by hers, except Lynn's action was deemed self-defense. It was hard for Nadirah to truly comprehend the calamity that would bring Lynn and Byron to that fateful moment where the decision to kill or be killed was determined.

It was a month before poor little Erin could sleep through the night and stop talking about the night her mother and father died.

"How come my daddy hurt Mommy?" she would often ask out of nowhere.

Erin's therapist said it was likely that Erin would, in time, forget that day, but Nadirah didn't think so. It seemed more likely that Erin would always bear the scar of Lynn's last hours on her soul. Fortunately, it was blessed sleep that spared Byron Junior and Liz such damnation. Of course, being so young, four and two, was also a blessing. Neither knew to shed a tear at their mother's funeral.

Often enough, Nadirah wondered if Lynn's last thoughts

were of her children and who would rear them in her stead. Never in a million years would Lynn imagine that her children would end up living in the very house she herself had grown up in. Surely, she must be turning in her grave. The coroner put Lynn's death at two minutes before Byron's which meant that, technically, Lynn predeceased Byron, giving his family the legal upper hand, but Aunt Stephanie fought like a bat out of proverbial hell to keep Byron's family from getting custody of Lynn's children. While Nadirah was mindful of the life she'd had with Aunt Stephanie and hated her alliance with BJ, she had to think about Lynn's children. She had no choice but to stand shoulder to shoulder with the woman she vowed to never even share a meal with, in an effort to do what was best for Erin, Byron Junior, and Liz. Besides, Byron's family wasn't the best—one of his sisters was raising five children on welfare; the other had only one child, but she said outright, "Unless a check comes with each of them kids, I'm not taking them." If she had any sense, she would have known that each child was entitled to a social security check. And then there was Byron's brother Craig. He was a security guard barely making it with his family of four. His wife nixed the idea of Byron's kids living with them under any circumstances. While Byron's parents were both retired, they each had health issues to deal with. But it didn't matter, Nadirah wasn't letting any of Byron's family get their hands on Lynn's children.

"I'll take the children," Nadirah had said the night Lynn died. She never considered once how she'd manage.

Stephanie stopped crying at that moment and looked at the picture she held of Lynn. "The kids are my responsibility."

"But, Aunt Stephanie, you're sixty five years old. You can't handle three small children. And speaking bluntly, why would you take Lynn's children when you never wanted Lynn and Les?"

Stephanie closed her eyes. The truth was never a sweet pill. "This is different."

"How? You took me in after my parents died and you treated me worse than you treated your own. So how are you going to do better by Lynn's children? You can't. Uncle Lester isn't here to bail you out."

"I'm not like I used to be."

Nadirah almost laughed. "Aunt Stephanie, you haven't changed.

You're no more loving than you were twenty, thirty years ago, or even a month ago. And what about tonight? BJ, the man you conspired with to hurt me, just left here three hours ago. You'd sleep with the devil himself to get what you want. How are you going to take in Lynn's children and miraculously become mother of the year?"

"I can do it."

Nadirah felt like she was talking to a wall. "Aunt Stephanie, I guarantee you, Lynn would want me to take her children, or maybe even Les. He might want them."

"I doubt it. Les has cut all ties to this family."

"Humph. I wonder why?"

"Nadirah, please don't make this worse than it already is."

"I'm not the problem, Aunt Stephanie, you are. Lynn's children need love. They need—"

"I can give them everything they need."

"Love? How? Aunt Stephanie, you're not capable of loving those children. I'm taking them!"

Tears rolled down Stephanie's cheeks. "They're my grandchildren! They belong with me! "

"No, no," Nadirah said, adamantly shaking her head. "I can't let you take them. I would never forgive myself if I allowed you to do to Lynn's children what you did to us." Nadirah teared. "If I have to fight you for them, I will." Nadirah got up to leave. "I'll be back when—"

"I'm sorry!"

Nadirah stopped cold. She looked back at Stephanie's tear-washed face.

"Forgive me. Please, forgive me."

Amazed, Nadirah stared at the woman who, so often when she was a little girl, made her feel like she wanted to die.

"Please give me another chance," Stephanie said softly. "Please."

When her own tears came Nadirah turned away. She didn't want to forgive or forget how she had been treated.

"Nadirah, please hear me out. I have to have another chance to do what's right by Lynn, by you. Please, I don't wanna fight with you. If you and I fight, what good will that do the children?"

"Why didn't you think about that when I was a child, when

Lynn and Les were kids? You fought with Uncle Lester all the time. This house wasn't a happy home, it was a miserable existence."

"But I can make up for that. I can do better. Just give me a chance."

Nadirah dried her eyes. "But I can't let—"

"You can help me, Nadirah. You can teach me to be better for Lynn's children."

"No...I can't—"

"I swear before God, Nadirah. I'll do everything you tell me to. God's giving me another chance. I need to do this. I need to do for Lynn's children what I didn't do for her." Stephanie slipped out of her chair onto her knees, shocking Nadirah.

"Please, help me do what's right. Please."

"Aunt Stephanie, get up." Nadirah went to her and took her arm. "Get up!"

Stephanie let Nadirah help her up off the floor, but then she threw her arms around Nadirah, hugging her for the first time in her life. Nadirah was so taken aback, she stood like statue. Her own arms hung at her side. In her head, she kept saying, *Oh, my God. Oh, my God.*

"Please forgive me," Stephanie held onto Nadirah and cried for the loss of the daughter she'd never even touched.

That unbelievable night is forever etched in Nadirah's mind. Seeing her aunt down on her knees amazed her, but when Aunt Stephanie hugged her and asked for her forgiveness, she was blown away. Never in a million years would she have foreseen such an extraordinarily humbling moment from such a cold woman. And what's more, when Aunt Stephanie began talking about her marriage to Uncle Lester, about his betrayal when she was pregnant, about how she got revenge on him, and about how she regretted disowning her own children, Nadirah was left with a great sense of understanding as to why Lynn had died. Lynn had died to save her mother. Until Lynn's death, Aunt Stephanie never cared about anyone but herself.

By the time Nadirah left her aunt's house, she had relented and agreed to help her get custody of Lynn's children, but not without a warning.

"Mistreat them, hurt them, abuse them, you lose them."

Stephanie considered the warning. "I won't do anything to harm

them, but if you're here to help me, I know they'll be okay."

"Oh, I won't be a stranger. I'll keep a close watch on those children and you, too."

In the weeks that followed, it was Les and his attorneys who took charge of Lynn's estate, what little there was. The house was all they had. Byron's family circled like vultures picking at anything and everything that wasn't nailed down. Even on the day of Lynn's funeral, they were at the house carrying out personal and household items like they'd hit the jackpot at a flea market. Thank God Les had acted fast in securing the Mercedes Byron had just bought. He returned the car to the dealer posthaste and put the refund in Nadirah's hand. Fortunately, Byron had put the money he and Lynn took from Nadirah in his and Lynn's joint savings account, which Les' attorneys were able to hold lien against, blocking Byron's family from laying claim. There was only two hundred and sixty thousand dollars left, but Nadirah didn't stress herself about it. Lynn and Byron had already paid a hefty fine for their crime against her. For all Nadirah knew, her money may have been the reason Lynn and Byron's lives ended so tragically.

As soon as the authorities released the house, Les put it on the market, and within a week he had a buyer. He was waiting now for the closing in early August. The proceeds would pay off the rest of Byron's debt and leave about two hundred thousand for Lynn's children.

Funny, no one ever referred to Lynn's children as Byron's children. He was their father, but his legacy was not going to be discussed in terms of how much he loved them because he didn't. If anything, what he took from them, their mother, is what he'd be remembered for.

Austin was Byron's best friend and he had a hard time understanding how he had not known the true soul of the man Lynn lived with. He knew nothing about the violent man who beat Lynn and, in the end, took her life. After returning to New York after Lynn's funeral, Austin put off going back to California for a week.

"Maybe if I had given Byron the money he needed," he said. "Lynn might be alive. They both might be alive."

"Austin, you don't own any part of Lynn's or Byron's death. It all belongs to Byron. Their problems went beyond finances. Byron was abusing Lynn. None of us knew this, and the truth is, even if we did, we might not have been able to save her. By keeping silent, Lynn gave

Byron the power to abuse her."

Still, Austin didn't understand. "Byron and I used to talk about everything. Until he got married, I knew everything about him. He didn't have the best childhood; his father and mother were both uneducated, minimum wage earners who struggled to bring Byron and his siblings up. He talked about his father beating his mother, beating them, about how he hated it."

"Yes, but that's probably why he turned out to be an abuser."

"No. Byron swore he'd never lay hand on his wife and children. He hated his father for hitting his mother. We talked about that at length. That's why I don't understand how—"

"Byron probably never dealt with what his father did to his mother. Did he ever talk to a therapist, a psychiatrist?"

Austin had to admit, "Byron said only crazy people went to shrinks."

"Then he should have gone to one. Byron and his whole family should have been in therapy. Austin, people just don't seem to realize that when children are abused, mentally and physically, wounds and scars form on their psyches that don't heal on their own. They don't fade away with time like the scars on our knees. Byron was wounded by his father, yet it was in his father's footsteps he tred. He knew no other way."

"He did. Byron knew better. Before he married Lynn, all he could talk about was having children with her, wanting a close-knit family. Nadirah, Byron loved Lynn. I know this. I remember when he first met her. He couldn't sleep without dreaming about her. He said once, being with Lynn was as close as he'd ever get to heaven."

"Well, he was right about that. God has the last say, but I'm sure he doesn't like that Byron killed Lynn."

Austin's eyes welled up. "Lynn was good people, and so was Byron—a long time ago."

Austin got up quickly from the sofa and started to leave the living room. Nadirah hurriedly got up herself.

"Austin."

Austin stopped, but he kept his back to Nadirah. "I need a minute," he said.

Nadirah went and stood in front of him. Austin didn't back away

and he didn't ask her what she wanted. They looked deep into each other's teary eyes and saw that they needed each other. They stepped into each other's arms and enclosed their pain up in a warm embrace of comfort. Together they cried, holding onto each other, siphoning the strength they each needed to understand what had gone wrong in Lynn and Byron's lives. Neither felt shame or embarrassment that they cried, but both felt a pulling of much more than the comfort they were getting and giving. Still holding on to each other, Austin and Nadirah again looked into each other's eyes and this time they saw and felt an intense desire. They kissed and that kiss confirmed a smothering desire to feel something sweeter, something more than pain.

"I will never hurt you," Austin said.

Kissing Austin again, Nadirah let him know that she believed him. As she and Austin climbed the stairs, they still held on to each other, letting go wasn't an option. Without questioning which bedroom to use, they both headed for his.

Chapter 34

How strange life was. Nadirah found herself spending more time at Aunt Stephanie's house than at the townhouse. Austin had long since gone back to California, but they talked every day. They had made love every day that he'd been in town, and talking to him was like making love without touching. Lynn's death had brought them together. Whether it was permanent or not, Nadirah didn't dare dwell on it. Austin's divorce was going to be final in December, but he might not want anything permanent again. Who could blame him? Erma Gray could make a fat man swear off of dessert.

With school out for the summer, Nadirah had more time to help out with the kids. While Bree and Erin had become the best of friends, Byron Junior and Liz cleaved to each other as if they understood they had to be each other's best friend. Aunt Stephanie hired Barbette full time, not as her home health aide, but as her housekeeper.

"I'm not doing laundry, I'm not cooking, and I'm not cleaning up behind all these kids," Stephanie said. "I never did it before, I won't do it now."

Nadirah let it go unsaid that Aunt Stephanie had never really been a mother before. Yet, surprisingly, she wasn't doing too badly with Lynn's children. Her acid tongue seemed to have disappeared. She was rather kind to the kids, especially Byron Junior and Liz. She doted on them, probably because they were so young. If anything, Nadirah worried that Aunt Stephanie would spoil Lynn's children beyond repair. As for Erin, Aunt Stephanie spoke to her more like she was a teenager and not so much like she was a little girl. She was nice to her, gave her everything she wanted, but Nadirah kept putting her in check to not let Erin grow up too fast or too spoiled.

It was amazing to observe Aunt Stephanie being a much better grandmother than she had been a mother. Too bad Lynn wasn't there to see for herself the rebirth of her own mother. Just as aston-

ishing to Nadirah was how well she and her aunt were getting along. Even when they disagreed, no sparks flew and the old Aunt Stephanie never resurfaced. Why did Lynn have to die for her mother to wake up and grow a heart?

When Nadirah first told Aunt Stephanie about Bree, she expected a negative response, but was floored when Aunt Stephanie said, "I'd like to meet her." Wow. If Nadirah learned anything since Lynn's death, it was never think for a minute that any one man or woman was a lost cause. Of course, she'd have to work at convincing herself that Erma Gray wasn't a lost cause. The woman was relentless. She was back to calling Austin every day asking for another chance.

"I'm moving on," Austin had said more than once.

Secretly, Nadirah hoped Austin meant he was moving on with her. They still hadn't talked about it, and she really didn't want to. The truth is she didn't see them moving on beyond where they were. She and Austin were on two different coasts and everyone knew that long distance relationships rarely worked. Even if there was the possibility of them coming together, Nadirah couldn't help but worry about the future. All relationships worked well in the beginning. Hadn't Lynn and Byron's? Hadn't Aunt Stephanie and Uncle Lester's? It was after the loving, after the newness that so many relationships went sour. Nadirah didn't know if she could handle a good thing going bad. Maybe it was best she left well enough alone.

For the time being, Nadirah's life was pretty busy helping out with Lynn's kids and taking care of Bree. ACS was moving slow in determining Bree's fate, but that was all the better for Nadirah. Mrs. Hamilton wasn't disclosing what her investigation had uncovered about Erma Gray, but whatever it was, Erma had not been given custody of Bree. At every opportunity, Nadirah reminded Mrs. Hamilton that she wanted to adopt Bree and, unbeknownst to Mrs. Hamilton, Nadirah made it her business to check on Dorothy Morrison to see if her prognosis had changed. It hadn't. If anything, Dorothy was pretty much the same. According to Beverly, Dorothy still ranted nonsensically while bitting down on her lip. In-between, she slipped into a cocoon of silence, sometimes staring, sometimes sleeping.

It was Beverly who volunteered to visit Dorothy at Bellevue once every two weeks since Nadirah was forbidden. Beverly combed

Dorothy's hair, helped feed her, and at times, helped change her clothes.

Beverly ate the last of her salad. "Today, one of the nurses told me that Dorothy is always a bit more relaxed after my visits. She doesn't bite down on her lip as much."

"That's a good thing," Nadirah said, "but I hope it doesn't change ACS's plans for putting Bree up for adoption."

"It won't. Aside from Dorothy being incapable of parenting Bree again, she doesn't want her. She says it all the time."

"Don't you think that's strange? Why would Dorothy have Bree if she didn't want her?"

Beverly shook her head. "Nadirah, a lot of women have babies they don't want."

"True."

"But from what little I can discern from Dorothy's rantings, something terrible happened in her life since having Bree. It's eating her up inside."

Nadirah picked up her empty salad bowl and carried it to the sink. On a rare night, she was having dinner with Beverly while William, Beverly's husband, was out of town and Bree was having a sleepover with Erin at Aunt Stephanie's.

"Beverly, unless Dorothy is so far gone her doctors can't pull her back, why can't they get her to tell them why she's so distressed?"

"They can't force her to talk." Beverly carried her own bowl to the sink. "Just like they can't glue her mouth shut to keep her from biting her lip."

"I wonder why she hurts herself like that."

"I think she's trying to punish herself."

"Because of what she did to Bree?"

"Perhaps. But whatever Dorothy has to say has to come in her own time. Which reminds me, the other day, she said something quite interesting."

"And that was?"

Beverly and Nadirah both started out of the kitchen, heading for the front of Beverly's tastefully decorated two-bedroom apartment.

"Well, first she asked if I knew Austin."

Sitting down on the sofa, Nadirah asked, "Out of the blue she asked you that?"

"Yep. She said, 'Do you know Austin'? I said, 'No, I don't, but I know someone who does.'" Beverly sat low on the hassock across from Nadirah.

"And she said?"

"She said, 'I gotta see Austin. Erma won't let me see Austin. Austin likes Bree. He'll take care of Bree.' Then she clammed up. She went back to that place she hides in. She went back to nibbling on her lip and rocking."

"Poor thing."

"Nadirah, I'm telling you, it was as if she had a moment of clarity. She was looking me straight in the eye when she talked about Austin, Erma, and Bree, but then that focus was gone in a flash."

"Yes, but in that moment, she remembered who really cared about her daughter—Austin. Not her sister."

"But why would her sister keep her from seeing Austin?"

"Probably being controlling and mean. Austin feels for Dorothy, but he deplores his wife."

"He is divorcing the woman. In fact, it wouldn't surprise me if Mrs. Gray wasn't at the root of her sister's problems."

"I'd bet on it," Nadirah said.

"Did you know when Dorothy was admitted, her sister visited her?"

"Erma was the one who found Dorothy at Bellevue, remember."

"Yes, but did you know she visited Dorothy three times and each of those times Dorothy lost it? She'd get hysterical and would have to be sedated."

"Who told you that?"

"The patient in the next bed. She said Dorothy didn't start biting her lip until her evil sister came to see her, which is why Dorothy's doctor banned Erma from seeing her."

"Mrs. Hamilton needs to know that."

"She may already know."

"We'll see because Erma's total focus is Austin and Bree. My fear is what she won't do to get them back."

Beverly sighed. "Too scary to think about, but I tell you what, Nadirah, my visits with Dorothy started as a favor to you, but I find

myself hoping that I can help her."

"That's not surprising, Beverly. That's who you are."

"Thanks, but each time I see Dorothy, I remind myself that, although she tried to hurt Bree, something had to have driven her to that act because, personally, I don't think she was as bad a mother as we first believed. There's more to her story, she just can't tell it."

Musingly, Nadirah agreed. "Part of it might be her guilt about not wanting Bree."

"That's possible." Beverly took a dinner mint from the candy bowl on the coffee table. "But speaking of Bree, I have to thank you."

"For what? You've done so much for me in these past months, it's you I need to be thanking."

"Well, you have, but I have to thank you for opening William's eyes."

"How did I do that?"

"By allowing me to bring Bree into our lives. William likes having Bree around so much, he told me to look into," Beverly began welling up, "adopting a child for us."

"Oh, Beverly, that's wonderful."

"William is so good with Bree. You should see him. He's patient, he's thoughtful, he's fun. Nadirah, he'd be such a good father."

"So are you looking to adopt a little girl, a baby?"

Beverly sighed. "No, I think I'm past the wanting the baby stage. Four years old and up is what I'm looking for, and not a girl, but a boy—William's special request. I think he has visions of watching basketball games with a son."

"Then by all means, get William a little boy."

"We're already in the process. We start our parenting classes in two weeks."

"Oh, Beverly." Nadirah got up. "I'm so happy for you."

Beverly and Nadirah embraced as better friends now than before Bree came into their lives.

"Okay," Beverly said, "my last thought on Dorothy—ask Austin to visit her. She might talk to him."

Nadirah agreed. "I'll mention it to him when he calls tonight, but I already know that he won't be back in New York for another three weeks. He's coming for Bree's birthday party."

Beverly smiled. "Was that a twinkle I saw in your eyes?"

"I think I'll take that as my cue to leave," Nadirah said, picking up her pocketbook. She hadn't said much about Austin to Beverly. Certainly not about them sleeping together. That was not a complication she needed to divulge, but she was ticking off every minute up to the second she could be with Austin again.

Chapter 35

Two weeks till the end of August and Nadirah was starting to breathe a whole lot easier as far as Bree was concerned. Making it to the end of each weekday with no call from Mrs. Hamilton was like waiting out a storm. It wasn't like she wasn't expecting to hear from Mrs. Hamilton, it was more like she was hoping ACS would forget about Bree and lose her paperwork. So many kids had slipped through the cracks of the system and stayed in foster homes for years, why not Bree? But Mrs. Hamilton didn't forget about Bree. Wednesday afternoon, at four-forty five P.M. the phone rang. The minute Nadirah heard Mrs. Hamilton's voice she knew immediately what she had to say wasn't going to be what she wanted to hear.

"I'll be picking Bree up Friday morning at ten. Please have her packed."

Nadirah's heart sank. "Packed? Why? Where is she going?"

"Miss Lewis, I believe I informed you that Bree could be moved at a moment's notice."

"But you can't just take her like that."

"Two days is sufficient notice."

"No, it's not. Mrs. Hamilton, Bree is fine here."

Sitting at the dining room table no longer interested in finishing her early dinner, Bree began listening to what Nadirah was saying.

"You can't just take her without—"

"We could go around in circles, Miss Lewis, and we'd come back full circle to ACS removing Bree from your home. I'm sure you'll do your best to prepare Bree for leaving your care, and I, of course, will speak with her also."

"Mrs. Hamilton, that's not the point. Why take Bree at all? I told you I wanted to adopt her."

Bree began to cry.

"And that's commendable, but ACS, as Bree's legal guardian,

has determined that Bree be placed in a different home more suited for her."

"Are you saying my home isn't suitable for Bree?"

"Miss Lewis, I won't argue with you over this matter. You allowed yourself to become too attached to her."

"Of course, I've become attached to Bree. I love her."

"That's all well and good, Miss Lewis, but you lost sight of your purpose in Bree's life. You were only temporarily housing her. ACS—"

"Mrs. Hamilton, ACS has to reconsider taking Bree from me for Bree's sake. She's happy with me. She's a different child from—"

"Miss Lewis, please have Bree ready. Good—"

"No, wait! Mrs. Hamilton, Saturday is Bree's birthday. I have a birthday party planned for her. She can't miss her own birthday party."

Crying more, Bree lay her head on top of her arms on the table.

"Miss Lewis, I'm sorry, but Friday is the day."

"But I'm getting ready to buy a house for myself and Bree. Mrs. Hamilton, Bree needs to stay with me."

"Miss Lewis, Friday morning at 10:00. You must comply."

"Where are you taking her? Where's she going?"

"Miss Lewis, I'm not at liberty to—"

"Please! Mrs. Hamilton, just tell me Bree hasn't been placed with Mrs. Gray."

Bree lifted her head at the mention of her aunt's name.

"Miss Lewis, do I need to remind you that ACS's goal is to first place children—"

"You can't put Bree in that woman's hands. She's—"

Bree got up from the table.

"Miss Lewis! Please have Bree ready Friday morning."

"Mrs. Hamilton, I need to speak with your supervisor! Who's your supervisor?"

Dead silence filled Nadirah's ear.

"Mrs. Hamilton?"

Silence.

"Mrs. Hamilton? Oh, come on! Please. Don't do this." Nadirah clutched the telephone to her chest as she slumped back against the wall to keep from falling to the floor. She felt powerless. When she took Bree she wanted to help, but she had no idea she'd end up loving her so much

she wasn't going to be able to let go.

Lost in her own anguish, Nadirah didn't hear Bree come into the living room until Bree was a foot away from her crying.

"Oh, sweetie." Nadirah hugged Bree close. She couldn't stop Bree from crying because she couldn't stop her own self. "It'll be all right. I promise, Bree, it'll be all right." Nadirah didn't believe her own words.

"I don't wanna go," Bree cried.

"I know, sweetie, and I don't want you to."

Riiiing!

Hoping against hope that Mrs. Hamilton was calling back, Nadirah quickly answered the telephone which was still in her hand.

"Hello!"

"What's wrong?" Austin asked.

"ACS is taking Bree. They're giving her to your wife."

"Oh, hell no! That's not happening."

"Austin, I don't know what to do. I can't let them take her."

"I can hear Bree crying."

"She's right here. Austin, what am I going to do?"

"When are they taking her?"

"Friday. Mrs. Hamilton knows I want to adopt Bree. If she hands Bree over to your wife, Bree's life is going to—"

"You need to talk to an attorney."

"I have one. He's—"

"No, I want you to talk to my attorney. William Bennett. He's downtown on Broadway. Twenty-five Broadway. I'll call him. He's the best. Maybe he can come up with a stay or something. Hang up, I'll call you back."

With her arms still around Bree, Nadirah took Bree over to the sofa and together they sat. Beginning to feel hopeful, she dried her own face and then Bree's. She gently rocked her as she waited anxiously for Austin to call her back. If there was a way, Austin would find it.

Riiii—

"Hello!"

"Take down this number."

"Wait a minute." Nadirah untangled herself from Bree. "You stay here," she said to Bree. "I'll be right back." With the phone still to her

ear, Nadirah raced upstairs to her bedroom. "Can he help me?"

"You have a pen?"

Nadirah dumped her pocketbook onto the bed. She grabbed a pen and the small writing pad that tumbled out. "What's his number?"

"William Bennett. (212) 555-4000. Call him now. Tell him everything. I'm taking a red-eye out tonight. I'll be there first thing in the morning. I'll go with you to meet with William."

"Austin, thank you."

"No, thank you for looking out for Dorothy's kid. I'll see you in the morning."

Although Nadirah disconnected herself from Austin by way of the phone line, she in no way felt disconnected from him in her heart. She was falling in love with Austin, but she didn't know if he felt the same way. But this was not the time to dwell on that matter, she had to take care of Bree. Punching in William Bennett's telephone number, Nadirah took a deep breath and said a silent prayer.

Chapter 36

By the close of business Thursday evening, Austin's attorney had secured a Temporary Restraining Order against ACS stopping them from taking Bree, along with a Notice of Motion to Show Cause as to why Bree should be removed from Nadirah's care at all. Once again Bree was assigned a court appointed guardian to protect her rights, which Nadirah had no problem with. The Family Court judge set a hearing date of September 20th to hear the case. For the moment Bree was safe. Friday morning, from Mrs. Hamilton Nadirah heard not a word, but from Erma she heard a number of choice curse words that would scorch and burn the ears of the angels watching over Bree. Nadirah responded to the assault the way she thought best—she hung up. Seconds later when Erma called back, Austin took the call.

"Shut up and listen for once in your life!"

Better him than me, Nadirah thought. She left the room, but she didn't go far.

"I don't know what game you're playing and why all of a sudden you want Bree when you and I both know, you don't give a da...listen! Dammit, Erma, listen! We both know you don't give a damn about Bree or me. You and I aren't together because of your lies, your games, and your craziness, but I'm telling you right now, cut this crap out! Stop calling here!" Austin disconnected the call and left the phone line open, making it impossible for any incoming calls to get through.

Nadirah stepped back into the room. "That's not going to stop her."

"A night in jail will. If she shows up here acting a fool, I'm

having her arrested."

"That'll make her real happy."

"I'll be real happy myself when December gets here. Our divorce will be final."

"How long were you married?"

"Nine damn years," Austin said grumpily. "I can't believe I hung in there that long. That woman seriously messed up my life."

Nadirah watched as Austin's face reflected the turmoil he was feeling inside. "Austin, if you don't want to talk about it, you—"

"Erma was so different when we met," Austin said. "She was fun, she was intelligent, she was loving, she was…she was—"

"Beautiful," Nadirah said, helping Austin out.

"Yeah, if you don't know her, she's still beautiful to look at, but, damn! Being married to Erma, living with her, was like living with Venus one minute and Medusa the next. For the life of me, I can't figure out how, for two years before we got married, she hid her true self from me. Each year after we got married, she steadily got worse."

Nadirah quietly wondered whether Austin had worn blinders those two years and simply chose to not see Erma's flaws.

"If I could take back the last nine years, God, I'd—" Austin couldn't go on. Emotionally weary, he hung his head. He closed his eyes and began to rewind the ugliness of his marriage to Erma.

Nadirah patiently waited for Austin to speak in his own time. After half a minute, she went to the kitchen and came back with a glass of ginger ale for each of them. Austin took his glass and took a hearty swig, while Nadirah again waited for him to continue talking.

"I've worked hard for everything I've ever wanted in life, but my marriage to Erma was the hardest I ever worked, and in the end, I failed."

"Austin, but it's not your failure," Nadirah said. "At least, not alone."

"Yeah, we both failed and I saw it coming six months after we got married."

"What did she do?"

Austin chuckled dryly. "Everything I didn't like. She stopped cooking. She demanded that I take her out to dinner every night and she wasn't talking about to Burger King. I went along with her for about a

week thinking she was hormonal or something. I figured she'd come to
her senses. She didn't. I put my foot down and told her money wasn't
flowing like that, and if need be, I'd cook dinner every night my damn
self. That lasted one night. Erma threw the steak and Spanish rice I prepared in the garbage."

"She didn't like your cooking?"

"She never tasted a morsel. And she even went for my plate, but
I dared her to touch it. I ate my dinner that night and started cooking for
myself every night thereafter."

"Did she ever eat with you?"

"Sure, when she brought in take-out."

"That sounds so disjointed."

"Nadirah, where Erma got her highfaluting ideas from, I don't
know, but, believe it or not, she got worse. Somebody must have told
her that a husband was supposed to lavish a high style of living on her.
Suddenly, she wanted a housekeeper, she wanted a car service to take
her to her job, which she didn't show up to half the time, and she wanted me to give her carte blanche to my bank accounts."

"Did you?"

"My mother and father didn't raise an idiot. Way before I got
married, my father used to tell me to wait two years before putting my
wife's name on anything. He said it would take that long to find out who
I was really married to. It took six months for Erma to go stupid on me.
When I saw how she was spending, I didn't put her name on a damn
thing, especially my bank accounts and this house."

"Something to be said about listening to one's parents?"

"Damn straight." Austin again drank from his glass, emptying
it. He set his glass down hard. "Erma spent every penny she earned and
was trying to work her way though my money. I got her straight on that,
but then she started clocking me. If I was a minute late calling her or
coming home, she went on the warpath accusing me of sleeping around.
It was a nightmare. She'd call my office; call my friends, anyone she
could think of to grill them about where I was. It was humiliating."

"Sounds like insecurity."

"She was unstable, Nadirah. When I look back, I can't believe I
didn't see it, and I can't believe I didn't end it sooner."

"Austin, you were trying to make your marriage work."

"No, I was laboring under some stupid fantasy that I could handle Erma, that our marriage was not so unique. Everyone had problems. I thought things would eventually get better, but after each miscarriage, things got progressively worse."

"But if things were so bad between you, why try to have a baby?"

"That's what I said at first. I tried to stop having sex with Erma to keep her from getting pregnant, but she wouldn't have it. If I tried to wear a condom, she'd throw a fit. It was hell. Finally, I gave her an ultimatum. See a psychiatrist or it's over. When she realized I was about to walk, she asked me to find her a doctor. I did. I went with her. That's when she was diagnosed as bipolar."

"But, Austin, how could she hide something like that when you were going with her? She had to have had episodes of depression or manic highs."

"She did. It was me. I didn't recognize what I thought were mood swings for what they really were—bipolar episodes, and to tell you the truth, Erma didn't know herself. When she was finally diagnosed, she couldn't accept it. She wouldn't stay on her medication or keep her appointments, which told me she was in denial."

"Maybe she was scared."

"Scared my ass!" Austin said irritably. "Erma was pigheaded. She was obstinate. She refused to follow directives, but in the process, she made my life a living hell. It just went from bad to worse at the speed of light. She started doing sneaky things like taking money from my wallet when I was asleep, and stealing my jewelry—my watch, my rings, oh, my cufflinks. I had a pair of ivory cufflinks left to me by my grandfather who got them from his father, my great-grandfather."

"You never got them back?"

"To this day, Erma denies ever seeing them, which is a lie."

Nadirah could only shake her head.

"And I'll tell you something else—I can't prove it, but I know it happened."

"What's that?"

"Erma was drugging me."

"Oh, come on."

Austin raised his right hand. "On my mother's grave."

"But how? You weren't eating her cooking."

"She brought in take-out, remember? Chinese food, pizza, whatever she felt like. We ate together then, that's when she was most tolerable."

"So are you saying when Erma brought in take-out, the two of you could sit down like normal husband and wife and talk and get along, but then she'd drug you?"

"I swear before God, Nadirah. I didn't think Erma could do anything to prepared take-out, and actually, I never considered the possibility of her drugging me. All I know is there were times when I would wake up thinking I had dozed while watching television or last remembered that I was eating dinner and it would be the next morning."

"I know you asked her about it."

"Damn right," Austin said. "And, of course, she denied my 'ludicrous,' as she called it, accusations. She said I fell asleep and she couldn't wake me because I was so tired. Nadirah, I've never been that sound a sleeper that I couldn't be awakened."

"You were suspicious of her, but you let her serve you food and drink a second time?"

"I didn't know. When it happened the third time, that's when I knew something was wrong. That's when I ended it. It was too much craziness for me."

"But why did she do it?"

"I don't know. She always denied doing it so I never got a reason."

"But what about her sister? Dorothy's in Bellevue." Nadirah was thinking about Bree. "Does mental illness run in the family?"

"Again, I don't know. They don't have much family, at least not in New York City. Their father walked out when Erma was fourteen and Dorothy was about one. Their mother was working out on Long Island as a live-in domestic and babysitter, but she died when Erma was seventeen and Dorothy was four."

"Were they brought up in the system?"

"They were supported by the system, but they lived with their grandmother and an uncle until the grandmother died, but Dorothy was twenty-three by then. She was able to hold onto the apartment and she convinced her social worker that she could take care of Dorothy who

was nine years old. The uncle was long gone somewhere so it was Erma and Dorothy."

Nadirah considered the impact on Dorothy at age nine being raised by her big sister. "They had each other, but it had to be rough."

"Erma said she handled it. She said she had always been in charge. Her grandmother was sick most of the time so she literally raised Dorothy by herself anyway."

"No wonder Dorothy's so messed up."

"Yes, but to be fair to Dorothy, she was never quite off the wall like Erma, but…"

Nadirah never liked anything that came behind the word "but."

"… she had her moments. She was moody."

"If Erma and Dorothy were so close, why did you see so little of Dorothy? She must have still been very young?"

"Erma was twenty-eight when we got married so Dorothy was about fifteen. After we were married, Erma still had her grandmother's apartment, which is where Dorothy was living. Erma didn't want Dorothy to live with us and refused to let me bring her in here. She said men couldn't be trusted around young girls."

"She didn't trust you?"

"Nope, and I didn't strain myself trying to convince her otherwise. Dorothy stayed at the apartment until Erma threw her out years later. She said she couldn't keep carrying Dorothy. She gave up the apartment."

"So she threw her out on the street?"

"For two weeks, I think. Then she put her in a studio apartment on 117th Street. Erma used to go there to see her, but they talked several times a day by phone. Once in a while, Erma brought Dorothy over here and I'd get to see them interact. Erma controlled Dorothy. I talked to Erma about it and she said I didn't understand their relationship. She said Dorothy couldn't function without her, and it was just as well because she knew what was best for her little sister. But I'm telling you, Nadirah, it was more than that. Erma got Dorothy to do anything she wanted her to."

"I kinda got that impression from things Dorothy said."

"I'm surprised she said anything at all about Erma. She always acted like she was afraid of Erma. She never said anything against her.

I remember coming in from work one evening and walking in on Erma browbeating Dorothy like she was a little kid being scolded by her mother. She had to be at least eighteen. It seems Erma wanted Dorothy to do something she didn't wanna do. Dorothy was crying. She was literally pleading with Erma to not make her do whatever it was. I tried to find out what was going on, but Erma and Dorothy both shut me out. I said the hell with it and didn't give it another thought, but I'm telling you, Dorothy is afraid of Erma."

"She's been victimized by her own sister. It's really sad. I can almost relate to her."

Austin remembered. "You're talking about your aunt?"

Nadirah nodded.

"Lynn told me about her mother," Austin said. "I met her only a few times. She didn't act out when I met her, but I know from Lynn how much of a terror she was. What was your life like with her?"

Thoughtfully, Nadirah pushed her hair back behind her ears. Talking about her years with Aunt Stephanie wasn't something she felt like reliving.

"Austin, I hope you understand, but talking about your wife is as much as I can stomach in one sitting. Can we save the discussion about my aunt for another time?"

"I do understand."

Nadirah was relieved. "So are you still going to see Dorothy tomorrow?"

"If you're going with me."

"I'd like to go, but Mrs. Hamilton told me to stay away from Dorothy."

"Tomorrow is Saturday. I doubt seriously if Mrs. Hamilton is doing overtime. Besides, at this point, she's the least of our concern."

"Well, I guess I'm going then, but let's go early. Bree's party is at three at my aunt's house. We can drop her off there on the way downtown."

Austin was perplexed. "Does Bree know about the party?"

"She helped plan it."

"Nadirah, don't you believe in surprise parties?"

Nadirah flashed back to the day she was told her parents had been killed. Her mother had a surprise for her that she never got, but

then again, she got the surprise of her life—her parents' deaths.

In Nadirah's eyes, Austin saw sadness. "Talk about it," he said.

Nadirah quickly pulled herself away from the saddest day of her life. "Actually, I don't like surprises. They're not always good. Besides, Bree really enjoyed planning and working on her own party. This way, it's what she wants."

"You have a point," Austin said. "However, speaking of surprises, don't be surprised when Erma shows up at the hospital tomorrow."

"Why are you so sure she'll show up?"

"Because Dorothy's not asking to see me on her own. Erma had to have put her up to it."

Nadirah thought about it. "But Beverly says Erma has been banned from visiting Dorothy."

"Does she know this as a fact? Did Dorothy tell her that?"

"I think a nurse told her. It seems Erma's visits were really stressful for Dorothy."

"Big surprise there, but who's really checking the visitor's roster?"

"You might be right. The day I visited, I simply walked in. No one questioned me."

"That's why I know Erma's behind Dorothy asking for me. Dorothy has no reason in the world to wanna see me."

"I don't know, Austin. Suppose, on her own, Dorothy wants to explain to you why she tried to kill Bree."

"I'm not the one she needs to explain it to. Bree is."

"That won't ever happen."

"Nadirah, I'm telling you, this is a set up and Erma is behind it. She hasn't been able to get to me any other way. I bet Erma shows up at the hospital."

Nadirah didn't take that bet. Where Erma Gray was concerned, she now knew to not put anything past her.

Austin exhaled loudly. "Wow, I'm hungry. What about you?"

"Austin, we've already eaten dinner."

Austin slid closer to Nadirah. He put his arm around her. "But we haven't had dessert." He smiled seductively at Nadirah and she knew immediately that it wasn't apple pie Austin wanted. His lips lightly

touched hers. His kiss was as soft as a breeze. They tasted of each other, exploring, savoring unhurriedly the flavor of their kiss. What more they wanted to do they would not do tonight, for Bree was home. Still, Nadirah tasted the sweetest dessert she'd ever had.

Chapter 37

Austin had been warned, but all the same, he was amazed when he saw Dorothy with his own two eyes. She was asleep so he was able to stare in astonishment at the bloated, bloody, black, crusty appendage that bulged in place of her lower lip. In contrast, evidencing her dehydration, Dorothy's crusty upper lip was white. At the corners of her mouth, thick, white mucus had formed. From her open mouth seeped fluids that she desperately needed to keep in her body. Standing alongside Austin, Nadirah watched his face as he silently scrutinized the skeletal form of his sister-in-law with a look of utter disbelief blazing from his eyes. It didn't surprise her when he began sniffing back tears. She put her hand on his arm to let him know that she was standing beside him.

"God,"Austin said in a hushed voice. "What brought her to this?"

While Nadirah had no answer, Austin had to hold strong to keep from walking out.

"She's so skinny, so haggard. My God, Nadirah. Dorothy's only twenty-four. She looks like an old woman." Austin pressed his finger beneath his nose to still the stinging that threatened. He was close to losing it.

Nadirah rubbed Austin's arm. She noticed that the other patient's bed was empty and made up.

"You here for that one?" The petite Asian nurse entering the room asked.

Austin said nothing. He kept his back to the nurse as he wiped his eyes.

"Yes, we are," Nadirah answered.

"She a bad one," the nurse said. She took Dorothy's arm and wrapped a blood pressure cup around it. "She no eat, she no drink, she no go to the bathroom. She give up."

Nadirah watched Dorothy's face as the nurse took her pres-

sure. Dorothy didn't open her eyes. When the nurse got her reading, Nadirah asked, "Can't she be fed intravenously?"

"We try. She pull out needle." The nurse took Dorothy's pulse reading. "We tie her hands, she scream, she throw tantrum. She bite her lip worse. We bandage her lip, she pull off bandage, she bite self more. She not let us help her."

Nadirah waited while the nurse wrote Dorothy's readings on her chart. "Is she sedated right now?"

"Yes, but she will wake up soon."

"Nurse," Austin said, stopping her at the door. "What is her doctor going to do for her? He can't just let her curl up and die."

"Her new doctor, Dr. Julian, he will try something he say. You talk to him. He tell you." The nurse went on about her rounds.

Again Austin sniffled. "Look, I have to get out of here." He turned away from Dorothy. He couldn't look at her anymore. "Let's come back when she's awake."

"Are you sure?" Nadirah asked. "We could wait—"

"Austin?" Dorothy asked feebly.

Austin quickly turned back. He and Nadirah both stared at Dorothy. Neither knew what to say. In Dorothy's eyes, Nadirah saw the most woeful sadness she'd ever seen. She focused on those eyes to keep from looking at Dorothy's disfigured lip and gaping, slobbery mouth that she could no longer close.

"Austin." Dorothy grimaced painfully. "Is that you, Austin?"

"It's me, Dorothy. I came to see you. Are you—" Before he finished the question, Austin knew it was stupid to ask Dorothy if she was all right when it was obvious she wasn't. "I'm here," he said. "You wanted to see me?"

Dorothy started to lift her head to sit up, but couldn't. She was too weak. Nadirah

stepped around Austin to get closer to Dorothy and immediately covered her nose with her hand. Dorothy smelled terrible.

Holding her breath, Nadirah quickly fluffed up and rearranged Dorothy's two pillows under her head and shoulders, raising her head higher. She then went to the foot of the bed and raised the top of the bed so that Dorothy was practically sitting up. Nadirah turned her head toward the door to inhale fresher air.

Dorothy disregarded Nadirah who stayed where she was at the foot of the bed. "I didn't mean to hurt Bree," Dorothy said with a thick, heavy tongue that slurred her speech. "I didn't mean to."

"I know," Austin said, catching a whiff of Dorothy's unpleasant body odor. He stepped back another foot from the bed. "Dorothy, I know you wouldn't intentionally hurt Bree. She's all right now. You don't have to worry about her. You have to worry about yourself now."

Dorothy started slowly rolling her head from side to side.

"You have to get better, Dorothy. You have to eat so you can get stronger."

"No…no."

"Dorothy, don't you wanna see Bree again?"

Dorothy rolled her head faster.

"Don't you want Bree to see you healthy and strong?"

"No! No! I don't ever wanna see Bree! Don't bring her here."

"But why, Dorothy? She's your daughter. She doesn't hate you."

"She's not my daughter. She's Erma's daughter."

Austin and Nadirah exchanged worried glances.

"Dorothy, Bree is Erma's niece. She's your daughter. You raised Bree all of her life. Don't you remember?"

Dorothy shook her head.

Austin couldn't take it. He walked to the door, leaving Nadirah looking from him to Dorothy who seemed to notice Nadirah for the first time.

"You're her teacher," Dorothy said.

"Yes, I am." Nadirah was surprised that Dorothy remembered her.

"She live with you?"

"I'm taking good care of Bree."

"She need somebody to take care of her. I don't. Erma don't. You love Bree?"

Nadirah nodded. "I do." Her heart ached for Dorothy. She could see how painful it was for Dorothy to speak, but she could also see how painful it was for her to say she didn't love her own child. Her eyes were crying, but no tears came. Her body was too dry.

"Austin hate me."

"No, Austin doesn't hate you, Dorothy. He's worried about

you."

"But I hurt Bree."

"Austin knows you didn't mean to hurt Bree. Austin, you don't hate Dorothy, do you?"

It wasn't hate Austin was feeling, it was pity.

"Austin," Nadirah said, calling him back from the door through which he wanted so badly to escape. "Dorothy wants to know if you hate her. Come back and talk to her."

Austin put both hands at his waist and stretched his neck before he could turn back to face Dorothy. He went to her bedside, this time closer.

"I don't hate you, Dorothy."

"You don't know what I did."

"Dorothy, Bree is okay. I just don't understand why you did it. I don't understand why you're in this condition. I hate seeing you like this."

Squeezing her eyes shut and grimacing painfully, Dorothy began deep in her throat groaning like she was an animal with a broken leg trapped deep in a black hole from which there was no way out. Her groaning terrified Austin.

"What did I say?"

Frightened, Nadirah latched onto Austin's arm. "Do something!"

"What?"

"I don't know, but get her to stop."

"Dorothy. Dorothy." Austin pushed the stomach wrenching smell to the back of his mind as he gently shook Dorothy by the shoulder, trying to get her to look at him. "Dorothy, I'm not blaming you for what you did to Bree. I know you couldn't help it, but I wanna help you. Nadirah and I both wanna help you. Dorothy, tell us how we can help you. We'll do anything. Just tell us—"

"Don't let Erma get Bree," Dorothy said in a tiny little voice.

"Don't worry about Bree or Erma," Austin said. "We have a lawyer. We won't let Erma get Bree. Bree will be fine. I promise you, Dorothy, Bree will be fine."

"I tried to stop Erma from getting Bree. I gave Bree something bad to drink."

Austin and Nadirah exchanged knowing glances.

"I was trying to save Bree. Erma wanted to take her. If Bree was dead then Erma couldn't take her. Erma's not a good mother. She's a bad mother. She was my mother."

Nadirah felt overwhelming pity for Dorothy.

"Dorothy," Austin said, "Erma's not your mother, she's your sister."

"No, Erma is my mother. I'm not supposed to tell nobody. Erma's my mother."

Austin looked at Nadirah who was just as confounded as he. But there was no point in trying to convince Dorothy who Erma truly was to her. In her mind, Erma was her mother, he couldn't do anything about that.

"Dorothy, why would Erma try to take Bree from you? Were you in trouble?"

Dorothy looked straight through Austin as if she didn't see him. "Erma wanted to take Bree. Bree's her baby. Erma said so."

Stumped, Austin shifted his eyes to Nadirah. Neither one knew what to make out of Dorothy's nonsensical statements.

"Dorothy," Nadirah said, "was Erma here?"

Dorothy suddenly looked at the door. "Don't let her come in! She'll make me do it again. I don't wanna do it again, Austin. Not to you. Not again."

"Do what, Dorothy?" Austin asked. "What will Erma make you do again?"

"I don't want to. It's wrong! I know it's wrong, but Erma said I better or she'll put me back on the street. She'll make me do bad things with a lot of men. I know she will. I don't want to do that no more. I don't."

Dorothy started to cry, but again no tears came, only anguish and pain poured from her.

Nadirah whispered, "Is she saying what I think she's saying?"

Austin was dumbfounded. He stared at Dorothy. He was beginning to understand so much now that was unclear before about Erma and Dorothy's relationship.

The sound of a woman's footfalls in heels suddenly sounded outside in the corridor. Dorothy gripped the side rails of her bed and sat

straight up.

Nadirah and Austin both looked at the open doorway. The sound of heavy footfalls was coming closer. Austin knew the sound of those footfalls all too well.

Nadirah sensed the fear around her. "Austin, that can't be her," she said. "She's not supposed to be here."

"I told you she would be."

Dorothy craned her neck looking toward the door. "Don't let her come in. Don't let her come in. She'll hurt me, she'll hurt me bad." Dorothy fell back and drew herself up into a tight, thin ball. She whimpered like a wounded animal.

Austin grabbed hold of Dorothy's bony shoulders and pulled her back upright. "What did Erma make you do to me, Dorothy? Tell me!"

"Erma made me have sex with you, Austin. I didn't want to!"

Austin's jaw dropped, and so did Nadirah's, but Austin quickly recovered.

"Dorothy, that's not true. We never had sex. You're wrong."

Dorothy began rolling her head from side to side. "I didn't want to, Austin. Erma made me."

"Dorothy, listen to me. I never had sex with you!"

"Bree's your baby, Austin! She's your baby."

Totally blown away, Austin gawked at Dorothy and so did Nadirah.

"Bastard!" Erma said sneeringly from the doorway. "I always said you were a dog."

"Miss!" A woman's voice called out in the corridor. "Miss, you're not supposed to be here."

Austin released Dorothy with a thrust. She fell back against her pillows like she didn't have a bone in her body. He faced Erma.

"What the hell have you done?"

Dorothy began biting hard down on her lip, drawing blood, tearing her lip from her mouth.

"What have I done?" Erma asked. "I need to be asking you that question, Austin. What have you done? Did you screw my sister?"

"You know damn well I've never touched Dorothy. I've never laid a hand on her."

"Seems it's not your hand she's talking about."

The Asian nurse came up to Erma. "Miss, you must leave."

"You better get out of my face!" Erma said. "I have every right to visit my sister."

The Asian nurse walked away. "Call security!"

"If they touch me, I'll call my lawyer and shut this place down!" Erma again focused on Austin. "Austin, you don't have to believe what a crazy person says, believe your own eyes. I think Bree looks an awful lot like you."

Austin stood stark still as he stared incomprehensibly at Erma. He couldn't believe Dorothy and he definitely didn't believe Erma.

"If Dorothy is crazy," Nadirah said, "what are you? If any of this is true, you're—"

"Bitch, you shut the hell up before I—"

Austin rushed at Erma, forcing her back into the corridor. He grabbed her. "What have you done?"

"Get your hands off me, Austin!"

"Security, security!" the nurse screamed.

Austin shook Erma. "What have you done?"

With all that was going on, Nadirah had forgotten about Dorothy until she heard the blood curdling howl that stood Nadirah's hairs up on her arms. She looked at Dorothy and couldn't believe her eyes. Dorothy was tearing her lip off of her face with her hand. Nadirah pounced on Dorothy, grabbing her hands, but Dorothy sank her teeth into Nadirah's hand, hurting her, not releasing her. Nadirah screamed.

Austin rushed back into the room and, seeing what was happening, grabbed Nadirah, but quickly realized it was not Nadirah he had to grab, it was Dorothy. He had to pry her mouth open to free Nadirah's hand. The nurses and orderlies, too, heard Nadirah's and Dorothy's screams and rushed into the room. They were prepared. They held Dorothy down while a needle was plunged into her emaciated rear end. Austin held Nadirah's throbbing, teeth-marked hand as he watched Dorothy put not her energy into resisting the hands that held her down, but into trying to completely bite off her lower lip. Even with a tongue depresser jammed into her mouth, Dorothy was still trying to bite down on her lip. In her frustration that she was being hindered, Dorothy howled, but it wasn't her screams that Austin heard, it was the words,

"Bree's your baby!" that sounded loudest in his ears, but Bree couldn't be his child; he had never slept with Dorothy. Ever.

Belatedly, Austin remembered Erma and looked back at the door. She was gone. He rushed out into the corridor. Erma was nowhere in sight.

"Go after her," Nadirah said behind Austin. She was holding onto her sore hand. "You have to get the truth from her."

"The truth will never come from Erma's mouth. She's a master liar. She got Dorothy to lie, too. She brainwashed her."

Nadirah wasn't sure about that. "Austin, as bazaar as it sounds, what Dorothy said could be true."

"Nadirah, I have never slept with Dorothy."

"But didn't you—"

"No! Don't you think I know who I've been with? I'm not senile. I don't have Alzheimer's."

"No, but you have been drugged. You said so yourself."

Austin fell back against the wall. Hadn't he just talked about his suspicions about being drugged by Erma and losing time? Still, wouldn't he know if he had sex with someone?

"How could I have sex with someone if I'm out cold?"

"Austin, I'm no doctor, and I'm certainly no man, but don't you guys get erections even when you're asleep?"

Austin's face fell. He looked back into the room at Dorothy, no longer screaming, but drugged and fading fast. Her arms were tied to the railing of the bed.

"And, Austin, don't men have wet dreams when they're asleep, ejaculating healthy sperm that could end up on a sheet or inside someone?"

"Oh, man. Please don't tell me I've been used like that. And for God's sake, please, please don't tell me I married someone as diabolical as Satan himself?"

"There's one way we can find out?"

"How? Dorothy's not talking anytime soon." Again Austin looked at Dorothy. "And if I catch up to Erma, I'm liable to kill her."

"Then don't go near her, we've already had one tragedy," Nadirah said. "Your focus should be on DNA."

Austin was stumped. "Are you serious?"

"Austin, think. A DNA test will tell the tale. Whatever the truth is, you'll know."

"You really believe I slept with Dorothy?"

"Actually, Austin, it's not what I believe, it's what you need to do to find out if Bree's your child or not."

Austin was shaking his head. It couldn't be.

"Austin, DNA does not lie. If Dorothy is speaking out of her head, or if Erma was low enough to drug you and force her sister to…to…screw you, then you need to know what the truth is. If Bree is your child by whatever means, you need to know."

"No." Austin locked his fingers behind his head and squeezed his arms snugly around his ears as he sank down to the floor into a tight squat. No part of his being would allow him to wrap his mind around the thought that he had literally been raped by Erma and Dorothy.

Nadirah forgot all about her sore hand. When Austin's shoulders began to shake, she got down close to him. When he put his arms around her, she held him to her bosom and let him relieve himself of the pain and confusion he felt.

"Miss," the Asian nurse said. "Are you hurt?"

"When can we see her again?" Nadirah asked about Dorothy.

"Today no good. She will sleep now for long time. Another day."

"Okay."

"I look at your hand now," the nurse said to Nadirah.

"Just give me a minute," she said, looking at Austin. "My friend needs me right now."

Chapter 38

For the life of Nadirah, she couldn't remember half of what happened at Bree's birthday party. After the surreal morning she and Austin had at the hospital, the afternoon was a blur. For Bree's sake, they both tried to smile and be entertaining when the truth was they were totally messed up. Every time Nadirah looked at Austin he was looking at Bree, studying her, wondering could it be true. He didn't see himself in her. He saw Dorothy. A few times, he would up and walk out, only to be found either on the front stoop or halfway down the block trying to walk off the rage boiling inside of him.

Austin said more times than Nadirah could count, "It's a lie. She's lying!"

Long after they were back home and Bree was put to bed, Austin still struggled with what might be. "I love that little girl," he said, "but I don't think—"

"What if it's true, Austin? Bree deserves to know also."

"Nadirah, if any part of this lie is true, I don't know what I'm gonna do." Austin began to pace. He kept clinching his jaw and his fists. "However it plays out, Erma has got to pay."

Nadirah agreed. "She's destroyed her sister. I called the hospital. Dorothy is still out."

Austin punched his right fist into his left hand. "Dorothy has to get better. If any part of this lie is true, I need to know how and why they did it. I need to know what drug they used on me?"

"I've been thinking about that," Nadirah said. "There are so many drugs, but more than likely they used a date rape drug."

"But date rape drugs are used on women."

"Actually, date rape drugs can be used on both men and women, and not just for rape, for any criminal activity. Austin, I did a term paper on date rape drugs several years back when I was going for my B.A. GHB, Rohypnol, and Ketamine are easy to get on the street, and from the side effects you described, Austin, you were

most definitely on one of those drugs."

"Goddammit!" Austin was beside himself. "Why? Why would they do that to me? Why did Erma want me to impregnate her own sister?"

"My guess? Because she couldn't have a baby of her own. Austin, that's the only plausible reason."

"If that's what happened, wasn't she supposed to claim Bree as her own?"

"That's what I would think."

"Then why didn't she? She was pregnant at the same time Dorothy was. I remember her saying that Dorothy was pregnant. I never saw her, but I didn't doubt it."

"Maybe she miscarried too soon before Dorothy delivered Bree. She couldn't pass a full-term baby off as her own if she miscarried too soon. Or maybe she changed her mind for some reason."

"No…no, that can't be. She probably wanted to accuse me of raping Dorothy."

"Then why didn't she?"

"Beats the hell out of me," Austin said. "I don't understand any of this. Why did she make Dorothy do something like that?" Again Austin punched his hand. "I don't believe it. It didn't happen."

Nadirah felt strongly that it did. "Do you think there's any truth to what Dorothy said about Erma being her mother?"

A jumble of thoughts raced through Austin's mind, but not one coherent thought leaped from his mouth. He was bewildered.

"But what if it's true?" Nadirah asked. "If it is, then everything Dorothy said is true."

"No, it can't be. I'm not Bree's father?"

Nadirah didn't want to upset Austin anymore than he already was so she said nothing more. Being drugged had never happened to her, but it had happened to so many other women who, when they awakened, had to come to grips with the fact that some man, maybe a friend, drugged her, and without her consent while she was unconscious, violated her and stole something that she alone had sole, absolute right to give. In kinship, Nadirah could imagine the degradation a female victim must feel, she couldn't even begin to imagine what Austin was feeling.

"It can't be true," Austin said again.

"Austin, years ago, I read a book called *The World According to Garp*. It was fiction, but in that book the main character, Garp, was conceived when his mother, a nurse, screwed a comatose patient who kept getting erections. If the patient was aware of what was going on, the reader never knew because the author never said. But, the bottom line, a man, unconscious, made a baby. Who says that can't happen in real life?"

Austin's stomach sank. He dropped his head back and closed his eyes. It was much too difficult to believe that he had been so vulnerable that Erma was able to take advantage of him like that. If it was true, he was going to kill Erma.

Austin didn't sleep the whole weekend, and neither did Nadirah. She sat up with Austin, listening to him, holding him, and praying in her heart that he would find out the truth. Much was discussed, but the one subject that Austin wouldn't talk about was the possibility of seeking custody of Bree if in fact it turned out that she was his.

"I'm not gonna set myself up to be let down. When I get the results of the DNA, I'll decide which path I take with Bree. Until then, I can't talk about it."

"But you have to think contingency. I think I know what you'd do if she was your child, my question is what will you do if she's not?"

Austin slowly popped, individually, each of the knuckles on each of his hands. He shook his head because he didn't know what he would do.

"I know you're scared, and—"

"I'm petrified," Austin said. "Nadirah, I really do care about that little girl. Knowing Bree, being with her, I wouldn't mind if she was mine, but I can't look at her without being reminded of Erma's deceptive manipulation. I'll never forgive Erma, and as sad as she is, I can't forgive Dorothy. She should have had more backbone to stand up to Erma. I hate them both."

That was early Sunday morning, and yet again Austin walked out of the house into a humid dawn. He didn't come back till late Sunday night. He said nothing about where he'd been or what he was planning to do, but Monday morning, he was up early ready to go to the DNA Diagnostic Center in midtown. He told Bree that it was a visit to a new doctor that they both needed to see.

"Why?" she asked. "I'm not sick. Are you?"

While Nadirah smiled to herself, Austin fumbled with an explanation he hadn't expected to have to give.

"You don't always have to be sick to go to the doctor. Sometimes you go to the doctor to make sure you're not sick."

"Oh," Bree said. "We're getting a checkup?"

"Yes," Austin said, relieved. "That's exactly what it is, a check up."

Carrying a small, blue cooler bag in his hand, Austin went to the front door and, opening it, looked out to see if the car service he'd called for had come as yet. It had not.

"Are you taking that with you?" Nadirah asked referring to the cooler bag Austin carried.

"Yeah."

"What's in it?"

"I'll tell you later."

"Okay. So when is that car getting here?" Nadirah asked.

"Any minute now."

"Uncle Austin," Bree said, "can I ask you something?"

Somewhat leery, Austin cautiously said, "Sure."

"Uncle Austin, I know I have a real mother even though I don't know where she is. But do I have a real father? Do you know who he is?"

Austin quickly looked to Nadirah for help.

"Bree," Nadirah said, "do you have a book to take with you to read?"

Bree wasn't easily diverted. "Don't Uncle Austin don't know my father?"

It was now Nadirah who looked to Austin for help, but he still looked like a deer caught in the headlights of an eighteen wheeler. Nadirah felt pretty much like that herself.

Wide-eyed, Bree waited for eitherAustin or Nadirah to answer her question.

The sudden tooting of a horn outside the townhouse signaled the arrival of the car service. While Nadirah and Austin both breathed a grateful sigh of relief, Austin rushed to the door.

"We'll be right out!" he called to the driver. "Okay, ladies, let's

go."

With her head down, walked past the book she had chosen to take with her on the coffee table.

"Bree, don't you want your book?" Nadirah asked.

Bree slipped her hand inside Austin's and lay her head against his side. Austin's troubled heart melted. As many times as he'd held Bree's hand, he'd never felt it like this before. Her hand felt so small, so smooth. Her head against his body had never felt so personal, so intimate, so right. Welling up, Austin was surprised at his own emotions.

Nadirah was touched by what she saw in Austin's eyes, but it hurt that Bree had so easily turned away from her. It was clear Bree preferred Austin. Their bond, whether biological or not, was strong. If it turned out that Bree was Austin's daughter, Bree may well forget about her. Austin will be all she'll ever need. They'll move to California, forget about her, and she'll be left behind.

The driver honked again. Within minutes they were on their way downdown in the bumper-to-bumper four-lane traffic snaking down Manhattan's Second Avenue. No one spoke, not even Bree. Maybe she sensed that the answer to her question was what they were going after. If Nadirah understood the look in Austin's eyes, she knew he was scared. He had made peace with what he was about to do, but whether he could handle the outcome either way was yet to be determined.

Epilogue

It's been three years since Dorothy died, but the day she died was the day Erma went to prison. Dorothy's nonsensical revelations proved to be truths that Erma couldn't lie her way around. There's something to be said about poetic justice. Dorothy, fragile in mind and soul, finally got peace while Erma, revengeful and evil to the core, finally got what was coming to her. Erma used and abused not her sister, but her own child. Dorothy didn't know herself until she was thirteen that Erma was her real mother, but by then she was used to Erma controlling her life and acting like her mother anyway. Erma had been a child herself when she had Dorothy. The boy Erma had gotten with was an eleventh grader whose parents sent him away to keep him from having to deal with an unwanted baby and a girl they didn't approve of.

Erma never forgot nor forgave her young lover for deserting her. Her mother made her keep the baby she didn't want as a punishment for her promiscuity. Erma couldn't love Dorothy as her baby, and told everyone Dorothy was her sister. After her mother died and she went with her grandmother, Erma told no one that Dorothy was her child. After her grandmother died, she raised Dorothy as her sister. If anyone in the neighborhood knew otherwise, no one ever said. The secret they shared held them close, but gave them no peace and no love for each other. Erma was always angry and often took her anger out on Dorothy. For the sake of peace, Dorothy often did whatever Erma wanted her to do, including deceiving Austin.

That long ago fateful day, Austin sat on his stoop with the DNA results in his hand, he cried. It was his blood, his DNA that coursed through Bree's veins. He was a father for eight whole years and didn't know it until Dorothy, in her mindless sputterings, revealed the secret that had long festered in her psyche, eating away at her until it destroyed her. Austin cried, too, because the DNA

report exposed even more. He was a perfect match with Bree, but Bree was not a perfect match with Dorothy.

"This has to be wrong," he said.

"It makes no sense," Nadirah said. "They have markers in common, but not enough to be a perfect match. Dorothy is not Bree's mother. How can that be?"

Wisely, because he was bothered by Dorothy's confusing admissions, on that Sunday when Austin disappeared for the day, he and his attorney had gotten an administrator at the hospital to authorize the drawing of a vial of Dorothy's blood for DNA testing. And that Monday when his and Bree's blood was tested, so was Dorothy's.

Austin reread the DNA report. For the life of him, he couldn't articulate the jumble of questions that were boggling his mind and tying his tongue.

"If Dorothy isn't a perfect maternal match for Bree," Nadirah said "then who is? It would?" It hit Nadirah like a volt of lightening. "It's Erma. Erma is Bree's mother."

Austin said not a word as he wrestled with Nadirah's revelation.

"Austin, that's the only thing that explains how you could be Bree's father and Dorothy not be Bree's mother, yet, Dorothy raised Bree with financing from Erma. Erma is Bree's mother."

All color drained from Austin's face. In a low, steady voice he said, "I'm gonna kill her."

Austin took out his cell phone. He called his attorney.

"I don't care what it takes or how long it takes, find a way. She's not getting away with this."

It was then, after Austin got off the phone that the dam of anger he had been holding back burst. He thew the cell phone against the far wall of the livingroom. "Every word she ever spoke was a lie!"

Nadirah stood back and watched Austin rile against the woman whom he had for years laid in bed with and professed to love. If all they suspected was true, Austin had every right in the world to want Erma dead. She had given his baby away. When Austin calmed down, only because he was drained and all cried out, Nadirah went to him. She hugged him, but he pulled away.

"How in the world did she do it?" he asked, but then it hit him. "That last pregnancy. That had to be the one Bree was born from. That

was the day Erma supposedly miscarried, the day my mother died. Oh God. I need to know what happened. I need to know why it happened."

"I can't begin to guess what Erma's motives were," Nadirah said. "but everything Dorothy said now makes sense. What doesn't make sense is why Erma gave Bree away and claimed she had a miscarriage?"

Feeling hopeless, Austin began to cry. He struggled with the realization that Bree was his child. He he had held her hand, read her stories, told her jokes and put her to bed without knowing that she shared his DNA. Erma had viciously robbed him of his child and hidden her in plain sight right under his nose.

Erma's brazenness, her contemptuousness set Austin on a path of retribution. Every day for a week he went to Erma's apartment and anywhere else he thought she might be. She was nowhere. Each day he grew angrier and more bitter and couldn't bring himself to even look at Bree.

"I can't be around her," he said. "All I feel is hate. I'm no good for Bree right now. I don't wanna look at her, I don't wanna touch her. I don't want her to feel from me not even an ounce of the hate I feel for the woman who gave birth to her."

"You just need some time," Nadirah said.

"I need you to keep taking care of Bree because before I can be of any good to her, I need answers. I need to know how and why. As soon as I can get in to see Dorothy, I am going to see her, but for now, I can't stay here."

"Will you go back to California?"

"I don't know. I have to take care of my urgent contracts for clients, but I need to take time off."

"What should I tell Bree?"

"Nothing."

"Okay, but should I contact ACS and tell them about you, about the DNA test?"

"My attorney will handle all of that."

Austin said nothing more about Bree. He moved out. He didn't call, he didn't come by. As much as it hurt Nadirah that he had shut her out, she understood. Austin had to go it alone. He had to find Erma, he had to know the whys because, until he did, he was not going to be any

good to her, to Bree or even to himself.

For the fourth day in a row, Austin solemnly walked down the corridor toward Dorothy's room praying that she was not only awake, but coherent.

"She want to see you," the Asian nurse said as Austin approached the nurse's station.

"She's awake?"

"Yes, but if she act up, she go back to sleep."

"I will keep her calm. She'll be all right."

"Good you come today. She transfer to Creedmore State Hospital tomorrow."

Austin hurried to Dorothy's room. She was laying in a fetal position with an IV in her arm. There was a bandage on her lip held there with white tape that ran around her neck and back behind her ears. Her eyes were closed.

Austin said softly. "Dorothy."

Dorothy slowly opened her eyes.

Austin quickly pulled a chair to the side of the bed close to Dorothy's head. He didn't smell her, but if he did he'd take it.

"I know Bree is my daughter."

"Not my daughter," Dorothy said weakly.

"She's Erma's daughter, right?" Austin held his breath.

"Erma's daughter."

Austin got lightheaded. He wanted to cry. He rolled his lips inward and pressed them together.

"Erma lied," Dorothy said.

Austin told himself to stay calm. "How, Dorothy? How did you get Erma's baby?"

"Erma gave her baby to me."

"When? Where was I? Wait. I know I was out of town, but Erma said she had a miscarriage."

"Erma had the baby."

"Erma had Bree? Where?"

"In her bed."

"Dorothy, where was my mother? My mother was there. Did she know Bree was born?"

"Yes."

"Is that why she had a heart attack?"

Dorothy closed her eyes.

"Dorothy, my mother had a heart attack. She died the day Bree was born."

"Erma called me. She didn't want Bree. Erma never wanted Bree."

"But Erma always wanted children, Dorothy. We tried many times to have children. Erma kept miscarrying."

"No. Erma never wanted children. Erma didn't want me."

"Dorothy, is Erma—"

"Erma hate children. Erma hate me. Erma said I messed up her life. Erma took drugs to kill her babies, Austin, but sometimes she stuck wire up in her belly and made her babies die."

Tears spilled over and Austin didn't bother to wipe them away.

"Erma kill all her babies except me and Bree. Me and Bree we sisters. I have to protect her. I have to save her from Erma."

Austin stifled his urge to cry. He hadn't imagined it would be this bad. "Dorothy, is Erma your real mother?"

"Erma is my real mother."

Austin dropped his arms atop his thighs and hung his head. It was just too much to comprehend. From the first hello, Erma had lied. Nothing about their life had ever been the truth.

"Erma tried to kill Bree, Austin. Erma hate Bree being born."

Austin sat back. "When did she try to kill Bree, Dorothy?"

"She made me poke Bree with a wire, but Bree wouldn't come out."

"When Dorothy? When?"

"The night Bree was born. I did it one time."

"Dorothy, are you sure. I didn't even know you were at my house that night."

"Erma called me. She said, 'Hurry up.' Was that all right, Austin? I got there fast."

"Dorothy, are you saying that Erma had you poking up inside her with a wire to make her miscarry?"

"She told me if I didn't, she never speak to me again. She won't help me anymore." Erma started to whimper.

"It's all right if Erma doesn't speak to you, Dorothy. You have me. You have Bree. We'll speak to you, but, Dorothy, I don't understand. Why did Erma want to kill Bree? Why did she want to get pregnant if she didn't want a baby?"

"Erma didn't want no baby. Never. Erma wanted you. She didn't want no baby. You wanted a baby, not Erma."

Austin couldn't believe what he was hearing. Erma had played him from the beginning. Having a baby was the trap she set to get him. How stupid he had been.

"Austin, tell Erma not to be mad at me. She's always mad at me. She won't help me no more."

"Dorothy, I'll take care of you. I'll help you get better."

"No. Erma won't like that. She told me to stay away from you."

"Don't worry about Erma, she won't bother you anymore. But tell me, Dorothy, if you poked Bree with a wire, why didn't she die?"

"Your mother wouldn't let her. Your mother saw me poking Erma. She was supposed to be at the store, but she came back too soon. She saw me. She screamed. She screamed loud. She scared me. She said, 'What are you doing?' She said, 'What in God's name are you doing?' She said she was gonna tell you. She ran. She called 911. Erma got mad."

"Did they argue? Is that when my mother had a heart attack?"

"No. No."

Austin rose up out of the chair. "What happened, Dorothy? What happened to my mother?"

Dorothy whined, "Erma made me."

Struck silent, Austin stared incredulously at Dorothy.

Dorothy began to cry. "I didn't want to, Austin. Erma made me. She said, I better."

Austin moved away from the bed.

"Erma said she'll make lots of men hurt me. She did that before. She made them hurt me, Austin."

His eyes never leaving Dorothy, Austin walked around the bed and back again. His head was spinning. He felt like he couldn't stand on his own so he held on to the bed railing.

"The coroner said my mother had a heart attack. How did she have a heart attack?"

Dorothy closed her eyes. Her mouth started to move as she began biting down on the bandage on her lip.

"No, Dorothy." Austin rushed back to Dorothy's side. He held the sides of her face. "Leave your lip alone. Open your eyes, Dorothy. Talk to me. I'm not mad at you. I need to know how my mother died. I'm not gonna hurt you. I'm not like Erma. You know that. I'm nothing like Erma. I won't even tell the police anything. I just need to know what happened to my mother and how Bree became your baby."

Dorothy stopped trying to bite on her lip. She opened her eyes. "If I tell you, you're gonna be mad."

"No, I won't." Austin let go of Dorothy's face. "I promise. Tell me about how my mother died."

Quiet for a minute, Dorothy finally raised her eyes and looked at Austin. "Erma made me hold your mother down. She put a pillow on her face."

A billowing fire burned in Austin's gut. He clinched his fists and clamped his jaw tight.

"She couldn't breathe, Austin. Her heart started hurting. I heard her say her heart. Her heart, Austin. Erma kept the pillow on her face but I let her go. And then she stopped moving and Erma took the pillow off. Your mother was trying to breath. Her face looked bad. It was real red. The ambulance came and they saw your mother on the floor and they said she was having a heart attack. That's what they said."

Austin sat. He cried openly and sorrowfully for his mother and the anguish of her last moments. Erma was going to pay for every minute his mother suffered and for the painful last beats of her heart.

"You mad at me?"

"No," he lied. He was mad as hell at her, at Erma, and at himself for ever laying eyes on Erma. "Tell me about the baby, Dorothy."

"What baby?"

"Bree, Dorothy. Tell me about how Bree was born. Did the paramedics deliver Bree at the house after they took my mother out?"

"Erma told me not to say anything about the baby. I didn't. I never did."

"Tell me about the baby, Dorothy. I need to help the baby."

"You'll help the baby?"

"Yes, I'll help the baby. Tell me how she was born."

"I'll tell you, but you can't tell nobody. Erma don't want nobody to know."

"I'll keep it to myself. Just tell me."

"Okay. The baby started coming. Erma was screaming because of the baby. The baby was hurting her and was taking a long time to come out. Babies hurt, Austin. Erma didn't like that. Erma was gonna kill the baby when it came out, but the ambulance came and I had to open the door. At the hospital, Erma told them her name was Dorothy and that she didn't know who the father was. They believed her, Austin. They believed her."

"Erma told the people in the hospital that her name was Dorothy?"

"Yes, she was me. She left the baby at the hospital so you wouldn't know. She told me to tell you she had a miscarriage. I told you that, Austin. I told you what Erma told me to tell you."

Austin remembered. Dorothy was the one who told him that Erma had miscarried their baby and that his mother was dead. God, he hated both of them.

"You took the baby home?"

"Erma went back with me to get the baby, but she made me take the baby with me. I didn't want to, but Erma made me. She said I should raise the baby because she had raised me. I had to do what she did."

"But what about your baby, Dorothy? What happened to your baby?"

"Bree died."

"No, Dorothy, Bree is alive. She's okay. Your baby, Dorothy? Where's the baby that you gave birth to?"

Dorothy slowly shook her head.

"Erma told me you were pregnant when she was pregnant. Weren't you pregnant? Didn't you have a baby?"

Dorothy groaned. She started to cry her waterless tears. She gripped her stomach.

"What Dorothy? What happened?"

"I didn't have no baby. I never had a baby."

Again, Austin was confused. He couldn't believe that so many

lies were told right to his face.

"Erma wanted me to have your baby but I never got pregnant. I couldn't."

Austin covered his face. Who in God's name did he marry?

"Austin," Dorothy said meekly. "Erma told me to never tell you you was Bree's father, but I had to tell you, Austin, I had to. Erma wants to take Bree back, but Bree is my baby. Erma gave her to me, but she wants her back so she can get you to come back."

"But I would never go back to Erma, Dorothy. I don't love her."

"You don't?"

"No, not anymore."

"Oh," Dorothy said, musingly. She closed her eyes and appeared to drift off to sleep.

"Dorothy, do you wanna rest now? I'll sit right here until you wake up."

Dorothy opened her eyes. "Erma loves you, Austin. She told me so. She came to get Bree from me. She said if I tell you I had sex with you and had Bree, you'd know she was your baby and if she had Bree, you'd come back to her. That's what Erma said, Austin."

"But I thought you said Erma told you to never tell me about Bree?"

"That was before. Austin, I don't want Bree to live with Erma. Erma is gonna raise Bree like she raised me. She'll do bad things to Bree. She'll let a lot of men do bad things to Bree. I know she will. That's why I tried to make Bree to to sleep with the angels. Erma can't get Bree if Bree is with the angels. Right, Austin? She can't get Bree if Bree is dead."

If someone had told Austin that such secrets, such ugliness lurked in his life, he would have called that person a liar. What Dorothy told him was too mind-blowing to be believed, but too preposterous to be ignored or dismissed as the nonsensical babblings of an unstable mind. The DNA report validated the story of Bree's birth, but it was only Dorothy's word about how his mother died. Did he believe Dorothy? He did.

"You mad at me, Austin?"

Dorothy sounded so much like a little girl; Austin couldn't help but feel sorry for her. He didn't like the role she played in killing his

mother, but the truth was, Erma was really the killer.

"No, Dorothy. I'm not mad at you. I feel sorry for you."

"Erma is gonna be mad at me. My grandmother told me to leave Erma alone. She said Erma was a bad seed. I don't want Erma to be mad at me. She's bad. My grandmother said so."

"Don't worry about Erma, Dorothy. She won't bother you again."

"You promise, Austin? You promise?"

"I promise."

Walking out of Bellevue, Austin was already on his cell phone talking to his attorney. Erma was about to come face to face with his reckoning.

❧❀❧❀❧

Erma was charged with kidnaping Bree and giving her away without Austin's knowledge of her birth or consent to give up his parental rights. Based solely on Dorothy's videotaped deposition from Creedmore State Hospital, Erma was also charged with one count of manslaughter in the death of Austin's mother. All the charges were brought before a grand jury, but Erma never went to trial. She fought hard to get the charges dropped, but after she was forced to take a DNA test and proven to be Bree's biological mother, Erma pleaded no contest to the charges and was sentenced to ten years in prison.

Austin last saw Erma from a distance. He never got within fifty feet of her because he didn't trust himself. When Erma was being led away in handcuffs she turned and saw Austin and Nadirah, shoulder to shoulder, hand-in-hand, looking at her not with satisfaction in their eyes, but anger.

Dorothy died without ever laying eyes on Erma again, which Nadirah hoped gave Dorothy some peace of mind. Austin never went back to visit Dorothy, he couldn't. He pitied her, but he had no love for her either. All the love he had to give, he gave to Nadirah and Bree. They were a family, husband and wife; father, mother, and child. Under their roof, there were no secrets or any lies.

However, under Stephanie's roof, there were still a few secrets and lies. It wasn't talked about, but Stephanie was still seeing BJ. Every

Saturday afternoon, when Nadirah brought Lynn's children back home, Stephanie always had a smile on her face, a spring in her walk, and a hug for everyone, including Nadirah. Lynn's children were happy and well cared for. Aunt Stephanie was doing remarkably well with them, and it still amazed Nadirah that this was the woman who had been incapable of loving her own. It was too bad that Lynn wasn't alive to bear witness herself. Nadirah was there, but she didn't know if it was BJ who was responsible for the miraculous change or, if in fact, Aunt Stephanie had been reborn. She went to church every Sunday and took the kids, including Bree, with her. But just in case BJ was the reason, Nadirah kept her opinion about their relationship to herself. Some secrets and some lies might not be so bad after all, especially if feeling good after the loving put love and compassion in the anemic soul of a scurrilous woman like her aunt, who had for so long not allowed herself to love or be loved.

Coming 2008

SASSY

A Novel